The
Random
House
Basic Dictionary

French-English
English-French

The Random House Basic Dictionary

French-English
English-French

Edited by
Francesca L.V. Langbaum
University of Virginia

Under the General Editorship of
Professor Robert A. Hall, Jr.
Cornell University

The Ballantine Reference Library
Ballantine Books · New York

Library of Congress Catalog Card Number: 54-5962
ISBN 0-345-29617-6
This edition published by arrangement with Random House, Inc.
Previously published as *The French Vest Pocket Dictionary* and *The Random
House French Dictionary*.

Manufactured in the United States of America
First Ballantine Books Edition: August 1981

Concise Pronunciation Guide

The following concise guide describes the approximate pronunciation of the letters and frequent combinations of letters occurring in the French language. A study of it will enable the reader to pronounce French adequately most of the time. While the guide cannot list all the exceptions to the established pronunciations, or cover the manner in which adjacent words affect each other in speech, such exceptions and variations will readily be learned as one develops facility in the language.

French Letter	Description of Pronunciation
a, à	Between *a* in *calm* and *a* in *hat*.
â	Like *a* in *calm*.
ai	Like *e* in *bed*.
au	Like *oa* in *coat*.
b	As in English. At end of words, usually silent.
c	Before *e, i, y*, like *s*. Elsewhere, like *k*. When *c* occurs at the end of a word and is preceded by a consonant, it is usually silent.
ç	Like *s*.
cc	Before *e, i*, like *x*. Elsewhere, like *k*.
ch	Usually like *sh* in *short*. *ch* is pronounced like *k* in words of Greek origin; before *a, o*, and *u;* and before consonants.
d	At beginning and in middle of words, as in English. At end of words, usually silent.
e	At end of words, normally silent; indicates that preceding consonant letter is pronounced. Between two single consonant sounds, usually silent. Elsewhere, like English *a* in *sofa*.
é	Approximately like *a* in *hate*.
è, ê, ei	Like *e* in *bed*.
eau	Like *au*.
ent	Silent when it is the third person plural ending.
er (end of words)	At end of words of more than one syllable, usually like *a* in *hate*, the *r* being silent; otherwise like *air* in *chair*.
es	Silent at end of words.
eu	A vowel sound not found in English; like French *e*, but pronounced with the lips rounded as for *o*.
ez	At end of words, almost always like English *a* in *hate*, the *z* being silent.
f	As in English; silent at the end of a few words.
g	Before *e, i, y*, like *z* in *azure*. Elsewhere, like *g* in *get*. At end of words, usually silent.
gn	Like *ni* in *onion*.
gu	Before *e, i, y*, like *g* in *get*. Elsewhere, like *g* in *get* plus French *u* (see below).
h	In some words, represents a slight tightening of the throat muscles (in French, called "aspiration"). In most words, silent.
i, î	Like *i* in *machine*.
ill	(-il at end of words) like *y*

French Letter	Description of Pronunciation	French Letter	Description of Pronunciation
	in *yes*, in many but not all words.		See above under *er*.
j	Like *z* in *azure*.	s	Generally, like *s* in *sea*. Single *s* between vowels, like *z* in *zone*. At end of words, normally silent.
k	As in English.		
l	As in English, but always pronounced "bright," with tongue in front of mouth.		
		sc	Before *e* or *i*, like *s*. Elsewhere, like *sk*.
m, n	When double, and when single between two vowel letters or at beginning of word, like English *m* and *n* respectively. When single at end of syllable (at end of word or before another consonant), indicates nasalization of preceding vowel.	t	Approximately like English *t*, but pronounced with tongue tip against teeth. At end of words, normally silent. When followed by *ie, ion, ium, ius,* and other diphthongs beginning with a vowel, *t* generally is like English *s* in *sea* (unless the *t* itself is preceded by an *s* or an *x*).
o	Usually like *u* in English *mud*, but rounder. When final sound in word, and often before *s* and *z*, like *ô*.	th	Like *t*.
		u, û	A vowel sound not found in English; like the *i* in *machine* but with lips rounded as for *ou*.
ô	Approximately like *oa* in *coat*.		
oe, oeu	Like *eu*.	ue	After *c* or *g* and before *il*, like *eu*.
oi	Approximately like a combination of the consonant *w* and the *a* of *calm*.	v	As in English.
		w	Usually like *v;* in some people's pronunciation, like English *w*.
ou, oû, où	Like *ou* in *tour*.		
p	At end of words, usually silent. Between *m* and *t*, *m* and *s*, *r* and *s*, usually silent. Elsewhere, as in English.	x	Generally sounds like *ks;* but when the syllable *ex* begins a word and is followed by a vowel, *x* sounds like *gz*. At end of words, usually silent.
pn, ps	Unlike English, when *pn* and *ps* occur at the beginning of words the *p* is usually sounded.		
		y	Generally like *i* in *machine;* but when between two vowels, like *y* in *yes*.
ph	Like *f*.		
qu	Usually like *k*.	z	Like *z* in *zone*. At end of words, often silent (see above under *ez*).
r	A vibration either of the uvula, or of the tip of the tongue, against the upper front teeth.		

Note on Pronunciation

A few minutes' study of the *Concise Pronunciation Guide* will enable you to pronounce most French words without having to look each word up in the dictionary. For the relatively few cases in which the pronunciation does not follow the usual pattern, this dictionary provides a transcription in simple and familiar symbols.

ă   bat

ā   cape

â   dare

ä   calm

à   [a vowel intermediate in quality between the *a* of *cat* and the *a* of *calm*, but closer to the former]

ĕ   set

ē   bee

ĭ   big

ī   bite

N   [a symbol used to indicate nasalized vowels. There are four such vowels in French, found in *un bon vin blanc* (œN bōN văN bläN)]

ŏ   hot

ŏ   no

ô   order

œ   [a vowel made with the lips rounded in position for *o* as in *over,* while trying to say *a* as in *able*]

oi   oil

o͝o   book

ōō   ooze

ou   loud

ŭ   up

ū   cute

û   burn

Y   [a vowel made with the lips rounded in position for *o͝o* as in *ooze,* while trying to say *e* as in *easy*]

ə   [indicates the sound of *a* in *alone, e* in *system, i* in *easily, o* in *gallop, u* in *circus*]

Irregular Verbs

Infinitive	Pres. Part.	Past Part.	Pres. Indic.	Future
aller	allant	allé	vais	irai
asseoir	asseyant	assis	assieds	assiérai
atteindre	atteignant	atteint	atteins	atteindrai
avoir	ayant	eu	ai	aurai
battre	battant	battu	bats	battrai
boire	buvant	bu	bois	boirai
conduire	conduisant	conduit	conduis	conduirai
connaître	connaissant	connu	connais	connaîtrai
courir	courant	couru	cours	courrai
craindre	craignant	craint	crains	craindrai
croire	croyant	cru	crois	croirai
devoir	devant	dû	dois	devrai
dire	disant	dit	dis	dirai
dormir	dormant	dormi	dors	dormirai
écrire	écrivant	écrit	écris	écrirai
envoyer	envoyant	envoyé	envoie	enverrai
être	étant	été	suis	serai
faire	faisant	fait	fais	ferai
falloir	———	fallu	(il) faut	(il) faudra
joindre	joignant	joint	joins	joindrai
lire	lisant	lu	lis	lirai
mettre	mettant	mis	mets	mettrai
mourir	mourant	mort	meurs	mourrai
naître	naissant	né	nais	naîtrai
ouvrir	ouvrant	ouvert	ouvre	ouvrirai
plaire	plaisant	plu	plais	plairai
pleuvoir	pleuvant	plu	(il) pleut	(il) pleuvra
pouvoir	pouvant	pu	peux	pourrai
prendre	prenant	pris	prends	prendrai
recevoir	recevant	reçu	reçois	recevrai
rire	riant	ri	ris	rirai
savoir	sachant	su	sais	saurai
suffire	suffisant	suffi	suffis	suffirai
suivre	suivant	suivi	suis	suivrai
tenir	tenant	tenu	tiens	tiendrai
valoir	valant	valu	vaux	vaudrai
venir	venant	venu	viens	veindrai
vivre	vivant	vécu	vis	vivrai
voir	voyant	vu	vois	verrai
vouloir	voulant	voulu	veux	voudrai

Abbreviations

abbr.	abbreviation	*med.*	medical
adj.	adjective	*mil.*	military
adv.	adverb	*n.*	noun
art.	article	*naut.*	nautical
comm.	commercial·	*pl.*	plural
conj.	conjunction	*pred.*	predicate
eccles.	ecclesiastical	*prep.*	preposition
f.	feminine	*pron.*	pronoun
fig.	figurative	*sg.*	singular
geom.	geometry	*tr.*	transitive (used only with
gramm.	grammar, grammatical		verbs which also have
interj.	interjection		reflexive use to indicate
intr.	intransitive		intransitive meaning)
lit.	literal, literally	*vb.*	verb
m.	masculine		

Useful Phrases

Good day. Bonjour.
Good evening. Bonsoir.
Good night. Bonne nuit.
Good bye. Au revoir.
How are you? Comment allez-vous?
Fine, thank you. Très bien, merci.
Glad to meet you. Enchanté de faire votre connaissance.
Thank you very much. Merci beaucoup.
You're welcome. Pas de quoi.
Please. S'il vous plaît.
Good luck. Bonne chance.
To your health. A votre santé.

Please help me. Aidez-moi, s'il vous plaît.
Do you understand? Comprenez-vous?
I don't understand. Je ne comprends pas.
Speak slowly, please. Parlez lentement, s'il vous plaît.
Please repeat. Répétez, s'il vous plaît.
I don't speak French. Je ne parle pas français.
Do you speak English? Parlez-vous anglais?
Does anyone here speak English? Y a-t-il quelqu'un qui parle anglais?
How do you say…in French? Comment dit-on…en français?

What is your name? Comment vous appelez-vous?
My name is… Je m'appelle…
I am an American. Je suis américain.

How is the weather?   Quel temps fait-il?
What time is it?   Quelle heure est-il?
What is it?   Qu'est-ce que c'est?

How much does this cost?   Combien est ceci?
It is too expensive.   C'est trop cher.
I want to buy...   Je voudrais acheter...

I want to eat.   Je voudrais manger.
Can you recommend a restaurant?   Pouvez-vous recommander un restaurant?
I am hungry.   J'ai faim.
Check, please.   L'addition, s'il vous plaît.
Is there a hotel here?   Y a-t-il un hôtel ici?

Where is...?   Où est...?
What is the way to...?   Quelle est la route de...?
Take me to...   Conduisez-moi à...
I need...   J'ai besoin de...
I am ill.   Je suis malade.
Please call a doctor.   Appelez un docteur, s'il vous plaît.
I want to send a telegram.   Je voudrais envoyer un télégramme.
Where can I change money?   Où puis-je changer de l'argent?
Will you accept checks?   Acceptez-vous des chèques?
What is the postage?   Quel est l'affranchissement?

Right away.   Tout de suite.
Help!   Au secours!
Come in.   Entrez.
Stop.   Arrêtez.
Hurry.   Dépêchez-vous.
Go on.   Continuez.
Right.   A droite.
Left.   A gauche.
Straight ahead.   Tout droit.

Signs

Attention Caution		**Ralentir** Go Slow	
Danger Danger		**Défense de fumer** No smoking	
Sortie Exit		**Défense d'entrer** No admittance	
Entrée Entrance		**Dames** Women	
Halte, Arrêtez Stop		**Hommes** Men	
Fermé Closed		**Lavabos, toilettes** Lavatory	
Ouvert Open			

Weights and Measures

The French use the *Metric System* of weights and measures, a decimal system in which multiples are shown by the prefixes **déci-** (one-tenth); **centi-** (one hundredth); **milli-** (one thousandth); **hecto-** (hundred); and **kilo-** (thousand).

1 centimètre	=	.3937 inch
1 mètre	=	39.37 inches
1 kilomètre	=	.621 mile
1 centigramme	=	.1543 grain
1 gramme	=	15.432 grains
100 grammes	=	3.527 ounces
1 kilogramme	=	2.2046 pounds
1 tonne	=	2,204 pounds
1 centilitre	=	.338 ounce
1 litre	=	1.0567 quart (liquid);
	=	.908 quart (dry)
1 kilolitre	=	264.18 gallons

Numerals

Cardinal

1 un, une	22 vingt-deux	77 soixante-dix-sept
2 deux	23 vingt-trois	78 soixante-dix-huit
3 trois	24 vingt-quatre	79 soixante-dix-neuf
4 quatre	25 vingt-cinq	80 quatre-vingts
5 cinq	26 vingt-six	81 quatre-vingt-un
6 six	27 vingt-sept	82 quatre-vingt-deux
7 sept	28 vingt-huit	90 quatre-vingt-dix
8 huit	29 vingt-neuf	91 quatre-vingt-onze
9 neuf	30 trente	92 quatre-vingt-douze
10 dix	31 trente et un	
11 onze	32 trente-deux	100 cent
12 douze	40 quarante	101 cent un
13 treize	50 cinquante	102 cent deux
14 quatorze	60 soixante	200 deux cents
15 quinze	70 soixante-dix	300 trois cents
16 seize	71 soixante et onze	301 trois cent un
17 dix-sept	72 soixante-douze	1,000 mille
18 dix-huit	73 soixante-treize	5,000 cinq mille
19 dix-neuf	74 soixante-quartorze	1,000,000 un million
20 vingt	75 soixante-quinze	
21 vingt et un	76 soixante-seize	

Ordinal

1st premier, première	19th dix-neuvième
2nd deuxième, second	20th vingtième
3rd troisième	21th vingt-et-unième
4th quatrième	22nd vingt-deuxième
5th cinquième	30th trentième
6th sixième	40th quarantième
7th septième	50th cinquantième
8th huitième	60th soixantième
9th neuvième	70th soixante-dixième
10th dixième	80th quatre-vingtième
11th onzième	90th quatre-vingt-dixième
12th douzième	
13th treizième	100th centième
14th quatorzième	101st cent-unième
15th quinzième	102nd cent-deuxième
16th seizième	300th trois-centième
17th dix-septième	1,000th millième
18th dix-huitième	1,000,000th millionième

Days of the Week

Sunday	dimanche
Monday	lundi
Tuesday	mardi
Wednesday	mercredi
Thursday	jeudi
Friday	vendredi
Saturday	samedi

Months

January	janvier	July	juillet
February	février	August	août
March	mars	September	septembre
April	avril	October	octobre
May	mai	November	novembre
June	juin	December	décembre

French-English

A

à, *prep.* at, in, to.

abaisser, *vb.* depress, lower.

abandon, *n.m.* desertion, abandonment.

abandonné, *adj.* forlorn.

abandonner, *vb.* forsake, leave (desert). **s'a.**, give up, resign oneself.

abasourdir, *vb.* astound.

abattage, *n.m.* slaughter.

abattement, *n.m.* depression, dejection.

abattre, *vb.* depress, reduce; slaughter. **s'a.**, alight.

abbaye, *n.f.* abbey.

abbé, *n.m.* abbot.

abbesse, *n.f.* abbess.

abcès, *n.m.* abscess.

abdiquer, *vb.* abdicate.

abdomen, *n.m.* abdomen.

abeille, *n.f.* bee.

aberration, *n.f.* aberration.

abîme, *n.m.* abyss.

abîmer, *vb.* injure, spoil.

abject, *adj.* abject, low.

aboiement, *n.m.* barking.

abolir, *vb.* abolish.

abolition, *n.f.* abolition.

abominable, *adj.* vile, objectionable.

abondamment, *adv.* fully.

abondance, *n.f.* plenty.

abondant, *adj.* plentiful. **peu a.**, scanty.

abonder de, *vb.* abound in.

abonnement, *n.m.* subscription.

abonner, *vb.* **s'a.**, subscribe.

abord, **1.** *n.m.* approach. **2.** *adv.* **d'a.**, at first.

aborder, *vb.* accost.

aboutir, *vb.* end (in).

aboyer, *vb.* bark.

abréger, *vb.* abridge, shorten, abbreviate.

abreuver, *vb.* water (animals).

abréviation, *n.f.* abbreviation.

abri, *n.m.* shelter. **à l'a. de**, safe from.

abricot, *n.m.* apricot.

abriter, *vb.* shelter.

abrupt (-pt), *adj.* steep.

absence, *n.f.* absence.

absent, *adj.* absent. **rester a.**, stay away.

absenter, *vb.* **s'a.**, go away.

abside, *n.f.* apse.

absinthe, *n.f.* absinthe.

absolu, *adj.* utter, absolute.

absolution, *n.f.* absolution.

absorbant, *adj. and n.m.* absorbent.

absorbé dans, *adj.* intent on.

absorber, *vb.* engross, absorb. **s'a. dans**, pore over.

absorption, *n.f.* absorption.

absoudre, *vb.* absolve.

abstenir, *vb.* forbear. **s'a. de**, abstain from.

abstinence, *n.f.* abstinence.

abstraction, *n.f.* abstraction.

abstrait, *adj.* abstract.

absurde, *adj.* absurd, preposterous.

absurdité, *n.f.* nonsense, absurdity.

abus, *n.m.* abuse.

abuser de, *vb.* abuse.

académie, *n.f.* academy.

académique, *adj.* academic.

acajou, *n.m.* mahogany.

accablant, *adj.* oppressive.

accabler, *vb.* overwhelm, burden.

accaparer, *vb.* get a corner on.

accélération, *n.f.* acceleration.

accélérer, *vb.* quicken, hurry.

accent, *n.m.* stress, emphasis, accent.

accentuer, *vb.* accentuate, accent, emphasize.

acceptable, *adj.* acceptable.

acceptation, *n.f.* acceptance.

accepter, *vb.* accept, admit.

accepteur, *n.m.* accepter.

accès, *n.m.* access, approach; fit (of anger); bout (of fever).

accessible, *adj.* accessible.

accessoire, *n.m. and adj.* accessory, adjunct.

accident, *n.m.* crash, accident.

accidentel, *adj.* accidental.

acclamation, *n.f.* acclamation.

acclamer, *vb.* acclaim, cheer.

accommoder, *vb.* accommodate.

accompagnement, *n.m.* accompaniment.

accompagner, *vb.* accompany, go with.

accompli, *adj.* accomplished, complete, perfect.

accomplir, *vb.* accomplish, achieve, fulfill, carry out, perform.

accomplissement, *n.m.* performance, fulfillment, achievement, accomplishment.

accord, *n.m.* agreement, harmony; settlement; chord, tune. **être d'a.**, agree, concur.

accorder, *vb.* grant, bestow; allow; tune. **s'a.**, agree.

accouchement, *n.m.* delivery.

accoucher, *vb.* deliver.

accoucheur, *n.m.* **médecin-a.**, obstetrician.

accouder, *vb.* **s'a.**, lean.

accourir, *vb.* flock, run up.

accoutumer, *vb.* accustom.

accréditer, *vb.* accredit.

accrocher, *vb.* hook, hitch.

accroissement, *n.m.* growth, addition.

accroître, *vb.* increase.

accroupir, *vb.* **s'a.**, squat, crouch.

accueil, *n.m.* reception, greeting.

accueillir, *vb.* receive, greet.

accumuler, *vb.* heap up.

accusateur, *n.m.* accuser.

accusatif, *n.m.* accusative.

accusation, *n.f.* accusation.

accusatrice, *n.f.* accuser.

accusé, *n.m.* defendant.

accuser, *vb.* arraign, accuse.

acharné, *adj.* eager, fanatical.

achat, *n.m.* purchase.

acheminer, *vb.* start (toward).

acheter, *vb.* buy.

acheteur, *n.m.* buyer.

achèvement, *n.m.* completion.

achever, *vb.* complete, finish, achieve.

acide, *adj. and n.m.* acid.

acidité, *n.f.* acidity.

acier, *n.m.* steel.

acoustique, *n.f.* acoustics.

acquérir, *vb.* acquire, get, obtain.

acquiescement, *n.m.* acquiescence, compliance.

acquiescer à, *vb.* acquiesce, consent.

acquisition, *n.f.* acquisition, purchase.

acquittement, *n.m.* acquittal.

acquitter, *vb.* acquit.

âcre, *adj.* sharp.

acrobate, *n.m.f.* acrobat.

acte, *n.m.* act. **a. notarié**, deed. **a. de naissance**, birth certificate.

acteur, *n.m.* actor.

actif, **1.** *n.m.* assets (*comm.*). **2.** *adj.* active.

action, *n.f.* action, deed, act; (*comm.*) share.

action de contrôle en retour, *n.f.* feedback.

actionnaire, *n.m.* shareholder.

actionner, *vb.* operate.

activement, *adv.* busily.

activer, *vb.* activate, fan, hurry.

activité, *n.f.* activity.

actrice, *n.f.* actress.

actuel, *adj.* present.

actualités, *n.f.pl.* newsreel.

actuellement, *adv.* now, at present.

acuponcture, *n.f.* acupuncture.

adaptation, *n.f.* adaptation.

adapter, *vb.* adapt, fit, adjust, suit.

addition, *n.f.* addition, bill.

additionnel, *adj.* additional.

additionner, *vb.* add.

adhérent, *n.m.* follower.

adhérer, *vb.* cleave, adhere.

adhésif, *adj.* adhesive.

adieu, *n.m. and interj.* goodbye, farewell. **faire ses adieux**, take one's leave.

adjacent, *adj.* adjacent.

adjectif, *n.m.* adjective.

adjoint, *n.m.* fellow-worker, associate.

adjuger, *vb.* grant.

admettre, *vb.* allow, admit, grant.

administrateur, *n.m.* administrator, director, manager.

administratif, *adj.* administrative.

administration, *n.f.* administration, direction.

administrer, *vb.* administer, manage.

admirable, *adj.* admirable.

admirateur, *n.m.* admirer.

admiration, *n.f.* admiration.

admirer, *vb.* admire.

admission, *n.f.* confession, admission.

adolescence, *n.f.* adolescence.

adolescent, *adj. and n.m.f.* adolescent.

adonner, *vb.* **s'a. à**, indulge in, become addicted to.

adopter, *vb.* adopt.

adoption, *n.f.* adoption.

adoration, *n.f.* adoration.

adorer, *vb.* worship, adore.

adosser, *vb.* **s'a. à**, lean on.

adoucir, *vb.* soothe.

adresse, *n.f.* address; skill, ability.

adresser, *vb.* address (a letter); direct. **s'a. à**, apply to.

adroit, *adj.* skillful, clever, handy.

adulte, *adj. and n.m.f.* adult.

adultère, *n.m.* adultery.

adultérer, *vb.* adulterate.

adverbe, *n.m.* adverb.

adversaire, *n.m.f.* opponent.

adverse, *adj.* adverse.

adversité, *n.f.* adversity.

aéré, *adj.* airy.

aérer, *vb.* air (a room).

aérien, *adj.* aerial.

aérogare, *n.f.* airline (city) station.

aeroglisseur, *n.m.* hovercraft.

aéroport, *n.m.* airport.

affable, *adj.* affable.

affaiblir, *vb.* weaken.

affaire, *n.f.* affair, matter; deal; *(pl.)* business. **se tirer d'a.**, manage (somehow). **homme d'a.s**, businessman.

affairé, *adj.* busy.

affaissement, *n.m.* collapse.

affaisser, *vb.* **s'a.**, collapse.

affamé, *adj.* hungry, famished.

affamer, *vb.* starve.

affectation, *n.f.* affectation.

affecter, *vb.* affect.

affection, *n.f.* affection.

affectueux, *adj.* affectionate.

affermir, *vb.* strengthen.

affété, *adj.* finicky.

affiche, *n.f.* poster.

afficher, *vb.* post.

affilier, *vb.* affiliate.

affinité, *n.f.* affinity.

affirmatif, *adj.* affirmative.

affirmation, *n.f.* statement.

affirmer, *vb.* assert, state, maintain, testify, affirm.

affliction, *n.f.* affliction.

affligé, *adj.* sorrowful.

affliger, *vb.* distress, afflict, grieve.

affluent, *n.m.* tributary.

affluer, *vb.* flow into.

affoler, *vb.* drive mad.

affranchir, *vb.* free.

affranchissement, *n.m.* postage.

affréter, *vb.* charter (boat).

affreusement, *adv.* terribly.

affreux, *adj.* dreadful, terrible, horrid, dire.

affront, *n.m.* affront, insult.

affronter, *vb.* confront, face.

afin, **1. a. de**, *prep.* in order to. **2.** *conj.* **a. que**, so that.

Africain, *n.m.* African.

africain, *adj.* African.

Afrique, *n.f.* Africa.

agacer, *vb.* vex, irritate.

âge, *n.m.* age. **d'un certain â.**, elderly. **le moyen â.**, the Middle Ages.

âgé, *adj.* aged.

agence, *n.f.* (comm.) agency.

agenouiller, *vb.* **s'a.**, kneel.

agent, *n.m.* agent. **a. de police**, policeman. **a. de change**, stockbroker.

aggraver, *vb.* aggravate.

agile, *adj.* nimble.

agir, *vb.* act. **s'a. de**, be a question of.

agitateur, *n.m.* agitator.

agitation, *n.f.* excitement, disturbance, commotion, flutter.

agité, *adj.* upset, excited.

agiter, *vb.* agitate, wave, wag, shake, stir. **s'a.**, toss, flutter.

agneau, *n.m.* lamb.

agonie, *n.f.* agony.

agrafe, *n.f.* clasp.

agrafer, *vb.* clasp.

agrandir, *vb.* enlarge.

agréable, *adj.* likable, pleasant, enjoyable, agreeable.

agréer, *vb.* accept, consent.

agrégation, *n.f.* aggregation, fellowship.

agrément, *n.m.* pleasure.

agresseur, *n.m.* aggressor.

agressif, *adj.* aggressive.

agression, *n.f.* aggression.

agricole, *adj.* agricultural.

agriculture, *n.f.* agriculture.

ahurir, *vb.* bewilder, fluster.

aide, *n.f.* help, aid.

aider, *vb.* help, aid.

aïeul (à yœl), *n.m.* grandfather.

aïeule (à yœl), *n.f.* grandmother.

aïeux, *n.m.pl.* ancestors.

aigle, *n.m.* eagle.

aiglefin, *n.m.* haddock.

aigre, *adj.* sour.

aigu, *adj.* shrill, keen, pointed.

aiguille, *n.f.* needle.

aiguisé, *adj.* keen.

aiguiser, *vb.* sharpen.

ail (à ê) *n.m.* garlic.

aile, *n.f.* wing.

ailleurs, *adv.* elsewhere. **d'a.**, in addition, anyhow.

aimable, *adj.* kind, pleasant, amiable.

aimant, *n.m.* magnet.

aimer, *vb.* love, like.

aine, *n.f.* groin.

aîné (è nä), **1.** *adj. and n.m.* elder. **2.** *adj.* eldest, senior.

ainsi, *adv.* thus, so.

air, *n.m.* air, looks. **en plein air**, in the open air.

aire, *n.f.* area.

aise, *n.f.* ease, comfort. **à l'a.**, comfortable.

aisé, *adj.* substantial, well-to-do; easy.

aisselle, *n.f.* armpit.

ajourner, *vb.* put off. **s'a.**, adjourn.

ajouter, *vb.* add.

ajustage, *n.m.* fitting.

ajuster, *vb.* fit, fix, adjust.

alarme, *n.f.* alarm.

alarmer, *vb.* alarm.

album, *n.m.* album.

alcool (-kôl), *n.m.* alcohol.

alcoolique (-kôl-), *adj.* alcoholic.

alcôve, *n.f.* alcove.

alentours, *n.m.pl.* neighborhood, surroundings.

alerte, *adj.* spry, active, alert.

algèbre, *n.f.* algebra.

aliéné, *n.m.* lunatic.

aliéner, *vb.* alienate.

aligner, *vb.* line up.

aliment, *n.m.* food.

alimentation, *n.f.* feeding.

alimenter, *vb.* feed.

alinéa, *n.m.* paragraph.

allaiter, *vb.* nurse.

allée, *n.f.* path, avenue, aisle.

allégation, *n.f.* allegation.

alléger, *vb.* lighten, soothe.

allégresse, *n.f.* glee, delight, mirth.

alléguer, *vb.* plead, allege.

Allemagne, *n.f.* Germany.

Allemand, *n.m.* German (person).

allemand, **1.** *n.m.* German (language). **2.** *adj.* German.

aller, *vb.* go. **s'en a.**, go away. **a. à**, fit. **se laisser a.**, drift. **a. bien**, fare well. **a. mal**, fare ill. **a. et retour**, round trip.

alliage, *n.m.* alloy.

alliance, *n.f.* alliance, union.

allié, **1.** *n.m.* ally, relation. **2.** *adj.* allied.

allier, *vb.* ally. **s'a. à**; join with.

allô, *interj.* hello.

allocation, *n.f.* allowance.

allonger, *vb.* lengthen, prolong.

allons, *interj.* well, come now.

allouer, *vb.* grant.

allumer, *vb.* light.

allumette, *n.f.* match.

allure, *n.f.* pace, gait.

allusion, *n.f.* hint, allusion. **faire a. à**, allude to.

almanach (-nä), *n.m.* almanac.

alors, **1.** *adv.* then. **2.** *conj.* **a. que**, when.

alouette, *n.f.* lark.

alphabet, *n.m.* alphabet.

altérer, *vb.* change.

alternatif, *adj.* alternate.

alternative, *n.f.* alternative.

alterner, *vb.* alternate.

Altesse, *n.f.* Highness (title).

altitude, *n.f.* altitude.

aluminium, *n.m.* aluminum.

amabilité, *n.f.* kindness.

amalgamer, *vb.* amalgamate.

amande, *n.f.* kernel; almond.

amant, *n.m.* lover.

amas, *n.m.* hoard, mass.

amasser, *vb.* hoard, gather, amass.

amateur, *n.m.* amateur.

ambassade, *n.f.* embassy.

ambassadeur, *n.m.* ambassador.

ambassadrice, *n.f.* ambassadress.

ambigu *m.*, ambiguë *f.* adj. ambiguous.

ambiguïté, *n.f.* ambiguity.

ambitieux, *adj.* ambitious.

ambition, *n.f.* ambition.

ambre, *n.m.* amber.

ambulance, *n.f.* ambulance.

âme, *n.f.* soul.

amélioration, *n.f.* improvement.

améliorer, *vb.* improve.

aménager, *vb.* fit up.

amende, *n.f.* fine. mettre à l'a., fine.

amendement, *n.m.* amendment.

amender, *vb.* amend.

amener, *vb.* bring, lead.

amer (-r), *adj.* bitter.

Américain, *n.m.* American.

américain, *adj.* American.

Amérique, *n.f.* America.

A. du Nord, North America.

A. du Sud, South America.

amertume, *n.f.* bitterness.

ameublement, *n.m.* furniture.

ami *m.*, amie *f. n.* friend.

amical, *adj.* friendly, amicable.

amidon, *n.m.* starch.

amiral, *n.m.* admiral.

amitié, *n.f.* friendship.

ammoniaque, *n.f.* ammonia.

amniocentèse, *n.f.* amniocentesis.

amoindrir, *vb.* lessen, reduce.

amollir, *vb.* soften.

amortir, *vb.* deaden, soften.

amour, *n.m.* love.

amoureux, 1. *n.m.* lover. 2. *adj.* in love, amorous.

amour-propre, *n.m.* vanity, pride, conceit.

ample, *adj.* ample, spacious.

ampleur, *n.f.* plenty, compass.

amplifier, *vb.* increase, enlarge, develop.

ampoule, *n.f.* blister; (electric) bulb.

amputer, *vb.* amputate.

amusement, *n.m.* fun, pastime, entertainment.

amuser, *vb.* entertain. s'a., have a good time.

amygdale, *n.f.* tonsil.

an, *n.m.* year.

analogie, *n.f.* analogy.

analogue, *adj.* similar, analogous.

analyse, *n.f.* analysis.

analyser, *vb.* analyze.

anarchie, *n.f.* anarchy.

anatomie, *n.f.* anatomy.

ancêtre, *n.m.* forefather, ancestor.

anche, *n.f.* reed.

anchois, *n.m.* anchovy.

ancien *m.*, ancienne *f.* adj. ancient, old, former.

ancre, *n.f.* anchor.

ancrer, *vb.* anchor.

âne *m.*, ânesse *f. n.* ass, donkey.

anéantir, *vb.* annihilate, destroy.

anecdote, *n.f.* anecdote.

anesthésique, *adj. and n.m.* anesthetic.

ange, *n.m.* angel.

Anglais, *n.m.* Englishman.

anglais, *adj. and n.m.* English.

Anglaise, *n.f.* Englishwoman.

angle, *n.m.* angle, corner.

Angleterre, *n.f.* England.

angoissant, *adj.* in anguish.

angoisse, *n.f.* agony, pang, anguish.

anguille, *n.f.* eel.

anguleux, *adj.* angular.

anicroche, *n.f.* hitch.

animal, *n.m. and adj.* animal.

animation, *n.f.* animation.

animer, *vb.* enliven, animate.

animosité, *n.f.* animosity.

anneau, *n.m.* ring, circle.

année, *n.f.* year; vintage.

annexe, *n.m.* annex.

annexer, *vb.* annex.

annexion, *n.f.* annexation.

anniversaire, *n.m.* anniversary, birthday.

annonce, *n.f.* advertisement, announcement.

annoncer, *vb.* advertise, announce.

annotation, *n.f.* annotation.

annoter, *vb.* annotate.

annuaire, *n.m.* directory.

annuel, *adj.* yearly, annual.

annulation, *n.f.* cancellation.

annuler, *vb.* cancel, void, annul.

ânonner, *vb.* stammer.

anonyme, *adj.* anonymous.

anormal, *adj.* irregular, abnormal.

anse, *n.f.* handle; bay.

antagonisme, *n.m.* antagonism.

antarctique, *adj.* antarctic.

antécédent, *adj. and n.m.* antecedent.

antécédents, *n.m.pl.* record.

antenne, *n.f.* antenna.

antérieur, *adj.* previous; fore, front.

anthracite, *n.m.* anthracite.

antichambre, *n.f.* entrance hall.

anticipation, *n.f.* anticipation.

anticiper, *vb.* anticipate.

antidote, *n.m.* antidote.

antilope, *n.f.* antelope.

antinucléaire, *adj.* antinuclear.

antipathie, *n.f.* antipathy.

antiquaire, *n.m.* antique dealer.

antique, *adj.* ancient, antiquated, antique.

antiquité, *n.f.* antiquity.

antiseptique, *adj. and n.m.* antiseptic.

antre, *n.m.* den.

anxiété, *n.f.* anxiety, worry.

anxieux, *adj.* anxious.

août (oo), *n.m.* August.

apaiser, *vb.* allay, quiet, appease.

apathie, *n.f.* apathy.

apercevoir, *vb.* perceive. s'a. de, realize.

aperçu, *n.m.* outline.

apéritif, *n.m.* appetizer.

apitoyer, *vb.* move (emotionally).

aplanir, *vb.* even off.

aplatir, *vb.* flatten.

aplomb, *n.m.* poise, boldness.

apoplexie, *n.f.* apoplexy.

apostolique, *adj.* apostolic.

apôtre, *n.m.* apostle.

apparaître, *vb.* appear.

appareil, *n.m.* gear, appliance, device. a. photographique, camera.

apparence, *n.f.* appearance, looks.

apparent, *adj.* noticeable, apparent.

apparition, *n.f.* appearance, ghost.

appartement, *n.m.* apartment.

appartenir, *vb.* belong, pertain.

appât, *n.m.* bait.

appel, *n.m.* call, appeal.

appeler, *vb.* call, summon, appeal. s'a., be named.

appendice, *n.m.* appendix.

appétit, *n.m.* appetite.

applaudir, *vb.* applaud.

applaudissements, *n.m.pl.* applause.

applicable, *adj.* applicable.

application, *n.f.* application, industry.

appliqué, *adj.* industrious.

appliquer, *vb.* apply (put on), stick. s'a., work hard.

appointements, *n.m.pl.* salary.

apporter, *vb.* bring, fetch.

apposer, *vb.* affix.

appréciable, *adj.* appreciable.

appréciation, *n.f.* appreciation.

apprécier, *vb.* appreciate, value.

appréhension, *n.f.* apprehension.

apprendre, *vb.* learn. a. à, teach (to). a. par cœur, memorize.

apprenti, *n.m.* apprentice.

apprentissage, *n.m.* apprenticeship.

apprêt, *n.m.* preparation.

apprêter, *vb.* s'a., prepare, get ready.

apprivoiser, *vb.* tame.

approbation, *n.f.* endorsement, approval, approbation.

approche, *n.f.* approach.

approcher, *vb.* s'a. de, approach, go toward.

approfondir, *vb.* deepen.

appropriation, *n.f.* appropri-

approprier, *vb.* **s'a.,** take over, appropriate.

approuver, *vb.* approve.

approvisionnement, *n.m.* supply.

approximatif, *adj.* approximate.

appui, *n.m.* support.

appuyer (-pwě-), *vb.* support, endorse, advocate. **a. sur,** emphasize.

après, 1. *adv., prep.* after. **2.** *conj.* **a. que,** after. **d'a.,** according to.

après-demain, *n.m.* day after tomorrow.

après-midi, *n.m.f.* afternoon.

âpreté, *n.f.* harshness, bitterness.

à-propos, *n.m.* fitness.

apte à, *adj.* apt, suitable for.

aptitude, *n.f.* fitness, ability, aptitude.

aqualit, *n.m.* waterbed.

aquarelle (-kwǎ-), *n.f.* water color.

aquarium (-kwǎ-), *n.m.* aquarium.

aquatique (-kwǎ-), *adj.* aquatic.

aqueux, *adj.* watery.

Arabe, *n.m.f.* Arab, Arabian.

arabe, 1. *n.m.* Arabic. **2.** *adj.* Arab, Arabian, Arabic.

arachide, *n.f.* peanut.

araignée, *n.f.* spider. **toile d'a.,** cobweb.

arbitrage, *n.m.* arbitration.

arbitraire, *adj.* arbitrary.

arbitre, *n.m.f.* umpire, arbitrator.

arbitrer, *vb.* arbitrate.

arbre, *n.m.* tree.

arbrisseau, *n.m.* shrub.

arc (-k), *n.m.* arc, arch, bow.

arcade, *n.f.* arcade.

arc-boutant, *n.m.* flying buttress.

arc-en-ciel, *n.m.* rainbow.

archaïque (àrk-), *adj.* archaic.

arche, *n.f.* arch (of bridge); ark.

archet, *n.m.* bow.

archevêque, *n.m.* archbishop.

archipel, *n.m.* archipelago.

architecte, *n.m.* architect.

architectural, *adj.* architectural.

architecture, *n.f.* architecture.

archives, *n.f.pl.* files, archives.

arctique, *adj.* arctic.

ardemment, *adv.* eagerly.

ardent, *adj.* eager, fiery, ardent.

ardeur, *n.f.* ardor.

ardoise, *n.f.* slate.

arène, *n.f.* arena, ring.

argent, *n.m.* silver, money.

argenterie, *n.f.* silverware.

Argentin, *n.m.* Argentine.

argentin, *adj.* Argentine.

argile, *n.f.* clay.

argot, *n.m.* slang.

argument, *n.m.* argument (reasoning).

argumenter, *vb.* argue (reason).

aride, *adj.* arid.

aristocrate, *n.m.f.* aristocrat.

aristocratie, *n.f.* aristocracy.

aristocratique, *adj.* aristocratic.

arithmétique, *n.f.* arithmetic.

arme, *n.f.* weapon; arm.

armée, *n.f.* army.

armement, *n.m.* armament.

arme nucléaire, *n.f.* nuclear weapon.

armer, *vb.* arm.

armistice, *n.m.* armistice.

armoire, *n.f.* cupboard, closet, wardrobe.

armure, *n.f.* armor.

aromatique, *adj.* aromatic.

arome, *n.m.* flavor, aroma.

arpenter, *vb.* pace.

arracher, *vb.* snatch.

arrangement, *n.m.* arrangement, settlement.

arranger, *vb.* settle, trim, fix, arrange.

arrestation, *n.f.* arrest, apprehension. **en état d'a.,** under arrest.

arrêt, *n.m.* stop.

arrêté, *n.m.* decree.

arrêter, *vb.* stop, check, halt, arrest.

arrière, *adv.* behind, back. **en a.,** backward. **marche a.,** reverse (gear).

arriéré, 1. *n.m.* arrear. **2.** *adj.* backward.

arrière-garde, *n.f.* rear guard.

arrivée, *n.f.* arrival.

arriver, *vb.* happen, reach, arrive.

arrogance, *n.f.* arrogance.

arrogant, *adj.* arrogant.

arroger, *vb.* arrogate, assume.

arrondir, *vb.* round off.

arrondissement, *n.m.* district.

arroser, *vb.* water, sprinkle; baste (meat).

arsenal, *n.m.* arsenal.

arsenic, *n.m.* arsenic.

art, *n.m.* art. **beaux-arts,** fine arts.

artère, *n.f.* artery.

artichaut, *n.m.* artichoke.

article, *n.m.* article, item, entry. **a. de fond,** editorial.

articulation, *n.f.* joint, articulation.

articuler, *vb.* articulate.

artifice, *n.m.* artifice.

artificiel, *adj.* artificial.

artificieux, *adj.* artful.

artillerie, *n.f.* artillery.

artisan, *n.m.* craftsman, artisan.

artiste, *n.m.* artist.

artistique, *adj.* artistic.

as (ǎs), *n.m.* ace.

ascenseur, *n.m.* elevator.

ascension, *n.f.* ascent (of a mountain).

Asiatique, *n.m.f.* Asian.

asiatique, *adj.* Asian.

Asie, *n.f.* Asia.

asile, *n.m.* haven, refuge, asylum.

aspect (-pě), *n.m.* looks, appearance, aspect.

asperger, *vb.* sprinkle.

asperges, *n.f.pl.* asparagus.

asphalte, *n.m.,* asphalt.

aspirateur, *n.m.* vacuum cleaner.

aspiration, *n.f.* aspiration, longing.

aspirer, *vb.* aspire, breathe.

assaillant, *n.m.* assailant.

assaillir, *vb.* assail, attack.

assaisonner, *vb.* season.

assassin, *n.m.* assassin, murderer.

assassinat, *n.m.* assassination, murder.

assassiner, *vb.* assassinate, murder.

assaut, *n.m.* assault, attack.

assemblage, *n.m.* collection.

assemblée, *n.f.* congregation, assembly.

assembler, *vb.* convene, gather. **s'a.,** assemble.

assentiment, *n.m.* assent.

asseoir, *vb.* seat. **s'a.,** sit down.

assertion, *n.f.* assertion.

asservir, *vb.* enslave.

assez (de), *n.* and *adv.* enough (of); pretty much.

assidu, *adj.* assiduous, industrious.

assiduité, *n.f.* industry.

assiéger, *vb.* besiege.

assiette, *n.f.* plate.

assigner, *vb.* assign.

assimiler, *vb.* assimilate.

assis, *adj.* seated.

assistance, *n.f.* those present.

assister à, *vb.* attend, be present at.

association, *n.f.* soccer; association, company; connection.

associé, 1. *n.m.* partner, associate. **2.** *adj.* associated.

associer, *vb.* associate.

assombrir, *vb.* **s'a.,** grow dark.

assommer, *vb.* murder, slaughter.

Assomption, *n.f.* Assumption (eccles.).

assortiment, *n.m.* assortment.

assortir, *vb.* match; tune.

assoupir, *vb.* **s'a.,** get drowsy.

assourdir, *vb.* deafen.

assujetti, *adj.* subject.

assujettir, *vb.* subject.

assumer, *vb.* assume.

assurance, *n.f.* assurance, insurance.

assuré, *adj.* sure.

assurer, *vb.* insure; assure. **s'a. de,** make certain.

assureur, *n.m.* insurer.

astérisque, *n.m.* asterisk.

astre, *n.m.* star.

astronaute, *n.m.* astronaut.

astronome, *n.m.* astronomer.

astronomie, *n.f.* astronomy.

astucieux, *adj.* tricky.

atelier, *n.m.* studio, (work)shop.

athée, *n.m.f.* atheist.
athlète, *n.m.f.* athlete.
athlétique, *adj.* athletic.
atlantique, *adj.* Atlantic.
atlas (-s), *n.m.* atlas.
atmosphère, *n.f.* atmosphere.
atmosphérique, *adj.* atmospheric.
atome, *n.m.* atom.
atomique, *adj.* atomic.
atroce, *adj.* atrocious, outrageous.
atrocité, *n.f.* atrocity.
attachement, *n.m.* attachment, affection.
attacher, *vb.* tie, fasten, join, attach.
attaque, *n.f.* attack.
attaquer, *vb.* attack.
attardé, *adj.* belated.
attarder, *vb.* s'a., linger, delay.
atteindre, *vb.* reach, attain; strike.
atteint, *adj.* stricken.
atteinte, *n.f.* reach. hors d'a., out of reach.
attelage, *n.m.* team.
atteler, *vb.* hitch up, harness.
attendre, *vb.* wait (for), await. s'a. à, expect.
attendrir, *vb.* soften, move. se laisser a., relent.
attendrissement, *n.m.* feeling, emotion.
attentat, *n.m.* criminal attack, outrage.
attente, *n.f.* expectation, wait.
attentif, *adj.* thoughtful, attentive.
attention, *n.f.* notice, heed, attention. faire a., heed, pay attention.
atténuer, *vb.* extenuate.
atterrir, *vb.* land.
attester, *vb.* attest.
attirer, *vb.* attract, entice, lure.
attitude, *n.f.* attitude.
attouchement, *n.m.* touch.
attraction, *n.f.* attraction.
attrait, *n.m.* charm.
attraper, *vb.* catch.
attrayant, *adj.* attractive.
attribuer, *vb.* ascribe, attribute.
attribut, *n.m.* attribute, characteristic.
attrister, *vb.* grieve.
au *m.*, à la *f.*, aux *pl. prep.* to the, in the.
aube, *n.f.* dawn.
auberge, *n.f.* inn.
aubergine, *n.f.* eggplant.
aubergiste, *n.m.* innkeeper.
aucun, *pron.* none.
aucunement, *adv.* not at all.
audace, *n.f.* audacity.
audacieux, *adj.* daring, bold.
au-dessous, 1. *adv.* below. 2. *prep.* au-d. de, beneath, under.
au-dessus, 1. *adv.* above. 2. *prep.* au-d. de, over, above.
audience, *n.f.* audience.
audiovisuel, *adj.* audiovisual.
auditoire, *n.m.* audience, assembly.

auge, *n.f.* trough.
augmentation, *n.f.* increase, raise, rise.
augmenter, *vb.* increase.
augure, *n.m.* omen, augury. de bon a., auspicious. de mauvais a., ominous.
augurer, *vb.* augur.
aujourd'hui, *adv.* today.
aumône, *n.f.* alms.
aumônier, *n.m.* chaplain.
auparavant, *adv.* before (time).
auprès de, *prep.* next, near, beside.
auréole, *n.f.* halo.
aurore, *n.f.* dawn.
auspice, *n.m.* auspice.
aussi, *adv.* too, also; so, as; therefore.
austère, *adj.* austere, severe.
austérité, *n.f.* austerity.
Australie, *n.f.* Australia.
Australien, *n.m.* Australian.
australien, *adj.* Australian.
autant, *adv.* so much, as much. a. que, as (so) much as. d'a. que, since. a. plus, so much the more.
autel, *n.m.* altar.
auteur, *n.m.* author, originator.
authentique, *adj.* true, genuine, authentic.
auto, *n.f.* auto.
autobus (-s), *n.m.* bus.
automatique, *adj.* automatic.
automne (-tôn), *n.m.* fall.
automobile, *n.f.* automobile.
autonomie, *n.f.* autonomy.
autorisation, *n.f.* license, authorization.
autoriser, *vb.* authorize.
autoritaire, *adj.* authoritative.
autorité, *n.f.* authority.
autour, 1. *adv.* around. 2. *prep.* a. de, around.
autre, 1. *adj.* other. 2. *pron.* other, else. l'un l'a., one another. quelqu'un d'a., someone else.
autrefois, *adv.* formerly.
autrement, *adv.* otherwise.
Autriche, *n.f.* Austria.
Autrichien, *n.m.* Austrian.
autrichien, *adj.* Austrian.
autruche, *n.f.* ostrich.
autrui, *pron.* someone else, others.
auxiliaire, *adj.* auxiliary.
avalanche, *n.f.* avalanche.
avaler, *vb.* swallow.
avance, *n.f.* advance. d'a., beforehand. en a., fast (clock).
avancé, *adj.* forward, advanced.
avancement, *n.m.* advance; advancement; promotion.
avancer, *vb.* proceed; come or go forward or onward.
avances, *n.f.pl.* advance. faire des a. à, make approaches to.
avant, 1. *n.m.* fore, bow. 2. *adv.*, *prep.* before. 3. *conj.* a. que, before. en a., forward, onward. en a. de, ahead of.
avantage, *n.m.* advantage.

avantageux, *adj.* advantageous; favorable; profitable.
avant-bras, *n.m.* forearm.
avant-garde, *n.f.* vanguard.
avant-hier (-yâr), *n.m.* day before yesterday.
avant-toit, *n.m.* eaves.
avare, 1. *n.m.f.* miser. 2. *adj.* miserly, stingy.
avarice, *n.f.* avarice.
avec, *prep.* with.
avenant, *adj.* comely. à l'a., accordingly.
avenir, *n.m.* future.
Avent, *n.m.* (*eccles.*) Advent.
aventure, *n.f.* adventure.
aventurer, *vb.* s'a., take a chance.
aventureux, *adj.* adventurous.
aventurier, *n.m.* adventurer.
avenue, *n.f.* avenue.
averse, *n.f.* shower.
aversion, *n.f.* aversion, dislike.
avertir, *vb.* notify, warn.
avertissement, *n.m.* warning.
avertisseur d'incendie, *n.m.* fire alarm.
aveu, *n.m.* admission, confession.
aveugle, *adj.* blind.
aveuglement, *n.m.* blindness.
aveuglément, *adv.* blindly.
aveugler, *vb.* blind.
aviateur, *n.m.* flier, aviator.
aviation, *n.f.* air force, aviation.
avide, *adj.* eager, greedy, avid.
avidité, *n.f.* greediness.
avilir, *vb.* debase, disgrace.
avion, *n.m.* airplane. a. de bombardement, bomber. par a., via air mail.
avis, *n.m.* notice, opinion, advice (*comm.*).
aviser, *vb.* inform, notify. s'a. (de), decide.
avocat, *n.m.* lawyer; advocate.
avoine, *n.f.* oat.
avoir, *vb.* have. il y a, ago.
avortement, *n.m.* abortion.
avoué, *n.m.* attorney, lawyer.
avouer, *vb.* confess, admit, avow.
avril (-l), *n.m.* April.
axe, *n.m.* axis.
ayatollah, *n.m.* ayatollah.
azur, *n.m.* azure, blue.
azuré, *adj.* azure.

B

babeurre, *n.m.* buttermilk.
babil, *n.m.* babble.
babiller, *vb.* babble.
bâbord, *n.m.* (*naut.*) port.
babouin, *n.m.* baboon.
bac, *n.m.* ferryboat. passage en b., ferry.
bachelier, *n.m.* graduate.
bacille (-l), *n.m.* bacillus.
bactérie, *n.f.* bacterium.
bactériologie, *n.f.* bacteriology.
badaud, *adj.* silly.

bagages, *n.m.pl.* luggage.

bagatelle, *n.f.* trifle.

bague, *n.f.* ring.

baguette, *n.f.* wand, stick; long, thin loaf of bread.

baie, *n.f.* bay, creek; berry.

baigner, *vb.* bathe.

baigneur, *n.m.* bather.

baignoire, *n.f.* bathtub.

bail, *n.m.* lease.

bâillement, *n.m.* yawn.

bâiller, *vb.* yawn.

bâillon, *n.m.* gag.

bain, *n.m.* bath.

baïonnette, *n.f.* bayonet.

baiser, *n.m. and vb.* kiss.

baissé, *adj.* downcast.

baisser, *vb.* lower, sink.

bal, *n.m.* ball.

balai, *n.m.* broom. **b. à laver,** mop.

balance, *n.f.* scales, balance.

balancement, *n.m.* rocking, swinging.

balancer, *vb.* rock, swing, sway. **se b.,** roll, hover.

balayer, *vb.* sweep.

balbutier, *vb.* stammer.

balcon, *n.m.* balcony.

baldaquin, *n.m.* canopy.

baleine, *n.f.* whale.

ballade, *n.f.* ballad.

balle, *n.f.* bullet, ball; bale.

ballet, *n.m.* ballet.

ballon, *n.m.* balloon.

ballot, *n.m.* bundle.

ballotter, *vb.* shake.

balsamique, *adj.* balmy.

bambou, *n.m.* bamboo.

ban, *n.m.* ban. **mettre au b.,** ban.

banal, *adj.* trite.

banane, *n.f.* banana.

banc, *n.m.* bench.

bandage, *n.m.* bandage.

bande, *n.f.* strip, stripe; pack, gang, band.

bande vidéo, *n.f.* videotape.

bandit, *n.m.* bandit, robber, knave.

banlieue, *n.f.* suburbs.

bannière, *n.f.* banner.

bannir, *vb.* banish.

bannissement, *n.m.* banishment.

banque, *n.f.* bank. **billet de b.,** banknote.

banqueroute, *n.f.* bankruptcy.

banqueroutier, *n.* bankrupt.

banquet, *n.m.* banquet, feast.

banquier, *n.m.* banker.

baptême (bä tĕm), *n.m.* christening, baptism.

baptiser (bä tē-), *vb.* christen, baptize.

Baptiste (bä tēst), *n.m.* Baptist.

baptistère (bä tēs-), *n.m.* baptistery.

bar, *n.m.* bar; bass (fish).

baraque, *n.f.* booth, stall.

baratter, *vb.* churn.

barbare, 1. *n.m.f.* barbarian. 2. *adj.* barbarian, barbarous, wild.

barbarie, *n.f.* cruelty.

barbe, *n.f.* beard.

barbouiller, *vb.* daub, blur.

baromètre, *n.m.* barometer.

baron, *n.m.* bàron.

barque, *n.f.* boat.

barrage, *n.m.* dam.

barre, *n.f.* bar, rail(ing). **b. du gouvernail,** helm.

barreau, *n.m.* bar.

barrer, *vb.* shut out.

barricade, *n.f.* barricade.

barrière, *n.f.* gate; bar, barrier; fence.

barrique, *n.f.* barrel, cask.

bas, *n.m.* stocking.

bas *m.,* **basse** *f. adj.* base, low, soft. **en b.,** down(ward); downstairs. **b. côté,** aisle.

bascule, *n.f.* seesaw. **chaise à b.,** rocking-chair.

base, *n.f.* base, basis.

basse, *n.f.* bass (voice).

basse-cour, *n.f.* barnyard.

bassesse, *n.f.* baseness.

bassin, *n.m.* basin, dock.

bataille, *n.f.* battle.

bataillon, *n.m.* battalion.

bâtard, *adj. and n.m.* bastard.

bateau, *n.m.* boat.

bâtiment, *n.m.* building.

bâtir, *vb.* build.

bâton, *n.m.* stick, staff.

battant, *n.m.* flap, door.

batte, *n.f.* bat.

battement, *n.m.* beat.

batterie, *n.f.* battery.

battre, *vb.* beat, strike; flap, pulsate. **se b.,** fight.

baume, *n.m.* balm.

bavard, *adj.* talkative, gossipy.

bavardage, *n.m.* gossip, chatter.

bavarder, *vb.* gossip, chat(ter).

bavette, *n.f.* bib.

bazar, *n.m.* bazaar.

béatitude, *n.f.* bliss.

beau, bel *m.,* **belle** *f. adj.* beautiful, handsome, fair, lovely, fine. **avoir beau,** (to do something) in vain. **faire beau,** be fine (weather).

beaucoup (de), *adj.* a lot, a great deal; much, many. **de b.,** by far.

beau-frère, *n.m.* brother-in-law.

beau-père, *n.m.* father-in-law.

beauté, *n.f.* beauty. **grain de b.,** mole.

bébé, *n.m.* baby.

bec, *n.m.* beak, bill; spot; burner.

bêche, *n.f.* spade.

bêcher, *vb.* dig.

becqueter, *vb.* peck.

bée, *adj.* **rester bouche b.,** stand gaping.

bégayer, *vb.* stammer.

bêler, *vb.* bleat.

Belge, *n.m.f.* Belgian.

belge, *adj.* Belgian.

Belgique, *n.f.* Belgium.

bélier, *n.m.* ram.

belle-fille, *n.f.* daughter-in-law.

belle-mère, *n.f.* mother-in-law; stepmother.

belligérant, *adj. and n.m.* belligerent.

bénédiction, *n.f.* blsessing, benediction.

bénéfice, *n.m.* benefit, advantage, profit.

bénéficier, *vb.* benefit, profit.

bénin *m.,* **bénigne** *f. adj.* benign.

bénir, *vb.* bless.

béquille, *n.f.* crutch.

berceau, *n.m.* cradle, bower.

bercer, *vb.* rock.

berge, *n.f.* bank.

berger, *n.m.* shepherd.

besogne, *n.f.* (piece of) work.

besoin, *n.m.* need, want. **avoir b.,** need.

bestiaux, *n.m.pl.* cattle.

bétail, *n.m.* cattle, animals.

bête, 1. *n.f.* beast, animal. 2. *adj.* stupid, dumb.

bêtise, *n.f.* nonsense.

béton, *n.m.* concrete.

betterave, *n.f.* beet.

beurre, *n.m.* butter.

bévue, *n.f.* blunder, boner.

biais, *n.m.* slant; bias. **en b.,** at an angle.

bibelot, *n.m.* trinket.

biberon, *n.m.* baby's bottle.

Bible, *n.f.* Bible.

bibliothèque, *n.f.* library; bookcase.

biblique, *adj.* biblical.

bicyclette, *n.f.* bicycle. **faire de la b.,** cycle.

bidon, *n.m.* can.

bien, *n.m.* good; *(pl.)* goods, property, estate. **faire du b. à,** benefit.

bien, *adv.* well. **b. entendu,** of course. **aller b.,** be well. **vouloir b.,** be willing. **b. que,** although.

bien-aimé, *n.m.f. and adj.* darling.

bien-être, *n.m.* welfare.

bienfaisant, *adj.* beneficent, kind, humane.

bienfait, *n.m.* benefit.

bienfaiteur, *n.m.* benefactor.

bienheureux, *adj.* blessed.

bientôt, *adv.* soon.

bienveillance, *n.f.* benevolence, kindness.

bienveillant, *adj.* benevolent, kindly.

bienvenu, *adj.* welcome.

bière, *n.f.* beer, ale.

biffer, *vb.* cancel, erase.

bifteck, *n.m.* beefsteak.

bigamie, *n.f.* bigamy.

bigot, *n.m.* bigot.

bigoterie, *n.f.* bigotry.

bijou, *n.m.* jewel.

bijouterie, *n.f.* jewelry.

bile, *n.f.* bile. **se faire de la b.,** worry.

billard, *n.m.* billiards.

bille, *n.f.* marble (toy).

billet, *n.m.* ticket, note. **b. de banque,** banknote.

billion (-l-), *n.m.* billion.
biographie, *n.f.* biography.
biologie, *n.f.* biology.
biscuit, *n.m.* biscuit.
bizarre, *adj.* queer, odd, strange, quaint.
blâme, *n.m.* blame.
blâmer, *vb.* blame.
blanc *m.,* **blanche** *f. adj.* white, blank. **en b.,** blank.
blancheur, *n.f.* whiteness.
blanchir, *vb.* whiten.
blanchisserie, *n.f.* laundry.
blasé, *adj.* sophisticated.
blasphème, *n.m.* blasphemy.
blasphémer, *vb.* curse, blaspheme.
blatte, *n.f.* cockroach.
blé, *n.m.* wheat.
blême, *adj.* pale.
blesser, *vb.* wound, hurt, injure.
blessure, *n.f.* wound, hurt, injury.
bleu, *adj.* blue.
bloc, *n.m.* pad, block.
blocus (-s), *n.m.* blockade.
blond, *adj.* fair, blond(e).
bloquer, *vb.* block.
blottir, *vb.* **se b.,** cower.
blouse, *n.f.* blouse.
blue jeans, *n.m.pl.* blue jeans.
bluff, *n.m.* bluff.
bluffeur, *n.m.* bluffer.
bobine, *n.f.* spool, reel.
bœuf (bœf), *n.m.* ox, beef. **jeune b.,** steer.
Bohème, *n.f.* Bohemia.
bohème, 1. *n.m.f.* bohemian, happy-go-lucky person. **2.** *n.f.* artistic underworld. **3.** *adj.* bohemian.
Bohémien, *n.m.* Bohemian; gypsy.
bohémien, *adj.* Bohemian.
boire, *vb.* drink. **b. à petits coups,** sip.
bois, *n.m.* wood, forest, lumber.
boiserie, *n.f.* woodwork.
boisseau, *n.m.* bushel.
boisson, *n.f.* beverage, drink.
boîte, *n.f.* box; can (food). **b. aux lettres,** mail-box.
boiter, *vb.* limp.
boiteux, *adj.* lame.
bol, *n.m.* bowl.
bombardement, *n.m.* bombardment.
bombarder, *vb.* bomb, bombard.
bombe, *n.f.* bomb, shell.
bombe à neutrons, *n.f.* neutron bomb.
bon *m.,* **bonne** *f. adj.* good, kind. **de b. heure,** early. **b. marché,** cheap.
bon, *n.m.* bond.
bonbon, *n.m.* candy, bonbon.
bond, *n.m.* bound, leap.
bonder, *vb.* overcrowd, jam.
bondir, *vb.* bound, leap, spring.
bonheur, *n.m.* happiness.
bonhomme, *n.m.* fellow.

bonjour, *interj. and n.m.* good morning.
bonne, *n.f.* maid.
bonnement, *adv.* simply.
bonnet, *n.m.* cap, hood.
bonsoir, *interj. and n.m.* good evening.
bonté, *n.f.* kindness, goodness.
bord, *n.m.* edge, rim, brim **b. du toit,** eaves.
border, *vb.* bound, edge, border, hem.
borne, *n.f.* bound, limit.
borner, *vb.* bound, limit.
bosquet, *n.m.* clump (trees).
bosse, *n.f.* bump.
bosselure, *n.f.* dent.
bossu, *adj.* hunchbacked.
botanique, *n.f.* botany.
botte, *n.f.* boot; bunch.
bottine, *n.f.* boot.
bouche, *n.f.* mouth.
boucher, *vb.* stop up.
boucher, *n.m.* butcher.
boucherie, *n.f.* butcher shop.
bouchon, *n.m.* cork.
boucle, *n.f.* curl, loop, buckle. **b. d'oreille,** earring.
boucler, *vb.* curl.
bouclier, *n.m.* shield.
bouder, *vb.* sulk.
boue, *n.f.* mud.
bouée, *n.f.* buoy.
boueur, *n.m.* scavenger.
boueux, *adj.* muddy.
bouffée, *n.f.* puff.
bouffon, *n.m.* clown, fool.
bouffonnerie, *n.f.* antic(s).
bouger, *vb.* stir, move, budge.
bougie, *n.f.* candle.
bouillir, *vb.* boil.
bouilloire, *n.f.* kettle.
bouillon, *n.m.* broth.
bouillonner, *vb.* bubble.
bouillotte, *n.f.* kettle.
boulanger, *n.m.* baker.
boulangerie, *n.f.* bakery.
boule, *n.f.* ball.
bouleau, *n.m.* birch.
bouledogue, *n.m.* bulldog.
boulevard, *n.m.* boulevard.
bouleversement, *n.m.* upset.
bouleverser, *vb.* upset, overturn.
bouquet, *n.m.* cluster, bunch, bouquet.
bouquiniste, *n.m.* (secondhand) bookseller.
bourbeux, *adj.* sloppy.
bourdon, *n.m.* bumblebee.
bourdonnement, *n.m.* buzz.
bourdonner, *vb.* hum, buzz.
bourg, *n.m.* borough, village.
bourgeois, *adj.* middle-class, bourgeois.
bourgeoisie, *n.f.* middle class.
bourgeon, *n.m.* bud.
bourgeonner, *vb.* bud.
bourre, *n.f.* stuffing.
bourreau, *n.m.* executioner, hangman; brute.
bourrelet, *n.m.* pad.
bourrer, *vb.* stuff, pad.
bourru, *adj.* gruff.
bourse, *n.f.* purse, bag; stock

exchange; scholarship, fellowship.
boursoufler, *vb.* bloat.
bousculer, *vb.* jostle.
bousiller, *vb.* bungle.
boussole, *n.f.* compass.
bout, *n.m.* end, tip, butt, stub.
bouteille, *n.f.* bottle.
boutique, *n.f.* shop.
bouton, *n.m.* button, bud; pimple.
boutonnière, *n.f.* buttonhole.
boxe, *n.f.* boxing.
boxeur, *n.m.* boxer.
boycotter, *vb.* boycott.
bracelet, *n.m.* bracelet.
braconnier, *n.m.* poacher.
brailler, *vb.* bawl.
braise, *n.f.* coals, embers.
brancard, *n.m.* stretcher.
branche, *n.f.* branch, bough, limb.
brandir, *vb.* brandish.
branler, *vb.* waver.
braquer, *vb.* aim, point.
bras, *n.m.* arm.
brasse, *n.f.* fathom.
brasser, *vb.* brew.
brasserie, *n.f.* brewery, beer-joint.
bravade, *n.f.* bravado.
brave, *adj.* fine, good, brave.
braver, *vb.* brave, face, defy.
bravoure, *n.f.* courage.
brebis, *n.f.* lamb.
brèche, *n.f.* breach, gap.
bref, 1. *adj.m.,* **brève** *f.* brief, short. **2.** *adv.* in short.
Brésil, *n.m.* Brazil.
brevet, *n.m.* commission. **b. d'invention,** patent.
bribe, *n.f.* scrap, bit.
bride, *n.f.* bridle.
brider, *vb.* curb.
bridge, *n.m.* bridge (game).
brièveté, *n.f.* brevity.
brigade, *n.f.* brigade.
brigadier, *n.m.* corporal.
brigand, *n.m.* robber, knave.
brillant, *adj.* brilliant, bright, glowing.
briller, *vb.* shine, glisten, glare.
brin, *n.m.* blade (grass).
brindille, *n.f.* twig.
brioche, *n.f.* bun.
brique, *n.f.* brick.
briquet, *n.m.* **pierre à b.,** flint.
brise, *n.f.* breeze.
briser, *vb.* break, shatter, smash.
britannique, *adj.* British.
brocart, *n.m.* brocade.
broche, *n.f.* spit, spindle; brooch.
brochure, *n.f.* pamphlet.
broder, *vb.* embroider.
broderie, *n.f.* embroidery.
bronchite, *n.f.* bronchitis.
bronze, *n.m.* bronze.
broquette, *n.f.* tack.
brosse, *n.f.* brush.
brouhaha, *n.m.* uproar.
brouillard, *n.m.* fog, mist.
brouiller, *vb.* jumble, embroil;

scramble (eggs). **se b.,** quarrel.
brouillon, *n.m.* (rough) draft.
broussailles, *n.f.pl.* brushwood.
brouter, *vb.* browse.
broyer, *vb.* crush.
bruine, *n.f.* drizzle.
bruiner, *vb.* drizzle.
bruissement, *n.m.* rustle.
bruit, *n.m.* noise, clatter; report, rumor.
brûler, *vb.* burn.
brume, *n.f.* mist. **b. légère,** haze.
brumeux, *adj.* foggy, misty.
brun, *adj.* brown.
brune, *adj. and n.f.* brunette.
brusque, *adj.* abrupt, curt, blunt, gruff, brusque.
brut, *adj.* crude, gross.
brutal, *adj.* brutal, savage.
brutalité, *n.f.* brutality.
brute, *n.f.* brute.
bruyant, *adj.* noisy, loud.
bruyère, *n.f.* heath, heather.
bûche, *n.f.* log.
bûcheron, *n.m.* wood-cutter.
budget, *n.m.* budget.
buffet, *n.m.* buffet.
buffle, *n.m.* buffalo.
buis, *n.m.* box (tree).
buisson, *n.m.* bush, shrub, thicket.
buissonneux, *adj.* bushy.
bulbe, *n.m.* bulb.
bulle, *n.f.* bubble; (papal) bull.
bulletin, *n.m.* bulletin, ticket.
bureau, *n.m.* office, bureau; desk. **b. de location,** box-office.
burin, *n.m.* chisel.
burlesque, *adj.* ludicrous.
buste, *n.m.* bust.
but, *n.m.* aim, goal, purpose.
butin, *n.m.* spoils, booty.
butte, *n.f.* hill, knoll.
buvard, *n.m.* blotter.

C

ça, *pron.* that.
cabane, *n.f.* cabin, hut.
cabaret, *n.m.* cabaret, tavern.
cabine, *n.f.* cabin, booth.
cabinet, *n.m.* closet; office. **c. de toilette,** lavatory. **c. de travail,** study.
câble, *n.m.* cable, rope.
câbler, *vb.* cable.
câblogramme, *n.m.* cablegram.
cacao, *n.m.* cocoa.
cacher, *vb.* hide, conceal. **se c.,** lurk.
cachet, *n.m.* seal.
cadavre, *n.m.* corpse.
cadeau, *n.m.* gift, present.
cadence, *n.f.* cadence.
cadet, 1. *n.m.* cadet. **2.** *adj.* junior.
cadran, *n.m.* dial.
cadre, *n.m.* frame.
café, *n.m.* coffee; café.
cage, *n.f.* cage.

cahier, *n.m.* notebook.
caille, *n.f.* quail.
caillot, *n.m.* clot.
caillou, *n.m.* pebble.
caisse, *n.f.* crate, case, box.
caissier, *n.m.* cashier, teller.
cajoler, *vb.* coax.
calamité, *n.f.* calamity.
calcium, *n.m.* calcium.
calcul, *n.m.* calculation.
calculer, *vb.* figure, reckon, calculate.
cale, *n.f.* hold.
calembour, *n.m.* pun.
calendrier, *n.m.* calendar.
calibre, *n.m.* caliber.
calicot, *n.m.* calico.
callosité, *n.f.* callus.
calme, *n.m. and adj.* quiet, calm.
calmer, *vb.* soothe, quiet, calm.
calomnie, *n.f.* slander.
calomnier, *vb.* slander.
calorie, *n.f.* calorie.
calotte, *n.f.* crown (of hat).
Calvaire, *n.m.* Calvary.
camarade, *n.m.f.* comrade, companion, mate.
camaraderie, *n.f.* companionship, fellowship.
cambrioleur, *n.m.* burglar.
camion, *n.m.* truck.
camoufler, *vb.* camouflage.
camp, *n.m.* camp.
campagnard, 1. *n.m.* countryman, peasant. **2.** *adj.* peasant.
campagne, *n.f.* country; campaign.
camper, *vb.* camp.
camphre, *n.m.* camphor.
Canada, *n.m.* Canada.
Canadien, *n.m.* Canadian.
canadien, *adj.* Canadian.
canaille, *n.f.* rabble; scoundrel.
canal, *n.m.* channel, canal.
canapé, *n.m.* sofa, couch; canapé.
canard, *n.m.* duck.
canari, *n.m.* canary.
cancer (-r), *n.m.* cancer.
cancérogène, *adj.* carcinogenic.
candeur, *n.f.* purity; candor.
candidat, *n.m.* candidate, applicant.
candidature, *n.f.* candidacy.
candide, *adj.* frank, open, candid.
canevas, *n.m.* canvas. **gros c.,** burlap.
canin, *adj.* canine.
canne, *n.f.* cane, stick.
canneberge, *n.f.* cranberry.
cannelle, *n.f.* cinnamon.
cannibale, *adj. and n.m.f.* cannibal.
canoë (-ô ã), *n.m.* canoe.
canon, *n.m.* cannon.
canot, *n.m.* boat, canoe. **c. automobile,** motorboat.
cantaloup, *n.m.* cantaloupe.
cantique, *n.m.* hymn.
canton, *n.m.* district, canton.
caoutchouc (-choo), *n.m.* rubber.

cap (-p), *n.m.* cape (headland).
capable, *adj.* efficient, fit, capable, competent.
capacité, *n.f.* capability, capacity.
cape, *n.f.* cape (clothing).
capitaine, *n.m.* captain.
capital, *n.m. and adj.* capital.
capitale, *n.f.* capital (city).
capitaliser, *vb.* capitalize.
capitalisme, *n.m.* capitalism.
capitaliste, *n.m.f.* capitalist.
caporal, *n.m.* corporal.
capote, *n.f.* hood.
câpre, *n.f.* caper.
caprice, *n.m.* whim, fancy.
capricieux, *adj.* fickle, capricious.
capsule, *n.f.* capsule.
captif, *adj. and n.m.* captive.
captiver, *vb.* captivate, charm.
captivité, *n.f.* captivity.
capture, *n.f.* capture.
capturer, *vb.* capture.
capuchon, *n.m.* hood.
car, *conj.* for.
caractère, *n.m.* character, nature, disposition; type.
caractériser, *vb.* characterize; distinguish; mark.
caractéristique, *adj.* characteristic.
carafe, *n.f.* decanter, waterbottle.
caramel, *n.m.* caramel.
carat, *n.m.* carat.
caravane, *n.f.* caravan.
carbone, *n.m.* carbon.
carboniser, *vb.* char.
carburateur, *n.m.* carburetor.
carcasse, *n.f.* shell; carcass.
cardinal, *n.m.* cardinal.
carême, *n.m.* Lent.
caresse, *n.f.* caress.
caresser, *vb.* fondle, stroke, caress.
cargaison, *n.f.* cargo.
caricature, *n.f.* caricature.
carie, *n.f.* decay.
carillon, *n.m.* chime.
carillonner, *vb.* chime.
carnaval, *n.m.* carnival.
carnet, *n.m.* notebook.
carnivore, *adj.* carnivorous.
carotte, *n.f.* carrot.
carré, *n.m. and adj.* square.
carreau, *n.m.* diamond (cards); pane; tile.
carrefour, *n.m.* crossroads.
carrière, *n.f.* career; scope; quarry.
carriole, *n.f.* (light) cart.
carrosse, *n.m.* coach.
carte, *n.f.* chart, map, card. **c. de crédit,** *n.f.* credit card. **c. du jour,** bill of fare.
carton, *n.m.* cardboard; box, carton.
cartouche, *n.f.* cartridge.
cas, *n.m.* case; event.
case, *n.f.* pigeonhole; hut, shed.
caserne, *n.f.* barracks.
casque, *n.m.* helmet.
casquette, *n.f.* cap.

cassable, adj. breakable.

casse-croûte, n.m. snack.

casser, vb. break, crack.

casserole, n.f. pan.

cassette, n.f. 1. casket. 2. cassette.

cassis, n.m. black currant.

caste, n.f. caste.

castor, n.m. beaver.

casuel, adj. casual.

catalogue, n.m. catalogue.

cataracte, n.f. cataract.

catarrhe, n.m. catarrh.

catastrophe, n.f. disaster, catastrophe.

catéchisme, n.m. catechism.

catégorie, n.f. category.

cathédrale, n.f. cathedral.

catholicisme, n.m. Catholicism.

catholique, adj. Catholic.

cauchemar, n.m. nightmare.

cause, n.f. case; cause.

causer, vb. chat; cause.

causerie, n.f. chat, talk.

causette, n.f. chat.

caution, n.f. bail, security.

cavalerie, n.f. cavalry.

cavalier, n.m. rider, horseman; escort.

cave, n.f. cellar, cavern.

cavité, n.f. cavity.

ce (sa), cet (sĕt) m., cette (sĕt) f., ces (sā) pl. adj. that, this.

ceci, pron. this.

cécité, n.f. blindness.

céder, vb. yield, give in, cede.

cèdre, n.m. cedar.

ceindre, vb. gird.

ceinture, n.f. belt, sash.

cela, pron. that.

célébration, n.f. celebration.

célèbre, adj. famous, noted.

célébrer, vb. celebrate.

célébrité, n.f. celebrity.

céleri, n.m. celery.

céleste, adj. heavenly, celestial.

célibataire, 1. n.m. bachelor. 2. adj. single.

celle, pron. f. See celui.

cellule, n.f. cell.

celluloïd (-lô ĕd), n.m. celluloid.

celtique, adj. Celtic.

celui m., celle f., ceux m.pl., celles f.pl. pron. the one. celui-ci, this one; the latter. celui-là, that one; the former.

cendre, n.f. ashes, cinders.

cendrier, n.m. ash-tray.

censeur, n.m. censor.

censure, n.f. censure.

censurer, vb. censor.

cent, adj. and n.m. hundred. pour c., percent.

centaine, n.f. hundred.

centenaire, adj. and n.m. centenary, centennial.

centième, adj. hundredth.

centigrade, adj. centigrade.

centimètre, n.m. centimeter.

central, adj. central.

centraliser, vb. centralize.

centre, n.m. center.

cependant, adv. however, still, yet.

cercle, n.m. circle, ring, hoop; club.

cercueil, n.m. coffin.

céréale, adj. and n.f. cereal.

cérémonial, adj. and n.m. ceremonial.

cérémonie, n.f. ceremony. sans c., informal.

cérémonieux, adj. formal, ceremonious.

cerf (sĕr), n.m. deer.

cerf-volant, n.m. kite.

cerise, n.f. cherry.

certain, adj. certain, sure; (pl.) some.

certes, adv. indeed.

certificat, n.m. credentials; certificate.

certifier, vb. certify.

certitude, n.f. certainty, assurance.

cerveau, n.m. brain.

cervelle, n.f. brains.

cessation, n.f. stopping, cessation.

cesser, vb. stop, desist, cease.

cession, n.f. assignment (law).

cet, cette, pron. See ce.

chacun, pron. everybody, everyone; each; apiece.

chagrin, 1. n.m. grief, vexation. 2. adj. fretful.

chagriner, vb. grieve.

chaîne, n.f. chain; range.

chaînon, n.m. link.

chair, n.f. flesh.

chaire, n.f. pulpit; chair (university).

chaise, n.f. chair.

chaland, n.m. barge.

châle, n.m. shawl.

chaleur, n.f. warmth, heat, glow.

chaloupe, n.f. launch.

chambre, n.f. room, chamber; House (parliament). c. à coucher, bedroom.

chameau, n.m. camel.

chamois, n.m. chamois.

champ, n.m. field.

champignon, n.m. mushroom.

champion, n.m. champion.

championnat, n.m. championship.

chance, n.f. luck, risk, chance.

chanceler, vb. stagger, reel.

chancelier, n.m. chancellor.

chandail, n.m. sweater.

chandelier, n.m. candlestick.

chandelle, n.f. candle.

change, n.m. exchange.

changeant, adj. changeable.

changement, n.m. change, shift.

changer, vb. alter, shift, change.

chanson, n.f. song.

chant, n.m. song, chant. c. du coq, cock-crow.

chantage, n.m. blackmail.

chanter, vb. sing, chant.

chanteur, n.m. singer.

chantier, n.m. (work)yard.

chaos (k-), n.m. chaos.

chaotique (k-), adj. chaotic.

chapeau, n.m. hat, bonnet.

chapelle, n.f. chapel.

chaperon, n.m. chaperon.

chapiteau, n.m. capital.

chapitre, n.m. chapter.

chapon, n.m. capon.

chaque, adj. every, each.

char, n.m. chariot. c. d'assaut, (military) tank.

charbon, n.m. coal. c. de bois, charcoal.

charge, n.f. load, charge.

charger, vb. load, burden, charge.

chariot, n.m. wagon; baggage cart.

charisme, n.m. charisma.

charitable, adj. charitable.

charité, n.f. charity.

charlatan, n.m. charlatan.

charmant, adj. delightful, lovely, charming.

charme, n.m. spell, charm.

charmer, vb. charm.

charnel, adj. carnal.

charnu, adj. fleshy.

charpente, n.f. framework.

charpentier, n.m. carpenter.

charretier, n.m. carter.

charrette, n.f. cart.

charrue, n.f. plow.

charte, n.f. charter.

chasse, n.f. hunt(ing), chase.

châsse, n.f. shrine.

chasser, vb. hunt, chase; drive away.

chasseur, n.m. hunter; bellboy.

châssis, n.m. (window) sash.

chaste, adj. chaste.

chasteté, n.f. chastity.

chat m., chatte f. n. cat.

châtaigne, n.f. chestnut.

château, n.m. mansion, castle.

châtier, vb. punish, chastise.

chatouiller, vb. tickle.

chatouilleux, adj. ticklish.

chaud, adj. hot, warm.

chaudière, n.f. boiler.

chauffage, n.m. heating.

chauffer, vb. heat, warm.

chauffeur, n.m. driver, chauffeur.

chaumière, n.f. cottage.

chaussée, n.f. road.

chausser, vb. wear shoes. se c., put on shoes.

chaussette, n.f. sock.

chaussure, n.f. footgear.

chauve, adj. bald.

chauve-souris, n.f. bat.

chaux, n.f. lime.

chavirer, vb. capsize.

chef, n.m. leader, chief.

chef-d'œuvre (shĕ-), n.m. masterpiece.

chemin, n.m. road. c. de fer, railway. à mi-c., halfway. c. de table, table-runner.

chemineau, n.m. tramp.

cheminée, n.f. fireplace, chimney; funnel.

chemise, n.f. shirt. c. de nuit, nightgown.

chêne, *n.m.* oak.

chenille, *n.f.* caterpillar.

chèque, *n.m.* check.

chèque de voyage, *n.m.* traveler's check.

cher (-r), *adj.* dear, expensive.

chercher, *vb.* seek, look for, search. **aller c.,** fetch.

chère, *n.f.* fare.

chéri, *adj. and n.m.* beloved, darling.

chérir, *vb.* cherish.

cheval, *n.m.* horse. **à c.,** on horseback. **monter à c.,** ride (horseback). **fer à c.,** horseshoe.

chevaleresque, *adj.* chivalrous.

chevalerie, *n.f.* chivalry.

chevalet, *n.m.* easel; knight.

chevalier, *n.m.* knight.

cheveu, *n.m., pl.* **cheveux,** hair.

cheville, *n.f.* ankle; peg.

chèvre, *n.f.* goat.

chevreau, *n.m.* kid.

chevreuil, *n.m.* roe.

chevron, *n.m.* rafter.

chevroter, *vb.* quaver.

chevrotine, *n.f.* buckshot.

chez, *prep.* at . . .'s (house, office, shop, etc.)

chic, *adj.* stylish.

chien, *n.m.* dog.

chienne, *n.f.* bitch.

chiffon, *n.m.* rag.

chiffonner, *vb.* crumple.

chiffre, *n.m.* figure.

chiffrer, *vb.* figure.

Chili, *n.m.* Chile.

Chilien, *n.m.* Chilean.

chilien, *adj.* Chilean.

chimie, *n.f.* chemistry.

chimiothérapie, *n.f.* chemotherapy.

chimique, *adj.* chemical.

chimiste, *n.m.f.* chemist.

Chine, *n.f.* China.

Chinois, *n.m.* Chinese (person).

chinois, 1. *n.m.* Chinese (language). **2.** *adj.* Chinese.

chiquenaude, *n.f.* flip.

chirurgie, *n.f.* surgery.

chirurgien, *n.m.* surgeon.

chloroforme (k-), *n.m.* chloroform.

choc, *n.m.* shock, clash, brunt.

chocolat, *n.m.* chocolate.

chœur (k-), *n.m.* choir, chorus.

choisir, *vb.* choose, select, pick.

choix, *n.m.* choice.

chômage, *n.m.* stoppage (of work).

choquer, *vb.* shock, clash.

choral (k-), *adj.* choral.

chose, *n.f.* thing, matter. **quelque c.,** anything.

chou, *n.m.* cabbage.

chou-fleur, *n.m.* cauliflower.

choyer, *vb.* pamper.

chrétien (k-), *adj. and n.m.* Christian.

chrétienté (k-), *n.f.* Christendom.

christianisme (k-), *n.m.* Christianity.

chronique (k-), **1.** *n.f.* chronicle. **2.** *adj.* chronic.

chronologique (k-), *adj.* chronological.

chrysanthème (k-), *n.m.* chrysanthemum.

chuchoter, *vb.* whisper.

chute, *n.f.* fall, drop, downfall.

cible, *n.f.* target.

cicatrice, *n.f.* scar.

cidre, *n.m.* cider.

ciel, *n.m., pl.* **cieux,** heaven, sky.

cierge, *n.m.* (church) candle.

cigale, *n.f.* locust.

cigare, *n.m.* cigar.

cigarette, *n.f.* cigarette.

cigogne, *n.f.* stork.

ci-joint, *adj.* enclosed.

cil (-l), *n.m.* eyelash.

cime, *n.f.* top, summit.

ciment, *n.m.* cement.

cimenter, *vb.* cement.

cimetière, *n.m.* churchyard, cemetery.

cinéma, *n.m.* cinema.

cinglant, *adj.* scathing.

cinq (-k), *adj. and n.m.* five.

cinquante, *adj. and n.m.* fifty.

cinquième, *adj. and n.m.* fifth.

cintre, *n.m.* semicircle; arch.

circonférence, *n.f.* circumference.

circonscription, *n.f.* **c. électorale,** borough.

circonscrire, *vb.* circumscribe.

circonstance, *n.f.* event, circumstance. **c. critique,** emergency.

circuit, *n.m.* circuit. **hors c.,** disconnected.

circulaire, *adj.* circular.

circulation, *n.f.* traffic, circulation.

circuler, *vb.* circulate, turn, revolve.

cire, *n.f.* wax.

cirer, *vb.* polish, shine.

cireur, *n.m.* bootblack.

cirque, *n.m.* circus.

cisailles, *n.f.pl.* shears.

ciseau, *n.m.* chisel; *(pl.)* scissors.

ciseler, *vb.* chisel.

citadelle, *n.f.* citadel.

citation, *n.f.* quotation, citation.

cité, *n.f.* city. **droit de c.,** citizenship.

citer, *vb.* quote, cite.

citoyen, *n.m.* citizen.

citron, *n.m.* lemon. **c. pressé,** lemonade.

citrouille, *n.f.* pumpkin.

civil (-l), **1.** *n.m.* civilian. **2.** *adj.* civil.

civilisation, *n.f.* civilization.

civilisé, *adj.* civilized.

civiliser, *vb.* civilize.

civique, *adj.* civic.

clair, *adj.* clear, bright. **c. de lune,** moonlight.

clairière, *n.f.* glade, clearing.

clairon, *n.m.* bugle.

clameur, *n.f.* clamor, outcry.

clandestin, *adj.* clandestine.

clapoteux, *adj.* choppy (sea).

claque, *n.f.* slap.

claquement, *n.m.* smack.

claquer, *vb.* slap, smack, chatter (teeth), bang.

clarifier, *vb.* clarify.

clarinette, *n.f.* clarinet.

clarté, *n.f.* clarity; light.

classe, *n.f.* class.

classement, *n.m.* classification.

classer, *vb.* classify, order, file, grade.

classeur, *n.m.* file.

classification, *n.f.* classification.

classifier, *vb.* classify.

classique, *adj.* classic, classical.

clause, *n.f.* clause.

clavicule, *n.f.* collarbone.

clef (klä), **clé,** *n.f.* key.

clémence, *n.f.* clemency.

clément, *adj.* merciful.

clerc, *n.m.* clerk.

clergé, *n.m.* clergy.

clérical, *adj.* clerical.

cliché, *n.m.* cliché; snapshot.

client, *n.m.* customer, patron, client.

clientèle, *n.f.* customers, practice.

cligner (de l'œil), *vb.* wink.

clignoter, *vb.* blink, wink.

climat, *n.m.* climate.

climatisation, *n.f.* air-conditioning.

climatiser, *vb.* air-condition.

clin, *n.m.* **c. d'œil,** wink.

clinique, 1. *n.f.* clinic. **2.** *adj.* clinical.

cloche, *n.f.* bell.

clocher, *n.m.* belfry. **de c.,** parochial.

cloison, *n.f.* partition.

cloître, *n.m.* cloister, convent.

clôture, *n.f.* fence.

clou, *n.m.* nail.

clouer, *vb.* nail, tack.

club (-b), *n.m.* club.

coaguler, *vb.* coagulate.

coalition, *n.f.* coalition.

coasser, *vb.* croak (frogs).

cocaïne, *n.f.* cocaine.

cochon, *n.m.* pig.

coco, *n.m.* **noix de c.,** coconut.

cocon, *n.m.* cocoon.

code, *n.m.* code; laws.

code postal, *n.m.* zip code.

cœur, *n.m.* heart.

coffre, *n.m.* bin; coffer.

cogner, *vb.* bump, strike, run into, knock (down).

cohérent, *adj.* coherent.

cohésion, *n.f.* cohesion.

coiffer, *vb.* dress (hair).

coiffeur, *n.m.* hairdresser, barber.

coiffure, *n.f.* hair-do.

coin, *n.m.* corner, wedge.

coïncidence (kŏ än-), *n.f.* coincidence.

coïncider (kŏ än-), *vb.* coincide.

col, *n.m.* collar; pass.

colère, *n.f.* anger, temper. en c., angry.

colimaçon, *n.m.* snail.

colis, *n.m.* parcel.

collaborateur, *n.m.* fellow-worker.

collaboration, *n.f.* assistance, collaboration.

collaborer, *vb.* work together, collaborate.

collant, *n.m.* panty hose.

collatéral, *adj.* and *n.m.* collateral.

colle, *n.f.* glue, paste.

collecte, *n.f.* collection.

collectif, *adj.* collective.

collection, *n.f.* collection.

collectionneur, *n.m.* collector.

collège, *n.m.* college.

collègue, *n.m.f.* colleague.

coller, *vb.* glue, paste, stick.

collier, *n.m.* necklace; collar (dog).

colline, *n.f.* hill.

collision, *n.f.* collision.

colombe, *n.f.* dove.

colon, *n.m.* settler, colonist.

colonel, *n.m.* colonel.

colonial, *adj.* colonial.

colonie, *n.f.* settlement, colony.

coloniser, *vb.* colonize.

colonne, *n.f.* column.

coloré, *adj.* colorful.

colorer, *vb.* color.

colossal, *adj.* huge, colossal.

colosse, *n.m.* giant, colossus.

colporter, *n.m.* peddle.

colporteur, *n.m.* peddler.

combat, *n.m.* fight, battle. hors de c., disabled.

combattant, *adj.* and *n.m.* combatant.

combattre, *vb.* fight.

combien (de), *adv.* how much, how many.

combinaison, *n.f.* combination, slip, B.V.D.'s.

combiner, *vb.* devise, combine.

comble, *n.m.* climax, top.

combler, *vb.* heap up, fill.

combustible, 1. *n.m.* fuel. 2. *adj.* combustible.

combustion, *n.f.* combustion.

comédie, *n.f.* comedy.

comédien, *n.m.* actor, comedian.

comestible, *adj.* edible.

comète, *n.f.* comet.

comique, *adj.* funny, comic(al).

comité, *n.m.* committee.

commandant, *n.m.* major, commander.

commande, *n.f.* order; commission.

commandement, *n.m.* command, commandment.

commander, *vb.* order, command.

commanditer, *vb.* finance.

comme, 1. *adv.* as, how. 2. *prep.* as, like. c. il faut, proper, decent.

commémoratif, *adj.* memorial.

commémorer, *vb.* commemorate.

commençant, *n.m.* beginner.

commencement, *n.m.* beginning, start.

commencer, *vb.* begin, start.

comment, *adv.* how.

commentaire, *n.m.* comment, commentary.

commentateur, *n.m.* commentator.

commenter, *vb.* comment on.

commerçant, *n.m.* trader.

commerce, *n.m.* trade, commerce.

commercer, *vb.* trade.

commercial, *adj.* commercial.

commettre, *vb.* commit.

commis, *n.m.* clerk.

commissaire, *n.m.* commissary, commissioner.

commission, *n.f.* errand, commission.

commode, 1. *n.f.* dresser, bureau. 2. *adj.* handy, convenient, comfortable.

commodité, *n.f.* convenience.

commun, *adj.* joint, common.

communauté, *n.f.* community.

commune, *n.f.* commune, town(ship).

communicatif, *adj.* communicative.

communication, *n.f.* communication.

communion, *n.f.* communion.

communiquer, *vb.* communicate.

communisme, *n.m.* communism.

communiste, *adj.* and *n.m.f.* communist.

compacité, *n.f.* compactness.

compact (-kt), *adj.* compact.

compagne, *n.f.* mate, companion.

compagnie, *n.f.* company.

compagnon, *n.m.* mate, fellow, companion.

comparable, *adj.* comparable.

comparaison, *n.f.* comparison.

comparaître, *vb.* appear.

comparatif, *adj.* and *n.m.* comparative.

comparer, *vb.* compare.

compartiment, *n.m.* compartment.

compas, *n.m.* compass.

compassion, *n.f.* sympathy, compassion.

compatible, *adj.* compatible.

compatissant, *adj.* sympathetic, compassionate.

compatriote, *n.m.f.* compatriot.

compensation, *n.f.* amends; compensation.

compenser, *vb.* compensate.

compétence, *n.f.* qualification, efficiency, competence.

compiler, *vb.* compile.

complaire, *vb.* please.

complaisance, *n.f.* kindness, compliance.

complaisant, *adj.* obliging, kind.

complément, *n.m.* object; complement.

complet, 1. *n.m.* suit. 2. *adj.* full, thorough, complete.

compléter, *vb.* complete.

complexe, *adj.* and *n.m.* complex.

complexité, *n.f.* complexity.

complication, *n.f.* complication.

complice, *n.m.f.* party to, accomplice.

compliqué, *adj.* intricate, involved, complicated.

compliquer, *vb.* complicate.

complot, *n.m.* plot.

comporter, *vb.* se c., act, behave.

composant, *adj.* and *n.m.* component.

composé, *adj.* and *n.m.* compound.

composer, *vb.* compound, compose.

compositeur, *n.m.* composer.

composition, *n.f.* essay, theme, composition.

compote, *n.f.* stewed fruit.

compréhensif, *adj.* comprehensive.

compréhension, *n.f.* comprehension.

comprendre, *vb.* understand, realize, comprise, include. c. mal, misunderstand.

compresse, *n.f.* compress.

compression, *n.f.* compression.

comprimer, *vb.* compress.

compromettre, *vb.* compromise.

compromis, *n.m.* compromise.

comptabilité, *n.f.* accounting, bookkeeping.

comptable, *n.m.* accountant.

compte, *n.m.* account, count. rendre c. de, account for: tenir c. de, allow for.

compter, *vb.* count, reckon. c. sur, rely on.

compteur, *n.m.* meter.

comptoir, *n.m.* counter.

comte, *n.m.* count.

comtesse, *n.f.* countess.

concave, *adj.* concave.

concéder, *vb.* grant, concede.

concentration, *n.f.* concentration.

concentrer, *vb.* condense, concentrate.

concept (-pt), *n.m.* concept.

conception, *n.f.* conception.

concernant, *prep.* concerning.

concerner, *vb.* concern.

concert, *n.m.* concert.

concession, *n.f.* grant, license, admission, concession.

concevable, *adj.* conceivable.

concevoir, *vb.* conceive, imagine.

concierge, *n.m.f.* janitor, doorkeeper, porter.

concile, *n.m.* council.

conciliation, *n.f.* conciliation.

concilier, vb. reconcile, conciliate.

concis, adj. concise.

concision, n.f. conciseness.

concluant, adj. conclusive.

conclure, vb. complete, conclude, infer.

conclusion, n.f. conclusion.

concombre, n.m. cucumber.

concourir, vb. concur, contribute, contend.

concours, n.m. contest.

concret, adj. concrete.

concurrence, n.f. competition.

concurrent, n.m. rival, competitor.

condamnation (-dă nă-), n.f. conviction, condemnation, sentence.

condamner (-dä nă), vb. convict, doom, condemn, sentence.

condensation, n.f. condensation.

condenser, vb. condense.

condescendance, n.f. condescension.

condescendre, vb. condescend.

condition, n.f. condition.

conditionnel, adj. and n.m. conditional.

conditionner, vb. condition.

condoléance, n.f. condolence. **faire ses c.s à,** condole with.

condominium, n.m. condominium.

conducteur, n.m. conductor.

conduire, vb. lead, take, drive, conduct. **se c.,** behave, act.

conduite, n.f. behavior, conduct.

cône, n.m. cone.

cône de charge n.m. warhead.

confection, n.f. making (e.g. clothes); ready-made garment.

confédération, n.f. confederacy, confederation.

confédéré, adj. and n.m. confederate.

conférence, n.f. lecture, talk, conference.

conférer, vb. confer, grant.

confesser, vb. confess, admit.

confesseur, n.m. confessor.

confession, n.f. denomination, confession.

confiance, n.f. trust, belief, confidence. **digne de c.,** dependable.

confiant, adj. confident.

confidence, n.f. confidence.

confident, n.m. confidant.

confidentiel, adj. confidential.

confier, vb. confide, entrust. **se c. à,** trust.

confiner, vb. confine, limit.

confirmation, n.f. confirmation.

confirmer, vb. confirm.

confiserie, n.f. confectionery.

confisquer, vb. confiscate.

confiture, n.f. jam, jelly.

conflit, n.m. conflict.

confondre, vb. confuse, confound.

conforme, adj. similar.

conformer, vb. conform. **se c. à,** comply with.

conformité, n.f. accordance.

confort, n.m. comfort.

confortable, adj. cozy, snug, comfortable.

confronter, vb. confront.

confus, adj. confused.

confusion, n.f. confusion.

congé, n.m. discharge; leave of absence.

congédier, vb. discharge, dismiss.

congélateur, n.m. freezer.

congeler, vb. congeal.

congestion, n.f. congestion.

conglomération, n.f. conglomeration.

congrès, n.m. congress, assembly, conference.

conjecture, n.f. guess, conjecture.

conjonction, n.f. conjunction.

conjugaison, n.f. conjugation.

conjuguer, vb. conjugate.

conjuration, n.f. conspiracy.

conjurer, vb. conspire, plot.

connaissance, n.f. knowledge, acquaintance. **sans c.,** unconscious. **faire la c. de,** meet.

connaisseur, n.m. connoisseur.

connaître, vb. be acquainted with, know.

connexion, n.f. connection.

conquérir, vb. conquer.

conquête, n.f. conquest.

consacrer, vb. consecrate, devote, dedicate, hallow.

conscience, n.f. conscience, consciousness.

consciencieux, adj. conscientious.

conscient, adj. conscious.

conscription, n.f. draft.

conscrit, adj. and n.m. conscript.

consécration, n.f. consecration.

consécutif, adj. consecutive.

conseil, n.m. advice, counsel; council, board; staff.

conseiller, 1. vb. advise, counsel, **2.** n.m. advisor.

consentement, n.m. consent.

consentir, vb. consent, assent, accede.

conséquence, n.f. outgrowth, result, consequence.

conséquent, adj. consequent, consistent. **par c.,** consequently.

conservateur, adj. and n.m. conservative.

conservation, n.f. conservation.

conserve, n.f. conserve, pickle.

conserver, vb. conserve, keep; preserve, can.

considérable, adj. considerable.

considération, n.f. consideration.

considérer, vb. consider.

consigne, n.m. check-room; (mil.) orders.

consigne automatique, n.f. (luggage) locker.

consigner, vb. consign.

consistance, n.f. consistency.

consistant, adj. consistent.

consister, vb. consist.

consolateur, n.m. comforter.

consolation, n.f. comfort, solace.

console, n.f. bracket.

consoler, vb. comfort, console.

consolider, vb. consolidate, strengthen.

consommateur, n.m. consumer.

consommation, n.f. consumption; end, consummation.

consommé, adj. consummate.

consommer, vb. consummate, complete, consume.

consomption, n.f. consumption.

consonne, n.f. consonant.

conspirateur, n.m. conspirator.

conspiration, n.f. conspiration.

conspirer, vb. conspire.

constamment, adv. continually, constantly.

constance, n.f. constancy, firmness.

constant, adj. constant, firm.

constater, vb. observe, state as a fact.

constellation, n.f. constellation.

consternation, n.f. dismay.

consterné, adj. aghast.

consterner, vb. dismay.

constipation, n.f. constipation.

constituant, adj. constituent.

constituer, vb. constitute.

constitution, n.f. constitution.

constitutionnel, adj. constitutional.

constructeur, n.m. builder.

constructif, adj. constructive.

construction, n.f. construction.

construire, vb. construct, build.

consul, n.m. consul.

consulat, n.m. consulate.

consultation, n.f. consultation.

consulter, vb. consult.

consumer, vb. consume.

contact (-kt), n.m. touch, contact.

contagieux, adj. contagious.

contagion, n.f. contagion.

contaminer, vb. contaminate.

conte, n.m. tale, story.

contemplation, n.f. contemplation.

contempler, vb. survey, observe, contemplate.

contemporain, adj. contemporary.

contenance, n.f. compass, capacity.

contenir, vb. hold, restrain, contain.

content de, adj. glad of, contented with. **c. de soi-même,** complacent.

contentement, n.m. content-

(ment), satisfaction. **c. de soi-même**, complacency.

contenter, *vb.* please, satisfy.

contenu, *n.m.* contents.

conter, *vb.* tell.

contester, *vb.* challenge (dispute), object to, contest.

contexte, *n.m.* context.

contigu, *adj.* adjoining.

continent, *n.m.* continent.

continental, *adj.* continental.

contingent, *n.m.* quota.

continu, *adj.* continuous.

continuation, *n.f.* continuation, continuance.

continuel, *adj.* continual.

continuer, *vb.* carry on, keep on, go on, continue.

continuité, *n.f.* continuity.

contour, *n.m.* outline.

contourner, *vb.* go round.

contracter, *vb.* contract.

contraction, *n.f.* contraction.

contradiction, *n.f.* discrepancy, contradiction.

contradictoire, *adj.* contradictory.

contraindre, *vb.* coerce, force.

contrainte, *n.f.* compulsion.

contraire, 1. *n.m.* reverse. 2. *adj.* contrary. **au c.**, on the contrary.

contrarier, *vb.* thwart, vex, annoy, oppose, keep (from).

contrariété, *n.f.* annoyance.

contraste, *n.m.* contrast.

contraster, *vb.* contrast.

contrat, *n.m.* contract.

contre, *prep.* against.

contre-balancer, *vb.* counterbalance.

contrebande, *n.f.* smuggling; contraband.

contre-cœur, *adv.* à c., unwillingly.

contredire, *vb.* contradict.

contrée, *n.f.* district, province.

contrefaire, *vb.* forge, counterfeit.

contrefort, *n.m.* buttress.

contremaître, *n.m.* foreman.

contre-partie, *n.f.* counterpart.

contrepoids (-pwä), *n.m.* counterbalance.

contribuer, *vb.* contribute.

contribution, *n.f.* share, contribution; tax.

contrôle, *n.m.* check.

contrôle des naissances, *n.m.* birth control, contraception.

contrôler, *vb.* control, check.

contrôleur, *n.m.* checker, collector.

controverse, *n.f.* controversy.

convaincre, *vb.* convince.

convaincu, *adj.* positive.

convalescence, *n.f.* convalescence.

convenable, *adj.* becoming, appropriate, suitable, congenial.

convenance, *n.f.* convenience.

convenir à, *vb.* suit, fit, befit, agree.

convention, *n.f.* convention; contract.

conventionnel, *adj.* conventional.

converger, *vb.* converge.

conversation, *n.f.* talk, conversation.

converser, *vb.* talk, converse.

conversion, *n.f.* conversion, change.

convertir, *vb.* convert, transform.

convexe, *adj.* convex.

conviction, *n.f.* conviction.

convive, *n.m.* guest, companion.

convoi, *n.m.* convoy, funeral procession.

convoiter, *vb.* covet.

convoitise, *n.f.* covetousness.

convoquer, *vb.* summon, call.

convulsion, *n.f.* convulsion.

coopératif (kŏ ŏ-), *adj.* coöperative.

coopération (kŏ ŏ-), *n.f.* coöperation.

coopérative (kŏ ŏ-), *n.f.* coöperative.

coopérer (kŏ ŏ-), *vb.* coöperate.

coordonner (kŏ ŏr-), *vb.* coördinate.

copie, *n.f.* copy.

copier, *vb.* copy.

copieux, *adj.* copious.

coq (-k), *n.m.* rooster.

coque, *n.f.* œuf à la c., boiled egg.

coquille, *n.f.* shell.

coquin, *adj. and n.m.* rogue, rascal.

cor, *n.m.* horn; corn.

corail, *n.m.*, *pl.* **coraux**, coral.

corbeau, *n.m.* raven, crow.

corbeille, *n.f.* basket.

corde, *n.f.* rope, string, cord.

cordial, *adj.* hearty, cordial.

cordon, *n.m.* rope.

cordonnier, *n.m.* shoemaker.

Corée, *n.f.* Korea.

corne, *n.f.* horn.

corneille, *n.f.* crow.

cornemuse, *n.f.* bagpipe.

cornichon, *n.m.* gherkin.

corporation, *n.f.* corporation.

corporel, *adj.* bodily.

corps, *n.m.* body.

corpulent, *adj.* burly.

corpuscule (-sk-), *n.m.* corpuscle.

correct (-kt), *adj.* right, correct.

correction, *n.f.* correction, correctness.

corrélation, *n.f.* correlation.

correspondance, *n.f.* (train) connection; similarity; correspondence.

correspondant, 1. *n.m.* correspondent. 2. *adj.* similar, corresponding.

correspondre, *vb.* correspond.

corriger, *vb.* mend, reclaim, correct.

corroborer, *vb.* corroborate.

corroder, *vb.* corrode.

corrompre, *vb.* bribe, corrupt.

corrompu, *adj.* corrupt.

corruption, *n.f.* bribery, graft, corruption.

corsage, *n.m.* bodice.

corset, *n.m.* corset.

cortège, *n.m.* procession.

cosmétique, *adj. and n.m.* cosmetic.

cosmopolite, *adj. and n.m.f.* cosmopolitan.

costume, *n.m.* attire, dress.

cote, *n.f.* quotation.

côte, *n.f.* rib; coast.

côté, *n.f.* side, way. **mettre de c.**, put to one side (save; discard). **à c. de**, beside.

côtelette, *n.f.* chop, cutlet.

coton, *n.m.* cotton.

cou, *n.m.* neck.

couche, *n.f.* layer, bed; stratum; diaper.

coucher, *vb.* put to bed. **se c.**, lie down; set.

couchette, *n.f.* bunk, berth.

coucou, *n.m.* cuckoo.

coude, *n.m.* elbow.

coudoyer, *vb.* jostle.

coudre, *vb.* sew, stitch.

couler, *vb.* flow, sink, run; cast (metal).

couleur, *n.f.* hue, color; suit (cards).

couloir, *n.m.* corridor.

coup (-k), *n.m.* blow, stroke, hit, bump, knock, cast. **c. de feu**, discharge (gun). **c. d'œil**, glance, look. **c. de pied**, kick. **c. de poing**, punch.

coupable, *adj.* guilty, to blame.

coupe, *n.f.* cut; goblet. **c. de cheveux**, haircut.

couper, *vb.* cut.

couple, *n.f.* couple, pair.

coupler, *vb.* couple.

coupon, *n.m.* remnant; coupon.

coupure, *n.f.* cut, clipping.

cour, *n.f.* court(yard).

courage, *n.m.* bravery, pluck, courage.

courageux, *adj.* brave.

couramment, *adv.* fluently.

courant, 1. *adj.* current. **peu c.**, unusual. **au c.**, well informed. 2. *n.m.* stream, current. **c. d'air**, draft.

courbe, *n.f.* curve, sweep.

courber, *vb.* bend, curve.

courbure, *n.f.* curvature.

coureur, *n.m.* runner.

courir, *vb.* run.

couronne, *n.f.* crown, wreath.

couronnement, *n.m.* coronation.

couronner, *vb.* crown.

courrier, *n.m.* mail.

courroie, *n.f.* strap.

courroux, *n.m.* wrath.

cours, *n.m.* course.

course, *n.f.* race, errand.

court, *adj.* short.

courtepointe, *n.f.* quilt.

courtier, *n.m.* broker.

courtisan, *n.m.* courtier.

courtois, *adj.* courteous.

courtoisie, *n.f.* courtesy.

cousin, *n.m.* cousin.

coussin, *n.m.* cushion.

coussinet, *n.m.* bearing.

coût, *n.m.* cost.

couteau, *n.m.* knife.

coutellerie, *n.f.* cutlery.

coûter, *vb.* cost.

coûteux, *adj.* expensive, costly.

coutume, *n.f.* custom.

couture, *n.f.* seam. **haute couture,** high fashion.

couturière, *n.f.* dressmaker.

couvée, *n.f.* brood.

couvent, *n.m.* convent.

couver, *vb.* brood, hatch; smolder.

couvercle, *n.m.* lid, cover.

couvert, 1. *n.m.* cover. 2. *adj.* covered, cloudy.

couverture, *n.f.* blanket, cover; (*pl.*) bedclothes.

couvrir, *vb.* cover.

crabe, *n.m.* crab.

crachat, *n.m.* spit.

cracher, *vb.* spit.

craie, *n.f.* chalk.

craindre, *vb.* fear.

crainte, *n.f.* fear, dread, awe.

craintif, *adj.* fearful, apprehensive.

cramoisi, *adj. and n.m.* crimson.

crampe, *n.f.* cramp.

crampon, *n.m.* cramp, crampiron.

cramponner, *vb.* **se c.,** cling.

crâne, *n.m.* skull.

crapaud, *n.m.* toad.

craquement, *n.m.* crack.

craquer, *vb.* crack.

cratère, *n.m.* crater.

cravate, *n.f.* necktie.

crayon, *n.m.* pencᵢl.

créance, *n.f.* belief. **lettres de c.,** credentials.

créancier, *n.m.* creditor.

créateur *m.,* créatrice *f.* 1. *adj.* creative. 2. *n.* creator.

création, *n.f.* creation.

créature, *n.f.* creature.

crédit, *n.m.* credit.

credo, *n.m.* creed.

crédule, *adj.* credulous.

créer, *vb.* create.

crème, *n.f.* cream, custard.

crêpe, *n.f.* pancake; crepe.

crépuscule (-sk-), *n.m.* dusk.

crête, *n.f.* ridge, crest.

crétin, *n.m.* dunce.

cretonne, *n.f.* cretonne.

creuser, *vb.* dig.

creuset, *n.m.* crucible.

creux, *adj. and n.m.* hollow.

crevasse, *n.f.* crevice.

crever, *vb.* burst; die.

crevette, *n.f.* shrimp.

cri, *n.m.* cry, call.

crible, *n.m.* sieve.

crier, *vb.* yell, shout.

crime, *n.m.* crime.

criminel, *adj.* criminal.

crinière, *n.f.* mane.

crise, *n.f.* crisis.

cristal, *n.m.* crystal.

cristallin, *adj.* crystalline.

cristalliser, *vb.* crystallize.

critérium, *n.m.* criterion.

critique, 1. *n.m.* critic. 2. *n.f.* criticism. 3. *adj.* critical.

critiquer, *vb.* criticize.

croasser, *vb.* croak.

croc (-ô), *n.m.* hook.

croche, *n.f.* quaver (music).

crochet, *n.m.* bracket, hook.

crochu, *adj.* hooked.

crocodile, *n.m.* crocodile.

croire, *vb.* believe.

croisade, *n.f.* crusade.

croisé, *n.m.* crusader.

croiser, *vb.* cross.

croiseur, *n.m.* cruiser.

croisière, *n.f.* cruise.

croissance, *n.f.* growth.

croissant, *n.m.* crescent.

croître, *vb.* grow.

croix, *n.f.* cross.

croquant, *adj.* crisp.

croquet, *n.m.* croquet.

croquis, *n.m.* sketch.

crosse, *n.f.* (golf) club.

crotale, *n.m.* rattlesnake.

crouler, *vb.* fall apart.

croup, *n.m.* croup.

croupir, *vb.* wallow.

croûte, *n.f.* crust.

croûton, *n.m.* crouton.

croyable, *adj.* believable.

croyance, *n.f.* belief.

croyant, *n.m.* believer.

cru, *adj.* raw.

cruauté, *n.f.* cruelty.

cruche, *n.f.* pitcher.

crucifier, *vb.* crucify.

crucifix, *n.m.* crucifix.

cruel, *adj.* cruel.

cryochirurgie, *n.f.* cryosurgery.

Cuba, *n.m.* Cuba.

Cubain, *n.m.* Cuban.

cubain, *adj.* Cuban.

cube, *n.m.* cube.

cubique, *adj.* cubic.

cueillir, *vb.* pick.

cuiller, *n.f.* spoon. **c. à thé,** teaspoon. **c. à bouche,** tablespoon.

cuillerée, *n.f.* spoonful.

cuir, *n.m.* leather.

cuirassé, *n.m.* battleship.

cuire, *vb.* cook; sting, smart.

cuisine, *n.f.* kitchen, cooking.

cuisinier, *n.m.* cook.

cuisse, *n.f.* thigh.

cuivre, *n.m.* copper **c. jaune,** brass.

cul-de-sac, *n.m.* blind alley.

culotte, *n.f.* breeches.

culpabilité, *n.f.* guilt.

culte, *n.m.* worship; cult.

cultiver, *vb.* cultivate; grow, raise.

culture, *n.f.* culture, cultivation; farming.

cure, *n.f.* cure.

curé, *n.m.* (parish) priest.

curieux, *adj.* curious.

curiosité, *n.f.* curiosity, curio.

cursif, *adj.* cursive.

cuticule, *n.f.* cuticle.

cuve, *n.f.* vat.

cuver, *vb.* ferment.

cuvette, *n.f.* (wash) basin.

cuvier, *n.m.* washtub.

cycle, *n.m.* cycle.

cycliste, *n.m.f.* cyclist.

cyclomoteur, *n.m.* moped.

cyclone, *n.m.* cyclone.

cygne, *n.m.* swan.

cylindre, *n.m.* cylinder.

cylindrique, *adj.* cylindrical.

cymbale, *n.f.* cymbal.

cynique, 1. *n.m.* cynic. 2. *adj.* cynical.

cynisme, *n.m.* cynicism.

cyprès, *n.m.* cypress.

czar, *n.m.* czar.

D

dactylographe, *n.m.f.* typist.

daigner, *vb.* deign.

daim, *n.m.* buck.

daine, *n.f.* doe.

dais, *n.m.* canopy.

dalle, *n.f.* slab, flag(stone).

dame, *n.f.* lady.

damner, (dä nā], *vb.* damn.

Danemark, *n.m.* Denmark.

danger, *n.m.* danger.

dangereux, *adj.* dangerous.

Danois, *n.m.* Dane.

danois, *adj. and n.m.* Danish.

dans, *prep.* in, into.

danse, *n.f.* dance.

danser, *vb.* dance.

danseur, *n.m.* dancer.

dard, *n.m.* dart.

date, *n.f.* date.

dater, *vb.* date.

datte, *n.f.* date.

davantage, *adv.* more, further.

de, *prep.* of, from, by, about; some.

dé, *n.m.* die; thimble.

débarquer, *vb.* land.

débarrasser, *vb.* rid.

débat, *n.m.* debate.

débattre, *vb.* canvass; debate.

débit, *n.m.* delivery (speech); sale; debit.

débiter, *vb.* sell (retail).

débiteur, *n.m.* debtor.

déblayer, *vb.* clear.

déborder, *vb.* overflow.

déboucher, *vb.* flow (into).

débourser, *vb.* disburse.

debout, *adv.* up. **être d.,** stand.

débris, *n.m.pl.* wreck, debris.

début, *n.m.* beginning, first appearance, debut.

débuter, *vb.* make one's first appearance; begin.

décadence, *n.f.* decay, decadence.

décaféiné, *adj.* decaffeinated.

décapiter, *vb.* behead.

décéder, *vb.* die.

décembre, *n.m.* December.

décence, *n.f.* decency.

décent, *adj.* decent.

déception, *n.f.* disappointment.

décerner, *vb.* award.

décès, *n.m.* death.

décevoir, *vb.* disappoint.

décharge, *n.f.* discharge.

décharger. *vb.* unload, discharge.

décharné, *adj.* gaunt.

déchausser, *vb.* take off shoes.

déchets (-ä), *n.m.pl.* waste.

déchets nucléaires, *n.m.pl.* nuclear waste.

déchiffrer, *vb.* decipher.

déchirer, *vb.* tear, rend.

déchirure, *n.f.* tear, rent.

décibel, *n.m.* decibel.

décider, *vb.* prevail upon, decide.

décimal, *adj.* decimal.

décisif, *adj.* decisive.

décision, *n.f.* decision.

déclamer, *vb.* recite.

déclaration, *n.f.* statement, declaration.

déclarer, *vb.* state, declare.

déclin, *n.m.* ebb.

décliner, *vb.* decline.

décolorer, *vb.* bleach, fade.

décomposer, *vb.* spoil, decompose.

déconcerter, *vb.* baffle, disconcert, embarrass.

décongestionnant, *adj.* decongestant.

décontracté, *adj.* relaxed.

décoratif, *adj.* decorative.

décoration, *n.f.* decoration, trimming.

décorer, *vb.* decorate.

décors, *n.m.pl.* scenery.

découper, *vb.* carve (meat).

découragé, *adj.* despondent.

découragement, *n.m.* discouragement.

décourager, *vb.* dishearten, discourage.

découverte, *n.f.* discovery.

découvreur, *n.m.* discoverer.

découvrir, *vb.* uncover detect, discover.

décrépit, *adj.* decrepit.

décret, *n.m.* decree.

décréter, *vb.* enact.

décrire, *vb.* describe.

dédaigneux, *adj.* scornful.

dédain, *n.m.* scorn, disdain.

dedans, *n.m.* inside, within.

dédicace, *n.f.* dedication.

dédier, *vb.* dedicate.

déduction, *n.f.* deduction.

déduire, *vb.* infer, deduce, deduct.

défaire, *vb.* undo.

défaite, *n.f.* defeat.

défaut, *n.m.* flaw, fault, failure, lack. **à d. de,** for want of.

défectueux, *adj.* faulty, defective.

défendeur, *n.m.* defendant.

défendre, *vb.* forbid, defend.

défense, *n.f.* prohibition, plea, defense.

défenseur, *n.m.* advocate, defender.

défensif, *adj.* defensive.

déférer, *vb.* defer.

défi, *n.m.* challenge, defiance.

défiance, *n.f.* mistrust.

déficit (-t), *n.m.* deficit.

défier, *vb.* challenge, defy. **se d. de,** mistrust.

défigurer, *vb.* deface.

défiler, *vb.* march off.

défini, *adj.* definite.

définir, *vb.* define.

définitif, *adj.* final, definitive.

définition, *n.f.* definition.

déformer, *vb.* distort, deform.

défraîchi, *adj.* dingy.

défricher, *vb.* reclaim.

défunt, *n.m. and adj.* deceased.

dégagé, *adj.* breezy.

dégât, *n.m.* damage.

dégénérer, *vb.* degenerate.

dégoût, *n.m.* distaste, disgust.

dégoûtant, *adj.* foul, disgusting.

dégoûter, *vb.* disgust.

dégoutter, *vb.* drip.

dégradation, *n.f.* degradation.

dégrader, *vb.* degrade.

degré, *n.m.* degree, step.

déguisement, *n.m.* disguise.

déguiser, *vb.* disguise.

dehors, *adv.* (out)doors, outside. **en d. de,** apart from.

déifier, *vb.* deify.

déité, *n.f.* deity.

déjà, *adv.* already.

déjeter, *vb.* make unsymmetrical.

déjeuner, *n.m. and vb.* lunch, breakfast. **petit d.,** breakfast.

déjouer, *vb.* foil, thwart.

delà, *adv.* beyond. **au d. de,** over, past, beyond.

délabrement, *n.m.* decay.

délabrer, *vb.* ruin, wreck.

délacer, *vb.* unlace.

délai, *n.m.* delay.

délaissement, *n.m.* desertion.

délaisser, *vb.* desert.

délassement, *n.m.* relaxation.

délasser, *vb.* refresh.

délateur, *n.m.* informer.

délavé, *adj.* faded, pallid.

délayer, *vb.* dilute with water.

délectable, *adj.* delicious.

délectation, *n.f.* enjoyment.

délecter, *vb.* delight.

délégation, *n.f.* delegation.

délégué, *n.m.* delegate.

déléguer, *vb.* delegate.

délester, *vb.* relieve of ballast.

délétère, *adj.* harmful; offensive.

délibératif, *adj.* deliberative.

délibération, *n.f.* deliberation.

délibéré, *adj.* deliberate.

délibérer, *vb.* deliberate.

délicat, *adj.* dainty, delicate.

délicatesse, *n.f.* delicacy.

délices, *n.f.pl.* delight.

délicieux, *adj.* delicious.

délié, *adj.* slender; keen.

délier, *vb.* untie.

délimiter, *vb.* mark the limits of.

délinéer, *vb.* delineate.

délinquant, 1. *n.m.* delinquent, offender. **2.** *adj.* delinquent.

délirant, *adj.* delirious.

délire, *n.m.* frenzy.

délirer, *vb.* rave.

délit, *n.m.* offense, crime.

délivrance, *n.f.* rescue, deliverance.

délivrer, *vb.* rescue, set free, deliver.

déloger, *vb.* dislodge.

déloyal, *adj.* disloyal.

déloyauté, *n.f.* disloyalty.

déluge, *n.m.* deluge.

déluré, *adj.* clever, cute.

démagogue, *n.m.* demagogue.

demain, *adv.* tomorrow.

demande, *n.f.* application, request, inquiry, claim. **d. en mariage,** proposal.

demander, *vb.* ask, request. **se d.,** wonder.

demandeur, *n.m.* plaintiff.

démangeaison, *n.f.* itch.

démanger, *vb.* itch.

démanteler, *vb.* dismantle.

démarcation, *n.f.* demarcation.

démarche, *n.f.* walk, bearing; step.

démarrage, *n.m.* start.

démarrer, *vb.* unmoor; start up.

démarreur, *n.m.* (self)-starter.

démasquer, *vb.* unmask; expose, reveal.

démêler, *vb.* disentangle.

démembrement, *n.m.* dismemberment.

démembrer, *vb.* dismember.

déménagement, *n.m.* moving.

déménager, *vb.* move.

déménageur, *n.m.* furniture mover.

démence, *n.f.* insanity.

démener, *vb.* struggle.

dément, *adj.* insane.

démenti, *n.m.* denial.

démentir, *vb.* give the lie to.

démesuré, *adj.* measureless, immense.

démettre, *vb.* **se d. (de),** resign.

demeure, *n.f.* abode.

demeurer, *vb.* dwell.

demi, *n.m. and adj.* half.

demi-cercle, *n.m.* semicircle.

demi-dieu, *n.m.* demigod.

demi-frère, *n.m.* stepbrother.

demi-heure, *n.f.* half an hour.

démilitariser, *vb.* demilitarize.

demi-place, *n.f.* half price; half fare.

demi-saison, *adj.* between-season.

demi-sœur, *n.f.* stepsister.

demi-solde, *n.f.* half-pay.

démission, *n.f.* resignation.

démobilisation, *n.f.* demobilization.

démobiliser, *vb.* demobilize.

démocrate, *n.m.f.* democrat.

démocratie, *n.f.* democracy.

démocratique, *adj.* democratic.

démodé, *adj.* old-fashioned.

demoiselle, *n.f.* young lady. **d. d'honneur,** bridesmaid.

démolir, vb. demolish.

démolition, n.f. demolition.

démon, n.m. demon.

démonétiser, vb. demonetize.

démoniaque, adj. demonic.

démonstratif, adj. effusive, demonstrative.

démonstration, n.f. demonstration.

démonter, vb. unhorse; dismantle.

démontrable, adj. demonstrable.

démontrer, vb. demonstrate.

démoralisation, n.f. demoralization.

démoraliser, vb. demoralize.

démouler, vb. remove from a mold.

démuni, adj. short of, lacking.

dénationaliser, vb. denationalize.

dénaturer, vb. denature.

dénégation, n.f. denial.

dénigrer, vb. disparage.

dénivelé, adj. not level.

dénombrement, n.m. enumeration; census.

dénombrer, vb. count.

dénomination, n.f. denomination.

dénommer, vb. name.

dénoncer, vb. report, denounce.

dénonciation, n.f. denunciation.

dénoter, vb. denote.

dénouement, n.m. result, outcome.

dénouer, vb. untie.

denrée, n.f. ware, produce.

dense, adj. dense.

densité, n.f. density.

dent, n.f. tooth. **mal de d.s,** toothache. **brosse à d.s,** toothbrush.

dental, adj. dental.

denté, adj. cogged.

dentelle, n.f. lace.

dentifrice, n.m. tooth paste or powder.

dentiste, n.m. dentist.

dentition, n.f. dentition.

denture, n.f. set of natural teeth.

dénuder, vb. denude.

dénué, adj. destitute, bare.

dénuement, n.m. destitution.

dénuer, vb. divest.

dépannage, n.m. emergency repairs.

dépareillé, adj. odd (unmatched).

départ, n.m. departure.

département, n.m. department.

départir, vb. divide in shares.

dépasser, vb. outrun, pass.

dépayser, vb. bewilder, confuse.

dépêche, n.f. dispatch.

dépêcher, vb. **se d.,** hurry.

dépeindre, vb. portray.

dépendance, n.f. annex (to a building).

dépendant, adj. dependent.

dépendre, vb. depend.

dépens, n.m.pl. expenses.

dépense, n.f. expenditure, expense.

dépenser, vb. spend, expend.

dépérir, vb. waste away; decline.

dépiécer, vb. dismember.

dépit, n.m. spite. **en d. de,** despite.

déplacement, n.m. displacement.

déplacer, vb. displace, move, shift.

déplaire à, vb. displease.

déplaisant, adj. displeasing.

déplanter, vb. transplant.

déplantoir, n.m. trowel.

déplier, vb. unfold.

déploiement, n.m. deployment.

déplorable, adj. wretched, deplorable.

déplorer, vb. deplore.

déployer, vb. deploy.

déplumer, vb. pluck.

déportation, n.f. deportation.

déportements, n.m.pl. misconduct.

déporter, vb. deport.

déposant, n.m. depositor.

déposer, vb. deposit, set down, depose.

dépositaire, n.m.f. trustee.

déposséder, vb. oust; dispossess.

dépôt, n.m. deposit, depot. **d. de vivres,** commissary.

dépouille, n.f. hide, skin, pelt.

dépouiller, vb. strip. **se d. de,** shed.

dépourvu, adj. devoid; needy.

dépoussiéreur, n.m. vacuum cleaner.

dépravation, n.f. depravity.

dépraver, vb. deprave.

dépréciation, n.f. depreciation.

déprécier, vb. depreciate, cheapen.

déprédation, n.f. depredation.

dépression, n.f. depression.

déprimer, vb. depress.

depuis, adv. and prep. since. **d. que,** conj. since.

députation, n.f. delegation.

député, n.m. representative, deputy.

déraciner, vb. uproot, eradicate.

déraison, n.f. unreason.

déraisonnable, adj. unreasonable.

dérangement, n.m. disturbance.

déranger, vb. disturb, trouble.

derechef, adv. once again.

dérégler, vb. upset, disorder.

dérider, vb. smooth; cheer up.

dérision, n.f. derision. **tourner en d.,** deride.

dérivation, n.f. derivation, etymology.

dérive, n.f. drift. **à la d.,** adrift.

dériver, vb. derive; drift.

dernier, adj. last, latter.

dernièrement, adv. lately.

dérober, vb. rob. **se d.,** steal away.

dérouiller, vb. remove the rust from.

dérouler, vb. unroll, unfold.

déroute, n.f. rout.

dérouter, vb. mislead; confuse.

derrière, n.m., adv. and prep. behind.

derviche, n.m. dervish.

dès, prep. since. **d. que,** conj. as soon as.

désabuser, vb. disillusion.

désaccord, n.m. disagreement.

désaccoutumer, vb. break of a habit.

désaffecter, vb. put (church) to secular use.

désagréable, adj. nasty, distasteful.

désagrégation, n.f. disintegration.

désaligné, adj. out of alignment.

désaltérer, vb. quench (one's) thirst.

désappointement, n.m. disappointment.

désappointer, vb. disappoint.

désapprobation, n.f. disapproval.

désapprouver, vb. disapprove.

désarmement, n.m. disarmament.

désarmer, vb. disarm.

désarroi, n.m. disorder.

désastre, n.m. disaster.

désastreux, adj. disastrous.

désavantage, n.m. disadvantage.

désaveu, n.m. denial.

désavouer, vb. disown.

descendance, n.f. descent.

descendant, 1. n.m. offspring, descendant. **2.** adj. downward, descending.

descendre, vb. go down, come down, alight; descend.

descente, n.f. raid; descent.

descriptif, adj. descriptive.

description, n.f. description.

désembarquer, vb. disembark, unload.

désenchanter, vb. disenchant.

désenivrer, vb. sober up.

désert, n.m. wilderness, desert.

déserter, vb. desert.

déserteur, n.m. deserter.

désertion, n.f. desertion.

désespéré, adj. hopeless, forlorn, desperate.

désespérer, vb. despair.

désespoir, n.m. desperation, despair.

déshabiller, vb. undress.

déshériter, vb. disinherit.

déshonnête, adj. improper, indecent.

déshonneur, n.m. disgrace, dishonor.

déshonorant, adj. dishonorable.

déshonorer, vb. disgrace, dishonor.

déshydrater, vb. dehydrate.

désignation, *n.f.* nomination.

désigner, *vb.* appoint, nominate; point out; designate.

désillusion, *n.f.* disillusion.

désinfectant, *n.m.* disinfectant.

désinfecter, *vb.* disinfect, fumigate.

désinfection, *n.f.* disinfection.

désintégration, *n.f.* disintegration.

désintegrer, *vb.* disintegrate.

désintéressé, *adj.* unselfish.

désintéressement, *n.m.* unselfishness.

désir, *n.m.* desire, wish.

désirable, *adj.* desirable.

désirer, *vb.* desire, wish.

désireux, *adj.* desirous.

désistement, *n.m.* withdrawal.

désobéir à, *vb.* disobey.

désobéissance, *n.f.* disobedience.

désobéissant, *adj.* disobedient.

désœuvré, *adj.* idle.

désolation, *n.f.* desolation.

désolé, *adj.* disconsolate; desolate.

désoler, *vb.* desolate.

désordonné, *adj.* disorderly.

désordonner, *vb.* upset, confuse.

désordre, *n.m.* disorder.

désorganisation, *n.f.* disorganization.

désorganiser, *vb.* disorganize.

désormais, *adv.* henceforth.

despote, *n.m.* despot.

despotique, *adj.* despotic.

despotisme, *n.m.* despotism.

dessécher, *vb.* dry out, parch; drain.

dessein, *n.m.* plan, intent.

desserrer, *vb.* loosen.

dessert, *n.m.* dessert.

dessin, *n.m.* drawing, design, sketch.

dessinateur, *n.m.* designer.

dessiner, *vb.* draw, design. se d., loom.

dessous, *n.m.* underside. en d., au-d. de, beneath, underneath.

dessus, *n.m.* top. en d., au-d. de, above. d. de lit, bedspread.

destin, *n.m.* fate, destiny.

destinataire, *n.m.f.* addressee.

destination, *n.f.* destination. à d. de, bound for.

destinée, *n.f.* destiny.

destiner, *vb.* destine, intend.

destituer, *vb.* dismiss.

destructif, *adj.* destructive.

destruction, *n.f.* destruction.

désuet, *adj.* obsolete.

désuétude, *n.f.* disuse.

désunion, *n.f.* disunion.

désunir, *vb.* disconnect.

détaché, *adj.* loose.

détachement, *n.m.* detachment.

détacher, *vb.* detach. se d., stand out.

détail, *n.m.* item, particular, detail. au d., at retail.

détective, *n.m.* detective.

déteindre, *vb.* run (of colors).

détenir, *vb.* detain.

détente, *n.f.* 1. trigger. 2. (politics) détente.

détention, *n.f.* custody, detention.

détérioration, *n.f.* deterioration.

détériorer, *vb.* deteriorate.

détermination, *n.f.* determination.

déterminer, *vb.* determine, fix.

détestable, *adj.* detestable, hateful.

détester, *vb.* abhor, loathe, detest.

détonation, *n.f.* detonation.

détoner, *vb.* detonate.

détour, *n.m.* turn; detour.

détourné, *adj.* devious.

détourner, *vb.* turn away; divert; avert; embezzle.

détresse, *n.f.* trouble, distress.

détriment, *n.m.* detriment.

détroit, *n.m.* strait.

détruire, *vb.* destroy.

dette, *n.f.* debt.

deuil, *n.m.* mourning.

deux, *adj. and n.m.* two. tous les d., both.

deuxième, *adj.* second.

deux-points, *n.m.* colon.

dévaliser, *vb.* rob.

dévaliseur, *n.m.* robber.

devancer, *vb.* be ahead of.

devant, 1. *n.m.* front. **2.** *prep.* before, in front of.

devanture, *n.f.* window, (shop) front.

dévastation, *n.* devastation.

dévaster, *vb.* devastate.

déveine, *n.f.* bad luck.

développement, *n.m.* development.

développer, *vb.* develop.

devenir, *vb.* become.

déverser, *vb.* divert.

dévêtir, *vb.* undress, disrobe.

déviation, *n.f.* deviation.

dévider, *vb.* unwind.

dévier, *vb.* turn away.

deviner, *vb.* guess.

devinette, *n.f.* puzzle, riddle.

devis, *n.m.* estimate.

devise, *n.f.* motto.

dévisser, *vb.* unscrew.

dévoiler, *vb.* unveil, disclose, reveal.

devoir, *n.m.* duty.

devoir, *vb.* owe; be supposed to; have to; (conditional) ought.

dévorer, *vb.* devour.

dévot, *adj.* devout.

dévotion, *n.f.* devotion.

dévoué, *adj.* devoted.

dévouement, *n.m.* devotion.

dévouer, *vb.* dedicate, devote.

dextérité, *n.f.* dexterity.

diabétique, *adj. and n.* diabetic.

diable, *n.m.* devil.

diablerie, *n.f.* mischief.

diabolique, *adj.* diabolic.

diacre, *n.m.* deacon.

diacritique, *adj.* diacritic.

diadème, *n.m.* diadem.

diagnostic, *n.m.* diagnosis.

diagnostiquer, *vb.* diagnose.

diagonal, *adj.* diagonal.

diagramme, *n.m.* diagram.

dialectal, *adj.* dialect.

dialecte, *n.m.* dialect.

dialogue, *n.m.* dialogue.

dialoguer, *vb.* converse, talk together.

diamant, *n.m.* diamond.

diamétral, *adj.* diametric.

diamètre, *n.m.* diameter.

diaphane, *adj.* diaphanous.

diaphragme, *n.m.* diaphragm.

diarrhée, *n.f.* diarrhea.

diathermie, *n.f.* diathermy.

diatribe, *n.f.* diatribe.

dictateur, *n.m.* dictator.

dictature, *n.f.* dictatorship.

dictée, *n.f.* dictation.

dicter, *vb.* dictate.

diction, *n.f.* diction.

dictionnaire, *n.m.* dictionary.

dicton, *n.m.* maxim, proverb.

didactique, *adj.* didactic.

dièse, *adj. and n.m.* sharp.

diète, *n.f.* diet.

diététique, *adj.* dietetic.

Dieu, *n.m.* God.

diffamant, *adj.* libelous.

diffamateur, *n.m.* libeler.

diffamation, *n.f.* libel.

diffamer, *vb.* defame.

différence, *n.f.* difference.

différenciation, *n.f.* differentiation.

différencier, *vb.* differentiate.

différend, *n.m.* difference, dispute.

différent, *adj.* different.

différer, *vb.* defer; differ.

difficile, *adj.* arduous, hard; difficult; fastidious.

difficilement, *adv.* with difficulty.

difficulté, *n.f.* trouble; difficulty.

difficulté psychologique, *n.f.* hangup.

difforme, *adj.* deformed.

difformité, *n.f.* deformity.

diffus, *adj.* diffuse.

diffusion, *n.f.* spread, diffusion.

digérer, *vb.* digest.

digestible, *adj.* digestible.

digestif, *adj. and n.m.* digestive.

digestion, *n.f.* digestion.

digital, *adj.* digital.

digitaline, *n.f.* digitalis.

digne, *adj.* worthy.

dignitaire, *n.m.* dignitary.

dignité, *n.f.* dignity.

digression, *n.f.* digression.

digue, *n.f.* dike, dam.

dilapidation, *n.f.* waste.

dilater, *vb.* expand, dilate.

dilemme, *n.m.* dilemma.

dilettante, *n.m.* amateur.

diligence, *n.f.* diligence.

diligent, *adj.* diligent.

diluer, *vb.* dilute.

dilution, *n.f.* dilution.
dimanche, *n.m.* Sunday.
dimension, *n.f.* dimension.
diminuer, *vb.* lessen, decrease, diminish.
diminutif, *adj. and n.m.* diminutive.
diminution, *n.f.* decrease.
dindon, *n.m.* turkey.
dîner, 1. *n.m.* dinner. **2.** *vb.* dine.
dîneur, *n.m.* diner.
diphtérie, *n.f.* diphtheria.
diphtongue, *n.f.* diphthong.
diplomate, *n.m.* diplomat.
diplomatie, *n.f.* diplomacy.
diplomatique, *adj.* diplomatic.
diplôme, *n.m.* diploma.
dipsomane, *n.* dipsomaniac.
dipsomanie, *n.f.* dipsomania.
dire, *vb.* say, tell. **vouloir d.**, mean. **c'est-à-d.**, namely; that is.
direct, *adj.* direct.
directement, *adv.* directly.
directeur, *n.m.* manager, director.
directif, *adj.* guiding.
direction, *n.f.* management, leadership, direction.
directorate, *n.m.* directorate.
dirigeable, *adj. and n.m.* dirigible.
dirigeant, *adj.* ruling.
diriger, *vb.* manage, boss, steer, direct.
discernable, *adj.* barely visible.
discernement, *n.m.* discernment, judgment.
discerner, *vb.* discern.
disciple, *n.m.* follower, disciple.
disciplinaire, *adj.* disciplinary.
discipline, *n.f.* discipline.
discipliner, *vb.* discipline.
disco, *adj.* disco.
discontinuer, *vb.* discontinue.
disconvenance, *n.f.* unsuitability.
discordance, *n.f.* discord.
discorde, *n.f.* discord.
discothèque, *n.f.* discotheque.
discourir, *vb.* speak one's views.
discours, *n.m.* speech, oration, talk, discourse.
discourtois, *adj.* discourteous.
discrédit, *n.m.* disrepute.
discréditer, *vb.* disparage.
discret, *adj.* discreet.
discrétion, *n.f.* discretion.
disculper, *vb.* exonerate.
discursif, *adj.* discursive.
discussion, *n.f.* argument, discussion.
discutable, *adj.* debatable.
discuter, *vb.* argue, debate, discuss.
disette, *n.f.* famine.
diseur, *n.m.* talker.
disgrâce, *n.f.* disgrace.
disgracier, *vb.* put out of favor.
disjoindre, *vb.* sever, disjoint.
dislocation, *n.f.* dislocation.
disloquer, *vb.* dislocate.

disparaître, *vb.* disappear.
disparate, *adj.* unlike; badly matched.
disparition, *n.f.* disappearance.
dispendieux, *adj.* expensive.
dispensaire, *n.m.* dispensary.
dispensation, *n.f.* dispensation.
dispense, *n.f.* military exemption.
dispenser, *vb.* dispense.
disperser, *vb.* scatter, disperse.
dispersion, *n.f.* dispersal.
disponible, *adj.* available.
disposé, *adj.* disposed. **d. d'avance**, predisposed. **peu d.**, reluctant.
disposer, *vb.* dispose, settle.
dispositif, *n.m.* device.
disposition, *n.f.* arrangement, disposal, disposition.
disproportionné, *adj.* disproportionate.
dispute, *n.f.* row, fight, quarrel, dispute.
disputer, *vb.* dispute. **se d.**, quarrel.
disqualifier, *vb.* disqualify.
disque, *n.m.* disk, record.
dissemblable, *adj.* unlike.
dissemblance, *n.f.* dissimilarity.
dissension, *n.f.* dissension.
dissentiment, *n.m.* dissent.
disséquer, *vb.* dissect.
dissertation, *n.f.* essay.
dissimulation, *n.f.* pretense.
dissimuler, *vb.* dissemble, pretend.
dissipation, *n.f.* dissipation.
dissiper, *vb.* dispel, waste, dissipate.
dissolu, *adj.* dissolute.
dissolution, *n.f.* dissolution.
dissoudre, *vb.* dissolve.
dissuader, *vb.* dissuade.
distance, *n.f.* distance.
distancer, *vb.* outdistance.
distant, *adj.* distant.
distillation (-l-), *n.f.* distillation.
distiller (-l-), *vb.* distill.
distillerie (-l-), *n.f.* distillery.
distinct (-kt), *adj.* distinct.
distinctif, *adj.* distinctive.
distinction, *n.f.* distinction.
distingué, *adj.* distinguished.
distinguer, *vb.* discriminate; make out; distinguish.
distraction, *n.f.* distraction, pastime.
distraire, *vb.* distract, amuse. **se d.**, have fun.
distrait, *adj.* absent-minded.
distribuer, *vb.* give out, deal out, distribute.
distributeur, *n.m.* distributor.
distribution, *n.f.* distribution; delivery; cast.
district (-trèk), *n.m.* district.
dit, *adj.* called.
divaguer, *vb.* ramble.
divan, *n.m.* davenport, couch.
divergence, *n.f.* divergence.
diverger, *vb.* diverge.
divers, *adj.* various.

diversion, *n.f.* diversion.
diversité, *n.f.* diversity.
divertir, *vb.* divert, entertain. **se d.**, enjoy oneself.
divertissement, *n.m.* diversion.
dividende, *n.m.* dividend.
divin, *adj.* divine.
divinateur, *n.m.* soothsayer.
divinité, *n.f.* divinity.
diviser, *vb.* part, divide.
divisible, *adj.* divisible.
division, *n.f.* division.
divorce, *n.m.* divorce.
divorcer, *vb.* divorce.
divulguer, *vb.* divulge.
dix (-s), *adj. and n.m.* ten.
dix-huit (-z-), *adj. and n.m.* eighteen.
dix-huitième (-z-), *adj. and n.m.f.* eighteenth.
dixième (-z-), *adj. and n.m.* tenth.
dix-neuf (-z-), *adj. and n.m.* nineteen.
dix-sept (-s-), *adj. and n.m.* seventeen.
dizaine, *n.f.* (group of) ten.
docile, *adj.* docile.
docilité, *n.f.* docility.
docte, *adj.* learned, wise.
docteur, *n.m.* doctor.
doctorat, *n.m.* doctorate.
doctrine, *n.f.* doctrine.
document, *n.m.* document.
documenter, *vb.* document.
dodu, *adj.* plump.
dogmatique, *adj.* dogmatic.
dogme, *n.m.* dogma.
dogue, *n.m.* watchdog.
doigt (dwä), *n.m.* finger. **d. de pied**, toe.
doit, *n.m.* debit.
dollar, *n.m.* dollar.
domaine, *n.m.* domain, property.
dôme, *n.m.* dome.
domestique, 1. *n.m.f.* servant. **2.** *adj.* domestic.
domicile, *n.m.* residence.
dominant, *adj.* dominant.
domination, *n.f.* sway, domination, dominion.
dominer, *vb.* rule, dominate.
domino, *n.m.* domino.
dommage, *n.m.* injury, damage. **c'est d.**, that's too bad. **quel d.!**, what a pity!
dompter, *vb.* tame, subdue.
don, *n.m.* gift.
donateur, *n.m.* donor.
donation, *n.f.* donation.
donc (-k), *adv.* therefore.
donjon, *n.m.* dungeon.
donne, *n.f.* deal (cards).
donner, *vb.* give.
donneur, *n.m.* giver.
dont, *pron.* whose.
dorénavant, *adv.* hereafter.
dorer, *vb.* gild.
dorloter, *vb.* coddle.
dormant, *adj.* dormant; asleep.
dormir, *vb.* sleep.
dos, *n.m.* back.
dose, *n.f.* dose.

doser, *vb.* decide the amount.
dossier, *n.m.* record.
dot (-t), *n.f.* dowry.
doter, *vb.* endow.
douaire, *n.m.* dowry.
douane, *n.f.* customs, custom house.
douanier, *n.m.* customs officer.
double, *adj. and n.m.* double. faire le d. de, duplicate.
doubler, *vb.* double.
doublure, *n.f.* lining.
doucement, *adv.* gently.
doucereux, *adj.* sugary; oversweet.
douceur, *n.f.* sweetness, gentleness, meekness.
douche, *n.f.* shower bath; douche.
douer, *vb.* endow.
douille, *n.f.* socket.
douleur, *n.f.* pain, ache, sorrow, grief.
douloureux, *adj.* painful.
doute, *n.m.* doubt.
douter, *vb.* doubt. se d. de, suspect.
douteux, *adj.* dubious, doubtful, questionable.
douve, *n.f.* ditch.
doux, *m.*, **douce** *f. adj.* soft, sweet, gentle, mild, meek.
douzaine, *n.f.* dozen.
douze, *adj. and n.m.* twelve.
douzième, *adj. and n.m.* twelfth.
doyen, *n.m.* dean.
dragon, *n.m.* dragon; dragoon.
draguer, *vb.* dredge.
drainage, *n.m.* drainage.
drainer, *vb.* drain.
dramatique, *adj.* dramatic.
dramatiser, *vb.* dramatize.
dramaturge, *n.m.* playwright.
drame, *n.m.* drama.
drap, *n.m.* sheet.
drapeau, *n.m.* flag.
draper, *vb.* drape.
draperie, *n.f.* drapery.
drapier, *n.m.* clothier.
dresser, *vb.* draw up.
dressoir, *n.m.* dresser.
drogue, *n.f.* drug.
droguer, *vb.* drug.
droit, 1. *n.m.* right; law; claim. **2.** *adj. and adv.* (up)right, straight, fair. d. d'auteur, copyright.
droite, *n.f.* right. à d., (to the) right.
drôle, *adj.* funny.
du, *m.*, **de la**, *f.*, **des**, *pl. prep.* some, any.
dû *m.*, **due** *f. adj.* due.
duc, *n.m.* duke.
duché, *n.m.* dukedom.
duchesse, *n.f.* duchess.
ductile, *adj.* ductile.
duel, *n.m.* duel.
duelliste, *n.m.* duellist.
dûment, *adv.* duly.
dune, *n.f.* dune.
duo, *n.m.* duo.
dupe, *n.f.* dupe.
duper, *vb.* trick.

duperie, *n.f.* trickery.
duplicité, *n.f.* duplicity.
dur, *adj.* hard, tough.
durabilité, *n.f.* durability.
durable, *adj.* lasting, durable.
durant, *prep.* during.
durcir, *vb.* harden.
durcissement, *n.m.* hardening.
durée, *n.f.* duration.
durement, *adv.* hard, harshly, strongly.
durer, *vb.* last.
dureté, *n.f.* hardness.
duvet, *n.m.* down.
duveté, *adj.* downy.
dynamique, *adj.* dynamic.
dynamite, *n.f.* dynamite.
dynamo, *n.f.* dynamo.
dynastie, *n.f.* dynasty.
dynastique, *adj.* dynastic.
dysenterie, *n.f.* dysentery.
dyslexie, *n.f.* dyslexia.
dyspepsie, *n.f.* dyspepsia.

E

eau, *n.f.* water. faire e., leak.
eau-de-vie, *n.f.* brandy.
eau-forte, *n.f.* nitric acid.
ébahir, *vb.* amaze.
ébahissement, *n.m.* amazement.
ébarber, *vb.* trim, clip.
ébauche, *n.f.* outline.
ébaucher, *vb.* outline.
ébène, *n.m.* ebony.
ébénisterie, *n.f.* cabinet work.
éblouir, *vb.* dazzle.
éboulement, *n.m.* cave-in.
ébouriffer, *vb.* ruffle.
ébranler, *vb.* shake.
ébriété, *n.f.* drunkenness.
écaille, *n.f.* scale.
écarlate, *adj. and n.f.* scarlet.
écart, *n.m.* separation. à l'é., aloof.
écarté, *adj.* isolated; lonely.
écartement, *n.m.* gap, separation.
écarter, *vb.* set aside.
ecclésiastique, *adj. and n.m.* ecclesiastic.
écervelé, *adj.* scatterbrained.
échafaud, *n.m.* scaffold.
échafaudage, *n.m.* scaffolding.
échancrer, *vb.* scallop, notch.
échange, *n.m.* exchange.
échangeable, *adj.* exchangeable.
échanger, *vb.* exchange.
échantillon, *n.m.* sample.
échappatoire, *n.f.* loophole.
échappement, *n.m.* exhaust.
échapper, *vb.* escape.
écharde, *n.f.* splinter.
écharpe, *n.f.* scarf, sling.
échasse, *n.f.* stilt.
échauder, *vb.* scald.
échauffer, *vb.* heat up.
échéance, *n.f.* maturity.
échecs (-shè), *n.m.pl.* chess.
échelle, *n.f.* ladder, scale.
échelon, *n.m.* step; echelon.

échevelé, *adj.* dishevelled.
échine, *n.f.* spine.
échiner, *vb.* work like a slave.
écho (-kò), *n.m.* echo.
échoir, *vb.* fall due.
échoppe, *n.f.* booth, stall.
échouer, *vb.* fail. faire é., frustrate.
éclabousser, *vb.* splash.
éclair, *n.m.* flash.
éclairage, *n.m.* lighting.
éclaircie, *n.f.* clearing.
éclaircir, *vb.* clear up.
éclairer, *vb.* (en)lighten, light, clear up, clarify.
éclaireur, *n.m.* scout.
éclat, *n.m.* chip, splinter; burst; brilliance, radiance, glamour.
éclatant, *adj.* bursting; loud; brilliant.
éclatement (de pneu), *n.m.* blowout.
éclater, *vb.* burst out.
éclectique, *adj.* eclectic.
éclipse, *n.f.* eclipse.
éclipser, *vb.* eclipse.
éclore, *vb.* hatch, open, blossom.
écluse, *n.f.* lock.
écœurer, *vb.* disgust.
école, *n.f.* school.
écolier, *n.m.* schoolboy.
écologie, *n.f.* ecology.
écologique, *adj.* ecological.
écologiste, *n.m.* ecologist; environmentalist.
économe, *adj.* economical.
économie, *n.f.* economy. é. politique, economics.
économique, *adj.* economic(al).
économiser, *vb.* economize.
économiste, *n.m.* economist.
écope, *n.f.* ladle.
écoper, *vb.* ladle or bail out.
écorce, *n.f.* bark.
écorcher, *vb.* skin.
écorchure, *n.f.* gall.
Écossais, *n.m.* Scotchman, Scotsman.
écossais, *adj.* Scotch, Scottish.
Écosse, *n.f.* Scotland.
écot, *n.m.* share.
écouler, *vb.* drain. s'é., flow, elapse.
écouter, *vb.* listen (to).
écouteur, *n.m.* listener.
écran, *n.m.* screen.
écraser, *vb.* crush.
écrémer, *vb.* skim.
écrevisse, *n.f.* crayfish.
écrier, *vb.* s'é., exclaim.
écrin, *n.m.* case, box.
écrire, *vb.* write. machine à é., typewriter.
écrit, *adj.* written.
écriteau, *n.m.* notice.
écritoire, *n.f.* inkstand.
écriture, *n.f.* writing, scripture.
écrivain, *n.m.* writer.
écrou, *n.m.* nut.
écrouler, *vb.* s'é., fall to pieces.
écru, *adj.* natural.
écu, *n.m.* shield.

écuelle, n.f. bowl, dish.
écume, n.f. lather, foam.
écuménique, adj. ecumenical.
écureuil, n.m. squirrel.
écurie, n.f. stable.
écusson, n.m. escutcheon.
écuyer (-kwĕ-), n.m. squire.
édenté, adj. toothless.
édifice, n.m. building.
édifier, vb. build; edify.
édit, n.m. edict.
éditeur, n.m. publisher.
édition, n.f. edition.
éditorial, adj. editorial.
éducateur, n.m. educator.
éducation, n.f. breeding, education.
éduquer, vb. educate.
effacer, vb. erase, efface.
effectif, adj. effective, actual.
effectivement, adv. effectively.
effectuer, vb. effect.
efféminé, adj. effeminate.
effet, n.m. effect; (pl.) belongings. **en e.**, as a matter of fact, indeed.
efficace, adj. effective.
efficacité, n.f. efficacy.
effigie, n.f. effigy.
effleurer, vb. skim, graze.
effondrement, n.m. collapse.
effondrer, vb. **s'é.**, collapse, sink.
efforcer, vb. **s'é.**, endeavor, try hard.
effort, n.m. endeavor, strain, exertion, effort.
effrayant, adj. fearful.
effrayer, vb. frighten, scare, startle.
effréné, adj. unrestrained; frantic.
effroi, n.m. fright.
effronté, adj. brazen.
effronterie, n.f. effrontery.
effusion, n.f. shedding.
égal, adj. even, equal, same.
également, adv. equally.
égaler, vb. equal.
égaliser, vb. equalize.
égalité, n.f. equality, evenness.
égard, n.m. regard, consideration, esteem. **à l'é. de**, as for. **plein d'é.s**, considerate.
égaré, adj. astray.
égarement, n.m. aberration.
égarer, vb. mislay, bewilder. **s'é.**, go astray, get lost.
égayer, vb. cheer up.
église, n.f. church.
égoïsme, n.m. selfishness, egoism.
égoïste, adj. selfish.
égorger, vb. kill.
égotisme, n.m. egotism.
égout, n.m. sewer.
égoutter, vb. drain; drip.
égratignure, n.f. scratch.
Égypte, n.m. Egypt.
Égyptien, n.m. Egyptian.
égyptien, adj. Egyptian.
éhonté, adj. brazen, shameless.
élaboration, n.f. working out, elaboration; data processing.
élaborer, vb. draft, elaborate.

élan, n.m. elk; zest.
élancer, vb. **s'é.**, dash.
élargir, vb. widen, increase, enlarge.
élasticité, n.f. elasticity.
élastique, adj. and n.m. elastic.
électeur, n.m. voter.
électif, adj. elective.
élection, n.f. election.
électoral, adj. electoral.
électricien, n.m. electrician.
électricité, n.f. electricity.
électrique, adj. electric, electrical.
électrocardiogramme, n.m. electrocardiogram.
électrocuter, vb. electrocute.
élégance, n.f. elegance.
élégant, adj. elegant, smart, stylish.
élégie, n.f. elegy.
élément, n.m. element.
élémentaire, adj. elementary.
éléphant, n.m. elephant.
élevage, n.m. breeding.
élévation, n.f. elevation.
élève, n.m.f. pupil.
élevé, adj. lofty.
élever, vb. raise. **s'é.**, arise, soar.
éleveur, n.m. breeder.
élider, vb. elide.
éligibilité, n.f. eligibility.
éligible, adj. eligible.
élimination, n.f. elimination.
éliminer, vb. eliminate.
élire, vb. elect.
élite, n.f. elite.
elle, pron.f. she, her; (pl.) they, them (f.).
elle-même, pron. herself.
éloge, n.m. praise.
éloigné, adj. remote.
éloignement, n.m. distance.
éloigner, vb. take away. **s'é.**, go away, recede.
éloquence, n.f. eloquence.
éloquent, adj. eloquent.
élu, adj. chosen.
éluder, vb. evade, elude.
émacié, adj. emaciated.
émail, n.m., pl. **émaux**, enamel.
émancipation, n.f. emancipation.
émanciper, vb. emancipate.
émaner, vb. emanate.
emballer, vb. pack.
embarcation, n.f. craft.
embargo, n.m. embargo.
embarquer, vb. embark.
embarras, n.m. embarrassment, trouble, fix.
embarrassant, adj. embarassing, awkward.
embarrasser, vb. embarrass.
embaumé, adj. balmy.
embaumer, vb. perfume, embalm.
embellir, vb. beautify.
embêter, vb. bore, irritate.
emblème, n.m. emblem.
embolie, n.f. embolism.
embouchure, n.f. mouth.
embourber, vb. bog.

embranchement, n.m. junction.
embrasser, vb. embrace, kiss.
embrayage, n.m. clutch.
embrouillement, n.m. tangle, mix-up.
embrouiller, vb. perplex, entangle.
embrun, n.m. spray.
embuscade, n.f. ambush.
émeraude, n.f. emerald.
émerger, vb. emerge.
émerveiller, vb. astonish.
émettre, vb. emit, send forth, issue.
émeute, n.f. riot.
émietter, vb. crumble.
émigrant, n.m. emigrant.
émigration, n.f. emigration.
émigré, n.m. political exile.
émigrer, vb. (e)migrate.
éminemment, adv. eminently.
éminence, n.f. eminence.
éminent, adj. eminent.
émission, n.f. issue.
emmagasinage, n.m. storage.
emmagasiner, vb. store.
emmener, vb. take away.
émotif, adj. emotional.
émotion, n.f. emotion, feeling.
émotionnable, adj. emotional.
émotionner, vb.-thrill.
émoussé, adj. blunt.
émouvant, adj. moving.
émouvoir, vb. move.
empaler, vb. impale.
empan, n.m. span.
emparer, vb. **s'e. de**, take possession of.
empêchement, n.m. prevention.
empêcher, vb. prevent, stop, hinder, inhibit.
empereur, n.m. emperor.
empêtrer, vb. entangle.
emphase, n.f. emphasis.
emphatique, adj. emphatic.
empiéter, vb. encroach, trespass.
empire, n.m. empire.
empirique, adj. empirical.
emplette, n.f. purchase. **faire des e.s**, shop.
emploi, n.m. employment, use; job.
employé, n.m. employee, clerk, (public) servant.
employer, vb. employ, use.
employeur, n.m. employer.
empois, n.m. starch.
empoisonné, adj. poisonous.
empoisonner, vb. poison.
emporter, vb. take away. **s'e.**, get angry.
empreinte, n.f. print, impression.
empressé, adj. solicitous.
empressement, n.m. eagerness.
empresser, vb. **s'e.**, be eager.
emprise, n.f. expropriation.
emprisonnement, n.m. imprisonment.
emprisonner, vb. imprison.
emprunt, n.m. loan.
emprunter à, vb. borrow from.
emprunteur, n.m. borrower.

ému, *adj.* touched, stirred.

émule, *n.* rival, competitor.

en, 1. *prep.* in, into. 2. *adv.* thence; of it; some, any.

encadrer, *vb.* frame.

en-cas, *n.m.* reserve.

enceinte, *adj.f.* pregnant.

encens, *n.m.* incense.

enchaîner, *vb.* chain.

enchantement, *n.m.* enchantment.

enchanter, *vb.* delight, charm, enchant.

enchère, *n.f.* bid. vente aux e.s, auction.

enclore, *vb.* fence in, enclose.

enclos, 1. *n.m.* enclosure. 2. *adj.* shut in.

enclume, *n.f.* anvil.

encoche, *n.f.* notch.

encoller, *vb.* paste.

encombrant, *adj.* cumbersome.

encombré, *adj.* crowded.

encombrement, *n.m.* congestion.

encombrer, *vb.* crowd, clutter, block up.

encontre, *adv.* à l'e., toward, counter (to).

encore, *adv.* still, yet, again.

encourageant, *adj.* encouraging.

encouragement, *n.m.* encouragement.

encourager, *vb.* encourage, urge, promote.

encourir, *vb.* incur.

encre, *n.f.* ink.

encrier, *n.m.* inkwell.

encyclopédie, *n.f.* encyclopedia.

endetté, *adj.* indebted.

endiguer, *vb.* dam up.

endive, *n.f.* chicory.

endolori, *adj.* painful.

endommager, *vb.* damage.

endormi, *adj.* asleep.

endormir, *vb.* put to sleep. s'e., go to sleep.

endossement, *n.m.* endorsement.

endosser, *vb.* endorse.

endroit, *n.m.* place.

enduire, *vb.* smear, daub.

endurance, *n.f.* endurance.

endurant, *adj.* patient.

endurcir, *vb.* harden.

endurcissement, *n.m.* hardening.

énergie, *n.f.* energy.

énergique, *adj.* energetic.

énervant, *adj.* enervating.

énervé, *adj.* nervous.

enfance, *n.f.* childhood. première e., infancy.

enfant, *n.m.f.* child.

enfantement, *n.m.* childbirth.

enfanter, *vb.* bear (children).

enfantillage, *n.m.* childishness.

enfantin, *adj.* childish.

enfariner, *vb.* coat with flour.

enfer (-r), *n.m.* hell.

enfermer, *vb.* shut in.

enfiévrer, *vb.* excite, inspire.

enfin, *adv.* finally, at last.

enflammer, *vb.* inflame.

enfler, *vb.* swell.

enflure, *n.f.* swelling.

enfoncer, *vb.* sink.

enfouir, *vb.* bury.

enfourchure, *n.f.* bifurcation; crotch of a tree.

enfreindre, *vb.* violate.

enfuir, *vb.* s'e., run away, flee, elope.

enfumer, *vb.* fill or cover with smoke.

engageant, *adj.* personable, charming.

engagement, *n.m.* pledge, agreement, engagement.

engager, *vb.* hire, engage. s'e., volunteer.

engelure, *n.f.* chilblain.

engendrer, *vb.* beget.

engin, *n.m.* machine; engine, motor.

englober, *vb.* include.

engloutir, *vb.* devour.

engorgement, *n.m.* choking.

engouement, *n.m.* infatuation.

engouffrer, *vb.* engulf.

engourdir, *vb.* dull.

engrais, *n.m.* fertilizer.

engraisser, *vb.* fatten.

engraver, *vb.* strand or ground (a ship).

engrenage, *n.m.* gear.

engrener, *vb.* engage (gears).

enhardir, *vb.* make bolder.

énigmatique, *adj.* enigmatic.

énigme, *n.f.* riddle, puzzle, enigma.

enivrant, *adj.* intoxicating.

enivrement, *n.m.* intoxication.

enivrer, *vb.* intoxicate. s'e., get drunk.

enjambée, *n.f.* stride.

enjamber, *vb.* stride.

enjeu, *n.m.* stake.

enjoindre, *vb.* enjoin; call upon.

enjôlement, *n.m.* cajolery.

enjôler, *vb.* cajole.

enjoliver, *vb.* beautify.

enjoué, *adj.* playful.

enjouement, *n.m.* playfulness.

enlacer, *vb.* entwine; interlace; embrace.

enlaidir, *vb.* make or become ugly.

enlevable, *adj.* detachable.

enlèvement, *n.m.* removal, abduction.

enlever, *vb.* take away, remove, abduct.

enneigé, *adj.* snow-covered.

ennemi, *adj. and n.m.* enemy.

ennoblir, *vb.* exalt; ennoble.

ennui (-nwè), *n.m.* nuisance, bore, bother; boredom.

ennuyer, *vb.* bore, annoy, vex, bother, irk.

ennuyeux, *adj.* boring, tedious, dull.

énoncer, *vb.* enunciate.

énonciation, *n.f.* enunciation.

énorme, *adj.* enormous.

énormité, *n.f.* enormity.

enquérir, *vb.* inquire.

enquête, *n.f.* inquiry.

enraciner, *vb.* root. s'e., take root.

enragé, *adj.* rabid.

enrageant, *adj.* infuriating.

enrager, *vb.* be, go mad. s'e., get angry.

enregistrement, *n.m.* registration, recording; checking.

enregistrer, *vb.* record, register, list; check (luggage).

enrichir, *vb.* enrich.

enrober, *vb.* coat, envelop.

enrôlement, *n.m.* enlistment, enrollment.

enrôler, *vb.* enlist, enroll.

enroué, *adj.* hoarse.

enrouement, *n.m.* hoarseness.

enrouler, *vb.* s'e., roll up, twist, wind.

enseigne, *n.f.* sign, ensign.

enseignement, *n.m.* teaching, instruction.

enseigner, *vb.* teach.

ensemble, 1. *n.m.* set. 2. *adv.* together.

ensevelir, *vb.* bury.

ensoleillé, *adj.* sunny.

ensommeillé, *adj.* sleepy.

ensuite, *adv.* then, next, afterwards.

ensuivre, *vb.* s'e., ensue.

entablement, *n.m.* entablature.

entacher, *vb.* taint, besmirch.

entailler, *vb.* hack (notch).

entamer, *vb.* begin.

entassement, *n.m.* accumulation.

entasser, *vb.* heap up.

ente, *n.f.* scion (horticulture).

entendement, *n.m.* understanding, sense.

entendre, *vb.* hear, understand. s'e., get on together.

entendu, *adj.* understood, agreed. bien e., of course.

enténébré, *adj.* gloomy.

entente, *n.f.* understanding, agreement.

enterrement, *n.m.* burial.

enterrer, *vb.* bury.

entêté, *adj.* perverse.

entêtement, *n.m.* stubbornness.

entêter, *vb.* s'e., be stubborn, insist.

enthousiasme, *n.m.* enthusiasm.

enthousiaste, 1. *n.m.f.* enthusiast. 2. *adj.* enthusiastic. e. de, keen on.

entichement, *n.m.* infatuation.

entier, *adj.* whole, complete, entire.

entité, *n.f.* entity.

entonnoir, *n.m.* funnel.

entorse, *n.f.* sprain.

entourage, *n.m.* circle of friends; surroundings.

entourer, *vb.* surround, encircle.

entournure, *n.f.* armhole.

entr'acte, *n.m.* intermission.

entr'aide, *n.f.* mutual assistance.

entrailles, *n.f.pl.* bowels.
entrain, *n.m.* zest.
entraîner, *vb.* draw along; involve, entail; coach, train.
entraîneur, *n.m.* coach.
entrant, *adj.* incoming.
entraver, *vb.* clog.
entre, *prep.* among, between.
entre-clos, *adj.* ajar.
entre-deux, *n.m.* interval.
entrée, *n.f.* admission, entry; main course.
entreface, *n.f.* interface.
entregent, *n.m.* tact; spirit.
entrelacer, *vb.* interlace.
entremets (-mě), *n.m.* (side) dish.
entremetteur, *n.m.* intermediary.
entreposer, *vb.* store.
entreposeur, *n.m.* warehouseman.
entrepôt, *n.m.* warehouse.
entreprenant, *adj.* enterprising.
entreprendre, *vb.* undertake.
entrepreneur, *n.m.* contractor. **e. de pompes funèbres,** undertaker.
entreprise, *n.f.* concern, undertaking.
entrer (dans), *vb.* enter, come in, go in. **laisser e.,** admit.
entretenir, *vb.* entertain. **s'e.,** converse.
entretien, *n.m.* maintenance; conference; talk, conversation.
entrevoir, *vb.* glimpse.
entrevue, *n.f.* interview.
entr'ouvert, *adj.* ajar.
entr'ouvrir, *vb.* open halfway.
énumération, *n.f.* enumeration.
énumérer, *vb.* enumerate.
envahir, *vb.* invade.
envahissement, *n.m.* invasion.
enveloppe, *n.f.* envelope, wrapping.
envelopper, *vb.* envelop, wrap, enfold.
envers, 1. *n.m.* wrong side. **2.** *prep.* toward.
enviable, *adj.* enviable.
envie, *n.f.* envy, desire. **avoir e. de,** want to, feel like.
envier, *vb.* envy.
envieux, *adj.* envious.
environ, *prep. and adv.* around, about; approximately.
environnement, *n.m.* surroundings.
environnementaliste, *n.m.* environmentalist.
environner, *vb.* surround.
envisager, *vb.* consider.
envoi, *n.m.* shipment, sending.
envoler, *vb.* **s'e.,** fly away.
envoyé, *n.m.* envoy.
envoyer, *vb.* send.
enzyme, *n.f.* enzyme.
éon, *n.m.* eon.
épais, *adj.* thick.
épaisseur, *n.f.* thickness.
épaissir, *vb.* thicken.
épancher, *vb.* shed (blood).
épanouir, *vb.* **s'é.,** bloom.

épargne, *n.f.* savings.
épargner, *vb.* save, spare.
éparpiller, *vb.* scatter.
épars, *adj.* scattered, sparse.
éparvin, *n.m.* spavin.
épatant, *adj.* (*colloq.*) grand.
épate, *n.f.* swagger.
épatement, *n.m.* amazement.
épater, *vb.* amaze.
épaule, *n.f.* shoulder.
épaulette, *n.f.* epaulette.
épée, *n.f.* sword.
épeler, *vb.* spell.
épellation, *n.f.* spelling.
éperdu, *adj.* distracted.
éperlan, *n.m.* smelt.
éperon, *n.m.* spur.
éperonner, *vb.* spur.
épervier, *n.m.* hawk.
épeuré, *adj.* frightened.
éphémère, *adj.* ephemeral, fleeting.
épice, *n.f.* spice.
épicé, *adj.* spicy.
épicerie, *n.f.* grocery.
épicier, *n.m.* grocer.
épidémie, *n.f.* epidemic.
épiderme, *n.m.* epidermis.
épidermique, *adj.* epidermal.
épier, *vb.* spy.
épigramme, *n.f.* epigram.
épilatoire, *n.m. and adj.* depilatory.
épilepsie, *n.f.* epilepsy.
épileptique, *adj. and n.* epileptic.
épilogue, *n.m.* epilogue.
épinards (-nar), *n.m.pl.* spinach.
épine, *n.f.* spine, thorn. **é. dorsale,** spinal column.
épinet, *n.m.* spinet.
épineux, *adj.* thorny.
épingle, *n.f.* pin. **é. à cheveux,** hairpin. **é. anglaise,** safety pin.
épingler, *vb.* pin.
épique, *adj.* epic.
épiscopal, *adj.* Episcopal.
épisode, *n.m.* episode.
épisodique, *adj.* episodic.
épistolaire, *adj.* epistolary.
épitaphe, *n.f.* epitaph.
épithète, *n.f.* epithet.
épitomé, *n.m.* epitome.
épitre, *n.f.* epistle.
éploré, *adj.* tearful.
épointé, *adj.* dull, blunted.
éponge, *n.f.* sponge.
éponger, *vb.* sponge up.
épopée, *n.f.* epic.
époque, *n.f.* epoch.
épouffé, *adj.* breathless, panting.
épouiller, *vb.* delouse.
épouse, *n.f.* wife.
épouser, *vb.* marry.
épouseur, *n.m.* suitor.
épousseter, *vb.* dust.
époussette, *n.f.* duster.
épouvantable, *adj.* terrible.
épouvante, *n.f.* fright.
épouvanter, *vb.* frighten.
époux, *n.m.* husband.
épreindre, *vb.* squeeze.

éprendre, *vb.* **s'é.,** fall in love.
épreuve, *n.f.* trial, test, ordeal, proof.
éprouver, *vb.* experience.
éprouvette, *n.f.* test tube.
épuisant, *adj.* exhausting.
épuisement, *n.m.* exhaustion.
épuiser, *vb.* exhaust.
épuration, *n.f.* purification.
épurer, *vb.* purify.
équanimité (-kwà-), *n.f.* equanimity.
équateur (-kwà-), *n.m.* equator.
équation (-kwà-), *n.f.* equation.
équatorial (-kwà-), *adj.* equatorial.
équestre, *adj.* equestrian.
équidistant, *adj.* equidistant.
équilibre, *n.m.* poise.
équilibrer, *vb.* balance.
équilibriste, *n.* tight-rope walker.
équinoxe, *n.m.* equinox.
équinoxial, *adj.* equinoctial.
équipage, *n.m.* crew.
équipe, *n.f.* team, crew, gang, shift.
équipement, *n.m.* equipment.
équiper, *vb.* equip.
équitable, *adj.* fair.
équité, *n.f.* equity.
équivalent, *adj. and n.m.* equivalent.
équivaloir, *vb.* equal in value.
équivoque, *adj.* equivocal.
érable, *n.m.* maple.
éradication, *n.f.* eradication.
éraflure, *n.m.* scratch; graze.
érailler, *vb.* unravel.
ère, *n.f.* era.
érection, *n.f.* erection; construction.
éreintant, *adj.* exhausting.
éreinter, *vb.* exhaust.
erg, *n.m.* erg.
ériger, *vb.* erect.
ermitage, *n.m.* hermitage.
ermite, *n.m.* hermit.
éroder, *vb.* erode.
érosif, *adj.* erosive.
érosion, *n.f.* erosion.
érotique, *adj.* erotic.
errant, *adj.* wandering.
erratique, *adj.* erratic.
errer, *vb.* wander; err.
erreur, *n.f.* mistake, error.
erroné, *adj.* erroneous.
éructation, *n.f.* belch.
éructer, *vb.* belch.
érudit, *adj.* learned, scholarly.
érudition, *n.f.* learning.
éruption, *n.f.* rash, eruption.
érysipèle, *n.m.* erysipelas.
escabeau, *n.m.* stool.
escadrille, *n.f.* (ships) flotilla; (airplanes) squadron.
escadron, *n.m.* squadron.
escalader, *vb.* scale; escalate.
escalier, *n.m.* stairs.
escalope, *n.f.* cutlet.
escamotage, *n.m.* legerdemain.
escamoteur, *n.m.* conjurer, magician.
escapade, *n.f.* escapade.
escarcelle, *n.f.* wallet.

escargot, n.m. snail.
escarole, n.f. endive.
escarpé, adj. abrupt.
escarpement, n.m. steepness.
eschare, n.f. scab; bedsore.
esclandre, n.m. slander.
esclavage, n.m. slavery.
esclave, n.m.f. slave.
escompte, n.m. discount.
escorte, n.f. escort.
escorter, vb. escort.
escouade, n.f. squad.
escrime, n.f. fencing.
escrimer, vb. fight.
escrimeur, n.m. swordsman.
escroc (-ô), n.m. swindler.
escroquer, vb. swindle.
escroquerie, n.f. swindle.
esculent, adj. esculent.
espace, n.m. space.
espacé, adj. at great intervals.
espacer, vb. space out.
espadon, n.m. swordfish.
Espagne, n.f. Spain.
Espagnol, n.m. Spaniard.
espagnol, adj. and n.m. Spanish.
espalier, n.m. espalier.
espèce, n.f. species, kind; (pl.)
cash.
espérance, n.f. hope.
espéranto, n.m. Esperanto.
espérer, vb. hope.
espiègle, adj. mischievous.
espièglerie, n.f. mischief.
espion, n.m. spy.
espionnage, n.m. espionage.
espionner, vb. spy on.
esplanade, n.f. esplanade.
espoir, n.m. hope.
esprit, n.m. spirit, mind, wit.
Saint-E., Holy Ghost.
esquif, n.m. skiff.
Esquimau n.m., Esquimaude
f.n. Eskimo.
esquimau, adj. Eskimo.
esquinancie, n.f. quinsy.
esquinter, vb. exhaust, tire out.
esquisse, n.f. sketch.
esquisser, vb. sketch.
esquiver, vb. shirk.
essai, n.m. essay, attempt; experiment; assay.
essaim, n.m. swarm.
essaimer, vb. swarm.
essayer, vb. try; assay.
essence, n.f. gasoline; essence.
essentiel, adj. essential.
esseulement, n.m. solitude.
essieu, n.m. axle.
essor, n.m. flight.
essorer, vb. dry.
essoufflé, adj. breathless.
essoufflement, n.m. breathless-
ness.
essuie-glace, n.m. windshield
wiper.
essuyer, vb. wipe.
est (-t), n.m. east.
estacade, n.f. stockade.
estafette, n.m. courier.
estafier, n.m. bodyguard.
estagnon, n.m. oil drum.
estaminet, n.m. bar, taproom.
estampe, n.f. engraving.

estampille, n.f. trademark.
esthète, n.m. esthete.
esthétique, adj. aesthetic.
estimable, adj. estimable.
estimateur, n.m. estimator; appraiser.
estimatif, adj. estimated.
estimation, n.f. estimate.
estime, n.f. esteem; estimation.
estimer, vb. esteem; estimate,
value, rate.
estival, adj. of summer.
estivant, n.m. summer tourist.
estiver, vb. spend the summer.
estoc, n.m. tree trunk.
estomac (má), n.m. stomach.
estourbir, vb. kill.
estrade, n.f. platform; stage.
estropié, 1. n.m. cripple. 2. adj.
crippled.
estropier, vb. cripple.
estuaire, n.m. estuary.
esturgeon, n.m. sturgeon.
et, conj. and.
étable, n.f. barn.
établi, adj. worktable.
établir, vb. settle, establish.
établissement, n.m. establishment.
étage, n.m. floor, story.
étagère, n.f. whatnot shelf.
étain, n.m. tin.
étal, n.m. butcher shop.
étalage, n.m. display.
étalager, vb. display.
étaler, vb. display, spread.
étalon, n.m. standard.
étameur, n.m. tinsmith.
étamine, n.f. coarse muslin;
stamen.
étampe, n.f. stamp.
étamper, vb. stamp.
étanche, adj. impervious.
étancher, vb. quench, stanch.
étang, n.m. pond.
étape, n.m. stage.
état, n.m. state.
état-major, n.m. staff.
États-Unis, n.m.pl. United
States.
été, n.m. summer.
éteindre, vb. extinguish, put
out.
éteint, adj. extinct.
étendage, n.m. clotheslines.
étendard, n.m. standard.
étendre, vb. extend, spread,
reach.
étendu, adj. extensive.
étendue, n.f. extent.
éternel, adj. everlasting.
éterniser, vb. perpetuate.
éternité, n.f. eternity.
éternuement, n.m. sneeze.
éternuer, vb. sneeze.
éther (-r), n.m. ether.
éthéré, adj. ethereal.
Éthiopie, n.f. Ethiopia.
éthique, n.f. ethics.
ethnique, adj. ethnic.
étinceler, vb. sparkle.
étincelle, n.f. spark, sparkle.
étincellement, n.m. sparkle,
glitter.
étiolement, n.m. atrophy.

étioler, vb. blanch.
étiqueter, vb. label.
étiquette, n.f. label, tag; etiquette.
étirer, vb. stretch out.
étoffe, n.f. stuff, material,
cloth.
étoffer, vb. stuff.
étoile, n.f. star.
étoiler, vb. bespangle.
étonnement, n.m. astonishment.
étonner, vb. astonish.
étouffé, adj. braised.
étouffer, vb. smother.
étourdi, adj. thoughtless.
étourdir, vb. daze.
étourdissant, adj. dazing.
étourdissement, n.m. dizziness.
étrange, adj. strange.
étranger, n. and adj. alien.
étranglement, n.m. strangula-
tion.
étrangler, vb. strangle.
étrave, n.f. stem, bow.
être, 1. n.m. being. 2. vb. be.
étrécir, vb. shrink.
étreindre, vb. clasp.
étreinte, n.f. clasp, hug, embrace.
étrier, n.m. stirrup.
étrille, n.f. currycomb.
étroit, adj. narrow.
Étrusque, n.m.f. Etruscan.
étrusque, adj. Etruscan.
étude, n.f. study.
étudiant, n.m. student.
étudier, vb. study.
étui, n.m. 1. case. 2. needle
case.
étuve, n.f. steam room.
étymologie, n.f. etymology.
étymologique, adj. etymologi-
cal.
eucalyptus, n.m. eucalyptus.
eucharistie, n.f. eucharist.
eunuque, n.m. eunuch.
euphémique, adj. euphemistic.
euphémisme, n.m. euphemism.
euphonie, n.f. euphony.
euphonique, adj. euphonic.
euphorie, n.f. euphoria.
Europe, n.f. Europe.
Européen, n.m. European.
européen, adj. European.
euthanasie, n.f. euthanasia.
eux, pron.m. them.
évacuable, adj. able to be
evacuated.
évacuation, n.f. evacuation.
évacuer, vb. evacuate.
évader, vb. s'é., escape.
évaluateur, n.m. appraiser.
évaluation, n.f. appraisal.
évaluer, vb. evaluate, rate, assess.
évangélique, adj. evangelic.
évangéliste, n.m. evangelist.
évangile, n.m. gospel.
évanouir, vb. s'é., fade away;
faint.
évaporation, n.f. evaporation.
évaporer, vb. evaporate.
évasif, adj. evasive.
évasion, n.f. escape.

évêché, n.m. bishopric.
éveil, n.m. alertness.
éveillé, adj. sprightly.
éveiller, vb. wake.
événement, n.m. event.
éventail, n.m. fan.
éventrer, vb. disembowel.
éventualité, n.f. eventuality.
éventuel, adj. possible.
éventuellement, adv. eventually.
évêque, n.m. bishop.
éviction, n.f. eviction.
évidemment, adv. evidently.
évidence, n.f. evidence. en é., conspicuous.
évident, adj. obvious, evident.
évider, vb. scoop out.
évier, n.m. sink.
évincer, vb. oust.
éviscérer, vb. eviscerate, disembowel.
évitable, adj. avoidable.
éviter, vb. avoid.
évocation, n.f. evocation.
évolution, n.f. evolution.
évoquer, vb. evoke.
exact (-kt), adj. exact, precise.
exactement, adv. exactly.
exactitude, n.f. precision.
exagération, n.f. exaggeration.
exagérer, vb. exaggerate.
exaltant, adj. exciting.
exaltation, n.f. exaltation.
exalté, adj. impassioned.
exalter, vb. exalt, elate.
examen, n.m. examination.
examiner, vb. examine.
exaspération, n.f. exasperation.
exaspérer, vb. exasperate, aggravate.
excavateur, n.m. steam shovel.
excavation, n.f. excavation.
excaver, vb. excavate.
excédent, n.m. excess; overweight.
excéder, vb. exceed.
excellence, n.f. excellence, excellency, highness.
excellent, adj. excellent.
exceller, vb. excel.
excentrique, adj. eccentric.
excepté, prep. except.
excepter, vb. except.
exception, n.f. exception.
exceptionnel, adj. exceptional.
excès, n.m. excess.
excessif, adj. excessive, extreme.
exciser, vb. excise; cut out.
excitabilité, n.f. excitability.
excitable, adj. excitable.
excitant, adj. exciting.
exciter, vb. excite.
exclamatif, adj. exclamatory.
exclamation, n.f. exclamation.
exclamer, vb. exclaim.
exclure, vb. exclude.
exclusif, adj. exclusive.
exclusion, n.f. exclusion.
excommunication, n.f. excommunication.
excommunier, vb. excommunicate.

excorier, vb. excoriate.
excrément, n.m. excrement.
excréter, vb. excrete.
excrétion, n.f. excretion.
excursion, n.f. excursion.
excursionniste, n. excursionist.
excusable, adj. excusable.
excuse, n.f. plea, excuse.
excuser, vb. excuse. s'e. de, apologize for.
exécuter, vb. perform, enforce.
exécuteur, n.m. executor.
exécutif, adj. and n.m. executive.
exécution, n.f. performance, enforcement, execution.
exemplaire, 1. n.m. copy. 2. adj. exemplary.
exemple, n.m. instance, example.
exempt, adj. exempt.
exempt de droits, adj. dutyfree.
exempter, vb. exempt.
exemption, n.f. exemption.
exerçant, adj. practicing.
exercer, vb. exercise, drill, train. s'e., practice.
exercice, n.m. exercise, drill, practice.
exhalaison, n.f. exhalation.
exhaler, vb. exhale.
exhaustion, n.f. exhaust.
exhiber, vb. show, present; exhibit.
exhibition, n.f. exhibition.
exhortation, n.f. exhortation.
exhorter, vb. exhort.
exhumer, vb. exhume.
exigence, n.f. requirement.
exiger, vb. require, exact, demand.
exil (-l), n.m. exile.
exilé, n.m. exile.
exiler, vb. banish.
existant, adj. existent.
existence, n.f. existence.
exister, vb. exist.
exode, n.m. exodus.
exonération, n.f. exoneration.
exonérer, vb. exonerate.
exorbitant, adj. exorbitant.
exorciser, vb. exorcise.
exotique, adj. exotic.
expansible, adj. expansible.
expansif, adj. expansive.
expansion, n.f. expansion.
expatriation, n.f. expatriation.
expatrié, n. exile, expatriate.
expectorant, n.m. and adj. expectorant.
expectorer, vb. expectorate.
expédient, n.m. makeshift.
expédier, vb. dispatch.
expéditif, adj. expeditious.
expédition, n.f. dispatch; expedition, shipment.
expérience, n.f. experience, experiment.
expérimental, adj. experimental.
expérimentation, n.f. experimentation.
expérimenté, adj. practiced, experienced.

expert, adj. and n.m. expert.
expiable, adj. expiable.
expiation, n.f. atonement.
expier, vb. atone for.
expiration, n.f. expiration.
expirer, vb. expire.
explétif, n. and adj. expletive.
explicatif, adj. explanatory.
explication, n.f. explanation.
explicite, adj. explicit, clear.
expliquer, vb. explain.
exploit, n.m. feat, exploit.
exploitation, n.f. exploitation, working.
exploiter, vb. exploit.
explorateur, n.m. explorer.
exploratif, adj. exploratory.
exploration, n.f. exploration.
explorer, vb. explore.
explosible, adj. explosive.
explosif, adj. and n.m. explosive.
explosion, n.f. blast, explosion.
exportation, n.f. export, exportation.
exporter, vb. export.
exposé, n.m. account, statement.
exposer, vb. expound, expose, exhibit.
exposition, n.f. exposition, exposure, show, display.
exprès, 1. n.m. special delivery. 2. adj. express. 3. adv. on purpose.
expressif, adj. expressive.
expression, n.f. expression.
exprimable, adj. expressible.
exprimer, vb. express.
exproprier, vb. expropriate.
expulser, vb. expel.
expulsion, n.f. expulsion.
expurgation, n.f. expurgation.
expurger, vb. expurgate.
exquis, adj. exquisite.
exsuder, vb. exude.
extase, n.f. ecstasy.
extasier, vb. s'e. sur, rave about.
extatique, adj. ecstatic.
extensif, adj. extensive.
extension, n.f. extension.
exténuation, n.f. extenuation.
exténuer, vb. extenuate, exhaust.
extérieur, 1. n.m. exterior. 2. adj. exterior, outer.
extérieurement, adv. externally.
extermination, n.f. extermination.
exterminer, vb. exterminate.
externat, n.m. day school.
externe, adj. external.
exterritorialité, n.f. extraterritoriality.
extincteur, n.m. fire extinguisher.
extinction, n.f. extinction.
extirper, vb. extirpate, root out.
extorquer, vb. extort.
extorsion, n.f. extortion.
extra-, prefix extra.

extraction, *n.m.* extraction; descent.

extrader, *vb.* extradite.

extradition, *n.f.* extradition.

extra-fin, *adj.* extremely fine.

extraire, *vb.* extract.

extrait, *n.m.* extract, abstract.

extraordinaire, *adj.* extraordinary, unusual.

extraordinairement, *adv.* extraordinarily.

extravagance, *n.f.* extravagance.

extravagant, *adj.* extravagant.

extrême, *adj. and n.m.* extreme.

extrémiste, *n.* extremist.

extrémité, *n.f.* extremity.

extrinsèque, *adj.* extrinsic.

extroverti, *n.* extrovert.

extrusion, *n.f.* extrusion.

exubérance, *n.f.* exuberance.

exubérant, *adj.* exuberant.

exultation, *n.f.* exultation.

exulter, *vb.* exult.

F

fable, *n.f.* fable.

fabliau, *n.m.* fabliau.

fabricant, *n.m.* maker, manufacturer.

fabricateur, *n.m.* forger.

fabrication, *n.f.* make.

fabriquer, *vb.* manufacture.

fabrique, *n.f.* factory.

fabuleux, *adj.* fabulous.

fabuliste, *n.m.* fabulist.

façade, *n.f.* front.

face, *n.f.* face. **en f. de,** opposite. **faire f. à,** confront.

facétie, *n.f.* joke, prank.

facétieux, *adj.* facetious.

facette, *n.f.* facet.

fâché, *j.* angry; sorry.

fâcher, *vb.* anger, offend, grieve. **se f.,** get angry.

fâcherie, *n.f.* quarrel, argument.

fâcheux, *adj.* upleasant.

facial, *adj.* facial.

facile, *adj.* easy.

facilité, *n.f.* fluency, ease.

faciliter, *vb.* facilitate, make easy.

façon, *n.f.* way, manner, fashion. **de f. à,** so as to.

faconde, *n.f.* glibness; fluency.

façonner, *vb.* shape, fashion.

facsimilé, *n.m.* facsimile.

facteur, *n.m.* factor, element; mailman.

factice, *adj.* artificial.

factieux, *adj.* factious; quarrelsome.

faction, *n.f.* faction, party.

factionnaire, *n.m.* sentry.

facture, *n.f.* invoice, bill.

facturer, *vb.* bill; send an invoice to.

facultatif, *adj.* optional.

faculté, *n.f.* faculty.

fadaise, *n.f.* nonsense.

fade, *adj.* insipid.

fadeur, *n.f.* insipidity.

fagot, *n.m.* bundle.

faible, *adj.* weak, faint, dim, feeble.

faiblement, *adv.* feebly, weakly.

faiblesse, *n.f.* weakness, frailty, dimness.

faiblir, *vb.* weaken.

failli, *adj. and n.m.* bankrupt.

faillibilité, *n.f.* fallibility.

faillible, *adj.* fallible.

faillir, *vb.* fail.

faillite, *n.f.* bankrupcy.

faim, *n.f.* hunger.

fainéant, *n.m.* loafer.

faire, *vb.* make, do. **f. part,** inform. **f. mal à,** hurt. **f. voir,** show.

faisable, *adj.* feasible.

faisan, *n.m.* pheasant.

fait, *n.m.* fact. **tout à f.,** wholly.

falaise, *n.f.* cliff.

fallacieux, *adj.* fallacious.

falloir, *vb.* be necessary. **comme il faut,** decent.

falot, *n.m.* lamp.

falsificateur, *n.* forger; falsifier.

falsification, *n.f.* falsification.

falsifier, *vb.* falsify.

fameux, *adj.* famous.

familiariser, *vb.* familiarize.

familiarité, *n.f.* familiarity.

familier, *adj.* familiar.

familièrement, *adv.* familiarly.

famille, *n.f.* family, household.

famine, *n.f.* famine.

fanatique, *adj. and n.m.* fanatic.

fanatisme, *n.m.* fanaticism.

faner, *vb.* fade.

fanfare, *n.f.* fanfare.

fanfaronnade, *n.f.* boast.

fange, *n.f.* filth; vice.

fantaisie, *n.f.* fancy, fantasy.

fantastique, *adj.* fantastic.

fantoche, *n.m.* puppet.

fantôme, *n.m.* phantom, ghost.

faon, *n.m.* fawn.

farce, *n.f.* stuffing; farce.

farceur, *n.m.* jokester.

farcir, *vb.* stuff.

fard, *n.m.* facial makeup.

fardeau, *n.m.* burden.

farinacé, *adj.* farinaceous.

farine, *n.f.* meal, flour.

farniente, *n.m.* idleness.

farouche, *adj.* fierce, sullen, shy.

fascinant, *adj.* fascinating.

fascination, *n.f.* fascination.

fascine, *n.f.* faggot (of wood).

fasciner, *vb.* fascinate.

fascisme, *n.m.* fascism.

fasciste, *n.m.* fascist.

faste, *n.m.* ostentation.

fastidieux, *adj.* dull.

fat, *adj.* foppish.

fatal, *adj.* mortal; fatal.

fatalisme, *n.m.* fatalism.

fataliste, *n.m.f.* fatalist.

fatalité, *n.f.* fatality; misfortune.

fatigant, *adj.* tiring.

fatigue, *n.f.* weariness.

fatiguer, *vb.* tire.

fatuité, *n.f.* smugness.

faubourg, *n.m.* suburb.

faubourien, *adj.* suburban.

faucher, *vb.* mow.

faucheur, *n.m.* reaper, mower.

faucille, *n.f.* sickle.

faucon, *n.m.* hawk.

fauconneau, *n.m.* young falcon.

fauconnerie, *n.f.* falconry.

faufil, *n.m.* basting thread.

faufiler, *vb.* baste.

faune, *n.f.* fauna; wildlife.

faussaire, *n.* forger; liar.

faussement, *adv.* falsely.

fausser, *vb.* pervert, warp, distort.

fausset, *n.m.* falsetto; spigot, faucet.

fausseté, *n.f.* falseness.

faute, *n.f.* fault, mistake. **f. de,** for want of.

fauteuil, *n.m.* armchair.

fautif, *adv.* faulty, wrong.

fauve, *adj.* wild.

faux, 1. *n.m.* forgery. **2.** *f.* scythe.

faux *m.,* **fausse** *f. adj.* false, wrong, spurious, counterfeit.

faux-filet, *n.m.* sirloin.

faveur, *n.f.* favor. **en f. de,** on behalf of

favorable, *adj.* conducive, favorable.

favorablement, *adv.* favorably.

favori, *n.m.* whisker.

favori *m.,* **favorite** *f. adj. and n.* favorite.

favoriser, *vb.* favor.

favoritisme, *n.m.* favoritism.

fayot, *n.m.* kidney bean.

féal, *adj.* faithful.

fébrile, *adj.* feverish.

fécal, *adj.* fecal.

fécond, *adj.* fertile.

féconder, *vb.* fertilize.

fécondité, *n.f.* fertility.

féculent, *adj.* starchy.

fédéral, *adj.* federal.

fédéraliser, *vb.* federalize.

fédéraliste, *n. and adj.* federalist.

fédération, *n.f.* confederacy, federation.

fédérer, *vb.* federate.

fée, *n.f.* fairy.

féerie, *n.f.* fairyland.

féerique, *adj.* fairylike.

feindre, *vb.* feign, pretend.

fêler, *vb.* crack.

félicitation, *n.f.* congratulation.

félicité, *n.f.* bliss.

féliciter (de), *vb.* congratulate (on).

félin, *adj.* feline.

félon, *adj.* disloyal.

femelle, *adj. and n.f.* female.

féminin, *adj.* female, feminine.

femme, *n.f.* woman, wife. **f. de chambre,** chambermaid.

fémoral, *adj.* femoral.

fendille, n.f. crack.
fendiller, vb. se f., crack.
fendoir, n.m. cleaver.
fendre, vb. split, rip.
fenêtre, n.f. window.
fenil, n.m. hayloft.
fente, n.f. crack, rip, split.
féodal, adj. feudal.
féodalité, n.f. feudalism.
fer (-r), n.m. iron. **chemin de f.,** railway. **fil de f.,** wire. **f. à cheval,** horseshoe.
fermail, n.m. brooch, clasp.
ferme, n.f. farm. **maison de f.,** farmhouse.
ferme, n.f. firm, steady, fast.
fermement, adv. firmly.
fermentation, n.f. fermentation.
fermenter, vb. ferment.
fermer, vb. close. **f. à clef,** lock.
fermeté, n.f. firmness.
fermier, n.m. farmer.
féroce, adj. fierce.
férocité, n.f. ferocity.
ferraille, n.f. old iron.
ferreux, adj. ferrous.
ferrique, adj. ferric.
fertile, adj. fertile.
fertilisant, n.m. fertilizer.
fertilisation, n.f. fertilization.
fertiliser, vb. fertilize.
fertilité, n.f. fertility.
férule, n.f. cane, rod.
fervemment, adv. fervently.
fervent, adj. fervent.
ferveur, n.f. fervor.
fesse, n.f. buttock.
fessée, n.f. spanking.
fesser, vb. spank.
festin, n.m. feast.
festiner, vb. feast.
feston, n.m. festoon.
fête, n.f. feast, party. **jour de f.,** holiday.
fêter, vb. fete.
fétiche, n.m. fetish.
fétide, adj. fetid.
feu, n.m. fire. **f. de joie,** bonfire. **f. d'artifice,** fireworks. **prendre f.,** catch fire. **coup de f.,** shot.
feu, adj. late (deceased).
feuillage, n.m. foliage.
feuille, n.f. leaf, sheet, foil.
feuilleter, vb. skim (book).
feutre, n.m. felt.
fève, n.f. bean.
février, n.m. February.
fez, n.m. fez.
fi, interj. fie!
fiacre, n.m. cab.
fiançailles, n.f.pl. engagement, betrothal.
fiancé, n.m. fiancé.
fiancer, vb. betroth.
fiasco, n.m. fiasco.
fibre, n.f. fiber.
fibreux, adj. fibrous.
ficelle, n.f. string, twine.
fiche, n.f. slip (of paper).
ficher, vb. se f. de, care nothing about.
fichier, n.m. card index.
fichu, adv. ruined.

fictif, adj. fictitious.
fiction, n.f. fiction.
fidèle, adj. faithful.
fidélité, n.f. fidelity, loyalty, allegiance.
fief, n.m. feud.
fiel, n.m. gall.
fiente, n.f. dung.
fier (-r), adj. proud.
fier, vb. se f., trust.
fierté, n.f. trust.
fièvre, n.f. fever.
fiévreux, adj. feverish.
fifre, n.m. fife(r).
figer, vb. coagulate.
figue, n.f. fig.
figuratif, adj. figurative.
figure, n.f. face, figure.
figurer, vb. figure, imagine. se f., fancy.
fil (-l), n.m. thread, string. **f. de fer,** wire.
filament, n.m. filament.
filature, n.f. spinning-mill.
file, n.f. file.
filer, vb. spin.
filet, n.m. net.
filial, adj. filial.
filin, n.m. rope.
fille, n.f. daughter. **jeune f.,** girl. **vieille f.,** old maid.
film, n.m. film.
filmer, vb. film.
filou, n.m. thief.
fils (fès), n.m. son.
filtrant, adj. filterable.
filtration, n.f. filtration.
filtre, n.m. filter.
filtrer, vb. filter.
fin, 1. n.f. end. 2. adj. fine; sharp; clever.
final, adj. final.
finaliste, n. finalist.
finalité, n.f. finality.
finance, n.f. finance.
financer, vb. finance.
financier, 1. n.m. financier. 2. adj. financial.
finasser, vb. finesse.
finir, vb. finish.
Finlande, n.f. Finland.
Finnois, n.m. Finn.
finnois, adj. and n.m. Finnish.
firmament, n.m. firmament.
firme, n.f. company.
fiscal, adj. fiscal.
fissure, n.f. fissure.
fixation, n.f. fixation.
fixe, adj. set, fixed.
fixer, vb. fix, secure, settle.
fixité, n.f. fixity.
flaccidité, n.f. flabbiness.
flacon, n.m. bottle.
flagellation, n.f. flagellation.
flageller, vb. flog.
flagrant, adj. flagrant.
flair, n.m. flair.
flairer, vb. smell.
flamand, adj. Flemish.
flambant, adj. flaming.
flambeau, n.m. torch.
flambée, n.f. blaze.
flamber, vb. blaze.
flamboyant, adj. flaming; flamboyant.

flamboyer, vb. flame, flare.
flamme, n.f. flame.
flanc, n.m. side, flank.
flanchet, n.m. flank (of beef).
flanelle, n.f. flannel.
flâner, vb. saunter, stroll, loiter, loaf.
flâneur, n.m. idler.
flanquer, vb. flank.
flaque, n.f. puddle.
flasque, adj. flabby.
flatter, vb. flatter.
flatterie, n.f. flattery.
flatteur, n.m. flatterer.
fléau, n.m. scourge, plague.
flèche, n.f. arrow.
fléchir, vb. bend.
flegmatique, adj. phlegmatic.
flegme, n.m. phlegm.
flet, n.m. flounder.
flétan, n.m. halibut.
flétrir, vb. wilt, wither.
fleur, n.f. flower, blossom, bloom.
fleuret, n.m. foil.
fleuri, adj. flowery.
fleurir, vb. flower, bloom, blossom.
fleuriste, n.m.f. florist.
fleuve, n.m. river.
flexibilité, n.f. flexibility.
flexible, adj. flexible.
flirt (-t), n.m. flirtation.
flirter, vb. flirt.
flocon, n.m. flake.
florissant, adj. prosperous, flourishing.
flot, n.m. wave. **à flot,** afloat.
flottant, adj. floating; irresolute.
flotte, n.f. fleet.
flottement, n.m. fluctuation; wavering.
flotter, vb. float.
flou, adj. hazy, indistinct.
fluctuation, n.f. fluctuation.
fluctuer, vb. fluctuate.
fluet m., **fluette** f. adj. thin, delicate.
fluide, adj. and n.m. fluid, liquid.
fluidité, n.f. fluidity.
flûte, n.f. flute.
flûté, adj. soft; flute-like.
flux, n.m. flow, flux.
fluxion, n.f. inflammation.
foi, n.f. faith; trust.
foie, n.m. liver.
foin, n.m. hay.
foire, n.f. fair.
fois, n.f. time. **à la f.,** at once.
foison, n.f. abundance.
foisonner, vb. abound.
folâtre, adj. frisky.
folâtrer, vb. frolic.
folichon, adj. playful.
folie, n.f. mania, madness, folly.
folklore, n.m. folklore.
follement, adv. foolishly.
follet, adj. merry, playful.
fomenter, vb. foment.
foncé, adj. dark.
foncer, vb. deepen.
fonction, n.f. function.

fonctionnaire, *n.m.* official, civil servant.
fonctionnement, *n.m.* operation, working.
fonctionner, *vb.* function, work.
fonctions, *n.f.pl.* office.
fond, *n.m.* bottom, (back)-ground. à f., thorough(ly). au f., fundamentally.
fondamental, *adj.* basic, fundamental.
fondateur, *n.m.* founder.
fondation, *n.f.* foundation, establishment.
fondé, *adj.* authentic; (*comm.*) funded.
fondement, *n.m.* foundation.
fonder, *vb.* found.
fonderie, *n.f.* foundry.
fondre, *vb.* melt, fuse.
fondrière, *n.f.* bog.
fonds, *n.m.* fund.
fongus (-s), *n.m.* fungus.
fontaine, *n.f.* fountain.
fonte, *n.f.* melting.
fonts, *n.m.pl.* font.
football, *n.m.* football.
footing, *n.m.* walking.
forain, *n.m.* peddler.
forçat, *n.m.* convict.
force, *n.f.* strength, force; emphasis.
forcé, *adj.* forced, far-fetched.
forcément, *adv.* of necessity.
forcené, *adj.* frantic.
forcer, *vb.* force, compel.
forcir, *vb.* thrive.
forer, *vb.* bore, drill.
forestier, *n.m.* forest ranger.
foret, *n.m.* drill.
forêt, *n.f.* forest.
foreuse, *n.f.* drill.
forfait, *n.m.* crime; forfeit; contract.
forfaiture, *n.f.* mishandling.
forfanterie, *n.f.* bragging.
forge, *n.f.* forge.
forger, *vb.* forge.
forgeron, *n.m.* blacksmith.
forgeur, *n.m.* forger; inventor.
formaliser, *vb.* offend.
formaliste, *adj.* formal; precise.
formalité, *n.f.* formality, ceremony.
formation, *n.f.* formation.
forme, *n.f.* shape, form.
formel, *adj.* formal.
former, *vb.* form, shape.
formidable, *adj.* terrible, formidable.
formule, *n.f.* formula, form.
formuler, *vb.* formulate, draw up.
fort, 1. *n.m.* fort. **2.** *adj.* strong, loud. **3.** *adv.* hard.
forteresse, *n.f.* fort(ress).
fortifiant, *adj.* strengthening.
fortification, *n.f.* fortification.
fortifier, *vb.* strengthen.
fortuit, *adj.* accidental.
fortuité, *n.f.* fortuitousness.
fortune, *n.f.* fortune.

fortuné, *adj.* lucky, fortunate.
fosse, *n.f.* pit.
fossé, *n.m.* ditch; dike.
fossette, *n.f.* dimple.
fossile, *n.m.* fossil.
fossoyer, *vb.* dig a trench.
fou *m.,* **folle** *f.* *adj.* mad, crazy, demented.
foudre, *n.m.* thunderbolt.
foudroyant, *adj.* terrifying, crushing.
foudroyer, *vb.* crush, blast.
fouet, *n.m.* whip, lash.
fouetter, *vb.* flog, whip.
fougère, *n.f.* fern.
fougue, *n.f.* dash.
fougueux, *adj.* fiery, impetuous.
fouille, *n.f.* excavation.
fouiller, *vb.* ransack.
fouillis, *n.m.* litter, mess.
fouir, *vb.* dig, burrow.
foulard, *n.m.* scarf.
foule, *n.f.* crowd, mob.
fouler, *vb.* trample.
foulure, *n.f.* sprain, wrench.
four, *n.m.* oven.
fourbe, 1. *n.m.* knave. **2.** *adj.* scheming.
fourberie, *n.f.* knavery.
fourbir, *vb.* polish.
fourche, *n.f.* fork.
fourchette, *n.f.* fork.
fourgon, *n.m.* wagon.
fourmi, *n.f.* ant.
fourmillement, *n.m.* swarming; tingling.
fourmiller, *vb.* mill; swarm.
fourneau, *n.m.* stove, furnace.
fournée, *n.f.* batch.
fourniment, *n.m.* equipment.
fournir de, *vb.* supply, furnish.
fournisseur, *n.m.* tradesman.
fournitures, *n.f.pl.* supplies.
fourrage, *n.m.* fodder, forage.
fourrager, *vb.* forage.
fourré, *adj.* lined (of clothing); thick; wooded.
fourreau, *n.m.* sheath.
fourrer, *vb.* thrust in. se f., interfere, meddle.
fourreur, *n.m.* furrier.
fourrure, *n.f.* fur.
fourvoyer, *vb.* mislead.
foyer, *n.m.* focus, hearth. f. domestique, home.
frac, *n.m.* dress coat.
fracas, *n.m.* crash; rattle; noise; ado.
fracasser, *vb.* se f., shatter.
fraction, *n.f.* fraction.
fracture, *n.f.* fracture.
fracturer, *vb.* break, fracture.
fragile, *adj.* brittle, delicate, frail, fragile.
fragilité, *n.f.* fragility.
fragment, *n.m.* fragment.
fragmenter, *vb.* divide up.
fraîcheur, *n.f.* freshness, coolness.
fraîchir, *vb.* freshen.
frais, *n.m.pl.* expense(s), cost, fee.
frais *m.* **fraîche** *f.* *adj.* fresh, cool.

fraise, *n.f.* strawberry; ruffle.
framboise, *n.f.* raspberry.
franc, 1. *n.m.* franc. **2.** *adj.m.,* **franche** *f.* frank, open.
Français, *n.m.* Frenchman.
français, *adj.* and *n.m.* French.
Française, *n.f.* Frenchwoman.
France, *n.f.* France.
franchement, *adv.* frankly.
franchir, *vb.* clear, cross.
franchise, *n.f.* frankness.
franciser, *vb.* make French.
franc-maçon, *n.m.* Freemason.
franc-parler, *n.m.* frankness.
franc-tireur, *n.m.* sniper; free-lancer.
frange, *n.f.* fringe.
frangible, *adj.* breakable.
frapper, *vb.* strike, hit, rap, knock. f. du pied, stamp.
frasque, *n.f.* prank.
fraternel, *adj.* brotherly.
fraterniser, *vb.* fraternize.
fraternité, *n.f.* brotherhood.
fraude, *n.f.* fraud.
frauder, *vb.* defraud.
fraudeur, *n.m.* smuggler.
frauduleux, *adj.* fraudulent.
frayer, *vb.* open up; rub.
frayeur, *n.f.* fright.
fredaine, *n.f.* prank.
fredonner, *vb.* hum.
frégate, *n.f.* frigate.
frein, *n.m.* brake, check.
freiner, *vb.* brake; restrain.
frelater, *vb.* adulterate.
frêle, *adj.* frail.
frelon, *n.m.* hornet.
frémir, *vb.* tremble. faire f., thrill.
frémissement, *n.m.* shiver, thrill.
frêne, *n.m.* ash (tree).
frénésie, *n.f.* frenzy.
frénétique, *adj.* frantic.
fréquemment, *adv.* often.
fréquence, *n.f.* frequency.
fréquent, *adj.* frequent.
fréquenter, *vb.* frequent, associate with.
frère, *n.m.* brother.
fresque, *n.f.* fresco.
fret, *n.m.* freight.
fréter, *vb.* charter (ship); freight.
frétillant, *adj.* lively.
frétiller, *vb.* wag; quiver.
fretin, *n.m.* young fish.
frette, *n.f.* hoop.
friand, *adj.* dainty; fond (of).
friandise, *n.f.* love of delicacies.
fricoter, *vb.* cook, stew.
friction, *n.f.* friction.
frictionner, *vb.* chafe.
frigo, *n.m.* frozen meat.
frigorifier, *vb.* freeze, refrigerate.
frileux, *adj.* chilly; susceptible to cold.
frime, *n.f.* pretense, sham.
fringant, *adj.* lively, frisky.
friper, *vb.* crush, rumple.
fripier, *n.m.* second-hand clothing dealer.

fripon, 1. *adj.* knavish. **2.** *n.m.* rascal.

friponnerie, *n.f.* roguery.

fripouille, *n.f.* rascal.

frire, *vb.* fry.

frisé, *adj.* curly.

friser, *vb.* curl.

frisoir, *n.m.* (hair) curler.

frisson, *n.m.* shudder, shiver.

frissonnement, *n.m.* shudder; shivering.

frissonner, *vb.* shudder, shiver.

frites, *n.f.pl.* (potato) chips.

friture, *n.f.* frying.

frivole, *adj.* frivolous.

frivolité, *n.f.* frivolity.

froc, *n.m.* (monk's) frock.

froid, *n.m. and adj.* cold. **un peu f.,** chilly. **avoir f.,** be cold.

froideur, *n.f.* coldness.

froissé, *adj.* bruised. **être f. de,** resent.

froissement, *n.m.* crumpling, rustling, jostling.

froisser, *vb.* crease, wrinkle; bruise, hurt.

frôler, *vb.* graze.

fromage, *n.m.* cheese.

froment, *n.m.* wheat.

froncement, *n.m.* puckering, contraction.

froncer, *vb.* pucker. **f. les sourcils,** frown.

frondaison, *n.f.* foliage.

fronde, *n.f.* sling.

fronder, *vb.* sling; censure.

front, *n.m.* forehead.

frontière, *n.f.* boundary, border, frontier.

frottement, *n.m.* rubbing.

frotter, *vb.* rub.

frou-frou, *n.m.* rustle.

fructueux, *adj.* fruitful.

frugal, *adj.* frugal.

frugalité, *n.f.* frugality.

fruit, *n.m.* fruit.

fruiterie, *n.f.* fruit store.

fruitier, *n.m.* fruit seller.

fugace, *adj.* fleeting.

fugitif, *adj.* fugitive.

fuir, *vb.* flee; shun; leak.

fuite, *n.f.* escape, flight; leak.

fumée, *n.f.* smoke.

fumer, *vb.* smoke.

fumeur, *n.m.* one who smokes.

fumeux, *adj.* smoky.

fumier, *n.m.* dung.

funèbre, *adj.* funereal.

funérailles, *n.f.pl.* funeral.

funeste, *adj.* disastrous.

fureter, *vb.* pry.

fureur, *n.f.* fury.

furie, *n.f.* fury.

furieux, *adj.* furious.

furtif, *adj.* sly.

fuseau, *n.m.* spindle.

fusée, *n.f.* rocket.

fuser, *vb.* melt, spread.

fusil, *n.m.* rifle.

fusiller (-zēl yā), *vb.* shoot.

fusion, *n.f.* merger; meltdown.

fusionner, *vb.* merge.

futé, *adj.* cunning, crafty.

futile, *adj.* futile.

futur, *n.m. and adj.* future.

futurologie, *n.f.* futurology.

fuyant, *adj.* passing, transitory, fugitive.

fuyard, *n.* fugitive.

G

gâcher, *vb.* mess.

gâchette, *n.f.* trigger.

gage, *n.m.* pledge, wage.

gageure, *n.f.* bet.

gagnant, *n.m.* winner.

gagner, *vb.* earn, gain, win, beat (in a game).

gai, *adj.* cheerful, cheery, merry, gay.

gaieté, *n.f.* mirth, cheer, merriment, gaiety.

gaillard, *adj.* hearty, sound.

gain, *n.m.* gain, profit.

gaine, *n.f.* girdle.

galant, 1. *n.m.* beau. **2.** *adj.* gallant, civil, courteous. **g. homme,** gentleman.

galanterie, *n.f.* courtesy, compliment.

galbe, *n.m.* outline, contour.

galère, *n.f.* galley, ship.

galerie, *n.f.* gallery, balcony (theater).

galet, *n.m.* boulder.

gallon, *n.m.* gallon.

galon, *n.m.* stripe, braid.

galop, *n.m.* gallop.

galoper, *vb.* gallop.

gambader, *vb.* frolic.

gamin, *n.m.* boy, urchin.

gamme, *n.f.* scale.

gangster (-r), *n.m.* gangster.

gant, *n.m.* glove.

ganterie, *n.f.* glove shop.

garage, *n.m.* garage.

garagiste, *n.m.* garage keeper.

garant, *n.m.* sponsor.

garantie, *n.f.* guarantee, pledge.

garantir, *vb.* guarantee, pledge, warrant.

garçon, *n.m.* boy; waiter; bachelor; flight attendant.

garçonnière, *n.f.* bachelor's apartment.

garde, *n.f.* watch, guard, custody. **prendre g. à,** beware of. **avant-g.,** vanguard. **g. du corps,** bodyguard.

garde-boue, *n.m.* fender.

garde-feu, *n.m.* fender (fireplace).

garde-manger, *n.m.* pantry.

garder, *vb.* guard, keep, mind.

gardeur, *n.m.* keeper.

gardien, *n.m.* keeper, guard, watchman, guardian.

gare, 1. *n.f.* station. **2.** *interj.* look out!

garer, *vb.* garage, park.

gargariser, *vb.* se g., gargle.

gargarisme, *n.m.* gargle.

garni, *adj.* furnished, garnished.

garnir, *vb.* trim, garnish.

garnison, *n.f.* garrison.

garniture, *n.f.* fittings.

gars, *n.m.* chap.

gaspillage, *n.m.* waste.

gaspiller, *vb.* waste, squander.

gâteau, *n.m.* cake. **g. de miel,** honeycomb. **g. sec,** cookie.

gâter, *vb.* spoil.

gâterie, *n.f.* excessive indulgence.

gâteux, *adj.* senile.

gauche, *adj. and n.f.* left. **à g.,** on or to the left. *adj.* awkward, clumsy.

gaucherie, *n.f.* clumsiness.

gaufre, *n.f.* waffle.

gaule, *n.f.* pole.

gausser, *vb.* se g. de, mock, banter.

gaz (-z), *n.m.* gas.

gaze, *n.f.* gauze.

gazeux, *adj.* gassy, gaseous.

gazon, *n.m.* turf, lawn.

gazouillement, *n.m.* warble, twitter.

géant, *n.m.* giant.

geindre, *vb.* moan, whine.

gel, *n.m.* frost.

gelé, *adj.* frozen.

gelée, *n.f.* jelly, frost.

geler, *vb.* freeze.

gémir, *vb.* groan, wail, moan.

gémissement, *n.m.* groan, moan.

gênant, *adj.* troublesome, bothersome.

gencive, *n.f.* gum.

gendarme, *n.m.* policeman.

gendarmerie, *n.f.* police force.

gendre, *n.m.* son-in-law.

gêne, *n.f.* trouble, uneasiness. **être à la g.,** be uneasy.

gêné, *adj.* uneasy.

généalogie, *n.f.* pedigree.

gêner, *vb.* hinder, be in the way, embarrass, bother.

général, *n.m. and adj.* general, overhead (*comm.*). **quartier g.,** headquarters.

généraliser, *vb.* generalize.

généralissime, *n.m.* commander-in-chief.

généralité, *n.f.* generality.

génération, *n.f.* generation.

généreusement, *adv.* generously.

généreux, *adj.* generous, liberal.

générosité, *n.f.* generosity.

génial, *adj.* of genius, highly original.

génie, *n.m.* genius; engineer corps. **soldat du g.,** engineer.

genièvre, *n.m.* gin.

génisse, *n.f.* heifer.

genou, *n.m.* knee; (*pl.*) lap.

genre, *n.m.* kind, gender.

gens, *n.m.f.pl.* people, persons, folk.

gentiane, *n.f.* gentian.

gentil, *n.m.*, **gentille** *f. adj.* pleasant, nice.

gentilhomme, *n.m.* nobleman, peer.

gentillesse, *n.f.* prettiness, gracefulness.

géographie, *n.f.* geography.

géographique, *adj.* geographical.

géologie, *n.f.* geology.

géométrie, *n.f.* geometry.

géométrique, *adj.* geometric.

gérance, *n.f.* managership.

géranium, *n.m.* geranium.

gérant, *n.m.* manager, director, superintendent.

gerbe, *n.f.* sheaf.

gerçure, *n.f.* chap.

gérer, *vb.* manage.

germain, *adj.* first (of cousins).

germe, *n.f.* germ.

germer, *vb.* sprout.

gésir, *vb.* lie.

geste, *n.m.* gesture.

gesticuler, *vb.* gesticulate.

gestion, *n.f.* management.

gibier, *n.m.* game.

giboulée, *n.f.* sudden storm, hailstorm.

gicler, *vb.* spurt.

gifler, *vb.* slap.

gigantesque, *adj.* great, huge.

gigue, *n.f.* leg; jig.

gilet, *n.m.* vest. g. de dessous, undershirt.

gingembre, *n.m.* ginger.

girofle, *n.m.* clou de g., clove.

giron, *n.m.* lap.

gitane, *n.m.f.* gypsy.

gîte, *n.m.* lodging, bed.

givre, *n.m.* frost.

glabre, *adj.* smooth-shaven.

glaçage, *n.m.* frosting.

glace, *n.f.* ice, ice cream; mirror.

glacer, *vb.* freeze.

glacial, *adj.* icy.

glacier, *n.m.* glacier.

glacière, *n.f.* icebox.

glacis, *n.m.* slope.

glaçon, *n.m.* block of ice.

glaise, *n.f.* clay.

gland, *n.m.* acorn.

glande, *n.f.* gland.

glaner, *vb.* glean.

glapir, *vb.* yelp; screech.

glas, *n.m.* knell.

glissade, *n.f.* slide, slip.

glissant, *adj.* slippery.

glisser, *vb.* slide, slip. se g., creep, sneak.

global, *adj.* entire.

globe, *n.m.* globe. g. de l'œil, eyeball.

gloire, *n.f.* glory.

glorieux, *adj.* glorious.

glorifier, *vb.* glorify.

glose, *n.f.* criticism; gloss.

glossaire, *n.m.* glossary.

glousser, *vb.* cluck.

gluant, *adj.* sticky.

gobelet, *n.m.* goblet.

gober, *vb.* swallow.

goéland, *n.m.* seagull.

golfe, *n.m.* gulf.

gomme, *n.f.* gum; eraser.

gommeux, *adj.* gummy.

gond, *n.m.* hinge.

gonfler, *vb.* inflate; swell.

gonfleur, *n.m.* tire pump.

gorge, *n.f.* throat; gorge.

gorger, *vb.* cram.

gosier, *n.m.* throat.

gosse, *n.m.f.* kid (child).

gothique, *adj.* Gothic.

goudron, *n.m.* tar.

gouffre, *n.m.* gulf, abyss.

goulu, *adj.* gluttonous.

gourde, *n.f.* flask.

gourmand, 1. *n.m.* glutton. **2.** *adj.* greedy.

gourmander, *vb.* scold.

gourmandise, *n.f.* greediness.

gourmer, *vb.* curb.

gourmet, *n.m.* epicure.

gourmette, *n.f.* curb (horse).

gourou, *n.m.* guru.

gousse, *n.f.* shell, pod.

goût, *n.m.* taste, relish.

goûter, 1. *n.m.* snack. **2.** *vb.* taste, relish.

goutte, *n.f.* drop; gout.

goutteux, *adj.* gouty.

gouttière, *n.f.* gutter.

gouvernail, *n.m.* rudder, helm.

gouvernante, *n.f.* governess, housekeeper.

gouvernement, *n.m.* government.

gouverner, *vb.* govern, rule, steer.

gouverneur, *n.m.* governor.

grabuge, *n.f.* squabble.

grâce, *n.f.* grace. faire g. de, spare.

gracier, *vb.* pardon.

gracieux, *adj.* graceful, gracious.

grade, *n.m.* grade, rank.

gradin, *n.m.* step, tier.

graduel, *adj.* gradual.

graduer, *vb.* graduate.

grain, *n.m.* grain, seed, berry, kernel. g. de beauté, mole.

graine, *n.f.* seed, berry.

graissage, *n.m.* greasing.

graisse, *n.f.* grease, fat.

graisser, *vb.* grease.

grammaire, *n.f.* grammar.

gramme, *n.m.* gram.

grand, *adj.* big, great, tall. grand'chose, much.

grandement, *adv.* grandly, greatly.

grandeur, *n.f.* size, height, greatness.

grandiose, *adj.* grand.

grandir, *vb.* grow.

grand'mère, *n.f.* grandmother.

grand-père, *n.m.* grandfather.

grange, *n.f.* barn.

granit (-t), *n.m.* granite.

graphique, *n.m.* chart.

grappe, *n.f.* bunch, cluster.

gras *m.,* **grasse** *f. adj.* fat, stout.

grassement, *adj.* plentifully.

grasset, *adj.* plump.

grassouillet, *adj.* plump.

gratification, *n.f.* bonus.

gratifier, *vb.* bestow.

gratin, *n.m.* burnt part.

gratitude, *n.f.* gratitude.

gratte-ciel, *n.m.* skyscraper.

gratter, *vb.* scrape, scratch.

gratuit, *adj.* free.

grave, *adj.* grave.

graveleux, *adj.* gritty.

graver, *vb.* engrave.

graveur, *n.m.* engraver.

gravier, *n.m.* gravel.

gravir, *vb.* climb.

gravité, *n.f.* gravity.

graviter, *vb.* gravitate.

gravure, *n.f.* engraving. g. à l'eau-forte, etching.

gré, *n.m.* pleasure.

Grec *m.,* **Grecque** *f. n.* Greek (person).

grec, *n.m.* Greek (language).

grec *m.,* **grecque** *f. adj.* Greek.

Grèce, *n.f.* Greece.

gréement, *n.m.* rig.

gréer, *vb.* rig.

greffier, *n.m.* clerk.

grêle, 1. *n.f.* hail. **2.** *adj.* thin, slight.

grêler, *vb.* hail.

grêlon, *n.m.* hailstone.

grelotter, *vb.* shiver.

grenier, *n.m.* attic.

grenouille, *n.f.* frog.

grève, *n.f.* strike. se mettre en g., strike, *vb.*

gréviste, *n.m.f.* striker.

gribouiller, *vb.* scribble.

grief, *n.m.* grievance.

grièvement, *adv.* seriously.

griffe, *n.f.* claw, clutch.

griffer, *vb.* seize; scratch.

griffonner, *vb.* scribble.

grignoter, *vb.* nibble.

gril, *n.m.* grill.

grillade, *n.f.* broiling.

grille, *n.f.* grate, gate.

griller, *vb.* broil, roast, toast.

grillon, *n.m.* cricket.

grimace, *n.f.* grimace.

grimacer, *vb.* make faces.

grimer, *vb.* make up.

grimper, *vb.* climb.

grincer, *vb.* creak, grate, grind.

gris, *adj.* gray; drab; drunk.

griser, *vb.* get drunk.

grive, *n.f.* thrush.

grogner, *vb.* growl, snarl, grumble.

grommeler, *vb.* mutter.

gronder, *vb.* scold, nag; roar, rumble.

gros *m.,* **grosse** *f. adj.* overly large; gross, stout, rough. en g., wholesale.

groseille, *n.f.* currant.

grosseur, *n.f.* size, thickness.

grossier, *adj.* coarse, crude, gross.

grossièreté, *n.f.* coarseness.

grossir, *vb.* magnify, grow.

grotesque, *adj.* grotesque.

grouiller, *vb.* stir, swarm.

groupe, *n.m.* group, party; cluster.

groupement, *n.m.* grouping.

grouper, *vb.* group.

grue, *n.f.* crane.

gué, *n.m.* ford. traverser à g., wade.

guêpe, *n.f.* wasp.

guère, *adv.* hardly.

guérir, *vb.* cure, heal.

guérison, *n.f.* cure.

guerre, *n.f.* war.

guerrier, *adj.* warlike.
guetter, *vb.* watch (for).
gueule, *n.f.* mouth.
gueux, *n.m.* beggar, tramp.
guichet, *n.m.* ticket-window.
guide, *n.m.* guide(book).
guider, *vb.* guide.
guillotine, *n.f.* guillotine.
guingan, *n.m.* gingham.
guirlande, *n.f.* garland.
guise, *n.f.* way, manner.
guitare, *n.f.* guitar.
gymnase, *n.m.* gymnasium.

H

habile, *adj.* clever, skillful, smart, able.
habileté, *n.f.* craft, ability.
habillement, *n.m.* apparel.
habillements masculins, *n.m.pl.* menswear.
habiller, *vb.* dress.
habilleur *m.,* **habilleuse** *f. n.* dresser.
habit, *n.m.* coat; attire; (*pl.*) clothes.
habitant, *n.m.* inhabitant, resident.
habitation, *n.f.* dwelling.
habiter, *vb.* inhabit, live.
habitude, *n.f.* habit, practice. **d'h.,** customarily. **avoir l'h. de,** be accustomed to.
habituel, *adj.* customary, usual.
habituer, *vb.* get used to.
hâbleur, *n.m.* boaster.
hache, *n.f.* ax.
hacher, *vb.* mince, chop, hack up.
hachette, *n.f.* hatchet.
hachis, *n.m.* hash.
hagard, *adj.* haggard.
haie, *n.f.* hedge.
haillon, *n.m.* rag.
haine, *n.f.* hatred.
haineux, *adj.* hating.
haïr, *vb.* hate.
haïssable, *adj.* hateful.
halage, *n.m.* towage.
hâle, *n.m.* tan, sunburn.
haleine, *n.f.* breath.
haler, *vb.* haul, tow.
hâler, *vb.* tan. **se h.,** become sunburned.
haleter, *vb.* pant, gasp.
halle, *n.f.* market.
halte, *n.f.* halt.
hamac, *n.m.* hammock.
hameau, *n.m.* hamlet.
hameçon, *n.m.* hook.
hampe, *n.f.* handle.
hanche, *n.f.* hip.
hangar, *n.m.* shed.
hanter, *vb.* haunt.
hantise, *n.f.* obsession.
happer, *vb.* snap.
harcèlement, *n.m.* hassle, harassment.
harceler, *vb.* worry, bother; hassle; harass.
hardes, *n.f.pl.* togs.

hardi, *adj.* bold.
hardiesse, *n.f.* boldness.
hareng, *n.m.* herring.
hargneux, *adj.* cross, snarling.
haricot, *n.m.* bean.
harmonie, *n.f.* harmony.
harmonieux, *adj.* harmonious.
harmoniser, *vb.* put in tune, harmonize.
harnacher, *vb.* harness.
harnais, *n.m.* harness.
harpe, *n.f.* harp.
harpin, *n.m.* boat hook.
hasard, *n.m.* chance. **au h. or par h.,** at random.
hasarder, *vb.* venture.
hasardeux, *adj.* hazardous, unsafe.
hâte, *n.f.* haste, hurry. **à la h.,** hastily.
hâter, *vb.* hasten, hurry.
hâtif, *adj.* early, hasty.
haussement, *n.m.* raising; shrug.
hausser, *vb.* raise; shrug.
haussier, *n.m.* bull (stock exchange).
haut, 1. *n.m.* top. **2.** *adj.* high, loud. **à haute voix,** aloud. **en haut,** up, above.
hautain, *adj.* haughty, lofty, proud.
hautbois, *n.m.* oboe.
haute fidélité, *n.f.* high fidelity.
hauteur, *n.f.* height; haughtiness. **être à la h. de,** be up to.
hauturier, *adj.* sea-going.
hâve, *adj.* wan, gaunt.
havre, *n.m.* haven.
havresac, *n.m.* knapsack.
hebdomadaire, *adj.* weekly.
héberger, *vb.* shelter.
bébété, *adj.* dull.
hébreu, 1. *n.m.* Hebrew (language). **2.** *adj.* Hebrew.
hein, *interj.* huh?
hélas (-s), *interj.* alas!
héler, *vb.* call, hail.
hélice, *n.f.* propeller.
hélicoptère, *n.m.* helicopter.
helvétique, *adj.* Swiss.
hémisphère, *n.m.* hemisphere.
hémorragie, *n.f.* hemorrhage.
hennir, *vb.* neigh.
héraut, *n.m.* herald.
herbage, *n.m.* grass, pasture.
herbe, *n.f.* grass, herb; marijuana. **mauvaise h.,** weed.
herbeux, *adj.* grassy.
héréditaire, *adj.* hereditary.
hérésie, *n.f.* heresy.
hérétique, 1. *n.m.f.* heretic. **2.** *adj.* heretic, heretical.
hérisser, *vb.* bristle.
hérisson, *n.m.* hedgehog.
héritage, *n.m.* inheritance.
hériter, *vb.* inherit.
héritier, *n.m.* heir.
hermétique, *adj.* (sealed) tight.
hermine, *n.f.* ermine.
hernie, *n.f.* hernia.
héroïne, *n.f.* heroine.
héroïque, *adj.* heroic.
héroïsme, *n.m.* heroism.
héros, *n.m.* hero.

hertz, *n.m.* hertz.
hésitation, *n.f.* hesitation.
hésiter, *vb.* hesitate, waver, falter.
hétérosexuel, *adj.* heterosexual.
hêtre, *n.m.* beech.
heure, *n.f.* hour; time. **de bonne h.,** early.
heureusement, *adv.* happily, luckily.
heureux, *adj.* glad, happy; lucky, fortunate; successful.
heurt, *n.m.* blow, shock.
heurter, *vb.* collide (with).
heurtoir, *n.m.* (door) knocker.
hibou, *n.m.* owl.
hideux, *adj.* hideous.
hier (-r), *adv.* yesterday.
hilare, *adj.* hilarious.
hilarité, *n.f.* hilarity.
Hindou, *n.m.* Hindu.
hindou, *adj.* Hindu.
hippodrome, *n.m.* race course.
hippopotame, *n.m.* hippopotamus.
hirondelle, *n.f.* swallow.
hispanique, *adj.* Hispanic.
hisser, *vb.* hoist.
histoire, *n.f.* history, story; to-do, fuss.
historien, *n.m.* historian.
historique, *adj.* historic.
hiver (-r), *n.m.* winter.
hiverner, *vb.* **s'h.,** hibernate.
hocher, *vb.* shake, nod.
hochet, *n.m.* rattle.
hoirie, *n.f.* inheritance.
Hollandais, *n.m.* Hollander, Dutchman.
hollandais, *adj. and n.m.* Dutch.
Hollande, *n.f.* Holland; the Netherlands.
hologramme, *n.m.* hologram.
holographie, *n.f.* holography.
homard, *n.m.* lobster.
hommage, *n.m.* homage.
hommasse, *adj.* mannish.
homme, *n.m.* man. **h. d'affaires,** businessman.
homogène, *adj.* of the same kind, homogeneous.
homosexuel, *adj.* homosexual.
Hongrie, *n.f.* Hungary.
Hongrois, *n.m.* Hungarian (person).
hongrois, 1. *n.m.* Hungarian (language). **2.** *adj.* Hungarian.
honnête, *adj.* honest.
honnêteté, *n.f.* honesty, fairness.
honneur, *n.m.* honor, credit.
honorable, *adj.* honorable.
honoraires, *n.m.pl.* fee.
honorer, *vb.* honor.
honte, *n.f.* shame. **avoir h. de,** be ashamed of. **faire h. à.,** shame.
honteux, *adj.* ashamed; shameful.
hôpital, *n.m.* hospital.
hoquet, *n.m.* hiccup.
horaire, *n.m.* timetable.

horde, n.f. horde.
horizon, n.m. horizon.
horizontal, adj. horizontal.
horloge, n.f. clock.
horloger, n.m. watchmaker.
hormis, prep. except.
horreur, n.f. horror.
horrible, adj. horrible, ghastly.
horrifier, vb. horrify.
horrifique, adj. hair-raising.
horripiler, vb. annoy.
hors-bord, n.m. outboard boat.
hors de, prep. out of, outside.
horticole, adj. horticultural.
hospice, n.m. refuge.
hospitalier, adj. hospitable.
hospitaliser, vb. hospitalize;
  shelter.
hospitalité, n.f. hospitality.
hostie, n.f. (eccles.) host.
hostile, adj. hostile.
hostilité, n.f. hostility.
hôte, n.m. host; guest.
hôtel, n.m. hotel; mansion. h.
  de ville, city hall.
hôtelier, n.m. innkeeper.
hôtesse, n.f. hostess.
hôtesse de l'air, n.f. stewardess, flight attendant.
hotte, n.f. basket carried on
  back.
houblon, n.m. hop.
houe, n.f. hoe.
houer, vb. hoe.
houille, n.f. coal.
houillère, n.f. coal mine.
houle, n.f. surge.
houleux, adj. stormy, rough.
houppe, n.f. tuft; powder puff.
hourra, n.m. cheer.
housse, n.f. covering.
houx, n.m. holly.
hublot, n.m. porthole.
huer, vb. shout, hoot.
huile, n.f. oil.
huiler, vb. oil.
huileux, adj. oily.
huissier, n.m. usher.
huit, adj. and n.m. eight.
huitième, adj. and n.m.f.
  eighth.
huître, n.f. oyster.
humain, adj. human, humane.
humanitaire, adj. humanitarian.
humanité, n.f. humanity.
humble, adj. lowly, humble.
humecter, vb. moisten.
humer, vb. suck up, sniff up.
humeur, n.f. humor; mood,
  temper.
humide, adj. damp, humid.
humidité, n.f. moisture.
humiliation, n.f. humiliation.
humilier, vb. humiliate, humble.
humilité, n.f. humility.
humoristique, adj. humorous.
humour, n.m. humor.
hune, n.f. (naut.) top.
huppe, n.f. tuft, crest.
hurlement, n.m. noise, howl-
  ing.
hurler, vb. howl, roar, yell.
hutte, n.f. hut, shed.

hybride, adj. and n.m. hybrid.
hydrogène, n.m. hydrogen.
hyène, n.f. hyena.
hygiène, n.f. sanitation, hygiene.
hygiénique, adj. hygienic.
hymne, n.m. hymn; n.f. church
  hymn.
hypnotiser, vb. hypnotize.
hypocondriaque, adj. and n.
  hypochondriac.
hypocrisie, n.f. hypocrisy.
hypocrite, 1. n.m.f. hypocrite.
  2. adj. hypocritical.
hypothèque, n.f. mortgage.
hypothéquer, vb. mortgage.
hypothèse, n.f. hypothesis.
hystérectomie, n.f. hysterectomy.
hystérie, n.f. hysteria.
hystérique, adj. hysterical.

I

ici, adv. here. d'i., hence.
ictère, n.m. jaundice.
idéal, adj. and n.m. ideal.
idéaliser, vb. idealize.
idéalisme, n.m. idealism.
idéaliste, n.m.f. idealist.
idée, n.f. idea, notion.
identification, n.f. identification.
identifier, vb. identify.
identique (à), adj. identical
  (with).
identité, n.f. identity.
idéologie, n.f. ideology.
idiome, n.m. idiom.
idiot, adj. and n.m. idiot(ic).
idiotie, n.f. idiocy.
idiotisme, n.m. idiom.
idolâtrer, vb. idolize.
idole, n.f. idol.
idyllique, adj. idyllic.
if, n.m. yew.
ignare, adj. ignorant.
ignoble, adj. ignoble.
ignorance, n.f. ignorance.
ignorant, adj. ignorant.
ignorer, vb. not know.
il (ěl), pron. he, it; (pl.) they.
île, n.f. island.
illégal (-l-), adj. illegal.
illégitime (-l-), adj. illegitimate.
illettré (-l-), adj. illiterate.
illicite (-l-), adj. illicit.
illimité (-l-), adj. boundless.
illogique (-l-), adj. illogical.
illuminer (-l-), vb. light, illuminate.
illusion (-l-), n.f. illusion, delusion.
illustration (-l-), n.f. illustration.
illustre (-l-), adj. illustrious, famous.
illustrer (-l-), vb. illustrate.
image, n.f. picture.
imaginaire, adj. fancied, imaginary.
imaginatif, adj. imaginative.

imagination, n.f. imagination.
imaginer, vb. imagine.
imam, n.m. imam.
imbattable, adj. unbeatable.
imbécillité, n.f. imbecility; stupidity.
imberbe, adj. beardless.
imbiber, vb. soak, steep.
imbu, adj. imbued; steeped.
imitation, n.f. imitation, copy.
imiter, vb. imitate, copy; mimic.
immaculé, adj. immaculate.
immangeable, adj. uneatable.
immatériel, adj. incorporeal.
immatriculer, vb. matriculate.
immédiat, adj. immediate.
immense, adj. immense, great,
  huge.
immensité, n.f. immensity.
immeuble, n.m. real estate.
imminent, adj. imminent.
immiscer, vb. s'i., meddle, interfere.
immixtion, n.f. mixing; interference.
immobile, adj. motionless.
immoler, vb. sacrifice. s'i., sacrifice oneself.
immonde, adj. filthy.
immoral, adj. immoral.
immortaliser, vb. immortalize.
immortalité, n.f. immortality.
immortel, adj. and n.m. immortal.
immuable, adj. unchangeable.
immunité, n.f. immunity.
impair, adj. odd.
impalpable, adj. intangible.
imparfait, adj. and n.m. imperfect.
impartial, adj. impartial.
impasse, n.f. dead end.
impassible, adj. impassive.
impatience, n.f. impatience.
impatient, adj. impatient.
impatienter, vb. provoke.
impayable, adj. invaluable;
  very funny.
impeccable, adj. faultless.
impécunieux, adj. impecu-
  nious.
impénétrable, adj. impenetrable.
impératif, adj. and n.m. imperative.
impératrice, n.f. empress.
imperceptible, adj. imperceptible.
impérial, adj. imperial.
impérialisme, n.m. imperialism.
impérieux, adj. domineering.
impérissable, adj. imperish-
  able.
imperméabiliser, vb. waterproof.
imperméable, 1. n.m. raincoat.
  2. adj. waterproof.
impertinence, n.f. impertinence.
impertinent, adj. saucy.
impétueux, adj. headlong, impetuous.
impie, adj. impious.

impitoyable, *adj.* merciless, pitiless, ruthless.

impliquer, *vb.* involve, imply.

implorer, *vb.* implore, beg.

impoli, *adj.* rude, impolite, discourteous.

impolitesse, *n.f.* discourtesy.

impopulaire, *adj.* unpopular.

importance, *n.f.* significance, importance.

important, *adj.* momentous, important.

importateur, *n.m.* importer.

importation, *n.f.* import.

importer, *vb.* matter; import.

importun, *adj.* tiresome, bothersome, importunate.

importuner, *vb.* pester, keep bothering.

importunité, *n.f.* importunity.

imposable, *adj.* taxable.

imposer (à), *vb.* impose (on); tax; enforce.

imposition, *n.f.* imposition.

impossibilité, *n.f.* impossibility. **dans l'i. de,** unable to.

impossible, *adj.* impossible.

imposteur, *n.m.* fraud (person), faker, impostor.

imposture, *n.f.* imposture, deception.

impôt, *n.m.* tax, tariff.

impotent, *adj.* weak, infirm.

impôt sur les ventes, *n.m.* sales tax.

imprécis, *adj.* imprecise.

imprégner, *vb.* impregnate, imbue.

imprenable, *adj.* impregnable.

impression, *n.f.* print, impression.

impressionnable, *adj.* sensitive, impressionable.

impressionnant, *adj.* impressive.

impressionner, *vb.* affect.

imprévoyance, *n.f.* improvidence.

imprévoyant, *adj.* not foresighted.

imprévu, *adj.* unexpected, unforeseen.

imprimé, *n.m.* printed matter.

imprimer, *vb.* impress; print.

imprimerie, *n.f.* printery, printing.

imprimeur, *n.m.* printer.

improbable, *adj.* improbable.

improbité, *n.f.* dishonesty.

improductif, *adj.* unproductive.

impromptu, *adv., adj* and *n.m.* impromptu.

impropre, *adv.* improper, unfit.

improviste, *adv.* **à l'i.,** all of a sudden.

imprudence, *n.f.* indiscretion.

impudence, *n.f.* impudence.

impudicité, *n.f.* lewdness.

impuissance, *n.f.* impotence.

impuissant, *adj.* impotent, powerless, helpless.

impulsif, *adj.* impulsive.

impulsion, *n.f.* impulse, spur.

impunément, *adv.* with impunity.

impunité, *n.f.* impunity.

impur, *adj.* impure.

impureté, *n.f.* impurity.

imputer, *vb.* impute.

inabordable, *adj.* inaccessible.

inaccoutumé, *adj.* unusual.

inachevé, *adj.* unfinished.

inactif, *adj.* inactive, indolent.

inadvertance, *n.f.* oversight.

inanimé, *adj.* lifeless.

inanité, *n.f.* uselessness.

inaperçu, *adj.* unperceived.

inattaquable, *adj.* unassailable.

inattendu, *adj.* unexpected.

inaugurer, *vb.* inaugurate.

inavouable, *adj.* unavowable, shameful.

incalculable, *adj.* countless, incalculable.

incapable, *adj.* unable.

incarcérer, *vb.* imprison.

incarnat, *adj.* flesh-colored, rosy.

incarner, *vb.* embody.

incartade, *n.f.* insult, prank.

incendie, *n.m.* fire.

incendier, *vb.* set fire to.

incertain, *adj.* uncertain.

incertitude, *n.f.* suspense.

incessamment, *adv.* incessantly; immediately.

inceste, *n.m.* incest.

incident, *n.m.* incident.

incinérer, *vb.* cremate; incinerate.

incision, *n.f.* incision.

inciter, *vb.* incite.

inclinaison, *n.f.* slope.

inclination, *n.f.* bow, nod; propensity.

incliner, *vb.* slant, nod, bow. **s'i.,** lean.

inclure, *vb.* include, enclose.

inclus, *adj.* included. **ci-inclus,** enclosed, herewith.

inclusif, *adj.* inclusive.

incolore, *adj.* colorless.

incomber, *vb.* devolve upon.

incommode, *adj.* uncomfortable, inconvenient.

incommoder, *vb.* inconvenience.

incomparable, *adj.* incomparable.

incompatible, *adj.* incompatible.

incompétence, *n.f.* incompetence.

incomplet, *adj.* imperfect, unfinished.

incompris, *adj.* unappreciated, not understood.

inconduite, *n.f.* misconduct.

inconnu, *adj.* unknown.

inconscient, *adj. and n.m.* unconscious.

inconséquent, *adj.* inconsistent.

inconsidéré, *adj.* thoughtless.

inconsistant, *adj.* weak, inconsistent.

inconstant, *adj.* inconstant.

incontestable, *adj.* unquestionable.

incontesté, *adj.* unquestioned.

incontinent, **1.** *adj.* incontinent. **2.** *adv.* immediately.

incontrôlable, *adj.* not verifiable.

inconvenance, *n.f.* impropriety.

inconvénient, *n.m.* inconvenience.

incorporer, *vb.* embody.

incorrect, *adj.* incorrect.

incriminer, *vb.* accuse.

incroyable, *adj.* incredible.

incroyant, *n.m.* unbeliever.

inculper, *vb.* charge, accuse.

inculte, *adj.* uncultivated, unkempt.

incurable, *adj.* incurable.

incurie, *n.f.* carelessness, neglect.

Inde, *n.f.* India.

indécis, *adj.* doubtful, vague, dim.

indéfini, *adj.* indefinite.

indéfinissable, *adj.* nondescript.

indéfrisable, *n.f.* permanent wave.

indélicat, *adj.* indelicate.

indélicatesse, *n.f.* indelicacy; blunder.

indépendance, *n.f.* independence.

indépendant, *adj.* independent.

index (-ks), *n.m.* index; forefinger.

indicateur, *n.m.* timetable.

indicatif, *adj. and n.m.* indicative.

indicatif interurbain, *n.m.* area code.

indication, *n.f.* indication.

indice, *n.m.* sign, proof.

indicible, *adj.* unspeakable, inexpressible.

Indien, *n.m.* Indian.

indien, *adj.* Indian.

indifférence, *n.f.* indifference.

indifférent, *adj.* indifferent.

indigène, *n.m.f.* native.

indigent, *adj.* destitute.

indigeste, *adj.* indigestible.

indignation, *n.f.* indignation, anger.

indigne, *adj.* worthless, unworthy.

indigné, *adj.* indignant.

indigner, *vb.* anger.

indiquer, *vb.* indicate, point out.

indirect, *adj.* indirect.

indiscret, *adj.* indiscreet.

indiscutable, *adj.* indisputable.

indispensable, *adj.* indispensable, essential.

indisposer, *vb.* indispose; set against.

indisposition, *n.f.* ailment.

indistinct, *adj.* indistinct.

individu, *n.m.* individual, person.

individuel, *adj.* individual.

indomptable, *adj.* adamant, unconquerable.

indu, *adj.* undue; not ordinary.

induire, *vb.* induce; infer.

indulgence, *n.f.* indulgence.
indulgent, *adj.* lenient, indulgent.
indûment, *adv.* unduly.
industrie, *n.f.* industry.
industriel, *adj.* industrial.
inébranlable, *adj.* immovable, firm.
inédit, *adj.* unpublished.
inefficace, *adj.* ineffectual.
inégal, *adj.* uneven, unequal.
inégalité, *n.f.* inequality, irregularity.
inepte, *adj.* inept, stupid.
ineptie, *n.f.* inept action.
inépuisable, *n.f.* inexhaustible.
inertie, *n.f.* inertia.
inestimable, *adj.* priceless.
inévitable, *adj.* inevitable.
inexact, *adj.* inexact.
inexécutable, *adj.* impracticable.
inexplicable, *adj.* inexplicable.
inexprimable, *adj.* inexpressible.
infaillible, *adj.* infallible.
infâme, *adj.* infamous.
infamie, *n.f.* infamy.
infanterie, *n.f.* infantry.
infatigable, *adj.* untiring.
inféconde, *adj.* barren, sterile.
infect, *adj.* infected, rotten.
infecter, *vb.* infect.
infection, *n.f.* infection.
inférieur, *adj. and n.m.* inferior, low(er).
infernal, *adj.* infernal.
infester, *vb.* infest.
infidèle, *adj.* disloyal, unfaithful, false.
infidélité, *n.f.* infidelity.
infime, *adj.* lowest; mean.
infini, *adj. and n.m.* infinite.
infinité, *n.f.* infinity.
infirme, *adj. and n.m.f.* invalid.
infirmer, *vb.* invalidate, weaken.
infirmière, *n.f.* nurse.
infirmité, *n.f.* infirmity.
inflammation, *n.f.* inflammation.
inflation, *n.f.* inflation.
infliger, *vb.* inflict.
influence, *n.f.* influence.
influent, *adj.* influential.
information, *n.f.* inquiry; (*pl.*) news.
informatique, *n.f.* computer science.
informatiser, *vb.* computerize.
informe, *adj.* shapeless.
informer, *vb.* inform. **i. de.** acquaint with.
infraction, *n.f.* breach.
infructueux, *adj.* fruitless.
infuser, *vb.* infuse. **faire i.,** brew.
ingambe, *adj.* nimble.
ingénieur, *n.m.* engineer.
ingénieux, *adj.* ingenious.
ingéniosité, *n.f.* ingenuity.
ingénu, *adj.* naïve, ingenuous.
ingrat, *adj.* ungrateful.
ingrédient, *n.m.* ingredient.
inguérissable, *adj.* incurable.

inhabile, *adj.* awkward, incapable.
inhiber, *vb.* inhibit.
inhospitalier, *adj.* inhospitable.
inhumain, *adj.* cruel, inhuman.
inimitié, *n.f.* enmity.
inique, *adj.* unfair.
initial, *adj.* initial.
initiale, *n.f.* initial.
initiative, *n.f.* initiative.
initier, *vb.* initiate.
injecté, *adj.* **i. de sang,** bloodshot.
injecter, *vb.* inject.
injection, *n.f.* injection.
injonction, *n.f.* injunction.
injures, *n.f.pl.* abuse.
injurier, *vb.* abuse, insult.
injurieux, *adj.* abusive, insulting, offensive.
injuste, *adj.* unfair.
injustice, *n.f.* injustice.
inlassable, *adj.* untiring.
inné, *adj.* innate.
innocence, *n.f.* innocence.
innocent, *adj.* innocent.
innocenter, *vb.* declare innocent.
innombrable, *adj.* countless.
innovation, *n.f.* innovation.
inoccupé, *adj.* idle; unoccupied.
inoculer, *vb.* inoculate.
inodore, *adj.* odorless.
inoffensif, *adj.* innocuous, harmless.
inondation, *n.f.* flood.
inonder, *vb.* flood.
inopiné, *adj.* unexpected.
inoubliable, *adj.* unforgettable.
inouï, *adj.* unheard-of.
inquiet, *adj.* restless, anxious, uneasy.
inquiéter, *vb.* trouble. **s'i.,** worry.
inquiétude, *n.f.* misgiving, worry.
insaisissable, *adj.* imperceptible.
insalubre, *adj.* unhealthy.
inscription, *n.f.* incription, entry.
inscrire, *vb.* inscribe; enter.
insecte, *n.m.* bug, insect.
insensé, *adj.* mad.
insensible, *adj.* insensible; unfeeling.
inséparable, *adj.* inseparable.
insérer, *vb.* insert.
insigne, *n.m.* badge, sign.
insignifiant, *adj.* petty, insignificant.
insinuer, *vb.* hint.
insipide, *adj.* tasteless, dull.
insistance, *n.f.* insistence.
insister, *vb.* insist.
insolation, *n.f.* susntroke.
insolence, *n.f.* insolence.
insolite, *adj.* unusual.
insomnie, *n.f.* insomnia.
insondable, *adj.* bottomless.
insouciant, *adj.* casual, careless.
insoumis, *adj.* unsubdued.

inspecter, *vb.* examine, survey.
inspecteur, *n.m.* inspector.
inspection, *n.f.* inspection.
inspiration, *n.f.* inspiration.
inspirer, *vb.* inspire.
instable, *adj.* temperamental, unsteady, unstable.
installer, *vb.* install.
instamment, *adv.* urgently.
instance, *n.f.* entreaty; instance.
instant, *n.m.* instant. **à l'i.,** at once.
instantané, *adj.* instantaneous.
instinct, *n.m.* instinct.
instinctif, *adj.* instinctive.
instituer, *vb.* institute.
instituteur, *n.m.* teacher.
institution, *n.f.* institution, institute.
institutrice, *n.f.* teacher.
instructeur, *n.m.* teacher.
instructif, *adj.* instructive.
instruction, *n.f.* education, instruction; (*pl.*) directions.
instruire, *vb.* educate, teach, intruct.
instrument, *n.m.* instrument.
instrumentation, *n.f.* orchestration.
insu, *n.m.* **à l'i. de,** unknown to.
insuccès, *n.m.* failure.
insuffisance, *n.f.* deficiency.
insuffisant, *adj.* deficient.
insulaire, **1.** *n.m.* islander. **2.** *adj.* insular.
insulte, *n.f.* affront, insult.
insulter, *vb.* affront, insult.
insurgé, *adj. and n.m.* insurgent.
insurger, *vb.* **s'i.,** revolt.
insurmontable, *adj.* insuperable.
intact (-kt), *adj.* intact.
intarissable, *adj.* inexhaustible.
intègre, *adj.* upright.
intégrité, *n.f.* integrity.
intellect, *n.m.* intellect.
intellectuel, *adj. and n.m.* intellectual.
intelligence, *n.f.* intelligence.
intelligent, *adj.* intelligent.
intelligible, *adj.* intelligible; audible.
intempérie, *n.f.* inclemency (of weather).
intempestif, *adj.* untimely.
intendance, *n.f.* administration.
intendant, *n.m.* director.
intendante, *n.f.* matron.
intense, *adj.* intense.
intensif, *adj.* intensive.
intensité, *n.f.* intensity.
intention, *n.f.* intention.
intentionné, *adj.* intentioned.
intentionnel, *adj.* intentional.
intercéder, *vb.* intercede.
intercepter, *vb.* intercept.
interdire, *vb.* forbid.
intéressant, *adj.* interesting.
intéresser, *vb.* interest, concern, affect.
intérêt, *n.m.* interest.

intérieur, adj. and n.m. interior.

interjection, n.f. interjection.

interloquer, vb. embarrass.

intermède, n.m. interlude.

intermédiaire, adj. and n.m.f. intermediate.

interminable, adj. interminable.

internat, n.m. boarding school.

international, adj. international.

interne, 1. adj. internal. **2.** n.m. resident student.

interner, vb. intern.

interpellation, n.f. questioning.

interpeller, vb. ask.

interposer, vb. interpose.

interprétation, n.f. interpretation.

interprète, n.m.f. interpreter.

interpréter, vb. interpret.

interrogateur, 1. n.m. examiner. **2.** adj. questioning.

interrogation, n.f. interrogation.

interrogatoire, n.m. cross-examination.

interroger, vb. question.

interrompre, vb. interrupt.

interrupteur, n.m. switch.

interruption, n.f. break, intermission, interruption.

intervalle, n.m. interval.

intervenir, vb. interfere.

intervention, n.f. interference.

intervertir, vb. transpose.

interview, n.m. or f. interview.

interviewer, vb. interview.

intestin, n.m. bowels.

intimation, n.f. notification.

intime, adj. intimate.

intimer, vb. notify.

intimider, vb. daunt, intimidate.

intimité, n.f. intimacy.

intituler, vb. entitle.

intolérance, n.f. intolerance.

intonation, n.f. intonation.

intoxication, n.f. poisoning.

intoxiquer, vb. poison.

intraitable, adj. intractable, difficult to deal with.

intrépide, adj. fearless.

intrigant, 1. adj. intriguing. **2.** n.m. schemer.

intrigue, n.f. plot, intrigue.

intriguer, vb. intrigue; puzzle.

introduction, n.f. introduction.

introduire, vb. introduce, insert.

introuvable, adj. unfindable.

intrus, n.m. intruder.

intrusion, n.f. intrusion; trespass.

intuitif, adj. intuitive.

intuition, n.f. intuition.

inusité, adj. unusual.

inutile, adj. useless, needless.

invalide, 1. n.m.f. invalid. **2.** adj. disabled, invalid.

invalider, vb. invalidate.

invasion, n.f. invasion.

invectiver, vb. abuse, revile.

inventaire, n.m. inventory.

inventer, vb. invent.

inventeur, n.m. inventor.

invention, n.f. invention.

inventorier, vb. inventory, catalogue.

inverse, adj. inverted, inverse.

investigateur, 1. adj. searching. **2.** n.m. investigator.

investigation, n.f. investigation, inquiry.

investir, vb. invest.

invétéré, adj. inveterate.

invincible, adj. invincible.

invisible, adj. invisible.

invitation, n.f. invitation.

invité, n.m. guest.

inviter, vb. invite, ask.

involontaire, adj. involuntary.

invoquer, vb. call upon.

invraisemblable, adj. improbable.

iode, n.m. iodine.

Irak, n.m. Iraq.

Iran, n.m. Iran.

iris (-s), n.m. iris.

irisé, adj. iridescent.

Irlandais, n.m. Irishman.

irlandais, adj. Irish.

Irlande, n.f. Ireland.

ironie, n.f. irony.

ironique, adj. ironical.

irradier, vb. radiate.

irraisonnable, adj. irrational.

irréfléchi, adj. thoughtless, rash.

irrégulier, adj. irregular.

irréligieux, adj. irreligious.

irrésistible, adj. irresistible.

irrésolu, adj. irresolute.

irrespectueux, adj. disrespectful.

irrévérence, n.f. direspect.

irrigation, n.f. irrigation.

irriguer, vb. irrigate.

irritation, n.f. irritation.

irriter, vb. irritate, anger, provoke.

Islam, n.m. Islam.

islamique, adj. Islamic.

isolateur, n.m. insulating.

isolement, n.m. isolation.

isoler, vb. isolate.

Israël, n.m. Israel.

Israëli, n.m. Israeli.

issue, n.f. issue, outlet, outcome.

isthme, n.m. isthmus.

Italie, n.f. Italy.

Italien, n.m. Italian (person).

italien, 1. n.m. Italian (language). **2.** adj. Italian.

italique, 1. n.m. italics. **2.** adj. italic.

itinéraire, n.m. route, itinerary.

ivoire, n.m. ivory.

ivre, adj. drunk, intoxicated.

ivresse, n.f. drunkenness, intoxication.

ivrogne, n.m. drunkard.

ivrognerie, n.f. drunkenness.

J

jaboter, vb. prattle.

jacasser, vb. chatter.

jachère, n.f. fallow.

jacinthe, n.f. hyacinth.

jadis (-s), adv. formerly.

jaillir, vb. gush, spurt.

jaillissement, n.m. gush, spurt.

jais, n.m. jet (mineral).

jalon, n.m. staff; landmark.

jalonner, vb. mark out.

jalouser, vb. envy.

jalousie, n.f. jealousy.

jaloux, adj. jealous.

jamais, adv. ever, never.

jambe, n.f. leg.

jambière, n.f. legging.

jambon, n.m. ham.

jante, n.f. rim.

janvier, n.m. January.

Japon, n.m. Japan.

Japonais, n.m. Japanese (person).

japonais, 1. n.m. Japanese (language). **2.** adj. Japanese.

japper, vb. yelp.

jaquette, n.f. jacket.

jardin, n.m. garden.

jardinage, n.m. gardening.

jardinier, n.m. gardener.

jarre, n.f. jar.

jarretière, n.f. garter.

jaser, vb. jabber.

jatte, n.f. bowl.

jaunâtre, adj. yellowish.

jaune, 1. adj. yellow. **2.** n.m. yolk (of egg).

jaunir, vb. turn yellow.

jaunisse, n.f. jaundice.

jazz, n.m. jazz.

je (jә), pron. I.

jeans, n.m.pl. jeans.

jésuite, n.m. Jesuit.

jet, n.m. jet (water, gas).

jetée, n.f. pier.

jeter, vb. throw.

jeton, n.m. token.

jeu, n.m. play, game. **mettre en j.,** stake.

jeudi, n.m. Thursday.

jeune, adj. young, youthful.

jeûne, n.m. fast.

jeûner, vb. fast.

jeunesse, n.f. youth.

joaillerie, n.f. jewelry.

joaillier, n.m. jeweler.

jobard, n.m. fool.

joie, n.f. joy.

joindre, vb. join.

joint, n.m. joint.

jointure, n.f. joint (esp. of the body).

joli, adj. pretty.

joliment, adv. prettily; awfully.

jonc, n.m. rush.

joncher, vb. scatter.

jonction, n.f. junction.

jongler, vb. juggle.

jongleur, n.m. juggler.

jonquille, n.f. jonquil.

joue, n.f. cheek.

jouer, vb. play.

jouet, n.m. toy.

joueur, n.m. player.

joufflu, adj. chubby.

joug, n.m. yoke.

jouir de, vb. enjoy.

jouissance, n.f. enjoyment.

jouisseur, *n.m.* pleasure-seeker.
jour, *n.m.* day, daylight. **j. de fête,** holiday. **point du j.,** dawn.
journal, *n.m.* newspaper, journal, diary.
journalier, *adj.* daily.
journalisme, *n.m.* journalism.
journaliste, *n.m.* journalist.
journée, *n.f.* day.
journellement, *adv.* daily.
joute, *n.f.* joust.
jovialité, *n.f.* jollity.
joyau, *n.m.* jewel.
joyeux, *adj.* joyful.
jubilé, *n.m.* jubilee.
jubiler, *vb.* exult.
judaïsme, *n.m.* Judaism.
judiciaire, *adj.* judicial, legal.
judicieux, *adj.* wise, judicious.
juge, *n.m.* judge.
jugement, *n.m.* judgment, reason. **mettre en j.,** try.
juger, *vb.* judge.
jugulaire, *adj.* jugular.
Juif *m.,* **Juive** *f. n.* Jew.
juif *m.,* **juive** *f. adj.* Jewish.
juillet, *n.m.* July.
juin, *n.m.* June.
jumeau *m.,* **jumelle** *f. adj. and n.* twin.
jumeler, *vb.* couple, join.
jumelles, *n.f.pl.* opera glasses.
jument, *n.f.* mare.
jupe, *n.f.* skirt.
jupon, *n.m.* petticoat.
jurer, *vb.* swear.
juridiction, *n.f.* jurisdiction.
juridique, *adj.* judicial.
jurisconsulte, *n.m.* jurist, lawyer.
jurisprudence, *n.f.* jurisprudence.
juriste, *n.m.* jurist.
juron, *n.m.* oath.
jury, *n.m.* jury.
jus, *n.m.* juice, gravy.
jusque, *prep.* up to. **jusqu'à,** as far as, until. **jusqu'ici,** hitherto.
juste, 1. *adj.* just, fair, right. **2.** *adv.* just.
justement, *adv.* precisely, exactly.
justesse, *n.f.* accuracy, precision.
justice, *n.f.* justice, fairness.
justifiant, *adj.* justifying.
justification, *n.f.* justification.
justifier, *vb.* justify.
juteux, *adj.* juicy.
juvénile, *adj.* juvenile.

K

kangourou, *n.m.* kangaroo.
karaté, *n.m.* karate.
képi, *n.m.* cap.
kermesse, *n.f.* fair.
kif, *n.m.* marijuana.
kilogramme, *n.m.* kilogram.
kilohertz, *n.m.* kilohertz.

kilométrage, *n.m.* mileage.
kilomètre, *n.m.* kilometer.
kilométrique, *adj.* kilometric.
kiosque, *n.m.* kiosk; newsstand; bandstand.
klaxon, *n.m.* car horn.
kyrielle, *n.f.* litany.

L

la, *pron.* her.
là, *adv.* there.
là-bas, *adv.* yonder, out there.
labeur, *n.m.* labor.
laboratoire, *n.m.* laboratory.
laborieux, *adj.* industrious, laborious.
labour, *n.m.* plowing.
labourer, *vb.* plow.
labyrinthe, *n.m.* maze.
lac, *n.m.* lake.
lacérer, *vb.* lacerate; tear up.
lacet, *n.m.* shoelace; winding.
lâche, 1. *n.m.f.* coward. **2.** *adj.* cowardly, loose.
lâchement, *adv.* loosely, shamefully.
lâcher, *vb.* loosen, let go. **l. pied,** give ground, flee.
lâcheté, *n.f.* cowardice.
lacis, *n.m.* network.
laconique, *adj.* laconic.
lacrymogène, *adj.* **gaz l.,** tear gas.
lacté, *adj.* milky.
lacune, *n.f.* gap, blank.
ladre, *adj.* stingy, mean.
lagune, *n.f.* lagoon.
laid, *adj.* ugly.
laideron, *n.m.* ugly person.
laideur, *n.f.* ugliness.
lainage, *n.m.* woolen goods.
laine, *n.f.* wool.
laineux, *adj.* wooly; downy.
laïque (lä ēk), *n.m.* layman.
laisse, *n.f.* leash.
laisser, *vb.* let, leave.
laisser-aller, *n.m.* freedom, negligence.
laissez-passer, *n.m.* pass.
lait, *n.m.* milk.
laitage, *n.m.* dairy foods.
laiterie, *n.f.* dairy.
laiteux, *adj.* milky.
laitier, *n.m.* milkman.
laiton, *n.m.* brass.
laitue, *n.f.* lettuce.
lambeau, *n.m.* rag.
lambin, *adj.* slow, dawdling.
lame, *n.f.* blade.
lamé, *adj.* gold- or silver-trimmed.
lamelle, *n.f.* (microscope) slide.
lamentable, *adj.* sad, grievous.
lamentation, *n.f.* lamentation.
lamenter, *vb.* mourn, lament.
laminer, *vb.* laminate.
lampe, *n.f.* lamp. **l. de poche,** flashlight.
lamper, *vb.* drink, gulp.
lampion, *n.m.* Chinese lantern.
lampiste, *n.m.* lamplighter.
lancé, *n.f.* lance.

lancer, *vb.* hurl; launch.
lanceur, *n.m.* pitcher.
lancinant, *adj.* throbbing (of pain).
lande, *n.f.* wasteland, moor.
langage, *n.m.* language.
langoureux, *adj.* languishing.
langue, *n.f.* tongue, language.
languette, *n.f.* tonguelike strip.
langueur, *n.f.* languor.
languir, *vb.* pine, languish.
languissant, *adj.* languid.
lanière, *n.f.* strap, thong.
lanterne, *n.f.* lantern.
lapider, *vb.* stone; abuse.
lapin, *n.m.* rabbit.
laps, *n.m.* lapse of time.
lapsus (-sYs), *n.m.* slip.
laquais, *n.m.* footman, lackey.
laque, *n.f.* shellac; hairspray.
larcin, *n.m.* larceny, theft.
lard, *n.m.* bacon, fat.
larder, *vb.* lard; pierce.
large, *adj.* wide.
largeur, *n.f.* width.
larguer, *vb.* loosen, let go.
larme, *n.f.* tear.
larmoyer, *vb.* weep, whimper.
larron, *n.m.* thief.
las, *adj.* weary.
lascif, *adj.* lewd, wanton.
laser, *n.m.* laser.
lasser, *vb.* weary.
latéral, *adj.* lateral.
Latin, *n.m.* Latin (person).
latin, 1. *n.m.* Latin (language). **2.** *adj.* Latin.
latte, *n.f.* lath.
laurier, *n.m.* bay, laurel.
lavabo, *n.m.* lavatory.
lavande, *n.f.* lavender.
lavandière, *n.f.* laundress.
lavement, *n.m.* enema.
laver, *vb.* wash.
lavette, *n.f.* dishrag.
laxatif, *n.m.* laxative.
le (lə), *m.,* **la** *f.,* **les** *pl.* **1.** *art.* the. **2.** *pron.* him, her, it.
lécher, *vb.* lick.
leçon, *n.f.* lesson.
lecteur, *n.m.* reader.
lecture, *n.f.* reading.
légal, *adj.* lawful, legal.
légaliser, *vb.* legalize.
légalité, *n.f.* legality.
légataire, *n.m.* legatee.
légation, *n.f.* legation.
légendaire, *adj.* legendary.
légende, *n.f.* legend; inscription.
léger, *adj.* light.
légèreté, *n.f.* lightness.
légion, *n.f.* legion.
législateur, *n.m.* legislator.
législatif, *adj.* legislative.
législation, *n.f.* legislation.
législature, *n.f.* legislature.
légitime, *adj.* legitimate, lawful.
legs, *n.m.* bequest.
léguer, *vb.* bequeath.
légume, *n.m.* vegetable.
lendemain, *n.m.* the next day.
lent, *adj.* slow.
lenteur, *n.f.* slowness.

lentille, n.f. lentil; lens.
lèpre, n.f. leprosy.
lépreux, 1. adj. leprous. 2. n. leper.
lequel, pron. which, who.
les, pron. them.
lesbien, adj. Lesbian.
lesbienne, n.f. Lesbian.
léser, vb. wrong, hurt.
lésine, n.f. stinginess.
lésion, n.f. wrong; lesion.
lessive, n.f. laundry.
lessiveuse, n.f. washing machine.
lest (-t), n.m. ballast.
leste, adj. nimble, clever.
lettre, n.f. letter.
lettré, adj. lettered, literate.
leur, 1. pron. to them; le leur, la leur, theirs. 2. leur m.f., leurs pl. adj. their.
leurre, n.m. lure, trap.
leurrer, vb. lure.
levain, n.m. yeast, leaven.
levée, n.m. embankment, levy.
lever, vb. raise. se l., get up.
levier, n.m. lever.
lèvre, n.f. lip.
lévrier, n.m. greyhound.
lexique, n.m. lexicon.
lézard, n.m. lizard.
lézarde, n.f. crevice.
liaison, n.f. connection, linkage.
liant, adj. supple; affable.
liasse, n.f. file.
libelle, n.m. libel.
libeller, vb. draw up, word.
libéral, adj. liberal.
libérateur, n.m. rescuer.
libérer, vb. free.
liberté, n.f. freedom, liberty.
libertin, 1. adj. wanton. 2. n. libertine.
libraire, n.m. bookseller.
librairie, n.f. bookstore.
libre, adj. free.
libre-échange, n.m. free trade.
licence, n.f. license.
licencié, n.m. licensee; holder of university degree.
licencieux, adj. licentious.
licite, adj. lawful.
licorne, n.f. unicorn.
licou, n.m. halter.
lie, n.f. dreg.
liège, n.m. cork.
lien, n.m. bond, link, tie.
lier, vb. bind, tie, link.
lierre, n.m. ivy.
lieu, n.m. place. au l. de, instead of.
lieu-commun, n.m. commonplace.
lieue, n.f. league.
lieutenant, n.m. lieutenant.
lièvre, n.m. hare.
ligne, n.f. line.
lignée, n.f. offspring.
ligoter, vb. bind up.
ligue, n.f. league.
liguer, vb. league.
lilas, n.m. lilac.
limaçon, n.m. snail.
lime, n.f. file; lime (fruit).

limer, vb. file.
limier, n.m. bloodhound.
limitation, n.f. limitation.
limitation des naissances, n.f. birth control, contraception.
limite, n.f. limit, border.
limiter, vb. limit, confine.
limon, n.m. mud, slime.
limonade, n.f. lemon soda.
limoneux, adj. muddy.
limpide, adj. clear, limpid.
lin, n.m. flax.
linceul, n.m. shroud.
linéaire, adj. lineal.
linge, n.m. linen, wash.
lingerie, n.f. linen goods, underwear.
linguistique, adj. linguistic.
linon, n.m. lawn (sheer linen).
linteau, n.m. lintel.
lion, n.m. lion.
lippu, adj. thick-lipped.
liqueur, n.m. liquid, liqueur.
liquidation, n.f. liquidation, settling.
liquide, adj. and n.m. liquid, fluid.
liquider, vb. liquidate.
liquoreux, adj. sweet.
lire, vb. read.
lis (-s), n.m. lily.
liséré, n.m. piping, border.
liseur, n.m. reader.
liseuse, n.f. bookmark.
lisible, adj. legible.
lisière, n.f. edge.
lisse, adj. smooth.
lisser, vb. smooth.
liste, n.f. list, roll.
lit, n.m. bed.
litanie, n.f. litany.
lit-cage, n.m. (folding) cot.
lit de la mer, n.m. seabed.
literie, n.f. bedding.
litière, n.f. litter.
litige, n.m. litigation.
litigieux, adj. litigious.
litre, n.m. liter.
littéraire, adj. literary.
littéral, adj. literal.
littérature, n.f. literature.
liturgie, n.f. liturgy.
livide, adj. livid.
livraison, n.f. delivery. l. contre remboursement, C.O.D.
livre, n.f. pound.
livre, n.m. book.
livre broché, n.m. paperback.
livrée, n.f. livery.
livrer, vb. deliver.
livresque, adj. bookish, from books.
livreur, n.m. delivery man.
local, adj. local.
localiser, vb. locate.
localité, n.f. locality.
locataire, n.m.f. tenant.
location, n.f. action or price of renting.
loch (-k), n.m. log.
locomotive, n.f. locomotive.
locuste, n.f. locust.
locution, n.f. locution, phrase.
loge, n.f. box.
logement, n.m. lodging.

loger, vb. lodge.
logique, 1. n.f. logic. 2. adj. logical.
logis, n.m. dwelling.
loi, n.f. law.
loin, adv. far, away.
lointain, adj. distant.
loir, n.m. dormouse.
loisible, adj. optional, allowable.
loisir, n.m. leisure.
Londres, n.m. London.
long m., longue f. adj. long.
longe, n.f. leash; loin (of veal).
longer, vb. go along.
longeron, n.m. beam, girder.
longitude, n.f. longitude.
longtemps, adv. long.
longueur, n.f. length.
lopin, n.m. small piece, plot.
loquace, adj. talkative.
loque, n.f. morsel, rag.
loquet, n.m. latch.
loqueteux, adj. tattered.
lorgner, vb. glance at; ogle.
lorgnon, n.m. glasses.
loriot, n.m. oriole.
lors, adv. then. l. de, at the time of.
lorsque, conj. when.
losange, n.m. diamond, lozenge.
lot, n.m. lot, prize.
loterie, n.f. raffle, lottery.
lotion, n.f. lotion.
lotir, vb. divide, apportion.
louable, adj. praiseworthy.
louage, n.m. hire.
louange, n.f. praise.
louche, adj. shady.
loucher, vb. squint.
louer, vb. praise; hire, rent.
loueur, n.m. one who rents.
loup, n.m. wolf.
loupe, n.f. magnifying glass.
louper, vb. spoil, botch.
loup-garou, n.m. werewolf.
lourd, adj. heavy.
lourdaud, n.m. clod.
lourdeur, n.f. heaviness, dullness.
loyal, adj. loyal.
loyauté, n.f. loyalty.
loyer, n.m. rent.
lubricité, n.f. lewdness.
lubrifier, vb. lubricate.
lucarne, n.f. attic window.
lucide, adj. lucid.
lucidité, n.f. clearness.
luciole, n.f. firefly.
lueur, n.f. gleam.
lugubre, adj. doleful, dismal, lugubrious.
lui, pron. he; to him, to her.
lui-même, pron. himself, itself.
luire, vb. gleam.
luisant, adj. shiny.
lumière, n.f. light.
lumineux, adj. luminous.
lunaire, adj. lunar.
lunatique, adj. whimsical.
lundi, n.m. Monday.
lune, n.f. moon. l. de miel, honeymoon. clair de l., moonlight.

lunetier, *n.m.* optician.
lunettes, *n.f.pl.* glasses.
lustre, *n.m.* chandelier; luster; five-year period.
lustrer, *vb.* polish, gloss.
luth, *n.m.* lute.
lutiner, *vb.* tease.
lutte, *n.f.* strife, struggle, contest.
lutter, *vb.* struggle, contend.
luxe, *n.m.* luxury.
luxer, *vb.* dislocate.
luxueux, *adj.* luxurious.
luxure, *n.f.* lust.
luzerne, *n.f.* alfalfa.
lycée, *n.m.* high school.
lycéen, *n.m.* high-school student.
lymphatique, *adj.* lymphatic.
lynchage, *n.m.* lynching.
lyncher, *vb.* lynch.
lyre, *n.f.* lyre.
lyrique, *adj.* lyric.

M

M. (abbr. for *Monsieur*), *n.m.* Mr.
macabre, *adj.* macabre, ghastly.
macédoine, *n.f.* salad; mixture.
macérer, *vb.* macerate, soak.
mâcher, *vb.* chew.
machin, *n.m.* thing, gadget.
machinal, *adj.* mechanical.
machination, *n.f.* plot, scheme.
machine, *n.f.* machine. **m. à copier**, copier. **m. à écrire**, typewriter.
machiner, *vb.* plot.
machiniste, *n.m.* machinist.
mâchoire, *n.f.* jaw.
mâchonner, *vb.* mumble, munch.
maçon, *n.m.* mason.
maculer, *vb.* spot, blot.
madame, *n.f.* madam, Mrs.
madeleine, *n.f.* light cake.
mademoiselle, *n.f.* Miss.
madone, *n.f.* Madonna.
mafia, *m.f.* mafia.
magasin, *n.m.* store.
mages, *n.m.pl.* wise men.
magicien, *n.m.* magician.
magie, *n.f.* magic.
magique, *adj.* magic.
magistrat, *n.m.* magistrate.
magnanime, *adj.* magnanimous.
magnat, *n.m.* magnate.
magnétique, *adj.* magnetic.
magnétophone, *n.m.* tape recorder.
magnificence, *n.f.* magnificence.
magnifique, *adj.* magnificent.
mahométan, *adj.* Mohammedan.
mai, *n.m.* May.
maigre, *adj.* lean, thin, meager.
maigrir, *vb.* lose weight.
maille, *n.f.* stitch; mesh.
maillot, *n.m.* shorts; T-shirt.

main, *n.f.* hand. **sous la m.**, handy.
main-d'œuvre, *n.f.* manpower.
maintenant, *adv.* now. **dès m.**, henceforth.
maintenir, *vb.* maintain.
maintien, *n.m.* upkeep; behavior.
maire, *n.m.* mayor.
mairie, *n.f.* city hall.
mais, *conj.* but.
maïs (mä ḗs), *n.m.* corn.
maison, *n.f.* house.
maisonnée, *n.f.* household.
maître, *n.m.* master, teacher.
maîtresse, *n.f.* mistress, teacher.
maîtrise, *n.f.* mastery.
maîtriser, *vb.* master, overcome.
majesté, *n.f.* majesty.
majestueux, *adj.* majestic.
majeur, *adj.* major.
majordome, *n.m.* majordomo.
majorer, *vb.* increase price, over-price.
majorité, *n.f.* majority.
majuscule, *n.f.* capital.
mal, **1.** *n.m.* harm, ill, evil. **2.** *adv.* badly. **faire m. à**, hurt. **avoir m. à**, have a pain in.
malade, **1.** *n.m.f.* sick person, patient. **2.** *adj.* sick.
maladie, *n.f.* disease, illness, sickness.
maladif, *adj.* sickly.
maladresse, *n.f.* awkwardness.
maladroit, *adj.* awkward.
malaise, *n.m.* discomfort.
malappris, *adj.* ill-bred.
malaria, *n.f.* malaria.
malavisé, *adj.* indiscreet, ill-advised.
malchance, *n.f.* bad luck, mishap.
maldonne, *n.f.* misdeal.
mâle, *adj.* and *n.m.* male.
malédiction, *n.f.* curse.
maléfice, *n.m.* witchery, evil spell.
malencontre, *n.f.* unlucky incident.
malencontreux, *adj.* unlucky.
malentendu, *n.m.* misunderstanding.
malfaiteur, *n.m.* malefactor.
malfamé, *adj.* ill-famed.
malgré, *prep.* despite.
malhabile, *adj.* awkward, dull.
malheur, *n.m.* misfortune, accident.
malheureux, *adj.* unfortunate, unhappy, miserable.
malhonnête, *adj.* dishonest.
malhonnêteté, *n.f.* dishonesty.
malice, *n.f.* mischief, malice.
malicieux, *adj.* malicious, roguish.
malin *m.*, **maligne** *f.* *adj.* malignant; sharp, sly.
malingre, *adj.* sickly, puny.
malintentionné, *adj.* ill-disposed.
malle, *n.f.* trunk.
mallette, *n.f.* small suitcase.

malotru, *n.m.* boor, lout.
malpropre, *adj.* messy.
malpropreté, *n.f.* messiness.
malsain, *adj.* unhealthy.
malséant, *adj.* improper.
maltraiter, *vb.* misuse.
malveillant, *adj.* malevolent.
malvenu, *adj.* without any right.
malversation, *n.f.* embezzlement.
maman, *n.f.* mamma.
mamelle, *n.f.* udder.
mammifère, *n.m.* mammal.
manche, *n.m.* handle. *f.* sleeve. **La M.**, the English Channel.
manchette, *n.f.* cuff.
manchon, *n.m.* muff.
mandarine, *n.f.* tangerine.
mandat, *n.m.* warrant, writ, mandate. **m.-poste**, money order.
mandataire, *n.m.* agent, proxy.
mander, *vb.* send for, inform.
manège, *n.m.* horsemanship.
manette, *n.f.* handle, lever.
mangeable, *adj.* eatable.
mangeoire, *n.f.* manger.
manger, *vb.* eat.
maniable, *adj.* manageable; easygoing.
maniaque, **1.** *n.m.* maniac. **2.** *adj.* maniac, maniacal.
manie, *n.f.* mania.
manier, *vb.* handle, wield.
manière, *n.f.* manner.
maniéré, *adj.* affected.
manière de vivre, *n.f.* life style.
manifestation, *n.f.* demonstration.
manifeste, *adj.* manifest, evident, overt.
manifester, *vb.* manifest, show.
manigance, *n.f.* trick, intrigue.
manipuler, *vb.* manipulate.
manivelle, *n.f.* crank; winch.
mannequin, *n.m.* dummy.
manœuvre, *n.f.* maneuver.
manoir, *n.m.* country house, estate.
manquant, **1.** *adj.* missing. **2.** *n.m.* absentee.
manque, *n.m.* lack.
manquer, *vb.* miss, lack, fail.
mansarde, *n.f.* attic.
mansuétude, *n.f.* mildness, kindness.
manteau, *n.m.* cloak, coat.
manucure, *n.m.f.* manicurist.
manuel, *adj.* and *n.m.* manual.
manufacture, *n.f.* manufacture.
manuscrit, *adj.* and *n.m.* manuscript.
manutention, *n.f.* management.
maquereau, *n.m.* mackerel.
maquette, *n.f.* preliminary sketch or model.
maquillage, *n.m.* make-up.
maquis, *n.m.* scrub land; guerrilla fighters.
maquisard, *n.m.* guerrilla fighter.
marais, *n.m.* marsh.
marâtre, *n.f.* stepmother.

maraude, *n.f.* marauding.
marbre, *n.m.* marble.
marchand, *n.m.* merchant.
marchander, *vb.* bargain, haggle.
marchandises, *n.f.pl.* goods.
marche, *n.f.* march, step.
marché, *n.m.* market, bargain. bon m., cheap.
marchepied, *n.m.* running-board.
marcher, *vb.* walk, step, march, run (machine).
marcheur, *n.m.* pedestrian.
mardi, *n.m.* Tuesday.
mare, *n.f.* pool.
marécage, *n.m.* bog.
marécageux, *adj.* marshy.
maréchal, *n.m.* marshal.
marée, *n.f.* tide.
mareyeur, *n.m.* fish seller.
margarine, *n.f.* margarine.
marge, *n.f.* margin.
margelle, *n.f.* edge, brink.
marguerite, *n.f.* daisy.
mari, *n.m.* husband.
mariage, *n.m.* marriage.
marié, 1. *n.m.* bridegroom. 2. *adj.* married.
mariée, *n.f.* bride.
marie-jeanne, *n.f.* marijuana.
marier, *vb.* marry.
marijuana, *n.f.* marijuana.
marin, 1. *n.m.* sailor. 2. *adj.* marine. fusilier m., marine.
marinade, *n.f.* mixture for pickling.
marine, *n.f.* navy.
mariner, *vb.* pickle.
marionnette, *n.f.* puppet.
maritime, *adj.* marine.
marmite, *n.f.* pot.
marmiter, *vb.* blast (with gunfire).
marmot, *n.m.* urchin, brat.
marmotter, *vb.* mumble.
marotte, *n.f.* fad.
marque, *n.f.* brand, mark.
marquer, *vb.* mark.
marqueur, *n.m.* marker, score-keeper.
marquis, *n.m.* marquis.
marraine, *n.f.* godmother; sponsor.
marron, *n.m.* chestnut; brown.
marronier, *n.m.* chestnut tree.
mars (-s), *n.m.* March.
marteau, *n.m.* hammer.
marteler, *vb.* hammer.
martial, *adj.* warlike.
martre, *n.m.* marten.
martyr, *n.m.* martyr.
martyre, *n.m.* martyrdom.
marxisme, *n.m.* marxism.
mascarade, *n.f.* masquerade.
mascotte, *n.f.* mascot.
masculin, *adj.* masculine.
masque, *n.m.* mask.
masquer, *vb.* mask.
massacre, *n.m.* slaughter.
massage, *n.m.* massage.
masse, *n.f.* mass.
masser, *vb.* mass; massage.
massif, *adj.* massive, solid.
massue, *n.f.* club.

mastiquer, *vb.* chew.
mat (-t), *adj.* dull.
mât (mä), *n.m.* mast.
matelas, *n.m.* mattress.
matelot, *n.m.* sailor.
matérialiser, *vb.* materialize.
matérialisme, *n.m.* materialism.
matérialiste, *adj. and n.m.f.* materialist, materialistic.
matériaux, *n.m.pl.* stuff, materials.
matériel, *adj.* material, real.
maternel, *adj.* native; maternal.
maternité, *n.f.* maternity.
mathématique, *adj.* mathematical.
mathématiques, *n.f.pl.* mathematics.
matière, *n.f.* matter. table des m.s, index.
matin, *n.m.* morning.
mâtin, *n.m.* big dog.
matinal, *adj.* early.
matinée, *n.f.* morning.
matineux, *adj.* rising early.
matois, *adj.* cunning, sly.
matou, *n.m.* tomcat.
matraque, *n.f.* heavy club.
matrice, *n.f.* womb.
matricule, *n.f.* roster, registration.
matriculer, *vb.* enroll, register.
matrimonial, *adj.* marital.
mâture, *n.f.* masts (of boats).
maturité, *n.f.* maturity.
maudire, *vb.* curse.
maudit, *adj.* cursed, miserable.
maugréer, *vb.* curse, grumble.
maussade, *adj.* glum, sullen, cross.
mauvais, *adj.* bad.
maxime, *n.f.* maxim.
maximum, *n.m.* maximum.
me (mo), *pron. me*, myself.
méandre, *n.m.* winding.
mécanicien, *n.m.* mechanic, engineer.
mécanique, *adj.* mechanical.
mécaniser, *vb.* mechanize.
mécanisme, *n.m.* mechanism, machinery.
mécano, *n.m.* mechanic.
méchamment, *adv.* maliciously.
méchanceté, *n.f.* wickedness, malice.
méchant, *adj.* wicked, malicious.
mèche, *n.f.* lock; wick, fuse.
mécompte, *n.m.* error, disappointment.
méconnaissable, *adj.* unrecognizable.
méconnaître, *vb.* fail to recognize.
mécontent, *adj.* discontented.
mécontentement, *n.m.* discontent.
mécontenter, *vb.* dissatisfy.
mécréant, *n.m.* unbeliever.
médaille, *n.f.* medal.
médaillon, *n.m.* locket.
médecin, *n.m.* physician.

médecine, *n.f.* medicine.
médiateur, *n.m.* mediator; ombudsman (in France).
médiation, *n.f.* mediation.
médical, *adj.* medical.
médicament, *n.m.* medicament.
médicinal, *adj.* medicinal.
médiéval, *adj.* medieval.
médiocre, *adj.* mediocre.
médiocrité, *n.f.* mediocrity.
médire, *vb.* slander, defame.
médisance, *n.f.* slander.
méditation, *n.f.* meditation.
méditer, *vb.* meditate, muse, brood.
méditerrané, *adj.* Mediterranean.
médium, *n.m.* medium.
méduse, *n.f.* jellyfish.
méduser, *vb.* stupefy.
méfait, *n.m.* crime, misdeed.
méfiance, *n.f.* distrust.
méfiant, *adj.* distrustful.
méfier, *vb.* se m. de, distrust.
mégarde, *n.f.* heedlessness.
mégère, *n.f.* vixen, shrew.
mégot, *n.m.* cigarette butt.
meilleur, *adj.* better, best.
mélancolie, *n.f.* melancholy.
mélancolique, *adj.* melancholy.
mélange, *n.m.* mixture.
mélasse, *n.f.* molasses.
mêlée, *n.f.* struggle.
mêler, *vb.* mix. se m. de, meddle in.
mélèze, *n.m.* larch.
mellifu, *adj.* sweet, honeyed.
mélodie, *n.f.* melody.
mélodieux, *adj.* melodious.
mélodique, *adj.* melodic.
mélodrame, *n.m.* melodrama.
mélomane, *n.m.* lover of music.
melon, *n.m.* melon.
membrane, *n.f.* membrane.
membre, *n.m.* member, limb.
membrure, *n.f.* frame, limbs.
même, 1. *adj.* same, very, self. moi-m., myself; lui-m., himself, etc. 2. *adv.* even. de m., likewise. tout de m., notwithstanding. mettre à m. de, enable to.
mémento, *n.m.* memento, notebook.
mémoire, *n.f.* memory, memoir.
mémorable, *adj.* memorable.
mémorandum, *n.m.* memorandum.
mémorial, *n.m.* memorial; memoirs.
menaçant, *adj.* threatening.
menace, *n.f.* threat.
menacer, *vb.* threaten.
ménage, *n.m.* household.
ménagement, *n.m.* discretion.
ménager, 1. *n.m.* manager. 2. *vb.* manage.
ménagère, *n.f.* housewife, housekeeper.
ménagerie, *n.f.* menagerie.
mendiant, *n.m.* beggar.
mendicité, *n.f.* begging.

mendier, vb. beg.

menées, n.f.pl. schemes.

mener, vb. lead.

ménestrel, n.m. minstrel.

ménétrier, n.m. country fiddler.

meneur, n.m. leader, ring-leader.

méningite, n.f. meningitis.

menottes, n.f.pl. handcuffs.

mensonge, n.m. falsehood, lie.

mensonger, adj. false, deceptive.

mensualité, n.f. remittance paid monthly.

mensuel, adj. monthly.

mensurable, adj. measurable.

mental, adj. mental.

mentalité, n.f. mentality.

menterie, n.f. lie.

menteur, n.m. liar.

menthe, n.f. mint.

mention, n.f. mention.

mentionner, vb. mention.

mentir, vb. lie.

menton, n.m. chin.

menu, 1. n.m. menu. 2. adj. little, minute.

menuet, n.m. minuet.

menuiserie, n.f. woodwork.

menuisier, n.m. carpenter.

méprendre, vb. **se m.,** be mistaken.

mépris, n.m. contempt, scorn.

méprisable, adj. mean, contemptible.

méprisant, adj. contemptuous.

méprise, n.f. mistake, misunderstanding.

mépriser, vb. scorn, despise.

mer (-r), n.f. sea. **mal de m.,** seasickness.

mercanti, n.m. profiteer.

mercantile, adj. mercantile.

mercenaire, adj. and n.m. mercenary.

mercerie, n.f. haberdashery.

merci, n.m. thanks, mercy.

mercredi, n.m. Wednesday.

mercure, n.m. mercury.

mère, n.f. mother.

méridien, n.m. meridian.

méridional, adj. southern.

meringue, n.f. meringue.

méritant, adj. meritorious.

mérite, n.m. merit, desert.

mériter, vb. merit, deserve.

méritoire, adj. meritorious.

merle, n.m. blackbird.

merveille, n.f. marvel.

merveilleux, adj. wonderful, marvelous.

mésalliance, n.f. misalliance.

mésallier, vb. marry badly.

mésaventure, n.f. accident, mishap.

mesdames, pl. of **madame.**

mesdemoiselles, pl. of **mademoiselle.**

mésestime, n.f. low opinion or repute.

mésintelligence, n.f. difficulty, discord.

mesquin, adj. shabby, mean, stingy.

mesquinerie, n.f. meanness.

message, n.m. message.

messager, n.m. messenger.

messe, n.f. Mass.

Messie, n.m. Messiah.

messieurs, pl. of **monsieur.**

mesurage, n.m. measurement.

mesure, n.f. measure. **à m. que,** as.

mesuré, adj. measured, cautious.

mesurer, vb. measure.

métairie, n.f. small farm.

métal, n.m. metal.

métallique, adj. metallic.

métallurgie, n.f. metallurgy.

métamorphose, n.f. transformation.

métaphore, n.f. metaphor.

métaphysique, 1. n.f. metaphysics. 2. adj. metaphysical.

métayer, n.m. small farmer.

météore, n.m. meteor.

météorologie, n.f. meteorology.

métèque, n.m. alien.

méthode, n.f. method.

méthodique, adj. methodical, systematic.

méticuleux, adj. meticulous.

métier, n.m. loom; craft, trade.

métis, adj. hybrid, crossbred.

métrage, n.m. measurement.

mètre, n.m. meter.

métrique, adj. metric.

métro, n.m. subway.

métropole, n.f. metropolis; native land.

métropolitain, adj. metropolitan.

mets, n.m. food, dish.

mettable, adj. wearable.

metteur, n.m. **m. en scène,** play director.

mettre, vb. put, place, set. **se m. à,** begin.

meuble, n.m. piece of furniture; (pl.) furniture.

meubler, vb. furnish, outfit.

meule, n.f. stack.

meunier, n.m. miller.

meurtre, n.m. murder.

meurtrier, n.m. murderer.

meurtrière, n.f. murderess.

meurtrir, vb. bruise.

meurtrissure, n.f. bruise.

meute, n.f. dog pack; mob.

Mexicain, n.m. Mexican.

mexicain, adj. Mexican.

Mexique, n.m. Mexico.

mezzanine, n.f. mezzanine.

mi, adj. mid, half.

miaou, n.m. mew.

miauler, vb. mew.

mica, n.m. mica.

miche, n.f. loaf of bread.

micro, n.m. microphone.

microbe, n.m. microbe.

microfiche, n.f. microfiche.

microforme, n.f. microform.

microphone, n.m. microphone.

microscope, n.m. microscope.

microscopique, adj. microscopic.

midi, n.m. noon; south.

midinette, n.f. young saleswoman, business woman.

mie, n.f. crumb.

miel, n.m. honey.

mielleux, adj. honeyed, sweet.

mien, pron. **le mien, la mienne,** mine.

miette, n.f. crumb.

mieux, adv. better, best.

mièvre, adj. affected.

mignard, adj. dainty, mincing.

mignon, 1. adj. delicate, dainty. 2. n.m.f. darling.

migraine, n.f. headache.

migration, n.f. migration.

mijoter, vb. cook slowly, simmer.

mil (mēl), num. thousand.

milice, n.f. militia.

milieu, n.m. middle, center, environment.

militaire, adj. military.

militant, adj. militant.

militarisme, n.m. militarism.

militer, vb. militate.

mille (-l), 1. n.m. mile. 2. adj. and n.m. thousand.

millet, n.m. millet.

millier (-l-), n.m. thousand.

milligramme (-l-), n.m. milligram.

million (-l-), n.m. million.

millionnaire (-l-), adj. and n.m.f. millionaire.

mime, n.m. mime, mimic.

mimique, adj. mimic.

minable, adj. shabby, poor.

minauder, vb. simper.

mince, adj. slender, slight, thin.

minceur, n.f. slimness.

mine, n.f. mine; mien; lead.

miner, vb. mine; wear away; weaken.

minerai, n.m. ore.

minéral, adj. and n.m. mineral.

mineur, 1. n.m. miner. 2. adj. and n.m. minor.

miniature, n.f. miniature.

miniaturiser, vb. miniaturize.

minier, adj. of mines.

minime, adj. very small.

minimum, n.m. minimum.

ministère, n.m. ministry, department, board.

ministériel, adj. ministerial.

ministre, n.m. minister. **premier m.,** premier.

minorité, n.f. minority.

minotier, n.m. miller.

minuit, n.m. midnight.

minuscule, adj. minute.

minute, n.f. minute.

minutie, n.f. trifle; care with details.

minutieux, adj. minute.

mioche, n.m.f. urchin.

miracle, n.m. miracle.

miraculeux, adj. miraculous.

mirage, n.m. mirage.

mirer, vb. aim at, look at.

mirifique, adj. wonderful.

miroir, n.m. mirror.

miroiter, vb. glisten.

misanthrope, 1. n.m. misanthrope. **2.** *adj.* misanthropic.

mise, *n.f.* putting; mode. **mise en scène,** setting.

miser, *vb.* bid.

misérable, *adj.* miserable, wretched, squalid.

misère, *n.f.* misery.

miséreux, *adj.* poor, miserable.

miséricorde, *n.f.* mercy.

miséricordieux, *adj.* merciful.

misogyne, 1. *n. m.* misogynist. **2.** woman-hating; misogynist.

missel, *n.m.* missal.

mission, *n.f.* mission.

missionnaire, *adj. and n.m.f.* missionary.

missive, *n.f.* missive.

mitaine, *n.f.* mitten.

mite, *n.f.* moth.

miteux, *adj.* shabby.

mitiger, *vb.* moderate.

mitoyen, *adj.* midway; jointly owned.

mitrailleuse, *n.f.* machine gun.

mixte, *adj.* mixed, joint.

Mlle. (abbr. for **Mademoiselle**), *n.f.* Miss.

Mme. (abbr. for **Madame**), *n.f.* Mrs.

mobile, *adj.* movable.

mobilier, *adj.* movable.

mobilisation, *n.f.* mobilization.

mobiliser, *vb.* mobilize.

mobilité, *n.f.* mobility; instability.

mode, *n.f.* fashion, mode, mood; *(pl.)* millinery. **à la m.,** fashionable.

modèle, *n.m.* model, pattern.

modeler, *vb.* model, shape.

modelliste, *n.m.f.* dress designer.

modérateur, *n.m.* moderator.

modération, *n.f.* moderation.

modéré, *adj.* moderate.

modérer, *vb.* check, moderate.

moderne, *adj.* modern.

moderniser, *vb.* modernize.

modernité, *n.f.* modernity.

modeste, *adj.* modest.

modestie, *n.f.* modesty.

modicité, *n.f.* small quantity.

modification, *n.f.* alteration.

modifier, *vb.* modify, qualify.

modique, *adj.* moderate, unimportant.

modiste, *n.f.* milliner.

modulation, *n.f.* modulation.

moduler, *vb.* modulate.

moelle, *n.f.* marrow.

moelleux (mwä ly), *adj.* mellow, soft.

mœurs (-s), *n.f.pl.* manner(s), custom.

moi, 1. *n.m.* ego. **2.** *pron.* me.

moignon, *n.m.* stump.

moindre, *adj.* less, lesser, least.

moine, *n.m.* monk.

moineau, *n.m.* sparrow.

moins, *adv.* less, least. **au m.,** at least. **à m. que,** unless.

moire, *n.f.* watered silk.

mois, *n.m.* month.

moisi, *adj.* moldy.

moisir, *vb.* mold.

moisissure, *n.f.* mold.

moisson, *n.f.* harvest, crop.

moissonner, *vb.* reap, harvest.

moissonneur, *n.m.* harvester.

moissonneuse, *n.f.* reaping machine.

moite, *adj.* moist.

moiteur, *n.m.* dampness.

moitié, *n.f.* half. **à m.,** half, *adv.*

molaire, *adj. and n.f.* molar.

môle, *n.m.* pier.

molécule, *n.f.* molecule.

molester, *vb.* molest.

mollah, *n.m.* mullah.

mollasse, *adj.* flabby, soft.

mollesse, *n.f.* softness, weakness.

mollet, 1. *adj.* soft. **œufs mollets,** soft-boiled eggs. **2.** *n.m.* calf of leg.

molletière, *n.f.* legging.

molleton, *n.m.* heavy flannel.

mollir, *vb.* soften, slacken.

mollusque, *n.m.* mollusc.

moment, *n.m.* moment.

momentané, *adj.* momentary.

mon *m.,* **ma** *f.,* **mes** *pl. adj.* my.

monacal, *adj.* pertaining to monks.

monarchie, *n.f.* monarchy.

monarchiste, *n.m.* monarchist.

monarque, *n.m.* monarch.

monastère, *n.m.* monastery.

monastique, *adj.* monastic.

monceau, *n.m.* pile.

mondain, *adj.* worldly.

monde, *n.m.* world, people. **tout le m.,** everybody, everyone. **mettre au m.,** bear.

mondial, *adj.* world-wide.

monétaire, *adj.* monetary.

moniteur, *n.m.* monitor.

monnaie, *n.f.* money, change, currency. **Hôtel de la M.,** mint.

monnayer, *vb.* mint.

monocle, *n.m.* monocle.

monogramme, *n.m.* monogram.

monologue, *n.m.* monologue.

monologuer, *vb.* soliloquize.

monoplan, *n.m.* monoplane.

monopole, *n.m.* monopoly.

monopoliser, *vb.* monopolize.

monosyllabe, *n.m.* monosyllable.

monosyllabique, *adj.* monosyllabic.

monotone, *adj.* monotonous.

monotonie, *n.f.* monotony, dullness.

monseigneur, *n.m.* title of honor; My Lord.

monsieur, *n.m.,* **messieurs,** *pl* gentleman, sir; Mr.

monstre, *n.m.* monster.

monstrueux, *adj.* monstrous.

monstruosité, *n.f.* monstrosity.

mont, *n.m.* mountain, hill.

montage, *n.m.* carrying up.

montagnard, *n.m.* mountaineer.

montagne, *n.f.* mountain.

montagneux, *adj.* mountainous.

montant, *n.m.* amount.

mont-de-piété, *n.m.* pawnshop.

monté, *adj.* mounted, supplied.

montée, *n.f.* ascent, rise, climb.

monter, *vb.* go up, mount, climb, rise.

montre, *n.f.* watch; display. **m.-bracelet,** wrist watch.

montrer, *vb.* show.

montreur, *n.m.* showman.

montueux, *adj.* hilly.

monture, *n.f.* mount.

monument, *n.m.* monument.

monumental, *adj.* monumental.

moquer, *vb.* **se m. de,** make fun of, mock, laugh at.

moquerie, *n.f.* mockery, ridicule.

moqueur, *adj.* mocking.

moral, *adj.* ethical, moral.

morale, *n.f.* morals, morality, morale.

moraliser, *vb.* moralize.

moraliste, *n.m.f.* moralist.

moralité, *n.f.* morals, morality.

morbide, *adj.* morbid.

morceau, *n.m.* piece, bit, morsel. **gros m.,** lump, chunk.

morceler, *vb.* cut up.

mordant, *adj.* pointed.

mordiller, *vb.* nibble.

mordre, *vb.* bite.

morfondre, *vb.* chill.

morgue, *n.f.* morgue.

moribond, *adj.* dying.

morne, *adj.* bleak, dismal, dreary.

morose, *adj.* morose.

morosité, *n.f.* moroseness.

morphine, *n.f.* morphine.

morphinomane, *n.* drug addict.

morphologie, *n.f.* morphology.

mors, *n.m.* horse's bit.

morse, *n.m.* walrus.

morsure, *n.f.* bite.

mort, 1. *n.m.* dummy, dead man. **2.** *n.f.* death. **3.** *adj.* dead.

mortaise, *n.f.* mortise.

mortalité, *n.f.* mortality.

mortel, 1. *adj.* deadly, mortal.

morte-saison, *n.f.* off season.

mortier, *n.m.* mortar.

mortifier, *vb.* mortify.

mort-né, *adj.* still-born.

mortuaire, *adj.* mortuary.

morue, *n.f.* cod.

mosaïque (-ä čk), *n.f.* mosaic.

Moscou, *n.m.* Moscow.

mosquée, *n.f.* mosque.

mot, *n.m.* word; cue.

moteur, *n.m.* motor.

motif, *n.m.* motive.

motion, *n.f.* motion.

motiver, *vb.* motivate, justify.

motocyclette, *n.f.* motorcycle.

motocycliste, *n.m.* motorcyclist.

motte, *n.f.* clod.

mou *m.,* **molle** *f. adj.* soft.

mouchard, *n.m.* spy.

moucharder, vb. spy.

mouche, n.f. fly.

moucher, vb. blow the nose.

moucheron, n.m. gnat.

moucheté, adj. spotted.

moucheture, n.f. spot.

mouchoir, n.m. handkerchief.

moudre, vb. grind.

moue, n.f. pout, wry face.

mouette, n.f. gull.

moufette, n.f. skunk.

moufle, n.f. mitten.

mouillage, n.m. wetting.

mouillé, adj. wet.

mouiller, vb. soak.

moulage, n.m. cast (from mold).

moule, n.m. mold.

mouler, vb. mold.

mouleur, n.m. molder.

moulin, n.m. mill.

moulure, n.f. molding.

mourant, adj. dying.

mourir, vb. die.

mouron, n.m. pimpernel.

mousquetaire, n.m. musketeer.

mousse, n.f. moss; foam, lather.

mousseline, n.f. muslin.

mousser, vb. foam, froth.

mousseux, adj. foaming.

mousson, n.m. monsoon.

moustache, n.f. mustache, whisker.

moustiquaire, n.f. mosquito net.

moustique, n.m. mosquito.

moutarde, n.f. mustard.

mouton, n.m. sheep; mutton.

moutonner, vb. curl; make wooly.

mouture, n.f. grinding.

mouvant, adj. moving, shifting.

mouvement, n.m. movement, stir.

mouvoir, vb. move.

moyen, 1. n.m. means, medium. 2. adj. middle, average.

moyennant, prep. by means of.

moyenne, n.f. average.

Moyen Orient, n.m. Middle East.

muabilité, n.f. changeability.

mue, n.f. molting; changing (esp. of voice).

muer, vb. molt (animals); break, change (voice).

muet m., muette f. adj. dumb, mute.

mufle, n.m. cad.

mugir, vb. roar, bellow.

mugissement, n.m. roaring, bellowing.

muguet, n.m. lily of the valley.

mulâtre, n.m. and adj. mulatto.

mulet, n.m. mule.

muletier, n.m. muleteer.

mulot, n.m. field mouse.

multinational, adj. multinational.

multiple, adj. multiple, manifold.

multiplicande, n.m. multiplicand.

multiplication, n.f. multiplication.

multiplicité, n.f. multiplicity.

multiplier, vb. multiply.

multitude, n.f. multitude.

municipal, adj. municipal.

municipalité, n.f. municipality.

munificence, n.f. munificence, liberality.

munificent, adj. very generous.

munir, vb. provide, supply.

munitionner, vb. provision, supply.

munitions (de guerre), n.f.pl. ammunition.

muqueux, adj. mucous.

mur, n.m. wall.

mûr, adj. ripe, mature.

muraille, n.f. wall.

mural, adj. mural.

mûre (de ronce), n.f. blackberry.

mûrier, n.m. mulberry tree.

mûrir, vb. ripen, mature.

murmure, n.m. murmur.

murmurer, vb. murmur.

musarder, vb. waste time, dawdle.

muscade, n.f. nutmeg.

muscle, n.m. muscle.

musculaire, adj. muscular.

musculeux, adj. muscular.

muse, n.f. muse.

museau, n.m. muzzle.

musée, n.m. museum.

museler, vb. muzzle; gag.

muselière, n.f. muzzle.

muser, vb. trifle, dawdle.

musical, adj. musical.

musicien, adj. and n.m. musical, musician.

musique, n.f. music.

musulman, adj. and n.m. Mohammedan.

mutabilité, n.f. mutability.

mutation, n.f. change, replacement.

mutilation, n.f. mutilation.

mutiler, vb. mutilate, mangle, mar.

mutin, adj. refractory, mutinous.

mutiner, vb. se m., mutiny, revolt.

mutinerie, n.f. mutiny.

mutisme, n.m. muteness, lack of speech.

mutuel, adj. mutual.

myope, adj. near-sighted.

myopie, n.f. near-sightedness.

myosotis, n.m. forget-me-not.

myriade, n.f. myriad.

myrrhe, n.f. myrrh.

myrte, n.m. myrtle.

mystère, n.m. mystery.

mystérieux, adj. mysterious, weird.

mysticisme, n.m. mysticism.

mystification, n.f. hoax.

mystifier, vb. mystify.

mystique, adj. mystic.

mythe, n.m. myth.

mythique, adj. mythical.

mythologie, n.f. mythology.

N

nabot, n.m. dwarf.

nacre, n.f. mother-of-pearl.

nacré, adj. pearly.

nage, n.f. act of swimming.

nageoire, n.f. fin.

nager, vb. swim.

nageur, n.m. swimmer.

naguère, adv. a short time ago.

naïf (nä ēf) m., naïve f. adj. naïve.

nain, adj. and n.m. dwarf.

naissance, n.f. birth.

naissant, adj. beginning, newborn.

naître, vb. be born.

naïveté (nä ēv-), n.f. simplicity.

nantir, vb. give as security; furnish.

nantissement, n.m. pledge, guarantee.

naphte, n.m. naphtha.

nappe, n.f. tablecloth.

narcisse, n.m. daffodil.

narcotique, n.m. narcotic.

narguer, vb. defy, flout.

narine, n.f. nostril.

narrateur, n.m. narrator, storyteller.

narration, n.f. narrative, recital.

narrer, vb. narrate, relate.

nasal, adj. nasal.

naseau, n.m. nostril.

nasiller, vb. talk with a nasal voice.

nasse, n.f. fish trap.

natal, adj. native.

natalité, n.f. rate of birth.

natation, n.f. swimming.

natif, n.m. and adj. native.

nation, n.f. nation.

national, adj. national.

nationalisation, n.f. nationalization.

nationaliser, vb. nationalize.

nationalisme, n.m. nationalism.

nationalité, n.f. nationality.

nativité, n.f. nativity.

naturaliser, vb. naturalize; (of animals) stuff.

naturalisme, n.m. naturalism, naturalness.

naturaliste, n.m. naturalist.

nature, n.f. nature.

naturel, 1. n.m. nature. 2. adj. natural.

naufrage, n.m. shipwreck.

naufragé, adj. shipwrecked.

nauséabond, adj. nauseous, offensive.

nausée, n.f. nausea.

nautique, adj. nautical.

naval, adj. naval.

navet, n.m. turnip.

navette spatiale, n.f. space shuttle.

navigable, adj. navigable.

navigateur, n.m. navigator, seaman.

navigation, n.f. seafaring, navigation.

naviguer, vb. sail, navigate.

navire, n.m. ship.

navrant, adj. distressing, causing grief.

navrer, vb. wound, grieve.

né, adj. born.

néanmoins, adv. yet, nevertheless, however.

néant, n.m. nothing(ness).

nébuleux, adj. cloudy; worried.

nécessaire, adj. requisite, necessary.

nécessité, n.f. necessity. n. préalable, prerequisite.

nécessiter, vb. make necessary or imperative.

nécessiteux, adj. needy.

nécrologe, n.m. obituary.

nef, n.f. nave.

néfaste, adj. ill-omened, unlucky.

négatif, adj. negative.

négation, n.f. negation; negative word.

négative, n.f. negative argument or opinion.

négligé, 1. adj. neglected, sloppy. 2. n.m. state of undress.

négligeable, adj. negligible.

négligence, n.f. neglect.

négligent, adj. negligent.

négliger, vb. overlook, neglect.

négoce, n.m. commerce, trade.

négociable, adj. negotiable.

négociant, n.m. merchant.

négociation, n.f. negotiation.

négocier, vb. negotiate.

nègre, adj. and n.m. Black.

négresse, n.f. Black.

neige, n.f. snow.

neiger, vb. snow.

neigeux, adj. snowy.

néon, n.m. neon.

néophyte, n.m. neophyte, convert.

néphrite, n.f. nephritis.

nerf (nèr), n.m. nerve.

nerveux, adj. nervous.

nervosité, n.f. nervousness.

net (-t) m., nette f. adj. net, clear, clean, neat.

netteté, n.f. clearness, neatness.

nettoyer, vb. clean, cleanse, scour.

nettoyeur, n.m. one who or that which cleans.

neuf, adj. and n.m. nine.

neuf m., neuve f. adj. brand-new.

neutraliser, vb. counteract.

neutralité, n.f. neutrality.

neutre, adj. and n.m. neutral.

neutron, n.m. neutron.

neuvième, adj. and n.m. ninth.

neveu, n.m. nephew.

névralgie, n.f. neuralgia.

névrite, n.f. neuritis.

névrose, n.f. neurosis.

névrosé, adj. and n.m. neurotic.

nez, n.m. nose.

ni, conj. nor. ni . . . ni . . ., neither . . . nor . . . .

niais, adj. foolish.

niaiserie, n.f. silliness, trifle.

niche, n.f. alcove.

nichée, n.f. brood.

nicher, vb. se n., nestle.

nickel, n.m. nickel.

nid, n.m. nest.

nièce, n.f. niece.

nielle, n.f. wheat blight.

nier, vb. deny.

nigaud, n.m. fool, simpleton.

nihilisme, n.m. nihilism.

nimbe, n.m. halo.

n'importe, interj. never mind.

nippes, n.f.pl. old clothes.

nitrate, n.m. nitrate.

niveau, n.m. level. au n. de, level with.

niveler, vb. make level; survey.

nivellement, n.m. leveling, surveying.

noble, 1. n.m. nobleman, peer. 2. adj. noble.

noblesse, n.f. nobility.

noce, n.f. wedding. faire la n., revel.

noceur, n.m. gay blade.

nocif, adj. harmful.

noctambule, n.m. sleep-walker, prowler.

nocturne, adj. nocturnal.

Noël (nô ěl), n.m. Christmas; carol.

nœud (nœ), n.m. knot.

noir, adj. and n.m. black.

noircir, vb. blacken.

noisetier, n.m. hazel (tree).

noisette, 1. n.f. hazelnut. 2. adj. light reddish brown.

noix, n.f. nut, walnut.

nolis, n.m. freight.

nom, n.m. name; noun.

nomade, adj. wandering, roaming.

nombre, n.m. number.

nombrer, vb. number.

nombreux, adj. numerous, manifold.

nombril, n.m. navel.

nominal, adj. nominal.

nominatif, adj. and n.m. nominative.

nomination, n.f. nomination, appointment.

nommément, adv. particularly, namely.

nommer, vb. name, nominate, appoint.

non, adv. no. non plus, neither.

non-aligné, adj., non-aligned.

nonchalamment, adv. carelessly, nonchalantly.

nonchalant, adj. nonchalant.

non-combattant, adj. and n.m. non-combatant.

nonne, n.f. nun.

nonobstant, prep. in spite of, notwithstanding.

nonpareil, adj. unequaled.

non-sens, n.m. nonsense.

nord, n.m. north.

normal, adj. normal.

normand, adj. Norman; equivocal.

norme, n.f. norm.

Norvège, n.f. Norway.

Norvégien, n.m. Norwegian (person).

norvégien, 1. n.m. Norwegian (language). 2. adj. Norwegian.

nostalgie, n.f. nostalgia.

notabilité, n.f. notability.

notable, 1. n.m. notable. 2. remarkable, notable.

notaire, n.m. lawyer, notary.

notamment, adv. particularly.

notation, n.f. notation.

note, n.f. note, bill.

noter, vb. note.

notice, n.f. notice, review.

notification, n.f. notification.

notifier, vb. notify.

notion, n.f. notion.

notoire, adj. notorious.

notoriété, n.f. notoriety.

notre sg., nos pl. adj. our.

nôtre, pron. le n., ours.

nouer, vb. tie.

noueux, adj. knotty.

nouilles, n.f.pl. noodles.

nourrice, n.f. (wet-)nurse.

nourricier, adj. nourishing; of nursing.

nourrir, vb. feed, nourish, foster.

nourriture, n.f. food, nourishment.

nous, pron. we, us, ourselves.

nouveau m., nouvelle f. adj. new, fresh. de n., anew.

nouveauté, n.f. novelty.

nouvel an, n.m. new year.

nouvelle, n.f. news.

nouvellement, adv. recently, newly.

novembre, n.m. November.

novice, n.m.f. novice.

noviciat, n.m. novitiate.

noyade, n.f. drowning.

noyau, n.m. kernel, nucleus.

noyer, vb. drown.

noyer, n.m. walnut (tree).

nu, adj. naked, bare.

nuage, n.m. cloud; gloom.

nuageux, adj. cloudy.

nuance, n.m. shade, degree.

nucléaire, adj. nuclear.

nudité, n.f. bareness.

nuire à, vb. injure, harm.

nuisible, adj. injurious, hurtful.

nuit, n.f. night.

nul, adj. no, none; void. nulle part, nowhere.

nullement, adv. not at all.

nullité, n.f. nonentity.

numéral, adj. and n.m. numeral.

numérique, adj. numerical.

numéro, n.m. number.

nu-pieds, adv. barefoot.

nuptial, adj. bridal.

nuque, n.f. nape.

nutritif, adj. nutritious.

nutrition, n.f. nutrition.

nylon, n.m. nylon.

nymphe, n.f. nymph.

O

oasis (-s), n.f. oasis.
obéir à, vb. obey.
obéissance, n.f. obedience.
obéissant, adj. obedient.
obélisque, n.m. obelisk.
obérer, vb. burden with debt.
obèse, adj. obese.
obésité, n.f. obesity.
objecter, vb. object.
objectif, adj. and n.m. objective.
objection, n.f. objection.
objet, n.m. object.
obligation, n.f. obligation.
obligatoire, adj. compulsory, mandatory, binding.
obligeance, n.f. obligingness.
obliger, vb. oblige, accommodate.
oblique, adj. slanting; devious.
oblitération, n.f. obliteration.
oblitérer, vb. obliterate.
oblong, adj. oblong.
obscène, adj. filthy, obscene.
obscénité, n.f. obscenity.
obscur, adj. obscure, dark, dim.
obscurcir, vb. darken, obscure.
obscurcissement, n.m. darkening, state of being obscure.
obscurément, adv. obscurely.
obscurité, n.f. darkness, dimness, obscurity.
obséder, vb. harass, haunt.
obsèques, n.f.pl. funeral.
obséquieusement, adv. obsequiously.
obséquieux, adj. obsequious.
observance, n.f. observance.
observateur, n.m. observer.
observation, n.f. observation, remark.
observer, vb. observe, watch.
obsession, n.f. obsession.
obstacle, n.m. obstacle, bar.
obstétrical, adj. obstetrical.
obstination, n.f. stubbornness.
obstiné, adj. obstinate, stubborn.
obstiner, vb. s'o., persist.
obstruction, n.f. obstruction.
obstruer, vb. obstruct, stop up.
obtempérer, vb. obey.
obtenir, vb. obtain, get.
obtention, n.f. obtaining.
obtus, adj. obtuse, dull, stupid.
obus (-s), n.m. shell.
obusier, n.m. howitzer.
occasion, n.f. opportunity, chance; bargain.
occasionnel, adj. occasional.
occasionner, vb. cause, bring about.
occident, n.m. west.
occidental, adj. western.
occulte, adj. occult.
occupant, n.m. occupant, tenant.
occupation, n.f. pursuit, occupation.
occupé, adj. busy.

occuper, vb. occupy, busy. s'o. de, attend to.
occurrence, n.f. occurrence.
océan, n.m. ocean.
océanique, adj. oceanic.
ocre, n.f. ochre.
octave, n.f. octave.
octobre, n.m. October.
octroyer, vb. grant.
oculaire, adj. ocular.
oculiste, n.m. oculist.
ode, n.f. ode.
odeur, n.f. odor, scent, perfume.
odieux, adj. hateful, obnoxious, odious.
odorant, adj. having a fragrant odor.
odorat, n.m. (sense of) smell.
œil, n.m., pl. yeux, eye. coup d'o., glance.
œillade, n.f. wink, quick look.
œillère, n.f. eyetooth.
œillet, n.m. carnation.
œuf, n.m. egg.
œuvre, n.f. work.
offensant, adj. offensive.
offense, n.f. offense.
offenser, vb. offend.
offenseur, n.m offender.
offensif, adj. offensive.
offensive, n.f. offensive.
offensivement, adv. offensively.
office, n.m. office, pantry; (church) service.
officiant, n.m. one who officiates.
officiel, adj. official.
officier, 1. n.m. officer; mate. 2. vb. officiate.
officieux, adj. officious.
offrande, n.f. offering.
offre, n.f. offer.
offrir, vb. offer, present.
offusquer, vb. obscure, shadow, irritate.
ogre, n.m. ogre.
oie, n.f. goose.
oignon (ô nyôN), n.m. onion, bulb.
oindre, vb. anoint.
oiseau, n.m. bird.
oiselet, n.m. small bird.
oiseux, adj. idle, empty, useless.
oisif, adj. idle.
oisillon, n.m. young bird.
oisiveté, n.f. idleness.
oléagineux, adj. oily.
olivâtre, adj. olive-colored.
olive, n.f. olive.
olivier, n.m. olive tree.
olympique, adj. Olympic.
ombilical, adj. umbilical.
ombrage, n.m. shade.
ombragé, adj. shady.
ombrager, vb. shade.
ombrageux, adj. suspicious, doubtful.
ombre, n.f. shade, shadow.
ombreux, adj. shady.
omelette, n.f. omelet.
omettre, vb. omit.
omission, n.f. omission.

omnibus (-s), n.m. bus.
omnipotent, adj. omnipotent.
omoplate, n.f. shoulder blade.
on, pron. one (indef. subj.).
once, n.f. ounce.
oncle, n.m. uncle.
onction, n.f. unction.
onctueux, adj. unctuous.
onde, n.f. wave.
ondé, adj. wavy.
ondoyer, vb. wave.
ondulation, n.f. wave. o. permanente, permanent wave.
onduler, vb. wave.
onéreux, adj. burdensome.
ongle, n.m. (finger)nail.
onglée, n.f. numb feeling.
onguent, n.m. salve, ointment.
onomatopée, n.f. onomatopœia.
onze, adj. and n.m. eleven.
onzième, adj. and n.m.f. eleventh.
opacité, n.f. opacity.
opale, n.f. opal.
opaque, adj. opaque.
opéra, n.m. opera.
opérateur, n.m. operator.
opération, n.f. operation, transaction.
opératoire, adj. operative.
opéré, n. patient undergoing surgery.
opérer, vb. operate.
opérette, n.f. operetta.
opiner, vb. hold or express an opinion.
opiniâtre, adj. stubborn.
opiniâtreté, n.f. stubbornness.
opinion, n.f. opinion.
opium, n.m. opium.
opportun, adj. timely.
opportunité, n.f. timeliness.
opposé, adj. opposite, averse.
opposer, vb. oppose. s'o. à, oppose, resist.
opposition, n.f. opposition.
oppresser, vb. weigh heavily on.
oppresseur, n.m. oppressor.
oppressif, adj. oppressive.
oppression, n.f. oppression.
opprimer, vb. oppress.
opprobre, n.m. disgrace, infamy.
opter, vb. select, decide.
opticien, n.m. optician.
optimisme, n.m. optimism.
optimiste, 1. adj. optimistic. 2. n.m.f. optimist.
option, n.f. option.
optique, adj. optic.
opulence, n.f. opulence, riches.
opuscule, n.m. small work.
or, 1. n.m. gold. 2. conj. now.
oracle, n.m. oracle.
orage, n.m. storm.
orageusement, adv. turbulently, stormily.
orageux, adj. stormy.
oraison, n.f. prayer, oration.
oral, adj. oral.
orange, n.f. orange.
oranger, n.m. orange tree.

orateur, n.m. speaker, orator.

oratoire, adj. oratorical. **art o.,** oratory.

orbe, n.m. orb, sphere.

orbite, n.m. orbit, socket (as of eye).

orchestre (-k-), n.m. orchestra, band.

orchestrer (-k-), vb. orchestrate.

orchidée, n.f. orchid.

ordinaire, adj. and n.m. ordinary.

ordinal, adj. and n.m. ordinal.

ordinateur, n.m. computer.

ordonnance, n.f. prescription, ordinance, decree.

ordonné, adj. orderly, tidy.

ordonner, vb. order, ordain, bid, command.

ordre, n.m. order. **de premier o.,** first-rate.

ordure, n.f. filth, garbage, refuse.

ordurier, adj. foul.

oreille, n.f. ear.

oreiller, n.m. pillow.

oreillons, n.m.pl. mumps.

orfèvrerie, n.f. gold or silver jewelry.

organdi, n.m. organdy.

organe, n.m. organ.

organique, adj. organic.

organisateur, 1. n.m. organizer. 2. adj. organizing.

organisation, n.f. organization, arrangement.

organiser, vb. organize.

organisme, n.m. organism.

organiste, n.m.f. organist.

orge, n.f. barley.

orgelet, n.m. sty (of eye).

orgie, n.f. orgy.

orgue, n.m. organ.

orgueil, n.m. pride.

orgueilleux,   adj.   proud, haughty.

Orient, n.m. Orient, East.

Oriental, n.m. Oriental.

oriental, adj. Oriental, eastern.

orienter, vb. orient.

orifice, n.m. orifice, hole.

originaire, adj. original, native.

originairement, adv. originally.

original, 1. n.m. queer person. 2. adj. original.

originalement, adv. originally; unusually.

originalité, n.f. originality.

origine, n.f. origin, source.

originel, adj. original.

oripeau, n.m. tinsel, showy clothes.

orme, n.m. elm.

orné, adj. ornate.

ornement,   n.m.   ornament, adornment, trimming.

ornemental, adj. ornamental.

ornementation, n.f. ornamentation.

orner, vb. adorn, trim.

ornière, n.f. rut, track.

ornithologie, n.f. ornithology.

orphelin, n.m. orphan.

orphelinat, n.m. orphanage.

orphéon, n.m. choral group.

orteil, n.m. toe.

orthodoxe, adj. orthodox.

orthodoxie, n.f. orthodoxy.

orthographe, n.f. spelling, orthography.

orthographier, vb. spell.

ortie, n.f. nettle.

os, n.m. bone.

oscillant, adj. oscillating.

oscillation, n.f. sway.

osciller, vb. fluctuate, oscillate.

osé, adj. attempted, bold.

oser, vb. dare.

osier, n.m. willow.

ossature, n.f. bony structure, skeleton.

ossements, n.m.pl. human remains.

osseux, adj. bony.

ossifier, vb. ossify.

ostensible, adj. ostensible.

ostentation, n.f. ostentation.

ostraciser, vb. ostracize.

otage, n.m. hostage.

ôter, vb. take off, take away.

ou, conj. or. **ou . . . ou . . .,** either . . . or . . . .

où, adv. where.

ouailles, n.f.pl. religious congregation.

ouater (wä-), vb. pad.

oubli,   n.m.   forgetfulness, oblivion.

oublier, vb. forget.

oublieux, adj. forgetful.

ouest (wĕst), n.m. west.

oui (wē), adv. yes.

ouï-dire, n.m. gossip, hearsay.

ouïe, n.f. gill.

ouïr, vb. hear.

ouragan, n.m. hurricane.

ourler, vb. hem.

ourlet, n.m. hem.

ours (-s), n.m. bear. **o. blanc,** polar bear.

ourson, n.m. bear cub.

outil, n.m. tool, implement.

outillage, n.m. quantity of tools, plant.

outiller, vb. supply with tools.

outrage, n.m. outrage.

outrageant, adj. outrageous.

outrager, vb. outrage, affront.

outrance, n.f. extreme degree. **à o.** to the very end.

outre, adv. and prep. beyond. **en o.,** besides, furthermore.

outré, adj. excessive, extreme.

outrecuidant, adj. excessively bold and forward.

outre-mer, adv. across the seas.

outrer, vb. overdo, irritate.

ouvert, adj. open.

ouverture, n.f. opening, gap; overture.

ouvrable, adj. work, workable.

ouvrage, n.m. work.

ouvrer, vb. work.

ouvreuse, n.f. usher or usherette.

ouvrier, n.m. workman; (pl.) labor.

ouvrir, vb. open.

ouvroir, n.m. work room or shop.

ovaire, n.m. ovary.

ovale, adj. and n.m. oval.

ovation, n.f. ovation.

oxygène, n.m. oxygen.

P

pacage, n.m. land used for pasture.

pacificateur, 1. adj. pacifying. 2. n.m. peacemaker.

pacification, n.f. peace-making.

pacifier, vb. pacify, appease, soothe.

pacifique, adj. pacific, peaceful, peaceable.

pacifisme, n.m. pacifism.

pacotille, n.f. small wares.

pacte, n.m. covenant, pact.

pactiser, vb. make a pact, compromise.

pagaie, n.f. paddle.

pagale, n.f. disorder, rush.

paganisme, n.m. paganism.

pagayer, vb. paddle.

pagayeur, n.m. paddle.

page, **1.** n.m. page (boy). **2.** n.f. page (in book).

pages centrales, n.f.pl. centerfold.

pagination, n.f. pagination.

paginer, vb. number pages.

pagode, n.f. pagoda.

paiement, payement, n.m. payment.

païen, adj. and n.m. pagan, heathen.

paillard, adj. lewd, indecent.

paillasse,   n.f.   mattress of straw, ticking.

paillasson, n.m. (door-)mat.

paille, n.f. straw; defect (in gems).

paillette, n.f. spangle; defect.

pain, n.m. bread, loaf. **petit p.,** roll.

pair, **1.** n.m. peer. **2.** adj. even, equal.

paire, n.f. pair.

pairesse, n.f. peeress.

pairie, n.f. peerage.

paisible, adj. peaceful.

paître, vb. graze.

paix, n.f. peace.

palabre, n.f. palaver.

palais, n.m. palace; palate.

palan, n.m. gear for hoisting.

palatal, adj. and n.f. palatal.

pale, n.f. blade, stake.

pâle, adj. pale.

palefrenier, n.m. groom.

palet, n.m. quoit.

paletot, n.m. overcoat.

pâleur, n.f. paleness.

palier, n.m. stair landing.

pâlir, vb. grow pale or dim.

palissade, n.f. paling, fence.

pâlissant, adj. becoming pale.

palme, n.f. palm.

palmier, n.m. palm (tree).

palpable, adj. palpable.

palper, vb. touch, feel.

palpitant, adj. fluttering, palpitating.

palpiter, vb. flutter, beat, palpitate.

paludéen, adj. marshy.

pâmer, vb. se p., faint.

pamphlet, n.m. pamphlet, satire.

pamphlétaire, n.m. pamphleteer.

pamplemousse, n.m. grapefruit.

pan, n.m. side, piece, flap.

panacée, n.f. panacea.

panache, n.m. plume.

panais, n.m. parsnip.

pandit, n.m. pundit.

pané, adj. dotted with bread crumbs.

panier, n.m. basket.

panique, n.f. and adj. panic.

panne, n.f. fat, lard; accident.

panneau, n.m. panel.

panse, n.f. paunch, cud.

pansement, n.m. dressing.

panser, vb. groom; dress.

pantalon, n.m. trousers.

panteler, vb. pant, gasp.

panthère, n.f. panther.

pantomime, n.f. pantomime.

pantoufle, n.f. slipper.

pantoufler, vb. act silly.

paon, (pän), n.m. peacock.

papal, adj. papal.

papauté, n.f. papacy.

pape, n.m. pope.

paperasse, n.f. waste paper; official documents.

paperassier, adj. scribbling, petty.

papeterie, n.f. stationery.

papetier, n.m. stationer.

papier, n.m. paper.

papier à notes, n.m. notepaper.

papier à tapisser, n.m. wallpaper.

papier peint, n.m. wallpaper.

papillon, n.m. butterfly.

papillonner, vb. flutter, trifle.

papoter, vb. prate, prattle.

pâque, n.f. Passover.

paquebot, n.m. small liner, packet.

pâquerette, n.f. daisy.

Pâques, n.m. Easter.

paquet, n.m. package, parcel, bundle; deck (cards).

par, prep. by; through.

parabole, n.f. parabola; parable.

parachute, n.m. parachute.

parade, n.f. parade, procession.

parader, vb. parade, show off.

paradis, n.m. paradise.

paradoxal, adj. paradoxical.

paradoxe, n.m. paradox.

paraffine, n.f. paraffin.

parage, n.m. ancestry, descent; locality.

paragraphe, n.m. paragraph.

paraître, vb. appear, seem.

parallèle, adj. and n.m.f. parallel.

paralyser, vb. paralyze.

paralysie, n.f. paralysis.

paralytique, adj. and n.m.f. paralytic.

paramètre, n.m. parameter.

parangon, n.m. model, paragon.

paraphraser, vb. paraphrase.

paraphrase, n.m. umbrella.

parasite, n.m. parasite.

paratonnerre, n.m. lightning rod.

paravent, n.m. screen.

parc (-k), n.m. park.

parcelle, n.f. part, instalment.

parce que, conj. because.

parchemin, n.m. parchment.

parcimonie, n.f. parsimony.

parcourir, vb. run through.

parcours, n.m. course, journey.

pardessus, n.m. overcoat.

par-dessus, adv. and prep. above, over.

pardon, 1. n.m. pardon, forgiveness. **2.** interj. sorry!

pardonner (à), vb. forgive, pardon.

pardonneur, n.m. pardoner.

pare-boue, n.m. mudguard.

pare-chocs, n.m. bumper.

pareil, adj. like.

parent, n.m. relative; (pl.) parents.

parenté, n.f. relationship.

parenthèse, n.f. parenthesis.

parer, vb. attire, deck out; parry.

paresse, n.f. sloth.

paresser, vb. laze, waste time.

paresseux, adj. lazy.

parfaire, vb. complete, finish up.

parfait, adj. perfect.

parfois, adv. sometimes.

parfum, n.m. perfume.

parfumé, adj. fragrant.

parfumer, vb. perfume.

parfumerie, n.f. perfumery.

pari, n.m. bet.

parier, vb. bet.

parieur, n.m. one who bets.

Parisien, n.m. Parisian.

parisien, adj. Parisian.

parité, n.f. equality, parity.

parjure, n.m. perjury.

parjurer, vb. se p., commit perjury.

parlant, adj. speaking, chatty.

parlement, n.m. parliament.

parlementaire, adj. parliamentary.

parlementer, vb. parley.

parler, vb. talk, speak.

parleur, n.m. one who speaks or talks.

parloir, n.m. parlor.

parmi, prep. among.

parodie, n.f. parody.

parodier, vb. parody, imitate.

paroi, n.f. wall lining.

paroisse, n.f. parish.

paroissial, adj. parochial.

parole, n.f. speech, word.

prendre la p., take the floor.

paroxysme, n.m. fit of violence.

parquer, vb. park, enclose.

parquet, n.m. floor.

parqueterie, n.f. parquetry.

parrain, n.m. godfather.

parsemer, vb. spread, strew.

part, n.f. share, part. **de la p. de,** on behalf of. **quelque p.,** somewhere. **nulle p.,** nowhere. **faire p. à,** share; inform.

partage, n.m. partition, sharing, share.

partager, vb. share, divide.

partance, n.f. going, sailing.

partant, n.m. one who leaves.

partenaire, n.m.f. partner.

parti, n.m. party.

partial, adj. partial.

partialité, n.f. bias, partiality.

participant, adj. and n.m. participant.

participation, n.f. participation, share.

participe, n.m. participle.

participer à, vb. partake of, take part in.

particularité, n.f. peculiarity.

particule, n.f. particle.

particulier, adj. particular, private, peculiar, special.

partie, n.f. part, party.

partiel, adj. partial.

partir, vb. depart, leave, go (come) away, sail.

partisan, n.m. partisan, follower.

partitif, adj. partitive.

partition, n.f. score.

partout, adv. everywhere, throughout. **p. où,** wherever.

parure, n.f. ornament.

parvenir, vb. reach.

parvenu, n.m. upstart.

pas, 1. n.m. step, pace. **faux p.,** slip. **2.** adv. not. **p. du tout,** not at all.

passable, adj. fair.

passage, n.m. aisle, passage, alley.

passager, 1. n.m. passenger. **2.** adj. passing, fugitive.

passant, n.m. passer-by.

passavant, n.m. permit.

passe, n.f. passing, permit.

passé, adj. and n.m. past.

passe-partout, n.m. skeleton key, passport.

passeport, n.m. passport.

passer, vb. pass; go by; spend; strain. **se p. de,** go without.

passereau, n.m. sparrow.

passerelle, n.f. bridge.

passe-temps, n.m. pastime.

passible, adj. capable of feeling.

passif, adj. and n.m. passive.

passion, n.f. passion.

passionné, adj. passionate.

passionnel, adj. concerning or due to passion.

passionner, vb. interest, excite.

se p., be eager or excited over.

passoire, *n.f.* device for straining.

pastel, *n.m.* crayon.

pastèque, *n.f.* watermelon.

pasteur, *n.m.* pastor.

pasteuriser, *vb.* pasteurize.

pastille, *n.f.* lozenge, cough drop.

pastoral, *adj.* pastoral.

pataud, *adj.* awkward.

patauger, *vb.* flounder.

pâte, *n.f.* paste, dough, batter.

pâté, *n.m.* block; pie.

patenôtre, *n.f.* (Lord's) prayer.

patent, *adj.* patent, evident.

patente, *n.f.* license.

patenter, *vb.* license.

paterne, *adj.* paternal.

paternel, *adj.* paternal.

paternité, *n.f.* fatherhood.

pâteux, *adj.* pasty, thick, muddy.

pathétique, *adj.* pathetic.

pathologie, *n.f.* pathology.

patience, *n.f.* patience.

patient, *adj. and n.m.* patient.

patin, *n.m.* skate.

patiner, *vb.* skate.

patineur, *n.m.* skater.

pâtir, *vb.* suffer.

pâtisserie, *n.f.* pastry.

patois, *n.m.* dialect, gibberish.

pâtre, *n.m.* shepherd.

patriarche, *n.m.* patriarch.

patricien, *adj. and n.m.* patrician.

patrie, *n.f.* native country, homeland.

patrimoine, *n.m.* patrimony.

patriote, *n.m.f.* patriot.

patriotique, *adj.* patriotic.

patriotisme, *n.m.* patriotism.

patron, *n.m.* employer; boss; model, pattern; patron.

patronat, *n.m.* management, employers.

patronner, *vb.* patronize, provide for.

patrouille, *n.f.* patrol

patrouiller, *vb.* patrol

patte, *n.f.* paw, leg, flap.

pâturage, *n.m.* pasture.

pâture, *n.f.* fodder, pasture.

paume, *n.f.* palm.

paupière, *n.f.* eyelid.

pause, *n.f.* pause.

pauvre, *adj.* poor.

pauvreté, *n.f.* poverty.

pavaner, *vb.* **se p.,** swagger, strut.

pavé, *n.m.* pavement.

paver, *vb.* pave.

pavillon, *n.m.* pavilion.

pavot, *n.m.* poppy.

paye, *n.f.* payment, salary.

payement, *n.m.* payment.

payer, *vb.* pay, settle.

payeur, *n.m.* payer.

pays, *n.m.* country.

paysage, *n.m.* landscape, scenery.

paysager, *adj.* of the country, rural.

paysan, *n.m.* peasant.

Pays-Bas, les, *n.m.pl.* Holland; the Netherlands.

péage, *n.m.* toll.

peau, *n.f.* skin, hide.

pêche, *n.f.* peach; fishing.

péché, *n.m.* sin.

pécher, *vb.* sin.

pêcher, 1. *vb.* fish. **2.** *n.m.* peach tree.

pêcherie, *n.f.* fishing place.

pêcheur *m.,* **pêcheresse** *f.* **1.** *n.* sinner. **2.** *adj.* sinful.

pêcheur, *n.m.* fisherman.

pécule, *n.f.* savings.

pécuniare, *adj.* pecuniary.

pédagogie, *n.f.* pedagogy.

pédale, *n.f.* pedal.

pédant, *adj. and n.m.f.* pedant, pedantic.

pédanterie, *n.f.* pedantry.

pédé(raste), *n.m.* homosexual.

pédestre, *adj.* pedestrian.

pédiatre, *n.m.* pediatrician.

pédicure, *n.m.* chiropodist.

peigne, *n.m.* comb.

peigner, *vb.* comb.

peignoir, *n.m.* dressing-gown.

peindre, *vb.* paint, portray, depict.

peine, *n.f.* pain, penalty. **à p.,** hardly, barely; **faire de la p. à,** pain, *vb.;* **valoir la p. de,** be worth while to; **se donner la p.,** take the trouble.

peiner, *vb.* labor; grieve.

peintre, *n.m.* painter.

peinture, *n.f.* paint, painting.

pelage, *n.m.* coat.

pelé, *adj.* bald, uncovered.

pêle-mêle, *adv.* pell-mell.

peler, *vb.* peel, pare.

pèlerin, *n.m.* pilgrim.

pèlerinage, *n.m.* pilgrimage.

pèlerine, *n.f.* cape.

pélican, *n.m.* pelican.

pelle, *n.f.* shovel.

pelletier, *n.m.* furrier.

pellicule, *n.f.* film.

pelote, *n.f.* ball, pellet.

peloton, *n.m.* ball; group of soldiers.

pelure, *n.f.* peel.

pénal, *adj.* penal.

pénalité, *n.f.* penalty.

penaud, *adj.* awkwardly bashful or embarrassed.

penchant, *n.m.* bent, liking, tendency.

pencher, *vb.* tilt, lean, droop. **se p.,** bend.

pendaison, *n.f.* hanging (execution).

pendant, *prep.* during, pending. **p. que,** as, while.

pendiller, *vb.* dangle.

pendre, *vb.* hang.

pendule, *n.m.* clock; pendulum.

pénétrable, *adj.* penetrable.

pénétrant, *adj.* keen.

pénétration, *n.f.* penetration.

pénétrer, *vb.* penetrate, pervade.

pénible, *adj.* painful.

péninsule, *n.f.* peninsula.

pénitence, *n.f.* penance.

pénitencier, *n.m.* penitentiary.

pénitent, *adj. and n.m.* penitent.

penne, *n.f.* feather.

pénombre, *n.f.* gloom, shadow.

pensée, *n.f.* thought; pansy.

penser (à), *vb.* think (of).

penseur, *n.m.* thinker.

pensif, *adj.* thoughtful, pensive.

pension, *n.f.* board, pension.

pensionnaire, *n.m.f.* boarder.

pensionnat, *n.m.* boarding school.

pente, *n.f.* slope, slant.

pénurie, *n.f.* penury, scarcity.

pépier, *vb.* chirp.

pépin, *n.m.* pip, kernel.

pépinière, *n.f.* nursery.

pépite, *n.f.* nugget.

perçant, *adj.* sharp.

perce, *n.f.* boring tool.

perce-neige, *n.f.* snowdrop.

percepteur, *n.m.* tax collector.

perception, *n.f.* perception, collecting.

percer, *vb.* pierce, bore.

percevoir, *vb.* collect, amass, perceive.

perche, *n.f.* pole, perch.

percher, *vb.* **se p.,** perch.

perchoir, *n.m.* perch.

perclus, *adj.* lame, crippled.

percussion, *n.f.* percussion.

percuter, *vb.* hit, strike.

perdition, *n.f.* perdition.

perdre, *vb.* lose; waste.

perdrix, *n.f.* partridge.

père, *n.m.* father.

péremptoire, *adj.* peremptory.

perfection, *n.f.* perfection.

perfectionnement, *n.m.* improvement, finishing.

perfectionner, *vb.* perfect, finish.

perfide, *adj.* treacherous.

perfidie, *n.f.* treachery.

perforation, *n.f.* perforation.

perforer, *vb.* perforate, drill.

péricliter, *vb.* be in danger, shake.

péril (-l), *n.m.* peril, danger.

périlleux, *adj.* perilous, dangerous.

périmètre, *n.m.* perimeter.

période, *n.f.* period, term, stage.

périodique, *adj.* periodic.

péripétie, *n.f.* shift of luck.

périr, *vb.* perish.

périscope, *n.m.* periscope.

périssable, *adj.* perishable.

perle, *n.f.* pearl, bead.

perlé, *adj.* pearly, perfect.

permanence, *n.f.* permanence.

permanent, *adj.* permanent.

perméable, *adj.* permeable.

permettre, *vb.* permit, allow.

permis, *n.m.* permit, license.

permission, *n.f.* permission, leave (of absence), furlough.

permissionnaire, *n.m.* one having a permit; one on leave.

permuter, *vb.* change, exchange.

pernicieux, *adj.* pernicious.

pérorer, *vb.* harangue, argue.

perpétrer, *vb.* commit.

perpétuel, *adj.* perpetual.

perpétuer, *vb.* perpetuate.

perplexe, *adj.* perplexed, undecided.

perplexité, *n.f.* perplexity.

perquisition, *n.f.* exploration, search.

perron, *n.m.* flight of steps.

perroquet, *n.m.* parrot.

perruque, *n.f.* wig.

perse, *adj.* Persian.

persécuter, *vb.* persecute.

persécution, *n.f.* persecution.

persévérance, *n.f.* perseverance.

persévérant, *adj.* persevering, resolute.

persévérer, *vb.* persevere.

persienne, *n.f.* blind, shutter.

persifler, *vb.* banter, ridicule.

persil, *n.m.* parsley.

persistance, *n.f.* persistence.

persistant, *adj.* persistent.

persister, *vb.* persist.

personnage, *n.m.* personage; character.

personnalité, *n.f.* personality.

personne, 1. *n.f.* person. **2.** *pron.* nobody.

personnel, 1. *n.m.* personnel, staff. **2.** *adj.* personal.

personnifier, *vb.* personify.

perspective, *n.f.* perspective, prospect.

perspicace, *adj.* discerning.

perspicacité, *n.f.* insight.

persuader, *vb.* persuade, convince, induce.

persuasif, *adj.* persuasive.

perte, *n.f.* loss, waste; (*pl.*) casualties.

pertinence, *n.f.* pertinence.

pertinent, *adj.* relevant, pertinent.

perturbateur, *n.m.* agitator, disturber.

pervers, *adj.* perverse, contrary.

pervertir, *vb.* pervert.

pesant, *adj.* heavy, ponderous.

pesanteur, *n.f.* weight, dullness.

peser, *vb.* weigh.

pessimisme, *n.m.* pessimism.

pessimiste, *n.m.* pessimist.

peste, *n.f.* pestilence; nuisance.

pestilence, *n.f.* pestilence, plague, nuisance.

pétale, *n.m.* petal.

pétiller, *vb.* twinkle, crackle.

petit, 1. *adj.* little, small, petty. **2.** *n.m.* cub.

petite-fille, *n.f.* granddaughter.

petitesse, *n.f.* smallness, pettiness.

petit-fils (-fès), *n.m.* grandson.

petit-gris, *n.m.* fur of the squirrel.

pétition, *n.f.* petition.

pétitionner, *vb.* request, ask.

petits-enfants, *n.m.pl.* grandchildren.

pétrifiant, *adj.* petrifying.

pétrifier, *vb.* petrify or (**se p.**) become petrified.

pétrir, *vb.* knead, mold.

pétrole, *n.m.* petroleum, kerosene.

pétulance, *n.f.* petulance.

peu, 1. *n.m.* little; few. **2.** *adv.* not. **p. à p.,** gradually.

peuplade, *n.f.* tribe, clan.

peuple, *n.m.* people.

peupler, *vb.* people.

peuplier, *n.m.* poplar.

peur, *n.f.* fear. **avoir p.,** be afraid. **de p. que . . . ne,** lest.

peureux, *adj.* shy, timid.

peut-être, *adv.* perhaps, maybe.

phallocratie, *n.f.* machismo.

phallocrate, *adj.* macho.

phare, *n.m.* beacon, lighthouse; headlight.

pharmacie, *n.f.* drug store, pharmacy.

pharmacien, *n.m.* druggist.

phase, *n.f.* phase.

phénix, *n.m.* phoenix; superior person.

phénoménal, *adj.* phenomenal.

phénomène, *n.m.* phenomenon; freak.

philanthrope, *n.m.* philanthropist.

philanthropie, *n.f.* philanthropy.

philatélie, *n.f.* stamp-collecting.

philosophe, *n.m.* philosopher.

philosophie, *n.f.* philosophy.

philosophique, *adj.* philosophical.

phobie, *n.f.* phobia.

phonéticien, *n.m.* phonetician.

phonétique, *adj. and n.f.* phonetic, phonetics.

phonographe, *n.m.* phonograph.

phoque, *n.m.* seal.

photocopie, *n.f.* photocopy.

photocopieur, *n.m.* photocopier.

photographe, *n.m.* photographer.

photographie, *n.f.* photograph, photography.

phrase, *n.f.* sentence.

phtisie, *n.f.* consumption.

phtisique, *adj. and n.m.* consumptive.

physicien, *n.m.* physical scientist.

physionomie, *n.f.* looks, expression.

physique, 1. *n.f.* physics. **2.** *adj.* physical.

piailler, *vb.* peep, squeal.

pianiste, *n.m.f.* pianist.

piano, *n.m.* piano.

pic, *n.m.* peak.

picoter, *vb.* prick, peck.

pièce, *n.f.* piece, coin, patch, room. **p. de théâtre,** play.

pied, *n.m.* foot. **aller à p.,** walk. **coup de p.,** kick.

pied-à-terre, *n.m.* temporary quarters.

piédestal, *n.m.* pedestal.

piège, *n.m.* snare, trap.

pierre, *n.f.* stone.

pierreries, *n.f.pl.* jewelry, gems.

pierreux, *adj.* full of stone or grit.

pierrot, *n.m.* clown in pantomime.

piété, *n.f.* piety.

piétiner, *vb.* trample.

piéton, *n.m.* pedestrian.

piètre, *adj.* pitiful, mean, wretched.

pieu, *n.m.* stake, pile.

pieuvre, *n.f.* octopus.

pieux, *adj.* pious.

pigeon, *n.m.* pigeon, dove.

pile, *n.f.* stack; battery.

piler, *vb.* crush, blast.

pilier, *n.m.* pillar, column.

pillage, *n.m.* plundering.

piller, *vb.* plunder.

pilotage, *n.m.* piloting; driving piles.

pilote, *n.m.* pilot.

piloter, *vb.* pilot, lead.

pilule, *n.f.* pill.

piment, *n.m.* chili.

pimenter, *vb.* flavor, season.

pimpant, *adj.* stylish, smart.

pin, *n.m.* pine.

pinacle, *n.m.* pinnacle.

pince, *n.f.* clip; (*pl.*) pliers.

pinceau, *n.m.* paint-brush.

pince-nez, *n.m.* eyeglasses.

pincer, *vb.* pinch, nip.

pinte, *n.f.* pint.

pioche, *n.f.* pickax.

piocher, *vb.* dig.

piocheur, *n.m.* digger.

pion, *n.m.* pawn, peon.

pioncer, *vb.* nap, sleep.

pionnier, *n.m.* pioneer.

pipe, *n.f.* pipe.

piper, *vb.* catch, decoy, trick.

piquant, *adj.* sharp. **mot p.,** quip.

pique, *n.m.* spade.

pique-nique, *n.m.* picnic.

piquer, *vb.* prick, sting.

piquet, *n.m.* picket, peg, stake.

piqûre, *n.f.* prick, sting, puncture.

pirate, *n.m.* pirate.

pirate de l'air, *n.m.* hijacker.

piraterie, *n.f.* piracy.

pire, *adj.* worse, worst.

pirouette, *n.f.* pirouette, shift.

pis, *adv.* worse, worst.

piscine, *n.f.* pool.

pissenlit, *n.m.* dandelion.

pistache, *n.f.* pistachio.

piste, *n.f.* track.

pistolet, *n.m.* pistol.

piston, *n.m.* piston.

pistonner, *vb.* help, push.

pitance, *n.f.* meager amount, as of food.

piteux, *adj.* pitiful.

pitié, *n.f.* pity, mercy.

pitoyable, *adj.* pitiful, miserable.

pitre, *n.m.* clown.

pittoresque, *adj.* picturesque, colorful.

pivoine, *n.f.* peony.

pivot, *n.m.* pivot.

pivoter, *vb.* turn, pivot, revolve.

pizza, *n.f.* pizza.

placard, *n.m.* closet; poster.

placarder, *vb.* post, display.

place, *n.f.* place, room.

placement, *n.m.* investment, placing.

placer, *vb.* invest, place.

placet, *n.m.* petition, demand.

placide, *adj.* placid.

placidité, *n.f.* placidness.

plafond, *n.m.* ceiling.

plage, *n.f.* beach.

plagiaire, *n.m.* one who plagiarizes.

plagiat, *n.m.* plagiarism.

plagier, *vb.* plagiarize.

plaid, *n.m.* plaid.

plaider, *vb.* plead.

plaideur, *n.m.* pleader.

plaidoirie, *n.f.* lawyer's speech.

plaie, *n.f.* wound, sore.

plaignant, *n.m.* plaintiff.

plaindre, *vb.* pity. **se p.,** complain.

plaine, *n.f.* plain.

plainte, *n.pl.* complaint.

plaintif, *adj.* mournful.

plaire à, *vb.* please. **s'il vous plaît,** if you please.

plaisance, *n.f.* pleasure, ease.

plaisant, *adj.* joking.

plaisanter, *vb.* joke.

plaisanterie, *n.f.* joke.

plaisir, *n.m.* pleasure.

plan, *n.m.* plan; plane; schedule, scheme. **premier p.,** foreground.

planche, *n.f.* board, shelf, plank.

planche à roulettes, *n.f.* skateboard.

plancher, *n.m.* floor.

planer, *vb.* glide; hover.

planétaire, 1. *adj.* planetary. **2.** *n.m.* planetarium.

planète, *n.f.* planet.

planeur, *n.m.* glider (plane).

plantation, *n.f.* plantation.

plante, *n.f.* plant; sole.

planter, *vb.* plant.

planteur, *n.m.* planter.

planton, *n.m.* military orderly.

plantureux, *adj.* fertile, rich.

plaque, *n.f.* plate, slab. **p. de projection,** lantern-slide.

plaquer, *vb.* plate; abandon.

plaquette, *n.f.* booklet, medal.

plastique, *adj.* plastic.

plastronner, *vb.* pose, strut jauntily.

plat, 1. *n.m.* dish, platter. **2.** *adj.* flat. **œuf sur le p.,** fried egg.

platane, *n.m.* plane-tree.

plat-bord, *n.m.* gunwale.

plateau, *n.m.* plateau, tray.

plate-bande, *n.f.* flower bed.

plate-forme, *n.f.* platform.

platine, 1. *n.f.* platen, plate. **2.** *n.m.* platinum.

platitude, *n.f.* flatness.

plâtras, *n.m.* rubbish, rubble.

plâtre, *n.m.* plaster.

plausible, *adj.* plausible.

plébéien, *adj.* ignoble.

plébiscite, *n.m.* plebiscite.

plein, *adj.* full, crowded.

plénier, *adj.* complete, plenary.

plénitude, *n.f.* fullness.

pleurer, *vb.* cry, weep, lament, mourn.

pleurésie, *n.f.* pleurisy.

pleurnicher, *vb.* complain, whine.

pleurs, *n.m.pl.* tears, weeping.

pleutre, *n.m.* cad, coward.

pleuvoir, *vb.* rain.

pli, *n.m.* fold, envelope, pleat, crease.

pliable, *adj.* pliable.

pliant, *n.m.* folding chair.

plier, *vb.* fold, bend.

plissement, *n.m.* fold, folding.

plisser, *vb.* pleat.

plomb, *n.m.* lead.

plomberie, *n.f.* plumbing.

plombier, *n.m.* plumber.

plongeon, *n.m.* plunge.

plonger, *vb.* plunge, dive, dip.

plongeur, *n.m.* diver; dishwasher.

plouf, *interj. and n.m.* splash, plop.

ploutocrate, *n.m.* plutocrat.

ployer, *vb.* incline, bend.

pluie, *n.f.* rain.

pluie radioactive, *n.f.* fallout.

plumage, *n.m.* feathers.

plume, *n.f.* pen, feather.

plumeau, *n.m.* feather duster.

plumer, *vb.* pluck.

plumet, *n.m.* plume.

plumeux, *adj.* feathery.

plumier, *n.m.* pen or pencil case.

plupart, *n.f.* greater part, majority. **pour la p.,** mostly.

pluralité, *n.f.* plurality.

pluriel, *adj. and n.m.* plural.

plus, *adv.* more, most. **ne . . . p.,** no more. **non p.,** neither. **en p.,** extra.

plusieurs, *adj. and pron.* several.

plus-que-parfait, *n.m. (gramm.)* pluperfect.

plutôt, *adv.* rather.

pluvieux, *adj.* rainy, wet.

pneumatique, *abbr.* **pneu,** *n.m.* tire.

pneumonie, *n.f.* pneumonia.

pochade, *n.f.* hasty sketch.

poche, *n.f.* pocket.

pocher, *vb.* poach.

pocheter, *vb.* pocket.

pochette, *n.f.* little pocket, handkerchief.

pochoir, *n.m.* stencil.

poêle, *n.m.* stove.

poème, *n.m.* poem.

poésie, *n.f.* poem, poetry.

poète, *n.f.* poet.

poétique, *adj.* poetic.

poids (pwä), *n.m.* weight.

poignant, *adj.* poignant, keen.

poignard, *n.m.* dagger.

poignarder, *vb.* stab.

poigne, *n.f.* grip, power.

poignée, *n.f.* handful; handle.

poignet, *n.m.* wrist; cuff.

poil (pwäl), *n.m.* hair.

poilu, 1. *adj.* hairy, strong. **2.** *n.m.* French soldier.

poinçon, *n.m.* punch.

poing, *n.m.* fist.

point, *n.m.* point, dot, period, stitch. **p. de vue,** point of view. **p. du jour,** dawn. **ne . . . p.,** none. **être sur le p. de,** be about to. **au p.,** in focus. **deux p.s,** colon. **p. d'interrogation,** question mark.

pointage, *n.m.* pointing; *(mil.)* sighting.

pointe, *n.f.* point, tip, touch (small amount).

pointer, *vb.* point, aim.

pointeur, *n.m.* pointer, checker.

pointillage, *n.m.* dotting.

pointiller, *vb.* dot; tease.

pointilleux, *adj.* fussy, precise.

pointu, *adj.* pointed.

pointure, *n.f.* size.

poire, *n.f.* pear.

poireau, *n.m.* leek.

poirier, *n.m.* pear tree.

pois, *n.m.* pea.

poison, *n.m.* poison.

poisser, *vb.* make gluey or sticky.

poisson, *n.m.* fish.

poissonnerie, *n.f.* fish store.

poissonneux, *adj.* filled with fish.

poissonnier, *n.m.* fish dealer.

poitrinaire, *adj. and n.m.* consumptive.

poitrine, *n.f.* chest.

poivre, *n.m.* pepper.

poivrer, *vb.* spice with pepper.

poivrier, *n.m.* pepper plant.

poix, *n.f.* pitch.

polaire, *adj.* polar.

pôle, *n.m.* pole.

polémique, *n.f.* argument.

poli, 1. *adj.* civil, polite. **2.** *n.m.* polish.

police, *n.f.* police; (insurance) policy.

policer, *vb.* refine.

polichinelle, *n.m.* Punch (puppet).

policier, *n.m.* policeman. **roman p.,** detective story.

polir, *vb.* polish.

polisseur, *n.m.* polisher.

polisson, 1. *n.m.* gamin, scamp. **2.** *adj.* running wild.

polissonnerie, *n.f.* naughty action or remark.

politesse, *n.f.* good manners.

politicien, *n.m.* politician.

politique, 1. *n.f.* policy, politics. **2.** *adj.* politic, political.

polka, *n.f.* polka.

pollen, *n.m.* pollen.
polluer, *vb.* pollute.
pollution, *n.f.* pollution.
Pologne, *n.f.* Poland.
Polonais, *n.m.* Pole.
polonais, *adj. and n.m.* Polish.
poltron, 1. *adj.* craven, cowardly. 2. *n.m.f.* coward.
poltronnerie, *n.f.* cowardly behavior.
polygame, 1. *n.m.* polygamist. 2. *adj.* polygamous.
polygamie, *n.f.* polygamy.
polygone, *n.m.* polygon.
pommade, *n.f.* pomade, salve.
pomme, *n.f.* apple. **p. de terre,** potato.
pommeau, *n.m.* pommel.
pommette, *n.f.* cheekbone.
pommier, *n.m.* apple tree.
pompe, *n.f.* pump; pomp.
pomper, *vb.* pump.
pompeux, *adj.* pompous.
pompier, *n.m.* fireman.
pompon, *n.m.* pompon, tuft.
ponce, *n.f.* pumice.
ponctualité, *n.f.* punctuality.
ponctuation, *n.f.* punctuation.
ponctuel, *adj.* punctual.
ponctuer, *vb.* punctuate.
poney, *n.m.* pony.
pont, *n.m.* bridge; deck.
pontife, *n.m.* pontiff.
pont-levis, *n.m.* drawbridge.
ponton, *n.m.* pontoon.
popeline, *n.f.* poplin.
popote, *n.f.* mess (military).
populace, *n.f.* mob.
populaire, *adj.* popular.
populariser, *vb.* popularize.
popularité, *n.f.* popularity.
population, *n.f.* population.
populeux, *adj.* populous.
porc, *n.m.* pig, pork.
porcelaine, *n.f.* china.
porc-épic, *n.m.* porcupine.
porche, *n.m.* porch.
porcherie, *n.f.* pigpen.
pore, *n.m.* pore.
poreux, *adj.* porous.
pornographie, *n.f.* pornography.
port, *n.m.* port, harbor; carrying; postage.
portable, *adj.* wearable.
portail, *n.m.* portal.
portatif, *adj.* portable.
porte, *n.f.* door, gate.
porte-affiches, *n.m.* billboard.
porte-avions, *n.m.* aircraft carrier.
portée, *n.f.* range, import, scope, reach; litter. **hors de p.,** out of reach.
portefaix, *n.m.* porter.
portefeuille, *n.m.* wallet, case, portfolio.
portemanteau, *n.m.* cloak rack.
portement, *n.m.* carrying.
porte-monnaie, *n.m.* purse.
porter, *vb.* carry, bear; wear. **se p.,** be (in health).
porte-rame, *n.m.* oarlock.
porteur, *n.m.* porter, bearer.

portier, *n.m.* doorman, porter.
portière, *n.f.* door-curtain.
portion, *n.f.* portion, share.
portique, *n.m.* portico, porch.
porto, *n.m.* port wine.
portrait, *n.m.* portrait.
portraitiste, *n.m.* painter of portraits.
Portugais, *n.m.* Portuguese (person).
portugais, 1. *n.m.* Portuguese (language). 2. *adj.* Portuguese.
Portugal, *n.m.* Portugal.
pose, *n.f.* pose, attitude.
posé, *adj.* poised, set.
poser, *vb.* place, stand, set, lay. **se p.,** settle, alight.
poseur, *n.m.* person or thing that places or applies; affected person.
positif, *adj. and n.m.* positive.
position, *n.f.* stand, place, position.
positiviste, *n.m.f.* positivist.
posséder, *vb.* own, possess.
possesseur, *n.m.* possessor.
possessif, *adj. and n.m.* possessive.
possession, *n.f.* possession.
possibilité, *n.f.* possibility.
possible, *adj.* possible. **tout son p.,** one's utmost.
postal, *adj.* postal.
poste, *n.f.* mail. **mettre à la p.,** mail. **p. restante,** general delivery.
poste, *n.m.* post. **p. d'essence,** gas station. **p. de secours,** first-aid station.
poster, *vb.* post (letter); place.
postérieur, *adj.* rear, posterior.
postérité, *n.f.* posterity.
posthume, *adj.* posthumous.
postiche, *adj.* false, unnecessary.
post-scriptum, *n.m.* postscript.
postulant, *n.m.* applicant.
postuler, *vb.* apply for.
posture, *n.f.* posture.
pot, *n.m.* pot, pitcher, jar.
potable, *adj.* drinkable.
potage, *n.m.* soup.
potager, *adj.* vegetable.
potasse, *n.f.* potash.
pot-de-vin, *n.m.* tip, bribe.
poteau, *n.m.* post.
potée, *n.f.* potful.
potence, *n.f.* gallows.
potentat, *n.m.* potentate.
potentiel, *adj. and n.m.* potential.
poterie, *n.f.* pottery.
poterne, *n.f.* postern.
potier, *n.m.* potter.
potion, *n.f.* potion.
potiron, *n.m.* pumpkin.
pou, *n.m.* louse.
pouce, *n.m.* thumb; inch.
pouding, *n.m.* pudding.
poudre, *n.f.* powder.
poudrer, *vb.* powder.
poudreux, *adj.* full of powder or dust.

poudrier, *n.m.* compact (cosmetic).
poudroyer, *vb.* be dusty.
pouilleux, *adj.* infected with lice.
poulailler, *n.m.* hen-house.
poulain, *n.m.* colt.
poule, *n.f.* hen, chicken.
poulet, *n.m.* chicken.
poulette, *n.f.* pullet.
poulie, *n.f.* pulley.
poulpe, *n.m.* octopus.
pouls, *n.m.* pulse.
poumon, *n.m.* lung.
poupe, *n.f.* poop (of ship).
poupée, *n.f.* doll.
poupin, *adj.* smart, chic.
pour, *prep.* for; in order to. **p. que,** so that.
pourboire, *n.m.* tip, gratuity.
pourceau, *n.m.* hog.
pour-cent, *n.m.* percent.
pourcentage, *n.m.* percentage.
pourchasser, *vb.* pursue.
pourfendeur, *n.m.* killer, bully.
pourparler, *n.m.* discussion, parley.
pourpoint, *n.m.* doublet.
pourpre, *adj.* purple.
pourquoi, *adv.* why.
pourri, *adj.* rotten.
pourrir, *vb.* rot, spoil.
pourriture, *n.f.* rot.
poursuite, *n.f.* pursuit.
poursuivant, *n.m.* one who sues or prosecutes.
poursuivre, *vb.* pursue, sue, prosecute.
pourtant, *adv.* however.
pourvoi, *n.m.* appeal (at court).
pourvoir (de), *vb.* provide (with), supply. **p. à,** cater to.
pourvoyeur, *n.m.* caterer, purveyor.
pourvu que, *conj.* provided that.
pousse, *n.f.* shoot, sprouting.
poussée, *n.f.* push.
pousser, *vb.* push, urge, drive; grow.
poussier, *n.m.* coal dust.
poussière, *n.f.* dust.
poussiéreux, *adj.* dusty.
poussin, *n.m.* newly-hatched chick.
poussoir, *n.m.* push-button.
poutre, *n.f.* beam.
pouvoir, 1. *vb.* be able, can, may. 2. *n.m.* power.
prairie, *n.f.* meadow.
praline, *n.f.* burnt almond.
praticable, *adj.* practicable.
praticien, *n.m.* practitioner.
pratique, 1. *n.f.* practice, exercise. 2. *adj.* practical.
pratiquer, *vb.* practice, exercise.
pré, *n.m.* meadow.
préalable, *adj.* preliminary.
préambule, *n.m.* preamble.
préau, *n.m.* yard, as of a prison.
préavis, *n.m.* advance notice.
précaire, *adj.* precarious.

précaution, *n.f.* precaution, discretion.

précédent, *n.m.* precedent.

précéder, *vb.* precede; come (go) before.

précepte, *n.m.* precept.

précepteur, *n.m.* tutor.

prêche, *n.m.* sermon; the Protestant religion.

prêcher, *vb.* preach.

précieux, *adj.* precious, valuable.

préciosité, *n.f.* preciosity.

précipice, *n.m.* precipice.

précipitamment, *adv.* headlong.

précipitation, *n.f.* hurry.

précipité, *adj.* hasty.

précipiter, *vb.* precipitate. se p., rush, hasten.

précis, *adj.* precise, exact, accurate.

précisément, *adv.* precisely, definitely, just so.

préciser, *vb.* state.

précision, *n.f.* accuracy, precision.

précité, *adj.* previously cited.

précoce, *adj.* precocious.

précocité, *n.f.* precociousness.

précompter, *vb.* deduct in advance.

préconçu, *adj.* preconceived.

préconiser, *vb.* extol, praise.

préconnaissance, *n.f.* foreknowledge.

précurseur, *n.m.* precursor.

prédécesseur, *n.m.* predecessor.

prédestination, *n.f.* predestination.

prédicateur, *n.m.* preacher.

prédiction, *n.f.* prediction.

prédilection, *n.f.* preference, predilection.

prédire, *vb.* foretell, predict.

prédisposer, *vb.* predispose.

prédisposition, *n.f.* predisposition.

prédominant, *adj.* predominant.

prééminence, *n.f.* preëminence.

préface, *n.f.* preface.

préfecture, *n.f.* prefecture, district.

préférable, *adj.* preferable.

préférence, *n.f.* preference.

préférer, *vb.* prefer.

préfet, *n.m.* prefect.

préfixe, *n.m.* prefix.

préfixer, *vb.* fix in advance.

prégnant, *adj.* pregnant.

préhistorique, *adj.* prehistoric.

préjudice, *n.m.* injury.

préjudiciel, *adj.* interlocutory (as in law).

préjugé, *n.m.* prejudice.

préjuger, *vb.* prejudge.

prélasser, *vb.* se p., bask, lounge.

prélat, *n.m.* prelate.

prélèvement, *n.m.* deduction in advance.

prélever, *vb.* deduct previously.

préliminaire, *adj.* preliminary.

prélude, *n.m.* prelude.

prématuré, *adj.* premature.

préméditation, *n.f.* premeditation.

préméditer, *vb.* premeditate.

prémices, *n.f.pl.* first fruits, first works.

premier, *adj.* first, foremost; early; former.

prémisse, *n.f.* premise.

prémunir, *vb.* warn, take precautions.

prendre, *vb.* take.

prénom, *n.m.* given name.

prénommé, *adj.* previously named.

préoccupation, *n.f.* care, worry.

préoccuper, *vb.* worry.

prépaiement, *n.m.* prepayment.

préparatifs, *n.m.pl.* preparation.

préparation, *n.f.* preparation.

préparatoire, *adj.* preparatory.

préparer, *vb.* prepare.

prépondérance, *n.f.* preponderance.

prépondérant, *adj.* preponderant.

préposé, *n.m.* one in charge.

préposition, *n.f.* preposition.

prérogative, *n.f.* prerogative.

près, 1. *adv.* near. **2.** *prep.* p. de, near. de p., nearby.

présage, *n.m.* omen.

présager, *vb.* (fore)bode.

presbyte, *adj.* far-sighted.

presbytère, *n.m.* parsonage, presbytery.

prescription, *n.f.* prescription.

prescrire, *vb.* prescribe.

préséance, *n.f.* precedence.

présélection, *n.f.* triage.

présence, *n.f.* presence, attendance.

présent, *adj. and n.m.* present.

présentable, *adj.* presentable.

présentation, *n.f.* presentation, introduction.

présentement, *adv.* now, at present.

présenter, *vb.* present, introduce. se p. à l'esprit, come to mind.

préservatif, *adj. and n.m.* preservative.

préservation, *n.f.* preservation.

préserver, *vb.* preserve.

présidence, *n.f.* presidency.

président, *n.m.* president, chairman.

présidente, *n.f.* chairwoman.

présidentiel, *adj.* presidential.

présider, *vb.* preside.

présomptif, *adj.* apparent, presumed.

présomptueux, *adj.* presumptuous.

presque, *adv.* almost, nearly.

presqu'île, *n.f.* peninsula.

pressage, *n.m.* pressing.

pressant, *adj.* urgent.

presse, *n.f.* press, crowd.

pressentiment, *n.m.* foreboding, misgiving.

pressentir, *vb.* foresee.

presse-papiers, *n.m.* paperweight.

presser, *vb.* press; urge; hurry.

pression, *n.f.* pressure.

pressoir, *n.m.* machine or device for squeezing.

pressurer, *vb.* squeeze, put pressure on.

prestance, *n.f.* imposing appearance.

preste, *adj.* dexterous, nimble.

prestesse, *n.f.* vivacity, nimbleness.

prestige, *n.m.* prestige, illusion.

prestigieux, *adj.* enchanting.

présumer, *vb.* presume.

présupposer, *vb.* presuppose.

prêt, 1. *n.m.* loan. **2.** *adj.* ready.

prêtable, *adj.* lendable.

prétendant, *n.m.* claimant.

prétendre, *vb.* claim.

prétendu, *adj.* supposed, so-called.

prétentieux, *adj.* pretentious.

prétention, *n.f.* claim.

prêter, *vb.* lend.

prêteur, *n.m.* lender.

prétexte, *n.m.* pretext.

prétexter, *vb.* pretend, feign.

prêtre, *n.m.* priest.

prêtresse, *n.f.* priestess.

preuve, *n.f.* proof.

preux, *adj. and n.m.* gallant, brave.

prévaloir, *vb.* prevail.

prévenance, *n.f.* attentiveness, obligingness.

prévenant, *adj.* prepossessing, obliging.

prévenir, *vb.* prevent; warn.

préventif, 1. *adj.* preventive. **2.** *n.m.* deterrent.

prévention, *n.f.* bias; prevention.

prévenu, *adj.* partial, biased.

prévision, *n.f.* forecast, expectation.

prévoir, *vb.* foresee.

prévôt, *n.m.* provost.

prévoyance, *n.f.* foresight.

prévoyant, *adj.* farseeing, prudent.

prier, *vb.* beg; pray.

prière, *n.f.* prayer.

prieur, *n.m.* prior.

prieuré, *n.m.* priory.

primaire, *adj.* primary.

primauté, *n.f.* preëminence, primacy.

prime, 1. *n.f.* premium, subsidy, **2.** *adj.* first; accented.

primer, *vb.* outdo, excel.

primeur, *n.f.* freshness, earliness.

primitif, *adj.* primitive; original.

primordial, *adj.* primordial.

prince, *n.m.* prince.

princesse, *n.f.* princess.

princier, *adj.* princely.

principal, *adj.* chief, main, principal.

principauté, *n.f.* principality.

principe, *n.m.* principle.

printanier, *adj.* of spring.

printemps, *n.m.* spring.

priorité, *n.f.* priority.

prisable, *adj.* estimable.

prise, *n.f.* grasp, hold, grip. **p. de courant,** (electric) plug.

prisée, *n.f.* appraisal.

priser, *vb.* appraise.

priseur, *n.m.* auctioneer, appraiser.

prisme, *n.m.* prism.

prison, *n.f.* jail, prison.

prisonnier, *n.m.* prisoner.

privation, *n.f.* privation, want, hardship.

privé, *adj.* private.

priver, *vb.* deprive.

privilège, *n.m.* privilege, license.

privilégier, *vb.* license.

prix, *n.m.* price, charge, fare; prize, award.

prix-courant, *n.m.* list of prices.

probabilité, *n.f.* probability, chances.

probable, *adj.* likely, probable.

probité, *n.f.* probity.

problématique, *adj.* problematical.

problème, *n.m.* problem.

procédé, *n.m.* procedure, process.

procéder, *vb.* proceed.

procédure, *n.f.* proceeding.

procès, *n.m.* trial; (law)suit.

procession, *n.f.* procession.

processionnel, *adj.* processional.

procès-verbal, *n.m.* minutes (of meeting).

prochain, 1. *n.m.* neighbor. 2. *adj.* next.

prochainement, *adv.* soon.

proche, *adj.* near, close.

proclamation, *n.f.* proclamation.

proclamer, *vb.* proclaim.

procréation, *n.f.* procreation.

procurer, *vb.* procure, get.

procureur, *n.m.* attorney.

prodigalement, *adv.* prodigally.

prodigalité, *n.f.* extravagance.

prodige, *n.m.* prodigy.

prodigieux, *adj.* wondrous.

prodigue, *adj.* extravagant, lavish, profuse.

prodiguer, *vb.* lavish.

producteur, *n.m.* producer.

productif, *adj.* productive.

production, *n.f.* production.

productivité, *n.f.* productivity.

produire, *vb.* produce, yield, breed.

produit, *n.m.* product, commodity.

proéminence, *n.f.* prominence.

proéminent, *adj.* prominent, standing out.

profane, *adj.* profane.

profaner, *vb.* misuse, debase, profane.

proférer, *vb.* say, utter.

professer, *vb.* profess.

professeur, *n.m.* professor, teacher.

profession, *n.f.* profession.

professionnel, *adj.* professional.

professoral, *adj.* professorial.

professorat, *n.m.* professorship.

profil (-1), *n.m.* profile.

profiler, *vb.* show a profile of.

profit, *n.m.* profit.

profitable, *adj.* profitable.

profiter, *vb.* profit.

profiteur, *n.m.* profiteer.

profond, *adj.* deep, profound; in-depth.

profondeur, *n.f.* depth.

profus, *adj.* profuse.

profusion, *n.f.* profusion, excess.

progéniture, *n.f.* offspring.

programme, *n.m.* program.

progrès, *n.m.* progress, advance.

progresser, *vb.* progress.

progressif, *adj.* progressive.

progressiste, *n.m.* progressive.

prohiber, *vb.* prohibit.

prohibitif, *adj.* prohibitive.

prohibition, *n.f.* prohibition.

proie, *n.f.* prey.

projecteur, *n.m.* projector.

projectile, *n.m.* missile.

projection, *n.f.* projection.

projet, *n.m.* project. **p. de loi,** bill.

projeter, *vb.* project, plan.

prolétaire, *adj.* and *n.m.* proletarian.

prolétariat, *n.m.* proletariat.

prolifération, *n.f.* proliferation.

prolifique, *adj.* prolific.

prolixe, *adj.* prolix, wordy.

prologue, *n.m.* prologue.

prolongation, *n.f.* extension, prolongation.

prolonger, *vb.* extend, prolong.

promenade, *n.f.* excursion; walk; ride.

promener, *vb.* take out. **se p.,** take a walk (ride).

promeneur, *n.m.* walker.

promesse, *n.f.* promise.

promettre, *vb.* promise.

promontoire, *n.m.* promontory.

promoteur, *n.m.* promoter.

promotion, *n.f.* promotion.

promouvoir, *vb.* promote.

prompt, *adj.* prompt.

promptitude, *n.f.* quickness.

promulguer, *vb.* promulgate.

prôner, *vb.* lecture to, praise.

pronom, *n.m.* pronoun.

prononcer, *vb.* pronounce, utter; deliver.

prononciation, *n.f.* pronunciation.

pronostic, *n.m.* prognosis, prediction.

propagande, *n.f.* propaganda.

propagandiste, *n.m.* propagandist.

propagateur, *n.m.* propagator.

propagation, *n.f.* propagation.

propager, *vb.* propagate.

propension, *n.f.* inclination, propensity.

prophète, *n.m.* prophet.

prophétie, *n.f.* prophecy.

prophétique, *adj.* prophetic.

prophétiser, *vb.* prophesy.

propice, *adj.* favorable. **peu p.,** unfavorable.

propitiation, *n.f.* propitiation, conciliation.

proportion, *n.f.* proportion.

proportionné, *adj.* proportionate.

proportionnel, *adj.* proportional.

proportionner, *vb.* keep in proportion.

propos, *n.m.* subject; discourse. **à p.,** relevant. **à p. de,** with regard to.

proposable, *adj.* suitable, appropriate.

proposer, *vb.* propose; move. **se p. de,** intend, mean.

proposition, *n.f.* proposal, proposition.

propre, *adj.* proper; clean, neat; own. **peu p.,** unfit.

propreté, *n.f.* cleanliness, neatness.

propriétaire, *n.m.f.* proprietor.

propriété, *n.f.* property (landed), estate.

propulser, *vb.* push, propel.

propulseur, *n.m.* propeller.

propulsion, *n.f.* propulsion.

proroger, *vb.* postpone, extend time limit.

prosaïque (-zä ĕk), *adj.* prosaic.

prosaïsme, *n.m.* prosaicness, dullness.

prosateur, *n.m.* writer of prose.

proscription, *n.f.* proscription.

proscrire, *vb.* outlaw, proscribe.

proscrit, *adj.* and *n.m.* exile(d); forbidden.

prose, *n.f.* prose.

prosodie, *n.f.* prosody.

prospecter, *vb.* search, as for gold.

prospecteur, *n.m.* prospector.

prospère, *adj.* prosperous.

prospérer, *vb.* flourish, thrive, prosper.

prospérité, *n.f.* prosperity.

prosterner, *vb.* prostrate.

prostituée, *n.f.* prostitute.

prostitution, *n.f.* prostitution.

protecteur, 1. *n.m.* protector; patron. 2. *adj.* protective.

protecteur du citoyen, *n.m.* ombudsman (in Quebec).

protection, *n.f.* protection.

protectorat, *n.m.* protectorate.

protéger, *vb.* protect, patronize, foster.

protéine, *n.f.* protein.

protestant, *adj.* and *n.m.* Protestant.

protestantisme, *n.m.* Protestantism.

protestation, *n.f.* protest.

protester. *vb.* protest.

protêt, *n.m.* protest.

prothèse, *n.f.* artificial aid, as a denture.

protocole, *n.m.* protocol.

protubérance, *n.f.* protuberance.

proue, *n.f.* prow, front.

prouesse, *n.f.* prowess.

prouver, *vb.* prove.

provenance, *n.f.* place of origin; product.

provençal, 1. *adj.* of Provence. **2.** *n.m.* language of Provence.

provende, *n.f.* provender, foodstuffs.

provenir, *vb.* come from.

proverbe, *n.m.* proverb, saying.

proverbial, *adj.* proverbial.

providence, *n.f.* providence.

providentiel, *adj.* providential.

province, *n.f.* province.

provincial, *adj.* and *n.m.* provincial.

provincialisme, *n.m.* provincialism.

provision, *n.f.* supply, store, provision.

provisoire, *adj.* temproary.

provocateur, *n.m.* one who provokes action.

provocation, *n.f.* provocation.

provoquer, *vb.* provoke.

proximité, *n.f.* closeness, proximity.

prude, 1. *n.f.* prude. **2.** *adj.* like a prude.

prudence, *n.f.* caution, prudence.

prudent, *adj.* cautious, prudent.

pruderie, *n.f.* prudishness.

prune, *n.f.* plum.

pruneau, *n.m.* prune.

prunelle, *n.f.* pupil (of eye).

prunier, *n.m.* plum tree.

Prusse, *n.f.* Prussia.

Prussien, *n.m.* Prussian.

prussien, *adj.* Prussian.

psalmiste, *n.m.* psalmist.

psaume, *n.m.* psalm.

psautier, *n.m.* psalm book.

pseudonyme, *n.m.* pseudonym.

psychanalyse (-k-), *n.f.* psychoanalysis.

psychédélique (-k-), *adj.* psychedelic.

psychiatre (-k-), *n.m.* psychiatrist.

psychiatrie (-k-), *n.f.* psychiatry.

psychique (-k), *adj.* psychic.

psychologie (-k-), *n.f.* psychology.

psychologique (-k-), *adj.* psychological.

psychologue (-k-), *n.m.* psychologist.

psychose (-k-), *n.f.* psychosis.

puant, *adj.* foul, shameful.

puberté, *n.f.* puberty.

public, 1. *adj. m.,* **publique** *f.* public. **2.** *n.m.* public.

publication, *n.f.* publication.

publiciste, *n.m.* publicist.

publicité, *n.f.* publicity, advertisement(s).

publier, *vb.* publish, issue.

puce, *n.f.* flea.

pucelle, *n.f.* young girl, virgin.

pudeur, *n.f.* modesty.

pudique, *adj.* modest.

puer, *vb.* smell, have an offensive odor.

puéril (-l), *adj.* childish.

pugiliste, *m.* boxer.

puîné, *adj.* younger (of a brother or sister).

puis, *adv.* then.

puisard, *n.m.* cesspool.

puisatier, *n.m.* well-digger.

puiser, *vb.* draw up, derive.

puisque, *conj.* since, as.

puissamment, *adv.* very, powerfully.

puissance, *n.f.* power.

puissant, *adj.* potent, powerful, mighty.

puits (pwè), *n.m.* well; shaft.

pulluler, *vb.* breed abundantly, multiply.

pulmonaire, *adj.* pulmonary.

pulpe, *n.f.* pulp.

pulpeux, *adj.* pulpy.

pulsar, *n.m.* pulsar.

pulsation, *n.f.* pulsation, beating.

pulvérisateur, *n.m.* vaporizer, spray.

pulvériser, *vb.* spray, pulverize.

punaise, *n.f.* bedbug.

punir, *vb.* punish.

punitif, *adj.* punitive.

punition, *n.f.* punishment.

pupille (-l), *n.m.f.* ward: pupil (of the eye).

pupitre, *n.m.* desk.

pur, *adj.* pure.

purée, *n.f.* mash.

purement, *adv.* purely, solely.

pureté, *n.f.* purity.

purgatoire, *n.m.* purgatory.

purge, *n.f.* purge.

purger, *vb.* purge.

purification, *n.f.* purification.

purifier, *vb.* purify, cleanse.

puritain, *adj.* and *n.m.* Puritan.

purulent, *adj.* purulent.

pustule, *n.f.* pimple.

putois, *n.m.* skunk, polecat.

putréfier, *vb.* corrupt, rot, spoil.

putride, *adj.* putrid.

pygmée, *n.m.* Pygmy.

pyjama, *n.m.* pajamas.

pyramidal, *adj.* pyramidal, overwhelming.

pyramide, *n.f.* pyramid.

Q

quadrangle (kw-), *n.m.* quadrangle.

quadrillé, *adj.* checked, ruled off.

quadriphonique (kw-), *adj.* quadraphonic.

quadrupède (kw-), *n.m.* and *adj.* quadruped.

quadruple (kw-), *adj.* quadruple.

quai, *n.m.* pier, dock; (station) platform.

qualification, *n.f.* qualification.

qualifier, *vb.* qualify.

qualité, *n.f.* quality, nature, grade.

quand, *adv.* when.

quant à, *prep.* as to, as for.

quantité, *n.f.* amount, quantity.

quarantaine, *n.f.* quarantine.

quarante, *adj.* and *n.m.* forty.

quart, *n.m.* fourth, quarter.

quartier, *n.m.* district, quarter. **q. général,** headquarters.

quartz (kw-), *n.m.* quartz.

quasar, (kw-), *n.m.* quasar.

quasi, *adv.* nearly, quasi.

quatorze, *adj.* and *n.m.* fourteen.

quatrain, *n.m.* quatrain.

quatre, *adj.* and *n.m.* four.

quatre-vingt-dix, *adj.* and *n.m.* ninety.

quatre-vingts, *adj.* and *n.m.* eighty.

quatrième, *adj.* and *n.m.* fourth.

quatuor (kw-), *n.m.* quartet.

que, 1. *pron.* whom, which, that. **2.** *conj.* that, than.

quel, *adj.* which, what; of what kind.

quelconque, *adj.* of any kind.

quelque, *adj.* some, any. **q. chose,** something. **q. part,** somewhere.

quelquefois, *adv.* sometimes.

quelques, *adj.* a few.

quelques-uns, *pron.* a few.

quelqu'un, *pron.* somebody.

querelle, *n.f.* quarrel.

quereller, *vb.* quarrel (with); scold.

querelleur, 1. *n.m.* quarreler. **2.** *adj.* inclined to quarrel.

question, *n.f.* question, issue, matter.

questionner, *vb.* question.

quête, *n.f.* quest, seeking.

queue (kœ), *n.f.* tail; line. **faire la q.,** stand in line.

qui, 1. *interr. pron.* who, whom. **2.** *rel. pron.* who, which. **q. que,** whoever.

quiconque, *pron.* whoever.

quignon, *n.m.* large piece of bread.

quincaillerie, *n.f.* hardware.

quinine, *n.f.* quinine.

quintal, *n.m.* unit of weight (100 kilograms).

quinze, *adj.* and *n.m.* fifteen.

quinzième, *adj.* and *n.m.* fifteenth.

quittance, *n.f.* receipt.

quitte, adj. free, quit, released.

quitter, vb. quit, leave.

quoi, pron. and interj. what.

quoique, conj. though.

quote-part, n.f. quota.

quotidien, adj. daily.

R

rabais, n.m. reduction.

rabaisser, vb. diminish, lower.

rabattre, vb. put down, suppress, quell.

rabbin, n.m. rabbi.

rabbinique, adj. rabbinical.

rabot, n.m. plane.

raboter, vb. plane, perfect.

roboteux, adj. rugged.

rabougri, adj. puny, stunted.

raccommodage, n.m. fixing, mending.

raccommoder, vb. mend.

raccorder, vb. join, bring together.

raccourcir, vb. shorten, curtail.

raccourcissement, n.m. shortening, curtailing.

raccrocher, vb. hook up; recover.

race, n.f. race.

rachat, n.m. redemption.

racheter, vb. redeem.

rachitique, adj. rickety, affected with rickets.

rachitisme, n.m. rickets.

racine, n.f. root.

raclage, n.m. action of scraping.

racler, vb. scrape.

racoler, vb. recruit, esp. by fraud.

raconter, vb. tell, narrate, recount.

raconteur, n.m. story-teller.

radar, n.m. radar.

radeau, n.m. raft.

radiant, adj. radiant.

radiateur, n.m. radiator.

radical, adj. and n.m. radical.

radier, vb. radiate; erase.

radieux, adj. radiant, beaming, glorious.

radio, n.f. radio; wireless.

radio-actif, adj. radioactive.

radiodiffuser, vb. broadcast.

radio-émission, n.f. broadcast.

radiogramme, n.m. radiogram.

radiographie, n.f. radiography.

radis, n.m. radish.

radium, n.m. radium.

radoter, vb. babble, drivel.

radoub, n.m. refitting (of ship).

radoucir, vb. quiet, soften, appease.

rafale, n.f. blast, gust, squall.

raffermir, vb. make stronger or more secure.

raffinement, n.m. refinement.

raffiner, vb. refine.

raffinerie, n.f. refinery.

raffoler, vb. dote on, be mad about.

rafistoler, vb. mend, patch.

rafler, vb. carry off.

rafraîchir, vb. refresh.

rafraîchissement, n.m. refreshment.

rage, n.f. rage, fury.

rager, vb. be angry, rage.

rageur, n.m. irritable person.

ragoût, n.m. stew.

ragoûtant, adj. tasty, pleasing.

ragréer, vb. refinish, renovate.

raid, n.m. raid.

raide, adj. stiff; taut; steep.

raideur, n.f. stiffness.

raidir, vb. stiffen.

raie, n.f. streak; part (in hair).

raifort, n.m. horseradish.

rail, n.m. rail.

railler, vb. make fun of.

raillerie, n.f. jesting.

railleur, n.m. scoffer, jester.

rainure, n.f. groove.

rais, n.m. ray, spoke.

raisin, n.m. grape(s). r. sec, raisin.

raison, n.f. reason, judgment. avoir r., be right.

raisonnable, adj. reasonable, rational.

raisonnement, n.m. reason, argument.

raisonner, vb. reason.

rajeunir, vb. rejuvenate.

rajuster, vb. readjust.

râle, vb. rail (bird); rattle in throat.

ralentir, vb. slacken, slow down.

râler, vb. rattle (in dying).

rallier, vb. rally.

rallonger, vb. make an addition to, lengthen.

ramage, n.m. flower pattern; chirping; babble.

ramassé, adj. thick-set, dumpy.

ramasser, vb. pick up.

ramasseur, n.m. collector.

rame, n.f. oar.

rameau, n.m. branch.

ramener, vb. bring (take) back.

rameneur, vb. restorer.

ramer, vb. row.

rameur, n.m. rower.

ramifier, vb. divide into branches, ramify.

ramille, n.f. twig.

ramollir, vb. soften, weaken.

rampe, n.f. banister; ramp.

ramper, vb. crawl, creep.

rance, adj. and n.m. rancid, rancidness.

rancœur, n.f. rancor.

rançon, n.f. ransom.

rancune, n.f. grudge, spite, rancor. garder de la r., bear a grudge.

rancunier, adj. rancorous, bitter.

rang, n.m. row; rank.

rangée, n.f. file, row.

ranger, vb. rank, array, (ar)range.

rapace, adj. predatory, greedy.

râpe, n.f. file, rasp.

râper, vb. grate.

rapide, 1. n.m. rapid. 2. adj. rapid, fast, quick.

rapidité, n.f. rapidity.

rapiécer, vb. patch.

rapière, n.f. rapier.

rapin, n.m. art student, pupil

rapiner, vb. plunder, rob.

rappel, n.m. recall, repeal, reminder.

rappeler, vb. recall, remind. se r., remember.

rapport, n.m. report; relation.

rapporter, vb. bring back; report. se r. à, relate to, refer to.

rapporteur, n.m. reporter, tattle-tale.

rapprochement, n.m. bringing close, junction.

rapprocher, vb. bring together. se r. de, approximate.

rapt, n.m. rape, kidnapping.

raquette, n.f. racket.

rare, adj. scarce, rare.

raréfier, vb. rarefy.

rarement, adv. seldom.

rareté, n.f. rarity, uniqueness, scarcity.

ras, adj. smooth-shaven, open.

raser, vb. shave.

rasoir, n.m. razor.

rassasier, vb. cloy, sate.

rassemblement, n.m. rally.

rassembler, vb. gather, congregate, muster.

rasseoir, vb. reseat. se r., be seated again.

rasséréner, vb. clear up (weather).

rassis, adj. stale.

rassurer, vb. reassure, comfort.

rat, n.m. rat.

ratatiner, vb. shrivel, shrink.

rate, n.f. spleen.

râteau, n.m. rake.

râteler, n.m. rake.

râtelier, n.m. rack.

rater, vb. miss.

ratière, n.f. rat trap.

ratifier, vb. ratify.

ration, n.f. ration.

rationnel, adj. rational.

rationnement, n.m. rationing.

rationner, vb. ration.

ratissoire, n.f. scraper, rake.

rattacher, vb. fasten.

rattraper, vb. overtake.

rature, n.f. erasure.

raturer, vb. erase, blot out.

rauque, adj. hoarse, raucous.

ravage, n.m. havoc.

ravager, vb. lay waste.

ravauder, vb. mend, patch.

ravigoter, vb. enliven, refresh.

ravin, n.m. ravine.

ravir, vb. ravish; delight.

ravissant, adj. ravishing, charming; ravenous.

ravissement, n.m. rapture.

ravisseur, n.m. ravisher, robber.

raviver, vb. revive.

rayer, vb. streak; cross out.

rayon, n.m. ray, beam; shelf. r. X, X-ray.

rayonnant, *adj.* beaming.

rayonne, *n.f.* rayon.

rayonnement, *n.m.* radiation; radiance.

rayonner, *vb.* radiate, beam.

rayure, *n.f.* streak, blemish.

re-, ré-, *prefix.* re-, again.

réabonnement, *n.m.* renewal of subscription.

réabonner, *vb.* renew, resubscribe.

réaction, *n.f.* reaction. **avion à r.**, jet-plane.

reactionnaire, *adj. and n.* reactionary.

réagir, *vb.* react.

réalisable, *adj.* realizable.

réalisation, *n.f.* attainment, carrying out.

réaliser, *vb.* realize. **se r.**, materialize.

réaliste, **1.** *n.m.f.* realist. **2.** *adj.* realist, realistic.

réalité, *n.f.* reality.

réassurer, *vb.* reinsure.

rébarbatif, *adj.* forbidding.

rebattre, *vb.* repeat, beat again.

rebattu, *adj.* trite.

rebelle, **1.** *n.m.f.* rebel. **2.** *adj.* rebel, rebellious.

rebeller, *vb.* **se r.**, rebel.

rébellion, *n.f.* rebellion.

rebondi, *adj.* plump.

rebondir, *vb.* bounce.

rebord, *n.m.* border, edge.

rebuffade, *n.f.* rebuff, rebuke.

rebut, *n.m.* trash, refuse, junk, rubbish.

rebuter, *vb.* rebuke, discard.

recéler, *vb.* accept stolen goods, hide.

récemment, *adv.* recently.

recensement, *n.m.* census.

recenser, *vb.* make a census.

récent, *adj.* recent.

réceptacle, *n.m.* receptacle.

récepteur, *n.m.* receiver.

réceptif, *adj.* receptive.

réception, *n.f.* reception, receipt.

recette, *n.f.* recipe; receipt; (*pl.*) returns.

receveur, *n.m.* conductor; receiver.

recevoir, *vb.* receive, get; entertain.

réchapper, *vb.* escape, get out.

réchaud, *n.m.* food warmer, chafing dish.

réchauffer, *vb.* warm again, excite.

recherche, *n.f.* inquiry, (re)search; quest.

rechercher, *vb.* seek again, investigate.

rechute, *n.f.* relapse.

récif, *n.m.* reef.

récipient, *n.m.* container.

réciproque, *adj.* mutual.

récit, *n.m.* account.

réciter, *vb.* recite, tell.

réclamation, *n.f.* complaint.

réclame, *n.f.* advertisement.

réclamer, *vb.* claim, demand.

reclus, **1.** *adj.* withdrawn, secluded. **2.** *n.m.* recluse.

réclusion, *n.f.* (solitary) confinement.

recoin, *n.m.* recess, corner.

récolte, *n.f.* crop, harvest.

récolter, *vb.* harvest, gather.

recommandable, *adj.* advisable.

recommandation, *n.f.* recommendation.

recommander, *vb.* recommend; register (letter).

recommencer, *vb.* start again.

récompense, *n.f.* reward.

récompenser, *vb.* reward.

réconcilier, *vb.* reconcile.

reconduire, *vb.* accompany, show out, dismiss.

reconnaissance, *n.f.* recognition; gratitude.

reconnaissant, *adj.* grateful.

reconnaître, *vb.* recognize; admit, acknowledge.

reconstituer, *vb.* rebuild, restore.

recourir, *vb.* resort (to).

recours, *n.m.* resort, recourse. **avoir r. à**, resort to; appeal to.

recouvrement, *n.m.* recovery.

recouvrer, *vb.* recover, retrieve.

recouvrir, *vb.* re-cover, cover completely.

récréation, *n.f.* amusement.

récréer, *vb.* entertain. **se r.**, amuse oneself.

recrue, *n.f.* recruit.

recruter, *vb.* recruit.

rectangle, *n.m.* rectangle.

recteur, *n.m.* rector.

rectifier, *vb.* rectify, correct.

reçu, *n.m.* receipt.

recueil, *n.m.* collection, compilation.

recueillir, *vb.* gather, collect, glean.

recul, *n.m.* kick, recoil.

reculade, *n.f.* backing, retreat.

reculer, *vb.* recoil, draw back, go back.

récuser, *vb.* challenge, reject.

recycler, *vb.* recycle.

rédacteur, *n.m.* editor.

rédaction, *n.f.* editorial staff.

reddition, *n.f.* surrendering.

rédemption, *n.f.* redemption.

rédiger, *vb.* draw up.

redingote, *n.f.* frock-coat.

redire, *vb.* repeat, echo, reveal.

redoutable, *adj.* redoubtable, alarming.

redouter, *vb.* dread.

redresser, *vb.* straighten.

réduction, *n.f.* reduction, decrease, cut.

réduire, *vb.* reduce. **se r. à**, amount to.

réduit, *n.m.* retreat, hovel.

réel, *adj.* real, actual.

réfection, *n.f.* reconstruction; refreshments.

réfectoire, *n.m.* dining-room.

référence, *n.f.* reference.

référer, *vb.* refer.

refermer, *vb.* close up or again.

réfléchir, *vb.* reflect, consider, ponder.

reflet, *n.m.* reflection.

refléter, *vb.* reflect.

réflexe, *adj. and n.m.* reflex.

réflexion, *n.f.* reflection, consideration, thought.

refluer, *vb.* return to source, ebb.

reflux, *n.m.* ebb.

refondre, *vb.* cast gain; remodel, improve.

réformateur, **1.** *adj.* reforming. **2.** *n.m.* reformer, crusader.

réforme, *n.f.* reform, reformation.

réformer, *vb.* reform.

refoulement, *n.m.* forcing back, retreat.

refouler, *vb.* drive back, repel.

réfractaire, *adj.* refractory.

rafraîchir, *vb.* freshen.

réfrigérant, *n.m.* refrigerator.

réfrigérer, *vb.* put under refrigeration.

refroidir, *vb.* chill, cool.

refroidissement, *n.m.* cooling, refrigeration, chill.

refuge, *n.m.* refuge.

réfugié, *n.m.* refugee.

réfugier, *vb.* **se r.**, take refuge.

refus, *n.m.* refusal, denial.

refuser, *vb.* refuse, withhold, deny.

réfutation, *n.f.* rebuttal.

réfuter, *vb.* disprove, refute.

regagner, *vb.* regain, recover.

regain, *n.m.* regrowth, renewal.

régal, *n.m.* feast, repast.

régaler, *vb.* entertain, treat.

regard, *n.m.* look.

regarder, *vb.* look (at); concern.

régence, *n.f.* regency.

régénérer, *vb.* regenerate.

régent, *adj. and n.m.* regent.

régenter, *vb.* direct, dominate.

régime, *n.m.* diet; government; direction.

régiment, *n.m.* regiment.

région, *n.f.* area, region.

régional, *adj.* regional.

régir, *vb.* rule.

régisseur, *n.m.* manager.

registre, *n.m.* register, record.

règle, *n.f.* rule; ruler.

règlement, *n.m.* regulation; settlement.

réglementaire, *adj.* according to regulations.

régler, *vb.* regulate; rule; settle.

règne, *n.m.* reign.

régner, *vb.* reign.

régression, *n.f.* regression.

regret, *n.m.* regret.

regrettable, *adj.* regrettable.

regretter, *vb.* regret, be sorry for.

régulariser, *vb.* regularize.

régularité, *n.f.* regularity.

régulateur, *n.m.* regulator.

régulier, *adj.* regular.

réhabiliter, *vb.* rehabilitate.

rehausser, *vb.* enhance.

rein, *n.m.* kidney; (*pl.*) loins, back.

reine, *n.f.* queen.

réitérer, *vb.* reiterate.

rejet, *n.m.* rejection.

rejeter, *vb.* reject.

rejeton, *n.m.* plant shoot; scion.

rejoindre, *vb.* rejoin; catch up with, overtake.

réjouir, *vb.* rejoice, delight, cheer up.

réjouissance, *n.f.* festivity.

relâché, *adj.* loose.

relâcher, *vb.* relax, slacken.

relais, *n.m.* relay.

relater, *vb.* relate.

relatif, *adj.* relative.

relation, *n.f.* relation, connection.

relaxation, *n.f.* relaxation, release.

relayer, *vb.* relay.

reléguer, *vb.* relegate, banish.

relève, *n.f.* (*mil.*) relief, replacement.

relèvement, *n.m.* bearing.

relever, *vb.* lift; relieve; point out.

relief, *n.m.* relief. **mettre en r.,** emphasize.

relier, *vb.* bind; link.

relieur, *n.m.* binder, esp. of books.

religieuse, *n.f.* nun.

religieux, *adj.* religious.

religion, *n.f.* religion.

reliquaire, *n.m.* receptacle for relic.

relique, *n.f.* relic.

reliure, *n.f.* binding.

reluire, *vb.* shine, glisten.

remanier, *vb.* redo, modify.

remarquable, *adj.* remarkable; noticeable.

remarque, *n.f.* remark.

remarquer, *vb.* remark; notice.

rembarrer, *vb.* drive back; put in one's place.

remblai, *n.m.* embankment.

remboursement, *n.m.* refund.

rembourser, *vb.* repay, refund.

remède, *n.m.* remedy, cure.

remédiable, *adj.* remediable.

remédier à, *vb.* remedy.

remerciement, *n.m.* thanks.

remercier, *vb.* thank.

remettre, *vb.* put back; restore; remit; pardon; deliver. **se r.,** recover.

remise, *n.f.* discount; delivery.

rémission, *n.f.* remmission.

remontrance, *n.f.* remonstrance.

remontrer, *vb.* show anew, point out error.

remords (-môr), *n.m.* remorse.

remorquer, *vb.* tow.

remorqueur, *n.m.* tug(boat).

rémouleur, *n.m.* sharpener, grinder.

remous, *n.m.* eddy.

rempart, *n.m.* bulwark, rampart.

remplaçant, *n.m.* substitute.

remplacer, *vb.* replace, substitute.

rempli, *n.m.* tuck, hitch.

remplier, *vb.* take a tuck in.

remplir, *vb.* fill; carry out; crowd.

remporter, *vb.* take away, bring back.

remuer, *vb.* stir. **se r.,** bustle.

renaissance, *n.f.* rebirth, revival.

renaître, *vb.* be reborn, get new life.

renard, *n.m.* fox; sly person.

rencontre, *n.f.* meeting. **aller à la r. de,** go to meet.

rencontrer, *vb.* meet; come across.

rendement, *n.m.* output.

rendez-vous, *n.m.* date, appointment.

rendre, *vb.* give back; repay; surrender. **se r. compte de,** realize.

rendu, *adj.* tired out, all in.

rêne, *n.f.* rein.

rené, *adj.* born-again.

renégat, *adj. and n.m.* renegade.

renfermer, *vb.* enclose.

renfler, *vb.* swell, inflate.

renforcer, *vb.* reinforce.

renfort, *n.m.* reinforcement, aid.

renfrogner, *vb.* **se r.** scowl, frown.

rengaine, *n.f.* often-told story.

renne, *n.m.* reindeer.

renom, *n.m.* renown, repute.

renommée, *n.f.* fame, renown.

renoncer à, *vb.* renounce, give up, forego.

renonciation, *n.f.* renunciation.

renouement, *n.m.* renewing, retying.

renouveau, *n.m.* springtime.

renouveler, *vb.* renew, renovate.

renouvellement, *n.m.* renewal.

renseignements, *n.m.pl.* information.

renseigner, *vb.* inform. **se r.,** inquire.

rente, *n.f.* income; interest; annuity.

rentier, *n.m.* one who lives off interest on investments.

rentrée, *n.f.* return.

rentrer, *vb.* go back, go home.

renversant, *adj.* amazing, overwhelming.

renverser, *vb.* overthrow, overturn; reverse.

renvoi, *n.m.* dismissal; return.

renvoyer, *vb.* send back, return; dismiss.

repaire, *n.m.* den, animal's lair.

repaître, *vb.* feed, feast.

répandre, *vb.* diffuse, scatter, spill.

répandu, *adj.* prevalent, widespread.

reparaître, *vb.* reappear.

réparateur, *n.m.* restorer, repairer.

réparation, *n.f.* repair; amends.

réparer, *vb.* repair, make up for, make amends for.

repartie, *n.f.* reply, quick retort.

repartir, *vb.* leave again; retort.

répartir, *vb.* apportion, allot, distribute.

repas, *n.m.* meal.

repasser, *vb.* press; pass; look over.

repentir, 1. *n.m.* repentance. **2.** *vb.* **se r.,** repent.

répercussion, *n.f.* repercussion.

répercuter, *vb.* reverberate, echo.

repère, *n.m.* guiding mark.

répertoire, *n.m.* list, repertory.

répéter, *vb.* repeat; rehearse.

répétition, *n.f.* repetition.

répit, *n.m.* respite.

replacer, *vb.* replace.

replier, *vb.* fold again or up.

réplique, *n.f.* rejoinder; cue.

répliquer, *vb.* rejoin.

répondant, *n.m.* respondent, bail.

répondre, *vb.* answer, reply. **r. de,** vouch for.

réponse, *n.f.* answer, reply.

report, *n.m.* (in bookkeeping) amount brought forward.

reportage, *n.m.* reporting.

reporter, 1. *n.m.* reporter. **2.** *vb.* carry or take back.

repos, *n.m.* rest.

reposer, *vb.* rest, repose.

repousser, *vb.* push back, repel; spurn.

repoussoir, *n.m.* foil.

répréhensible, *adj.* objectionable.

répréhension, *n.f.* reprehension, censure.

reprendre, *vb.* take back, resume.

représailles, *n.f.pl.* retaliation.

représentant, *n.m.* representative.

représentatif, *adj.* representative.

représentation, *n.f.* representation, performance.

représenter, *adj.* represent.

répressif, *adj.* repressive.

répression, *n.f.* repression.

réprimande, *n.f.* reproof, rebuke, reprimand.

réprimander, *vb.* chide, reprove, reprimand.

réprimer, *vb.* quell.

reprise, *n.f.* recovery; turn; darn. **à plusieurs r.s,** repeatedly.

repriser, *vb.* darn.

réprobation, *n.f.* reprobation.

reproche, *n.m.* reproach.

reprocher, *vb.* reproach.

reproduction, *n.f.* reproduction.

reproduction exacte, *n.f.* clone.

reproduire, *vb.* reproduce.

réprouver, *vb.* censure.

reptile, *n.m.* reptile.

républicain, *adj. and n.m.* republican.

république, *n.f.* republic.

répudier, *vb.* repudiate.

répugnance, *n.f.* repugnance.

répulsion, *n.f.* repulsion.

réputation, *n.f.* reputation.

réputer, *vb.* consider, esteem.

requête, *n.f.* request, plea.

requin, *n.m.* shark.

requis, *adj.* required, necessary.

réquisition, *n.f.* requisition.

rescousse, *n.f.* rescue.

réseau, *n.m.* network.

réserve, *n.f.* reserve, reservation; qualification. **de r.,** spare, extra.

réservé, *adj.* aloof, reticent.

réserver, *vb.* reserve.

réserviste, *n.f.* reservist *(mil.).*

réservoir, *n.m.* tank, reservoir.

résidant, *adj.* resident.

résidence, *n.f.* residence, dwelling.

résider, *vb.* reside.

résidu, *n.m.* residue.

résignation, *n.f.* resignation.

résigner, *vb.* resign.

résiliation, *n.f.* cancelling.

résine, *n.f.* resin.

résistance, *n.f.* endurance, resistance.

résister (à), *vb.* resist.

résolu, *adj.* resolute.

résolument, *adv.* resolutely.

résolution, *n.f.* resolution.

résonnance, *n.f.* resonnance.

résonnant, *adj.* resonant.

résonner, *vb.* resound.

résoudre, *vb.* resolve, solve.

respect (-spè), *n.m.* respect.

respectable, *adj.* decent, respectable.

respecter, *vb.* respect.

respectif, *adj.* respective.

respectueux, *adj.* respectful.

respiration, *n.f.* respiration, breathing.

respirer, *vb.* breathe.

resplendir, *vb.* gleam resplendently.

responsabilité, *n.f.* responsibility.

responsable, *adj.* responsible; accountable, liable.

ressaisir, *vb.* regain possession.

ressemblance, *n.f.* likeness.

ressembler (à), *vb.* resemble. **se r.,** look alike.

ressentiment, *n.m.* resentment.

ressentir, *vb.* feel, resent, show.

resserrer, *vb.* tighten, compress.

ressort, *n.m.* spring, elasticity.

ressortir, *vb.* stand out.

ressource, *n.f.* resort, resource.

ressusciter, *vb.* revive, resuscitate.

restaurant, *n.m.* restaurant.

restaurateur, *n.m.* restorer; restaurant man.

restauration, *n.f.* restoration.

restaurer, *vb.* restore.

reste, *n.m.* remainder, rest, remnant.

rester, *vb.* remain, stay.

restituer, *vb.* give back, restore.

restreindre, *vb.* restrict.

restrictif, *adj.* restrictive.

restriction, *n.f.* restriction.

résultat, *n.m.* outcome, upshot, result.

résulter, *vb.* result.

résumé, *n.m.* summing up.

résumer, *vb.* sum up.

rétablir, *vb.* restore, reëstablish. **se r.,** recover.

rétablissement, *n.m.* recovery.

retard, *n.m.* delay. **en r.,** late; slow.

retarder, *vb.* delay, retard; be slow.

retenir, *vb.* retain; keep; hold (back); detain. **se r. de,** refrain from.

rétentif, *adj.* retentive.

retentir, *vb.* resound.

retentissant, *adj.* reëchoing.

réticence, *n.f.* silence, reticence.

retirer, *vb.* withdraw. **se r.,** retire, retreat.

retoucher, *vb.* retouch, alter.

retour, *n.m.* return. **de r.,** back.

retourner, *vb.* go back, invert, return. **se r.,** turn around.

retrait, *n.m.* contraction, retraction.

retraite, *n.f.* retreat; privacy.

retrancher, *vb.* cut off, curtail.

rétrécir, *vb.* shrink, contract.

rétribution, *n.f.* salary, recompense.

retrousser, *vb.* turn up.

retrouver, *vb.* find; recover.

réunion, *n.f.* meeting, convention, reunion.

réunir, *vb.* unite. **se r.,** assemble.

réussir, *vb.* succeed.

réussite, *n.f.* successful outcome.

revanche, *n.f.* revenge. **en r.,** in return.

rève, *n.m.* dream.

réveil, *n.m.* awaking; revival.

réveiller, *vb.* wake (up), rouse, arouse.

révélateur, 1. *adj.* revealing. **2.** *n.m.* revealer.

révélation, *n.f.* revelation.

révéler, *vb.* disclose, reveal.

revenant, *n.m.* ghost, specter.

revendeur, *n.m.* retailer, old-clothes dealer.

revendiquer, *vb.* claim.

revenir, *vb.* come back, return, recur; amount to.

revenu, *n.m.* income, revenue.

rêver, *vb.* dream.

réverbérer, *vb.* reverberate.

révéremment, *adv.* reverently.

révérence, *n.f.* reverence; bow, curtsy.

révérend, *adj.* reverend.

révérer, *vb.* revere.

rêverie, *n.f.* dreaming, reverie.

revers, *n.m.* reverse, wrong side; lapel.

revêtir, *vb.* clothe; assume.

rêveur, 1. *n.m.* dreamer. **2.** *adj.* pensive.

réviser, *vb.* revise.

réviseur, *n.m.* reviser, inspector.

révision, *n.f.* revision, review.

revivre, *vb.* revive.

révocation, *n.f.* revocation, annulment.

revoir, *vb.* see again. **au r.,** good-bye.

révolte, *n.f.* revolt.

révolter, *vb.* **se r.,** revolt.

révolution, *n.f.* revolution, turn.

révolutionnaire, *adj. and n.m.* revolutionary.

revolver, *n.m.* revolver.

révoquer, *vb.* revoke.

revue, *n.f.* review, magazine.

rez-de-chaussée, *n.m.* ground floor.

rhétorique, *n.f.* rhetoric.

rhinocéros, *n.m.* rhinoceros.

rhubarbe, *n.f.* rhubarb.

rhum, *n.m.* rum.

rhumatisme, *n.m.* rheumatism.

rhume, *n.m.* cold.

ricaner, *vb.* laugh objectionably.

riche, *adj.* rich, wealthy.

richesse, *n.f.* wealth.

ricocher, *vb.* ricochet, spring back.

rictus, *n.m.* grin.

ride, *n.f.* wrinkle, ripple.

rideau, *n.m.* curtain.

rider, *vb.* ripple, wrinkle.

ridicule, 1. *n.m.* ridicule. **2.** *adj.* ridiculous.

ridiculiser, *vb.* ridicule.

rien, *pron.* nothing.

rieur, *n.m.* laugher.

rigide, *adj.* rigid.

rigidité, *n.f.* rigidity.

rigole, *n.f.* ditch, gutter.

rigoureux, *adj.* rigorous.

rigueur, *n.f.* rigor.

rime, *n.f.* rhyme.

rimer, *vb.* rhyme.

rince-doigts, *n.m.* finger bowl.

rincer, *vb.* rinse.

ripaille, *n.f.* feasting, revelry.

riposte, *n.f.* retort.

rire, 1. *n.m.* laugh, laughter. **2.** *vb.* laugh.

ris, *n.m.* laugh; reef in a sail; sweetbread.

risée, *n.f.* laugh, mocking.

risible, *adj.* laughable.

risque, *n.m.* risk.

risquer, *vb.* risk.

risque-tout, *n.m.* daredevil.

rissoler, *vb.* brown, as in cooking.

rite, *n.m.* rite.

rituel, *adj.* ritual.

rivage, *n.m.* shore, bank.

rival, *adj. and n.m.* rival.

rivaliser, *vb.* compete, rival.

rivalité, *n.f.* rivalry.

rive, *n.f.* bank.

river, vb. clinch.
rivet, n.m. rivet.
rivière, n.f. river.
rixe, n.f. brawl.
riz, n.m. rice.
rizière, n.f. rice field.
robe, n.f. dress, gown, frock, robe.
robinet, n.m. faucet, tap.
robuste, adj. hardy, strong, robust.
roc, n.m. rock.
rocailleux, adj. rocky, rough.
rocher, n.m. rock.
rocheux, adj. rocky.
rock, adj. rock (music).
rôder, vb. prowl.
rôdeur, n.m. prowler.
rogner, vb. pare, trim down.
rognon, n.m. kidney.
rogue, adj. proud, arrogant.
roi, n.m. king.
rôle, n.m. role, part.
Romain, n.m. Roman.
romain, adj. Roman.
roman, n.m. novel.
romance, n.f. ballad.
romancier, n.m. novelist.
romanesque, adj. romantic.
roman-feuilleton, n.m. serial.
romanichel, n.m. gypsy.
romantique, adj. romantic.
romarin, n.m. rosemary.
rompre, vb. break.
ronce, n.f. bramble.
rond, 1. n.m. round; circle. 2. adj. round.
ronde, n.f. round, patrol.
rondeur, n.f. roundness.
ronflement, n.m. snoring, roar.
ronfler, vb. snore.
ronger, vb. gnaw; fret.
rongeur, adj. and n.m. rodent.
ronronner, vb. purr, murmur.
rosaire, n.m. rosary.
rosbif, n.m. roast beef.
rose, 1. n.f. rose. 2. adj. pink.
roseau, n.m. reed.
rosée, n.f. dew.
rosier, n.m. rosebush.
rossignol, n.m. nightingale.
rôt, n.m. roast (meat).
rotation, n.f. rotation.
rotatoire, adj. rotary.
roter, vb. belch.
rôti, n.m. roast.
rôtir, vb. roast.
rotondité, n.f. rotundity.
rotule, n.f. kneecap.
roturier, adj. commonplace, vulgar.
roublardise, n.f. cunningness.
roue, n.f. wheel.
roué, 1. n.m. rake, debauchee. 2. adj. crafty.
rouge, 1. n.m. rouge. 2. adj. red. r. foncé, maroon.
rouge-gorge, n.m. robin.
rougeole, n.f. measles.
rougeur, n.f. flush, blush.
rougir, vb. blush.
rouille, n.f. rust.
rouiller, vb. rust.
rouir, vb. soak.

rouleau, n.m. roll, roller, scroll, coil.
roulement, n.m. rolling, winding; rotation.
rouler, vb. roll, wind.
roulette, n.f. little wheel, caster.
roulis, n.m. roll.
Roumain, n.m. Rumanian (person).
roumain, 1. n.m. Rumanian (language). 2. adj. Rumanian.
Roumanie, n.f. Rumania.
rousseur, n.f. redness. tache de r., freckle.
roussir, vb. scorch.
route, n.f. road, way, course, route. en r., under way. en r. de, on the way to.
routine, n.f. routine.
routinier, adj. routine.
roux, adj. and n.m. red, reddish-brown.
royal, adj. royal, regal.
royaliste, adj. and n.m.f. royalist.
royaume, n.m. kingdom.
royauté, n.f. royalty.
ruban, n.m. ribbon, tape.
rubis, n.m. ruby.
rubrique, n.f. red ocher; heading.
ruche, n.f. hive.
rude, adj. rough, gruff, harsh; rugged.
rudesse, n.f. harshness.
rudiment, n.m. rudiment, element.
rudimentaire, adj. rudimentary.
rudoyer, vb. bully.
rue, n.f. street, road.
ruée, n.f. rush.
ruelle, n.f. lane, alley.
ruer, vb. se r., rush.
rugir, vb. roar.
rugissement, n.m. roar.
rugueux, adj. rugged, harsh.
ruine, n.f. ruin.
ruiner, vb. ruin.
ruineux, adj. ruinous.
ruisseau, n.m. brook, creek, gutter.
ruisseler, vb. stream, flow.
rumeur, n.f. rumor, noise.
ruminant, adj. and n.m. ruminant.
ruminer, vb. chew the cud.
rupture, n.f. break, rupture.
rural, adj. rural.
ruse, n.f. trick; cunning.
rusé, adj. sly, cunning.
Russe, n.m.f. Russian (person).
russe, 1. n.m. Russian (language). 2. adj. Russian.
Russie, n.f. Russia.
rusticité, n.f. rusticity, uncouthness.
rustique, adj. rustic.
rustre, adj. and n.m. boor, boorish.
rythme, n.m. rhythm.
rythmique, adj. rhythmical.

S

sabbat, n.m. Sabbath.
sable, n.m. sand.
sabler, vb. sand; quaff.
sablier, n.m. sandbox, sandman; hourglass.
sablonneux, adj. sandy.
sablonnière, n.f. sand pit.
sabord, n.m. porthole.
sabot, n.m. hoof; wooden shoe.
sabotage, n.m. sabotage.
saboter, vb. sabotage.
saboteur, n.m. saboteur; awkward bungler.
sabre, n.m. saber.
sac, n.m. sack, bag. s. à main, pocketbook. s. à air, airbag.
saccade, n.f. jerk.
saccager, vb. ransack, sack, plunder.
sacerdoce, n.m. priesthood.
sachet, n.m. sachet.
sacre, n.m. consecration, coronation.
sacré, adj. sacred.
sacrement, n.m. sacrament.
sacrer, vb. crown, consecrate; curse.
sacrifice, n.m. sacrifice.
sacrifier, vb. sacrifice.
sacrilège, n.m. sacrilege.
sacristain, n.m. sexton.
sac tyrolien, n.m. backpack.
sadisme, n.m. sadism.
sagace, adj. shrewd.
sagacité, n.f. sagacity.
sage, 1. n.m. sage. 2. adj. wise, good.
sage-femme, n.f. midwife.
sagesse, n.f. wisdom.
saignée, n.f. bleeding.
saigner, vb. bleed.
saillant, adj. prominent, projecting.
saillie, n.f. projection.
saillir, vb. protrude.
sain, adj. healthy, sound, wholesome. s. d'esprit, sane.
saindoux, n.m. lard.
saint, 1. n.m. saint. 2. adj. holy.
Saint-Esprit, n.m. Holy Ghost.
sainteté, n.f. holiness.
saisie, n.f. seizure.
saisir, vb. seize, grasp, snatch, grab.
saisissement, n.m. chill, seizure.
saison, n.f. season.
salade, n.f. salad.
saladier, n.m. salad bowl or dish.
salaire, n.m. wages, earnings, pay.
salarié, 1. adj. salaried. 2. n.m.f. person earning a salary.
sale, adj. dirty.
saler, vb. salt.
saleté, n.f. dirt.
salière, n.f. saltcellar.
salin, adj. salt, salty.
salir, vb. get dirty.

salive, *n.f.* saliva.

salle, *n.f.* (large) room, hall, auditorium, (hospital) ward. **s. de. classe,** classroom. **s. de bain,** bathroom.

salon, *n.m.* parlor.

saltimbanque, *n.m.* charlatan, buffoon.

salubre, *adj.* healthful.

salubrité, *n.f.* healthfulness.

saluer, *vb.* bow, greet, salute.

salut, *n.m.* bow, salute; salvation.

salutaire, *adj.* wholesome, beneficial.

salutation, *n.f.* greeting.

salve, *n.f.* salvo, salute.

samedi, *n.m.* Saturday.

sanctifier, *vb.* hallow.

sanction, *n.f.* sanction.

sanctionner, *vb.* sanction, countenance.

sanctuaire, *n.m.* sanctuary.

sandale, *n.f.* sandal.

sang, *n.m.* blood.

sang-froid, *n.m.* calmness, composure.

sanglant, *adj.* bloody.

sangler, *vb.* strap, fasten.

sanglier, *n.m.* (wild) boar.

sanglot, *n.m.* sob.

sangloter, *vb.* sob.

sangsue, *n.f.* leech.

sanguin, *adj.* pertaining to blood.

sanguinaire, *adj.* bloodthirsty.

sanitaire, *adj.* sanitary.

sans, *prep.* without, out of. **s. doute,** without doubt. **s. plomb,** unleaded. **s. repos,** restless. **s. valeur,** worthless. **s. nom,** nameless.

sans-souci, *adj.* carefree, careless.

santé, *n.f.* health.

saper, *vb.* sap, weaken.

saphir, *n.m.* sapphire.

sapin, *n.m.* fir.

sarcasme, *n.m.* sarcasm.

sarcastique, *adj.* sarcastic.

sarcler, *vb.* weed, root out.

sardine, *n.f.* sardine.

sardonique, *adj.* sardonic.

satanique, *adj.* satanic.

satellite, *n.m.* satellite.

satin, *n.m.* satin.

satire, *n.f.* satire.

satiriser, *vb.* satirize.

satisfaction, *n.f.* satisfaction.

satisfaire, *vb.* satisfy.

satisfaisant, *adj.* satisfactory.

saturer, *vb.* saturate.

satyre, *n.m.* satyr.

sauce. *n.f.* sauce, **s. piquante,** catsup.

saucisse, *n.f.* sausage.

sauf, 1. *prep.* but. **2.** *adj.* safe. **sain et sauf,** safe and sound.

sauf-conduit, *n.m.* safe-conduct pass.

sauge, *n.f.* sage.

saugrenu, *adj.* absurd, preposterous.

saule, *n.f.* willow.

saumon, *n.m.* salmon.

saumure, *n.f.* brine.

saut, *n.m.* spring, jump.

saute, *n.f.* wind shift.

sauter, *vb.* spring, jump, leap, skip. **faire s.,** blow up.

sauterelle, *n.f.* grasshopper.

sautiller, *vb.* hop.

sauvage, 1. *n.m.f.* savage. **2.** *adj.* wild, savage.

sauvegarde, *n.f.* safeguard.

sauvegarder, *vb.* safeguard.

sauve-qui-peut, *n.m.* stampede, panic.

sauver, *vb.* save. **se s.,** run away.

sauvetage, *n.m.* salvage.

sauveteur, *n.m.* rescuer, saver.

sauveur, *n.m.* savior, Saviour.

savane, *n.f.* prairie.

savant, 1. *n.m.* scholar. **2.** *adj.* learned.

saveur, *n.f.* flavor, savor, zest.

savoir, 1. *vb.* know, be aware, have knowledge. **vouloir s.,** wonder. **2.** *n.m.* knowledge.

savoir-faire, *n.m.* poise, ability.

savoir-vivre, *n.m.* breeding, manners.

savon, *n.m.* soap.

savonner, *vb.* soap, lather.

savourer, *vb.* relish.

savoureux, *adj.* tasty.

scabreux, *adj.* rough, harsh, indelicate.

scalper, *vb.* scalp.

scandale, *n.m.* scandal.

scandaleux, *adj.* scandalous.

scandaliser, *vb.* shock.

scander, *vb.* scan.

Scandinave, *n.m.f.* Scandinavian.

scandinave, *adj.* Scandinavian.

Scandinavie, *n.f.* Scandinavia.

scarabée, *n.m.* beetle.

scarlatine, *n.f.* scarlet fever.

sceau, *n.m.* seal.

scélérat, *n.m.* villain, criminal, knave, ruffian.

sceller, *vb.* seal.

scénario, *n.m.* scenario.

scène, *n.f.* scene, stage.

scénique, *adj.* scenic.

scepticisme, *n.m.* skepticism.

sceptique, 1. *n.m.f.* skeptic. **2.** *adj.* skeptical.

sceptre, *n.m.* scepter.

schampooing, *n.m.* shampoo.

schisme, *n.m.* schism.

sciatique, *n.f.* sciatica.

scie, *n.f.* saw.

science, *n.f.* science.

science-fiction, *n.f.* science fiction.

scientifique, *adj.* scientific.

scier, *vb.* saw.

scinder, *vb.* divide.

scintiller, *vb.* twinkle.

scission, *n.f.* cutting, division.

sclérose, *n.f.* sclerosis.

scolaire, *adj.* scholastic. **système s.,** school system.

scolastique, *adj.* scholastic.

scrofule, *n.f.* scrofula.

scrupule, *n.m.* scruple.

scrupuleux, *adj.* scrupulous.

scruter, *vb.* scan, scrutinize.

scrutin, *n.m.* ballot, poll.

sculpter (-lt-), *vb.* carve.

sculpteur (-lt-), *n.f.* sculptor.

sculpture (-lt-), *n.f.* sculpture.

se (sə), *pron.* himself, herself, itself, oneself, themselves, each other.

séance, *n.f.* sitting; session; meeting.

séant, *adj.* sitting, proper.

seau, *n.m.* pail, bucket.

sec *m.,* **sèche** *f. adj.* dry.

sécession, *n.f.* secession.

sécher, *vb.* dry.

sécheresse, *n.f.* dryness, drought.

second (-g-), *adj.* second.

secondaire (-g-), *adj.* secondary.

seconde (-g-), *n.f.* second.

seconder (-g-), *vb.* second, help.

secouer, *vb.* shake, rouse.

secourir, *vb.* relieve, succor, help.

secours, *n.m.* help, relief. **premiers s.,** first aid. **poste de s.,** first aid station. **au s.!,** help!

secousse, *n.f.* jar, shock.

secret, *adj. and n.m.* secret.

secrétaire, *n.m.f.* secretary.

sécréter, *vb.* secrete.

sécrétion, *n.f.* secretion.

sectaire, *adj.* sectarian.

secte, *n.f.* sect.

secteur, *n.m.* district, sector.

section, *n.f.* section.

sectionner, *vb.* cut into sections.

séculaire, *adj.* secular.

séculier, *adj.* secular, lay.

sécurité, *n.f.* safety.

sédatif, *adj. and n.m.* sedative.

sédentaire, *adj.* sedentary, stationary.

séditieux, *adj.* seditious.

sédition, *n.f.* sedition.

séduction, *n.f.* seduction.

séduire, *vb.* seduce, attract, allure.

séduisant, *adj.* attractive.

segment, *n.m.* segment.

ségrégation, *n.f.* segregation.

seigle, *n.m.* rye.

seigneur, *n.m.* lord, peer.

seigneurie, *n.f.* lordship.

sein, *n.m.* bosom, breast.

seize, *adj. and n.m.* sixteen.

seizième, *adj. and n.m.* sixteenth.

séjour, *n.m.* stay. **lieu de s.,** resort.

séjourner, *vb.* sojourn.

sel, *n.m.* salt.

sélection, *n.f.* selection.

selle, *n.f.* saddle.

seller, *vb.* saddle.

sellette, *n.f.* little stool or saddle.

selon, *prep.* according to.

seltz, *n.m.* **eau de s.,** soda water.

semailles, *n.f.pl.* sowing.

semaine, *n.f.* week; weekly pay.

semblable, *adj.* similar, alike.

semblant, *n.m.* show; appearance. **faire s.,** make believe.

sembler, *vb.* seem, appear.

semelle, *n.f.* sole.

semence, *n.f.* seed.

semer, *vb.* sow.

semestre, *n.m.* semester.

semeur, *n.m.* sower.

sémillance, *n.f.* briskness, liveliness.

sémitique, *adj.* Semitic.

semoncer, *vb.* lecture, scold.

sénat, *n.m.* senate.

sénateur, *n.m.* senator.

sénile, *adj.* senile.

sénilité, *n.f.* senility.

sens (-s), *n.m.* meaning, sense; direction.

sensation, *n.f.* sensation, feeling.

sensationnel, *adj.* sensational.

sensé, *adj.* sensible.

sensibilité, *n.f.* sensitivity.

sensible, *adj.* sensible, sensitive; conscious (of).

sensitif, *adj.* sensitive.

sensualisme, *n.m.* sensualism.

sensualité, *n.f.* sensuality.

sensuel, *adj.* sensual.

sentence, *n.f.* sentence.

sentencieux, *adj.* sententious.

senteur, *n.f.* smell.

sentier, *n.m.* path.

sentiment, *n.m.* feeling.

sentimental, *adj.* sentimental.

sentimentalité, *n.f.* sentimentality.

sentinelle, *n.f.* sentry.

sentir, *vb.* feel; smell.

séparable, *adj.* separable.

séparation, *n.f.* separation, parting.

séparé, *adj.* separate.

séparer, *vb.* separate, segregate. **se s.,** part.

sept (sĕt), *adj. and n.m.* seven.

septembre, *n.m.* September.

septième (sĕt-), *adj. and n.m.* seventh.

septique, *adj.* septic.

sépulcre, *n.m.* sepulcher.

séquestrer, *vb.* withdraw, remove.

serein, *adj.* serene, placid.

sérénade, *n.f.* serenade.

sérénité, *n.f.* serenity.

serf, 1. *n.m.* serf. 2. *adj.* in serfdom or the like.

sergent, *n.m.* sergeant.

série, *n.f.* series.

sérieux, 1. *adj.* serious, sober, grave. 2. *n.m.* gravity.

serin, *n.m.* canary.

seringue, *n.f.* syringe.

serment, *n.m.* oath.

sermon, *n.m.* sermon.

sermonner, *vb.* lecture, preach.

serpent, *n.m.* snake, serpent.

serpenter, *vb.* wind, wander.

serre, *n.f.* green-house; claw.

serré, *adj.* tight.

serre-joint, *n.m.* clamp.

serrer, *vb.* tighten, squeeze, press, crowd, shake (hands). **s. dans ses bras,** hug.

serrure, *n.f.* lock.

sérum, *n.m.* serum.

servage, *n.m.* servitude.

servant, 1. *adj.* serving. 2. *n.m.* server, gunner.

servante, *n.f.* maid.

serviable, *adj.* helpful.

service, *n.m.* service, favor. **être de s.,** be on duty.

serviette, *n.f.* napkin; towel; brief case.

servile, *adj.* menial.

servilité, *n.f.* servility.

servir, *vb.* serve. **se s. de,** use. **ne s. à rien,** be of no use.

serviteur, *n.m.* attendant, servant.

servitude, *n.f.* slavery.

session, *n.f.* session.

seuil, *n.m.* threshold.

seul, *adj.* alone, only, single.

seulement, *adv.* only, solely.

sève, *n.f.* sap.

sévère, *adj.* severe, stern.

sévérité, *n.f.* severity, rigor.

sévir, *vb.* punish, rage.

sevrer, *vb.* wean, withhold.

sexe, *n.m.* sex.

sexisme, *n.m.* sexism.

sexiste, *adj.* sexist.

sexuel, *adj.* sexual.

seyant, *adj.* becoming.

shrapnel, *n.m.* shrapnel.

si, 1. *adv.* so, so much, yes. **si . . . que,** however (+*adj.*). 2. *conj.* if, whether.

siècle, *n.m.* century.

siège, *n.m.* seat; siege.

siéger, *vb.* sit, convene, reside.

sien, *pron.* **le sien, la sienne,** his, hers, its.

sieste, *n.f.* siesta.

siffler, *vb.* whistle, hiss.

sifflerie, *n.f.* hissing, whistling.

sifflet, *n.m.* whistle.

signal, *n.m.* signal.

signalement, *n.m.* description, details.

signaler, *vb.* point out.

signature, *n.f.* signature.

signe, *n.m.* sign. **s. de la tête,** nod. **faire s. à,** beckon.

signer, *vb.* sign. **se s.,** cross oneself.

significatif, *adj.* significant, meaningful.

signification, *n.f.* significance, meaning.

signifier, *vb.* signify, mean.

silence, *n.m.* silence.

silencieux, *adj.* noiseless, silent.

silex, *n.m.* flint.

sillage, *n.m.* wake, course.

sillon, *n.m.* furrow.

sillonner, *vb.* plow.

similaire, *adj.* similar.

simple, *adj.* plain, simple, mere; no-frills.

simplicité, *n.f.* simplicity.

simplifier, *vb.* simplify.

simulation, *n.f.* simulation.

simuler, *vb.* pretend.

simultané, *adj.* simultaneous.

sincère, *adj.* candid, sincere.

sincérité, *n.f.* candor, sincerity.

singe, *n.m.* monkey; imitator.

singularité, *n.f.* singularity; peculiar trait.

singulier, *adj. and n.m.* singular; peculiar, strange.

sinistre, 1. *n.m.* disaster. 2. *adj.* sinister.

sinon, *conj.* otherwise.

sinueux, *adj.* winding, sinuous.

sirène, *n.f.* siren.

sirop, *n.m.* syrup.

siroter, *vb.* sip.

site, *n.m.* site.

sitôt, *adv.* as soon (as).

situation, *n.f.* situation, position, location, office.

situer, *vb.* situate, locate.

six (sês), *adj. and n.m.* six.

sixième (-z-), *adj. and n.m.* sixth.

ski, *n.m.* ski. **faire du s.,** ski, *vb.*

skieur, *n.m.* skier.

smoking, *n.m.* dinner-jacket, tuxedo.

sobre, *adj.* temperate, sober.

sobriété, *n.f.* moderation, temperance.

sobriquet, *n.m.* nickname.

soc, *n.m.* plowshare.

sociable, *adj.* sociable.

social, *adj.* social.

socialisme, *n.m.* socialism.

socialiste, *adj. and n.m.f.* socialist.

société, *n.f.* society; company.

sociologie, *n.f.* sociology.

sociologiste, *n.m.* sociologist.

sœur, *n.f.* sister.

soi-disant, *adj.* so-called.

soie, *n.f.* silk; bristle.

soierie, *n.f.* silk goods.

soif, *n.f.* thirst. **avoir s.,** be thirsty.

soigné, *adj.* trim. **mal s.,** sloppy.

soigner, *vb.* tend, look after, take care of.

soigneux, *adj.* careful.

soi-même, *pron.* oneself.

soin, *n.m.* care. **prendre s. de,** take care of.

soir, *n.m.* evening. **hier s.,** last night. **ce s.,** tonight. **le s.,** at night.

soirée, *n.f.* evening.

soit, *vb.* so be it. **s. . . . s.,** whether . . . or. **s. que,** whether.

soixante (-s-), *adj. and n.m.* sixty.

soixante-dix, *adj. and n.m.* seventy.

sol, *n.m.* earth, soil, ground.

solaire, *adj.* solar.

soldat, *n.m.* soldier.

solde, *n.f.* balance.

sole, *n.f.* sole.

solécisme, *n.m.* solecism.

soleil, *n.m.* sun, sunshine. **coucher du s.,** sunset. **lever du s.,** sunrise.

solennel, adj. solemn.
solenniser, vb. solemnize.
solennité, n.f. solemnity.
solidaire, adj. jointly binding.
solidariser, vb. se s., unite, join together.
solidarité, n.f. joint responsibility.
solide, adj. and n.m. solid.
solidifier, vb. solidify.
solidité, n.f. solidity.
soliloque, n.m. soliloquy.
soliste, n.m. soloist.
solitaire, adj. lonely, lonesome.
solitude, n.f. solitude.
solliciter, vb. solicit, ask, apply.
sollicitude, n.f. solicitude.
soluble, adj. soluble.
solution, n.f. solution.
solvable, adj. solvent.
sombre, adj. dark, dim, gloomy, somber.
sombrer, vb. sink.
sommaire, n.m. summary.
sommation, n.f. appeal, summons.
somme, 1. n.f. amount, sum. **2.** n.m. nap.
sommeil, n.m. sleep. **avoir s.,** be sleepy.
sommeiller, vb. doze, slumber.
sommer, vb. summon.
sommet, n.m. top, peak, summit.
somnolence, n.f. drowsiness.
somnolent, adj. drowsy, sleepy.
somptueux, adj. lavish, sumptuous.
son m., **sa** f., **ses** pl. adj. his, her, its.
son, n.m. sound, ring; bran.
sonate, n.f. sonata.
sonder, vb. fathom; probe.
songe, n.m. dream.
songer à, vb. think of, dream.
songeur, 1. adj. dreamy, thoughtful. **2.** n.m. dreamer.
sonner, vb. sound, ring, strike.
sonnerie, n.f. ringing.
sonnette, n.f. bell.
sonore, adj. sonorous.
sophiste, n.m. sophist.
soprano, n.m. soprano.
sorcellerie, n.f. sorcery.
sorcier, n.m. wizard.
sorcière, n.f. witch.
sordide, adj. sordid.
sort, n.m. lot.
sorte, n.f. sort, kind. **de s. que,** so that.
sortie, n.f. exit, way out.
sortilège, n.m. sorcery.
sortir, vb. go (come, get) out.
sot m., **sotte** f. adj. silly, stupid, foolish, dumb.
sottise, n.f. foolishness.
sou, n.m. cent. **sans le s.,** penniless.
soubassement, n.m. basement.
soubresaut, n.m. bound, jerk.
souche, n.f. stub, stump.
souci, n.m. care, worry, concern.

soucier, vb. se s. (de), care, worry (about).
soucieux, adj. anxious.
soucoupe, n.f. saucer.
soudain, adj. sudden.
soudaineté, n.f. suddenness.
soude, n.f. soda.
souder, vb. solder, fuse.
souffle, n.m. breath.
souffler, vb. blow.
soufflet, n.m. bellows; blow, slap.
souffleter, vb. slap one's face.
souffrance(s), n.f. (pl.) misery, pain, suffering.
souffrir, vb. suffer, bear.
soufre, n.m. sulphur.
souhait, n.m. wish.
souhaiter, vb. wish for.
souiller, vb. soil, defile.
souillure, n.f. stain, dirt.
soulager, vb. relieve, alleviate.
soûler, vb. fill with food and drink, inebriate.
soulever, vb. lift, raise, arouse.
soulier, n.m. shoe.
souligner, vb. underline.
soumettre, vb. submit, subdue.
soumis, adj. obedient, submissive.
soumission, n.f. submission.
soupape, n.f. valve.
soupçon, n.m. suspicion.
soupçonner, vb. suspect.
soupçonneux, adj. suspicious.
soupe, n.f. soup.
souper, n.m. supper.
soupir, n.m. sigh.
soupirer, vb. sigh. **s. après,** yearn for.
souple, adj. flexible.
souplesse, n.f. suppleness, pliability.
source, n.f. source; spring.
sourcil, n.m. eyebrow.
sourciller, vb. frown.
sourcilleux, adj. haughty, disdainful.
sourd, adj. deaf.
sourd-muet, n.m. deaf mute.
souricière, n.f. (mouse)trap.
sourire, n.m. and vb. smile.
souris, n.f. mouse.
sournois, adj. sly.
sous, prep. under.
souscription, n.f. subscription.
souscrire, vb. subscribe.
sous-estimer, vb. underestimate.
sous-louer, vb. sublet.
sous-marin, n.m. submarine.
sous-produit, n.m. by-product.
soussigné, adj. undersigned.
sous-sol, n.m. basement.
sous-titre, n.m. subtitle.
soustraction, n.f. subtraction.
soustraire, vb. subtract.
soutane, n.f. cassock.
soute, n.f. storeroom.
soutenir, vb. support, uphold, maintain; claim; back up.
soutenu, adj. steady.
souterrain, adj. underground.
soutien, n.m. support.
soutien-gorge, n.m. brassière.

souvenance, n.f. recall, recollection.
souvenir, 1. n.m. remembrance, memory. **2.** vb. **se s. de,** remember.
souvent, adv. often.
souverain, n.m. ruler, sovereign.
souveraineté, n.f. sovereignty.
soyeux, adj. silky.
spacieux, adj. spacious.
spasme, n.m. spasm.
spatule, n.f. spatula.
spécial, adj. special.
spécialiser, vb. specialize.
spécialiste, n.m.f. specialist.
spécialité, n.f. specialty.
spécifier, vb. specify.
spécifique, adj. specific.
spécimen, n.m. specimen.
spectacle, n.m. sight, show.
spectaculaire, adj. spectacular.
spectateur, n.m. spectator.
spectre, n.m. ghost; spectrum.
spéculation, n.f. speculation.
spéculer, vb. speculate.
sphère, n.f. sphere.
spinal, adj. spinal.
spiral, adj. spiral.
spirale, n.f. spiral.
spirite, n.m.f. spiritualist.
spiritisme, n.m. spiritualism.
spirituel, adj. spiritual; witty.
spiritueux, adj. pertaining to alcohol.
splendeur, n.f. splendor.
splendide, adj. splendid.
spolier, vb. plunder, pillage.
spontané, adj. spontaneous.
spontanéité, n.f. spontaneity.
sporadique, adj. sporadic.
sport, n.m. sport.
sportif, adj. of sport.
squelette, n.m. skeleton.
stabiliser, vb. stabilize.
stabilité, n.f. stability.
stable, adj. stable, steady.
stage, n.m. period of probation.
stagflation, n.f. stagflation.
stagnant, adj. stagnant.
stalle, n.f. stall.
stance, n.f. stanza.
station, n.f. stand, stop, station (subway).
stationnaire, adj. stationary.
stationner, vb. park.
statique, adj. static.
statistique, n.f. statistics.
statue, n.f. statue.
statuer, vb. decree, decide.
stature, n.f. stature.
statut, n.m. statute.
sténographe, n.m.f. stenographer.
sténographie, n.f. stenography.
stéréophonique, adj. stereophonic.
stérile, adj. barren.
stériliser, vb. sterilize.
stéthoscope, n.m. stethoscope.
stigmatiser, vb, mark, stigmatize.
stimulant, n.m. stimulus.
stimuler, vb. stimulate.

stipuler, vb. stipulate.

stoïque, adj. and n.m.f. stoic.

store, n.m. (window) shade, blind.

stratagème, n.m. stratagem.

stratégie, n.f. strategy.

stratégique, adj. strategic.

strict (-kt), adj. severe, strict.

strier, vb. mark, streak, make grooves.

structure, n.f. structure.

stuc, n.m. stucco.

studieux, adj. studious.

stupéfait, adj. astounded.

stupéfiant, n.m. narcotic, dope.

stupéfier, vb. astound.

stupeur, n.f. amazement.

stupide, adj. stupid.

stupidité, n.f. stupidity.

style, n.m. style.

styler, vb. train, teach.

stylet, n.m. stiletto.

stylographe, stylo, n.m. fountain pen.

suavité, n.f. suavity.

subalterne, adj. and n.m.f. junior (rank).

subdiviser, vb. subdivide.

subir, vb. undergo, bear.

subit, adj. sudden.

subjectif, adj. subjective.

subjonctif, adj. and n.m. subjunctive.

subjuguer, vb. subdue, overcome.

sublime, adj. sublime, exalted.

submerger, vb. submerge, flood.

subordonné, adj. and n.m. subordinate.

subordonner, vb. subordinate.

subreptice, adj. surreptitious.

subséquent, adj. subsequent.

subside, n.m. subsidy.

subsister, vb. subsist, live.

substance, n.f. substance.

substantiel, adj. substantial.

substantif, n.m. noun.

substituer, vb. substitute.

substitution, n.f. substitution.

subtil (-l), adj. subtle.

subtilité, n.f. subtlety.

subvention, n.f. grant, subsidy.

subventionner, vb. subsidize.

subversif, adj. subversive.

suc, n.m. juice.

succéder à, vb. succeed, follow.

succès, n.m. success; hit.

successeur, n.m. successor.

successif, adj. successive.

succession, n.f. succession.

succion, n.f. suction.

succomber, vb. succumb.

succursale, n.f. branch office.

sucer, vb. suck.

sucre, n.m. sugar.

sucrer, vb. add sugar.

sud (-d), n.m. south.

sudation, n.f. sweating.

sud-est, n.m. southeast.

sud-ouest, n.m. southwest.

Suède, n.f. Sweden.

Suédois, n.m. Swede.

suédois, adj. and n.m. Swedish.

suer, vb. sweat.

sueur, n.m. sweat.

suffire, vb. suffice.

suffisance, n.f. adequacy, conceit.

suffisant, adj. sufficient, adequate; conceited.

suffixe, n.m. suffix.

suffoquer, vb. suffocate.

suffrage, n.m. suffrage.

suggérer, vb. suggest.

suggestion, n.f. suggestion.

suicide, n.m. suicide.

suicider, vb. se s., kill oneself.

suie, n.f. soot.

suif, n.m. tallow.

suinter, vb. seep.

Suisse, 1. n.m. Swiss. **2.** n.f. Switzerland.

suisse, adj. Swiss.

suite, n.f. sequence; retinue; (pl.) results, aftermath. **et ainsi de s.,** and so on. **tout de s.,** at once.

suivant, 1. n.m. follower. **2.** adj. next, following, subsequent. **3.** prep. by, according to.

suivi, adj. followed, coherent.

suivre, vb. follow; attend. **faire s.,** forward.

sujet, 1. n.m. subject; topic. **2.** adj. subject. **s. à,** liable to.

sujétion, n.f. subjection, slavery.

superbe, adj. superb, magnificent.

superficie, n.f. surface.

superficiel, adj. superficial, shallow.

superflu, adj. superfluous.

supérieur, adj. and n.m. superior, higher, upper; senior.

supériorité, n.f. superiority.

superlatif, adj. and n.m. superlative.

superstar, n.m. superstar.

superstitieux, adj. superstitious.

superstition, n.f. superstition.

suppléant, adj. and n.m. assistant, substitute.

suppléer, vb. substitute.

supplément, n.m. supplement.

supplémentaire, adj. extra. **heures s.s,** overtime.

supplice, n.m. punishment, torture.

supplier, vb. beseech, entreat, beg, supplicate.

support, n.m. support, stand.

supporter, vb. support, bear, stand, endure.

supposer, vb. suppose, assume.

supposition, n.f. assumption, conjecture, supposition.

suppôt, n.m. implement, tool, agent.

suppression, n.f. suppression.

supprimer, vb. suppress, put down, take out.

supputation, n.f. computation.

supputer, vb. compute.

suprématie, n.f. supremacy.

suprême, adj. supreme.

sur, prep. on, upon, over.

sûr, adj. safe, sure, secure.

surabonder, vb. be very abundant.

suranné, adj. out-of-date.

surcroît, n.m. addition.

surdité, n.f. deafness.

suret, adj. sour.

sûreté, n.f. safety, security, reliability.

surface, n.f. surface, area.

surgélateur, n.m. deep freeze.

surgir, vb. spring up, arise.

surhumain, adj. superhuman.

surintendant, n.m. superintendent.

sur-le-champ, adv. at once, immediately.

surmener, vb. overwork.

surmonter, vb. overcome, surmount.

surnaturel, adj. and n.m. supernatural.

surnom, n.m. nickname.

surpasser, vb. 'surpass.

surplis, n.m. surplice.

surplomber, vb. overhang.

surplus, n.m. surplus, excess.

surprendre, vb. surprise.

surprise, n.f. surprise.

sursaut, n.m. start.

sursauter, vb. give a start.

sursis, n.m. delay, putting off.

surtaxe, n.f. surtax.

surtout, 1. n.m. overcoat. **2.** adv. above all.

surveillance, n.f. supervision, watch.

surveillant, n.m. superintendent.

surveiller, vb. supervise, watch over.

survenir, vb. happen.

survie, n.f. survival.

survivance, n.f. survival.

survivre, vb. survive.

susceptible, adj. susceptible; liable.

suspect (-kt), adj. suspicious.

suspecter, vb. suspect.

suspendre, vb. suspend, hang, sling.

suspension, n.f. suspension.

suspicion, n.f. suspicion.

sustenter, vb. sustain, bulwark.

svelte, adj. slender, slim.

syllabe, n.f. syllable.

sylphide, n.f. sylph.

sylvestre, adj. sylvan, woody.

sylviculture, n.f. forestry.

symbole, n.m. symbol.

symboliser, vb. symbolize.

symétrie, n.f. symmetry.

sympathie, n.f. sympathy. **avoir de la s. pour,** like.

sympathique, adj. congenial, likeable.

sympathiser, vb. sympathize.

symphonie, n.f. symphony.

symptôme, n.m. symptom.

synchroniser, vb. synchronize.

syndical, adj. of a trade-union.

syndicat, n.m. syndicate **s. ouvrier,** trade-union.

syndrome, n.m. syndrome.

synonyme, n.m. synonym.

syntaxe, n.f. syntax.

synthèse, *n.f.* synthesis.
synthétique, *adj.* synthetic.
systématique, *adj.* systematic.
système, *n.m.* system.

T

tabac (-bå), *n.m.* tobacco.
tabernacle, *n.m.* tabernacle.
table, *n.f.* table. **t. des matières,** index.
tableau, *n.m.* picture. **t. noir,** blackboard.
tabler, *vb.* count on, depend.
tablette, *n.f.* tablet.
tablier, *n.m.* apron.
tabou, *n.m.* taboo.
tabouret, *n.m.* stool.
tache, *n.f.* spot, stain, blot, smear.
tâche, *n.f.* task; assignment.
tacher, *vb.* spot, stain, blot.
tâcher, *vb.* try.
tacite, *adj.* tacit, silent.
taciturne, *adj,* unspeaking.
tact (-kt), *n.m.* tact.
tacticien, *n.m.* tactician.
tactique, 1. *adj.* of tactics, tactical. **2.** *n.f.* tactics.
taffetas, *n.m.* taffeta.
taie, *n.f.* pillowcase.
taillade, *n.f.* slash.
taille, *n.f.* waist, figure, size.
tailler, *vb.* trim, cut.
tailleur, *n.m.* tailor.
taire, *vb.* keep quiet. **se t.,** be silent.
talent, *n.m.* ability, talent.
talon, *n.m.* heel.
talus, *n.m.* slope.
tambour, *n.m.* drum.
tambourin, *n.m.* tambourine.
tamis, *n.m.* sieve.
tampon, *n.m.* plug, pad.
tamponner, *vb.* plug; run together.
tan, *n.m.* tan (leather).
tandis que, *conj.* while, whereas.
tangible, *adj.* tangible.
tanguer, *vb.* cover with pitch.
tant, *adv.* so much, so many. **t. que,** as long as.
tante, *n.f.* aunt.
tantième, *n.m.* part, percentage.
tantôt, *adv.* presently, soon.
tapage, *n.m.* din.
tapageur, *adj.* rowdy.
taper, *vb.* pat, knock, tap; type.
tapir, *vb.* **se t.,** squat, cower, lurk.
tapis, *n.m.* carpet, rug.
tapisserie, *n.f.* tapestry.
tapissier, *n.m.* upholsterer.
taquiner, *vb.* tease.
taquinerie, *n.f.* teasing.
tard, *adv.* late.
tarder, *vb.* delay.
tardif, *adj.* slow, tardy, late.
tarière, *n.f.* auger.
tarif, *n.m.* scale of charges;

rate; fare. **t. douanier,** tariff.
tartan, *n.m.* plaid.
tarte, *n.f.* pie.
tartre, *n.m.* tartar.
tas, *n.m.* heap, pile.
tasse, *n.f.* cup.
tasser, *vb.* pack, fill up.
tâter, *vb.* feel.
tâtonner, *vb.* grope.
taudis, *n.m.* hovel.
taupe, *n.f.* mole.
taureau, *n.m.* bull.
taux, *n.m.* rate.
taverne, *n.f.* tavern.
taxe, *n.f.* tax. **t. (à la) valeur ajoutée,** value-added tax.
taxer, *vb.* tax, assess.
taxi, *n.m.* cab, taxi.
te (ta), *pron.* you, yourself.
technicien, *n.m.* technician.
technique, 1. *n.f.* technique. **2.** *adj.* technical.
technologie, *n.f.* technology.
teindre, *vb.* dye.
teint, *n.m.* complexion.
teinte, *n.f.* tint, shade.
teinter, *vb.* tint, stain.
teinture, *n.f.* dye.
teinturier, *n.m.* dry-cleaner, dyer.
tel, *adj.* such.
télégramme, *n.m.* telegram.
télégraphe, *n.m.* telegraph.
télégraphie, *n.f.* telegraph. **t. sans fil,** *abbrev.* T.S.F., radio, wireless.
télégraphier, *vb.* telegraph.
téléphone, *n.m.* telephone. **coup de t.,** ring.
téléphoner, *vb.* telephone.
télescope, *n.m.* telescope.
télescoper, *vb.* crash, run together.
télévision, *n.f.* television.
tellement, *adv.* so much.
téméraire, *adj.* rash.
témoignage, *n.m.* testimony, token.
témoigner, *vb.* testify.
témoin, *n.m.* witness.
tempe, *n.f.* temple.
tempérament, *n.m.* temper, temperament.
tempérance, *n.f.* temperance.
tempérant, *adj.* temperate.
température, *n.f.* temperature.
tempéré, *adj.* temperate.
tempérer, *vb.* moderate, calm, lessen.
tempête, *n.f.* storm, tempest.
tempétueux, *adj.* tempestuous.
temple, *n.m.* temple.
temporaire, *adj.* temporary.
temporiser, *vb.* temporize, evade.
temps (tän), *n.m.* time; weather.
tenace, *adj.* tenacious.
ténacité, *n.f.* tenacity.
tenailles, *n.f.pl.* tongs.
tendance, *n.f.* tendency, trend, leaning.
tendre, 1. *adj.* tender, fond, loving. **2.** *vb.* tend, extend.

tendresse, *n.f.* tenderness, fondness.
tendu, *adj.* tense; uptight.
ténèbres, *n.f.pl.* gloom, darkness.
ténébreux, *adj.* dismal.
teneur, *n.m.* **t. de livres,** bookkeeper.
tenir, *vb.* hold.
tennis (-s), *n.m.* tennis.
ténor, *n.m.* tenor.
tension, *n.f.* strain; stress.
tentacule, *n.m.* tentacle.
tentatif, *adj.* tentative.
tentation, *n.f.* temptation.
tentative, *n.f.* attempt.
tente, *n.f.* tent; awning.
tenter, *vb.* tempt, try, attract.
tenture, *n.f.* wallcovering.
tenue, *n.f.* rig; conduct, manners.
ténuité, *n.f.* tenuity, unimportance.
térébenthine, *n.f.* turpentine.
terme, *n.m.* term, period; end.
terminaison, *n.f.* ending.
terminer, *vb.* end.
terminologie, *n.f.* terminology.
terminus, *n.m.* terminus.
terne, *adj.* drab, dull, dim, dingy.
ternir, *vb.* tarnish, dull.
terrain, *n.m.* ground(s).
terrasse, *n.f.* terrace.
terrasser, *vb.* heap up, embank; knock down, conquer.
terre, *n.f.* earth, ground, land. **pomme de t.,** potato. **à t.,** ashore.
terrestre, *adj.* earthly.
terreur, *n.f.* terror, fright, fear.
terrible, *adj.* terrible, awful, tremendous.
terrifier, *vb.* terrify.
territoire, *n.m.* territory.
terroir, *n.m.* soil.
terroriser, *vb.* terrorize.
tertre, *n.m.* mound.
tesson, *n.m.* broken piece, fragment.
testament, *n.m.* testament, will.
testateur, *n.m.* testator.
tête, *n.f.* head. **tenir t. à,** cope with.
téter, *vb.* suck.
téton, *n.m.* breast.
texte, *n.m.* text.
textile, *adj.* textile.
textuel, *adj.* textual.
texture, *n.f.* texture.
thé, *n.m.* tea.
théâtral, *adj.* theatrical.
théâtre, *n.m.* theater.
théière, *n.f.* teapot.
thème, *n.m.* theme.
théologie, *n.f.* theology.
théorie, *n.f.* theory.
théorique, *adj.* theoretical.
thermomètre, *n.m.* thermometer.
thésauriser, *vb.* hoard.
thèse, *n.f.* thesis.
thym, *n.m.* thyme.

ticket, n.m. check, ticket, coupon.

tiède, adj. lukewarm.

tiédir, vb. make or become cool.

tien, pron. le tien, la tienne, yours.

tiers, n.m. third.

Tiers Monde, n.m. Third World.

tige, n.f. stem, stalk.

tigre, n.m. tiger.

tilleul, n.m. linden, limetree.

timbre, n.m. stamp. t.-poste, postage stamp.

timbrer, vb. stamp.

timide, adj. timid, shy, coy, bashful.

timidité, n.f. timidity.

timoré, adj. timorous.

tintamarre, n.m. racket.

tinter, vb. ring, knell, tinkle.

tirailleur, n.m. sharpshooter.

tire, n.f. pull, yank.

tire-bouchon, n.m. corkscrew.

tirer, vb. draw, pull; shoot.

tiret, n.m. blank.

tiroir, n.m. drawer.

tisane, n.f. drink, broth.

tisser, vb. weave.

tisserand, n.m. weaver.

tissu, n.m. web; cloth, fabric.

titre, n.m. title, right.

titrer, vb. invest with a title.

toast (-t), n.m. toast.

toaster, vb. toast.

toile, n.f. web; canvas; linen.

toilette, n.f. toilet; dressing, dress.

toison, n.f. fleece.

toit, n.m. roof.

toiture, n.f. roofing.

tolérance, n.f. tolerance.

tolérer, vb. tolerate, bear.

tomate, n.f. tomato.

tombe, n.f. grave.

tombeau, n.m. tomb.

tombée, n.f. fall, decline.

tomber, vb. fall. laisser t., drop.

ton, n.m. tone, pitch.

ton m., ta f., tes pl. adj. your.

tondeuse, n.f. (lawn) mower.

tondre, vb. shear; mow.

tonique, adj. and n.m. tonic.

tonne, n.f. ton; barrel.

tonneau, n.m. cask, barrel.

tonner, vb. thunder.

tonnerre, n.m. thunder.

topaze, n.f. topaz.

topographie, n.f. topography.

torche, n.f. torch.

tordre, vb. twist, wrench, wring. se t., writhe.

torpeur, n.f. torpor.

torpille, n.f. torpedo.

torrent, n.m. torrent.

torride, adj. torrid.

torse, n.m. torso.

tort, n.m. wrong. avoir t., be wrong.

tortiller, vb. twist, wiggle.

tortu, adj. crooked.

tortue, n.f. turtle, tortoise.

torture, n.f. torture.

torturer, vb. torture.

tôt, adv. soon, early.

total, adj. and n.m. total.

totalisateur, n.m. adding machine.

totaliser, vb. total, add up.

totalitaire, adj. totalitarian.

totalité, n.f. entirety.

touchant, prep. concerning.

touche, n.f. key.

toucher, 1. n.m. touch. 2. vb. touch; collect; affect; border on.

touffe, n.f. tuft, bunch.

touffu, adj. bushy.

toujours, adv. always, still, ever, yet.

toupie, n.f. top (child's toy).

tour, 1. n.m. turn; trick; stroll. faire le t. de, go around. 2. n.f. tower.

tourbe, n.f. rabble.

tourbillon, n.m. whirl. t. d'eau, whirlpool. t. de vent, whirlwind.

tourbillonner, vb. whirl.

tourelle, n.f. turret.

touriste, n.m.f. tourist.

tourment, n.m. torment.

tourmenter, vb. torment.

tourne-disques, n.m. record player.

tournedos, n.f. beefsteak.

tournée, n.f. round.

tourner, vb. turn, revolve, spin.

tournesol, n.m. sunflower.

tournevis, n.m. screwdriver.

tournoi, n.m. tournament.

tournure, n.f. figure.

tousser, vb. cough.

tout, 1. adj.m. toute f., tous m.pl., toutes f.pl. all, each every. 2. pron. everything. t. les deux, both. t. d'un coup, all at once. t. de même, all the same. pas du t., not at all.

toutefois, adv. however.

tout-puissant, adj. almighty.

toux, n.f. cough.

toxique, adj. toxic.

tracasser, vb. worry.

trace, n.f. trace, step, track, footprint.

tracer, vb. outline, trace.

tracteur, n.m. tractor.

traction, n.f. traction.

tradition, n.f. tradition.

traditionnel, adj. traditional.

traducteur, n.m. translator.

traduction, n.f. translation.

traduire, vb. translate.

trafic, n.m. traffic.

trafiquer, vb. traffic, carry on dealings.

tragédie, n.f. tragedy.

tragique, adj. tragic.

trahir, vb. betray.

trahison, n.f. treason.

train, n.m. train.

traînard, n.m. loiterer, dawdler.

traîne, n.f. train of dress.

traîneau, n.m. sled, sleigh.

traîner, vb. drag, haul.

traire, vb. milk.

trait, n.m. feature; draft; shot. t. d'union, hyphen.

traité, n.m. treaty.

traitement, n.m. treatment.

traiter, vb. treat, deal.

traître, n.m. traitor.

traîtrise, n.f. treachery.

trajet, n.m. crossing.

trame, n.f. web (woof); plan, plot.

tramer, vb. devise.

tramway, n.m. streetcar.

tranchant, adj. sharp, crisp.

tranche, n.f. slice.

tranchée, n.f. trench.

trancher, vb. cut.

tranquille (-l), adj. quiet. laisser t., leave alone.

tranquilliser (-l-), vb. soothe, make tranquil.

tranquillité (-l-), n.f. quiet, stillness.

transaction, n.f. transaction.

transe, n.f. fright, fear.

transférer, vb. transfer.

transformer, vb. transform.

transfuser, vb. transfuse.

transfusion, n.f. transfusion.

transition (-z-), n.f. transition.

transitoire (-z-), adj. transitory.

transmettre, vb. transmit, convey, send.

transparent, adj. transparent.

transpiration, n.f. perspiration.

transpirer, vb. perspire.

transplanter, vb. transplant.

transport, n.m. transfer, transport, transportation; bliss, ecstasy.

transporter, vb. transport, transfer, convey.

transposer, vb. transpose.

transsexuel, adj. transsexual.

travail, n.m. work, job, labor.

travailler, vb. work.

travailleur, 1. n.m. worker, laborer. 2. adj. industrious.

travée, n.f. span.

travers, n.m. breadth. à t., across, through. de t., askance, awry.

traversée, n.f. crossing.

traverser, vb. cross.

traversin, n.m. bolster.

travesti, adj. transvestite.

travestir, vb. disguise.

trébucher, vb. stumble, trip.

trèfle, n.m. clover; club (cards).

treillis, n.m. denim.

treize, adj. and n.m. thirteen.

tréma, n.m. dieresis.

tremblement, n.m. trembling. t. de terre, earthquake.

trembler, vb. tremble, shake, quake.

trembloter, vb. quiver.

trémousser, vb. flutter.

trempe, n.f. temper, cast.

tremper, vb. soak, drench, temper.

trente, adj. and n.m. thirty.

trépasser, vb. die.

trépied, n.m. tripod, trivet.

très, *adv.* very.

trésor, *n.m.* treasure, treasury; darling.

trésorier, *n.m.* treasurer.

tressaillement, *n.m.* thrill; start.

tressaillir, *vb.* thrill; start.

tresse, *n.f.* braid.

tresser, *vb.* braid.

tréteau, *n.m.* trestle.

trêve, *n.f.* truce.

triangle, *n.m.* triangle.

tribade, *n.f.* Lesbian.

tribu, *n.f.* tribe.

tribulation, *n.f.* tribulation.

tribut, *n.m.* tribute.

tributaire, *adj.* tributary.

tricher, *vb.* cheat.

tricherie, *n.f.* cheating.

tricoter, *vb.* knit.

trier, *vb.* sort.

trimestre, *n.m.* term.

trimestriel, *adj.* quarterly.

trinquer, *vb.* touch glasses in making a toast.

triomphant, *adj.* triumphant.

triomphe, *n.m.* triumph.

triompher, *vb.* triumph.

triple, *adj. and n.m.* triple.

tripoter, *vb.* fiddle with, dabble in; bother.

triste, *adj.* sad.

tristesse, *n.f.* sadness.

trivial, *adj.* trivial.

trivialité, *n.f.* triviality.

troc, *n.m.* barter.

trois, *adj. and n.m.* three.

troisième, *adj.* third.

trompe, *n.f.* horn, trumpet, elephant's trunk.

trompe l'œil, *n.m.* make-believe, sham.

tromper, *vb.* deceive, cheat. **se t.,** be wrong, make a mistake.

tromperie, *n.f.* deceit.

trompette, *n.f.* trumpet.

trompeur, *adj.* deceitful.

tronc, *n.m.* trunk.

trône, *n.m.* throne.

trop, *adv.* too; too much, too many.

trophée, *n.m.* trophy.

tropical, *adj.* tropical.

tropique, *n.m.* tropic.

troquer, *vb.* barter, dicker, trade.

trot, *n.m.* trot.

trotter, *vb.* trot.

trottiner, *vb.* trot, jog.

trottoir, *n.m.* sidewalk.

trou, *n.m.* hole.

trouble, *n.m.* disturbance, riot.

troublé, *adj.* anxious, worried.

troubler, *vb.* perturb.

trouer, *vb.* pierce, bore.

troupe, *n.f.* troop.

troupeau, *n.m.* herd, flock, drove.

troupier, *n.m.* soldier, trooper.

trousseau, *n.m.* bunch; outfit.

trousser, *vb.* truss up, turn up.

trouvaille, *n.f.* discovery.

trouver, *vb.* find. **se t.,** be located.

truc, *n.m.* trick; thing.

truelle, *n.f.* trowel.

truite, *n.f.* trout.

truquer, *vb.* fake.

trust, *n.m.* trust.

T.S.F., *n.f.* radio.

tu, *pron.* you.

tube, *n.m.* tube, pipe.

tuberculeux, *adj.* tuberculous.

tuberculose, *n.f.* tuberculosis.

tuer, *vb.* kill.

tuerie, *n.f.* slaughter, massacre.

tuile, *n.f.* tile.

tulipe, *n.f.* tulip.

tuméfier, *vb.* make swollen.

tumulte, *n.m.* tumult, turmoil, uproar.

tunique, *n.f.* tunic.

tunnel, *n.m.* tunnel.

Turc *m.,* **Turque** *f.n.* Turk.

turc, *n.m.* Turkish (language).

turc *m.,* **turque** *f. adj.* Turkish.

Turquie, *n.f.* Turkey.

tutelle, *n.f.* tutelage, protection.

tuteur, *n.m.* guardian.

tutoyer, *vb.* use "tu" (familiar form) to.

tuyau, *n.m.* pipe; hose.

tympan, *n.m.* eardrum.

type, *n.m.* type; fellow, guy.

typique, *adj.* typical.

tyran, *n.m.* tyrant.

tyrannie, *n.f.* tyranny.

tyranniser, *vb.* tyrannize.

tzigane, *n.* gypsy.

U

ubiquité, *n.f.* ubiquity.

ulcère, *n.m.* ulcer.

ultérieur, *adj.* ulterior, further.

ultime, *adj.* ultimate, last.

un *m.,* **une** *f.* **1.** *art.* a. **2.** *adj. and n.m.* one.

unanime, *adj.* unanimous.

unanimité, *n.f.* unanimity.

unifier, *vb.* unify.

uniforme, *adj. and n.m.* uniform.

union, *n.f.* union.

unique, *adj.* unique; only.

unir, *vb.* unite.

unisexuel, *adj.* unisex.

unisson, *n.m.* unison.

unité, *n.f.* unit, unity.

univers, *n.m.* universe.

universel, *adj.* universal.

université, *n.f.* university, college.

urbain, *adj.* urban.

urgence, *n.f.* urgency.

urgent, *adj.* urgent, pressing.

urne, *n.f.* urn; ballot box.

urticaire, *n.f.* hives.

usage, *n.m.* use; custom.

usager, *adj.* for daily use.

usé, *adj.* shabby, worn-out.

user, *vb.* wear out.

usine, *n.f.* factory.

ustensile, *n.f.* utensil.

usuel, *adj.* usual.

usure, *n.f.* wear and tear; usury; interest.

usurper, *vb.* usurp.

utile, *adj.* helpful, useful.

utilisation, *n.f.* use.

utiliser, *vb.* use.

utilité, *n.f.* utility.

utopie, *n.f.* utopia.

V

vacance, *n.* vacancy; *(pl.)* vacation.

vacarme, *n.m.* uproar.

vaccin, *n.m.* vaccine.

vacciner, *vb.* vaccinate.

vache, *n.f.* cow.

vaciller (-l-), *vb.* waver.

vacuité, *n.f.* emptiness, vacuity.

vagabond, *adj.* vagrant.

vagabonder, *vb.* roam, tramp.

vague, 1. *n.f.* wave. **2.** *adj.* vague.

vaguer, *vb.* wander.

vaillant, *adj.* valiant, brave, gallant.

vain, *adj.* idle, vain, futile.

vaincre, *vb.* defeat.

vainqueur, *n.m.* victor.

vaisseau, *n.m.* ship.

vaisselle, *n.f.* dishes.

valeur, *n.f.* valor; value, worth; *(pl.)* securities.

valeureux, *adj.* brave, valorous.

valide, *adj.* valid.

valise, *n.f.* suitcase.

vallée, *n.f.* valley.

vallon, *n.m.* valley, vale.

valoir, *vb.* be worth. **v. mieux,** be better.

valse, *n.f.* waltz.

vandale, *n.m.f.* vandal.

vanille, *n.f.* vanilla.

vanité, *n.f.* conceit, vanity.

vaniteux, *adj.* vain.

vantard, *adj.* boastful.

vanter, *vb.* extol. **se v.,** boast, brag.

vapeur, 1. *n.m.* steamship. **2.** *n.f.* vapor, steam.

vaporisateur, *n.f.* vaporizer, spray.

variation, *n.f.* variation, change.

varicelle, *n.f.* chicken-pox.

varier, *vb.* vary.

variété, *n.f.* variety.

variole, *n.f.* smallpox.

vase, *n.m.* vase, jar, pot.

vasectomie, *n.f.* vasectomy.

vaseux, *adj.* slimy.

vassal, *n.f.* vassal.

vaste, *adj.* vast, spacious.

vaurien, *n.m.* worthless person, idler.

veau, *n.m.* calf.

végéter, *vb.* vegetate.

véhicule, *n.m.* vehicle.

veille, *n.f.* eve, day before.

veiller, *vb.* watch over, sit up.

veine, *n.f.* vein; luck.

velours, *n.m.* velvet. **v. côtelé,** corduroy.

velouté, *adj.* like velvet.
velu, *adj.* hairy.
vendange, *n.f.* vintage.
vendeur, *n.m.* seller; clerk, salesman.
vendre, *vb.* sell.
vendredi, *n.m.* Friday.
vénéneux, *adj.* poisonous.
vénérer, *vb.* venerate.
vengeance, *n.f.* revenge.
venger, *vb.* avenge. **se v.**, get revenge.
venimeux, *adj.* poisonous.
venin, *n.m.* poison.
venir, *vb.* come. **v. de**, have just. . . . **/ à v.**, forthcoming.
vent, *n.m.* wind.
vente, *n.f.* sale.
venteux, *adj.* windy.
ventilateur, *n.m.* fan.
ventiler, *vb.* ventilate.
ventre, *n.m.* belly.
venue, *n.f.* advent, arrival.
vêpres, *n.f.pl.* vespers.
ver (-r), *n.m.* worm.
veracité, *n.f.* veracity.
véranda, *n.f.* porch.
verbe, *n.m.* verb.
verbeux, *adj.* wordy, verbose.
verdeur, *n.f.* greenness, sharpness, vigor.
verdict (-kt), *n.m.* verdict.
verdir, *vb.* make or become green.
verge, *n.f.* rod.
verger, *n.m.* orchard.
vérification, *n.f.* check.
vérifier, *vb.* check, confirm.
véritable, *adj.* genuine, real.
verité, *n.f.* truth.
vermine, *n.f.* vermin.
vernir, *vb.* varnish.
vernis, *n.m.* varnish.
vérole, *n.f.* **petite v.**, smallpox.
verre, *n.m.* glass.
verrou, *n.m.* bolt.
verrouiller, *vb.* bolt.
vers, **1.** *n.m.* verse. **2.** *prep.* toward.
verse, *adj.* green.
verser, *vb.* pour, shed.
versifier, *vb.* versify.
version, *n.f.* version, translation.
vert, *adj.* green.
vertical, *adj.* upright, vertical.
vertige, *n.m.* dizziness.
vertigineux, *adj.* dizzy.
vertu, *n.f.* virtue.
vertueux, *adj.* virtuous.
verveux, *adj.* lively, animated.
vessie, *n.f.* bladder.
veste, *n.f.* jacket.
vestiaire, *n.m.* cloak-room.
vestibule, *n.m.* hall, lobby.
vestige, *n.m.* vestige, remains.
veston, *n.m.* jacket, coat.
vêtement, *n.m.* garment; *(pl.)* clothes.
vétéran, *n.m.* veteran.
vétérinaire, *n.m.* veterinary.
vêtir, *vb.* clothe.
véto, *n.m.* veto.
veuf, *n.m.* widower.
veuve, *n.f.* widow.

vexation, *n.f.* vexation.
vexer, *vb.* vex.
viaduc, *n.m.* viaduct.
viande, *n.f.* meat.
vibrant, *adj.* vibrant, vibrating.
vibration, *n.f.* vibration.
vibrer, *vb.* vibrate.
vicaire, *n.m.* vicar.
vice, *n.m.* vice.
vice-roi, *n.m.* viceroy.
vicieux, *adj.* vicious.
vicomte, *n.m.* viscount.
victime, *n.f.* victim.
victoire, *n.f.* victory.
victorieux, *adj.* victorious.
vidange, *n.f.* emptying, cleaning.
vide, **1.** *n.m.* emptiness, vacuum, blank, gap. **2.** *adj.* empty, void, vacant, blank.
vidéodisque, *n.m.* videodisc.
vider, *vb.* empty, drain.
vie, *n.f.* life.
vieil, *adj.* old.
vieillard, *n.m.* old man.
vieille, **1.** *n.f.* old woman. **2.** *adj.* (*f.*) old.
vieillesse, *n.f.* old age.
vieillir, *vb.* age.
vierge, *n.f.* virgin.
vieux, *adj.m.* old.
vif *m.*, **vive** *f.*, lively, quick, brisk, bright, vivacious.
vif-argent, *n.m.* quicksilver.
vigie, *n.f.* lookout man or station.
vigilance, *n.f.* vigilance.
vigilant, *adj.* watchful.
vigne, *n.f.* vine; vineyard.
vigoureux, *adj.* lusty, hardy, vigorous.
vigueur, *n.f.* vigor, force.
vil (-l), *adj.* vile.
vilain, *adj.* ugly, mean, wicked.
village (-l-), *n.m.* village.
ville (-l-), *n.f.* city, town.
villégiature (-l-), *n.f.* country holiday.
vin, *n.m.* wine.
vinaigre, *n.m.* vinegar.
vindicatif, *adj.* vindictive.
vingt (văn), *adj. and n.m.* twenty.
vingtaine (văn-), *n.f.* score.
vingtième (văn-), *adj. and n.m.* twentieth.
violateur, *n.m.* violator.
violation, *n.f.* violation.
violemment, *adj.* violently.
violence, *n.f.* violence.
violent, *adj.* violent.
violer, *vb.* violate.
violet, *adj.* purple, violet.
violette, *n.f.* violet.
violon, *n.m.* violin.
vipère, *n.f.* viper.
virgule, *n.f.* comma.
viril (-l), *adj.* manly.
virilité, *n.f.* manhood.
virtuel, *adj.* virtual.
virtuose, *n.m.f.* virtuoso.
virus (-s), *n.m.* virus.
vis (-s), *n.f.* screw.
visa, *n.m.* visa.
visage, *n.m.* face.

vis-à-vis, *adv.* opposite, across from.
viser, *vb.* aim.
visibilité, *n.f.* visibility.
visible, *adj.* visible.
visière, *n.f.* visor; keenness.
vision, *n.f.* vision.
visionnaire, *adj. and n.m.f.* visionary.
visite, *n.f.* call, visit.
visiter, *vb.* visit.
visiteur, *n.m.* visitor.
visqueux, *adj.* viscous, sticky.
visser, *vb.* screw.
visuel, *adj.* visual.
vital, *adj.* vital.
vitalité, *n.f.* vitality.
vitamine, *n.f.* vitamin.
vite, *adv.* quick, fast.
vitesse, *n.f.* speed, rate; gear. **changer de v.**, shift gears.
vitrail, *n.m.* (church) window.
vitre, *n.f.* pane.
vitrine, *n.f.* display case, shop-window.
vitupération, *n.f.* vituperation.
vivace, *adj.* long-lived; perennial (of plant).
vivacité, *n.f.* vivacity.
vivant, *adj.* alive.
vivement, *adv.* quickly, smartly, vividly.
vivre, *vb.* live.
vocabulaire, *n.m.* vocabulary.
vocal, *adj.* vocal.
vocation, *n.f.* vocation.
vœu (vœ), *n.m.* vow.
vogue, *n.f.* vogue.
voici, *vb.* here is, behold.
voie, *n.f.* track, road. **v. d'eau**, leak.
voilà, *vb.* there is; behold.
voile, *n.m.* veil; sail.
voiler, *vb.* veil, hide.
voilure, *n.f.* sails.
voir, *vb.* see. **faire v.**, show.
voirie, *n.m.* dump.
voisin, **1.** *n.m.* neighbor. **2.** *adj.* nearby, adjoining.
voisinage, *n.m.* neighborhood.
voisiner, *vb.* act like a neighbor.
voiture, *n.f.* car, carriage. **en v.!**, all aboard!
voix, *n.f.* voice.
vol, *n.m.* flight; theft, robbery; ripoff.
volage, *adj.* fickle.
volaille, *n.f.* fowl, poultry.
volatil, *adj.* volatile.
volcan, *n.m.* volcano.
volcanique, *adj.* volcanic.
volée, *n.f.* flight, covey; herd.
voler, *vb.* fly; steal, rob; rip off.
volet, *n.m.* shutter, blind.
voleur, *n.m.* thief, robber.
vol frété, *n.m.* charter flight.
volontaire, **1.** *n.m.* volunteer. **2.** *adj.* voluntary, volunteer.
volonté, *n.f.* will.
volontiers, *adv.* gladly, willingly.
voltigement, *n.m.* flutter.
voltiger, *vb.* flutter; hover.

volubilité, *n.f.* volubility, glibness.

volume, *n.m.* volume.

volumineux, *adj.* bulky.

volupté, *n.f.* pleasure, voluptuousness.

vomir, *vb.* vomit.

vorace, *adj.* voracious.

votant, *n.m.* voter.

vote, *n.m.* vote.

voter, *vb.* vote.

votre *sg.,* **vos** *pl. adj.* your.

vôtre, *pron.* **le v.,** yours.

vouer, *vb.* vow.

vouloir, *vb.* want, wish, will. **v. dire,** mean. **v. savoir,** wonder. **v. bien,** be willing. **en v. à,** bear a grudge against.

vous, *pron.* you, yourself.

voûte, *n.f.* vault.

voûter, *vb.* arch.

voyage, *n.m.* journey, trip.

voyager, *vb.* travel.

voyageur, *n.m.* traveler, passenger.

voyageur de banlieue, *n.m.* commuter.

voyant, 1. *n.m.* clairvoyant. **2.** *adj.* gaudy, flashy.

voyelle, *n.f.* vowel.

vrai, *adj.* true, real.

vraisemblable, *adj.* probable, likely.

vraisemblance, *n.f.* probability.

vue, *n.f.* view, sight.

vue d'ensemble, *n.f.* overview.

vulcaniser, *vb.* vulcanize.

vulgaire, *adj.* vulgar, coarse, rude.

vulgarité, *n.f.* vulgarity.

vulnérable, *adj.* vulnerable.

W, X, Y, Z

wagon, *n.m.* coach, car.

wagon-lits, *n.m.* sleeping car.

wagon-restaurant, *n.m.* diner, dining-car.

watt, *n.m.* watt.

xérès (ks-), *n.m.* sherry.

xylophone (ks-), *n.m.* xylophone.

y, *adv.* there, in it, to it.

yacht, *n.m.* yacht.

zèbre, *n.m.* zebra.

zèle, *n.m.* zeal.

zélé, *adj.* zealous.

zénith, *n.m.* zenith.

zéro, *n.m.* zero.

zézayer, *vb.* lisp.

zibeline, *n.f.* sable.

zigzaguer, *vb.* zigzag.

zodiaque, *n.m.* zodiac.

zone, *n.f.* zone, district.

zoologie, *n.f.* zoology.

zoologique, *adj.* zoological. **jardin z.,** zoo.

English-French

A

a, *art.* un *m.,* une *f.*
aardvark, *n.* aardvark *m.*
abacus, *n.* abaque *m.*
abandon, *vb.* abandonner.
abandon, *n.* abandon *m.*
abandoned, *adj.* abandonné.
abandonment, *n.* abandon *m.*
abase, *vb.* abaisser; avilir.
abasement, *n.* abaissement *m.;* avilissement *m.*
abash, *vb.* déconcerter.
abate, *vb.* diminuer.
abatement, *n.* diminution *f.*
abbess, *n.* abbesse *f.*
abbey, *n.* abbaye *f.*
abbot, *n.* abbé *m.*
abbreviate, *vb.* abréger.
abbreviation, *n.* abréviation *f.*
abdicate, *vb.* abdiquer.
abdication, *n.* abdication *f.*
abdomen, *n.* abdomen *m.*
abdominal, *adj.* abdominal.
abduct, *vb.* enlever.
abduction, *n.* enlèvement *m.*
abductor, *n.* ravisseur *m.*
aberrant, *adj.* aberrant, égaré.
aberration, *n.* égarement *m.*
abet, *vb.* aider, encourager, appuyer.
abetment, *n.* encouragement *m.,* appui *m.*
abettor, *n.* aide *m.,* complice *m.*
abeyance, *n.* suspension *f.*
abhor, *vb.* détester.
abhorrence, *n.* aversion extrême *f.,* horreur *f.*
abhorrent, *adj.* odieux, répugnant (à).
abide, *vb.* (tolerate) supporter; (remain) demeurer; (a. by the law) respecter la loi.
abiding, *adj.* constant, durable.
ability, *n.* talent *m.*
abject, *adj.* abject.
abjuration, *n.* abjuration *f.*
abjure, *vb.* abjurer, renoncer à.
abjurer, *n.* personne *f.* qui abjure.
ablative, *adj. and n.* ablatif *m.*
ablaze, *adj.* en feu, en flammes.
able, *adj.* capable; (to be a.) pouvoir.
able-bodied, *adj.* fort, robuste.
able-bodied seaman, *n.* marin de première classe *m.*
ablution, *n.* ablution *f.*
ably, *adv.* capablement.
abnegate, *vb.* nier.
abnegation, *n.* abnégation *f.*
abnormal, *adj.* anormal.
abnormality, *n.* irrégularité *f.*
abnormally, *adv.* anormalement.
aboard, 1. *adv.* (naut.) à bord; (all a.) en voiture. 2. *prep.* à bord de.
abode, *n.* demeure *f.*
abolish, *vb.* abolir.

abolishment, *n.* abolissement *m.*
abolition, *n.* abolition *f.*
abominable, *adj.* abominable.
abominate, *vb.* abominer.
abomination, *n.* abomination *f.*
aboriginal, *adj.* aborigène, primitif.
abortion, *n.* avortement *m.*
abortive, *adj.* abortif, manqué.
abound, *vb.* abonder (en).
about, 1. *adv.* (approximately) à peu près; (around) autour; (to be a. to) être sur le point de. 2. *prep.* (concerning) au sujet de; (near) auprès de; (around) autour de.
about-face, *n.* volte-face *f.*
above, 1. *adv.* au-dessus. 2. *prep.* (higher than) au-dessus de; (more than) plus de.
aboveboard, *adj. and adv.* ouvertement, franchement.
abrasion, *n.* abrasion *f.*
abrasive, *adj.* abrasif.
abreast, *adv.* de front.
abridge, *vb.* abréger.
abridgment, *n.* abrégé *m.,* réduction *f.*
abroad, *adv.* à l'étranger.
abrogate, *vb.* abroger.
abrogation, *n.* abrogation *f.*
abrupt, *adj.* brusque; (steep) escarpé.
abruptly, *adv.* brusquement, subitement.
abruptness, *n.* brusquerie *f.,* précipitation *f.*
abscess, *n.* abcès *m.*
abscond, *vb.* disparaître, se dérober.
absence, *n.* absence *f.*
absent, *adj.* absent.
absentee, *n.* absent *m.,* manquant *m.*
absinthe, *n.* absinthe *f.*
absolute, *adj.* absolu.
absolutely, *adv.* absolument.
absoluteness, *n.* pouvoir absolu *m.;* arbitraire *m.*
absolution, *n.* absolution *f.*
absolutism, *n.* absolutisme *m.*
absolve, *vb.* absoudre.
absorb, *vb.* absorber.
absorbed, *adj.* absorbé, préoccupé.
absorbent, *n. and adj.* absorbant *m.*
absorbing, *adj.* absorbant, préoccupant.
absorption, *n.* absorption *f.*
abstain from, *vb.* s'abstenir de.
abstemious, *adj.* abstème.
abstinence, *n.* abstinence *f.*
abstract, 1. *n.* (book) extrait *m.* 2. *adj.* abstrait.
abstracted, *adj.* détaché, pensif.
abstraction, *n.* abstraction *f.*
abstruse, *adj.* caché, abstrus.
abundance, *n.* abondance *f.*
abundant, *adj.* abondant.

abundantly, *adv.* abondamment.
absurd, *adj.* absurde.
absurdity, *n.* absurdité *f.*
absurdly, *adv.* absurdement.
abuse, 1. *n.* (misuse) abus *m.;* (insult) injures *f.pl.* 2. *vb.* abuser de, injurier.
abusive, *adj.* (insulting) injurieux.
abusively, *adv.* abusivement, injurieusement.
abut, *vb.* s'embrancher (sur), aboutir (à).
abutment, *n.* contrefort *m.;* (of a bridge) culée *f.*
abyss, *n.* abîme *m.*
academic, *adj.* académique.
academic freedom, *n.* liberté de l'enseignement.
academy, *n.* académie *f.*
acanthus, *n.* acanthe *f.*
accede, *vb.* consentir.
accelerate, *vb.* accélérer.
acceleration, *n.* accélération *f.*
accelerator, *n.* accélérateur *m.*
accent, *n.* accent *m.*
accentuate, *vb.* accentuer.
accept, *vb.* accepter.
acceptability, *n.* acceptabilité *f.*
acceptable, *adj.* acceptable.
acceptably, *adv.* agréablement.
acceptance, *n.* acceptation *f.*
access, *n.* accès *m.*
accessible, *adj.* accessible.
accessory, *n. and adj.* accessoire *m.*
accident, *n.* accident *m.*
accidental, *adj.* accidentel.
accidentally, *adv.* accidentellement, par hasard.
acclaim, *vb.* acclamer.
acclamation, *n.* acclamation *f.*
acclimate, *vb.* acclimater.
acclivity, *n.* montée *f.,* rampe *f.*
accolade, *n.* accolade *f.*
accommodate, *vb.* (lodge) loger; (oblige) obliger.
accommodating, *adj.* accommodant, obligeant.
accommodation, *n.* (lodging) logement *m.*
accompaniment, *n.* accompagnement *m.*
accompanist, *n.* accompagnateur *m.,* accompagnatrice *f.*
accompany, *vb.* accompagner.
accomplice, *n.* complice *m.f.*
accomplish, *vb.* accomplir.
accomplished, *adj.* accompli, achevé.
accord, *n.* accord *m.*
accordance, *n.* conformité *f.*
accordingly, *adv.* (correspondingly) à l'avenant; (therefore) donc.
according to, *prep.* selon.
accordion, *n.* accordéon *m.*
accost, *vb.* aborder.
account, *n.* (comm.) compte *m.;* (narrative) récit *m.*
accountable for, *adj.* responsable de.

accountant, n. comptable m.

account for, vb. rendre compte de.

accounting, n. comptabilité f.

accouter, vb. habiller, équiper.

accouterments, n. équipements m.pl., accoutrements m.pl.

accredit, vb. accréditer.

accretion, n. accroissement m.

accrual, n. accroissement m.

accrue, vb. provenir.

accumulate, vb. entasser.

accumulation, n. entassement m.

accumulative, adj. (thing) qui s'accumule, (person) qui accumule.

accumulator, n. accumulateur m., accumulatrice f.

accuracy, n. précision f.

accurate, adj. précis.

accursed, adj. maudit, exécrable.

accusation, n. accusation f.

accusative, n. and adj. accusatif m.

accuse, vb. accuser.

accused, n. and adj. accusé m., accusée f.

accuser, n. accusateur m., accusatrice f.

accustom, vb. accoutumer.

accustomed, adj. accoutumé, habituel.

ace, n. as m.

acerbity, n. acerbité f., âpreté f.

acetate, n. acétate m.

acetic acid, n. acide acétique m.

acetylene, n. acétylène m.

ache, 1. n. douleur f. 2. vb. faire mal à.

achieve, vb. accomplir.

achievement, n. accomplissement m.

acid, adj. and n. acide m.

acidify, vb. acidifier.

acidity, n. acidité f.

acidosis, n. acidose f.

acid test, n. épreuve concluante f.

acidulous, adj. acidulé.

acknowledge, vb. reconnaître; (a. receipt of) accuser réception de.

acme, n. comble m., apogée m.

acne, n. acné f.

acolyte, n. acolyte m.

acorn, n. gland m.

acoustics, n. acoustique f.

acquaint, vb. informer (de); (be a.d with) connaître.

acquaintance, n. connaissance f.

acquainted, adj. connu, familier (avec).

acquiesce in, vb. acquiescer à.

acquiescence, n. acquiescement m.

acquire, vb. acquérir.

acquirement, n. acquis m., acquisition f.

acquisition, n. acquisition f.

acquisitive, adj. porté à acquérir.

acquit, vb. acquitter.

acquittal, n. acquittement m.

acre, n. arpent m., acre f.

acreage, n. superficie f.

acrid, adj. âcre.

acrimonious, adj. acrimonieux.

acrimony, n. acrimonie f., aigreur f.

acrobat, n. acrobate m.f.

across, 1. prep. à travers; (on the other side of) de l'autre côté de. 2. adv. en travers.

acrostic, n. acrostiche m.

act, 1. n. acte m. 2. vb. (do) agir; (play) jouer; (behave) se conduire.

acting, 1. n. (theater) jeu m.; feinte f. 2. adj. (taking the place of) suppléant; (comm.) gérant.

actinism, n. actinisme m.

actinium, n. actinium m.

action, n. action f.

activate, vb. activer.

activation, n. activation f.

activator, n. activateur m.

active, adj. actif.

activity, n. activité f.

actor, n. acteur m.

actress, n. actrice f.

actual, adj. réel.

actuality, n. réalité f., actualité f.

actually, adv. réellement, véritablement, en effet.

actuary, n. actuaire m.

actuate, vb. mettre en action, animer.

acumen, n. finesse f., pénétration f.

acupuncture, n. acuponcture f.

acute, adj. (geom.) aigu m., aiguë f.; (mind) fin.

acutely, adv. vivement, d'une manière poignante.

acuteness, n. finesse f., vivacité f.

adage, n. adage m., proverbe m.

adamant, adj. indomptable.

Adam's apple, n. pomme d'Adam f.

adapt, vb. adapter.

adaptable, adj. adaptable.

adaptability, n. faculté d'adaptation f.

adaptation, n. adaptation f.

adapter, n. qui adapte.

adaptive, adj. adaptable.

add, vb. (join) ajouter; (arith.) additionner.

adder, n. vipère f.

addict, n. personne adonnée à f.

addict oneself to, vb. s'adonner à.

addition, n. addition f.

additional, adj. additionel.

addle, 1. vb. corrompre, rendre couvi (of eggs). 2. adj. couvi, pourri.

address, 1. n. (on letters, etc.) adresse f.; (speech) discours

m. 2. vb. (a letter) adresser; (a person) adresser la parole à.

addressee, n. destinataire m.f.

adduce, vb. alléguer, avancer.

adenoid, adj. and n. adénoïde f.

adeptly, adv. habilement, adeptement.

adeptness, n. habileté f.

adequacy, n. suffisance f.

adequate, adj. suffisant.

adequately, adv. suffisamment, convenablement.

adhere, vb. adhérer.

adherence, n. adhérence f., attachement m.

adherent, n. adhérent m.

adhesion, n. adhésion f.

adhesive, adj. adhésif.

adhesiveness, n. propriété d'adhérer f.

adieu, n. and adv. adieu m.

adjacent, adj. adjacent.

adjective, n. adjectif m.

adjoin, vb. adjoindre, être contigu (à).

adjourn, vb. ajourner, tr. s'ajourner, intr.

adjournment, n. ajournement m.

adjunct, n. and adj. adjoint m., accessoire m.

adjust, vb. ajuster, arranger, régler.

adjuster, n. ajusteur m.

adjustment, n. ajustement m., accommodement m.

adjutant, n. capitaine adjudant major m.

administer, vb. administrer.

administration, n. administration f.

administrative, adj. administratif.

administrator, n. administrateur m.

admirable, adj. admirable.

admirably, adv. admirablement.

admiral, n. amiral m.

admiralty, n. amirauté f.

admiration, n. admiration f.

admire, vb. admirer.

admirer, n. admirateur m.

admiringly, adv. avec admiration.

admissible, adj. admissible.

admission, n. (entrance) entrée f.; (confession) aveu m.

admit, vb. (let in) laisser entrer; (confess) avouer.

admittance, n. entrée f.

admittedly, adv. de l'aveu de tout le monde.

admixture, n. mélange m.

admonish, vb. réprimander.

admonition, n. admonition f., avertissement m.

ado, n. fracas m.

adolescence, n. adolescence f.

adolescent, adj. and n. adolescent m.f.

adopt, vb. adopter.

adoption, n. adoption f.

adorable, adj. adorable.

adoration, n. adoration f.

adore, *vb.* adorer.

adorn, *vb.* orner.

adornment, *n.* ornement *m.*

adrenal glands, *n.pl.* capsules surrénales *f.pl.*

adrenalin, *n.* adrénaline *f.*

adrift, *adv. (naut.)* à la dérive.

adroit, *adj.* adroit.

adulate, *vb.* aduler.

adulation, *n.* adulation *f.*

adult, *adj. and n.* adulte *m.f.*

adulterant, *n.* adultérant *m.*

adulterate, *vb.* adultérer; (of wines, milk, etc.) frelater.

adulterer, *n.* adultère *m.*

adulteress, *n.* femme adultère *f.*

adultery, *n.* adultère *m.*

advance, 1. *n.* (motion forward) avancement *m.;* (progress) progrès *m.;* (pay) avances *f.pl.;* (in a.) d'avance. 2. *vb.* avancer.

advanced, *adj.* avancé.

advancement, *n.* avancement *m.,* progrès *m.*

advantage, *n.* avantage *m.*

advantageous, *adj.* avantageux.

advantageously, *adv.* avantageusement.

advent, *n.* venue *f.; (eccles.)* Avent *m.*

adventitious, *adj.* adventice, fortuit.

adventure, *n.* aventure *f.*

adventurer, *n.* aventurier *m.*

adventurous, *adj.* aventureux.

adventurously, *adv.* aventureusement.

adverb, *n.* adverbe *m.*

adverbial, *adj.* adverbial.

adversary, *n.* adversaire *m.*

adverse, *adj.* adverse.

adversely, *adv.* défavorablement, d'une manière hostile.

adversity, *n.* adversité *f.*

advert, *vb.* faire allusion (à).

advertise, *vb.* annoncer; (a. a product) faire de la réclame pour un produit.

advertisement, *n.* publicité *f.;* (in a paper) annonce *f.;* (on a wall) affiche *f.*

advertiser, *n.* personne qui fait de réclame *f.*

advertising, *n.* publicité *f.,* annonce (newspaper) *f.*

advice, *n.* conseil *m.; (comm.)* avis *m.*

advisability, *n.* convenance *f.,* utilité *f.*

advisable, *adj.* recommandable.

advisably, *adv.* convenablement.

advise, *vb.* conseiller.

advisedly, *adv.* de propos délibéré.

advisement, *n.* délibération.

advocacy, *n.* défense *f.,* plaidoyer *m.*

advocate, 1. *n.* (law) avocat *m.;* (supporter) défenseur *m.* 2. *vb.* appuyer.

aegis, *n.* égide *f.*

aerate, *vb.* aérer.

aeration, *n.* aération *f.*

aerial, *adj.* aérien.

aerially, *adv.* d'une manière aérienne.

aerie, *n.* aire *f.*

aeronautics, *n.* aéronautique *f.*

aesthetic, *adj.* esthétique.

afar, *adv.* loin, de loin.

affability, *n.* affabilité *f.*

affable, *adj.* affable.

affably, *adv.* affablement.

affair, *n.* affair *f.*

affect, *vb.* (move) toucher; (concern) intéresser; (pretend) affecter.

affectation, *n.* affectation *f.*

affected, *adj.* maniéré.

affecting, *adj.* touchant, émouvant.

affection, *n.* affection *f.*

affectionate, *adj.* affectueux.

affectionately, *adv.* affectueusement.

afferent, *adj.* afférent.

affiance, *vb.* fiancer.

affidavit, *n.* attestation (sous serment) *f.*

affiliate, *vb.* affilier.

affiliation, *n.* affiliation *f.*

affinity, *n.* affinité *f.*

affirm, *vb.* affirmer.

affirmation, *n.* affirmation *f.*

affirmative, *adj.* affirmatif.

affirmatively, *adv.* affirmativement.

affix, *vb.* apposer.

afflict, *vb.* affliger (de).

affliction, *n.* affliction *f.*

affluence, *n.* affluence *f.,* opulence *f.*

affluent, *adj.* affluent, opulent.

afford, *vb.* (have the means to) avoir les moyens de.

affray, *n.* bagarre *m.,* tumulte *m.*

affront, 1. *n.* affront *m.* 2. *vb.* insulter.

afield, *adv.* aux champs, en campagne.

afire, *adv.* en feu.

afloat, *adv.* à flot, en train.

aforementioned, *adj.* mentionné plus haut, susdit.

aforesaid, *adj.* susdit, ledit.

afraid, *pred. adj.* (be afraid) avoir peur.

Africa, *n.* Afrique *f.*

African, 1. *n.* Africain *m.* 2. *adj.* africain.

aft, *adv.* à l'arrière.

after, 1. *adj. and prep.* après. 2. *conj.* après que.

aftereffect, *n.* effet *m.*

aftermath, *n.* suites *f. pl.*

afternoon, *n.* après-midi *m. or f.*

afterthought, *n.* réflexion tardive *f.*

afterward, *adv.* ensuite.

again, *adv.* de nouveau, encore; (again and again) maintes et maintes fois.

against, *prep.* contre.

agape, *adv.* bouche bée.

agate, *n.* agate *f.*

age, 1. *n.* âge *m.* 2. *vb.* vieillir.

aged, *adj.* vieux, âgé.

ageism, *n.* attitude discriminative basée sur l'âge *f.*

ageless, *adj.* qui ne vieillit jamais.

agency, *n. (comm.)* agence *f.*

agenda, *n.* ordre du jour *m.,* agenda *m.*

agent, *n.* agent *m.*

agglutinate, *vb.* agglutiner.

agglutination, *n.* agglutination *f.*

aggrandize, *vb.* agrandir.

aggrandizement, *n.* agrandissement *m.*

aggravate, *vb.* (intensify) aggraver; (exasperate) exaspérer.

aggravation, *n.* aggravation *f.,* agacement *m.*

aggregate, *n.* masse *f.*

aggregation, *n.* agrégation *f.,* assemblage *m.*

aggression, *n.* agression *f.*

aggressive, *adj.* agressif.

aggressively, *adv.* agressivement.

aggressiveness, *n.* caractère agressif *m.*

aggressor, *n.* agresseur *m.*

aghast, *adj.* consterné.

agile, *adj.* agile.

agility, *n.* agilité *f.*

agitate, *vb.* agiter.

agitation, *n.* agitation *f.*

agitator, *n.* agitateur *m.*

agnostic, *n. and adj.* agnostique *m.*

ago, *adv.* il y a *(always precedes).*

agonized, *adj.* torturé, déchirant.

agony, *n.* (anguish) angoisse *f.;* (death agony) agonie *f.*

agrarian, *adj.* agraire, agrarien.

agree, *vb.* être d'accord.

agreeable, *adj.* agréable.

agreeably, *adv.* agréablement.

agreement, *n.* accord *m.*

agriculture, *n.* agriculture *f.*

ahead, 1. *adv. and interj.* en avant. 2. *prep.* (ahead of) en avant de.

aid, 1. *n.* aide *f.;* (first aid) premiers secours; (first-aid station) poste de secours. 2. *vb.* aider.

aide, *n.* aide *m.,* assistant *m.*

ail, *vb. intr.* être souffrant.

ailment, *n.* indisposition *f.*

aim, 1. *n.* (fig.) but *m.* 2. *vb.* viser.

aimless, *adj.* sans but.

aimlessly, *adv.* sans but, à la dérive.

air, 1. *n.* air *m.;* (a force) aviation *f.;* (by a. mail) par avion; (in the open a.) en plein air. 2. *vb.* aérer.

airbag, *n.* (in automobiles) sac à air *m.*

air base, *n.* champs d'aviation *m.*

airborne, adj. par voie de l'air.
air-condition, vb. climatiser.
air-conditioning, n. climatisation f.
aircraft, n. avions m.pl.; (aircraft carrier) porte-avions m.
air fleet, n. aéroflotte.
air gun, n. fusil à vent.
airing, n. aérage m., tour m.
air line, n. ligne aérienne f.
air liner, n. avion m.
air mail, n. poste aérienne f.
airplane, n. avion m.
air pollution, n. pollution de l'air f.
airport, n. aéroport m.
air pressure, n. pression d'air f.
air raid, n. raid aérien m.
airsick, adj. (to be a.) avoir le mal d'air.
airtight, adj. imperméable à l'air, étanche.
airy, adj. (well aired) aéré; (light) léger.
aisle, n. (passageway) passage m.; (arch.) bas côté m.
ajar, adv. entr'ouvert.
akin, adj. allié (à), parent (de).
alacrity, n. empressement m.
alarm, n. alarme f.
alarmist, n. alarmiste f.
albino, n. albinos m.
album, n. album m.
alcohol, n. alcool m.
alcoholic, adj. alcoolique.
alcove, n. (recess) niche f.; (sleeping alcove) alcôve f.
ale, n. bière f.
alert, adj. alerte.
alfalfa, n. luzerne f.
algebra, n. algèbre f.
alias, 1. n. nom d'emprunt m. 2. adv. autrement nommé, dit.
alibi, n. alibi m.
alien, adj. étranger.
alienate, vb. aliéner.
alight, vb. (descend) descendre; (stop after descent) s'abattre.
align, vb. aligner.
alike, 1. adj. semblable; (be alike) se ressembler. 2. adv. également.
alimentary canal, n. canal alimentaire m.
alive, adj. vivant.
alkali, n. alcali m.
alkaline, adj. alcalin.
all, 1. adj. tout m.sg., toute f.sg., tous m.pl., toutes f.pl. 2. adv. and pron. (everything) tout; (above all) surtout; (all at once) tout d'un coup; (all the same) tout de même; (that's all) c'est tout; (not at all) pas du tout; (everybody) tous; (all of you) vous tous.
allay, vb. apaiser.
allegation, n. allégation f.
allege, vb. alléguer.
allegiance, n. fidélité f.
allegory, n. allégorie f.
allergy, n. allergie f.
alleviate, vb. soulager.

alley, n. (in town) ruelle f.; (blind alley) cul-de-sac m.
alliance, n. alliance f.
allied, adj. allié.
alligator, n. alligator m.
allocate, vb. assigner.
allot, vb. (grant) accorder; (distribute) répartir.
allotment, n. partage m., lot m.
allow, vb. (permit) permettre; (admit) admettre; (grant) accorder; (allow for) tenir compte de.
allowance, n. (money granted) allocation f.; (food) ration f.; (tolerance) tolérance f.; (pension) rente f.; (weekly allowance) semaine f.
alloy, n. alliage m.
all right, adv. très bien.
allude to, vb. faire allusion à.
allure, vb. séduire.
allusion, n. allusion f.
ally, 1. n. allié m. 2. vb. allier.
almanac, n. almanach m.
almighty, adj. tout-puissant.
almond, n. amande f.
almost, adv. presque.
alms, n. aumône f.
aloft, adv. en haut.
alone, adj. seul; (let alone) laisser tranquille.
along, 1. prep. le long de. 2. adv. (come along!) venez donc!
alongside, prep. le long de.
aloof, 1. adj. à l'écart. 2. adj. réservé.
aloud, adv. à haute voix.
alpaca, n. alpaga (fabric) m.; alpaca (animal) m.
alphabet, n. alphabet m.
alphabetical, adj. alphabétique.
alphabetize, vb. alphabétiser.
Alps, n.pl. Alpes f.pl.
already, adv. déjà.
also, adv. aussi.
altar, n. autel m.
alter, vb. changer.
alteration, n. modification f.
alternate, 1. n. remplaçant m. 2. adj. alternatif. 3. vb. alterner.
alternative, n. alternative f.
although, conj. bien que.
altitude, n. altitude f.
altogether, adv. tout à fait.
altruism, n. altruisme m.
alum, n. alun m.
aluminum, n. aluminium m.
always, adv. toujours.
amalgam, n. amalgame n.
amalgamate, vb. amalgamer.
amass, vb. amasser.
amateur, n. amateur m.
amaze, vb. étonner.
amazement, n. stupeur f.
amazing, adj. étonnant.
ambassador, n. ambassadeur m., ambassadrice f.
amber, n. ambre m.
ambidextrous, adj. ambidextre.
ambiguity, n. ambiguïté f.
ambiguous, adj. ambigu m., ambiguë f.

ambition, n. ambition f.
ambitious, adj. ambitieux.
ambulance, n. ambulance f.
ambulatory, adj. ambulatoire.
ambush, n. embuscade f.
ameliorate, vb. améliorer.
amenable, adj. responsable, soumis (à), sujet (à).
amend, vb. amender.
amendment, n. amendement m.
amenity, n. aménité f., agrément m.
America, n. Amérique f.; (North A.) A. du Nord; (South A.) A. du Sud.
American, 1. n. Américain m. 2. adj. américain.
amethyst, n. améthyste f.
amiable, adj. aimable.
amicable, adj. amical.
amid, prep. au milieu de.
amidships, adv. par le travers.
amiss, adv. de travers.
amity, n. amitié f.
ammonia, n. ammoniaque f.
ammunition, n. munitions (f.pl.) de guerre.
amnesia, n. amnésie f.
amnesty, n. amnistie f.
amniocentesis, n. amniocentèse f.
amoeba, n. amibe f.
among, prep. parmi, entre.
amoral, adj. amoral.
amorous, adj. amoureux.
amorphous, adj. amorphe.
amortize, vb. amortir.
amount, 1. n. (sum) somme f.; (quantity) quantité f. 2. vb. (amount to) se réduire à.
ampere, n. ampère m.
amphibian, n. amphibie m.
amphibious, adj. amphibie.
amphitheater, n. amphithéâtre m.
ample, adj. ample.
amplify, vb. amplifier.
amputate, vb. amputer.
amputee, n. amputé m.
amuse, vb. amuser.
amusement, n. amusement m.
an, art. un m., une f.
anachronism, n. anachronisme m.
analogous, adj. analogue.
analogy, n. analogie f.
analysis, n. analyse f.
analyst, n. analyste m.
analytic, adj. analytique.
analyze, vb. analyser.
anarchy, n. anarchie f.
anatomy, n. anatomie f.
ancestor, n. ancêtre m.
ancestral, adj. d'ancêtres, héréditaire.
ancestry, n. aïeux, m.pl.
anchor, 1. vb. ancrer. 2. n. ancre f.
anchorage, n. mouillage m., ancrage m.
anchovy, n. anchois m.
ancient, adj. ancien m., ancienne f.
and, conj. et.

anecdote, n. anecdote f.

anemia, n. anémie f.

anesthetic, adj. and n. anesthésique m.

anesthetist, n. anesthésiste m.

anew, adv. de nouveau.

angel, n. ange m.

anger, n. colère f.

angle, 1. n. angle m.; (at an angle) en biais. 2. vb. (fish) pêcher à la ligne.

angry, adj. fâché; (to get angry) se fâcher.

anguish, n. angoisse f.

angular, adj. anguleux.

aniline, n. aniline f.

animal, n. and adj. animal m.

animate, vb. animer.

animated, adj. animé.

animated cartoon, n. dessin animé m.

animation, n. animation f.

animosity, n. animosité f.

anise, n. anis m.

ankle, n. cheville f.

annals, n.pl. annales f.pl.

annex, n. (to a building) dépendance f.

annexation, n. annexion f.

annihilate, vb. anéantir.

anniversary, n. anniversaire m.

annotate, vb. annoter.

annotation, n. annotation f.

announce, vb. annoncer.

announcement, n. annonce f.

announcer, n. speaker m.

annoy, vb. (vex) contrarier; (bore) ennuyer.

annoyance, n. contrariété f.

annual, adj. annuel.

annuity, n. annuité f., rente annuelle f.

annul, vb. annuler.

anode, n. anode f.

anoint, vb. oindre.

anomalous, adj. anomal, irrégulier.

anonymous, adj. anonyme.

another, adj. and pron. un autre m., une autre f.; (one another) l'un l'autre.

answer, vb. répondre.

answer, n. réponse f.

answerable, adj. responsable (de), susceptible de réponse.

ant, n. fourmi f.

antacid, adj. antiacide.

antagonism, n. antagonisme m.

antagonist, n. antagoniste m.

antagonistic, adj. en opposition (à), hostile (à), opposé (à).

antagonize, vb. s'opposer à.

antarctic, adj. antarctique.

antecedent, adj. and n. antécédent m.

antedate, vb. antidater.

antelope, n. antilope f.

antenna, n. antenne f.

anterior, adj. antérieur.

anteroom, n. antichambre m. or f.

anthem, n. (national) hymne national m.

anthology, n. anthologie f.

anthracite, n. anthracite m.

anthrax, n. anthrax m.

anthropology, n. anthropologie f.

antiaircraft, adj. contre-avion.

antibody, n. anticorps m.

antic, n. bouffonerie f.

anticipate, vb. (advance) anticiper; (expect) s'attendre à; (foresee) prévoir.

anticipation, n. anticipation f.

anticlerical, adj. anticlérical.

anticlimax, n. anticlimax m.

antidote, n. antidote m.

antimony, n. antimoine m.

antinuclear, adj. antinucléaire.

antipathy, n. antipathie f.

antiquated, adj. antique.

antique, n. antique m.; (antique dealer) antiquaire m.

antiquity, n. antiquité f.

antiseptic, adj. and n. antiseptique m.

antisocial, adj. antisocial.

antitoxin, n. antitoxine f.

antler, n. andouiller m.

anvil, n. enclume f.

anxiety, n. anxiété f.

anxious, adj. inquiet m., inquiète f.

any, 1. adj. (in questions, for "some") du m.sg., de la f.sg., des pl.; (not . . . any) ne . . . pas de; (no matter which) n'importe quel; (every) tout. 2. pron. (any of it or them, with verb) en.

anybody, pron. (somebody) quelqu'un; (somebody, implying negation) personne; (not . . . anybody) ne . . . personne; (no matter who) n'importe qui.

anyhow, adv. en tout cas; d'une manière quelconque.

anyone, pron. see anybody.

anything, pron. (somebody) quelque chose; (something, implying negation) rien; (not . . . anything) ne . . . rien; (no matter what) n'importe quoi.

anyway, adv. see anyhow.

anywhere, adv. n'importe où.

apart, 1. adv. à part. 2. prep. (apart from) en dehors de.

apartheid, n. ségrégation des populations noire et blanche, f.

apathetic, adj. apathique.

apathy, n. apathie f.

ape, 1. n. singe m. 2. vb. singer.

aperture, n. ouverture f.

apex, n. sommet m.

aphorism, aphorisme m.

apiary, n. rucher m.

apiece, adv. chacun.

apologetic, adj. use verb s'excuser.

apologist, n. apologiste m.

apologize for, vb. s'excuser de.

apology, n. excuses f. pl.

apoplexy, n. apoplexie f.

apostate, n. apostat m.

apostle, n. apôtre m.

apostolic, adj. apostolique.

appall, vb. épouvanter.

apparatus, n. appareil m.

apparel, n. habillement m.

apparent, adj. apparent.

apparition, n. apparition f.

appeal, 1. n. appel m. 2. vb. (a. to) en appeler à.

appear, vb. (become visible) apparaître; (seem) sembler.

appearance, n. (apparition) apparition f.; (semblance) apparence f.; (aspect) aspect m.

appease, vb. apaiser.

appeaser, n. personne qui apaise.

appellant, n. appelant m.

appellate, adj. d'appel.

appendage, n. accessoire m., apanage m.

appendectomy, n. appendéctomie f.

appendicitis, n. appendicite f.

appendix, n. appendice m.

appetite, n. appétit m.

appetizer, n. (drink) apéritif m.

appetizing, adj. appétissant.

applaud, vb. applaudir.

applause, n. applaudissements m.pl.

apple, n. pomme f.

applesauce, n. compote (f.) de pommes.

appliance, n. appareil m.

applicable, adj. applicable.

applicant, n. postulant m.

application, n. (request) demande f.

applied, adj. appliqué.

apply, vb. (a. to somebody) s'adresser à; (a. for a job) solliciter; (put on) appliquer; (a. oneself) s'appliquer.

appoint, vb. (a person) nommer; (time, place) désigner.

appointment, n. (meeting) rendez-vous m.; (make an a. with) donner un rendezvous à; (nomination) nomination f.

apportion, vb. répartir.

apposition, n. apposition f.

appraisal, n. évaluation f.

appraise, vb. priser.

appreciable, adj. appréciable.

appreciate, vb. apprécier.

appreciation, n. appréciation f.

apprehend, vb. saisir.

apprehension, n. (seizure) arrestation f.; (understanding) compréhension f.; (fear) appréhension f.

apprehensive, adj. craintif.

apprentice, n. apprenti m.

apprise, vb. prévenir, informer.

approach, 1. n. approche f.; (make approaches to) faire des avances à. 2. vb. s'approcher de.

approachable, adj. abordable, accessible.

approbation, n. approbation f.

appropriate, 1. adj. convenable. 2. vb. s'approprier.

appropriation, n. appropriation f.

approval, n. approbation f.

approve, vb. approuver.

approximate, 1. adj. approximatif. **2.** vb. se rapprocher (de).

approximately, adv. approximativement, à peu près.

approximation, n. approximation f.

appurtenance, n. appartenance f., dépendance f.

apricot, n. abricot m.

April, n. avril m.

apron, n. tablier m.

apropos, adj. à propos.

apse, n. abside f.

apt, adj. (likely to) sujet à; (suitable for) apte à; (appropriate) à propos; (clever) habile.

aptitude, n. aptitude f.

aquarium, n. aquarium m.

aquatic, adj. aquatique.

aqueduct, n. aqueduc m.

aqueous, adj. aqueux.

aquiline, adj. aquilin.

Arab, 1. n. Arabe m.f. **2.** adj. arabe.

Arabic, adj. and n. arabe m.

arable, adj. arable, labourable.

arbiter, n. arbitre m.

arbitrary, adj. arbitraire.

arbitrate, vb. arbitrer.

arbitration, n. arbitrage m.

arbitrator, n. arbitre m.

arbor, n. (bower) berceau m.

arboreal, adj. arboricole.

arc, n. arc m.

arcade, n. arcade f.

arch, 1. n. arc m.; (of bridge) arche f. **2.** adj. espiègle.

archaeology, n. archéologie f.

archaic, adj. archaïque.

archbishop, n. archevêque m.

archdiocese, n. archidiocèse m.

archduke, n. archiduc m.

archer, n. archer m.

archery, n. tir à l'arc m.

archipelago, n. archipel m.

architect, n. architecte m.

architectural, adj. architectural.

architecture, n. architecture f.

archives, n. archives f.pl.

archway, n. voûte f., passage (sous une voûte) m.

arctic, adj. arctique.

ardent, adj. ardent.

ardor, n. ardeur f.

arduous, adj. difficile.

area, n. (geom.) aire f.; (locality) région f.; (surface) surface f.

area code, n. indicatif interurbain m.

arena, n. arène f.

argentine, adj. argentin.

argue, vb. (reason) argumenter; (indicate) prouver; (discuss) discuter.

argument, n. (reasoning) argument m.; (dispute) discussion f.

argumentative, adj. disposé à argumenter, raisonneur.

aria, n. air m., chanson f.

arid, adj. aride.

arise, vb. (move upward) s'élever; (originate from) provenir de.

aristocracy, n. aristocratie f.

aristocrat, n. aristocrate m.f.

aristocratic, adj. aristocratique.

arithmetic, n. arithmétique f.

ark, n. arche f.

arm, 1. n. (limb) bras m.; (weapon) arme f. **2.** vb. armer.

armament, n. armement m.

armchair, n. fauteuil m.

armed forces, n. forces armées f.pl.

armful, n. brassée f.

armhole, n. emmanchure f., entournure f.

armistice, n. armistice m.

armor, n. armure f.

armory, n. (drill hall) salle (f.) d'exercice.

armpit, n. aisselle f.

arms, n. armes f.pl.

army, n. armée f.

arnica, n. arnica f.

aroma, n. arome m.

aromatic, adj. aromatique.

around, 1. adv. autour. **2.** prep. autour de.

arouse, vb. (stir) soulever; (awake) réveiller.

arraign, vb. accuser, poursuivre en justice.

arrange, vb. arranger.

arrangement, n. arrangement m.

array, n. (military) rangs m.pl.; (display) étalage m.

array, vb. ranger.

arrear, n. arriéré m.

arrest, 1. n. (capture) arrestation f.; (military) arrêts m.pl.; (halt) arrêt m. **2.** vb. arrêter.

arrival, n. arrivée f.

arrive, vb. arriver.

arrogance, n. arrogance f.

arrogant, adj. arrogant.

arrogate, vb. usurper, (to oneself) s'arroger.

arrow, n. flèche f.

arrowhead, n. pointe de flèche f.; (plant) sagittaire f.

arsenal, n. arsenal m.

arsenic, n. arsenic m.

arson, n. crime d'incendie m.

art, n. art m.; (fine arts) beaux-arts.

arterial, adj. artériel.

arteriosclerosis, n. artériosclérose f.

artery, n. artère f.

artesian well, n. puits artésien m.

artful, adj. (crafty) artificieux; (skillful) adroit.

arthritis, n. arthrite f.

artichoke, n. artichaut m.

article, n. article m.

articulate, vb. articuler.

articulation, n. articulation f.

artifice, n. artifice m.

artificial, adj. artificiel.

artificiality, n. nature artificielle f.

artillery, n. artillerie f.

artisan, n. artisan m.

artist, n. artiste m.

artistic, adj. artistique.

artistry, n. habileté f.

artless, adj. ingénu, naïf.

as, 1. adv. comme; (as . . . as) aussi . . . que; (as much as) autant que; (such as) tel que. **2.** conj. (so . . . as) de façon à; (while) pendant que; (since) puisque; (progress) à mesure que. **3.** prep. (as to) quant à.

asbestos, n. asbeste m.

ascend, vb. monter.

ascendancy, n. ascendant m.

ascendant, adj. ascendant, supérieur.

ascent, n. montée f.; (of a mountain) ascension f.

ascertain, vb. s'assurer (de).

ascetic, n. ascétique m.

ascribe, vb. attribuer.

ash, n. cendre f.; (tree) frêne m.

ashamed, adj. honteux; (be a. of) avoir honte de.

ashen, adj. cendré, gris pâle.

ashes, n. cendres f.pl.

ashore, adv. à terre; (go a.) débarquer.

ash-tray, n. cendrier m.

Asia, n. Asie f.

Asian, 1. n. Asiatique m.f. **2.** adj. asiatique.

aside, adv. de côté.

ask, vb. demander à; (invite) inviter.

askance, adv. de travers, obliquement.

asleep, adj. endormi.

asparagus, n. asperges f.pl.

aspect, n. aspect m.

asperity, n. aspérité f., rudesse f.

aspersion, n. aspersion f.

asphalt, n. asphalte m.

asphyxia, n. asphyxie f.

asphyxiate, vb. asphyxier.

aspirant, n. aspirant m., candidat m.

aspirate, vb. aspirer.

aspiration, n. aspiration f.

aspirator, n. aspirateur m.

aspire, vb. aspirer.

ass, n. âne m., ânesse f.

assail, vb. assaillir.

assailable, adj. attaquable.

assailant, n. assaillant m.

assassin, n. assassin m.

assassinate, vb. assassiner.

assassination, n. assassinat m.

assault, n. assaut m.

assay, 1. n. essai m., vérification f., épreuve f. **2.** vb. essayer.

assemblage, n. assemblage m.

assemble, vb. assembler, tr.; s'assembler, intr.

assembly, n. assemblée f.

assent, 1. *n.* assentiment *m.* **2.** *vb.* consentir.

assert, *vb.* affirmer.

assertion, *n.* assertion *f.*

assertive, *adj.* assertif.

assertiveness, *n.* qualité d'être assertif.

assess, *vb.* (tax) taxer; (evaluate) évaluer.

assessor, *n.* assesseur *m.*

assets, *n.pl. (comm.)* actif *m.;* (property) biens *m.pl.*

asseverate, *vb.* affirmer solennellement.

asseveration, *n.* affirmation *f.*

assiduous, *adj.* assidu.

assiduously, *adv.* assidûment.

assign, *vb.* assigner.

assignable, *adj.* assignable, transférable.

assignation, *n.* assignation *f.,* rendez-vous *m.*

assignment, *n.* (law) cession *f.;* (school) tâche *f.*

assimilate, *vb.* assimiler, *tr.;* s'assimiler, *intr.*

assimilation, *n.* assimilation *f.*

assimilative, *adj.* assimilatif, assimilateur.

assistance, *n.* aide *f.*

assistant, *n.* aide *m.f.*

assist in, *vb.* aider à.

associate, *vb.* associer, *tr.;* s'associer, *intr.*

association, *n.* association *f.*

assonance, *n.* assonance *f.*

assort, *vb.* assortir.

assorted, *adj.* assorti.

assortment, *n.* assortiment *m.*

assuage, *vb.* adoucir, apaiser.

assume, *vb.* (take) prendre; (appropriate) s'arroger; (feign) simuler; (suppose) supposer.

assuming, *adj.* prétentieux, arrogant.

assumption, *n.* supposition *f.;* (eccles.) Assomption *f.*

assurance, *n.* assurance *f.*

assure, *vb.* assurer.

assured, *adj.* assuré.

assuredly, *adv.* assurément.

aster, *n.* aster *m.*

asterisk, *n.* astérisque *m.*

astern, *adv.* à l'arrière, de l'arrière.

asteroid, *n.* astéroïde *m.*

asthma, *n.* asthme *m.*

astigmatism, *n.* astigmatisme *m.*

astir, *adj.* agité, debout.

astonish, *vb.* étonner.

astonishment, *n.* étonnement *m.*

astound, *vb.* stupéfier.

astral, *adj.* astral.

astray, *adj.* égaré; (go a.) s'égarer.

astride, *adv.* à califourchon.

astringent, *n. and adj.* astringent *m.*

astrology, *n.* astrologie *f.*

astronaut, *n.* astronaute *m.*

astronomy, *n.* astronomie *f.*

astute, *adj.* fin.

asunder, *adv.* (apart) écartés; (to pieces) en morceaux.

asylum, *n.* asile *m.*

asymmetry, *n.* asymétrie *f.*

at, *prep.* (time, place, price) à; (someone's house, shop, etc.) chez.

ataxia, *n.* ataxie *f.*

atheist, *n.* athée *m.f.*

athlete, *n.* athlète *m.f.*

athletic, *adj.* athlétique.

athletics, *n.* sports *m.pl.*

athwart, *adv.* de travers.

Atlantic, *adj.* atlantique.

Atlantic Ocean, *n.* océan Atlantique *m.*

atlas, *n.* atlas *m.*

atmosphere, *n.* atmosphère *f.*

atmospheric, *adj.* atmosphérique.

atoll, *n.* atoll *m.*

atom, *n.* atome *m.*

atomic, *adj.* atomique.

atomic bomb, *n.* bombe atomique *f.*

atomic energy, *n.* énergie atomique *f.*

atomic theory, *n.* théorie atomique *f.*

atomic warfare, *n.* guerre atomique *f.*

atomic weight, *n.* poids atomique *m.*

atonal, *adj.* atonal.

atone for, *vb.* expier.

atonement, *n.* expiation *f.*

atrocious, *adj.* atroce.

atrocity, *n.* atrocité *f.*

atrophy, *n.* atrophie *f.*

atropine, *n.* atropine *f.*

attach, *vb.* attcher.

attaché, *n.* attaché *m.*

attachment, *n.* attachement *m.;* (device) accessoire *m.*

attack, 1. *n.* attaque *f.* **2.** *vb.* attaquer.

attacker, *n.* agresseur *m.*

attain, *vb.* atteindre.

attainable, *adj.* qu'on peut atteindre.

attainment, *n.* (realization) réalisation *f.;* (knowledge) connaissance *f.*

attempt, *n.* tentative *f.*

attend, *vb.* (give heed to) faire attention à; (medical) soigner; (serve) servir; (meeting) assister à; (lectures) suivre; (see to) s'occuper de.

attendance, *n.* service *m.;* présence *f.*

attendant, *n.* serviteur *m.;* (retinue) suite *f.*

attention, *n.* attention *f.;* (pay attention to) faire attention à.

attentive, *adj.* attentif.

attentively, *adv.* attentivement.

attenuate, *vb.* atténuer.

attest, *vb.* attester.

attic, *n.* grenier *m.*

attire, 1. *n.* costume *m.* **2.** *vb.* parer, *tr.;* se parer, *intr.*

attitude, *n.* attitude *f.*

attorney, *n.* avoué *m.*

attract, *vb.* attirer.

attraction, *n.* attraction *f.*

attractive, *adj.* attrayant.

attributable, *adj.* attributable, imputable.

attribute, *n.* attribut *m.*

attrition, *n.* attrition *f.*

attune, *vb.* accorder, mettre à l'unisson.

auction, *n.* vente (*f.*) aux enchères.

auctioneer, *n.* commissaire-priseur *m.*

audacious, *adj.* audacieux.

audacity, *n.* audace *f.*

audible, *adj.* intelligible.

audience, *n.* (listeners) auditoire *m.;* (interview) audience *f.*

audiovisual, *adj.* audiovisuel.

audit, 1. *vb.* vérifier (des comptes). **2.** *n.* vérification (des comptes) *f.*

audition, *n.* audition *f.*

auditor, *n.* vérificateur *m.,* censeur *m.*

auditorium, *n.* salle *f.*

auditory, *adj.* auditif.

auger, *n.* tarière *f.*

augment, *vb.* augmenter.

augur, *vb.* augurer.

August, *n.* août *m.*

aunt, *n.* tante *f.*

auspice, *n.* auspice *m.*

auspicious, *adj.* de bon augure.

austere, *adj.* austère.

austerity, *n.* austérité *f.*

Australia, *n.* Australie *f.*

Australian, 1. *n.* Australien *m.* **2.** *adj.* australien.

Austria, *n.* Autriche *f.*

Austrian, 1. *n.* Autrichien *m.* **2.** *adj.* autrichien.

authentic, *adj.* authentique.

authenticate, *vb.* authentiquer, valider.

authenticity, *n.* authenticité *f.*

author, *n.* auteur *m.*

authoritarian, *adj.* autoritaire.

authoritative, *adj.* autoritaire.

authoritatively, *adv.* avec autorité, en maître.

authority, *n.* autorité *f.*

authorization, *n.* autorisation *f.*

authorize, *vb.* autoriser.

auto, *n.* auto *f.*

autobiography, *n.* autobiographie *f.*

autocracy, *n.* autocratie *f.*

autocrat, *n.* autocrate *m.*

autograph, 1. *n.* autographe *m.* **2.** *vb.* autographier.

automatic, *adj.* automatique.

automatically, *adv.* automatiquement.

automobile, *n.* automobile *f.*

automotive, *adj.* automoteur.

autonomously, *adv.* d'une manière autonome.

autonomy, *n.* autonomie *f.*

autopsy, *n.* autopsie *f.*

autumn, *n.* automne *m.*

auxiliary, *adj.* auxiliaire.

avail, *vb.* servir; (be of no a.) ne servir à rien.

available, adj. disponible.
avalanche, n. avalanche f.
avarice, n. avarice f.
avariciously, adv. avec avarice.
avenge, vb. venger.
avenger, n. vengeur m., vengeresse f.
avenue, n. avenue f.
average, 1. n. moyenne f. 2. adj. moyen.
averse, adj. opposé.
aversion, n. aversion f.
avert, vb. détourner.
aviary, n. volière f.
aviation, n. aviation f.
aviator, n. aviateur m.
aviatrix, n. aviatrice f.
avid, adj. avide.
avocation, n. distraction f., profession f., métier m.
avoid, vb. éviter.
avoidable, adj. évitable.
avoidance, n. action d'éviter f.
avow, vb. avouer.
avowal, n. aveu m.
avowed, adj. avoué, confessé.
avowedly, adj. de son propre aveu, ouvertement.
await, vb. attendre.
awake, vb. éveiller, tr.; s'éveiller, intr.
awaken, vb. see awake.
award, 1. n. (prize) prix m.; (law) sentence f. 2. vb. décerner.
aware, adj. (be a.) savoir; (not to be a.) ignorer.
awash, adv. dans l'eau.
away, adv. loin; (go a.) s'en aller; (a. from) absent de.
awe, n. crainte f.
awesome, adj. inspirant du respect.
awful, adj. terrible.
awhile, adv. pendant quelque temps.
awkward, adj. (clumsy) gauche; (embarrassing) embarrassant.
awning, n. tente f.
awry, adv. de travers.
ax, n. hache f.
axiom, n. axiome m.
axis, n. axe m.
axle, n. essieu m.
ayatollah, n. ayatollah m.
azure, n. azur m.
azure, adj. azuré.

B

babble, vb. babiller.
babbler, n. babillard m.
babe, n. enfant m. or f.
baboon, n. babouin m.
baby, n. bébé m.
babyish, adj. enfantin.
bachelor, n. célibataire m.
bacillus, n. bacille m.
back, 1. n. dos m. 2. vb. (b. up, go b.) reculer; (uphold) soutenir. 3. adv. en arrière.
backbone, n. épine dorsale f.

backer, n. partisan m.
backfire, vb. donner des retours de flamme, retomber (sur).
background, n. fond m.
backhand, adj. donné avec le revers de la main.
backing, n. soutien m.
backlash, n. réaction conservatrice f.
backlog, n. réserve f.
back out, vb. se retirer.
backpack, n. sac tyrolien m.
backstage, adv. dans les coulisses.
backward, adj. en arrière.
backwardness, n. retard m.
backwards, adv. en arrière.
backwater, 1. n. eau stagnante f. 2. vb. aller en arrière (dans l'eau).
backwoods, n. forêts vierges f.pl.
bacon, n. porc (m.) salé et fumé.
bacteriologist, n. bactériologue m.
bacteriology, n. bactériologie f.
bacterium, n. bactérie f.
bad, adj. mauvais; (wicked) méchant.
badge, n. insigne m.
badger, vb. ennuyer.
badness, n. mauvaise qualité f.; (wickedness) méchanceté f.
baffle, vb. déconcerter.
bafflement, n. confusion f., frustration f.
bag, n. sac m.; (suitcase) valise f.
baggage, n. bagage m.
baggage cart, n. (airport) chariot m.
baggy, adj. bouffant.
bagpipe, n. cornemuse f.
bail, 1. n. (law) caution f. 2. vb. (b. out water) vider (l'eau).
bailiff, n. huissier m.
bait, n. appât m.
bake, vb. faire cuire au four, tr.
baker, n. boulanger m.
bakery, n. boulangerie f.
baking, n. boulangerie f.
balance, 1. n. (equilibrium) équilibre m.; (bank) solde m.; account, scales) balance f. 2. vb. balancer, tr.
balcony, n. balcon m.; (theater) galerie f.
bald, adj. chauve.
baldness, n. calvitie f.; (fig.) sécheresse f.
bale, n. balle f.
balk, vb. frustrer.
balky, adj. regimbé.
ball, n. (games, bullet) balle f.; (round object) boule f.; (dance) bal m.
ballad, n. (song) romance f.; (poem) ballade f.
ballast, n. lest m.
ball bearing, n. roulement à billes m.
ballerina, n. ballérina f.

ballet, n. ballet m.
balloon, n. ballon m.
ballot, n. scrutin m.
ballroom, n. salon de bal m.
balm, n. baume m.
balmy, adj. embaumé; doux m., douce f.
balsa, n. balsa f.
balsam, n. baume m.
balustrade, n. balustrade f.
bamboo, n. bambou m.
ban, 1. n. ban m. 2. vb. mettre au ban, tr.
banal, adj. banal.
banana, n. banane f.
band, n. bande f.; (music) orchestre m.
bandage, n. bandage m.
bandanna, n, foulard (de soie de couleur) m.
bandbox, n. carton (de modiste) m.
bandit, n. bandit m.
bandmaster, n. chef de musique m.
bandsman, n. musicien m.
bandstand, n. kiosque m.
baneful, adj. pernicieux.
bang, vb. frapper.
bang, n. coup m.
banish, vb. bannir.
banishment, n. bannissement m.
banister, n. rampe f.
bank, n. banque f.; (river) rive f.
bankbook, n. livret de banque m.
banker, n. banquier m.
banking, n. banque f., affaires de banque f.pl.
bank note, n. billet de banque m.
bankrupt, adj. and n. failli m.
bankruptcy, n. faillite f.
banner, n. bannière f.
banquet, n. banquet m.
banter, 1. n. badinage m. 2. vb. badiner, railler.
baptism, n. baptême m.
baptismal, adj. baptismal.
Baptist, n. Baptiste m.
baptistery, n. baptistère m.
baptize, vb. baptiser.
bar, n. (drinks) bar m.; (metal) barre f.; (law) barreau m.
barb, n. barbillon m.
barbarian, barbarous, adj. and n. barbare m.f.
barbarism, n. barbarie f.; (gramm.) barbarisme m.
barber, n. coiffeur m.
barbiturate, n. barbiturat m.
bare, 1. adj. nu. 2. vb. découvrir.
bareback, adv. à dos nu.
barefoot, adv. nu-pieds.
barely, adv. à peine.
bareness, n. nudité f.
bargain, n. marché m.
bargain, vb. marchander.
barge, n. chaland m.
barium, n. barium m.
bark, 1. n. (tree) écorce f.;

(dog) aboiement *m.* **2.** *vb.* (dog) aboyer.

barley, *n.* orge *f.*

barn, *n.* (grain) grange *f.;* (livestock) étable *f.*

barnacle, *n.* anatife (shellfish) *m.;* barnache (goose) *f.*

barnyard, *n.* basse-cour *f.*

barometer, *n.* baromètre *m.*

barometric, *adj.* barométrique.

baron, *n.* baron *m.*

baroness, *n.* baronne *f.*

baronial, *adj.* baronnial, seigneurial.

baroque, *adj.* baroque.

barracks, *n.* caserne *f.*

barrage, *n.* barrage *m.*

barred, *adj.* barré, empêché, exclus, défendu.

barrel, *n.* tonneau *m.*

barren, *adj.* stérile.

barrenness, *n.* stérilité *f.*

barricade, *n.* barricade *f.*

barrier, *n.* barrière *f.*

barroom, *n.* buvette *f.,* comptoir *m.,* bar *m.*

bartender, *n.* barman *m.*

barter, *n.* troc *m.*

base, 1. *n.* base *f.* **2.** *adj.* bas *m.,* basse *f.*

baseball, *n.* baseball *m.*

baseboard, *n.* moulure de base *f.*

basement, *n.* sous-sol *m.*

baseness, *n.* bassesse *f.*

bashful, *adj.* timide.

bashfully, *adv.* timidement, modestement.

bashfulness, *n.* timidité *f.,* modestie *f.*

basic, *adj.* fondamental.

basin, *n.* (wash) cuvette *f.;* (river) bassin *m.*

basis, *n.* base *f.*

bask, se chauffer *intr.*

basket, *n.* (with handle) panier *m.;* (without handle) corbeille *f.*

bass, *n.* (music) basse *f.;* (fish) bar *m.*

bassinet, *n.* bercelonnette *f.*

bassoon, *n.* basson *m.*

bastard, *n.* bâtard *m., (law)* enfant naturel *m.*

baste, 1. *vb.* (cooking) arroser; (sewing) faufiler.

bat, *n.* (animal) chauve-souris *f.;* (baseball) batte *f.*

batch, *n.* fournée *f.*

bate, *vb.* rabattre, diminuer.

bath, *n.* bain *m.*

bathe, *vb.* se baigner.

bather, *n.* baigneur *m.*

bathrobe, *n.* peignoir (*m.*) de bain.

bathroom, *n.* salle (*f.*) de bain.

bathtub, *n.* baignoire *f.*

baton, *n.* bâton *m.*

battalion, *n.* bataillon *m.*

batter, *n.* (cooking) pâte *f.*

battery, *n.* (military) batterie *f.;* (electric) pile *f.*

battle, *n.* bataille *f.*

battle, *vb.* lutter.

battlefield, *n.* champ (*m.*) de bataille.

battleship, *n.* cuirassé *m.*

bauxite, *n.* bauxite *f.*

bawl, *vb.* brailler.

bay, *n.* (geography) baie *f.;* (plant) laurier *m.*

bayonet, *n.* baïonnette *f.*

bazaar, *n.* bazar *m.*

be, *vb.* être.

beach, *n.* plage *f.*

beachhead, *n.* (haut de) plage *f.*

beacon, *n.* phare *m.*

bead, *n.* perle *f.*

beading, *n.* ornement de grains *m.*

beady, *adj.* comme un grain, couvert de grains.

beak, *n.* bec *m.*

beaker, *n.* gobelet *m.,* coupe *f.*

beam, 1. *n.* (construction) poutre *f.;* (light) rayon *m.* **2.** *vb.* rayonner.

beaming, *adj.* rayonnant.

bean, *n.* haricot *m.*

bear, 1. *n.* ours *m.* **2.** *vb.* (carry) porter; (endure) supporter; (birth) enfanter.

bearable, *adj.* supportable.

beard, *n.* barbe *f.*

bearded, *adj.* barbu.

beardless, *adj.* imberbe.

bearer, *n.* porteur *m.*

bearing, *n.* (person) maintien *m.;* (machinery) coussinet *m.;* (naut.) relèvement *m.*

bearskin, *n.* peau d'ours *f.*

beast, *n.* bête *f.*

beat, 1. *vb.* battre. **2.** *n.* battement *m.*

beaten, *adj.* battu.

beatify, *vb.* béatifier.

beating, *n.* battement *m.,* rossée *f.*

beau, *n.* galant *m.*

beautiful, *adj.* beau (bel) *m.,* belle *f.*

beautifully, *adv.* admirablement.

beautify, *vb.* embellir

beauty, *n.* beauté *f.*

beaver, *n.* castor *m.*

becalm, *vb.* calmer, apaiser; (naut.) abriter.

because, *conj.* parce que.

beckon, *vb.* faire signe (à).

become, *vb.* devenir.

becoming, *adj.* convenable; (dress) seyant.

bed, *n.* lit *m.*

bedbug, *n.* punaise *f.*

bedclothes, *n.* couvertures *f.pl.*

bedding, *n.* literie *f.*

bedfellow, *n.* camarade de lit *m.*

bedizen, *vb.* parer, attifer.

bedridden, *adj.* alité.

bedrock, *n.* roche solide *f.*

bedroom, *n.* chambre (*f.*) à coucher.

bedside, *n.* bord du lit *m.*

bedspread, *n.* dessus (*m.*) de lit.

bedstead, *n.* bois de lit *m.,* couchette *f.*

bedtime, *n.* heure (*f.*) de se coucher.

bee, *n.* abeille *f.*

beef, *n.* bœuf *m.*

beefsteak, *n.* bifteck *m.,* tournedos *m.*

beehive, *n.* ruche *f.*

beer, *n.* bière *f.*

beeswax, *n.* cire jaune *f.*

beet, *n.* betterave *f.*

beetle, *n.* scarabée *m.*

befall, *vb.* arriver (à).

befit, *vb.* convenir (à).

befitting, *adj.* convenable.

before, 1. *adv.* (place) en avant; (time) avant. **2.** *prep.* (place) devant; (time) avant. **3.** *conj.* avant que.

beforehand, *adv.* d'avance.

befriend, *vb.* aider; traiter en ami.

befuddle, *vb.* embrouiller, déconcerter.

beg, *vb.* (of beggar) mendier; (ask) prier.

beget, *vb.* engendrer, produire.

beggar, *n.* mendiant *m.*

beggarly, *adj.* chétif, misérable.

begin, *vb.* commencer.

beginner, *n.* commençant *m.*

beginning, *n.* commencement *m.*

beguile, *vb.* tromper, séduire.

behalf, *n.* (on b. of) de la part de; (in b. of) en faveur de.

behave, *vb.* se conduire.

behavior, *n.* conduite *f.*

behead, *vb.* décapiter.

behind, *adv. and prep.* derrière.

behind, *n.* derrière *m.*

behold, 1. *vb.* voir. **2.** *interj.* voici.

beige, *adj.* beige.

being, *n.* être *m.*

bejewel, *vb.* orner de bijoux.

belated, *adj.* attardé.

belch, *vb.* éructer.

belfry, *n.* clocher *m.,* beffroi *m.*

Belgian, 1. *n.* Belge *m.f.* **2.** *adj.* belge.

Belgium, *n.* Belgique *f.*

belie, *vb.* démentir.

belief, *n.* croyance *f.;* (confidence) confiance *f.*

believable, *adj.* croyable.

believe, *vb.* croire.

believer, *n.* croyant *m.*

belittle, *vb.* rabaisser.

bell, *n.* (house) sonnette *f.;* (church) cloche *f.*

bellboy, *n.* chasseur *m.*

bell buoy, *n.* bouée sonore *f.*

belligerence, *n.* belligérance *f.*

belligerent, *adj.* belligérant *m.*

belligerently, *adv.* d'une manière belligérante.

bellow, *vb.* mugir.

bellows, *n.* soufflet *m.*

bell-tower, *n.* clocher *m.*

belly, *n.* ventre *m.*

belongings, *n.* effets, *m.pl.*

belong to, *vb.* appartenir (à).

beloved, *adj. and n.* chéri *m.*

below, 1. *adv.* en bas. **2.** *prep.* au-dessous de.

belt, *n.* ceinture *f.*

bench, *n.* banc *m.*

bend, *vb.* plier; (curve) courber *tr.*

beneath, *see* below.

benediction, *n.* bénédiction *f.*

benefactor, *n.* bienfaiteur *m.*

benefactress, *n.* bienfaitrice *f.*

beneficent, *adj.* beinfaisant.

beneficial, *adj.* salutaire.

beneficiary, *n.* bénéficiare *m.*

benefit, *n.* (favor) bienfait *m.;* (advantage) bénéfice *m.* .

benevolence, *n.* bienveillance *f.*

benevolent, *adj.* bienveillant.

benevolently, *adv.* bénévolement.

benign, *adj.* bénin *m.* bénigne *f.*

benignity, *n.* bénignité *f.*

bent, *n.* penchant *m.*

benzene, *n.* benzène *m.*

benzine, *n.* benzine *f.*

bequeath, *vb.* léguer.

bequest, *n.* legs *m.*

berate, *vb.* gronder.

bereave, *vb.* priver (de).

bereavement, *n.* privation *f.,* perte *f.,* deuil *m.*

beriberi, *n.* béribéri *m.*

berry, *n.* baie *f.*

berth, *n.* couchette *f.*

beseech, *vb.* supplier.

beseechingly, *adv.* en suppliant.

beset, *vb.* attaquer, presser, assiéger.

beside, *prep.* à côté de.

besides, *adv.* en outre.

besiege, *vb.* assiéger.

besieged, *adj.* assiégé.

besieger, *n.* assiégeant *m.*

besmirch, *vb.* tacher, salir.

best, 1. *adj.* (le) meilleur. **2.** *adv.* (le) mieux.

bestial, *adj.* bestial.

bestir, *vb.* remuer.

best man, *n.* garcon d'honneur (at weddings) *m.*

bestow, *vb.* accorder.

bestowal, *n.* dispensation *f.*

bet, 1. *n.* pari *m.* **2.** *vb.* parier.

betake (oneself), *vb.* se rendre.

betray, *vb.* trahir.

betroth, *vb.* fiancer.

betrothal, *n.* fiançailles *f.pl.*

better, 1. *adj.* meilleur. **2.** *adv.* mieux.

between, *prep.* entre.

bevel, 1. *adj.* en biseau. **2.** *vb.* biaiser.

beverage, *n.* boisson *f.*

bewail, *vb.* lamenter, pleurer.

beware of, *vb.* prendre garde à.

bewilder, *vb.* égarer.

bewildered, *adj.* égaré.

bewildering, *adj.* déconcertant.

bewilderment, *n.* égarement *m.*

bewitch, *vb.* ensorceler.

beyond, 1. *adv.* au delà. **2.** *prep.* au delà de.

biannual, *adj.* semestriel.

bias, *n.* (slant) biais *m.;* (prejudice) prévention *f.*

bib, *n.* bavette *f.*

Bible, *n.* Bible *f.*

biblical, *adj.* biblique.

bibliography, *n.* bibliographie *f.*

bicarbonate, *n.* bicarbonat *m.*

bicentennial, *n.* and *adj.* bicentenaire *m.*

biceps, *n.* biceps *m.*

bicker, *vb.* se quereller, se chamailler.

bicycle, *n.* bicyclette *f.*

bicyclist, *n.* cycliste *m.*

bid, 1. *n.* (auction) enchère *f.;* (bridge) appel *m.* **2.** *vb.* (order) ordonner; (invite) inviter.

bidder, *n.* enchérisseur *m.*

bide, *vb.* (live) demeurer; (wait) attendre.

bier, *n.* corbillard *m.,* civière *f.*

bifocal, *adj.* bifocal.

big, *adj.* grand.

bigamy, *n.* bigamie *f.*

bigot, *n.* bigot *m.*

bigotry, *n.* bigoterie *f.*

bilateral, *adj.* bilatéral.

bile, *n.* bile *f.*

bilingual, *adj.* bilingue.

bilious, *adj.* bilieux.

bill, *n.* (restaurant) addition *f.;* (hotel, profession) note *f.;* (money) billet *(m.)* de banque; (poster) affiche *f.;* (politics) projet *(m.)* de loi; **(b. of fare)** carte *(f.)* du jour; (bird) bec *m.*

billet, *n.* (mil.) billet de logement *m.*

billfold, *n.* portefeuille *m.*

billiard balls, *n.pl.* billes *n.pl.*

billiards, *n.* billard *m.*

billion, *n.* billion *m.*

bill of health, *n.* patente de santé *f.*

bill of lading, *n.* connaissement *m.*

bill of sale, *n.* lettre de vente *f.,* acte de propriété *m.*

billow, *n.* grande vague *f.,* lame *f.*

bimetallic, *adj.* bimétallique.

bimonthly, *adj.* *and* *adv.* bimensuel.

bin, *n.* coffre *m.*

bind, *vb.* lier; (books) relier.

bindery, *n.* atelier de reliure *m.*

binding, 1. *n.* (book) reliure *f.* **2.** *adj.* obligatoire.

binocular, *adj.* binoculaire.

biochemistry, *n.* biochimie *f.*

biodegradable, *adj.* sujet à la putréfaction.

biofeedback, *n.* biofeedback *m.,* information reçue par un organisme pendant un processus biologique *f.*

biographer, *n.* biographe *m.*

biographical, *adj.* biographique.

biography, *n.* biographie *f.*

biological, *adj.* biologique.

biologically, *adv.* biologiquement.

biology, *n.* biologie *f.*

bipartisan, *adj.* représentant les deux partis.

biped, *n.* bipède *m.*

bird, *n.* oiseau *m.*

birdlike, *adj.* comme un oiseau.

bird of prey, *n.* oiseau de proie *m.*

birth, *n.* naissance *f.*

birth control, *n.* contrôle des naissances *m.*

birthday, *n.* anniversaire *(m.)* de naissance.

birthmark, *n.* tache de naissance *f.*

birthplace, *n.* lieu *(m.)* de naissance.

birth rate, *n.* natalité *f.*

birthright, *n.* droit d'aînesse *m.*

biscuit, *n.* (hard) biscuit *m.;* (soft) petit pain *(m.)* au lait.

bisect, *vb.* couper en deux.

bishop, *n.* évêque *m.*

bishopric, *n.* évêché *m.*

bismuth, *n.* bismuth *m.*

bison, *n.* bison *m.*

bit, *n.* (piece) morceau *m.;* **(a b. of)** un peu (de); (harness) mors *m.;* unité unique d'information *f.*

bitch, *n.* chienne *f.*

bite, 1. *n.* morsure *f.* **2.** *vb.* mordre.

biting, *adj.* mordant.

bitter, *adj.* amer.

bitterly, *adv.* amèrement, avec amertume.

bitterness, *n.* amertume *f.*

bivouac, *n.* bivouac *m.*

biweekly, *adj.* and *adv.* tous les quinze jours.

black, *adj.* noir.

Black, *n.* and *adj.* (for person) nègre *m.;* négresse *f.*

blackberry *n.* mûre *(f.)* de ronce.

blackbird, *n.* merle *m.*

blackboard, *n.* tableau *(m.)* noir.

blacken, *vb.* noircir.

black eye, *n.* oeil poché *m.*

blackguard, *n.* gredin *m.,* polisson *m.,* salaud *m.*

blackmail, *n.* chantage *m.*

black market, *n.* marché noir *m.*

blackout, *n.* blackout *m.*

blacksmith, *n.* forgeron *m.*

bladder, *n.* vessie *f.*

blade, *n.* (sword, knife) lame *f.;* (grass) brin *m.*

blame, 1. *n.* blâme *m.* **2.** *vb.* blâmer.

blameless, *adj.* innocent, sans tache.

blanch, *vb.* blanchir, palir.

bland, *adj.* doux *m.,* douce *f.*

blank, 1. *n.* (space) blanc *m.;* (void) vide *m.;* (printing) tiret *m.* **2.** *adj.* (page) blanc *m.,* blanche *f.;* (empty) vide.

blanket, *n.* couverture *f.*

blare, *n.* son (de la trompette) *m.*, rugissement *m.*

blare, *vb.* retentir, *intr.*

blaspheme, *vb.* blasphémer.

blasphemer, *n.* blasphémateur *m.*

blasphemous, *adj.* blasphématoire.

blasphemy, *n.* blasphème *m.*

blast, 1. *n.* (wind) rafale *f.;* (mine) explosion *f.*

blatant, *adj.* criard, bruyant.

blaze, 1. *n.* flambée *f.* 2. *vb.* flamber.

blazing, *adj.* enflammé, flamboyant.

bleach, *vb.* décolorer, *tr.*

bleak, *adj.* morne.

bleakness, *n.* froidure *f.*

bleed, *vb.* saigner.

blemish, *n.* défaut *m.*

blend, 1. *n.* mélange *m.* 2. *vb.* mêler *tr.*

blended, *adj.* mélangé.

bless, *vb.* bénir.

blessed, *adj.* béni.

blessing, *n.* bénédiction *f.*

blight, 1. *vb.* flétrir, détruire, nieller, brouir. 2. *n.* brouissure *f.*, flétrissure *f.*

blind, 1. *n.* store *m.* 2. *adj.* aveugle; (**b. alley**) cul-de-sac *m.*

blindfold, *adj. and adv.* les yeux bandés.

blinding, *adj.* aveuglant.

blindly, *adv.* aveuglément.

blindness, *n.* cécité *f.*

blink, *vb.* clignoter.

bliss, *n.* béatitude *f.*

blissful, *adj.* bienheureux.

blissfully, *adv.* heureusement.

blister, *n.* ampoule *f.*

blithe, *adj.* gai, joyeux.

blizzard, *n.* tempête (*f.*) de neige.

bloat, *vb.* boursoufler.

bloc, *n.* bloc *m.*

block, 1. *n.* bloc *m.;* (houses) pâté *m.* 2. *vb.* bloquer.

blockade, *n.* blocus *m.*

blond, *adj. and n.* blond *m.*

blood, *n.* sang *m.*

bloodhound, *n.* limier *m.*

bloodless, *adj.* exsangue, sans effusion de sang.

blood plasma, *n.* plasma du sang *m.*

blood poisoning, *n.* empoisonnement du sang *m.*

blood pressure, *n.* tension artérielle *f.*

bloodshed, *n.* effusion (*f.*) de sang.

bloodshot, *adj.* injecté de sang.

bloodthirsty, *adj.* sanguinaire.

bloody, *adj.* sanglant.

bloom, 1. *n.* fleur *f.* 2. *vb.* fleurir.

blooming, 1. *n.* floraison *f.* 2. *adj.* fleurissant.

blossom, *see* bloom.

blot, 1. *n.* tache *f.* 2. *vb.* (spot) tacher; (dry ink) sécher l'encre.

blotch, *n.* tache *f.*

blotchy, *adj.* couvert de taches.

blotter, *n.* buvard *m.*

blouse, *n.* blouse *f.*

blow, 1. *n.* coup *m.* 2. *vb.* souffler; (**b. out**) éteindre; (**b. over**) passer; (**b. up**) faire sauter, *tr.*

blowout, *n.* éclatement (*m.*) de pneu.

blubber, 1. *vb.* pleurer comme un veau. 2. *n.* graisse de baleine *f.*

bludgeon, 1. *n.* matraque *f.* 2. *vb.* donner des coups de matraque.

blue, *adj.* bleu.

blue jeans, *n.* blue jeans *m.pl.*

blueprint, *n.* dessin négatif *m.*

bluff, *n.* bluff *m.*

bluffer, *n.* bluffeur *m.*

blunder, *n.* bévue *f.*

blunderer, *n.* maladroit *m.*

blunt, *adj.* (blade) émoussé; (person) brusque.

bluntly, *adv.* brusquement.

bluntness, *n.* brusquerie *f.*

blur, *vb.* (smear) barbouiller.

blush, 1. *n.* rougeur *f.* 2. *vb.* rougir.

bluster, *n.* rodomontade *f.*, fanfaronnade *f.*

boar, *n.* (wild) sanglier *m.*

board, 1. *n.* (plank) planche *f.;* (daily meals) pension *f.;* (boat) bord *m.;* (politics) ministère *m.;* (administration) conseil *m.*

boarder, *n.* pensionnaire *m.f.*

boast (of), *vb.* se vanter (de).

boaster, *n.* vantard *m.*

boastful, *adj.* vantard.

boastfulness, *n.* vantardise *f.*

boat, *n.* bateau *m.*

boathouse, *n.* garage (à bateaux) *m.*

boatswain, *n.* maître d'équipage *m.*

bob, *vb.* (hair) couper court.

bobbin, *n.* bobine *f.*

bode, *vb.* présager.

bodice, *n.* corsage *m.*

bodily, *adj.* corporel.

body, *n.* corps *m.*

bodyguard, *n.* garde (*f.*) du corps.

bog, 1. *n.* marécage *m.* 2. *vb.* embourber.

Bohemia, *n.* (geographical) Bohème *f.;* (fig.) bohème *f.*

Bohemian, 1. *n.* (geographical) Bohémien *m.;* (fig.) bohème *m.f.* 2. *adj.* (geographical) bohémien; (fig.) bohème.

boil, 1. *vb.* bouillir, *intr.;* faire bouillir, *tr.* 2. *n.* (med.) furoncle *m.*, (popular) clou *m.*

boiler, *n.* chaudière *f.*

boisterous, *adj.* (person) bruyant.

boisterously, *adv.* bruyamment.

bold, *adj.* hardi.

boldface, *adj.* (type) caractères gras *m.pl.*

boldly, *adv.* hardiment, avec audace.

boldness, *n.* hardiesse *f.*

bologna, *n.* saucisson (*m.*) de Bologne.

bolster, *n.* traversin *m.*

bolster up, *vb.* soutenir.

bolt, 1. *n.* verrou *m.* 2. *vb.* verrouiller.

bomb, *n.* bombe *f.*

bombard, *vb.* bombarder.

bombardier, *n.* bombardier *m.*

bombardment, *n.* bombardement *m.*

bomber, *n.* avion (*m.*) de bombardement.

bombproof, *adj.* à l'épreuve des bombes.

bombshell, *n.* bombe *f.*

bombsight, *n.* viseur de lancement *m.*

bonbon, *n.* bonbon *m.*

bond, *n.* lien *m.;* (law, finance) obligation *f.*

bondage, *n.* servitude *f.*

bonded, *adj.* entreposé.

bone, *n.* os *m.*

boneless, *adj.* sans os.

bonfire, *n.* feu (*m.*) de joie.

bonnet, *n.* chapeau *m.*

bonus, *n.* gratification *f.*

bony, *adj.* osseux.

book, *n.* livre *m.*

bookbindery, *n.* atelier de reliure *m.*

bookcase, *n.* bibliothèque *f.*

bookkeeper, *n.* teneur (*m.*) de livres.

bookkeeping, *n.* comptabilité *f.*

booklet, *n.* opuscule *m.*

bookseller, *n.* libraire *m.;* (second-hand) bouquiniste *m.*

bookstore, bookshop, *n.* librairie *f.*

boon, *n.* bienfait *m.*, don *m.*

boor, *n.* rustre *m.*

boorish, *adj.* rustre.

boost, *vb.* (push) pousser; (praise) louer.

boot, *n.* bottine *f.*

bootblack, *n.* cireur *m.*

booth, *n.* (fair) baraque *f.;* (telephone) cabine *f.*

booty, *n.* butin *m.*

border, *n.* bord *m.;* (of country) frontière *f.*

borderline, *adj.* touchant (à), avoisinant.

bore, *vb.* (make a hole) forer; (annoy) ennuyer.

boredom, *n.* ennui *m.*

boric acid, *n.* acide borique *m.*

boring, *adj.* ennuyeux.

born, 1. *adj.* né. 2. *vb.* (**be b.**) naître.

born-again, *adj.* réné.

borough, *n.* (administration) circonscription électorale *f.;* (large village) bourg *m.*

borrower, *n.* emprunteur *m.*

borrow from, *vb.* emprunter à.

bosom, *n.* sein *m.*

boss, 1. *n.* patron *m.* 2. *vb.* diriger.

bossy, *adj.* comme un patron, impérieux.

botanical, *adj.* botanique.

botany, *n.* botanique *f.*

botch, 1. *n.* ravaudage *m.* **2.** *vb.* ravauder, faire une mauvaise besogne.

both, *adj. and pron.* tous (les) deux *m.,* toutes (les) deux *f.*

bother, 1. *n.* ennui *m.* **2.** *vb.* gêner.

bothersome, *adj.* gênant.

bottle, *n.* bouteille *f.*

bottom, *n.* fond *m.*

bottomless, *adj.* sans fond.

bough, *n.* branche *f.*

bouillon, *n.* bouillon *m.*

boulder, *n.* galet *m.*

boulevard, *n.* boulevard *m.*

bounce, *vb.* (ball) rebondir.

bound, 1. *n.* (limit) borne *f.;* (jump) bond *m.* **2.** *vb.* (limit) borner; (jump) bondir.

boundary, *n.* frontière *f.*

bound for, *adj.* en route pour.

boundless, *adj.* sans bornes, illimité.

boundlessly, *adv.* sans bornes.

bounteous, *adj.* généreux, bienfaisant.

bounty, *n.* largesse *f.;* (premium) prime *f.*

bouquet, *n.* bouquet *m.*

bourgeois, *adj.* bourgeois.

bout, *n.* (fever) accès *m.*

bovine, *n.* bovine *f.; adj.* bovin.

bow, *n.* (weapon) arc *m.;* (violin) archet *m.;* (curtsy) révérence *f.;* (ship) avant *m.*

bow, *vb.* incliner, *tr.*

bowels, *n.* entrailles *f.pl.*

bowl, 1. *n.* bol *m.* **2.** *vb.* jouer aux boules.

bowlegged, *adj.* à jambes arquées.

bowler, *n.* joueur de boule *m.*

box, *n.* boîte *f.;* (theater) loge *f.*

boxcar, *n.* wagon de marchandises *m.*

boxer, *n.* boxeur *m.*

boxing, *n.* boxe *f.*

box office, *n.* bureau (*m.*) de location.

boy, *n.* garçon *m.*

boycott, *vb.* boycotter.

boyhood, *n.* première jeunesse *f.*

boyish, *adj.* enfantin, puéril.

boyishly, *adv.* comme un gamin.

brace, 1. *vb.* fortifier. **2.** *n.* vilebrequin (tool) *m.,* paire *f.,* couple *m.*

bracelet, *n.* bracelet *m.*

bracket, *n.* (wall) console *f.;* (printing) crochet *m.*

brag, *vb.* se vanter.

braggart, *n.* fanfaron *m.*

braid, *n.* (hair) tresse *f.;* (sewing) galon *m.*

brain, *n.* cerveau *m.;* (brains) cervelle *f.*

brainy, *adj.* intelligent.

brake, *n.* frein *m.*

bran, *n.* son *m.*

branch, *n.* branche *f.*

brand, *n.* marque *f.*

brandish, *vb.* brandir.

brand-new, *adj.* tout neuf.

brandy, *n.* eau-de-vie *f.*

brash, *adj.* impertinent.

brass, *n.* cuivre (*m.*) jaune.

brassiere, *n.* soutien-gorge *m.*

brat, *n.* gosse *m.f.*

bravado, *n.* bravade *f.*

brave, *adj.* courageux.

bravery, *n.* courage *m.*

brawl, *n.* rixe *f.*

brawn, *n.* partie charnue *f.,* muscles *m.pl.*

bray, *vb.* braire.

brazen, *adj.* (person) effronté.

Brazil, *n.* Brésil *m.*

breach, *n.* infraction *f.; (mil.)* brèche *f.*

bread, *n.* pain *m.*

breadth, *n.* largeur *f.*

break, 1. *n.* rupture *f.;* (pause) interruption *f.* **2.** *vb.* rompre, briser, casser.

breakable, *adj.* cassable.

breakage, *n.* cassure *f.,* rupture *f.*

breakfast, *n.* (petit) déjeuner *m.*

breakwater, *n.* brise-lames *m.,* jetée *f.*

breast, *n.* poitrine *f.,* sein *m.*

breath, *n.* haleine *f.; (fig.,* wind) souffle *m.*

breathe, *vb.* respirer.

breathless, *adj.* (out of breath) essoufflé.

breathlessly, *adv.* hors d'haleine.

bred, *adj.* élevé.

breeches, *n.* pantalon *m.sg.*

breed, *vb.* produire; (livestock) élever.

breeder, *n.* (raiser) éleveur *m.*

breeding, *n.* (manners) éducation *f.;* (animals) élevage *m.*

breeze, *n.* brise *f.*

breezy, *adj.* (windy) venteux; (manner) dégagé.

brevity, *n.* brièveté *f.*

brew, *vb.* (beer) brasser; (tea) faire infuser, *tr.*

brewery, *n.* brasserie *f.*

briar, *n.* ronce *f.*

bribe, *vb.* corrompre.

briber, *n.* corrupteur *m.*

bribery, *n.* corruption *f.*

brick, *n.* brique *f.*

bricklaying, *n.* maçonnerie *f.*

bricklike, *adj.* comme une brique.

bridal, *adj.* nuptial.

bride, *n.* mariée *f.*

bridegroom, *n.* marié *m.*

bridesmaid, *n.* demoiselle (*f.*) d'honneur.

bridge, *n.* pont *m.;* (boat) passerelle *f.;* (cards) bridge *m.*

bridged, *adj.* lié.

bridgehead, *n.* tête de pont *f.*

bridle, *n.* bride *f.*

brief, *adj.* bref *m.,* brève *f.*

brief case, *n.* serviette *f.*

briefly, *adv.* brièvement.

briefness, *n.* brièveté *f.*

brier, *n.* bruyère *f.,* ronces *f.pl.*

brig, *n.* brick *m.*

brigade, *n.* brigade *f.*

bright, *adj.* vif *m.,* vive *f.;* intelligent.

brighten, *vb.* faire briller, *tr.*

brightness, *n.* éclat *m.*

brilliance, *n.* éclat *m.*

brilliant, *adj.* brillant.

brim, *n.* bord *m.*

brine, *n.* saumure *f.*

bring, *vb.* (thing) apporter; (person) amener; **(b. about)** amener, causer.

brink, *n.* bord *m.*

briny, *adj.* salé.

brisk, *adj.* vif *m.,* vive *f.*

brisket, *n.* poitrine (meat) *f.*

briskly, *adv.* vivement.

briskness, *n.* vivacité *f.*

bristle, *n.* soie *f.*

bristly, *adj.* hérissé (de), poilu.

British, *adj.* britannique.

British Empire, *n.* Empire Britannique *m.*

British Isles, *n.* Îles Britanniques *f.pl.*

brittle, *adj.* fragile.

broad, *adj.* large.

broadcast, *vb.* radiodiffuser.

broadcast, *n.* radio-émission *f.*

broadcaster, *n.* speaker *m.*

broadcloth, *n.* drap (*m.*) fin.

broaden, *vb.* élargir.

broadly, *adv.* largement.

broadminded, *adj.* large d'esprit.

broadside, *n.* côte *f.,* bordée *f.*

brocade, *n.* brocart *m.*

brocaded, *adj.* de brocart.

broil, *vb.* griller.

broiler, *n.* gril *m.*

broken-hearted, *adj.* qui a le coeur brisé.

broker, *n.* courtier *m.;* (stock-**b.**) agent (*m.*) de change.

brokerage, *n.* courtage *m.*

bronchial, *adj.* bronchique.

bronchitis, *n.* bronchite *f.*

bronze, *n.* bronze *m.*

brooch, *n.* broche *f.*

brood, 1. *n.* couvée *f.* **2.** *vb.* couver.

brook, *n.* ruisseau *m.*

broom, *n.* balai *m.*

broomstick, *n.* manche à balai *m.*

broth, *n.* bouillon *m.*

brothel, *n.* bordel *m.,* maison mal famée *f.*

brother, *n.* frère *m.*

brotherhood, *n.* fraternité *f.*

brother-in-law, *n.* beau-frère *m.*

brotherly, *adj.* fraternel.

brow, *n.* front *m.*

brown, *adj.* brun.

browse, *vb.* (animals) brouter; (books) feuilleter (des livres).

bruise, 1. *n.* meurtrissure *f.* **2.** *vb.* meurtrir.

brunette, *adj. and n.* brune *f.*

brunt, *n.* choc *m.*

brush, n. brosse f.; (paint-b.) pinceau m.

brushwood, n. broussailles f.pl.

brusque, adj. brusque.

brusquely, adv. brusquement.

brutal, adj. brutal.

brutality, n. brutalité f.

brutalize, vb. abrutir.

brute, n. brute f.

bubble, 1. n. bulle f. 2. vb. bouillonner.

buck, n. daim m.; (male) mâle m.

bucket, n. seau m.

buckle, n. boucle f.

buckram, n. bougran m.

buckshot, n. chevrotine f.

buckwheat, n. sarrasin m., blé noir m.

bud, 1. n. bourgeon m. 2. vb. bourgeonner.

budding, adj. en herbe.

budge, vb. bouger.

budget, n. budget m.

buffalo, n. buffle m.

buffer, n. tampon m.

buffet, n. (sideboard) buffet m.

buffoon, n. bouffon m.

bug, n. insecte m.

bugle, n. clairon m.

build, vb. bâtir.

builder, n. (buildings) entrepreneur m.; (ships) constructeur m.

building, n. bâtiment m.

bulb, n. (electricity) ampoule f.; (botany) bulbe m.

bulge, n. bosse f.

bulk, n. masse f.

bulkhead, n. cloison étanche f.

bulky, adj. volumineux.

bull, n. taureau m.

bulldog, n. bouledogue m.

bulldozer, n. machine à refouler f.

bullet, n. balle f.

bulletin, n. bulletin m.

bulletproof, adj. à l'épreuve des balles.

bullfinch, n. bouvreuil m.

bullion, n. lingot m.

bully, vb. rudoyer.

bulwark, n. rempart m.

bum, n. fainéant m.

bumblebee, n. bourdon m.

bump, 1. n. (blow) coup m.; (protuberance) bosse f. 2. vb. cogner.

bumper, n. (auto) pare-chocs m.

bun, n. brioche f.

bunch, n. (flowers) bouquet m.; (grapes) grappe f.; (keys) trousseau m.

bundle, n. paquet m.

bungle, vb. bousiller.

bunion, n. cor m.

bunk, n. couchette f.

bunny, n. lapin m.

bunting, n. drapeaux m.pl.

buoy, n. bouée f.

buoyant, adj. qui a du ressort.

burden, n. fardeau m.

burdensome, adj. onéreux.

bureau, n. (office) bureau m.;

(chest of drawers) commode f.

burglar, n. cambrioleur m.

burglarize, vb. cambrioler.

burglary, n. vol (m.) avec effraction.

burial, n. enterrement m.

burlap, n. gros canevas m.

burly, adj. corpulent.

burn, vb. brûler.

burner, n. bec m.

burning, adj. brûlant.

burnish, vb. brunir, polir.

burrow, n. terrier m.

burst, vb. éclater.

bury, vb. enterrer.

bus, n. autobus m.

bush, n. buisson m.

bushel, n. boisseau m.

bushy, adj. buissonneux; (hair) touffu.

busily, adv. activement.

business, n. affaire f.; (comm.) affaires f.pl.

businesslike, adj. pratique.

businessman, n. homme (m.) d'affaires.

business-woman, n. femme (f.) d'affaires.

bust, n. buste m.

bustle, vb. se remuer.

busy, adj. occupé.

busybody, n. officieux m.

but, conj. mais; (only) ne . . . que; (except) sauf.

butcher, n. boucher m.

butchery, n. tuerie f., massacre m.

butler, n. maître (m.) d'hôtel.

butt, n. bout m., (of jokes) plastron m.

butter, n. beurre m.

buttercup, n. bouton d'or m.

butterfly, n. papillon m.

buttermilk, n. babeurre m.

butterscotch, n. caramel au beurre m.

buttock, n. fesse f.

button, n. bouton m.

buttonhole, n. boutonnière f.

buttress, n. contrefort m.; (flying b.) arc-boutant m.

buxom, adj. (of women) aux formes rebondies.

buy, vb. acheter.

buyer, n. acheteur m.

buzz, 1. n. bourdonnement m. 2. vb. bourdonner.

buzzard, n. buse f.

buzzer, n. trompe f., sirène f.

by, prep. (through) par; (near) près de.

by-and-by, adv. bientôt.

bygone, adj. passé, d'autrefois.

bylaw, n. règlement local m.

by-pass, 1. n. route d'évitement f. 2. vb. faire un détour.

by-product, n. sous-produit m.

bystander, n. spectateur m.

byte, n. unité fondamentale de données f.

byway, n. sentier détourné m.

C

cab, n. (taxi) taxi m.; (horse) fiacre m.

cabaret, n. cabaret m.

cabbage, n. chou m.

cabin, n. (hut) cabane f.; (boat) cabine f.

cabinet, n. cabinet m.

cabinetmaker, n. ébéniste m.

cable, 1. n. câble m. 2. vb. câbler.

cablegram, n. câblogramme m.

cackle, 1. n. caquet m. 2. vb. caqueter.

cacophony, n. cacophonie f.

cactus, n. cactus m.

cad, n. mufle m.

cadaver, n. cadavre m.

cadaverous, adj. cadavérique.

cadence, n. cadence f.

cadet, n. cadet m.

cadmium, n. cadmium m.

cadre, n. cadre m.

café, n. café, (-restaurant) m.

cafeteria, n. restaurant m.

caffeine, n. caféine f.

cage, n. cage f.

caged, adj. mis en cage.

caisson, n. caisson m.

cajole, vb. cajoler.

cake, n. gâteau m.

calamitous, adj. calamiteux, désastreux.

calamity, n. calamité f.

calcify, vb. calcifier.

calcium, n. calcium m.

calculable, adj. calculable.

calculate, vb. calculer.

calculating, adj. qui fait des calculs.

calculation, n. calcul m.

calculus, n. calcul m.

caldron, n. chaudron m.

calendar, n. calendrier m.

calender, n. calandre f.

calf, n. veau m.

calfskin, adj. en peau de veau.

caliber, n. calibre m.

calico, n. calicot m.

calisthenic, adj. callisthénique.

calisthenics, n. callisthénie f.

calk, vb. ferrer à glace.

call, 1. n. appel m.; (visit) visite f. 2. vb. appeler; (call on) faire visite à.

calligraphy, n. calligraphie f.

calling, n. vocation f., profession f.

calling card, n. carte de visite f.

callously, adv. d'une manière insensible.

callousness, n. insensibilité f.

callow, adj. blanc-bec.

callus, n. callosité f.

calm, 1. adj. calme. 2. vb. calmer.

calmly, adv. calmement.

calmness, n. calme m., tranquillité f.

caloric, adj. calorique.

calorie, n. calorie f.

calorimeter, n. calorimètre m.
calumniate, vb. calomnier.
calumny, n. calomnie f.
Calvary, n. Calvaire m.
calve, vb. vêler.
calyx, n. calice m.
camaraderie, n. camaraderie f.
cambric, n. batiste f.
camel, n. chameau m.
camellia, n. camélia m.
camel's hair, n. poil de chameau m.
cameo, n. camée m.
camera, n. appareil photographique m.
camouflage, vb. camoufler.
camouflaged, adj. camouflé.
camouflaging, adj. camouflant.
camp, 1. n. camp m.; (holiday camp) camping m. 2. vb. camper.
campaign, n. campagne f.
camper, n. qui fait du camping.
camphor, n. camphre m.
camphor ball, n. balle de camphre f.
campus, n. terrains (m.pl.) de l'université.
can, 1. n. (food) boîte f.; (general) bidon m. 2. vb. (be able) pouvoir; (put in a can) conserver.
Canada, n. Canada m.
Canadian, 1. n. Canadien m. 2. adj. canadien.
canal, n. canal m.
canalize, vb. canaliser.
canapé, n. canapé m.
canard, n. canard m.
canary, n. serin m.
Canary Islands, n. Îles Canaries f.pl.
cancel, vb. annuler; (erase) biffer.
cancellation, n. annulation f.
cancer, n. cancer m.
candelabrum, n. candélabre m.
candid, adj. sincère.
candidacy, n. candidature f.
candidate, n. candidat m.
candidly, adv. franchement.
candidness, n. candeur f.
candied, adj. candi.
candle, n. bougie f.; (church) cierge m.
candier, n. fabricant de chandelles m.
candlestick, n. chandelier m.
candor, n. sincérité f.
candy, n. bonbon m.
cane, n. canne f.
canine, adj. canin.
canister, n. boîte à thé f.
canker, n. chancre m.
cankerworm, n. ver rongeur m.
canned, adj. conservé en boîtes (de fer blanc).
canner, n. travailleur dans une conserverie m.
cannery, n. conserverie f.
cannibal, adj. and n. cannibale m.f.
canning, n. mise en conserve, en boîtes (de fer blanc) f.

cannon, n. canon m.
cannonade, n. cannonnade f.
cannoneer, n. cannonier m.
cannot, vb. ne peut pas.
canny, adj. avisé, rusé.
canoe, n. canot m.
canon, n. chanoine m.; canon (rule) m.
canonical, adj. canonique.
canonize, vb. canoniser.
canopy, n. dais m.
cant, n. hypocrisie f.
can't, vb. ne peut pas.
cantaloupe, n. melon m., cantaloup m.
canteen, n. cantine f.; bidon m.
canter, 1. n. petit galop f. 2. vb. aller au petit galop.
cantonment, n. cantonnement m.
canvas, n. toile f.
canvass, 1. n. sollicitation f. 2. vb. solliciter; (discuss) débattre.
canyon, n. gorge f., défilé m.
cap, n. bonnet m.; (peaked) casquette f.
capability, n. capacité f.
capable, adj. capable.
capably, adv. capablement.
capacious, adj. ample, spacieux.
capacity, n. capacité f.
caparison, 1. n. caparaçon m. 2. vb. caparaçonner.
cape, n. (geography) cap m.; (cloak) cape f.
caper, 1. n. bond m.; (plant) câpre f. 2. vb. bondir.
capillary, adj. capillaire.
capital, adj. capital.
capital, n. (finance) capital m.; (city) capitale f.; (letter) majuscule f.; (architecture) chapiteau m.
capitalism, n. capitalisme m.
capitalist, n. capitaliste m.f.
capitalistic, adj. capitaliste.
capitalization, n. capitalisation f.
capitalize, vb. capitaliser.
capitulate, vb. capituler.
capon, n. chapon m.
caprice, n. caprice m.
capricious, adj. capricieux.
capriciously, adv. capricieusement.
capriciousness, n. caractère capricieux m., humeur fantasque f.
capsize, vb. chavirer, intr.; faire chavirer, tr.
capsule, n. capsule f.
captain, n. capitaine m.
caption, n. en-tête m.
captious, adj. chicaneur.
captivate, vb. captiver.
captivating, adj. séduisant.
captive, adj. and n. captif m.
captivity, n. captivité f.
captor, n. capteur m.
capture, 1. n. capture f. 2. vb. capturer.
car, n. (auto) voiture f.; (train) wagon m.

caracul, n. caracul m.
carafe, n. carafe f.
caramel, n. caramel m.
carat, n. carat m.
caravan, n. caravane f.
caraway, n. carvi m., cumin (des près) m.
carbide, n. carbure m.
carbine, n. carabine f.
carbohydrate, n. carbohydrate m.
carbon, n. carbone m.
carbon dioxide, n. acide carbonique m.
carbon monoxide, n. oxyde de carbone m.
carbon paper, n. papier carbone m.
carbuncle, n. escarboucle f., charbon (med.) m.
carburetor, n. carburateur m.
carcass, n. carcasse f.
carcinogenic, adj. cancérogène.
card, n. carte f.
cardboard, n. carton m.
cardiac, adj. cardiaque.
cardigan, n. gilet de tricot m.
cardinal, n. cardinal m.
care, 1. n. (worry) souci m.; (attention) attention f.; (take c.!) faites attention!; (charge) soin m.; (take c. of) prendre soin de. 2. vb. (c. about) se soucier de; (c. for) aimer; (look after) soigner.
careen, vb. caréner.
career, n. carrière f.
carefree, adj. insouciant.
careful, adj. soigneux.
carefully, adv. soigneusement, attentivement.
carefulness, n. soin m., attention f.
careless, adj. insouciant.
carelessly, adv. nonchalamment, négligemment.
carelessness, n. insouciance f., négligence f.
caress, 1. n. caresse f. 2. vb. caresser.
caretaker, n. concierge m.f.
cargo, n. cargaison f.
caricature, n. caricature f.
caries, n. carie f.
carillon, n. carillon m.
carload, n. voiturée f.
carnal, adj. charnel.
carnation, n. œillet m.
carnival, n. carnaval m.
carnivorous, adj. carnivore.
carol, n. (Xmas c.) noël m.
carouse, vb. faire la fête.
carpenter, n. charpentier m.
carpet, n. tapis m.
carpeting, n. pose de tapis f.
car pool, n. groupe de personnes qui voyagent régulièrement ensemble en auto m.
carriage, n. (vehicle) voiture f.; (bearing) maintien m.; (transport) transport m.
carrier, n. porteur m., messager m.
carrier pigeon, n. pigeon voyageur m.

carrot, n. carotte m.
carrousel, n. carrousel m.
carry, vb. porter; (c. on) continuer; (c. out) exécuter; (c. through) mener à bonne fin.
cart, n. charrette f.
cartage, n. charriage m., transport m.
cartel, n. cartel m.
carter, n. charretier m.
cartilage, n. cartilage m.
carton, n. carton m.
cartoon, n. dessin satirique m.
cartoonist, n. caricaturiste m.
cartridge, n. cartouche f.
carve, vb. (art) sculpter; (meat) découper.
carver, n. découpeur m., sculpteur m.
carving, n. découpage m., sculpture f.
cascade, n. cascade f.
case, n. (instance, state of things) cas m.; (law) cause f.; (packing) caisse f.; (holder) étui m.; (in any c.) en tout cas.
cash, 1. n. espèces f.pl.; (C.O.D.) livraison contre remboursement f. 2. vb. (c. a check) toucher.
cashier, n. caissier m.
cashmere, n. cachemire m.
casing, n. revêtement m., enveloppe f.
casino, n. casino m.
cask, n. tonneau m.
casket, n. cassette f.
casserole, n. casserole f.
cassette, n. cassette f.
cast, 1. n. (throw) coup m.; (characteristic) trempe f.; (theater) distribution f.; (c. from mold) moulage m.; (hue) nuance f. 2. vb. (throw) jeter; (metal) couler.
castaway, n. naufragé m., rejeté m.
caste, n. caste f.
caster, n. fondeur m.
castigate, vb. châtier, punir.
cast iron, n. fonte f.
castle, n. château m.
castoff, adj. abandonné.
casual, adj. (accidental) casuel; (person) insouciant.
casually, adv. fortuitement, en passant.
casualness, n. nonchalance f.
casualties, n. (mil.) pertes f.pl.
cat, n. chat m., chatte f.
cataclysm, n. cataclysme m.
catacomb, n. catacombe f.
catalogue, n. catalogue f.
catapult, n. catapulte f.
cataract, n. cataracte f.
catarrh, n. catarrhe m.
catastrophe, n. catastrophe f.
catch, vb. attraper; (seize, understand) saisir.
catcher, n. qui attrape.
catchword, n. mot d'ordre m.
catchy, adj. (musical air) facile à retenir; (question) insidieuse.

catechism, n. catéchisme m.
catechize, vb. catéchiser.
categorical, adj. catégorique.
category, n. catégorie f.
cater, vb. pourvoir à.
caterpillar, n. chenille f.
catgut, n. corde à boyau f.
catharsis, n. catharsis f., (med.) purgation f.
cathartic, adj. cathartique, purgatif.
cathedral, n. cathédrale f.
cathode, n. cathode f.
Catholic, adj. catholique.
Catholic Church, n. Église catholique f.
Catholicism, n. catholicisme m.
cat nap, n. somme m.
catsup, n. sauce piquante f.
cattle, n. bétail m., bestiaux m.pl.
cattleman, n. éleveur de bétail m.
catwalk, n. coursive f.
cauliflower, n. chou-fleur m.
causation, n. causation f.
cause, n. cause f.
causeway, n. chaussée f.
caustic, adj. caustique.
cauterize, vb. cautériser.
cautery, n. cautère m.
caution, n. prudence f.
caution, vb. avertir.
cautious, adj. prudent.
cavalcade, n. cavalcade f.
cavalier, adj. and n. cavalier m.
cavalry, n. cavalerie f.
cave, n. caverne f.
cave-in, n. effondrement m.
cavern, n. caverne f.
caviar, n. caviar m.
cavity, n. cavité f.
cease, vb. cesser (de).
ceaseless, adj. incessant, continuel.
cedar, n. cèdre m.
cede, vb. céder.
ceiling, n. plafond m.
celebrant, n. célébrant m.
celebrate, vb. célébrer.
celebration, n. célébration f.
celebrity, n. célébrité f.
celerity, n. célérité f., vitesse f.
celery, n. céleri m.
celestial, adj. céleste.
celibacy, n. célibat m.
celibate, adj. célibataire.
cell, n. cellule f.
cellar, n. cave f.
cellist, n. violoncelliste m.
cello, n. violoncelle m.
cellophane, n. cellophane f.
cellular, adj. cellulaire.
celluloid, n. celluloïd m.
cellulose, n. cellulose f.
Celtic, adj. celtique.
cement, 1. n. ciment m. 2. vb. cimenter.
cemetery, n. cimetière m.
censor, 1. n. censeur m. 2. vb. censurer.
censorious, adj. critique, hargneux.
censorship, n. censure f.

censure, n. censure f.
census, n. recensement m.
cent, n. cent m.; (per c.) pour cent.
centenary, centennial, adj. and n. centenaire m.
center, n. centre m.
centerfold, n. pages centrales f.pl.
centerpiece, n. pièce de milieu f.
centigrade, adj. centigrade.
centigrade thermometer, n. thermomètre centigrade m.
central, adj. central.
centralize, vb. centraliser.
century, n. siècle m.
century plant, n. agave d'Amérique m.
ceramic, adj. céramique.
ceramics, n. céramique f.
cereal, adj. and n. céréale f.
cerebral, adj. cérébral.
ceremonial, adj. and n. cérémonial m.
ceremonious, adj. cérémonieux.
ceremony, n. cérémonie f.
certain, adj. certain.
certainly, adv. certainement.
certainty, n. certitude f.
certificate, n. certificat m.; (birth c.) acte de naissance.
certification, n. certification f.
certified, adj. certifié, diplômé, breveté.
certifier, n. (personne) qui certifie.
certify, vb. certifier.
certitude, n. certitude f.
cervical, adj. cervical.
cervix, n. cervix m.
cessation, n. cessation f., suspension f.
cession, n. cession f.
cesspool, n. fosse d'aisances f.
chafe, vb. frictionner.
chaff, 1. n. menue paille f.; (colloq.) blague f. 2. vb. blaguer.
chafing dish, n. réchaud m.
chagrin, n. chagrin m.
chain, n. chaîne f.
chain reaction, n. réaction caténaire f.
chain store, n. succursale de grand magasin f.
chair, n. chaise f.; (arm-c.) fauteuil m.
chairman, n. président m.
chairmanship, n. présidence f.
chairperson, n. président m.; présidente f.
chairwoman, n. présidente f.
chalice, n. calice m.
chalk, n. craie f.
chalky, adj. de craie, calcaire.
challenge, n. défi m.
challenge, vb. défier; (dispute) contester.
challenger, n. qui fait un défi, prétendant m.
chamber, n. chambre f.
chamberlain, n. chambellan m.

chambermaid, *n.* femme de chambre *f.*

chamber music, *n.* musique de chambre *f.*

chameleon, *n.* caméléon *m.*

chamois, *n.* chamois *m.*

champ, *vb.* ronger, mâcher.

champion, *n.* champion *m.*

championship, *n.* championnat *m.*

chance, *n.* chance *f.; (by c.)* par hasard.

chancel, *n.* sanctuaire *m.,* choeur *m.*

chancellery, *n.* chancellerie *f.*

chancellor, *n.* chancelier *m.*

chandelier, *n.* lustre *m.*

change, 1. *n.* changement *m.; (money)* monnaie *f.; (exchange)* change *m.* **2.** *vb.* changer.

changeable, *adj.* changeant.

changeability, *n.* variabilité *f.*

changer, *n.* changeur *m.*

channel, *n.* canal *m.; (the English C.)* la Manche *f.*

chant, 1. *n.* chant *m.* **2.** *vb.* chanter.

chaos, *n.* chaos *m.*

chaotic, *adj.* chaotique.

chap, *n.* (on skin) gerçure *f.; (young man)* gars *m.*

chapel, *n.* chapelle *f.*

chaperon, *n.* (person) duègne *f.; chaperon m.*

chaplain, *n.* aumônier *m.*

chapman, *n.* colporteur *m.*

chapped, *adj.* gercé.

chapter, *n.* chapitre *m.*

char, *vb.* carboniser.

character, *n.* caractère *m.; (in fiction)* personnage *m.; (role)* rôle *m.*

characteristic, 1. *n.* trait caractéristique *m.* **2.** *adj.* caractéristique.

characteristically, *adv.* d'une manière caractéristique.

characterization, *n.* action de caractériser *f.*

characterize, *vb.* caractériser.

charcoal, *n.* charbon *(m.)* de bois.

charge, 1. *n.* (guns, legal, office) charge *f.; (price)* prix *m.; (care)* soin *m.* **2.** *vb.* charger; **(c. with)** charger de; (price) demander.

charger, *n.* grand plat *m.; cheval de bataille m.*

chariot, *n.* char *m.,* chariot *m.*

charioteer, *n.* conducteur de chariot *m.*

charisma, *n.* charisme *m.*

charitable, *adj.* charitable.

charitableness, *n.* bienveillance *f.*

charitably, *adv.* charitablement.

charity, *n.* charité *f.*

charlatan, *n.* charlatan *m.*

charlatanism, *n.* charlatanisme *m.*

charm, 1. *n.* charme *m.* **2.** *vb.* charmer.

charmer, *n.* charmeur *m.,* enchanteur *m.*

charming, *adj.* charmant.

charred, *adj.* carbonisé.

chart, *n.* (map) carte *f.; (graph)* graphique *m.*

charter, 1. *n.* charte *f.* **2.** *vb.* (boat) affréter.

charter flight, *n.* vol frété *m.; charter m.*

charwoman, *n.* femme de journée *f.,* femme de ménage *f.*

chase, 1. *n.* chasse *f.* **2.** *vb.* chasser.

chaser, *n.* chasseur *m.; ciseleur m.*

chasm, *n.* abîme *m.*

chassis, *n.* chassis *m.*

chaste, *adj.* chaste.

chasten, *vb.* châtier, corriger.

chasteness, *n.* pureté *f.*

chastise, *vb.* châtier.

chastisement, *n.* châtiment *m.*

chastity, *n.* chasteté *f.*

chat, 1. *n.* causette *f.* **2.** *vb.* causer.

chateau, *n.* château *m.*

chattel, *n.* bien *m.,* meuble *m.*

chatter, 1. *n.* bavardage *m.* **2.** *vb.* bavarder.

chatterbox, *n.* bavard *m.*

chauffeur, *n.* chauffeur *m.*

cheap, *adj.* (inexpensive) bon marché, (mean) de peu de valeur.

cheapen, *vb.* déprécier.

cheaply, *adv.* à bon marché.

cheapness, *n.* bon marché *m.,* bas prix *m.;* basse qualité *f.*

cheat, *vb.* tromper; (at games) tricher.

cheater, *n.* tricheur *m.,* trompeur *m.*

check, 1. *n.* (restraint) frein *m.; (verification)* vérification *f.; (stub)* ticket *m.; (bill)* addition *f.; (bank draft)* chèque *m.* **2.** *vb.* (stop) arrêter; (restrain) modérer; (verify) vérifier; (luggage) enregistrer.

checker, *n.* enregistreur *m.,* contrôleur *m.*

checkers, *n.* jeu de dames *m.*

checkmate, 1. *n.* échec et mat *m.* **2.** *vb.* mater.

cheek, *n.* joue *f.*

cheer, 1. *n.* (applause) hourra *m.* **2.** *vb.* (acclaim) acclamer; **(c. up,** *tr.)* réjouir.

cheerful, cheery, *adj.* gai.

cheerfully, *adv.* gaiement, de bon cœur.

cheerfulness, *n.* gaieté *f.,* bonne humeur *f.*

cheerless, *adj.* triste, morne, sombre.

cheery, *adj.* gai, joyeux.

cheese, *n.* fromage *m.*

cheesecloth, *n.* gaze *f.*

cheesy, *adj.* fromageux.

chemical, *adj.* chimique.

chemically, *adv.* chimiquement.

chemist, *n.* chimiste *m.f.*

chemistry, *n.* chimie *f.*

chemotherapy, *n.* chimiothérapie *f.*

chenille, *n.* chenille *f.*

cherish, *vb.* chérir.

cherry, *n.* cerise *f.*

cherub, *n.* chérubin *m.*

chess, *n.* échecs *m.pl.*

chessman, *n.* pièce *f.*

chest, *n.* (box) coffre *m.; (body)* poitrine *f.; (c.* **of drawers)** commode *f.*

chestnut, *n.* châtaigne *f.*

chevron, *n.* chevron *m.*

chew, *vb.* mâcher.

chewer, *n.* mâcheur *m.*

chic, *adj.* chic.

chicanery, *n.* chicane *f.,* chicanerie *f.*

chick, *n.* poussin *m.*

chicken, *n.* poulet *m.*

chicken-hearted, *adj.* peureux.

chicken-pox, *n.* varicelle *f.*

chicle, *n.* chiclé *m.*

chicory, *n.* chicorée *f.*

chide, *vb.* gronder, réprimander.

chief, 1. *n.* chef *m.* **2.** *adj.* principal.

chiefly, *adv.* surtout, principalement.

chieftain, *n.* chef de clan *m.*

chiffon, *n.* chiffon *m.*

chilblain, *n.* engelure *f.*

child, *n.* enfant *m.f.*

childbirth, *n.* enfantement *m.*

childhood, *n.* enfance *f.*

childish, *adj.* enfantin.

childishness, *n.* puérilité *f.,* enfantillage *m.*

childless, *adj.* sans enfant.

childlessness, *n.* l'état d'être sans enfants.

childlike, *adj.* comme un enfant, en enfant.

Chile, *n.* Chili *m.*

Chilean, 1. *n.* Chilien *m.* **2.** *adj.* chilien.

chili, *n.* piment *m.*

chill, 1. *n.* froid *m.; (shiver)* frisson *m.* **2.** *vb.* refroidir.

chilliness, *n.* froid *m.,* frisson *m.*

chilly, *adj.* un peu froid.

chime, 1. *n.* carillon *m.* **2.** *vb.* carillonner.

chimney, *n.* cheminée *f.*

chimney sweep, *n.* ramoneur *m.*

chimpanzee, *n.* chimpanzé *m.*

chin, *n.* menton *m.*

China, *n.* Chine *f.*

china, *n.* (ware) porcelaine *f.*

chinchilla, *n.* chinchilla *m.*

Chinese, 1. *n.* (person) Chinois *m.; (language)* chinois *m.* **2.** *adj.* chinois.

chink, *n.* fente *f.,* crevasse *f.*

chintz, *n.* perse *f.*

chip, *n.* éclat *m.; (potato c.s)* frites *f.pl.*

chipmunk, *n.* tamias *m.*

chiropodist, *n.* pédicure *m.*

chiropractor, *n.* chiropracteur *m.*

chirp, *vb.* pépier, gazouiller.

chisel, 1. vb. ciseler. 2. n. ciseau m.

chivalrous, adj. chevaleresque.

chivalry, n. chevalerie f.

chive, n. ciboulette f.

chloride, n. chlorure m.

chlorine, n. chlore m.

chloroform, n. chloroforme m.

chlorophyll, n. chlorophylle m.

chockfull, adj. plein comme un œuf.

chocolate, n. chocolat m.

choice, n. choix m.

choir, n. chœur m.

choke, vb. étouffer.

choker, n. foulard m.

cholera, n. choléra m.

choleric, adj. cholérique.

choose, vb. choisir.

chop, 1. n. (meat) côtelette f. 2. vb. couper.

chopper, n. couperet m.

choppy, adj. (sea) clapoteux.

chopstick, n. baguette f., bâtonnet m.

choral, adj. choral.

chord, n. (music) accord m.

chore, n. travail (m.) de ménage.

choreography, n. chorégraphie f.

chorister, n. choriste m. enfant de chœur m.

chortle, vb. glousser de joie.

chorus, n. chœur m.

chowder, n. (sorte de) bouillabaisse f.

christen, vb. baptiser.

Christendom, n. chrétienté f.

christening, n. baptême m.

Christian, adj. and n. chrétien m.

Christianity, n. christianisme m.

Christmas, n. Noël m.

chromatic, adj. chromatique.

chromium, n. chrome m.

chromosome, n. chromosome m.

chronic, adj. chronique.

chronically, adv. chronologiquement.

chronicle, n. chronique f.

chronological, adj. chronologique.

chronology, n. chronologie f.

chrysalis, n. chrysalide f.

chrysanthemum, n. chrysanthème m.

chubby, adj. joufflu.

chuck, n. petite tape f., gloussement (de volaille) m.

chuckle, vb. rire tout bas.

chug, 1. n. souffle m. (d'une machine à vapeur). 2. vb. souffler.

chum, n. camarade m., copain m.

chummy, adj. familier, intime.

chunk, n. gros morceau m.

chunky, adj. en gros morceaux.

church, n. église f.

churchman, n. homme d'église m., ecclésiastique m.

churchyard, n. cimetière m.

churn, vb. baratter.

chute, n. glissière f.

chutney, n. chutney m.

cicada, n. cigale f.

cider, n. cidre m.

cigar, n. cigare m.

cigarette, n. cigarette f.

cilia, n. cils m.pl.

ciliary, adj. ciliaire.

cinch, n. (it's a c.) c'est facile.

cinchona, n. quinquina m.

cinder, n. cendre f.

cinema, n. cinéma m.

cinematic, adj. cinématographique.

cinnamon, n. cannelle f.

cipher, n. chiffre m.; (nought) zéro m.

circle, 1. n. cercle n. 2. vb. entourer (de).

circuit, n. circuit m.

circuitous, adj. détourné, sinueux.

circuitously, adv. d'une manière détournée, par des détours.

circular, adj. circulaire.

circularize, vb. envoyer des circulaires.

circulate, vb. circuler, tr.; faire circuler, intr.

circulation, n. circulation f.

circulator, n. circulateur m.

circulatory, adj. circulaire, circulatoire.

circumcise, vb. circoncire.

circumcision, n. circoncision f.

circumference, n. circonférence f.

circumlocution, n. circonlocution f.

circumscribe, vb. circonscrire.

circumspect, adj. circonspect.

circumstance, n. (condition) circonstance f.; (financial) moyens m.pl.

circumstantial, adj. circonstancié.

circumstantially, adv. en détail.

circumvent, vb. circonvenir.

circumvention, n. circonvention f.

circus, n. cirque m.

cirrhosis, n. cirrhose f.

cistern, n. citerne f.

citadel, n. citadelle f.

citation, n. citation f.

cite, vb. citer.

citizen, n. citoyen m.

citizenry, n. tous les citoyens m.pl.

citizenship, n. droit (m.) de cité.

citric acid, n. acide citrique m.

city, n. ville f.; cité f.

civic, adj. civique.

civics, n. instruction (f.) civique.

civil, adj. civil; (polite) poli; (c. servant) fonctionnaire m.

civilian, n. civil m.

civility, n. civilité f., politesse f.

civilization, n. civilisation f.

civilize, vb. civiliser.

civilized, adj. civilisé.

civil service, n. administration (civile) f.

civil war, n. guerre civile f.

clad, adj. habillé, vêtu.

claim, 1. n. (demand) demande f.; (right) droit m. 2. vb. (demand) réclamer, prétendre; (insist) soutenir.

claimant, n. réclamateur m., prétendant m.

clairvoyance, n. clairvoyance f.

clairvoyant, n. voyant m.

clam, n. palourde f., mollusque m.

clamber, vb. grimper.

clammy, adj. visqueux, moite.

clamor, n. clameur f.

clamorous, adj. bruyant.

clamp, 1. n. (metal) crampon m.; (carpentry) serre-joint m. 2. vb. cramponner, serrer.

clan, n. clan m., clique f., coterie f.

clandestine, adj. clandestin.

clandestinely, adv. clandestinement.

clang, 1. n. cliquetis m., son métallique m. 2. vb. résonner.

clangor, n. cliquetis m.

clannish, adj. de clan.

clap, vb. (applaud) applaudir.

clapboard, n. bardeau m.

clapper, n. claqueur m., battant (of a bell) m.

claque, n. claque f.

claret, n. vin rouge de Bordeaux m.

clarification, n. clarification f.

clarify, vb. (lit.) clarifier; (fig.) éclaircir.

clarinet, n. clarinette f.

clarinetist, n. clarinettiste m.

clarion, n. clairon m.

clarity, n. clarté f.

clash, 1. vb. choquer, tr.; s'entre-choquer, intr. 2. n. choc m.

clasp, 1. n. agrafe f.; (embrace) étreinte f. 2. vb. agrafer, étreindre.

class, n. classe f.

classic, classical, adj. classique.

classicism, n. classicisme m.

classifiable, adj. classifiable.

classification, n. classification f.

classify, vb. classifier, classer.

classmate, n. camarade (m.) de classe.

classroom, n. salle (f.) de classe.

clatter, n. bruit m.

clause, n. clause f.

claustrophobia, n. claustrophobie f.

claw, n. griffe f.

claw-hammer, n. marteau à dent m.

clay, n. argile f., glaise f.

clean, 1. adj. propre. 2. vb. nettoyer.

clean-cut, adj. net, fin.

cleaner, n. (dry-c.) teinturier m.

cleanliness, cleanness, n. propreté f.

cleanse, vb. nettoyer, curer.

cleanser, n. chose qui nettoie f., détersif m., cureur m.

clear, 1. adj. clair. **2.** vb. (c. up) déblayer; (profit) gagner; (get over) franchir; (weather, intr.) s'éclaircir.

clear-cut, adj. nettement dessiné.

clearing, n. (open place) clairière f., éclaircissement m. (comm.) acquittement m., (woods) éclaircie f.

clearing house, n. banque de virement f., chambre de compensation f.

clearly, adv. clairement, nettement, évidemment.

clearness, n. clarté f., netteté f.

cleat, n. fer m., (naut.) taquet m.

cleavage, n. fendage m., scission f.

cleave, vb. (split) fendre; (adhere) adhérer.

cleaver, n. fendeur (person) m.; fendoir m., couperet (instrument) m.

cleft, n. fente f.

clemency, n. clémence f.

clench, vb. serrer.

clergy, n. clergé m.

clergyman, n. ecclésiastique m.

clerical, adj. (clergy) clérical; (business) de bureau.

clericalism, n. cléricalisme m.

clerk, n. (business) employé m.; (store) commis m.; (law, eccles.) clerc m.

clerkship, n. place de clerc f., place de commis f.

clever, adj. habile.

cleverly, adv. habilement.

cleverness, n. adresse f.

clew, n. fil m.

cliché, n. cliché m.

click, 1. n. cliquetis m., déclic m. **2.** vb. cliqueter.

client, n. client m.

clientele, n. clientèle f.

cliff, n. falaise f.

climactic, adj. arrivé à son apogée.

climate, n. climat m.

climatic, adj. climatique.

climax, n. comble m.

climb, 1. n. montée f. **2.** vb. monter, grimper.

climber, n. grimpeur m., ascensioniste m.

clinch, vb. river; (settle) conclure.

cling, vb. s'accrocher.

clinging, adj. qui se cramponne, qui s'accroche (à).

clinic, n. clinique f.

clinical, adj. clinique.

clinically, adv. d'une manière clinique.

clip, 1. vb. couper. **2.** n. pince f.

clipper, n. rogneur m., tondeuse (instrument) f., (naut.) fin voilier m.

clipping, n. coupure f.

clique, n. clique f.

cloak, n. manteau m.; (cloakroom) vestiaire m.

clock, n. horloge f.; (two o'clock) deux heures.

clockwise, adv. dans le sens des aiguilles d'une montre.

clockwork, n. mouvement (m.) d'horlogerie.

clod, n. motte (f.) de terre; (person) lourdaud m.

clog, vb. entraver.

cloister, n. cloître m.

clone, n. reproduction exacte f.

close, 1. adj. (closed) fermé; (narrow) étroit; (near) proche; (secret) réservé. **2.** vb. fermer. **3.** adv. tout près. **4.** prep. (c. to) près de.

closely, adv. de près, étroitement.

closeness, n. proximité f., lourdeur (of the weather) f., réserve f.

closet, n. (room) cabinet m.; (clothes) placard m.

clot, n. (blood) caillot m.

cloth, n. étoffe f.

clothe, vb. vêtir (de); habiller.

clothes, n. habits m.pl.

clothespin, n. pince f.

clothier, n. drapier m., tailleur m.

clothing, n. vêtements m.pl.

cloud, n. nuage m.

cloudburst, n. trombe f., rafale de pluie f.

cloudiness, n. état nuageux m., obscurité f.

cloudless, adj. sans nuage.

cloudy, adj. nuageux, couvert.

clout, n. gifle f., tape f. **2.** vb. gifler, taper.

clove, n. clou (m.) de girofle.

clover, n. trèfle m.

clown, n. bouffon m.

clownish, adj. rustre, grossier, de payan.

cloy, vb. rassasier.

club, n. (society) club m., société f., cercle m.; (stick) massue f.; (golf) crosse f.; (cards) trèfle m.

clubfoot, n. pied bot m.

clue, n. fil m.

clump, n. (trees) bosquet m.; massif m.

clumsiness, n. gaucherie f., maladresse f.

clumsy, adj. gauche.

cluster, 1. n. (people) groupe m.; (fruit) grappe f.; (flowers, trees) bouquet m. **2.** vb. se grouper.

clutch, 1. n. (claw) griffe f.; (auto) embrayage m. **2.** vb. saisir.

clutter, vb. encombrer.

coach, 1. n. (carriage) carrosse m.; (train) wagon m.; (sports) entraîneur m. **2.** vb. (sports) entraîner; (school) donner des leçons particulières à.

coachman, n. cocher m.

coagulate, vb. se coaguler.

coagulation, n. coagulation f.

coal, n. charbon (m.) de terre, houille f.

coalesce, vb. se fondre, se fusionner, s'unir.

coalition, n. coalition f.

coal tar, n. goudron de houille m.

coarse, adj. grossier.

coarsen, vb. rendre plus grossier.

coarseness, n. grossièreté f.

coast, n. côte f.

coastal, adj. de la côte, littoral.

coaster, n. caboteur m., dessous de carafe m.

coast guard, n. garde-côtes m.

coat, 1. n. (man) pardessus m.; (woman) manteau m.; (paint) couche f. **2.** vb. (c. with) revêtir de.

coating, n. couche f., enduit m., étoffe pour habits f.

coat of arms, n. écusson m., cotte d'armes f.

coax, vb. cajoler.

cobalt, n. cobalt m.

cobbler, n. savetier m., cordonnier m.

cobblestone, n. pierre du pavé f.

cobra, n. cobra m.

cobweb, n. toile (f.) d'araignée.

cocaine, n. cocaïne f.

cock, 1. n. (fowl) coq m.; (male) mâle m. **2.** vb. faire de l'œil.

cocker spaniel, n. épagneul cocker m.

cockeyed, adj. louche.

cockhorse, n. dada m.

cockroach, n. blatte f.

cocksure, adj. sûr et certain.

cocktail, n. cocktail m.

cocky, adj. suffisant.

cocoa, n. cacao m.

coconut, n. noix (f.) de coco; coco m.

cocoon, n. cocon m.

cod, n. morue f.

coddle, vb. dorloter.

code, n. code m.

codeine, n. codéine f.

codfish, n. morue f.

codify, vb. codifier.

cod-liver oil, n. huile de foie de morue f.

coeducation, n. enseignement mixte m.

coequal, adj. égal.

coerce, vb. contraindre.

coercion, n. coercition f., contrainte f.

coercive, adj. coercitif.

coexist, vb. coexister.

coffee, n. café m.

coffer, n. coffre m.

coffin, n. cercueil m.

cog, n. dent f.

cogent, adj. puissant, fort.

cogitate, vb. méditer, penser.

cognizance, n. connaissance f.

cognizant, adj. instruit, (law) compétent.

cogwheel, n. roue d'engrenage f.

coherent, adj. cohérent.

cohesion, n. cohésion f.

cohesive, adj. cohésif.

cohort, n. cohorte f.

coiffure, n. coiffure f.

coil, n. rouleau m.

coin, n. pièce (f.) de monnaie.

coinage, n. monnayage m., monnaie f.

coincide, vb. coïncider.

coincidence, n. coïncidence f.

coincident, adj. coïncident.

coincidental, adj. coïncident, d'accord (avec).

coincidentally, adv. par coïncidence.

colander, n. passoire f.

cold, 1. n. (temperature) froid m.; (medical) rhume m. 2. adj. froid; (it is cold) il fait froid; (feel cold) avoir froid.

cold-blooded, adj. de sang froid.

coldly, adv. froidement.

coldness, n. froideur f.

collaborate, vb. collaborer.

collaboration, n. collaboration f.

collaborator, n. collaborateur m.

collapse, 1. n. effondrement m.; (med.) affaissement m. 2. vb. s'effondrer; (med.) s'affaisser.

collar, n. col m.; (dog) collier m.

collarbone, n. clavicule f.

collate, vb. collationner, comparer.

collateral, adj. and n. collatéral m.

collation, n. collation f., comparaison f., repas froid m.

colleague, n. collègue m.f.

collect, vb. rassembler.

collection, n. collection f.; (money) collecte f.

collective, adj. collectif.

collectively, adv. collectivement.

collector, n. (art) collectionneur m.; (tickets) contrôleur m.

college, n. collège m.; (higher education) université f.

collegiate, adj. de collège, collégial.

collide, vb. se heurter (contre).

colliery, n. houillère f., mine de charbon f.

collision, n. collision f.

colloquial, adj. familier.

colloquialism, n. expression de style familier f.

colloquially, adv. en style familier.

colloquy, n. colloque m., entretien m.

collusion, n. collusion f., connivence f.

colon, n. (gramm.) deux points m.pl.

colonel, n. colonel m.

colonial, adj. colonial.

colonist, n. colon m.

colonization, n. colonisation f.

colonize, vb. coloniser.

colony, n. colonie f.

color, 1. n. couleur f. 2. vb. colorer, tr.

coloration, n. coloris m.

colored, adj. coloré, de couleur, colorié.

colorful, adj. coloré, pittoresque.

coloring, n. coloris m., couleur f.

colorless, adj. sans couleur, incolore, terne.

colossal, adj. colossal.

colt, n. poulain m.

colter, n. coutre m.

column, n. colonne f.

columnist, n. journaliste (qui a sa rubrique à lui) m.

coma, n. coma m.

comb, 1. n. peigne m. 2. vb. peigner.

combat, n. combat m.

combatant, adj. and n. combattant m.

combative, adj. combatif.

combination, n. combinaison f.

combination lock, n. serrure à combinaisons f.

combine, vb. combiner, tr.

combustible, adj. and n. combustible m.

combustion, n. combustion f.

come, vb. venir; (c. about) arriver; (c. across) rencontrer; (c. away) partir; (c. back) revenir; (c. down) descendre; (c. in) entrer; (c. out) sortir; (c. up) monter.

comedian, n. comédien m.

comedienne, n. comédienne f.

comedy, n. comédie f.

comely, adj. avenant.

comet, n. comète f.

comfort, 1. n. (mental) consolation f.; (material) confort m. 2. vb. consoler.

comfortable, adj. commode.

comfortably, adv. confortablement, commodément.

comforter, n. consolateur m.

comfortingly, adv. d'une manière réconfortante.

comfortless, adj. sans consolation, inconsolable, désolé.

comic, comical, adj. comique.

comic strip, n. dessein comique m.

coming, n. venue f., arrivée f., approche f.

comma, n. virgule f.

command, 1. n. commandement m. 2. vb. commander (à).

commandeer, vb. réquisitionner.

commander, n. commandant m.

commander in chief, n. généralissime m.

commandment, n. commandement m.

commemorate, vb. commémorer.

commemoration, n. célébration f., commémoration f.

commemorative, adj. commémoratif.

commence, vb. commencer.

commencement, n. (school) distribution (f.) des diplômes.

commend, vb. (entrust) recommander; (praise) louer.

commendable, adj. louable, recommandable.

commendably, adv. d'une manière louable.

commendation, n. louange f.

commensurate, adj. proportionné.

comment, 1. n. commentaire m. 2. vb. commenter.

commentator, n. commentateur m.

commerce, n. commerce m.

commercial, adj. commercial.

commercialism, n. commercialisme m.

commercialize, vb. commercialiser.

commercially, adv. commercialement.

commiserate, vb. plaindre, avoir pitié de.

commissary, n. (person) commissaire m.; (supply store) dépôt (m.) de vivres.

commission, n. (assignment) commande f.; (officer) brevet m.; (committee, percentage) commission f.

commissioner, n. commissaire m.

commit, vb. commettre.

commitment, n. engagement m.

committee, n. comité m.

commodious, adj. spacieux.

commodity, n. produit m., commodité f., denrée f.

common, adj. commun; (vulgar) vulgaire.

common law, n. droit coutumier m.

commonly, adv. communément, ordinairement.

commonness, n. vulgarité f.

commonplace, n. lieu-commun m.

commonwealth, n. état m.

commotion, n. agitation f.

communal, adj. communal.

commune, n. commune f.

communicable, adj. communicable.

communicant, n. communiant m.

communicate, vb. communiquer.

communication, n. communication f.

communicative, adj. communicatif.

communion, n. communion f.

communiqué, n. communiqué m.

communism, *n.* communisme *m.*

communist, *adj. and n.* communiste *m.f.*

communistic, *adj.* communiste.

community, *n.* communauté *f.*

commutation, *n.* commutation *f.*

commute, *vb.* changer, *(law)* commuer.

commuter, *n.* voyageur de banlieue *m.*

compact, 1. *n.* (agreement) accord *m.; (cosmetic)* poudrier *m.* **2.** *adj.* compact.

compactness, *n.* compacité *f.*

companion, *n.* compagnon *m.,* compagne *f.*

companionable, *adj.* sociable.

companionship, *n.* camaraderie *f.*

company, *n.* compagnie *f.*

comparable with, *adj.* comparable à.

comparative, *adj. and n.* comparatif *m.*

comparatively, *adv.* comparativement, relativement.

compare, *vb.* comparer.

comparison, *n.* comparaison *f.*

compartment, *n.* compartiment *m.*

compass, *n.* (naut.) boussole *f.; (geom.)* compas *m.*

compassion, *n.* compassion *f.*

compassionate, *adj.* compatissant.

compassionately, *adv.* avec compassion.

compatible, *adj.* compatible.

compatriot, *n.* compatriote *m.f.*

compel, *vb.* forcer.

compensate, *vb.* compenser.

compensation, *n.* compensation *f.*

compensatory, *adj.* compensateur.

compete, *vb.* rivaliser.

competence, *n.* compétence *f.*

competent, *adj.* capable.

competently, *adv.* convenablement, avec compétence.

competition, *n.* concurrence *f.*

competitor, *n.* concurrent *m.*

compile, *vb.* compiler.

complacency, *n.* contentement *(m.)* de soi-même.

complacent, *adj.* content de soi-même.

complacently, *adv.* avec un air (un ton) suffisant.

complain, *vb.* se plaindre.

complainer, *n.* plaignant *m.,* réclameur *m.*

complainingly, *adv.* d'une manière plaignante.

complaint, *n.* plainte *f.*

complement, *n.* complément *m.*

complete, *adj.* complet.

completely, *adv.* complètement, tout à fait.

completeness, *n.* état complet *m.,* perfection *f.*

completion, *n.* achèvement *m.*

complex, *adj. and n.* complexe *m.*

complexion, *n.* teint *m.*

complexity, *n.* complexité *f.*

compliance, *n.* acquiescement *m.*

compliant, *adj.* complaisant, accommodant.

complicate, *vb.* compliquer.

complicated, *adj.* compliqué.

complication, *n.* complication *f.*

complicity, *n.* complicité *f.*

compliment, *n.* compliment *m.*

complimentary, *adj.* flatteur, de félicitations.

comply with, *vb.* se conformer à.

component, *adj. and n.* composant *m.*

comport, *vb.* s'accorder (avec), convenir (à).

compose, *vb.* composer.

composed, *adj.* composé, calme, tranquille.

composer, *n.* compositeur *m.*

composite, *adj.* composé.

composition, *n.* composition *f.*

compost, *n.* compost *m.,* terreau *m.*

composure, *n.* calme *m.,* tranquillité *f.,* sang-froid *m.*

compote, *n.* compote *f.*

compound, 1. *adj. and n.* composé *m.* **2.** *vb.* composer.

comprehend, *vb.* comprendre.

comprehensible, *adj.* compréhensible, intelligible.

comprehension, *n.* compréhension *f.*

comprehensive, *adj.* compréhensif.

compress, 1. *n.* compresse *f.* **2.** *vb.* comprimer, *tr.*

compressed, *adj.* comprimé.

compression, *n.* compression *f.*

compressor, *n.* compresseur *m.*

comprise, *vb.* comprendre.

compromise, 1. *n.* compromis *m.* **2.** *vb.* compromettre.

compromiser, *n.* comprometteur *m.*

compulsion, *n.* contrainte *f.*

compulsive, *adj.* coercitif, obligatoire.

compulsory, *adj.* obligatoire.

compunction, *n.* componction *f.*

computation, *n.* supputation *f.*

compute, *vb.* supputer.

computer, *n.* ordinateur *m.*

computerize, *vb.* informatiser.

computer science, *n.* informatique *f.*

comrade, *n.* camarade *m.f.*

comradeship, *n.* camaraderie *f.*

concave, *adj.* concave.

conceal, *vb.* cacher.

concealment, *n.* action *(f.)* de cacher.

concede, *vb.* concéder.

conceit, *n.* vanité *f.*

conceited, *adj.* vaniteux, suffisant.

conceivable, *adj.* concevable.

conceivably, *adv.* d'une manière concevable.

conceive, *vb.* concevoir.

concentrate, *vb.* concentrer *tr.*

concentration camp, *n.* camp de concentration *m.*

concept, *n.* concept *m.*

conception, *n.* conception *f.*

concern, 1. *n.* (what pertains to one) affaire *f.; (comm.)* entreprise *f.; (solicitude)* souci *m.* **2.** *vb.* concerner; (c. oneself with) s'intéresser à; (be c.ed about) s'inquiéter de.

concerning, *prep.* concernant.

concert, *n.* concert *m.*

concerted, *adj.* concerté.

concession, *n.* concession *f.*

conciliate, *vb.* concilier.

conciliation, *n.* conciliation *f.*

conciliator, *n.* conciliateur *m.*

conciliatory, *adj.* conciliant, conciliatoire.

concise, *adj.* concis.

concisely, *adv.* avec concision, succinctement.

conciseness, *n.* concision *f.*

conclave, *n.* conclave *m.*

conclude, *vb.* conclure.

conclusion, *n.* conclusion *f.*

conclusive, *adj.* concluant.

conclusively, *adv.* d'une manière concluante.

concoct, *vb.* préparer.

concomitant, 1. *adj.* concomitant. **2.** *n.* accessoire *m.*

concord, *n.* concorde *f.*

concordat, *n.* concordat *m.*

concourse, *n.* concours *m.,* affluence *f.*

concrete, 1. *n.* béton *m.* **2.** *adj.* concret.

concretely, *adv.* d'une manière concrète.

concreteness, *n.* état concret *m.*

concubine, *n.* concubine *f.*

concur, *vb.* (events) concourir; (persons) être d'accord.

concurrence, *n.* assentiment *m.,* concours *m.*

concurrent, *adj.* concourant.

concussion, *n.* secousse *f.,* ébranlement *m.*

condemn, *vb.* condamner.

condemnable, *adj.* condamnable.

condemnation, *n.* condamnation *f.*

condensation, *n.* condensation *f.*

condense, *vb.* condenser, *tr.*

condenser, *n.* condenseur *m.*

condescend, *vb.* condescendre.

condescendingly, *adv.* avec condescendance.

condescension, *n.* condescendance *f.*

condiment, *n.* condiment *m.,* assaisonnement *m.*

condition, 1. *n.* condition *f.* **2.** *vb.* conditionner.

conditional, *adj. and n.* conditionnel *m.*

conditionally, adv. conditionnellement.

condolence, n. condoléance f.

condole with, vb. faire ses condoléances à.

condominium, n. condominium m.

conducive, adj. favorable.

conduct, 1. n. conduite f. 2. vb. conduire.

conductivity, n. conductivité f.

conductor, n. conducteur m.; (bus) receveur m.; (rail) chef (m.) de train; (music) chef (m.) d'orchestre.

conduit, n. conduit m., tuyau m.

cone, n. cône m.

confection, n. confection f.; (sweet) bonbon m.

confectioner, n. confiseur m.

confectionery, n. confiserie f.

confederacy, confederation, n. confédération f.

confederate, adj. and n. confédéré m.

confer, vb. conférer.

conference, n. (meeting) entretien m.; (congress) congrès m.

confess, vb. avouer; (eccles.) confesser, tr.

confession, n. confession f.

confessional, n. confessional m.

confessor, n. confesseur m.

confetti, n. confetti m.

confidant, n. confident m.

confidante, n. confidente f.

confide, vb. confier (à), tr.

confidence, n. (trust) confiance f.; (secret) confidence f.

confident, adj. confiant.

confidential, adj. confidentiel.

confidentially, adv. confidentiellement.

confidently, adv. avec confiance.

confine, vb. (banish) confiner; (limit) limiter.

confirm, vb. confirmer.

confirmation, n. confirmation f.

confirmed, adj. invétéré, incorrigible.

confiscate, vb. confisquer.

confiscation, n. confiscation f.

conflagration, n. conflagration f., incendie m.

conflict, n. conflit m.

conform, vb. conformer, tr.

conformation, n. conformation f., conformité f.

conformer, n. conformiste m.

conformist, n. conformiste m.

conformity, n. conformité f.

confound, vb. confondre; (c. him!) que le diable l'emporte!

confront, vb. confronter.

confuse, vb. confondre.

confusion, n. confusion f.

congeal, vb. congeler, tr.

congealment, n. congélation f.

congenial, adj. (person) sympathique; (thing) convenable f.

congenital, adj. congénital.

congenitally, adv. d'une manière congénitale.

congestion, n. (med.) congestion f.; (traffic) encombrement m.

conglomerate, adj. congloméré.

conglomeration, n. conglomération f.

congratulate, vb. féliciter (de).

congratulation, n. félicitation f.

congratulatory, adj. de félicitation.

congregate, vb. rassembler, tr.

congregation, n. assemblée f.

congress, n. congrès m.

congressional, adj. congressionnel.

conic, adj. conique.

conjecture, n. conjecture f.

conjugal, adj. conjugal.

conjugate, vb. conjuguer.

conjugation, n. conjugaison f.

conjunction, n. conjonction f.

conjunctive, adj. conjonctif.

conjunctivitis, n. conjonctivite f.

conjure, vb. conjurer.

connect, vb. joindre.

connection, n. connexion f.; (social) relations f.pl.; (train) correspondance f.

connivance, n. connivence f.

connive, vb. conniver (à).

connoisseur, n. connaisseur m.

connotation, n. connotation f.

connote, vb. signifier, vouloir dire.

connubial, adj. conjugal, du mariage.

conquer, vb. conquérir.

conquerable, adj. qui peut être vaincu, domptable.

conqueror, n. conquérant m.

conquest, n. conquête f.

conscience, n. conscience f.

conscientious, adj. consciencieux.

conscientiously, adv. consciencieusement.

conscious, adj. conscient.

consciously, adv. sciemment, en parfaite connaissance.

consciousness, n. conscience f.

conscript, adj. and n. conscrit m.

conscription, n. conscription f.

consecrate, vb. consacrer.

consecration, n. consécration f.

consecutive, adj. consécutif.

consecutively, adv. consécutivement, de suite.

consensus, n. consensus m., assentiment général m.

consent, 1. n. consentement m. 2. vb. consentir.

consequence, n. conséquence f.

consequent, adj. conséquent.

consequential, adj. conséquent, logique.

consequently, adv. par conséquent.

conservation, n. conservation f.

conservatism, n. conservatisme m.

conservative, adj. (politics) conservateur; (comm.) prudent.

conservatively, adv. d'une manière conservatrice.

conservatory, n. conservatoire m.

conserve, vb. conserver.

consider, vb. considérer.

considerable, adj. considérable.

considerably, adv. considérablement.

considerate, adj. plein d'égards.

considerately, adv. avec égards, avec indulgence.

consideration, n. considération f.

considering, prep. vu que, attendu que.

consign, vb. consigner.

consignment, n. expédition f., consignation f.

consistency, n. consistance f.

consistent, adj. consistant.

consist of, vb. consister en.

consolation, n. consolation f.

console, vb. consoler.

consolidate, vb. consolider.

consommé, n. consommé m.

consonant, n. consonne f.

consort, 1. n. compagnon m., époux m. 2. vb. s'associer (à).

conspicuous, adj. en évidence.

conspicuously, adv. visiblement, éminemment.

conspicuousness, n. éclat m., position éminente f.

conspiracy, n. conspiration f.

conspirator, n. conspirateur m.

conspire, vb. conspirer.

conspirer, n. conspirateur m.

constancy, n. constance f., fermeté f.

constant, adj. constant.

constantly, adv. constamment.

constellation, n. constellation f.

consternation, n. consternation f.

constipation, n. constipation f.

constituency, n. circonscription électorale f.

constituent, adj. constituant.

constitute, vb. constituer.

constitution, n. constitution f.

constitutional, adj. constitutionnel.

constrain, vb. contraindre.

constrained, adj. contraint.

constraint, n. contrainte f., gêne f.

constrict, vb. resserrer.

construct, vb. construire.

construction, n. construction f.

constructive, adj. constructif.

constructively, adv. constructivement, par induction.

constructor, n. constructeur m.

construe, vb. interpréter.

consul, n. consul m.

consular, adj. consulaire.

consulate, *n.* consulat *m.*

consult, *vb.* consulter.

consultant, *n.* conseiller *m.*

consultation, *n.* consultation *f.*

consume, *vb.* consumer.

consumer, *n.* consommateur *m.*

consummate, **1.** *adj.* consommé. **2.** *vb.* consommer.

consummation, *n.* consommation *f.*

consumption, *n.* consommation *f.; (med.)* phtisie *f.*

consumptive, *adj.* poitrinaire, tuberculeux.

contact, *n.* contact *m.*

contagion, *n.* contagion *f.*

contagious, *adj.* contagieux.

contain, *vb.* contenir.

container, *n.* récipient *m.*

contaminate, *vb.* contaminer.

contaminated, *adj.* contaminé.

contemplate, *vb.* contempler.

contemplation, *n.* contemplation *f.*

contemplative, *adj.* contemplatif.

contemporary, *adj.* contemporain.

contempt, *n.* mépris *m.*

contemptible, *adj.* méprisable.

contemptuous, *adj.* méprisant.

contemptuously, *adv.* avec mépris, dédaigneusement.

contend, *vb.* (struggle) lutter; (maintain) soutenir.

contender, *n.* compétiteur *m.,* concurrent *m.*

content, *n.* (satisfaction) contentement *m.; (c.s)* contenu *m.*

contented with, *adj.* content de.

contention, *n.* contention *f.,* lutte *f.*

contentment, *n.* contentement *m.*

contest, **1.** *n.* (struggle) lutte *f.; (competition) concours *m.* **2.** *vb.* contester.

contestable, *adj.* contestable.

contestant, *n.* concurrent *m.,* disputant *m.*

context, *n.* contexte *m.*

contiguous, *adj.* contigu.

continence, *n.* continence *f.,* retenue *f.*

continent, *adj. and n.* continent *m.*

continental, *adj.* continental.

contingency, *n.* contingence *f.*

contingent, *adj.* contingent.

continual, *adj.* continuel.

continuation, *n.* continuation *f.*

continue, *vb.* continuer.

continuity, *n.* continuité *f.*

continuous, *adj.* continu.

continuously, *adv.* continûment, sans interruption.

contort, *vb.* tordre, défigurer.

contortionist, *n.* contortionniste *m.*

contour, *n.* contour *m.*

contraband, *n.* contrebande *f.*

contraception, *n.* limitation des naissances *f.*

contract, **1.** *n.* contrat *m.* **2.** *vb.* contracter, *tr.*

contracted, *adj.* contracté, resserré.

contraction, *n.* contraction *f.*

contractor, *n.* entrepreneur *m.*

contradict, *vb.* contredire.

contradictable, *adj.* qui peut être contredit.

contradiction, *n.* contradiction *f.,* démenti *m.*

contradictory, *adj.* contradictoire.

contraption, *n.* machin *m.*

contrary, *adj. and n.* contraire *m.; (on the c.)* au contraire.

contrast, **1.** *n.* contraste *m.* **2.** *vb.* mettre en contraste, *tr.; contraster, *intr.*

contribute, *vb.* contribuer.

contribution, *n.* contribution *f.*

contributive, *adj.* contributif.

contributor, *n.* contribuant *m.*

contributory, *adj.* contribuant.

contrite, *adj.* contrit, pénitent.

contrition, *n.* contrition *f.*

contrivance, *n.* combinaison *f.,* invention *f.,* artifice *m.*

contrive, *vb.* inventer, imaginer, arranger.

control, **1.** *n.* autorité *f.; (machinery) commande *f.* **2.** *vb.* gouverner; (check) contrôler.

controllable, *adj.* vérifiable, gouvernable.

controller, *n.* contrôleur *m.*

controversial, *adj.* de controverse, polémique.

controversy, *n.* controverse *f.*

contusion, *n.* contusion *f.*

conundrum, *n.* devinette *f.,* énigme *f.*

convalescence, *n.* convalescence *f.*

convalescent, *adj.* convalescent.

convene, *vb.* assembler, *tr.*

convenience, *n.* convenance *f.; (comfort) commodité *f.*

convenient, *adj.* commode.

conveniently, *adv.* commodément.

convent, *n.* couvent *m.*

convention, *n.* convention *f.*

conventional, *adj.* conventionnel.

conventionally, *adv.* par convention.

converge, *vb.* converger.

convergence, *n.* convergence *f.*

convergent, *adj.* convergent.

conversant, *adj.* versé (dans), familier (avec).

conversation, *n.* conversation *f.*

conversational, *adj.* de conversation.

conversationalist, *n.* causeur *m.*

converse, *vb.* converser.

conversely, *adv.* réciproquement.

convert, *vb.* convertir, *tr.*

converter, *n.* convertisseur *m.*

convertible, *adj.* convertible (of things), convertissable (of persons).

convex, *adj.* convexe.

convey, *vb.* (transport) transporter; (transmit) transmettre.

conveyance, *n.* transport *m.*

conveyor, *n.* transporteur *m.,* conducteur (électrique) *m.*

convict, **1.** *n.* forçat *m.* **2.** *vb.* condamner.

conviction, *n.* (condemnation) condamnation *f.; (persuasion) conviction *f.*

convince, *vb.* convaincre.

convincing, *adj.* convaincant.

convincingly, *adv.* d'une manière convaincante.

convivial, *adj.* jovial, joyeux.

convocation, *n.* convocation *f.*

convoke, *vb.* convoquer.

convoy, *n.* convoi *m.*

convulse, *vb.* convulser, bouleverser.

convulsion, *n.* convulsion *f.*

convulsive, *adj.* convulsif.

cook, **1.** *n.* cuisinier *m.* **2.** *vb.* cuire, (intr.); faire cuire, *tr.*

cookbook, *n.* livre de cuisine *m.*

cookie, *n.* gâteau sec *m.*

cool, *adj.* frais *m.,* fraîche *f.*

cooler, *n.* rafraîchissoir *m.,* réfrigérant *m.,* (motor) radiateur *m.*

coolness, *n.* fraîcheur *f.*

coop, **1.** *n.* cage *(f.)* à poules.

coöperate, *vb.* coopérer.

coöperation, *n.* coopération *f.*

coöperative, **1.** *n.* coopérative *f.* **2.** *adj.* coopératif.

coöperatively, *adj.* d'une manière coopérative.

coördinate, *vb.* coordonner.

coördination, *n.* coordination *f.*

coördinator, *n.* coordinateur *m.*

cop, **1.** *n.* (slang) flic *m.* **2.** *vb.* (colloquial) attraper, pincer.

cope with, *vb.* tenir tête à.

copier, *n.* machine à copier *f.*

copious, *adj.* copieux.

copiously, *adv.* copieusement.

copiousness, *n.* abondance *f.*

copper, *n.* cuivre *m.*

copperplate, *n.* cuivre plané *m.; taille-douce *f.*

copy, **1.** *n.* copie *f.* **2.** *vb.* copier.

copyist, *n.* copiste *m.,* imitateur *m.*

copyright, *n.* droit *(m.)* d'auteur.

coquetry, *n.* coquetterie *f.*

coquette, *n.* coquette *f.*

coral, *n.* corail *m.; pl.* coraux.

cord, *n.* corde *f.*

cordial, *adj. and n.* cordial *m.*

cordiality, *n.* cordialité *f.*

cordially, *adv.* cordialement.

cordon, *n.* cordon *m.*

cordovan, *adj.* cordovan.

corduroy, *m.* velours côtelé *m.*

core, *n.* cœur *m.*

cork, *n.* (botany) liège *m.;* (stopper) bouchon *m.*

corkscrew, *n.* tire-bouchon *m.*

corn, *n.* maïs *m.*

cornea, *n.* cornée *f.*

corner, *n.* coin *m.*

cornerstone, *n.* pierre angulaire *f.*

cornet, *n.* cornet *m.*

cornetist, *n.* cornettiste *m.*

cornice, *n.* corniche *f.*

cornucopia, *n.* corne d'abondance *f.*

corollary, *n.* corollaire *m.*

coronary, *adj.* coronaire *m.*

coronation, *n.* couronnement *m.*

coroner, *n.* coroner *m.*

coronet, *n.* (petite) couronne *f.*

corporal, *n.* (mil.) caporal *m.*

corporate, *adj.* de corporation.

corporation, *n.* corporation *f.*

corps, *n.* corps *m.*

corpse, *n.* cadavre *m.*

corpulent, *adj.* corpulent, gros.

corpuscle, *n.* corpuscule *m.*

corral, *n.* corral *m.*

correct, 1. *adj.* correct. 2. *vb.* corriger.

correction, *n.* correction *f.*

corrective, 1. *adj.* correctif. 2. *n.* correctif *m.*

correctly, *adv.* correctement, justement.

correctness, *n.* correction *f.*

correlate, *vb.* être en corrélation, *intr.;* mettre en corrélation, *tr.*

correlation, *n.* corrélation *f.*

correspond, *vb.* correspondre.

correspondence, *n.* correspondance *f.*

correspondent, *n.* correspondant *m.*

corridor, *n.* couloir *m.*

corroborate, *vb.* corroborer.

corroboration, *n.* corroboration *f.*, confirmation *f.*

corroborative, *adj.* coroboratif.

corrode, *vb.* corroder.

corrosion, *n.* corrosion *f.*

corrugate, *vb.* rider, plisser.

corrupt, 1. *adj.* corrompu. 2. *vb.* corrompre.

corruptible, *adj.* corruptible.

corruption, *n.* corruption *f.*

corruptive, *adj.* corruptif.

corsage, *n.* corsage *m.*

corset, *n.* corset *m.*

corvette, *n.* corvette *f.*

cosmetic, *adj. and n.* cosmétique *m.*

cosmic, *adj.* cosmique.

cosmic rays, *n.* rayons cosmiques *m.pl.*

cosmopolitan, *adj. and n.* cosmopolite *m.f.*

cosmos, *n.* cosmos *m.*

cost, 1. *n.* coût *m.* 2. *vb.* coûter.

costliness, *n.* haut prix *m.*, somptuosité *f.*

costly, *adj.* coûteux.

costume, *n.* costume *m.*

costumer, *n.* costumier *m.*

cot, *n.* (berth) couchette *f.;* (folding) lit-cage *m.*

coterie, *n.* coterie *f.*, clique *f.*

cotillion, *n.* cotillon *m*

cottage, *n.* chaumière *f.*

cotton, *n.* coton *m.*

cottonseed, *n.* graine de coton *f.*

couch, *n.* divan *m.*

cougar, *n.* couguar *m.*

cough, 1. *n.* toux *f.* 2. *vb.* tousser.

could, *vb.* pouvait, pourrait.

council, *n.* conseil *m.*

councilman, *n.* conseiller *m.*

counsel, 1. *n.* conseil *m.* 2. *vb.* conseiller.

counselor, *n.* conseiller *m.*

count, 1. *n.* (calculation) compte *m.;* (title) comte *m.* 2. *vb.* compter.

countenance, *n.* expression *f.*

counter, 1. *n.* (shop) comptoir *m.* 2. *adv.* (c. to) à l'encontre de.

counteract, *vb.* neutraliser.

counteraction, *n.* action contraire *f.*

counterattack, *n.* contre-attaque *f.*

counterbalance, 1. *n.* contre-poids *m.* 2. *vb.* contre-balancer.

counterfeit, 1. *adj.* (money) faux *m.*, fausse *f.* 2. *vb.* contrefaire.

countermand, *vb.* contremander.

counteroffensive, *n.* contre-offensive *f.*

counterpart, *n.* contre-partie *f.*

countess, *n.* comtesse *f.*

countless, *adj.* innombrable.

country, *n.* (nation) pays *m.;* (opposed to town) campagne *f.;* (native c.) patrie *f.*

countryman, *n.* (of same c.) compatriote *m.f.;* (rustic) campagnard *m.*

county, *n.* comté *m.*

coupé, *n.* coupé *m.*

couple, 1. *n.* couple *f.* 2. *vb.* coupler.

coupon, *n.* coupon *m.*

courage, *n.* courage *m.*

courageous, *adj.* courageux.

courier, *n.* courrier *m.*

course, *n.* cours *m.;* (of c.) bien entendu; (route) route *f.;* (meal) service *m.*

court, 1. *n.* cour *f.* 2. *vb.* faire la cour à.

courteous, *adj.* courtois.

courtesy, *n.* courtoisie *f.*

courthouse, *n.* palais de justice *m.*

courtier, *n.* courtisan *m.*

courtly, *adj.* de cour, élégant, courtois.

courtmartial, *n.* conseil de guerre *m.*

courtroom, *n.* salle d'audience *f.*

courtship, *n.* cour *f.*

courtyard, *n.* cour *f.*

cousin, *n.* cousin *m.*, cousine *f.*

covenant, *n.* pacte *m.*

cover, 1. *n.* (book, comm., blanket) couverture *f.;* (pot) couvercle *m.;* (shelter) abri *m.;* (envelope) pli *m.; (mil.)* couvert *m.* 2. *vb.* couvrir.

coverage, *n.* couverture *f.*

covering, *n.* couverture *f.*, enveloppe *f.*

covet, *vb.* convoiter.

covetous, *adj.* avide, avaricieux.

cow, *n.* vache *f.*

coward, *adj.* lâche.

cowardice, *n.* lâcheté *f.*

cowboy, *n.* (U.S.A.) cowboy *m.*

cower, *vb.* se blottir.

cow hand, *n.* vacher *m.*

cowhide, *n.* peau (*f.*) de vache.

coxswain, *n.* patron de chaloupe *m.*, barreur *m.*

coy, *adj.* timide.

cozy, *adj.* confortable.

crab, *n.* crabe *m.*

crab apple, *n.* pomme sauvage *f.*

crack, 1. *n.* (fissure) fente *f.;* (noise) craquement *m.* 2. *vb. tr.* (glass, china) fêler; (nuts) casser; (noise) faire craquer. 3. *vb. intr.* (split) se fendiller; (noise) craquer.

cracked, *adj.* fendu, fêlé.

cracker, *n.* biscuit *m.*

cracking, *n.* craquement *m.*, claquement *m.*

crackup, *n.* crach *m.*

cradle, *n.* berceau *f.*

craft, *n.* (skill) habileté *f.;* (trade) métier *m.;* (boat) embarcation *f.*

craftsman, *n.* artisan *m.*

craftsmanship, *n.* habileté, technique *f.*

crafty, *adj.* rusé, astucieux.

crag, *n.* rocher à pic *m.*, rocher escarpé *m.*

cram, *vb.* remplir, farcir.

cramp, *n. (med.)* crampe *f.;* (mechanical) crampon *m.*

cranberry, *n.* canneberge *f.*, airelle *f.*

crane, *n.* grue *f.*

cranium, *n.* crâne *m.*

crank, *n.* manivelle *f.*

cranky, *adj.* d'humeur difficile.

cranny, *n.* crevasse *f.*, fente *f.*

craps, *n.* (slang) jeu de dés *m.*

crapshooter, *n.* (slang) joueur aux dés *m.*

crash, 1. *n.* (noise) fracas *m.;* (accident) accident *m.* 2. *vb.* tomber avec fracas, *intr.*

crate, *n.* caisse *f.*

crater, *n.* cratère *m.*

crave for, *vb.* désirer ardemment.

craven, *adj.* lâche, poltron.

craving, *n.* désir ardent *m.*, besoin impérieux *m.*

crawl, *vb.* (reptiles) ramper; (persons) se traîner.

crayon, n. pastel m.
crazed, adj. fou, dément.
crazy, adj. fou m., folle f.
creak, vb. grincer.
creaky, adj. qui crie, qui grince.
cream, n. crème f.
creamery, n. crêmerie f.
creamy, adj. crémeux, de crème.
crease, 1. n. pli m. 2. vb. froisser, tr.
create, vb. créer.
creation, n. création f.
creative, adj. créateur m., créatrice f.
creator, n. créateur m., créatrice f.
creature, n. créature f.
credence, n. créance f., croyance f.
credentials, n. lettres (f.pl.) de créance; (student, servant) certificat m.
credibility, n. crédibilité f.
credible, adj. croyable.
credit, n. crédit m.; (merit) honneur m.
creditable, adj. estimable.
creditably, adv. honorablement.
credit card, n. carte de crédit f.
creditor, n. créancier m.
credo, n. credo m.
credulity, n. crédulité f.
credulous, adj. crédule.
creed, n. (belief) croyance f., (theology) credo m.
creek, n. ruisseau m.
creep, vb. (reptiles, insects, plants) ramper; (persons) se glisser.
cremate, vb. incinérer.
crematory, n. crématorium m.
creosote, n. créosote f.
crepe, n. crêpe m.
crescent, n. croissant m.
crest, n. crête f.
crestfallen, adj. abattu, découragé.
cretonne, n. cretonne f.
crevice, n. crevasse f.
crew, n. (boat) équipage m.; (gang) équipe f.
crib, n. (child's bed) lit (m.) d'enfant; (manger) mangeoire f.
cricket, n. (insect) grillon m.; (game) cricket m.
crier, n. crieur m., huissier m.
crime, n. crime m.
criminal, adj. criminel.
criminologist, n. criminologue m.
criminology, n. criminologie f.
crimson, adj. and n. cramoisi m.
cringe, vb. faire des courbettes, se tapir, s'humilier.
crinkle, 1. n. pli m., sinuosité f. 2. vb. serpenter, former en zigzag.
cripple, 1. n. estropié m. 2. vb. estropier.
crisis, n. crise f.

crisp, adj. (food) croquant; (manner) tranchant.
crispness, n. frisure f.
crisscross, adj. and adv. entrecroisé.
criterion, n. critérium m.
critic, n. critique m.
critical, adj. critique.
criticism, n. critique f.
criticize, vb. critiquer.
critique, n. critique f.
croak, vb. (frogs) coasser; (crows, persons) croasser.
crochet, 1. vb. broder au crochet. 2. m. crochet m.
crock, n. pot (m.) de terre.
crockery, n. faïence f.
crocodile, n. crocodile m.
crocodile tears, n. larmes de crocodiles f.pl.
crone, n. vieille femme f.
crony, n. vieux camarade m., compère m.
crook, n. (thief) escroc m., voleur m.
crooked, adj. tortu.
croon, vb. chantonner, fredonner.
crop, n. récolte f.
croquet, n. (jeu de) croquet m.
croquette, n. croquette f.
cross, 1. n. croix f. 2. adj. maussade. 3. vb. croiser, tr.; (c. oneself) se signer; (c. out) rayer; (go across) traverser.
crossbreed, n. race croisée f.
cross-examine, vb. contre-examiner.
cross-eye, adj. louche.
cross-fertilization, n. croisement m.
cross-purpose, n. opposition f., contradiction f., malentendu m.
cross section, n. coupe en travers f.
crossword puzzle, n. mots croisés m.pl.
crotch, n. fourche f., fourchet m.
crouch, vb. s'accroupir.
croup, n. croupe f.; (med.) croup m.
croupier, n. croupier m.
crouton, n. crouton m.
crow, 1. n. (bird) corneille f.; (cock-c.) chant (m.) du coq. 2. vb. chanter.
crowd, n. foule f.
crowd, vb. serrer, tr.; (c. with) remplir de.
crowded, adj. (streets, etc.) encombré.
crown, 1. n. couronne f.; (of head) sommet m.; (of hat) calotte f. 2. vb. couronner.
crown prince, n. prince héritier m.
crow's-foot, n. patte d'oie (near the eye) f.; (naut.) araignée f.
crucial, adj. crucial.
crucible, n. creuset m.
crucifix, n. crucifix m.

crucifixion, n. crucifixion f., crucifiement m.
crucify, vb. crucifier.
crude, adj. (unpolished) grossier; (metals, etc.) brut.
crudeness, n. crudité f.
cruel, adj. cruel.
cruelty, n. cruauté f.
cruet, n. burette f.
cruise, n. croisière f.
cruiser, n. croiseur m.
crumb, n. (small piece) miette f.; (not crust) mie f.
crumble, vb. émietter, tr.
crumple, vb. chiffonner, tr.
crunch, 1. vb. croquer, broyer, 2. n. grincement m.
crusade, n. croisade f.
crusader, n. croisé m.
crush, vb. écraser.
crust, n. croûte f.
crustacean, adj. crustacé.
crusty, adj. couvert d'une croûte; (fig.) bourru, maussade.
crutch, n. béquille f.
cry, 1. n. cri m. 2. vb. (shout) crier; (weep) pleurer.
crying, adj. criant.
cryosurgery, n. cryochirurgie f.
crypt, n. crypte f.
cryptic, adj. occulte, secret.
cryptography, n. cryptographie f.
crystal, n. cristal m.
crystalline, adj. cristallin.
crystallize, vb. cristalliser, tr.
cub, n. petit m. (d'un animal).
Cuba, n. Cuba m.
Cuban, 1. n. Cubain m. 2. adj. cubain.
cubbyhole, n. retraite f., cachette f., placard m.
cube, n. cube m.
cubic, adj. cubique.
cubicle, n. compartiment m., cabine f.
cubic measure, n. mesures de volume f.pl.
cubism, n. cubisme m.
cuckoo, n. coucou m.; (fig.) niais m.
cucumber, n. concombre m.
cud, n. bol alimentaire m., panse f., chique (of tobacco) f.
cuddle, vb. serrer (dans ses bras), tr.
cudgel, 1. n. bâton m., gourdin m., trique f. 2. vb. bâtonner.
cue, n. (theater) réplique f.; (hint) mot m.
cuff, n. poignet m.
cuisine, n. cuisine f.
culinary, adj. culinaire, de cuisine.
cull, vb. cueillir, recueillir.
culminate, vb. culminer.
culmination, n. point culminant m.
culpable, adj. coupable.
culprit, n. coupable m.f.
cult, n. culte m.
cultivate, vb. cultiver.
cultivated, adj. cultivé.

cultivation, n. culture f.
cultivator, n. cultivateur m.
cultural, adj. cultural.
culture, n. culture f.
cumbersome, adj. encombrant.
cumulative, adj. cumulatif.
cunning, 1. n. (guile) ruse f.; (skill) adresse f. 2. adj. rusé; (attractive) charmant.
cup, n. tasse f.
cupboard, n. armoire f.
cupidity, n. cupidité f.
curable, adj. guérissable.
curator, n. conservateur m.
curb, 1. n. (horse) gourmette f.; (pavement) bord m. 2. vb. (horse) gourmer; (fig.) brider.
curbstone, n. garde-pavé m.
curd, n. lait caillé m.
curdle, vb. cailler.
cure, 1. n. (healing) guérison f.; (remedy) remède m. 2. vb. guérir.
curfew, n. couvre-feu m.
curio, n. curiosité f.
curiosity, n. curiosité f.
curious, adj. curieux.
curl, 1. n. boucle f. 2. vb. friser.
curly, adj. frisé.
currant, n. groseille f.
currency, n. monnaie f.
current, adj. and n. courant m.
currently, adv. couramment.
curriculum, n. programme d'études m., plan d'études m.
curry, n. cari m.
curse, 1. n. (malediction) malédiction f.; (oath) juron m.; (scourge) fléau m. 2. vb. maudire; (swear) jurer.
cursed, adj. maudit.
cursory, adj. rapide, superficiel.
curt, adj. brusque.
curtail, vb. raccourcir.
curtain, n. rideau m.
curtsy, n. révérence f.
curvature, n. courbure f.
curve, 1. n. courbe f. 2. vb. courber, tr.
cushion, n. coussin m.
cuspidor, n. crachoir m.
custard, n. crème f.
custodian, n. gardien m.
custody, n. (care) garde f.; (arrest) détention f.
custom, n. coutume f.
customary, adj. habituel.
customer, n. client m.
custom-house, customs, n. douane f.
customs-officer, n. douanier m.
cut, 1. n. (wound) coupure f.; (clothes, hair) coupe f.; (reduction) réduction f. 2. vb. couper.
cutaneous, adj. cutané.
cute, adj. gentil m., gentille f.
cut glass, n. cristal m.
cuticle, n. cuticule f.
cutlery, n. coutellerie f.
cutlet, n. côtelette f.
cutout, n. découpage m., coupe f.

cutter, n. coupeur m., coupeuse f.
cutthroat, n. coupe-jarret m.
cutting, 1. n. incision f. 2. adj. incisif, tranchant.
cyclamate, n. cyclamate m.
cycle, 1. n. cycle m. 2. vb. faire de la bicyclette.
cyclist, n. cycliste m.
cyclone, n. cyclone m.
cyclotron, n. cyclotron m.
cylinder, n. cylindre m.
cylindrical, adj. cylindrique.
cymbal, n. cymbale f.
cynic, n. cynique m.
cynical, adj. cynique.
cynicism, n. cynisme m.
cypress, n. cyprès m.
cyst, n. kyste m.

D

dab, 1. n. coup léger m., tape f. 2. vb. toucher légèrement.
dabble, vb. humecter, faire l'amateur.
dad, n. papa m.
daffodil, n. narcisse m.
daffy, adj. niais, sot.
dagger, n. poignard m.
dahlia, n. dahlia m.
daily, adj. quotidien.
daintiness, n. délicatesse f.
dainty, adj. délicat.
dairy, n. laiterie f.
dairyman, n. crémier m.
dais, n. estrade f.
daisy, n. marguerite f.
dale, n. vallon m., vallée f.
dam, n. digue f.
damage, 1. n. dommage m. 2. vb. endommager.
damask, n. damas m.
damnation, n. damnation f.
damp, adj. humide.
dampen, vb. humecter.
dampness, n. humidité f., moiteur f.
damsel, n. demoiselle f., jeune fille f.
dance, 1. n. danse f. 2. vb. danser.
dancer, n. danseur m.
dandelion, n. pissenlit m.
dandruff, n. pellicules f.pl.
dandy, 1. n. dandy m. 2. adj. élégant.
danger, n. danger m.
dangerous, adj. dangereux.
dangle, vb. pendiller, intr.
Dane, n. Danois m.
Danish, adj. and n. danois m.
dapper, adj. pimpant, petit et vif.
dappled, adj. pommelé.
dare, vb. oser.
daredevil, n. casse-cou m.
daring, adj. audacieux.
dark, adj. sombre.
darken, vb. obscurcir, tr.
dark horse, n. tocard m.
darkness, n. obscurité f.

darkroom, n. chambre noire f.
darling, adj. and n. chéri m.
darn, 1. n. reprise f. 2. vb. repriser.
darning needle, n. aiguille à repriser f.
dart, 1. n. dard m.; (sewing) pince f. 2. vb. se précipiter.
dash, 1. n. (energy) fougue f.; (pen) trait m. 2. vb. (throw) lancer; (destroy) détruire; (rush) se précipiter.
dashboard, n. tablier m.
dashing, adj. fougueux, brillant, superbe.
data, n. données f.pl.
data processing, n. élaboration f.
date, 1. n. date f.; (appointment) rendez-vous m.; (fruit) datte f. 2. vb. dater.
date line, n. ligne de changement de date f.
daub, 1. n. barbouillage m. 2. vb. barbouiller.
daughter, n. fille f.
daughter-in-law, n. belle-fille f.
daunt, vb intimider.
dauntless, adj. intrépide, indomptable.
dauntlessly, adv. d'une manière intrépide.
davenport, n. divan m.
dawdle, vb. flâner, muser.
dawn, n. aube f.
day, n. jour m.; (span of day) journée f.
daydream, n. rêverie f.
daylight, n. lumière (f.) du jour.
daylight-saving time, n. l'heure d'été f.
daze, vb. étourdir.
dazzle, vb. éblouir.
deacon, n. diacre m.
dead, adj. mort.
deaden, vb. amortir.
dead end, n. cul de sac m., impasse f.
dead letter, n. lettre morte f.
deadline, n. ligne de délimitation f.
deadlock, n. impasse f.
deadly, adj. mortel.
deadwood, n. bois mort m.
deaf, adj. sourd.
deafen, vb. assourdir.
deaf-mute, adj. sourd-muet.
deafness, n. surdité f.
deal, 1. n. (great d.) beaucoup; (business) affair f.; (cards) donne f. 2. vb. (d. with) traiter; (d. out) distribuer.
dealer, n. marchand m.
dean, n. doyen m.
dear, adj. and n. cher m.
dearly, adv. chèrement.
dearth, n. disette f.
death, n. mort f.
deathless, adj. impérissable.
deathly, adj. mortel.
debacle, n. débâcle f.
debase, vb. avilir.
debatable, adj. discutable.

debate, 1. n. débat m. **2.** vb. discuter.

debater, n. orateur parlementaire m., argumentateur m.

debauch, 1. n. débauche f. **2.** vb. débaucher, corrompre.

debenture, n. obligation f.

debilitate, vb. débiliter, affaiblir.

debit, n. débit m.

debonair, adj. courtois et jovial.

debris, n. débris m.pl.

debt, n. dette f.

debtor, n. débiteur m.

debunk, vb. dégonfler.

debut, n. début m.

debutante, n. débutante f.

decade, n. période (f.) de dix ans.

decadence, n. décadence f.

decadent, adj. décadent.

decaffeinated, adj. décafféiné.

decalcomania, m. décalcomanie f.

decanter, n. carafe f.

decapitate, vb. décapiter.

decay, 1. n. décadence f.; (state of ruin) délabrement m.; (teeth) carie f. **2.** vb. tomber en décadence.

deceased, adj. défunt.

deceit, n. tromperie f.

deceitful, adj. trompeur.

deceive, vb. tromper.

deceiver, n. imposteur.

December, n. décembre m.

decency, n. décence f.

decent, adj. décent.

decentralization, n. décentralisation f.

decentralize, vb. décentraliser.

deception, n. tromperie f., duperie f.

deceptive, adj. décevant, trompeur.

decibel, n. décibel m.

decide, vb. décider.

decided, adj. décidé, prononcé.

deciduous, adj. à feuillage caduc.

decimal, adj. décimal.

decimate, vb. décimer.

decipher, vb. déchiffrer.

decision, n. décision f.

decisive, adj. décisif.

deck, n. (boat) pont m.; (cards) paquet m.

deck hand, n. matelot de pont m.

declaim, vb. déclamer.

declamation, n. déclamation f.

declaration, n. déclaration f.

declarative, adj. explicatif, (law) déclaratif.

declare, vb. déclarer.

declension, n. déclinaison f.

decline, vb. décliner.

decode, vb. déchiffrer.

décolleté, adj. décolleté.

decompose, vb. décomposer, tr.

decongestant, adj. décongestionnant.

decor, n. décor m.

decorate, vb. décorer.

decoration, n. décoration f.

decorative, adj. décoratif.

decorator, n. décorateur m.

decorous, adj. bienséant, convenable.

decorum, n. décorum m.

decoy, 1. n. leurre m. **2.** vb. leurrer.

decrease, 1. n. diminution f. **2.** vb. diminuer.

decree, n. décret m.

decrepit, adj. décrépit.

decry, vb. décrier, dénigrer.

dedicate, vb. dédier.

dedication, n. dédicace f.

deduce, vb. déduire.

deduct, vb. déduire.

deduction, n. déduction.

deductive, adj. déductif.

deed, n. action f.; (law) acte (m.) notarié.

deem, vb. juger.

deep, adj. profond.

deepen, vb. approfondir, tr.

deep freeze, n. surgélateur m.

deeply, adv. profondément.

deep-rooted, adj. enraciné.

deer, n. cerf m.

deerskin, n. peau de daim f.

deface, vb. défigurer.

defamation, n. diffamation f.

defame, vb. diffamer.

default, n. défaut m.

defeat, 1. n. défaite f. **2.** vb. vaincre.

defeatism, n. défaitisme m.

defect, n. défaut m.

defection, n. défection f.

defective, adj. défectueux.

defend, vb. défendre.

defendant, n. défendeur n.

defender, n. défenseur m.

defense, n. défense f.

defenseless, adj. sans défense.

defensible, adj. défendable, soutenable.

defensive, adj. défensif.

defer, vb. (put off) différer; (show deference) déférer.

deference, n. déférence f.

deferential, adj. plein de déférence, respectueux.

defiance, n. défi m.

defiant, adj. de défi.

deficiency, n. insuffisance f.

deficient, adj. insuffisant.

deficit, n. déficit m.

defile, vb. souiller.

define, vb. définir.

definite, adj. défini.

definitely, adv. d'une manière déterminée.

definition, n. définition f.

definitive, adj. définitif.

deflate, vb. dégonfler.

deflation, n. dégonflement m.

deflect, vb. faire dévier, détourner.

deform, vb. déformer.

deformity, n. difformité f.

defraud, vb. frauder.

defray, vb. payer.

defrost, vb. déglacer.

defroster, n. dégiaceur m.

deft, adj. adroit.

defy, vb. défier.

degenerate, vb. dégénérer.

degeneration, n. dégénérescence f.

degradation, n. dégradation f.

degrade, vb. dégrader.

degree, n. degré m.

dehydrate, vb. déshydrater.

deify, vb. déifier.

deign, vb. daigner.

deity, n. divinité f.

dejected, adj. abattu.

dejection, n. abattement m.

delay, 1. n. retard m. **2.** vb. retarder, tr.; tarder, intr.

delectable, adj. délectable.

delegate, 1. n. délégué m. **2.** vb. déléguer.

delegation, n. délégation f.

delete, vb. rayer, biffer.

deliberate, 1. adj. délibéré. **2.** vb. délibérer.

deliberately, adv. de propos délibéré.

deliberation, n. délibération f.

deliberative, adj. délibératif.

delicacy, n. délicatesse f.

delicate, adj. délicat.

delicious, adj. délicieux.

delight, 1. n. délices f.pl. **2.** vb. enchanter.

delightful, adj. charmant.

delineate, vb. esquisser, dessiner.

delinquency, n. délit m.

delinquent, adj. and n. délinquant m.

delirious, adj. délirant.

deliver, vb. délivrer; (speech) prononcer.

deliverance, n. délivrance f.

delivery, n. (child) accouchement m.; (speech) débit m.; (goods) livraison f.; (letters) distribution f.; **(general d.)** poste restante f.

delouse, vb. épouiller.

delude, vb. tromper.

deluge, n. déluge m.

delusion, n. illusion f.

de luxe, adv. de luxe.

delve, vb. creuser, pénétrer.

demagogue, n. démagogue m.

demand, 1. n. demande f. **2.** vb. demander; (as right or by force) exiger.

demarcation, n. démarcation f.

demean, vb. comporter.

demeanor, n. maintien m.

demented, adj. fou m., folle f.

demerit, n. démérite m.

demigod, n. demi-dieu m.

demilitarize, vb. démilitariser.

demise, n. décès m., mort f.

demobilization, n. démobilisation f.

demobilize, vb. démobiliser.

democracy, n. démocratie f.

democrat, n. démocrate m.f.

democratic, adj. démocratique.

demolish, vb. démolir.

demolition, n. démolition f.

demon, n. démon m.

demonstrable, *adj.* démonstrable.

demonstrate, *vb.* démontrer.

demonstration, *n.* démonstration *f.*

demonstrative, *adj.* démonstratif.

demonstrator, *n.* démonstrateur *m.*

demoralize, *vb.* démoraliser.

demote, *vb.* réduire à un grade inférieur.

demur, *vb.* hésiter, s'opposer à.

demure, *adj.* posé, d'une modestie affectée.

den, *n.* antre *m.*, repaire *m.*

denaturalize, *vb.* dénaturaliser.

denature, *vb.* dénaturer.

denial, *n.* dénégation *f.*; (refusal) refus *m.*

denim, *n.* treillis *m.*

Denmark, *n.* Danemark *m.*

denomination, *n.* dénomination *f.*; (religion) confession *f.*

denominator, *n.* dénominateur *m.*

denote, *vb.* dénoter.

denouement, *n.* dénouement *m.*

denounce, *vb.* dénoncer.

dense, *adj.* dense; (stupid) bête.

density, *n.* densité *f.*

dent, *n.* bosselure *f.*

dental, *adj.* dentaire; (gramm.) dental.

dentifrice, *n.* dentifrice *m.*

dentist, *n.* dentiste *m.*

dentistry, *n.* art du dentiste *m.*, dentisterie *f.*

denture, *n.* dentier *m.*, râtelier *m.*

denude, *vb.* dénuder.

denunciation, *n.* dénonciation *f.*

deny, *vb.* nier.

deodorant, *n.* désodorisant *m.*

deodorize, *vb.* désodoriser, désinfecter.

depart, *vb.* partir, s'en aller, quitter.

department, *n.* département *m.*; (government) ministère *m.*; (d. store) grand magasin *m.*

departmental, *adj.* départemental.

departure, *n.* départ *m.*

depend on, *vb.* dépendre de; (rely) compter sur.

dependability, *n.* confiance que l'on inspire *f.*

dependable, *adj.* digne de confiance.

dependence, *n.* dépendance *f.*, confiance *f.*

dependent, *adj.* dépendant.

depict, *vb.* peindre.

depiction, *n.* description *f.*

deplete, *vb.* épuiser.

deplorable, *adj.* déplorable.

deplore, *vb.* déplorer.

depopulate, *vb.* dépeupler.

deport, *vb.* déporter.

deportation, *n.* déportation *f.*

deportment, *n.* maintien *m.*

depose, *vb.* déposer.

deposit, 1. *n.* dépôt *m.* 2. *vb.* déposer.

depositor, *n.* déposant *m.*

depository, *n.* dépôt *m.*, dépositaire *m.*

depot, *n.* dépôt *m.*, gare *f.*

deprave, *vb.* dépraver, corrompre.

depravity, *n.* dépravation *f.*, corruption *f.*

deprecate, *vb.* désapprouver, s'opposer à.

depreciate, *vb.* déprécier.

depreciation, *n.* dépréciation *f.*

depredation, *n.* déprédation *f.*, pillage *m.*

depress, *vb.* (lower) abaisser; (fig.) abattre.

depressed, *adj.* abattu, bas.

depression, *n.* dépression *f.*; (personal) abattement *m.*; (comm.) crise *f.*

deprive, *vb.* priver.

depth, *n.* profondeur *f.*

depth charge, *n.* grenade sous-marine *f.*

deputy, *n.* délégué *m.*; (politics) député *m.*

derail, *vb.* dérailler.

derange, *vb.* déranger.

deranged, *adj.* dérangé, troublé.

derelict, 1. *n.* vaisseau abandonné *m.*, épave *f.* 2. *adj.* abandonné, délaissé.

dereliction, *n.* abandon *m.*

deride, *vb.* tourner en dérision.

derision, *n.* dérision *f.*

derisive, *adj.* dérisoire.

derivation, *n.* dérivation *f.*, origine *f.*

derivative, *n.* dérivatif.

derive, *vb.* dériver.

dermatology, *n.* dermatologie *f.*

derogatory, *adj.* dérogatoire.

derrick, *n.* grue *f.*

descend, *vb.* descendre.

descendant, *n.* descendant *m.*

descent, *n.* descente *f.*

describe, *vb.* décrire.

description, *n.* description *f.*

descriptive, *adj.* descriptif.

desecrate, *vb.* profaner.

desensitize, *vb.* désensibiliser.

desert, 1. *n.* (place) désert *m.*; (merit) mérite *m.* 2. *vb.* déserter.

deserter, *n.* déserteur *m.*

desertion, *n.* abandon *m.*; (military) désertion *f.*

deserve, *vb.* mériter.

deserving, *adj.* méritoire, de mérite.

design, 1. *n.* (project) dessein *m.*; (architecture) projet *m.* 2. *vb.* dessiner; (d. for) destiner à.

designate, *vb.* désigner.

designation, *n.* désignation *f.*

designedly, *adv.* à dessein.

designer, *n.* dessinateur *m.*

designing, *adj.* intrigant, artificieux.

desirable, *adj.* désirable.

desire, 1. *n.* désir *m.* 2. *vb.* désirer.

desirous, *adj.* désireux.

desist, *vb.* cesser.

desk, *n.* (office) bureau *m.*; (school) pupitre *m.*

desolate, *adj.* désolé.

desolation, *n.* désolation *f.*

despair, 1. *n.* désespoir *m.* 2. *vb.* désespérer.

desperado, *n.* désespéré *m.*, cerveau brûlé *m.*

desperate, *adj.* désespéré.

desperation, *n.* désespoir *m.*

despicable, *adj.* méprisable.

despise, *vb.* mépriser.

despite, *prep.* en dépit de.

despondent, *adj.* découragé.

despot, *n.* despote *m.*

despotic, *adj.* despotique.

despotism, *n.* despotisme *m.*

dessert, *n.* dessert *m.*

destination, *n.* destination *f.*

destine, *vb.* destiner.

destiny, *n.* destin *m.*

destitute, *adj.* (deprived) dénué; (poor) indigent.

destitution, *n.* destitution *f.*

destroy, *vb.* détruire.

destroyer, *n.* destructeur *m.*; (naval) contre-torpilleur *m.*

destructible, *adj.* destructible.

destruction, *n.* destruction *f.*

destructive, *adj.* destructif.

desultory, *adj.* à bâtons rompus, décousu.

detach, *vb.* détacher.

detachment, *n.* détachement *m.*

detail, *n.* détail *m.*

detain, *vb.* retenir; (in prison) détenir.

detect, *vb.* découvrir.

detection, *n.* découverte *f.*

detective, *n.* agent (*m.*) de la police secrète; (d. novel) roman policier.

detente, *n.* détente *f.*

detention, *n.* détention *f.*

deter, *vb.* détourner, empêcher (de), dissuader (de).

detergent, *n.* détersif *m.*

deteriorate, *vb.* détériorer, *tr.*

deterioration, *n.* détérioration *f.*

determination, *n.* détermination *f.*

determine, *vb.* déterminer.

determined, *adj.* déterminé.

determinism, *n.* déterminisme *m.*

deterrence, *n.* préventif *m.*

deterrent, *n. and adj.* préventif *m.*

detest, *vb.* détester.

dethrone, *vb.* détrôner.

detonate, *vb.* détoner.

detour, *n.* détour *m.*

detract, *vb.* enlever, ôter (à), dénigrer, déroger (à).

detriment, *n.* détriment *m.*, préjudice *m.*

detrimental, adj. préjudiciable, nuisible (à).

devaluate, vb. dévaluer, déprécier.

devastate, vb. dévaster.

develop, vb. développer, tr.

developer, n. (photography) révélateur m.

developing nation, n. nation en cours de développement f.

development, n. développement m.

deviate, vb. dévier, s'écarter (de).

deviation, n. déviation f., écart m.

device, n. expédient m.

devil, n. diable m.

devilish, adj. diabolique.

devious, adj. détourné.

devise, vb. (plan) combiner; (plot) tramer.

devitalize, vb. dévitaliser.

devoid, adj. dépourvu.

devote, vb. consacrer.

devoted, adj. dévoué.

devotee, n. dévot m., dévote f.

devotion, n. (religious) dévotion f.; (to person or thing) dévouement m.

devour, vb. dévorer.

devout, adj. dévot.

dew, n. rosée f.

dewy, adj. de rosée.

dexterity, n. dextérité f.

dexterous, adj. adroit.

diabetes, n. diabète m.

diabolic, adj. diabolique.

diadem, n. diadème m.

diagnose, vb. diagnostiquer.

diagnosis, n. diagnose f.

diagnostic, adj. diagnostique.

diagonal, adj. diagonal.

diagonally, adv. diagonalement.

diagram, n. diagramme m.

dial, 1. n. cadran m. 2. vb. (d. a number) composer.

dialect, n. dialecte m.

dialogue, n. dialogue m.

diameter, n. diamètre m.

diametrical, adj. diamétral.

diamond, n. diamant m.; (shape) losange m.; (cards) carreau m.

diaper, n. (babies) couche f.

diaphragm, n. diaphragme m.

diarrhea, n. diarrhée f.

diary, n. journal m.

diathermy, n. diathermie f.

diatribe, n. diatribe f.

dice, n. dés m.pl.

dicker, vb. marchander.

dictaphone, n. machine à dicter f.

dictate, vb. dicter.

dictation, n. dictée f.

dictator, n. dictateur m.

dictatorial, adj. dictatorial.

dictatorship, n. dictature f.

diction, n. diction f.

dictionary, n. dictionnaire m.

didactic, adj. didactique.

die, 1. n. dé m. 2. vb. mourir.

die-hard, n. intransigeant m., ultra m.

diet, n. régime m.

dietary, adj. diététique.

dietetics, n. diététique f.

dietitian, n. diététicien m.

differ, vb. différer.

difference, n. différence f.

different, adj. différent.

differential, adj. différentiel f.

difficult, adj. difficile.

difficulty, n. difficulté f.

diffident, adj. hésitant, timide.

diffuse, adj. diffus.

diffusion, n. diffusion f.

dig, vb. bêcher; (hole) creuser.

digest, vb. digérer.

digestible, adj. digestible.

digestion, n. digestion f.

digestive, adj. and n. digestif m.

digital, adj. (in watches, etc.) digital.

digitalis, n. digitaline f.

dignified, adj. plein de dignité.

dignify, vb. honorer, élever.

dignitary, n. dignitaire m.

dignity, n. dignité f.

digress, vb. faire une digression.

digression, n. digression f.

dike, n. (ditch) fossé m.; (dam) digue f.

dilapidated, adj. délabré.

dilapidation, n. délabrement m.

dilate, vb. dilater.

dilatory, adj. dilatoire, lent, négligent.

dilemma, n. dilemme m.

dilettante, n. dilettante m., amateur m.

diligence, n. diligence f.

diligent, adj. diligent.

dill, n. aneth m.

dilute, vb. diluer.

dim, adj. (light, sight) faible; (color) terne.

dime, n. un dixième de dollar m.

dimension, n. dimension f.

diminish, vb. diminuer.

diminution, n. diminution f.

diminutive, 1. adj. tout petit. 2. n. (gramm.) diminutif m.

dimness, n. (weakness) faiblesse f.; (darkness) obscurité f.

dimple, n. (face) fossette f.

din, n. tapage m.

dine, vb. dîner.

diner, dining-car, n. wagon-restaurant m.

dingy, adj. défraîchi; (color) terne.

dinner, n. dîner m.; (d. jacket) smoking m.

dinosaur, n. dinosaurien m.

diocese, n. diocèse m.

dip, vb. plonger.

diphtheria, n. diphtérie f.

diploma, n. diplôme m.

diplomacy, n. diplomatie f.

diplomat, n. diplomate m.

diplomatic, adj. diplomatique.

dipper, n. cuiller (f.) à pot.

dire, adj. affreux.

direct, vb. (guide) diriger; (address) adresser.

direct, adj. direct.

direct current, n. courant continu m.

direction, n. direction f.; (orders) instructions f.pl.

directional, adj. de direction.

directive, 1. n. directif m. 2. adj. dirigeant.

directly, adv. directement.

directness, n. rectitude f.; (frankness) franchise f.

director, n. directeur m.

directorate, n. conseil d'administration m.

directory, n. annuaire m.

dirge, n. chant funèbre m.

dirigible, adj. and n. dirigeable m.

dirt, n. saleté f.

dirty, adj. sale.

disability, n. incapacité f., impuissance f.

disable, vb. mettre hors de combat, tr.

disabled, adj. invalide.

disabuse, vb. désabuser.

disadvantage, n. désavantage m.

disagree, vb. être en désaccord.

disagreeable, adj. désagréable.

disagreement, n. désaccord m.

disappear, vb. disparaître.

disappearance, n. disparition f.

disappoint, vb. désappointer.

disappointment, n. désappointement m.

disapproval, n. désapprobation f.

disapprove, vb. désapprouver.

disarm, vb. désarmer.

disarmament, n. désarmement m.

disarray, n. désarroi m., désordre m.

disassemble, vb. démonter, désassembler.

disaster, n. désastre m.

disastrous, adj. désastreux.

disavow, vb. désavouer.

disavowal, n. désaveu m.

disband, vb. congédier, tr.; se débander, intr.

disbar, vb. rayer du tableau des avocats.

disbelieve, vb. ne pas croire, refuser de croire.

disburse, vb. débourser.

discard, vb. mettre de côté.

discern, vb. discerner.

discerning, adj. judicieux, éclairé.

discernment, n. discernement m.

discharge, 1. n. décharge f.; (mil.) congé m. **2.** vb. décharger; (mil.) congédier.

disciple, n. disciple m.

disciplinarian, n. disciplinaire m.

disciplinary, adj. disciplinaire.

discipline, n. discipline f.

disclaim, vb. désvouer, nier.

disclaimer, n. désaveu m.

disclose, vb. révéler.

disclosure, n. révélation f.

disco, adj. disco.

discolor, vb. décolorer.

discomfiture, n. défaite f., déroute f.

discomfort, n. malaise m.

disconcert, vb. déconcerter.

disconnect, vb. désunir.

disconnected, adj. (electricity) hors circuit.

disconsolate, adj. désolé.

discontent, n. mécontentement m.

discontented, adj. mécontent.

discontinue, vb. discontinuer.

discord, n. discorde f.

discordant, adj. discordant, en désaccord.

discotheque, n. discothèque f.

discount, n. escompte m.; (reduction) remise f.

discourage, vb. décourager.

discouragement, n. découragement m.

discourse, n. discours m.

discourteous, adj. impoli.

discourtesy, n. impolitesse f.

discover, vb. découvrir.

discoverer, n. découvreur m.

discovery, n. découverte f.

discredit, 1. n. discrédit m. 2. vb. discréditer.

discreditable, adj. déshonorant, peu honorable.

discreet, adj. discret.

discrepancy, n. contradiction f.

discretion, n. discrétion f.

discriminate, vb. distinguer.

discrimination, n. discernement m., jugement m.

discursive, adj. discursif, sans suite.

discuss, vb. discuter.

discussion, n. discussion f.

disdain, n. dédain m.

disdainful, adj. dédaigneux.

disease, n. maladie f.

disembark, vb. débarquer.

disembody, vb. dépouiller du corps.

disenchantment, n. désenchantement m.

disengage, vb. dégager.

disentangle, vb. démêler.

disfavor, n. défaveur f.

disfigure, vb. défigurer, enlaidir.

disfranchise, vb. priver du droit de vote.

disgorge, vb. dégorger.

disgrace, n. disgrâce f.

disgraceful, adj. honteux.

disgruntled, adj. mécontent, de mauvaise humeur.

disguise, 1. n. déguisement m. 2. vb. dégoûter.

dish, n. plat m.; (wash the dishes) laver la vaisselle.

dishcloth, n. torchon m.

dishearten, vb. décourager.

dishonest, adj. malhonnête.

dishonesty, n. malhonnêteté f.

dishonor, n. déshonneur m.

dishonorable, adj. (action) déshonorant.

disillusion, n. désillusion f.

disinfect, vb. désinfecter.

disinfectant, n. désinfectant m.

disinherit, vb. déshériter.

disintegrate, vb. désagréger.

disinterested, adj. désintéressé.

disjointed, adj. désarticulé, disloqué.

disk, n. disque m.

dislike, 1, n. aversion f. 2. vb. ne pas aimer.

dislocate, vb. disloquer.

dislodge, vb. déloger.

disloyal, adj. infidèle.

disloyalty, n. infidélité f., perfidie f.

dismal, adj. sombre.

dismantle, vb. dépouiller (de).

dismay, n. consternation f.

dismember, vb. démembrer.

dismiss, vb. congédier.

dismissal, n. renvoi m.

dismount, vb. descendre.

disobedience, n. désobéissance f.

disobedient, adj. désobéissant.

disobey, vb. désobéir à.

disorder, n. désordre m.

disorderly, adj. désordonné.

disorganize, vb. désorganiser.

disown, vb. désavouer.

disparage, vb. déprécier, dénigrer.

disparate, adj. disparate.

disparity, n. inégalité f.

dispassionate, adj. calme.

dispatch, 1. n. (business) expédition f.; (speed) promptitude f.; (message) dépêche f. 2. vb. expédier.

dispatcher, n. expéditeur m.

dispel, vb. dissiper.

dispensable, adj. dont on peut se passer.

dispensary, n. dispensaire m.

dispensation, n. dispensation f.

dispense, vb. distribuer, dispenser.

dispersal, n. dispersion f.

disperse, vb. disperser.

displace, vb. déplacer.

displaced person, n. réfugié m.

displacement, n. déplacement m.

display, 1. n. (show) exposition f.; (shop, ostentation) étalage m. 2. vb. étaler.

displease, vb. déplaire à.

disposable, adj. disponible.

disposal, n. disposition f.

dispose, vb. disposer.

disposition, n. disposition f.; (character) caractère m.

dispossess, vb. déposséder, exproprier.

disproportion, n. disproportion f.

disproportionate, adj. disproportionné.

disprove, vb. réfuter.

disputable, adj. contestable, disputable.

dispute, 1. n. (discussion) discussion f.; (quarrel) dispute f. 2. vb. (se) disputer.

disqualify, vb. (sports) disqualifier.

disregard, vb. ne tenir aucun compte de.

disrepair, n. délabrement m.

disreputable, adj. déshonorant, honteux.

disrespect, n. irrévérence f.

disrespectful, adj. irrespectueux.

disrobe, vb. déshabiller, dévêtir.

disrupt, vb. faire éclater, rompre.

dissatisfaction, n. mécontentement m.

dissatisfy, vb. mécontenter.

dissect, vb. disséquer.

dissemble, vb. dissimuler.

disseminate, vb. disséminer.

dissension, n. dissension f.

dissent, vb. différer.

dissertation, n. dissertation f., discours m.

disservice, n. mauvais service rendu m.

dissimilar, adj. dissemblable.

dissimulation, n. dissimulation f.

dissipate, vb. dissiper.

dissipated, adj. dissipé.

dissipation, n. dissipation f.

dissociate, vb. désassocier, dissocier.

dissolute, adj. dissolu.

dissolution, n. dissolution f.

dissolve, vb. dissoudre, tr.

dissonance, n. dissonance f., désaccord m.

dissonant, adj. dissonant.

dissuade, vb. dissuader.

distance, n. distance f.

distant, adj. distant.

distaste, n. dégoût m.

distasteful, adj. désagréable.

distemper, 1. n. maladie des chiens f. 2. vb. peindre en détrempe.

distend, vb. dilater, gonfler.

distill, vb. distiller.

distillation, n. distillation f.

distiller, n. distillateur m.

distillery, n. distillerie f.

distinct, adj. distinct.

distinction, n. distinction f.

distinctive, adj. distinctif.

distinctly, adv. distinctement, clairement.

distinguish, vb. distinguer.

distinguished, adj. distingué.

distort, vb. déformer.

distract, vb. (divert) distraire; (upset) affoler.

distracted, adj. affolé, bouleversé.

distraction, n. (diversion) distraction f.; (madness) folie f.

distraught, adj. affolé, éperdu, hors de soi.

distress, 1. n. détresse f. 2. vb. affliger.

distressing, adj. affligeant, pénible, désolant.

distribute, vb. distribuer.

distribution, n. distribution f.

distributor, n. distributeur m.
district, n. (region) contrée f.; (administration) district m.; (town) quartier m.
distrust, 1. n. méfiance f. **2.** vb. se méfier de.
distrustful, adj. méfiant.
disturb, vb. déranger.
disturbance, n. dérangement m.
disunite, vb. désunir.
disuse, n. désuétude f.
ditch, n. fossé m.
ditto, adv. idem, de même.
diva, n. diva f.
divan, n. divan m.
dive, vb. plonger.
dive bomber, n. avion de bombardement qui fait des vols piqués m.
diver, n. plongeur m.
diverge, vb. diverger.
divergence, n. divergence f.
divergent, adj. divergent.
diverse, adj. divers.
diversion, n. (amusement) divertissement m.
diversity, n. diversité f.
divert, vb. (turn aside) détourner; (amuse) divertir.
divest, vb. ôter, dépouiller, priver.
divide, vb. diviser.
divided, adj. divisé, séparé.
dividend, n. dividende m.
divine, adj. divin.
divinity, n. divinité f.
divisible, adj. divisible.
division, n. division f.
divisive, adj. qui divise, qui sépare.
divorce, 1. n. divorce m. **2.** vb. divorcer.
divorcee, n. divorcé m., divorcée f.
divulge, vb. divulguer.
dizziness, n. vertige m.
dizzy, adj. pris de vertige.
do, vb. faire; **(how d. you d.?)** comment allez-vous?
docile, adj. docile.
dock, n. bassin m.
docket, n. registre m., bordereau m.
dockyard, n. chantier de construction de navires m.
doctor, n. docteur m.
doctorate, n. doctorat m.
doctrinaire, adj. doctrinaire.
doctrine, n. doctrine f.
document, n. document m.
documentary, adj. documentaire.
documentation, n. documentation f.
dodge, vb. esquiver, éluder.
doe, n. daine f.
doeskin, n. peau de daim f.
dog, n. chien m.
dogfight, n. combat de chiens m., mêlée générale f.
dogged, adj. obstiné, tenace.
doggerel, n. poésie burlesque f.
doghouse, n. chenil m.
dogma, n. dogme m.

dogmatic, adj. dogmatique.
dogmatism, n. dogmatisme m.
doily, n. petit napperon m.
doldrum, n. (naut.) zone des calmes f., cafard m.
dole, 1. n. pitance f.; aumone f. **2.** vb. distribuer parcimonieusement.
doleful, adj. lugubre.
doll, n. poupée f.
dollar, n. dollar m.
dolorous, adj. douloureux.
dolphin, n. dauphin m.
domain, n. domaine m.
dome, n. dôme m.
domestic, adj. domestique.
domesticate, vb. domestiquer, apprivoiser.
domicile, n. domicile m.
dominance, n. dominance f., prédominance f.
dominant, adj. dominant.
dominate, vb. dominer.
domination, n. domination f.
domineer, vb. se montrer tyrannique.
domineering, adj. impérieux.
dominion, n. domination f.; (territory) possessions f.pl.
domino, n. domino m.
don, vb. endosser, revêtir.
donate, vb. donner.
donation, n. donation f.
done, vb. fait.
donkey, n. âne m.
don't, vb. ne faites pas!, ne sais pas!
doom, vb. condamner.
doomsday, n. (jour du) jugement dernier m.
door, f. porte f.; **(d.-keeper)** concierge m.f.
doorman, n. portier m.
doorstep, n. seuil m., pas de la porte m.
doorway, n. (baie de) porte f., encadrement de la porte m.
dope, n. stupéfiant m.
dormant, adj. endormi, assoupi.
dormer, n. lucarne f.
dormitory, n. maison (f.) d'étudiants.
dosage, n. dosage m.
dose, n. dose f.
dossier, n. dossier m.
dot, n. point m.
dotage, n. radotage m.
dote, vb. radoter; **(d. on)** aimer excessivement.
double, 1. adj. and n. double m. **2.** vb. doubler.
double-breasted, adj. croisé.
double-cross, vb. duper, tromper.
double-dealing, n. duplicité f.
double time, n. pas gymnastique m.
doubly, adv. doublement.
doubt, 1. n. doute m. **2.** vb. douter (de).
doubtful, adj. douteux.
doubtless, adv. sans doute.
dough, n. pâte f.

doughnut, n. pet (m.) de nonne.
dour, adj. austère.
douse, vb. plonger, tremper.
dove, n. colombe f.
dowager, n. douairère f.
dowdy, adj. dans élégance, qui manque de chic.
dowel, n. 1. n. goujon m. 2. vb. goujonner.
down, 1. n. duvet m. **2.** adv. en bas. **3.** prep. (along) le long de.
downcast, adj. (look) baissé.
downfall, n. chute f.
downhearted, adj. découragé, déprimé.
downhill, 1. n. descente f. **2.** adj. en pente, incliné.
downpour, n. averse f.
downright, adv. tout à fait.
downstairs, adv. en bas.
downtown, adv. en ville.
downtrodden, adj. opprimé, piétiné.
downward, adj. descendant.
downy, adj. duveteux.
dowry, n. dot f.
doze, vb. sommeiller.
dozen, n. douzaine f.
drab, adj. (color) gris; (dull) terne.
draft, 1. n. (drawing) dessin m.; (mil.) conscription f.; (air) courant (m.) d'air. **2.** vb. (mil.) appeler sous le drapeau.
draftee, n. conscrit m.
draftsman, n. dessinateur m.
drafty, adj. plein de courante d'air.
drag, vb. traîner.
dragnet, n. drague f., seine f., chalut m.
dragon, n. dragon m.
drain, vb. drainer, tr.; s'écouler, intr.
drainage, n. drainage m.
dram, n. drachme f., goutte f.
drama, n. drame m.
dramatic, adj. dramatique.
dramatics, n. théâtre m.
dramatist, n. dramaturge m.
dramatize, vb. dramatiser.
dramaturgy, n. dramaturgie f.
drape, vb. draper.
drapery, n. draperie f.
drastic, adj. drastique.
draught, n. traction f.; trait m.
draw, vb. (pull) tirer; (sketch) dessiner.
drawback, n. inconvénient m.
drawbridge, n. pont-levis m.
drawer, n. tiroir m.
drawing, n. dessin m.
drawl, 1. n. voix (f.) traînante. **2.** vb. traîner la voix.
dray, n. camion m.
drayman, n. camionneur m.
dread, 1. n. crainte f. **2.** vb. redouter.
dreadful, adj. affreux.
dreadfully, adv. terriblement, affreusement.
dream, n. rêve m.

dreamer, n. rêveur m.

dreamy, adj. rêveur m., rêveuse f.

dreary, adj. morne.

dredge, vb. draguer.

dreg, n. lie f.

drench, vb. tremper.

dress, 1. n. robe f. 2. vb. habiller, tr.; s'habiller, intr.

dresser, n. commode f.

dressing, n. toilette f.; (surgical) pansement m.

dressing gown, n. robe de chambre f., peignoir m.

dressmaker, n. couturière f.

dress rehearsal, n. répétition générale f.

drier, n. sécheur m., dessécheur m.

drift, 1. n. (boat) dériver; (person) se laisser aller.

driftwood, n. bois flottant m.

drill, 1. n. (tool) foret m.; (exercise) exercice m. 2. vb. (hole) forer; (exercise) exercer, tr.; faire l'exercice, intr.

drink, 1. n. boisson f. 2. vb. boire.

drinkable, adj. potable.

drip, vb. dégoutter.

dripping, 1. n. dégouttement m. 2. adj. ruisselant.

drive, 1. n. promenade (f.) en voiture; (energy) énergie f. 2. vb. (auto, animals) conduire; (force) pousser.

drivel, n. bave f.

driver, n. (auto) chauffeur m.

drizzle, 1. n. bruine f. 2. vb. bruiner.

dromedary, n. dromadaire m.

drone, n. (bird) abeille mâle f.; bourdonnement m. 2. vb. bourdonner.

droop, vb. pencher.

drop, 1. n. goutte f.; (fall) chute f. 2. vb. tomber, intr.; laisser tomber, tr.

dropout, n. étudiant qui quitte l'école avant de recevoir son diplôme m.

dropper, n. compte-gouttes m.

dropsy, n. hydropisie f.

drought, n. sécheresse f.

drove, n. troupeau m.

drown, vb. noyer, tr.

drowse, vb. s'assoupir.

drowsiness, n. somnolence f.

drowsy, adj. somnolent.

drudge, vb. s'éreinter.

drug, n. drogue f.

druggist, n. pharmacien m.

drug store, n. pharmacie f.

drum, n. tambour m.; (ear) tympan m.

drum major, n. tambour-major m.

drummer, n. tambour m.

drumstick, n. baguette de tambour f.

drunk, adj. ivre.

drunkard, n. ivrogne m.

drunkenness, n. ivresse f.; (habitual) ivrognerie f.

dry, 1. adj. sec m., sèche f. 2. vb. sécher.

dry-clean, vb. nettoyer à sec.

dry dock, 1. n. cale sèche f. 2. vb. mettre en cale sèche.

dry goods, n. articles de nouveautés m.pl.

dryness, n. sécheresse f.

dual, adj. double.

dualism, n. dualité f., dualisme m.

dubious, adj. douteux.

duchess, n. duchesse f.

duchy, n. duché m.

duck, n. canard m.

duct, n. conduit m.

ductile, adj. ductile.

dud, 1. adj. incapable. 2. n. obus qui a raté m.

due, adj. dû m., due f.

duel, n. duel m.

duelist, n. duelliste m.

duet, n. duo m.

duffel bag, n. sac pour les vêtements de rechange m.

dugout, n. abri-caverne m.

duke, n. duc m.

dukedom, n. duché m.

dulcet, adj. doux, suave.

dull, adj. (boring) ennuyeux.

dullard, n. lourdaud m.

dullness, n. (monotony) monotonie f.

duly, adv. dûment.

dumb, adj. muet m., muette f.; (stupid) sot m., sotte f.

dumbwaiter, n. monte-plats m.

dumfound, vb. abasourdir, interdire.

dummy, n. (dressmaking) mannequin m.; (cards) mort m.

dump, n. voirie f.

dumpling, n. boulette (de pâte) f.

dun, vb. importuner, talonner.

dunce, n. crétin m.

dunce cap, n. bonnet d'âne m.

dune, n. dune f.

dung, n. fiente f.; (agriculture) fumier m.

dungaree, n. salopette f., bleus m.pl.

dungeon, n. cachot m.

dupe, 1. n. dupe f. 2. vb. duper.

duplex, adj. double.

duplicate, 1. n. double m. 2. vb. faire le double de.

duplication, n. duplication f.

duplicity, n. duplicité f.

durable, adj. durable.

durability, n. durabilité f.

duration, n. durée f.

duress, n. contrainte f., coercition f.

during, prep. pendant.

dusk, n. crépuscule m.

dusky, adj. sombre.

dust, 1. n. poussière f. 2. vb. épousseter.

dustpan, n. ramasse-poussière m.

dust storm, n. tourbillon de poussière m.

dusty, adj. poussiéreux.

Dutch, adj. and n. hollandais m.

Dutchman, n. Hollandais m.

dutiful, adj. respectueux, fidèle.

dutifully, adv. avec soumission.

duty, n. (moral, legal) devoir m.; (tax) droit m.; (be on d.) être de service.

duty-free, adj. exempt de droits.

dwarf, adj. and n. nain m.

dwell, vb. demeurer.

dwindle, vb. diminuer.

dye, 1. n. teinture f. 2. vb. teindre.

dyer, n. teinturier m.

dyestuff, n. matière colorante f.

dynamic, adj. dynamique.

dynamics, n. dynamique f.

dynamite, n. dynamite f.

dynamo, n. dynamo f.

dynasty, n. dynastie f.

dysentery, n. dysenterie f.

dyslexia, n. dyslexie f.

dyspepsia, n. dyspepsie f.

dyspeptic, adj. dyspeptique.

E

each, 1. adj. chaque. 2. pron. chacun m., chacune f.; (e. other) l'un l'autre.

eager, adj. ardent.

eagerly, adv. ardemment, avidement.

eagerness, n. empressement m.

eagle, n. (bird) aigle m.; (mil.) aigle f.

eaglet, n. aiglon m.

ear, n. oreille f.

earache, n. mal d'oreille m.

eardrum, n. tympan m.

earl, n. comte m.

early, 1. adj. (of morning) matinal; (first) premier. 2. adv. de bonne heure; tôt.

earmark, 1. n. marque distinctive f. 2. vb. marquer, assigner.

earn, vb. gagner.

earnest, adj. sérieux.

earnestly, adv. sérieusement, sincèrement.

earnestness, n. gravité f., sérieux m.

earnings, n. salaire m.

earphone, n. casque (téléphonique) m.

earring, n. boucle (f.) d'oreille.

earshot, n. portée de voix f.

earth, n. terre f.

earthenware, n. poterie f., argile cuite f.

earthly, adj. terrestre.

earthquake, n. tremblement (m.) de terre.

earthworm, n. ver de terre m.

earthy, adj. terreux.

ease, n. aise f.; (with e.) avec facilité.

easel, n. chevalet m.

easily, adv. facilement.

easiness, n. facilité f.

east, n. est m.

Easter, n. Pâques m.

easterly, adj. d'est, vers l'est.

eastern, adj. de l'est, oriental.

eastward, adv. vers l'est.

easy, adj. facile; (of manners) aisé.

easygoing, adj. insouciant, peu exigeant, accommodant.

eat, vb. manger.

eaves, n. avant-toit m.

eavesdrop, vb. écouter aux portes.

ebb, n. (water) reflux m.; (decline) déclin m.

ebony, n. ébène m.

ebullient, adj. bouillonnant.

eccentric, adj. excentrique.

eccentricity, n. excentricité f.

ecclesiastic, adj. and n. ecclésiastique m.

ecclesiastical, adj. ecclésiastique.

echelon, n. échelon m.

echo, n. écho m.

eclipse, n. éclipse f.

ecological, adj. écologique.

ecology, n. écologie f.

economic, adj. économique.

economical, adj. (person) économe.

economics, n. économie (f.) politique.

economist, n. économiste m.

economize, vb. économiser.

economy, n. économie f.

ecru, n. écru m.

ecstasy, n. (religious) extase f.; (fig.) transport m.

ecumenical, adj. œcuménique.

eczema, n. eczéma m.

eddy, n. remous m.

edge, n. bord m.; (blade) fil m.

edging, n. pose f., bordure f.

edgy, adj. d'un air agacé.

edible, adj. comestible.

edict, n. édit m.

edifice, n. édifice m.

edify, vb. édifier.

edition, n. édition f.

editor, n. (text) éditeur m.; (paper) rédacteur m.

editorial, n. article (m.) de fond.

educate, vb. (upbringing) élever; (knowledge) instruire.

education, n. éducation f.; (schooling) instruction f.

educator, n. éducateur m.

eel, n. anguille f.

efface, vb. effacer.

effect, 1. n. effet m. 2. vb. effectuer.

effective, adj. (having effect) efficace; (in effect) effectif.

effectively, adv. efficacement, effectivement.

effectiveness, n. efficacité f.

effectual, adj. efficace.

effeminate, adj. efféminé.

effervesce, vb. être en effervescence, pétiller d'animation.

effete, adj. epuisé, caduc.

efficacious, adj. efficace.

efficacy, n. efficacité f.

efficiency, n. (person) compétence f.; (machine) rendement m.

efficient, adj. (person) capable.

efficiently, adv. efficacement, avec compétence.

effigy, n. effigie f.

effort, n. effort m.

effortless, adj. sans effort.

effrontery, n. effronterie f.

effulgent, adj. resplendissant.

effusive, adj. démonstratif.

egg, n. œuf m.; (boiled e.) œuf à la coque; (fried e.) œuf sur le plat; (poached e.) œuf poché; (scrambled e.) œuf brouillé.

eggplant, n. aubergine f.

egoism, n. égoïsme m.

egotism, n. égotisme m.

egotist, n. égotiste m.

Egypt, n. Égypte m.

Egyptian, 1. n. Égyptien m. 2. adj. égyptien.

eight, adj. and n. huit m.

eighteen, adj. and n. dix-huit m.

eighteenth, adj. and n. dix-huitième m.f.

eighth, adj. and n. huitième m.f.

eightieth, adj. quatre-vingt-ième.

eighty, adj. and n. quatre-vingts m.

either, 1. adj. (each of two) chaque; (one or other) l'un ou l'autre. 2. pron. chacun; l'un ou l'autre. 3. conj. (e. . . . or) ou . . . ou . . .

ejaculate, vb. éjaculer, prononcer.

eject, vb. (throw) jeter.

ejection, n. jet m., éjection f., expulsion f.

eke, vb. suppléer à, subsister pauvrement.

elaborate, 1. adj. minutieux. 2. vb. élaborer.

elapse, vb. (time) s'écouler.

elastic, adj. and n. élastique m.

elasticity, n. élasticité f.

elate, vb. exalter, transporter.

elated, adj. exalté.

elation, n. exaltation f.

elbow, n. coude m.

elbowroom, n. aisance des coudes f.

elder, adj. and n. aîné m.

elderberry, n. baie de sureau f.

elderly, adj. d'un certain âge.

eldest, adj. aîné.

elect, vb. élire.

election, n. élection f.

electioneer, vb. faire une campagne électorale.

elective, adj. électif.

electorate, n. électorat m., les votants m.pl.

electric, electrical, adj. électrique.

electric chair, n. fauteuil électrique m.

electric eel, n. anguille électrique f.

electrician, n. électricien m.

electricity, n. électricité f.

electrocardiogram, n. électrocardiogramme m.

electrocute, vb. électrocuter.

electrode, n. électrode f.

electrolysis, n. électrolyse f.

electron, n. électron m.

electronics, n. électronique f.

electroplate, 1. vb. plaquer. 2. adj. plaqué.

elegance, n. élégance f.

elegant, adj. élégant.

elegiac, adj. élégiaque.

elegy, n. élégie f.

element, n. élément m.

elemental, elementary, adj. élémentaire.

elephant, n. éléphant m.

elephantine, adj. éléphantin.

elevate, vb. élever.

elevation, n. élévation f.

elevator, n. ascenseur m.

eleven, adj. and n. onze m.

eleventh, adj. and n. onzième m.f.

elf, n. elfe m.

elfin, adj. d'elfe.

elicit, vb. tirer, faire jaillir.

eligibility, n. éligibilité f.

eligible, adj. éligible.

eliminate, vb. éliminer.

elimination, n. élimination f.

elixir, n. élixir m.

elk, n. élan m.

elm, n. orme m.

elocution, n. élocution f.

elongate, vb. allonger, étendre.

elope, vb. s'enfuir.

eloquence, n. éloquence f.

eloquent, adj. éloquent.

eloquently, adv. d'une manière éloquente.

else, 1. adj. autre; (someone e.) quelqu'un d'autre. 2. adv. autrement.

elsewhere, adv. ailleurs.

elucidate, vb. élucider, éclaircir.

elude, vb. éluder.

elusive, adj. évasif, insaisissable.

emaciated, adj. émacié.

emanate, vb. émaner.

emancipate, vb. émanciper.

emancipation, n. émancipation f.

emancipator, n. émancipateur m.

emasculate, vb. émasculer.

embalm, vb. embaumer.

embankment, n. levée f.

embargo, n. embargo m.

embark, vb. embarquer, tr.

embarrass, vb. embarrasser.

embarrassing, adj. embarrassant.

embarrassment, n. embarras m.

embassy, n. ambassade f.

embellish, vb. embellir.

embellishment, *n.* embellissement *m.*

ember, *n.* braise *f.*, charbon ardent *m.*

embezzle, *vb.* détourner.

embitter, *vb.* aigrir, envenimer.

emblazon, *vb.* blasonner.

emblem, *n.* emblème *m.*

emblematic, *adj.* emblématique.

embody, *vb.* incarner, incorporer.

emboss, *vb.* graver en relief, travailler en bosse.

embrace, 1. *n.* étreinte *f.* 2. *vb.* embrasser.

embroider, *vb.* broder.

embroidery, *n.* broderie *f.*

embroil, *vb.* embrouiller.

embryo, *n.* embryon *m.*

embryology, *n.* embryologie *f.*

embryonic, *adj.* embryonnaire.

emerald, *n.* émeraude *f.*

emerge, *vb.* émerger.

emergency, *n.* circonstance (*f.*) critique.

emergent, *adj.* émergent.

emery, *n.* émeri *m.*

emetic, *n.* émétique *m.*

emigrant, *n.* émigrant *m.*

emigrate, *vb.* émigrer.

emigration, *n.* émigration *f.*

eminence, *n.* éminence *f.*

eminent, *adj.* éminent.

emissary, *n.* émissaire *m.*

emission control, *n.* appareil pour limiter l'émission de vapeurs nuisibles *m.*

emit, *vb.* émettre.

emollient, *adj.* émollient.

emolument, *n.* traitement *m.*

emotion, *n.* émotion *f.*

emotional, *adj.* émotif; (excitable) émotionnable.

emperor, *n.* empereur *m.*

emphasis, *n.* (impressiveness) force *f.*; (stress) accent *m.*

emphasize, *vb.* mettre en relief.

emphatic, *adj.* (manner) énergique.

empire, *n.* empire *m.*

empirical, *adj.* empirique.

employ, *vb.* employer.

employee, *n.* employé *m.*

employer, *n.* patron *m.*

employment, *n.* emploi *m.*

empower, *vb.* autoriser.

empress, *n.* impératrice *f.*

emptiness, *n.* vide *m.*

empty, 1. *adj.* vide. 2. *vb.* vider.

emulate, *vb.* émuler.

emulsion, *n.* émulsion *f.*

enable, *vb.* mettre à même (de).

enact, *vb.* (law) décréter; (play) jouer.

enactment, *n.* promulgation *f.*, acte législatif *m.*

enamel, *n.* émail *m.*, *pl.* émaux.

enamor, *vb.* amouracher.

encamp, *vb.* camper, faire camper.

encampment, *n.* campement *m.*, camp *m.*

encephalitis, *n.* encéphalite *f.*

encephalon, *n.* encéphale *m.*

enchant, *vb.* enchanter.

enchanting, *adj.* ravissant.

enchantment, *n.* enchantement *m.*

encircle, *vb.* entourer.

enclose, *vb.* enclore; (in letter) joindre.

enclosure, *n.* enclos *m.*; (in letter) pièce (*f.*) jointe.

encompass, *vb.* entourer.

encounter, *vb.* rencontrer.

encourage, *vb.* encourager.

encouragement, *n.* encouragement *m.*

encroach, *vb.* empiéter.

encumber, *vb.* encombrer.

encyclical, *n.* encyclique *f.*

encyclopedia, *n.* encyclopédie *f.*

end, 1. *n.* fin *f.*; (extremity) bout *m.*; (aim) but *m.* 2. *vb.* finir.

endanger, *vb.* mettre en danger.

endear, *vb.* rendre cher.

endearment, *n.* charme *m.*, attrait *m.*

endeavor, 1. *n.* effort *m.* 2. *vb.* s'efforcer.

endemic, *adj.* endémique.

ending, *n.* terminaison *f.*

endless, *adj.* sans fin.

endocrine gland, *n.* glande endocrine *f.*

endorse, *vb.* (sign) endosser; (support) appuyer.

endorsement, *n.* (signing) endossement *m.*; (approval) approbation *f.*

endow, *vb.* doter.

endowment, *n.* dotation *f.*, fondation *f.*

endurance, *n.* résistance *f.*

endure, *vb.* supporter.

enduring, *adj.* durable.

enema, *n.* lavement *m.*

enemy, *adj.* and *n.* ennemi *m.*

energetic, *adj.* énergique.

energy, *n.* énergie *f.*

enervate, *vb.* énerver, affaiblir.

enervation, *n.* affaiblissement *m.*

enfold, *vb.* envelopper.

enforce, *vb.* imposer; (law) exécuter.

enforcement, *n.* exécution *f.*

enfranchise, *vb.* affranchir, accorder le droit de vote.

engage, *vb.* engager, *tr.*; (become e.d, to be married) se fiancer.

engaged, *adj.* occupé, pris; fiancé.

engagement, *n.* engagement *m.*; (marriage) fiançailles *f.pl.*

engaging, *adj.* attrayant, séduisant.

engender, *vb.* engendrer.

engine, *n.* machine *f.*; (train) locomotive *f.*; (motor) moteur *m.*

engineer, *n.* (profession) ingénieur *m.*; (engine operator)

mécanicien *m.*; (mil.) soldat (*m.*) du génie.

engineering, *n.* génie *m.*

England, *n.* Angleterre *f.*

English, *adj.* and *n.* anglais *m.*

Englishman, *n.* Anglais *m.*

Englishwoman, *n.* Anglaise *f.*

engrave, *vb.* graver.

engraver, *n.* graveur *m.*

engraving, *n.* gravure *f.*

engross, *vb.* (absorb) absorber.

engrossing, *adj.* absorbant.

enhance, *vb.* rehausser.

enigma, *n.* énigme *f.*

enigmatic, *adj.* énigmatique.

enjoin, *vb.* enjoindre.

enjoy, *vb.* jouir de; (e. oneself) s'amuser.

enjoyable, *adj.* agréable.

enjoyment, *n.* jouissance *f.*

enlace, *vb.* enlacer.

enlarge, *vb.* agrandir, *tr.*

enlargement, *n.* agrandissement *m.*

enlarger, *n.* agrandisseur *m.*, amplificateur *m.*

enlighten, *vb.* éclairer.

enlightenment, *n.* éclaircissement *m.*

enlist, *vb.* enrôler, *tr.*

enlisted man, *n.* gradé *m.*

enlistment, *n.* enrôlement *m.*

enliven, *vb.* animer.

enmesh, *vb.* engrener, embarrasser.

enmity, *n.* inimitié *f.*

ennoble, *vb.* anoblir.

ennui, *n.* ennui *m.*

enormity, *n.* énormité *f.*

enormous, *adj.* énorme.

enough, *adj.* and *adv.* assez (de).

enrage, *vb.* faire enrager.

enrapture, *vb.* ravir, enchanter.

enrich, *vb.* enrichir.

enroll, *vb.* enrôler.

enrollment, *n.* enrôlement *m.*

ensemble, *n.* ensemble *m.*

enshrine, *vb.* enchâsser.

ensign, *n.* (navy) enseigne *m.*

enslave, *vb.* asservir.

ensnare, *vb.* prendre au piège.

ensue, *vb.* s'ensuivre.

entail, *vb.* (involve) entraîner; (law) substituer.

entangle, *vb.* empêtrer.

enter, *vb.* entrer (dans).

enterprise, *n.* entreprise *f.*

enterprising, *adj.* entreprenant.

entertain, *vb.* (amuse) amuser; (receive) recevoir.

entertainment, *n.* amusement *m.*

enthrall, *vb.* captiver, ensorceler.

enthusiasm, *n.* enthousiasme *m.*

enthusiast, *n.* enthousiaste *m.f.*

enthusiastic, *adj.* enthousiaste.

entice, *vb.* attirer.

entire, *adj.* entier.

entirely, *adv.* entièrement.

entirety, *n.* totalité *f.*

entitle, *vb.* donner droit à; (book) intituler.

entity, n. entité f.
entomb, vb. enterrer, ensevelir.
entrails, n. entrailles f.pl.
entrain, vb. embarquer en chemin de fer.
entrance, n. entrée f.
entrant, n. débutant m., inscrit m.
entrap, vb. attraper, prendre au piège.
entreat, vb. supplier.
entreaty, n. instance f.
entrench, vb. retrancher.
entrust to, vb. confier à.
entry, n. (entrance) entrée f.; (recording) inscription f.
enumerate, vb. énumérer.
enumeration, n. énumération f.
enunciate, vb. énoncer.
enunciation, n. énonciation f.
envelop, vb. envelopper.
envelope, n. enveloppe f.
enviable, adj. enviable.
envious, adj. envieux.
environment, n. milieu m.
environmentalist, n. écologiste m.; environnementaliste m.
environmental protection, n. protection de l'environnement f.
environs, n. environs m.pl., alentours m.pl.
envisage, vb. envisager.
envoy, n. envoyé m.
envy, 1. n. envie f. **2.** vb. envier.
eon, n. éon m.
ephemeral, adj. éphémère.
epic, 1. n. épopée f. **2.** adj. épique.
epicure, n. gourmet m.
epidemic, n. épidémie f.
epidermis, n. épiderme m.
epigram, n. épigramme f.
epilepsy, n. épilepsie f.
epilogue, n. épilogue m.
episode, n. épisode m.
epistle, n. épître f.
epitaph, n. épitaphe f.
epithet, n. épithète f.
epitome, n. épitomé m., résumé m.
epitomize, vb. résumer, abréger.
epoch, n. époque f.
equable, adj. uniforme, régulier.
equal, adj. égal; (be e. to) être à la hauteur de.
equality, n. égalité f.
equalize, vb. égaliser, tr.
equanimity, n. tranquillité d'esprit f., équanimité f., sérénité f.
equate, vb. égaler, mettre en équation.
equation, n. équation f.
equator, n. équateur m.
equatorial, adj. équatorial.
equestrian, adj. équestre.
equidistant, adj. équidistant.
equilateral, adj. équilatéral.
equilibrium, n. équilibre m.
equinox, n. équinoxe m.
equip, vb. équiper.
equipment, n. équipement m.

equitable, adj. équitable, juste.
equity, n. équité f.
equivalent, adj. and n. équivalent m.
equivocal, adj. équivoque.
equivocate, vb. équivoquer.
era, n. ère f.
eradicate, vb. déraciner.
eradicator, n. effaceur m., grattoir m.
erase, vb. effacer.
eraser, n. gomme f.
erasure, n. rature f.
erect, adj. droit.
erection, n. érection f., construction f.
erectness, n. attitude droite f.
ermine, n. hermine f.
erode, vb. éroder, ronger.
erosion, n. érosion f.
erosive, adj. érosif.
erotic, adj. érotique.
err, vb. errer.
errand, n. course f.
errant, adj. errant.
erratic, adj. irrégulier, excentrique.
erring, adj. égaré, dévoyé.
erroneous, adj. erroné.
error, n. erreur f.
erudite, adj. érudit.
erudition, n. érudition f.
erupt, vb. entrer en éruption.
eruption, n. éruption f.
escalate, vb. escalader.
escalator, n. escalier roulant m.
escapade, n. escapade f.
escape, 1. n. fuite f. **2.** vb. échapper.
escapism, n. évasion f., échappement m.
eschew, vb. éviter, s'abstenir.
escort, n. (mil.) escorte f.; (to a lady) cavalier m.
esculent, adj. comestible.
escutcheon, n. écusson m.
esoteric, adj. ésotérique.
especial, adj. spécial.
espionage, n. espionnage m.
espousal, n. adoption f., adhésion (à) f.
espouse, vb. épouser, embrasser (une cause).
Eskimo, 1. n. Esquimau m., Esquimaude f. **2.** adj. esquimau m., esquimaude f.
esquire, n. écuyer m.; titre honorifique d'un "gentleman" m.
essay, 1. n. essai m.; (school) composition f. **2.** vb. essayer.
essayist, n. essayiste m.
essence, n. essence f.
essential, adj. essentiel.
essentially, adv. essentiellement.
establish, vb. établir.
establishment, n. établissement m.
estate, n. (condition, class) état m.; (wealth) biens m.pl.; (land) propriété f.
esteem, 1. n. estime f. **2.** vb. estimer.

estimable, adj. estimable.
estimate, 1. n. estimation f.; (comm.) devis m. **2.** vb. estimer.
estimation, n. (opinion) jugement m.
estrange, vb. aliéner.
estuary, n. estuaire m.
etching, n. gravure (f.) à l'eau-forte.
eternal, adj. éternel.
eternity, n. éternité f.
ether, n. éther m.
ethereal, adj. éthéré.
ethical, adj. moral.
ethics, n. éthique f.
Ethiopia, n. Éthiopie f.
ethnic, adj. ethnique.
etiquette, n. étiquette f.
Etruscan, 1. n. Étrusque m.f. **2.** adj. étrusque.
etymology, n. étymologie f.
eucalyptus, n. eucalyptus m.
eugenic, adj. eugénésique.
eugenics, n. eugénisme m., eugénique f.
eulogize, vb. faire l'éloge de.
eulogy, n. panégyrique m.
eunuch, n. eunuque m.
euphonious, adj. mélodieux, euphonique.
Europe, n. Europe f.
European, 1. n. Européen m. **2.** adj. européen.
euthanasia, n. euthanasie f.
evacuate, vb. évacuer.
evacuee, n. évacué m.
evade, vb. éluder.
evaluate, vb. évaluer.
evaluation, n. évaluation f.
evanescent, adj. évanescent, éphémère.
evangelist, n. évangéliste m.
evaporate, vb. évaporer, tr.
evaporation, n. évaporation f.
evasion, n. subterfuge f.
evasive, adj. évasif.
eve, n. veille f.
even, 1. adj. égal; (number) pair. **2.** adv. même.
evening, n. soir m.; (span of e.) soirée f.
evenness, n. égalité f.
event, n. événement m.; (eventuality) cas m.
eventful, adj. plein d'événements.
eventual, adj. (ultimate) définitif; (contingent) éventuel.
ever, adv. (at all times) toujours; (at any time) jamais.
everglade, n. région marécageuse (de la Floride) f.
evergreen, adj. à feuilles persistantes, toujours vert.
everlasting, adj. éternel.
every, adj. (each) chaque; (all) tous les m.; toutes les f.
everybody, everyone, pron. tout le monde; chacun.
everyday, adj. de tous les jours.
everything, pron. tout.
everywhere, adv. partout.
evict, vb. évincer.

eviction, n. éviction f., expulsion f.

evidence, n. évidence f.; (proof) preuve f.

evident, adj. évident.

evidently, adv. évidemment.

evil, n. mal m.

evil, adj. mauvais.

evince, vb. démontrer.

eviscerate, vb. éviscérer.

evoke, vb. évoquer.

evolution, n. évolution f.

evolutionist, n. évolutionniste m.

evolve, vb. évoluer, développer.

ewe, n. agnelle f.

exact, adj. exact.

exacting, adj. (person) exigeant.

exactly, adv. exactement.

exaggerate, vb. exagérer.

exaggerated, adj. exagéré.

exaggeration, n. exagération f.

exalt, vb. exalter; (raise) élever.

exaltation, n. exaltation f.

examination, n. examen m.

examine, vb. examiner.

example, n. exemple m.

exasperate, vb. exaspérer.

exasperation, n. exaspération f.

excavate, vb. creuser.

exceed, vb. excéder.

exceedingly, adv. extrêmement.

excel, vb. exceller, intr.

excellence, excellency, n. excellence f.

excellent, adj. excellent.

excelsior, n. copeaux d'emballage m.pl.

except, 1. vb. excepter. 2. prep. excepté, sauf.

exception, n. exception f.

exceptional, adj. exceptionnel.

excerpt, n. extrait m.

excess, n. excès m.; (surplus) excédent m.

excessive, adj. excessif.

exchange, 1. n. échange m.; (money) change m. 2. vb. échanger.

exchangeable, adj. échangeable.

excise, n. contribution indirecte f., régie f.

excitable, adj. émotionnable, excitable.

excite, vb. exciter.

excitement, n. agitation f.

exclaim, vb. s'écrier.

exclamation, n. exclamation f.

exclamation point or mark, n. point d'exclamation m.

exclude, vb. exclure.

exclusion, n. exclusion f.

exclusive, adj. exclusif; (stylish) sélect.

excommunicate, vb. excommunier.

excommunication, n. excommunication f.

excoriate, vb. excorier, écorcher.

excrement, n. excrément m.

excruciating, adj. atroce, affreux.

exculpate, vb. disculper, exonérer.

excursion, n. excursion f.

excusable, adj. excusable.

excuse, 1. n. excuse f. 2. vb. excuser.

execrable, adj. exécrable, abominable.

execute, vb. exécuter.

execution, n. exécution f.

executioner, n. bourreau m.

executive, adj. and n. exécutif m.

executive mansion, n. maison présidentielle f.

executor, n. exécuteur m.

exemplary, adj. exemplaire.

exemplify, vb. expliquer par des exemples.

exempt, 1. adj. exempt. 2. vb. exempter.

exercise, 1. n. exercice m. 2. vb. exercer.

exert, vb. employer; (e. oneself) s'efforcer de.

exertion, n. effort m.

exhale, vb. exhaler.

exhaust, 1. n. (machines) échappement m. 2. vb. épuiser.

exhaustion, n. épuisement m.

exhaustive, adj. complet, approfondi.

exhibit, vb. (pictures, etc.) exposer; (show) montrer.

exhibition, n. exposition f.

exhibitionism, n. exhibitionnisme m.

exhilarate, vb. égayer.

exhort, vb. exhorter.

exhortation, n. exhortation f.

exhume, vb. exhumer.

exigency, n. exigence f.

exile, 1. n. exil m.; (person) exilé m. 2. vb. exiler.

exist, vb. exister.

existence, n. existence f.

existent, adj. existant.

exit, n. sortie f.

exodus, n. exode m.

exonerate, vb. exonérer.

exorbitant, adj. exorbitant.

exorcise, vb. exorciser.

exotic, adj. exotique.

expand, vb. étendre, tr.; (dilate) dilater, tr.

expanse, n. étendue f.

expansion, n. expansion f.

expansive, adj. expansif.

expatiate, vb. discourir.

expatriate, vb. expatrier.

expect, vb. s'attendre à; (await) attendre.

expectancy, n. attente f.

expectant, n. attente f.; (hope) espérance f.

expectorate, vb. expectorer.

expediency, n. convenance f.

expedient, n. expédient m.

expedite, vb. activer, accélérer.

expedition, n. expédition f.

expel, vb. expulser.

expend, vb. (money) dépenser; (use up) épuiser.

expenditure, n. dépense f.

expense, n. dépense f.; (expenses) frais m.pl.

expensive, adj. coûteux, cher.

expensively, adv. coûteusement.

experience, 1. n. expérience f. 2. vb. éprouver.

experienced, adj. expérimenté.

experiment, n. expérience f.

experimental, adj. expérimental.

expert, adj. and n. expert m.

expiate, vb. expier.

expiration, n. expiration f.

expire, vb. expirer.

explain, vb. expliquer.

explanation, n. explication f.

explanatory, adj. explicatif.

expletive, n. explétif m.

explicit, adj. explicite.

explode, vb. (burst) éclater, intr.

exploit, 1. n. exploit m. 2. vb. exploiter.

exploitation, n. exploitation f.

exploration, n. exploration f.

exploratory, adj. exploratif.

explore, vb. explorer.

explorer, n. explorateur m.

explosion, n. explosion f.

explosive, adj. and n. explosif m.

exponent, n. interprète m.

export, 1. n. (exportation) exportation f.; (exported object) article (m.) d'exportation. 2. vb. exporter.

exportation, n. exportation f.

expose, vb. exposer.

exposé, n. exposé m.

exposition, n. exposition f.

expository, adj. expositoire.

expostulate, vb. faire des remontrances à.

exposure, n. exposition f.

expound, vb. exposer.

express, 1. adj. exprès. 2. vb. exprimer.

expressage, n. frais d'expédition m.pl.

expression, n. expression f.

expressive, adj. expressif.

expressly, adv. expressément.

expressman, n. agent de messageries m.

expropriate, vb. exproprier.

expulsion, n. expulsion f.

expunge, vb. effacer, rayer.

expurgate, vb. expurger, épurer.

exquisite, adj. exquis.

extant, adj. existant.

extemporaneous, adj. improvisé, impromptu.

extend, vb. étendre; (prolong) prolonger.

extension, n. extension f.

extensive, adj. étendu.

extensively, adv. largement, considérablement.
extent, n. étendue f.; (to some e.) jusqu'à un certain point.
extenuate, vb. (tire out) exténuer; (diminish) atténuer.
exterior, adj. and n. extérieur m.
exterminate, vb. exterminer.
extermination, n. extermination f.
external, adj. externe.
extinct, adj. éteint.
extinction, n. extinction f.
extinguish, vb. éteindre.
extirpate, vb. extirper.
extol, vb. vanter.
extort, vb. extorquer.
extortion, n. extorsion f.
extortioner, n. extorqueur m.
extra, adj. (additional) supplémentaire; (spare) de réserve.
extra-, prefix. (outside of) en dehors de; (intensive) extra-.
extract, 1. n. extrait m. 2. vb. extraire.
extraction, n. extraction f., origine f.
extradite, vb. extrader.
extraneous, adj. étranger à.
extraordinary, adj. extraordinaire.
extravagance, n. extravagance f.; (money) prodigalité f.
extravagant, adj. extravagant; (money) prodigue.
extravaganza, m. œuvre fantaisiste f.
extreme, adj. and n. extrême m.
extremity, n. extrémité f.
extricate, vb. dégager, tirer.
extrovert, n. extroverti m.
exuberant, adj. exubérant.
exude, vb. exsuder.
exult, vb. exulter.
exultant, adj. exultant, joyeux.
eye, n. œil m.pl. yeux.
eyeball, n. globe (m.) de l'œil.
eyebrow, n. sourcil m.
eyeglass, n. lorgnon m.
eyeglasses, n. lunettes f.pl.
eyelash, n. cil m.
eyelet, n. œillet m.
eyelid, n. paupière f.
eyesight, n. vue f.
eyewitness, n. témoin oculaire m.

F

fable, n. fable f.
fabric, n. (structure) édifice m.; (cloth) tissu m.
fabricate, vb. fabriquer.
fabrication, n. fabrication f.
fabulous, adj. fabuleux.
façade, n. façade f.
face, 1. n. figure f. 2. vb. faire face à.
facet, n. facette f.
facetious, adj. facétieux.

face value, n. valeur nominale f.
facial, adj. facial.
facile, adj. facile.
facilitate, vb. faciliter.
facility, n. facilité f.
facing, n. revêtement m., revers m.
facsimile, n. fac-similé m.
fact, n. fait m.; (as a matter of f.) en effet.
faction, n. faction f.
factor, n. facteur m.
factory, n. fabrique f.
factual, adj. effectif, positif.
faculty, n. faculté f.
fad, n. marotte f.
fade, vb. intr. se faner; (color) se décolorer; (f. away) s'évanouir.
fagged, adj. épuisé, fatigué.
fail, vb. manquer; (not succeed) échouer.
failing, 1. n. manquement m. 2. adj. faiblissant. 3. prep. au défaut de.
faille, n. faille f.
failure, n. (lack) défaut m.; (want of success) insuccès m.
faint, 1. adj. faible. 2. vb. s'évanouir.
faintly, adv. faiblement, timidement, légèrement.
fair, 1. n. foire m. 2. adj. (beautiful) beau m., belle f.; (blond) blond; (honest) juste; (pretty good) passable.
fairly, adv. honnêtement, impartialement.
fairness, n. (honesty) honnêteté f.
fairy, n. fée f.
fairyland, n. pays des fées m.
faith, n. foi f.
faithful, adj. fidèle.
faithless, adj. infidèle.
fake, vb. truquer.
faker, n. truqueur m.
falcon, n. faucon m.
falconry, n. fauconnerie f.
fall, 1. n. chute f.; (autumn) automne m. 2. vb. tomber.
fallacious, adj. fallacieux.
fallacy, n. fausseté f.
fallen, adj. tombé, déchu.
fallible, adj. faillible.
fallout, n. pluie radioactive f.
fallow, adj. en jachère.
false, adj. faux m., fausse f.
falsehood, n. mensonge m.
falseness, n. fausseté f.
falsetto, n. and adj. fausset m.
falsification, n. falsification f.
falsify, vb. falsifier.
falter, vb. hésiter.
fame, n. renommée f.
famed, adj. célèbre, renommé, fameux.
familiar, adj. familier.
familiarity, n. familiarité f.
familiarize, vb. familiariser.
family, n. famille f.
famine, n. (food) disette f.; (general) famine f.
famished, adj. affamé.

famous, adj. célèbre.
fan, n. éventail m.; (mechanical) ventilateur m.
fanatic, adj. and n. fanatique m.
fanatical, adj. fanatique.
fanaticism, n. fanatisme m.
fanciful, adj. fantastique, fantaisiste.
fancy, 1. n. fantaisie f. 2. vb. se figurer.
fanfare, n. fanfare f.
fang, n. croc (of a dog) m., crochet (of a snake) m.
fantastic, adj. fantastique.
fantasy, n. fantaisie f.
far, adv. loin; (so f.) jusqu'ici; (as f. as) autant que; (much) beaucoup; (by f.) de beaucoup.
faraway, adj. lointain.
farce, n. farce f.
farcical, adj. bouffon.
fare, 1. n. (price) prix m.; (food) chère f. 2. vb. aller.
farewell, interj. and n. adieu m.
far-fetched, adj. forcé.
far-flung, adj. très étendu, vaste.
farina, n. farine f.
farm, n. ferme f.
farmer, n. fermier m.
farmhouse, n. maison (f.) de ferme.
farming, n. culture f.
farmyard, n. cour de ferme f.
far-reaching, adj. de grande envergure.
far-sighted, adj. clairvoyant.
farther, 1. adj. plus éloigné. 2. adv. plus loin.
farthest, adj. and adv. le plus lointain.
fascinate, vb. fasciner.
fascination, n. fascination f.
fascism, n. fascisme m.
fashion, n. mode f.; (manner) manière f.
fashionable, adj. à la mode.
fast, 1. n. jeûne m. 2. adj. (speedy) rapide; (firm) en avance; (of clock) en avance. 3. vb. jeûner. 4. adv. (quickly) vite; (firmly) ferme.
fasten, vb. attacher, tr.
fastener, n. fermeture f.
fastening, n. attache f.
fastidious, adj. difficile.
fat, adj. gras m., grasse f.
fatal, adj. fatal; (deadly) mortel.
fatality, n. fatalité f.
fatally, adv. fatalement, mortellement.
fate, n. destin m.
fateful, adj. fatal.
father, n. père m.
fatherhood, n. paternité f.
father-in-law, n. beau-père m.
fatherland, n. patrie f.
fatherless, adj. sans père.
fatherly, adj. paternel.
fathom, 1. n. (naut.) brasse f. 2. vb. sonder.
fatigue, n. fatigue f.

fatten, vb. engraisser.

fatty, adj. graisseux.

fatuous, adj. sot.

faucet, n. robinet m.

fault, n. (mistake) faute f.; (defect) défaut m.

faultfinding, n. disposition à critiquer f.

faultless, adj. sans défaut.

faultlessly, adv. d'une manière impeccable.

faulty, adj. défectueux.

favor, 1. n. faveur f. **2.** vb. favoriser.

favorable, adj. favorable.

favored, adj. favorisé.

favorite, adj. and n. favori m., favorite f.

favoritism, n. favoritisme m.

fawn, n. faon m.

faze, vb. bouleverser.

fear, 1. n. crainte f. **2.** vb. craindre.

fearful, adj. (person) craintif; (thing) effrayant.

fearless, adj. intrépide.

fearlessness, n. intrépidité f.

feasible, adj. faisable.

feast, n. fête f.; (banquet) festin m.

feat, n. exploit m.

feather, n. plume f.

feathered, adj. emplumé.

feathery, adj. plumeux.

feature, n. trait m.

February, n. février m.

fecund, adj. fécond.

federal, adj. fédéral.

federation, n. fédération f.

fedora, n. chapeau mou m.

fee, n. (for professional services) honoraires m.pl.; (school) frais m.pl.

feeble, adj. faible.

feeble-minded, adj. d'esprit faible.

feebleness, n. faiblesse f.

feed, 1. n. nourriture f. **2.** vb. nourrir, tr.

feedback, n. action de contrôle en retour f.

feel, vb. sentir, tr.; (touch) tâter.

feeling, n. sentiment m.

feign, vb. feindre.

felicitate, vb. féliciter.

felicitous, adj. heureux.

felicity, n. félicité f.

feline, adj. félin.

fell, adj. funeste.

fellow, n. (general) homme m., garçon m.; (companion) compagnon m.

fellowship, n. camaraderie f.; (university) bourse (f.) universitaire.

felon, n. criminel m.

felony, n. crime m.

felt, n. feutre m.

female, 1. n. (person) femme f.; (animals, plants) femelle f. **2.** adj. féminin, femelle.

feminine, adj. féminin.

femininity, n. féminéité f.

fence, 1. n. clôture f. **2.** vb. (en-

close) enclore; (sword, foil) fair de l'escrime.

fencer, n. escrimeur m.

fencing, n. escrime f.

fender, n. garde-boue m.; (fireplace) garde-feu m.

ferment, vb. fermenter.

fermentation, n. fermentation f.

fern, n. fougère f.

ferocious, adj. féroce.

ferociously, adv. d'une manière féroce.

ferocity, n. férocité f.

ferry, n. passage (m.) en bac; (f. boat) bac m.

fertile, adj. fertile.

fertility, n. fertilité f.

fertilization, n. fertilisation f.

fertilize, vb. fertiliser.

fervency, n. ardeur f.

fervent, adj. fervent.

fervently, adv. ardemment.

fervid, adj. fervent.

fervor, n. ferveur f.

fester, vb. suppurer.

festival, n. fête f.

festive, adj. de fête.

festivity, n. réjouissance f.

festoon, 1. n. feston m. **2.** vb. festonner.

fetal, adj. foetal.

fetch, vb. (go and get) aller chercher; (bring) apporter.

fetching, adj. attrayant.

fete, vb. fêter.

fetid, adj. fétide.

fetish, n. fétiche m.

fetlock, n. fanon m.

fetter, 1. n. lien m., chaîne f. **2.** vb. enchaîner.

fetus, n. foetus m.

feud, n. inimitié f.; (historical) fief m.

feudal, adj. féodal.

feudalism, n. régime féodal m.

fever, n. fièvre f.

feverish, adj. fiévreux.

feverishly, adv. fébrilement, fiévreusement.

few, 1. adj. peu de; (a f.) quelques. **2.** pron. peu; (a f.) quelques-uns.

fiancé, n. fiancé m.

fiasco, n. fiasco m.

fiat, n. décret m.

fib, n. petit mensonge m.

fiber, n. fibre f.

fiberboard, n. fibre de bois m.

fibrous, adj. fibreux.

fickle, adj. volage.

fickleness, n. inconstance f.

fiction, n. fiction f.; (literature) romans m.pl.

fictional, adj. de romans.

fictitious, adj. fictif, imaginaire.

fictitiously, adv. d'une manière factice.

fiddle, 1. n. violon m. **2.** vb. jouer du violon.

fiddlesticks, interj. quelle blague!

fidelity, n. fidélité f.

fidget, vb. se remuer.

field, n. champ m.

fiend, n. démon m.

fiendish, adj. diabolique, infernal.

fierce, adj. féroce.

fiery, adj. ardent.

fiesta, n. fête f.

fife, n. fifre m.

fifteen, adj. and n. quinze m.

fifteenth, adj. and n. quinzième m.

fifth, adj. and n. cinquième m.

fifty, adj. and n. cinquante m.

fig, n. figue f.

fight, 1. n. combat m.; (struggle) lutte f.; (quarrel) dispute f. **2.** vb. combattre; se disputer.

fighter, n. combattant m.

figment, n. invention f.

figurative, adj. figuré.

figuratively, adv. au figuré.

figure, 1. n. figure f.; (of body) tournure f.; (math.) chiffre m. **2.** vb. figurer; calculer.

figured, adj. à dessin.

figurehead, n. homme de paille m.

figure of speech, n. façon de parler f.

figurine, n. figurine f.

filament, n. filament m.

filch, vb. escamoter.

file, 1. n. (tool) lime f.; (row) file f.; (papers) liasse f.; (for papers, etc.) classeur m.; (f.s) archives f.pl. **2.** vb. (tool) limer; (papers) classer; (f. off) défiler.

filial, adj. filial.

filigree, n. filigrane m.

filings, n. limaille f.

fill, vb. remplir, tr.

fillet, n. (band) bandeau m.; (meat, fish) filet m.

filling, n. remplissage m.

filling station, n. poste d'essence m.

film, n. (cinema) film m.; (photo) pellicule f.

filmy, adj. couvert d'une pellicule.

filter, 1. n. filtre m. **2.** vb. filtrer.

filth, n. ordure f.

filthy, adj. immonde; obscène.

fin, n. nageoire f.

final, adj. final.

finale, n. finale m.

finalist, n. finaliste m.

finality, n. finalité f.

finally, adv. finalement, enfin.

finance, 1. n. finance f. **2.** vb. financer.

financial, adj. financier.

financier, n. financier m.

find, vb. trouver.

fine, 1. n. amende f. **2.** adj. (beautiful) beau m., belle f.; (pure, thin) fin. **3.** vb. mettre à l'amende.

fine arts, n. beaux arts m.pl.

finery, n. parure f.

finesse, 1. n. finesse f. **2.** vb. finasser.

finger, n. doigt m.

finger bowl, n. rince-bouche m.

fingernail, n. ongle m.

fingerprint, n. empreinte digitale f.

finicky, adj. affété.

finish, vb. finir.

finished, adj. fini, achevé.

finite, adj. fini.

Finland, n. Finlande f.

Finn, n. Finlandais, Finnais m.

Finnish, 1. n. finnois m. 2. adj. finlandais, finnois.

fir, n. sapin m.

fire, 1. n. feu m.; (burning of house, etc.) incendie m. 2. vb. (weapon) tirer.

fire alarm, n. avertisseur d'incendie m.

firearm, n. arme (f.) à feu.

firedamp, n. grisou m.

fire engine, n. pompe à incendie f.

fire escape, n. échelle de sauvetage f.

fire extinguisher, n. extincteur m.

firefly, n. luciole f.

fireman, n. pompier m.

fireplace, n. cheminée f.

fireproof, adj. à l'épreuve du feu.

fireside, n. coin du feu m.

firewood, n. bois de chauffage m.

fireworks, n. feu (m.) d'artifice.

firm, 1. n. maison (f.) de commerce. 2. adj. ferme.

firmness, n. fermeté f.

first, 1. adj. premier. 2. adv. d'abord.

first-aid, n. premiers secours m.pl.

first-class, adj. de premier ordre.

first-hand, adj. de première main.

first-rate, adj. de premier ordre.

fiscal, adj. fiscal.

fish, 1. n. poisson m. 2. vb. pêcher.

fisherman, n. pêcheur m.

fishery, n. pêcherie f.

fishhook, n. hameçon m.

fishing, n. pêche f.

fishmonger, n. marchand de poisson m.

fishwife, n. marchande de poisson f.

fishy, adj. de poisson; (slang) louche.

fission, n. fission f.

fissure, n. fente f.

fist, n. poing m.

fistic, adj. au poing.

fit, 1. n. accès m. 2. adj. (suitable) convenable; (capable) capable; (f. for) propre à. 3. vb. (befit) convenir à; (clothes) aller à; (adjust) ajuster, tr.

fitful, adj. agité, irrégulier.

fitness, n. à-propos m.; (person) aptitude f.

fitting, 1. n. ajustage m. 2. adj. convenable.

five, adj. and n. cinq m.

fix, 1. n. embarras m. 2. vb. fixer; (repair) réparer.

fixation, n. fixation f.

fixed, adj. fixe.

fixture, n. object (m.) d'attache.

flabby, adj. flasque.

flaccid, adj. flasque.

flag, n. drapeau m.; (stone) dalle f.

flagellate, vb. flageller.

flagging, 1. n. relâchement m. 2. adj. qui s'affaiblit.

flagon, n. flacon m.

flagpole, n. mât de drapeau m.

flagrant, adj. flagrant.

flagrantly, adv. d'une manière flagrante.

flagship, n. vaisseau amiral m.

flagstone, n. dalle f.

flail, 1. n. fléau m. 2. vb. battre au fléau.

flair, n. flair m.

flake, n. (snow) flocon m.

flamboyant, adj. flamboyant.

flame, 1. n. flamme f. 2. vb. flamboyer.

flame thrower, n. lanceur de flammes m.

flaming, adj. flamboyant.

flamingo, n. flamant m.

flank, n. flanc m.

flannel, n. flanelle f.

flap, 1. n. (wing) coup m.; (pocket) patte f.; (table) battant m. 2. vb. battre.

flare, vb. flamboyer.

flare-up, 1. n. emportement m. 2. vb. s'emporter.

flash, n. éclair m.

flashcube, n. flash-cube m.

flashiness, n. faux brillant m., éclat superficiel m.

flashlight, n. (lighthouse) feu (m.) à éclats; (pocket) lampe (f.) de poche.

flashy, adj. voyant.

flask, n. gourde f.

flat, 1. n. appartement m. 2. adj. plat m., platte f.

flatcar, n. wagon en plateforme m.

flatness, n. (evenness) égalité f.; (dullness) platitude f.

flatten, vb. aplatir.

flatter, vb. flatter.

flatterer, n. flatteur m.

flattery, n. flatterie f.

flattop, n. porte-avion m.

flaunt, vb. parader, étaler.

flavor, n. (taste) saveur f.; (fragrance) arome m.

flavoring, n. assaisonnement m.

flavorless, adj. fade.

flaw, n. défaut m.

flawless, adj. sans défaut, parfait.

flawlessly, adv. d'une manière impeccable.

flax, n. lin m.

flay, vb. écorcher.

flea, n. puce f.

fleck, 1. n. tache f. 2. vb. tacheter (de).

fledgling, n. oisillon m.

flee, vb. s'enfuir.

fleece, n. toison f.

fleecy, adj. laineux, moutonneux.

fleet, n. flotte f.

fleeting, adj. fugitif.

flesh, n. chair f.

fleshy, adj. charnu.

flex, vb. fléchir.

flexibility, n. flexibilité f.

flexible, adj. flexible.

flicker, 1. n. lueur (f.) vacillante. 2. vb. trembloter.

flier, n. aviateur m.

flight, n. (flying) vol m.; (fleeing) fuite f.

flight attendant, n. hôtesse de l'air f.

flighty, adj. étourdi.

flimsy, adj. sans solidité.

flinch, vb. reculer, broncher.

fling, vb. jeter.

flint, n. (lighter) pierre (f.) à briquet; (mineral) silex m.

flippant, adj. léger.

flippantly, adv. légèrement.

flirt, vb. flirter.

flirtation, n. flirt m.

float, vb. flotter.

flock, 1. n. troupeau m. 2. vb. accourir.

flog, vb. fouetter.

flood, n. inondation f.

floodgate, n. écluse f.

floodlight, n. lumière à grand flots f.

floor, n. plancher m.; (take the f.) prendre la parole; (story) étage m.

flooring, n. plancher m., parquet m.

floorwalker, n. inspecteur du magasin m.

flop, 1. vb. faire plouf, s'effondrer. 2. n. fiasco m.

floral, adj. floral.

florid, adj. fleuri, vermeil.

florist, n. fleuriste m.f.

flounce, 1. n. volant m. 2. vb. se démener.

flounder, n. flet m.

flour, n. farine f.

flourish, vb. prospérer.

flow, vb. couler.

flower, 1. n. fleur f. 2. vb. fleurir.

flowerpot, n. pot à fleurs m.

flowery, adj. fleuri.

fluctuate, vb. osciller.

fluctuation, n. fluctuation f.

flue, n. tuyau de cheminée m.

fluency, n. facilité f.

fluent, adj. (be a f. speaker of . . .) parler . . . couramment.

fluid, adj and n fluide m.

fluidity, n. fluidité f.

flunk, vb. coller, recaler.

flunkey, n. laquais m.

fluorescent lamp, n. lampe fluorescente f.

fluoroscope, n. fluoroscope m.

flurry, 1. *n.* agitation *f.* 2. *vb.* agiter.

flush, *n.* (redness) rougeur *f.;* (plumbing) chasse *f.*

flute, *n.* flûte *f.*

flutter, 1. *n.* (bird) voltigement *m.;* (agitation) agitation *f.* 2. *vb.* s'agiter; (heart) palpiter.

flux, *n.* flux *m.*

fly, 1. *n.* mouche *f.* 2. *vb.* voler.

foam, *n.* écume *f.*

focal, *adj.* focal.

focus, 1. *n.* foyer *m.;* (in f.) au point. 2. *vb.* (photo) mettre au point.

fodder, *n.* fourrage *m.*

foe, *n.* ennemi *m.*

fog, *n.* brouillard *m.*

foggy, *adj.* brumeux.

foil, *n.* (sheet) feuille *f.;* (set-off) repoussoir *m.;* (fencing) fleuret *m.*

foist, *vb.* fourrer.

fold, 1. *n.* pli *m.* 2. *vb.* plier.

folder, *n.* (booklet) prospectus *m.*

foliage, *n.* feuillage *m.*

folio, *n.* in-folio *m.*

folk, *n.* gens *m.f.pl.*

folklore, *n.* folk-lore *m.*

follicle, *n.* follicule *m.*

follow, *vb.* suivre.

follower, *n.* disciple *m.*

folly, *n.* folie *f.*

foment, *vb.* fomenter.

fond, *adj.* tendre; (be f. of) aimer.

fondant, *n.* fondant *m.*

fondle, *vb.* caresser.

fondly, *adv.* tendrement.

fondness, *n.* tendresse *f.*

food, *n.* nourriture *f.*

foodstuff, *n.* comestible *m.*

fool, *n.* sot *m.,* sotte *f.;* (jester) bouffon *m.*

foolhardiness, *n.* témérité *f.*

foolhardy, *adj.* téméraire.

foolish, *adj.* sot *m.,* sotte *f.*

foolproof, *adj.* à toute épreuve.

foolscap, *n.* papier écolier *m.*

foot, *n.* pied *m.*

footage, *n.* métrage *m.*

football, *n.* football *m.,* ballon *m.*

foothill, *n.* colline basse *f.*

foothold, *n.* point d'appui *m.*

footing, *n.* pied *m.,* point d'appui *m.*

footlights, *n.* rampe *f.*

footnote, *n.* note *f.*

footprint, *n.* empreinte de pas *f.*

footsore, *adj.* aux pieds endoloris.

footstep, *n.* pas *m.*

footstool, *n.* tabouret *m.*

footwork, *n.* jeu de pieds *m.*

fop, *n.* fat *m.*

for, 1. *prep.* pour. 2. *conj.* car.

forage, 1. *n.* fourrage *m.* 2. *vb.* fourrager.

foray, *n.* razzia *f.*

forbear, *vb.* (avoid) s'abstenir de; (be patient) montrer de la patience.

forbearance, *n.* patience *f.*

forbid, *vb.* défendre (à).

forbidding, *adj.* rébarbatif.

force, 1. *n.* force *f.* 2. *vb.* forcer.

forced, *adj.* forcé.

forceful, *adj.* énergique.

forcefulness, *n.* énergie *f.,* vigueur *f.*

forceps, *n.* forceps *m.*

forcible, *adj.* forcé.

ford, 1. *n.* gué *m.* 2. *vb.* traverser à gué.

fore, *adj.* antérieur, de devant.

fore, *n.* avant *m.*

fore and aft, *adv.* de l'avant à l'arrière.

forearm, *n.* avant-bras *m.*

forebears, *n.* ancêtres *m.pl.*

forebode, *vb.* présager.

foreboding, 1. *n.* mauvais augure *m.,* pressentiment *m.* 2. *adj.* qui présage le mal.

forecast, 1. *n.* prévision *f.* 2. *vb.* prévoir.

forecaster, *n.* pronostiqueur *m.*

forecastle, *n.* gaillard *m.*

foreclose, *vb.* exclure, forclore.

forefather, *n.* ancêtre *m.*

forefinger, *n.* index *m.*

forefront, *n.* premier rang *m.*

foregone, *adj.* décidé d'avance.

foreground, *n.* premier plan *m.*

forehead, *n.* front *m.*

foreign, *adj.* étranger.

foreign aid, *n.* aide aux pays étrangers *f.*

foreigner, *n.* étranger *m.*

foreleg, *n.* jambe antérieure *f.*

foreman, *n.* contremaître *m.*

foremost, *adj.* premier.

forenoon, *n.* matinée *f.*

forensic, *adj.* judiciaire.

forerunner, *n.* avant-coureur *m.*

foresee, *vb.* prévoir.

foreseeable, *adj.* que l'on peut prévoir.

foreshadow, *vb.* présager.

foresight, *n.* prévoyance *f.*

forest, *n.* forêt *f.*

forestall, *vb.* anticiper, devancer.

forester, *n.* forestier *m.*

forestry, *n.* sylviculture *f.*

foretaste, *n.* avant-goût *m.*

foretell, *vb.* prédire.

forever, *adv.* pour toujours.

forevermore, *adv.* à jamais.

forewarn, *vb.* prévenir.

foreword, *n.* avant-propos *m.*

forfeit, *vb.* forfaire.

forfeiture, *n.* perte par confiscation *f.,* forfaiture *f.*

forgather, *vb.* se réunir.

forge, 1. *n.* forge *f.* 2. *vb.* forger; (signature, money) contrefaire.

forger, *n.* faussaire *m.,* falsificateur *m.*

forgery, *n.* faux *m.*

forget, *vb.* oublier.

forgetful, *adj.* oublieux.

forget-me-not, *n.* myosotis *m.*

forgive, *vb.* pardonner (à).

forgiveness, *n.* pardon *m.*

forgo, *vb.* renoncer à.

fork, *n.* fourchette *f.;* (tool, road) fourche *f.*

forlorn, *adj.* (hopeless) désespéré; (forsaken) abandonné.

form, 1. *n.* forme *f.;* (blank) formule *f.* 2. *vb.* former.

formal, *adj.* formel.

formaldehyde, *n.* formaldéhyde *f.*

formality, *n.* formalité *f.*

formally, *adv.* formellement.

format, *n.* format *m.*

formation, *n.* formation *f.*

formative, *adj.* formatif.

former, 1. *adj.* précédent; (with latter) premier. 2. *pron.* le premier.

formerly, *adv.* autrefois, jadis, auparavant.

formidable, *adj.* formidable.

formless, *adj.* informe.

formula, *n.* formule *f.*

formulate, *vb.* formuler.

formulation, *n.* formulation *f.*

forsake, *vb.* abandonner.

forsythia, *n.* forsythie *f.*

fort, *n.* fort *m.*

forte, *n.* fort *m.*

forth, *adv.* en avant; (and so f.) et ainsi de suite.

forthcoming, *adv.* à venir.

forthright, 1. *adj.* tout droit. 2. *adv.* carrément, nettement.

forthwith, *adv.* sur-le-champ, tout de suite.

fortieth, *adj. and n.* quarantième *m.*

fortification, *n.* fortification *f.*

fortify, *vb.* fortifier, renforcer.

fortissimo, *adv.* fortissimo.

fortitude, *n.* courage *m.*

fortnight, *n.* quinzaine *f.*

fortress, *n.* forteresse *f.*

fortuitous, *adj.* fortuit.

fortunate, *adj.* heureux.

fortune, *n.* fortune *f.*

fortuneteller, *n.* diseur de bonne aventure *m.*

forty, *adj. and n.* quarante *m.*

forum, *n.* (Roman) forum *m.*

forward, 1. *adj.* en avant; (advanced) avancé; (bold) hardi. 2. *adv.* en avant. 3. *vb.* (letter) faire suivre.

forwardness, *n.* empressement *m.,* effronterie *f.*

fossil, *n.* fossile *m.*

fossilize, *vb.* fossiliser.

foster, *vb.* nourrir.

foundling, *n.* enfant trouvé.

foul, *adj.* (dirty) sale; (disgusting) dégoûtant; (obscene) ordurier; (abominable) infâme.

found, *vb.* fonder.

foundation, *n.* fondation *f.;* (theory) fondement *m.*

founder, *n.* fondateur *m.*

foundling, *n.* enfant trouvé.

foundry, *n.* fonderie *f.*

fountain, *n.* fontaine *f.*

fountainhead, *n.* source *f.*

fountain pen, *n.* stylo-(graphe) *m.*

four, *adj. and n.* quatre *m.*

four-in-hand, *n.* attelage à quatre *m.*

fourscore, *adj.* quatre-vingts.

foursome, *n.* à quatre.

fourteen, *adj. and n.* quatorze *m.*

fourth, *adj. and n.* quatrième *m.;* (fraction) quart *m.*

fourth estate, *n.* quatrième état *m.*

fowl, *n.* volaille *f.*

fox, *n.* renard *m.*

foxglove, *n.* digitale *f.*

foxhole, *n.* renardière *f.*

fox terrier, *n.* fox-terrier *m.*

fox trot, *n.* fox-trot *m.*

foxy, *adj.* rusé.

foyer, *n.* foyer *m.*

fracas, *n.* fracas *m.*

fraction, *n.* fraction *f.*

fracture, *n.* fracture *f.*

fragile, *adj.* fragile.

fragment, *n.* fragment *m.*

fragmentary, *adj.* fragmentaire.

fragrance, *n.* parfum *m.*

fragrant, *adj.* parfumé.

frail, *adj.* frêle.

frailty, *n.* faiblesse *f.*

frame, *n.* (picture) cadre *m.;* (structure) structure *f.*

frame-up, **1.** *n.* coup monté *m.* **2.** *vb.* monter un coup.

framework, *n.* charpente *f.*

France, *n.* France *f.*

franchise, *n.* droit (*m.*) électoral.

frank, *adj.* franc *m.,* franche *f.*

frankfurter, *n.* saucisse (*f.*) de Francfort.

frankincense, *n.* encens *m.*

frankly, *adv.* franchement.

frankness, *n.* franchise *f.*

frantic, *adj.* frénétique.

fraternal, *adj.* fraternel.

fraternally, *adv.* fraternellement.

fraternity, *n.* fraternité *f.*

fraternization, *n.* fraternisation *f.*

fraternize, *vb.* fraterniser.

fratricide, *n.* fratricide *m.*

fraud, *n.* fraude *f.;* (person) imposteur *m.*

fraudulent, *adj.* frauduleux.

fraudulently, *adv.* frauduleusement.

fraught, *adj.* chargé (de), plein, gros.

fray, **1.** *n.* bagarre *f.* **2.** *vb.* érailler.

freak, *n.* (whim) caprice *m.;* (abnormality) phénomène *m.*

freckle, *n.* tache de rousseur *f.*

freckled, *adj.* taché de rousseur.

free, **1.** *adj.* libre; (without cost) gratuit. **2.** *vb.* libérer, affranchir.

freedom, *n.* liberté *f.*

free lance, **1.** journaliste ou politicien indépendant *m.* **2.** *vb.* faire du journalisme indépendant.

freestone, *n.* pêche dont la

chair n'adhère pas au noyau *f.*

free verse, *n.* vers libre *m.*

free will, *n.* libre arbitre *m.*

freeze, *vb.* geler.

freezer, *n.* glacière *f.;* congélateur *m.*

freezing point, *n.* point de congélation *m.*

freight, *n.* fret *m.*

freightage, *n.* frêtement *m.*

freighter, *n.* affréteur *m.*

French, *adj. and n.* français *m.*

French leave, *n.* filer à l'anglaise.

Frenchman, *n.* Français *m.*

French toast, *n.* tranche de pain frite *f.*

Frenchwoman, *n.* Française *f.*

frenzied, *adj.* affolé, frénétique.

frenzy, *n.* frénésie *f.*

frequency, *n.* fréquence *f.*

frequent, **1.** *adj.* fréquent. **2.** *vb.* fréquenter.

frequently, *adv.* fréquemment.

fresco, *n.* fresque *f.*

fresh, *adj.* frais *m.,* fraîche *f.;* (new, recent) nouveau; nouvel *m.,* nouvelle *f.*

freshen, *vb.* refraîchir.

freshman, *n.* étudiant de première année *m.*

freshness, *n.* fraîcheur *f.*

fresh-water, *adj.* d'eau douce.

fret, *vb.* ronger, *tr.*

fretful, *adj.* chagrin.

fretfully, *adv.* avec irritation.

fretfulness, *n.* irritabilité *f.*

friar, *n.* moine *m.,* frère religieux *m.*

fricassee, *n.* fricassée *f.*

friction, *n.* friction *f.*

Friday, *n.* vendredi *m.*

friend, *n.* ami *m.,* amie *f.*

friendless, *adj.* sans amis.

friendliness, *n.* disposition (*f.*) amicale.

friendly, *adj.* amical.

friendship, *n.* amitié *f.*

fright, *n.* effroi *m.*

frighten, *vb.* effrayer.

frightful, *adj.* affreux.

Frigid Zone, *n.* zone glaciale *f.*

frill, **1.** *n.* volant *m.;* affectation *f.* **2.** *vb.* plisser.

frilly, *adj.* froncé, ruché.

fringe, *n.* frange *f.*

frisky, *adj.* folâtre.

frivolity, *n.* frivolité *f.*

frivolous, *adj.* frivole.

frivolousness, *n.* frivolité *f.*

frock, *n.* robe *f.;* (monk's) froc *m.*

frog, *n.* grenouille *f.*

frolic, *vb.* folâtrer.

from, *prep.* de; (time) depuis.

front, *n.* front *m.;* (front part) devant *m.;* (in f. of) devant.

frontage, *n.* étendue de devant *f.*

frontal, *adj.* frontal, de face.

frontier, *n.* frontière *f.*

frost, *n.* gelée *f.*

frostbite, *n.* gelure *f.*

frosting, *n.* glaçage *m.*

frosty, *adj.* gelé, glacé.

froth, **1.** *n.* écume *f.* **2.** *vb.* écumer.

frown, *vb.* froncer les sourcils.

frowzy, *adj.* mal tenu, peu soigné.

frozen, *adj.* gelé.

fructify, *vb.* fructifier.

frugal, *adj.* frugal.

frugality, *n.* frugalité *f.*

fruit, *n.* fruit *m.*

fruitful, *adj.* fructueux.

fruition, *n.* réalisation *f.,* jouissance *f.,* fructification *f.*

fruitless, *adj.* infructueux.

frustrate, *vb.* faire échouer.

frustration, *n.* frustration *f.*

fry, *vb.* frire, *intr.;* faire frire, *tr.*

fryer, *n.* casserole *f.*

fuchsia, *n.* fuchsia *m.*

fudge, **1.** *n.* espèce de fondant américain *m.* **2.** *interj.* bah!

fuel, *n.* combustible *m.*

fugitive, *adj.* fugitif.

fugue, *n.* fugue *f.*

fulcrum, *n.* pivot *m.,* point d'appui *m.*

fulfill, *vb.* accomplir.

fulfillment, *n.* accomplissement *m.*

full, *adj.* plein.

fullback, *n.* arrière *m.*

full dress, *adj.* en tenue de cérémonie.

fullness, *n.* plénitude *f.*

fully, *adv.* pleinement.

fulminate, *vb.* fulminer.

fulmination, *n.* fulmination *f.*

fumble, *vb.* tâtonner.

fume, *n.* fumée *f.*

fumigate, *vb.* désinfecter.

fumigator, *n.* fumigateur *m.*

fun, *n.* (amusement) amusement *m.;* (have f.) s'amuser; (joke) plaisanterie *f.;* (make f. of) se moquer de.

function, *n.* fonction *f.*

functional, *adj.* fonctionnel.

functionary, *n.* fonctionnaire *m.*

fund, *n.* fonds *m.*

fundamental, *adj.* fondamental.

funeral, *n.* funérailles *f.pl.*

funereal, *adj.* funèbre, funéraire.

fungicide, *n.* fongicide *m.*

fungus, *n.* fongus *m.*

funnel, *n.* entonnoir *m.;* (smoke-stack) cheminée *f.*

funny, *adj.* drôle.

fur, *n.* fourrure *f.*

furious, *adj.* furieux.

furlong, *n.* furlong *m.*

furlough, *n.* permission *f.*

furnace, *n.* fourneau *m.*

furnish, *vb.* fournir; (house) meubler.

furnishings, *n.* ameublement *m.*

furniture, *n.* meubles *m.pl.*

furor, *n.* fureur *f.*

furred, *adj.* fourré.

furrier, *n.* fourreur *m.*

furrow, *n.* sillon *m.*

furry, *adj.* qui ressemble à la fourrure.

further, 1. *adj.* ultérieur. **2.** *adv.* (distance) plus loin; (extent) davantage.

furtherance, *n.* avancement *m.*

furthermore, *adv.* en outre.

fury, *n.* furie *f.*

fuse, *vb.* fondre.

fuselage, *n.* fuselage *m.*

fusillade, *n.* fusillade *f.*

fusion, *n.* fusion *f.,* fusionnement *m.*

fuss, *n.* **(make a f.)** faire des histoires.

fussy, *adj.* difficile.

futile, *adj.* futile.

futility, *n.* futilité *f.*

future, 1. *n.* avenir *m.;* *(gramm.)* futur *m.* **2.** *adj.* futur.

futurity, *n.* avenir *m.*

futurology, *n.* futurologie *f.*

fuzz, *n.* duvet *m.,* flou *m.*

fuzzy, *adj.* flou, frisotté.

G

gab, *vb.* jaser.

gabardine, *n.* gabardine *f.*

gable, *n.* pignon *m.*

gadabout, *n.* coureur *m.*

gadfly, *n.* taon *m.*

gadget, *n.* truc *m.*

gag, 1. *vb.* bâillonner. **2.** *n.* blague *f.,* bobard *m.;* bâillon *m.*

gaiety, *n.* gaieté *f.*

gaily, *adv.* gaiement.

gain, 1. *n.* gain *m.* **2.** *vb.* gagner.

gainful, *adj.* profitable, rémunérateur.

gainfully, *adv.* profitablement.

gainsay, *vb.* contredire.

gait, *n.* allure *f.*

gala, *n.* fête de gala *f.*

galaxy, *n.* galaxie *f.,* assemblée brillante *f.*

gale, *n.* grand vent *m.*

gall, *n.* (bile) fiel *m.;* (sore) écorchure *f.*

gallant, *adj.* (brave) vaillant; (with ladies) galant.

gallantly, *adv.* galamment.

gallantry, *n.* vaillance *f.,* galanterie *f.*

gall bladder, *n.* vésicule biliaire *f.*

galleon, *n.* galion *m.*

gallery, *n.* galerie *f.*

galley, *n.* galère *f.,* (naut.) cuisine *f.,* (typographic) galée *f.*

galley proof, *n.* épreuve en première *f.*

Gallic, *adj.* gaulois.

gallivant, *vb.* courailler.

gallon, *n.* gallon *m.*

gallop, 1. *n.* galop *m.* **2.** *vb.* galoper.

gallows, *n.* potence *f.*

gallstone, *n.* calcul biliaire *m.*

galore, *adv.* à foison, à profusion.

galosh, *n.* galoche *f.*

galvanize, *vb.* galvaniser.

gamble, 1. *n.* jeu *(m.)* de hasard. **2.** *vb.* jouer.

gambler, *n.* joueur *m.*

gambling, *n.* jeu *m.*

gambol, 1. *n.* gambade *f.* **2.** *vb.* gamboler.

game, *n.* jeu *m.;* (hunting) gibier *m.*

gamely, *adv.* courageusement, crânement.

gameness, *n.* courage *m.,* crânerie *f.*

gamin, *n.* gamin *m.*

gamut, *n.* gamme *f.*

gamy, *adj.* giboyeux.

gander, *n.* jars *m.*

gang, *n.* bande *f.;* (workers) équipe *f.*

gangling, *adj.* dégingandé.

gangplank, *n.* passerelle *f.*

gangrene, *n.* gangrène *f.*

gangrenous, *adj.* gangreneux.

gangster, *n.* gangster *m.*

gangway, *n.* passage *m.,* passavant *m.*

gap, *n.* (opening) ouverture *f.;* (empty space) vide *m.*

gape, *vb.* rester bouche bée.

garage, *n.* garage *m.*

garb, 1. *n.* vêtement *m.,* costume *m.* **2.** *vb.* vêtir, habiller.

garbage, *n.* ordures *f.pl.*

garble, *vb.* tronquer, altérer.

garden, *n.* jardin *m.*

gardener, *n.* jardinier *m.*

gardenia, *n.* gardénia *m.*

gargle, 1. *n.* gargarisme *m.* **2.** *vb.* se gargariser.

gargoyle, *n.* gargouille *f.*

garish, *adj.* voyant.

garland, *n.* guirlande *f.*

garlic, *n.* ail *m.*

garment, *n.* vêtement *m.*

garner, *vb.* mettre en grenier.

garnet, *n.* grenat *m.*

garnish, *vb.* garnir.

garnishee, *n.* tiers-saisi *m.*

garnishment, *n.* saisie-arrêt *f.*

garret, *n.* mansarde *f.*

garrison, *n.* garnison *f.*

garrote, 1. *n.* garrotte *f.* **2.** *vb.* garrotter.

garrulous, *adj.* bavard, loquace.

garter, *n.* jarretière *f.*

gas, *n.* gaz *m.*

gaseous, *adj.* gazeux.

gash, 1. *n.* coupure *f.,* entaille *f.* **2.** *vb.* couper, entailler.

gasket, *n.* garcette *f.*

gasless, *adj.* sans gaz.

gas mask, *n.* masque à gaz *m.*

gasohol, *n.* essence *(f.)* fabriquée avec de l'alcool.

gasoline, *n.* essence *f.*

gasp, *vb.* (astonishment) sursauter; (lack of breath) haleter.

gassy, *adj.* gazeux, bavard.

gastric, *adj.* gastrique.

gastric juice, *n.* suc gastrique *m.*

gastritis, *n.* gastrite *f.*

gastronomically, *adv.* d'une manière gastronomique.

gastronomy, *n.* gastronomie *f.*

gate, *n.* (city) porte *f.;* (with bars) barrière *f.;* (wrought-iron) grille *f.*

gateway, *n.* porte *f.,* entrée *f.*

gather, *vb.* rassembler, *tr.;* recueillir, *tr.*

gathering, *n.* rassemblement *m.*

gaudily, *adv.* de manière voyante.

gaudiness, *n.* éclat criard *m.,* ostentation *f.*

gaudy, *adj.* voyant.

gaunt, *adj.* décharné.

gauntlet, *n.* gantelet *m.*

gauze, *n.* gaze *f.*

gavel, *n.* marteau *m.*

gavotte, *n.* gavotte *f.*

gawky, *adj.* dégingandé.

gay, 1. *adj.* gai. **2.** homosexuel *n.* **3.** pédé(raste) *m.*

gaze, *vb.* regarder fixement.

gazelle, *n.* gazelle *f.*

gazette, *n.* gazette *f.*

gazetteer, *n.* gazetier *m.,* répertoire géographique *m.*

gear, *n.* (implements, device) appareil *m.;* (machines) engrenage *m.;* (in g.) engrené; **(g. change)** changement *(m.)* de vitesse.

gearing, *n.* engrenage *m.*

gearshift, *n.* changement de vitesse *m.*

gelatin, *n.* gélatine *f.*

gelatinous, *adj.* gélatineux.

geld, *vb.* châtrer.

gelding, *n.* animal châtré *m.*

gem, *n.* pierre *(f.)* précieuse.

gender, *n.* genre *m.*

gene, *n.* déterminant d'hérédité *m.*

genealogical, *adj.* généalogique.

genealogy, *n.* généalogie *f.*

general, *adj.* and *n.* général *m.*

generality, *n.* généralité *f.*

generalization, *n.* généralisation *f.*

generalize, *vb.* généraliser.

generally, *adv.* généralement.

generalship, *n.* stratégie *f.*

generate, *vb.* engendrer, générer.

generation, *n.* génération *f.*

generic, *adj.* générique.

generosity, *n.* générosité *f.*

generous, *adj.* généreux.

generously, *adv.* généreusement.

genetic, *adj.* génétique.

genetics, *n.* génétique *f.*

genial, *adj.* sympathique.

geniality, *n.* jovialité *f.,* bienveillance *f.*

genially, *adv.* affablement.

genital, *adj.* génital.

genitals, *n.* organes génitaux *m.pl.*

genitive, *n. and adj.* génitif *m.*

genius, *n.* génie *m.*

genocide, *n.* génocide *m.*

genre, *n.* genre *m.*

genteel, *adj.* de bon ton.

gentian, *n.* gentiane *f.*

gentile, *n.* gentil *m.*

gentility, *n.* prétention à la distinction *f.*

gentle, *adj.* doux *m.*, douce *f.*

gentleman, *n.* monsieur *m. pl.* messieurs; (character) galant homme *m.*

gentlemanly, *adj.* comme il faut, bien élevé.

gentlemen's agreement, *n.* convention verbale *f.*

gentleness, *n.* douceur *f.*

gently, *adv.* doucement.

gentry, *n.* petite noblesse *f.*

genuflect, *vb.* faire des génuflexions.

genuine, *adj.* véritable.

genuinely, *adv.* véritablement.

genuineness, *n.* authenticité *f.*

genus, *n.* genre *m.*

geographer, *n.* géographe *m.*

geographical, *adj.* géographique.

geography, *n.* géographie *f.*

geometric, *adj.* géométrique.

geometry, *n.* géométrie *f.*

geopolitics, *n.* géopolitique *f.*

geranium, *n.* géranium *m.*

germ, *n.* germe *m.*

German, 1. *n.* (person) Allemand *m.;* (language) allemand *m.* **2.** *adj.* allemand.

germane, *adj.* approprié.

Germanic, *adj.* allemand, germanique.

German measles, *n.* rougeole bénigne *f.*

Germany, *n.* Allemagne *f.*

germicide, *n.* microbicide *m.*

germinal, *adj.* germinal.

germinate, *vb.* germer.

gestate, *vb.* enfanter.

gestation, *n.* gestation *f.*

gesticulate, *vb.* gesticuler.

gesticulation, *n.* gesticulation *f.*

gesture, *n.* geste *m.*

get, *vb.* (obtain) obtenir; (receive) recevoir; (take) prendre; (become) devenir; (arrive) arriver; **(g. in)** entrer; **(g. off)** descendre; **(g. on,** agree) s'entendre; **(g. on,** go up) monter; **(g. out)** sortir; **(g. up)** se lever.

getaway, *n.* fuite *f.*

geyser, *n.* geyser *m.*

ghastly, *adj.* horrible.

ghost, *n.* (specter) revenant *m.;* (Holy G.) Saint-Esprit *m.*

ghost writer, *n.* collaborateur anonyme *m.*, nègre *m.*

ghoul, *n.* goule *f.*, vampire *m.*

giant, *n.* géant *m.*

gibberish, *n.* baragouin *m.*

gibbon, *n.* gibbon *m.*

gibe, 1. *n.* raillerie *f.* **2.** *vb.* railler.

giblet, *n.* abatis (de volaille) *m.*

giddy, *adj.* étourdi.

gift, *n.* don *m.;* (present) cadeau *m.*

gifted, *adj.* doué.

gigantic, *adj.* géant, gigantesque.

giggle, *vb.* rire nerveusement, glousser.

gigolo, *n.* gigolo *m.*

gild, *vb.* dorer.

gill, *n.* ouïes (of fish) *f.pl.*

gilt, 1. *n.* dorure *f.* **2.** *adj.* doré.

gilt-edged, *adj.* doré sur tranche.

gimcrack, 1. *n.* camelote *f.* **2.** *adj.* de camelote.

gimlet, *n.* vrille *f.*

gin, *n.* genièvre *m.*

ginger, *n.* gingembre *m.*

ginger ale, *n.* boisson gazeuse au gingembre *f.*

gingerly, *adv.* avec précaution.

gingersnap, *n.* biscuit au gingembre *m.*

gingham, *n.* guingan *m.*

giraffe, *n.* girafe *f.*

gird, *vb.* ceindre.

girder, *n.* support *m.*

girdle, *n.* gaine *f.*

girl, *n.* jeune fille *f.*

girlish, *adj.* de jeune fille.

girth, *n.* sangle *f.*, circonférence *f.*, corpulence *f.*

gist, *n.* fond *m.*, essence *f.*

give, *vb.* donner; **(g. back)** rendre; **(g. in)** céder; **(g. out)** distribuer; **(g. up)** renoncer à.

give-and-take, *adv.* donnant donnant.

given, *adj.* donné.

given name, *n.* nom de baptême *m.*

giver, *n.* donneur *m.*

gizzard, *n.* gésier *m.*

glace, *adj.* glacé.

glacial, *adj.* glaciaire.

glacier, *n.* glacier *m.*

glad, *adj.* heureux.

gladden, *vb.* réjouir.

glade, *n.* clairère *f.*, éclaircie *f.*

gladiolus, *n.* glaïeul *m.*

gladly, *adv.* volontiers.

gladness, *n.* joie *f.*

Gladstone bag, *n.* sac américain *m.*

glamour, *n.* éclat *m.*

glance, *n.* coup (*m.*) d'œil.

gland, *n.* glande *f.*

glandular, *adj.* glandulaire.

glare, 1. *n.* (light) clarté *f.;* (stare) regard (*m.*) enflammé. **2.** *vb.* (shine) briller; (look) jeter des regards enflammés.

glaring, *adj.* éclatant, flagrant, voyant, manifeste.

glass, *n.* verre *m.*

glass-blowing, *n.* soufflage *m.*

glasses, *n.* lunettes *f.pl.*

glassful, *n.* verre *m.*, verrée *f.*

glassware, *n.* verrerie *f.*

glassy, *adj.* vitreux.

glaucoma, *n.* glaucome *m.*

glaze, 1. *n.* lustre *m.* **2.** *vb.* vitrer.

glazier, *n.* vitrier *m.*

gleam, 1. *n.* lueur *f.* **2.** *vb.* luire.

glee, *n.* allégresse *f.*

glee club, *n.* chœur d'hommes *m.*

gleeful, *adj.* joyeux, allègre.

glen, *n.* vallon *m.*, ravin *m.*

glib, *adj.* spécieux.

glide, *vb.* glisser; (plane) planer.

glider, *n.* planeur *m.*

glimmer, 1. *n.* faible lueur *f.* **2.** *vb.* jeter une faible lueur.

glimmering, *adj.* faible, vacillant.

glimpse, *vb.* entrevoir.

glint, 1. *n.* éclair *m.*, reflet *m.* **2.** *vb.* entreluire, étinceler.

glitter, *vb.* étinceler.

gloat, *vb.* se régaler de.

global, *adj.* global.

globe, *n.* globe *m.*

globetrotter, *n.* globe trotter *m.*

globular, *adj.* globulaire, globuleux.

globule, *n.* globule *m.*

glockenspiel, *n.* glockenspiel *m.*

gloom, *n.* (darkness) ténèbres *f.pl.;* (sadness) tristesse *f.*

gloomy, *adj.* sombre.

glorification, *n.* glorification *f.*

glorify, *vb.* glorifier.

glorious, *adj.* glorieux; (weather) radieux.

glory, *n.* gloire *f.*

gloss, 1. lustre *m.*, vernis *m.*, glose *f.* **2.** *vb.* lustrer, glacer.

glossary, *n.* glossaire *m.*

glossy, *adj.* lustré, glacé.

glove, *n.* gant *m.*

glow, *n.* (light) lumière *f.;* (heat) chaleur *f.*

glowing, *adj.* embrasé, rayonnant.

glowingly, *adv.* en termes chaleureux.

glowworm, *n.* ver luisant *m.*

glucose, *n.* glucose *f.*

glue, 1. *n.* colle (*f.*) forte. **2.** *vb.* coller.

glum, *adj.* maussade.

glumness, *n.* air maussade *m.*, tristesse *f.*

glut, 1. *n.* assouvissement *m.*, excès *m.*, pléthore *f.* **2.** *vb.* assouvir, rassasier, gorger.

glutinous, *adj.* glutineux.

glutton, *n.* gourmand *m.*

gluttonous, *adj.* gourmand, goulu.

glycerin, *n.* glycérine *f.*

gnarl, *n.* loupe *f.*, nœud *m.*

gnash, *vb.* grincer.

gnat, *n.* moucheron *m.*

gnaw, *vb.* ronger.

gnu, *n.* gnou *m.*

go, *vb.* aller; **(g. away)** s'en aller; **(g. back)** retourner; **(g. by)** passer; **(g. down)** descendre; **(g. in)** entrer; **(g. on)** continuer; **(g. out)** sortir; **(g. up)** monter; **(g. without)** se passer de.

goad, 1. *n.* aiguillon *m.* **2.** *vb.* aiguillonner, piquer.

goal, *n.* but *m.*

goat, *n.* chèvre *f.*

goatee, *n.* barbiche *f.*

goatherd, *n.* chevrier *m.*

goatskin, *n.* peau de chèvre *f.*

gobble, *vb.* avaler goulûment, dévorer.

gobbler, *n.* avaleur *m.; dindon m.*

go-between, *n.* intermédiaire *m.*

goblet, *n.* gobelet *m.*

goblin, *n.* gobelin *m.,* lutin *m.*

God, *n.* Dieu *m.*

godchild, *n.* filleul *m.*

goddess, *n.* déesse *f.*

godfather, *n.* parrain *m.*

godless, *adj.* athée, impie, sans Dieu.

godlike, *adj.* comme un dieu, divin.

godly, *adj.* dévot, pieux, saint.

godmother, *n.* marraine *f.*

godsend, *n.* aubaine *f.,* bienfait du ciel *m.*

Godspeed, *interj.* bon voyage!

go-getter, *n.* homme d'affaires énergique *m.,* arriviste *m.*

goiter, *n.* goitre *m.*

gold, *n.* or *m.*

gold brick, *n.* attrape-niais *m.*

golden, *adj.* d'or.

goldenrod, *n.* solidage *m.*

golden rule, *n.* règle par excellence *f.*

gold-filled, *adj.* aurifié, en (or) doublé.

goldfinch, *n.* chardonneret *m.*

goldfish, *n.* poisson rouge *m.*

gold leaf, *n.* feuille d'or *f.,* or battu *m.*

goldsmith, *n.* orfèvre *m.*

gold standard, *n.* étalon or *m.*

golf, *n.* golf *m.*

gondola, *n.* gondole *f.*

gondolier, *n.* gondolier *m.*

gone, *adj.* disparu, parti.

gong, *n.* gong *m.*

gonorrhea, *n.* gonorrhée *f.,* blennorrhagie *f.*

good, *adj.* bon *m.,* bonne *f.*

good, *n.* bien *m.; (goods)* marchandises *f.pl.*

good-bye, *n. and interj.* adieu *m.*

Good Friday, *n.* Vendredi Saint *m.*

good-hearted, *adj.* qui a bon cœur, compatissant.

good-humored, *adj.* de bonne humeur, plein de bonhomie.

good-looking, *adj.* beau, joli.

good-natured, *adj.* au bon naturel, accommodant.

goodness, *n.* bonté *f.*

good will, *n.* bonne volonté *f.*

goose, *n.* oie *f.*

gooseberry, *n.* groseille verte *f.*

gooseneck, *n.* col de cygne *m.*

goose step, *n.* pas d'oie *m.*

gore, 1. *n.* (dress) chanteau *m.,* soufflet *m.; (blood)* sang coagulé *m.* **2.** *vb.* corner.

gorge, *n.* gorge *f.*

gorgeous, *adj.* splendide.

gorilla, *n.* gorille *f.*

gory, *adj.* sanglant, ensanglanté.

gosling, *n.* oison *m.*

gospel, *n.* évangile *m.*

gossamer, *n.* filandre *f.,* gaze légère *f.*

gossip, 1. *n.* bavardage *m.* **2.** *vb.* bavarder.

Gothic, *adj.* gothique.

gouge, 1. *n.* gouge *f.* **2.** *vb.* gouger.

gourd, *n.* gourde *f.,* courge *f.*

gourmand, *n.* gourmand *m.*

gourmet, *n.* gourmet *m.*

govern, *vb.* gouverner.

governess, *n.* gouvernante *f.*

government, *n.* gouvernement *m.*

governmental, *adj.* gouvernemental.

governor, *n.* gouvernant *m.*

governorship, *n.* fonctions de gouverneur *f.pl.,* temps de gouvernement *m.*

gown, *n.* robe *f.*

grab, *vb.* saisir.

grace, *n.* grâce *f.*

graceful, *adj.* gracieux.

gracefully, *adv.* avec grâce.

graceless, *adj.* sans grâce, gauche.

gracious, *adj.* gracieux; (merciful) miséricordieux.

grackle, *n.* mainate *m.*

grade, 1. *n.* grade *m.; (quality)* qualité *f.* **2.** *vb.* classer.

grade crossing, *n.* passage à niveau *m.*

gradual, *adj.* graduel.

gradually, *adv.* graduellement.

graduate, *vb.* graduer; (school) prendre ses grades.

graft, *n.* corruption *f.*

grail, *n.* graal *m.*

grain, *n.* grain *m.*

gram, *n.* gramme *m.*

grammar, *n.* grammaire *f.*

grammarian, *n.* grammairien *m.*

grammar school, *n.* école primaire *f.*

grammatical, *adj.* grammatical.

gramophone, *n.* phonographe.

granary, *n.* grenier *m.*

grand, *adj.* grandiose; (in titles) grand; (fine, *colloq.*) épatant.

grandchild, *n.* petit-fils *m.;* petite-fille *f.;* petits-enfants *m.pl.*

granddaughter, *n.* petite-fille *f.*

grandee, *n.* grand *m.*

grandeur, *n.* grandeur *f.*

grandfather, *n.* grand-père *m.*

grandiloquent, *adj.* grandiloquent.

grandiose, *adj.* grandiose.

grand jury, *n.* jury d'accusation *m.*

grandly, *adv.* grandement, magnifiquement.

grandmother, *n.* grand'mère *f.*

grand opera, *n.* grand opéra *m.*

grandson, *n.* petit-fils *m.*

grandstand, *n.* grande tribune *f.*

granger, *n.* régisseur *m.*

granite, *n.* granit *m.*

granny, *n.* bonne-maman *f.*

grant, 1. *n.* concession *f.; (money)* subvention *f.* **2.** *vb.* accorder; (admit) admettre.

granular, *adj.* en grains, granulé.

granulate, *vb.* granuler, grener.

granulation, *n.* granulation *f.*

granule, *n.* granule *m.*

grape, *n.* raisin *m.*

grapefruit, *n.* pamplemousse *f.*

grapeshot, *n.* mitraille *f.*

grapevine, *n.* treille *f.*

graph, *n.* courbe *f.*

graphic, *adj.* graphique, pittoresque.

graphite, *n.* graphite *m.*

graphology, *n.* graphologie *f.*

grapple, 1. *n.* grappin *m.;* lutte *f.* **2.** *vb.* accrocher; en venir aux prises.

grasp, 1. *n.* (hold) prise *f.* **2.** *vb.* saisir.

grasping, *adj.* avide, cupide.

grass, *n.* herbe *f.*

grasshopper, *n.* sauterelle *f.*

grassy, *adj.* herbeux, verdoyant.

grate, 1. *n.* grille *f.* **2.** *vb.* (cheese, etc.) râper; (make noise) grincer.

grateful, *adj.* reconnaissant.

gratify, *vb.* contenter, satisfaire.

grating, 1. *n.* grille *f.* **2.** *adj.* grinçant, discordant.

gratis, *adv.* gratis, gratuitement.

gratitude, *n.* gratitude *f.*

gratuitous, *adj.* gratuit.

gratuity, *n.* (tip) pourboire *m.*

grave, 1. *n.* tombe *f.* **2.** *adj.* grave.

gravel, *n.* gravier *m.*

gravely, *adv.* gravement, sérieusement.

gravestone, *n.* pierre sépulcrale *f.,* tombe *f.*

graveyard, *n.* cimetière *m.*

gravitate, *vb.* graviter.

gravitation, *n.* gravitation *f.*

gravity, *n.* gravité *f.*

gravure, *n.* gravure *f.*

gravy, *n.* jus *m.*

gray, *adj.* gris.

grayish, *adj.* grisâtre.

gray matter, *n.* substance grise *f.,* cendrée *f.*

graze, *vb.* paître.

grazing, *n.* pâturage *m.*

grease, 1. *n.* graisse *f.* **2.** *vb.* graisser.

great, *adj.* grand.

Great Dane, *n.* grand Danois *m.*

greatness, *n.* grandeur *f.*

Greece, *n.* Grèce *f.*

greediness, *n.* gourmandise *f.*

greedy, *adj.* gourmand.

Greek, 1. *n.* (person) Grec *m.,* Grecque *f.;* (language) grec

m. 2. adj. grec m., grecque f.

green, adj. vert.

greenery, n. verdure f.

greenhouse, n. serre f.

greet, vb. saluer.

greeting, n. salutation f.; (reception) accueil m.

gregarious, adj. grégaire.

grenade, n. grenade f.

grenadine, n. grenadine f.

greyhound, n. lévrier m.

grid, n. gril m.

griddle, n. gril m.

gridiron, n. gril m.

grief, n. chagrin m.

grievance, n. grief m.

grieve, vb. affliger, tr.; chagriner, tr.

grievous, adj. douloureux.

grill, 1. n. gril m. 2. vb. griller.

grillroom, n. grill-room f.

grim, adj. sinistre.

grimace, n. grimace f.

grime, n. saleté f., noirceur f.

grimy, adj. sale, noirci, encrassé.

grin, n. large sourire m.

grind, vb. (crush) moudre; (sharpen) aiguiser.

grindstone, n. meule f.

gringo, n. Anglo-américain m.

grip, n. prise f.

gripe, vb. saisir, empoigner; grogner.

grisly, adj. hideux, horrible.

grist, n. blé à moudre m., mouture f.

gristle, n. cartilage m.

grit, n. grès m., sable m.; (fig.) cran m., courage m.

grizzled, adj. grison, grisonnant.

groan, 1. n. gémissement m. 2. vb. gémir.

grocer, n. épicier m.

grocery, n. épicerie f.

grog, n. grog m.

groggy, adj. gris, titubant.

groin, n. aine f.

groom, 1. n. (horses) palefrenier m.; (bridegroom) nouveau marié m. 2. vb. (horses) panser.

groove, n. rainure f.

grope, vb. tâtonner.

grosgrain, adj. de grosgrain.

gross, adj. (bulky) gros m., grosse f.; (coarse) grossier; (comm.) brut.

grossly, adv. grossièrement.

grossness, n. grossièreté f., énormité f.

grotesque, adj. and n. grotesque m.

grotto, n. grotte f.

grouch, 1. n. maussaderie f.; grogneur m. 2. vb. grogner.

ground, n. (earth) terre f.; (territory) terrain m.; (reason) raison f.; (background) fond m.

ground hog, n. marmotte d'Amérique f.

groundless, adj. sans fondement.

ground swell, n. houle f., lame de fond f.

groundwork, n. fondement m., fond m., base f.

group, 1. n. groupe m. 2. vb. grouper, tr.

groupie, n. groupie f.; membre d'un groupe de jeunes filles m.

grouse, 1. n. tétras m. 2. vb. grogner.

grove, n. bocage m., bosquet m.

grovel, vb. ramper, se vautrer.

grow, vb. croître; (persons) grandir; (become) devenir; (cultivate) cultiver.

growl, vb. grogner.

grown, adj. fait, grand.

grownup, adj. and n. grand m., adulte m.f.

growth, n. croissance f.; (increase) accroissement m.

grub, 1. n. larve f., ver blanc m.; (slang) nourriture f. 2. vb. défricher, fouiller.

grubby, adj. véreux, (fig.) sale.

grudge, n. rancune f.

gruel, n. gruau m.

gruesome, adj. lugubre, terrifiant.

gruff, adj. bourru.

grumble, vb. grommeler.

grumpy, adj. bourru, morose.

grunt, 1. n. grognement m. 2. vb. grogner.

guarantee, 1. n. garantie f. 2. vb. garantir.

guarantor, n. garant m.

guaranty, n. garantie f.

guard, 1. n. garde f. 2. vb. garder.

guarded, adj. prudent, circonspect, réservé.

guardhouse, n. corps de garde m., poste m.

guardian, n. gardien m.; (law) tuteur m.

guardianship, n. tutelle f.

guardsman, n. garde m.

guava, n. goyave f.

gubernatorial, adj. du gouverneur, du gouvernement.

guerrilla, n. guérilla f.

guess, 1. n. conjecture f. 2. vb. deviner.

guesswork, n. conjecture f.

guest, n. invité m.

guffaw, 1. n. gros rire m. 2. vb. s'esclaffer.

guidance, n. direction f.

guide, 1. n. guide m. 2. vb. guider.

guidebook, n. guide m.

guidepost, n. poteau indicateur m.

guild, n. corporation f., corps de métier m.

guile, n. astuce f., artifice m.

guillotine, n. guillotine f.

guilt, n. culpabilité f.

guiltily, adv. criminellement.

guiltless, adj. innocent.

guilty, adj. coupable.

guimpe, n. guimpe f.

guinea fowl, n. pintade f.

guinea pig, n. cobaye m.

guise, n. guise f., façon f.

guitar, n. guitare f.

gulch, n. ravin m.

gulf, n. (geog.) golfe m.; (fig.) gouffre m.

gull, n. mouette f.

gullet, n. gosier m.

gullible, adj. crédule, facile à duper.

gully, n. ravin m.

gulp, 1. n. goulée f., gorgée f., trait m. 2. vb. avaler, gober.

gum, n. gomme f.; (teeth) gencive f.

gumbo, n. gombo m.

gummy, adj. gommeux.

gun, n. (cannon) canon m.; (rifle) fusil m.

gunboat, n. canonnière f.

gunman, n. partisan armé m., voleur armé m., bandit m.

gunner, n. artilleur m.

gunpowder, n. poudre (f.) à canon.

gunshot, n. portée de fusil f.

gunwale, n. plat-bord m.

gurgle, vb. faire glouglou, gargouiller.

guru, n. gourou m.

gush, 1. n. jaillissement m. 2. vb. jaillir.

gusher, n. source jaillissante f., personne exubérante f.

gusset, n. gousset m., soufflet m.

gust, n. (wind) rafale f.

gustatory, adj. gustatif.

gusto, n. goût m., délectation f., verve f.

gusty, adv. venteux, orageux.

gut, 1. n. boyau m., intestin m. 2. vb. éventrer, vider.

gutter, n. (roof) gouttière f.; (street) ruisseau m.

guttural, adj. guttural.

guy, 1. n. type m., individu m. 2. vb. se moquer de.

guzzle, vb. ingurgiter, boire avidement.

gym, n. gymnase m.

gymnasium, n. gymnase m.

gymnast, n. gymnaste m.

gymnastic, adj. gymnastique.

gymnastics, n. gymnastique f.

gynecology, n. gynécologie f.

gypsum, n. gypse m.

gypsy, n. gitane m.f.

gyrate, vb. tournoyer.

gyroscope, n. gyroscope m.

H

habeas corpus, n. habeas corpus m.

haberdasher, n. chemisier m., mercier m.

haberdashery, n. chemiserie f., mercerie f.

habiliment, n. habillement m., apprêt m.

habit, n. habitude f.

habitable, *adj.* habitable.

habitat, *n.* habitat *m.*

habitation, *n.* habitation *f.*

habitual, *adj.* habituel.

habituate, *vb.* habituer, accoutumer.

habitué, *n.* habitué *m.*

hack, 1. *n.* (tool) pioche *f.;* (horse) cheval (*m.*) de louage; (vehicle) voiture (*f.*) de louage. **2.** *vb.* (**h. up**) hacher; (notch) entailler.

hackneyed, *adj.* banal, rebattu.

hacksaw, *n.* scie à métaux *f.*

haddock, *n.* aigle fin *m.*

haft, *n.* manche *m.,* poignée *f.*

hag, *n.* vielle sorcière *f.*

haggard, *adj.* hagard.

haggle, *vb.* marchander.

hagridden, *adj.* tourmenté par le cauchemar.

hail, 1. *n.* grêle *f.* **2.** *vb.* (weather) grêler; (salute) saluer; (come from) venir de. **3.** *interj.* salut.

Hail Mary, *n.* Ave Maria *m.*

hailstone, *n.* grêlon *m.*

hailstorm, *n.* tempête de grêle *f.*

hair, *n.* cheveux *m.pl.;* (single, on head) cheveu *m.;* (on body, animals) poil *m.*

haircut, *n.* coupe (*f.*) de cheveux.

hairdo, *n.* coiffure *f.*

hairdresser, *n.* coiffeur *m.*

hairline, *n.* délié *m.*

hairpin, *n.* épingle (*f.*) à cheveux.

hair-raising, *adj.* horripilant, horrifique.

hair's-breadth, *n.* l'épaisseur d'un cheveu *f.*

hairspray, *n.* laque *f.*

hairy, *adj.* velu, poilu.

halcyon, 1. *n.* alcyon *m.* **2.** *adj.* calme.

hale, *adj.* sain.

half, 1. *n.* moitié *f.* **2.** *adj.* demi. **3.** *adv.* à moitié.

half-and-half, *n.* moitié de l'un, moitié de l'autre *f.*

halfback, *n.* demi-arrière *m.*

half-baked, *adj.* à moitié cuit, inexpérimenté, incomplet.

half-breed, *n.* métis *m.*

half brother, *n.* frère de père *m.,* frère de mère *m.*

half dollar, *n.* demi-dollar *m.*

half-hearted, *adj.* sans enthousiasme.

half-mast, *adv.* à mi-mât.

halfpenny, *n.* petit sou *m.*

halfway, *adv.* à mi-chemin.

half-wit, *n.* niais *m.,* sot *m.*

halibut, *n.* flétan *m.*

hall, *n.* (large room) salle *f.;* (entrance) vestibule *m.*

hallmark, *n.* contrôle *m.*

hallow, *vb.* sanctifier.

Halloween, *n.* la veille de la Toussaint *f.*

hallucination, *n.* hallucination *f.*

hallway, *n.* corridor *m.,* vestibule *m.*

halo, *n.* auréole *f.*

halt, 1. *n.* halte *f.* **2.** *vb.* arrêter, *tr.*

halter, *n.* licou *m.,* longe *f.,* corde *f.*

halve, *vb.* diviser en deux, partager en deux.

halyard, *n.* drisse *f.*

ham, *n.* jambon *m.*

hamlet, *n.* hameau *m.*

hammer, 1. *n.* marteau *m.* **2.** *vb.* marteler.

hammock, *n.* hamac *m.*

hamper, 1. *n.* pannier *m.* **2.** *vb.* embarrasser, gêner.

hamstring, *vb.* couper le jarret à, couper les moyens à.

hand, *n.* main *f.*

handball, *n.* balle *f.*

handbook, *n.* manuel *m.*

handcuff, 1. *n.* menotte *f.* **2.** *vb.* mettre les menottes à.

handful, *n.* poignée *f.*

handicap, 1. *n.* handicap *m.,* désavantage *m.*

handicraft, *n.* métier *m.*

handiwork, *n.* main-d'œuvre *f.*

handkerchief, *n.* mouchoir *m.*

handle, 1. *n.* manche *m.* **2.** *vb.* manier.

handle bar, *n.* guidon *m.*

handmade, *adj.* fait à la main, fabriqué à la main.

handmaid, *n.* servante *f.*

hand organ, *n.* orgue portatif *m.,* orgue de Barbarie *m.*

handout, *n.* aumône *f.;* compte rendu communiqué à la presse *m.*

hand-pick, *vb.* trier à la main, éplucher à la main.

handsome, *adj.* beau *m.,* belle *f.*

hand-to-hand, *adj.* corps à corps.

handwriting, *n.* écriture *f.*

handy, *adj.* (person) adroit; (thing) commode; (at hand) sous la main.

handy man, *n.* homme à tout faire *m.,* bricoleur *m.,* factotum *m.*

hang, *vb.* pendre.

hangar, *n.* hangar *m.*

hangdog, *adj.* avec une mine patibulaire, avec un air en dessous.

hanger-on, *n.* dépendant *m.,* parasite *m.*

hang glider, *n.* glisseur duquel l'usager pend *m.*

hanging, 1. *n.* suspension *f.,* pendaison *f.* **2.** *adj.* suspendu, pendant.

hangman, *n.* bourreau *m.*

hangnail, *n.* envie *f.*

hangout, *n.* repaire *m.,* nid *m.*

hang-over, *n.* reste *m.,* reliquat *m.*

hangup, *n.* difficulté psychologique *f.*

hank, *n.* écheveau *m.,* torchette *f.*

hanker, *vb.* désirer vivement, convoiter.

haphazard, *adv.* au hasard.

happen, *vb.* (take place) arriver; (chance to be) se trouver.

happening, *n.* évènement *m.*

happily, *adv.* heureusement.

happiness, *n.* bonheur *m.*

happy, *adj.* heureux.

happy-go-lucky, *adj.* sans souci, insouciant.

harakiri, *n.* hara-kiri *m.*

harangue, 1. *n.* harangue *f.* **2.** *vb.* haranguer.

harass, *vb.* harceler, tracasser.

harbinger, *n.* avant-coureur *m.,* précurseur *m.*

harbor, *n.* (refuge) asile *m.;* (port) port *m.*

hard, 1. *adj.* dur; (difficult) difficile. **2.** *adv.* fort.

hard-bitten, *adj.* tenace dur à cuire.

hard-boiled, *adj.* dur, tenace, boucané.

hard coal, *n.* anthracite *m.*

harden, *vb.* durcir.

hard-headed, *adj.* pratique, positif.

hard-hearted, *adj.* insensible, impitoyable, au cœur dur.

hardiness, *n.* robustesse *f.,* vigueur *f.*

hardly, *adv.* (in a hard manner) durement; (scarcely) à peine; (h. ever) presque jamais.

hardness, *n.* dureté *f.;* (difficulty) difficulté *f.*

hardship, *n.* privation *f.*

hardtack, *n.* galette *f.,* biscuit de mer *m.*

hardware, *n.* quincaillerie *f.*

hardwood, *n.* bois dur *m.*

hardy, *adj.* robuste.

hare, *n.* lièvre *m.*

harebrained, *adj.* écervelé, étourdi.

harelip, *n.* bec-de-lièvre *m.*

harem, *n.* harem *m.*

hark, *vb.* prêter l'oreille à. **2.** *interj.* écoutez!

Harlequin, *n.* Arlequin *m.*

harlot, *n.* prostituée *f.,* fille de joie *f.*

harm, 1. *n.* mal *m.* **2.** *vb.* nuire à.

harmful, *adj.* nuisible.

harmless, *adj.* inoffensif.

harmonic, *adj.* harmonique.

harmonica, *n.* harmonica *m.*

harmonious, *adj.* harmonieux.

harmonize, *vb.* harmoniser.

harmony, *n.* harmonie *f.*

harness, 1. *n.* harnais *m.* **2.** *vb.* harnacher.

harp, *n.* harpe *f.*

harpoon, 1. *n.* harpon *m.* **2.** *vb.* harponner.

harridan, *n.* vieille sorcière *f.,* vieille mégère *f.*

harrow, *vb.* herser; (fig.) tourmenter.

harry, *vb.* harceler.

harsh, *adj.* rude.

harshness, n. rudesse f.

harvest, 1. n. moisson f. 2. vb. moissoner.

hash, 1. n. hachis m., émincé m. 2. vb. hacher (de la viande).

hashish, n. hachisch m.

hasn't, vb. n'a pas.

hassle, 1. vb. harceler. 2. n. harcèlement m.

hassock, n. agenouilloir m.

haste, n. hâte f.

hasten, vb. hâter, tr.

hastily, adv. à la hâte.

hasty, adj. précipité.

hat, n. chapeau m.

hatch, vb. (hen) couver; (egg) éclore.

hatchery, n. établissement de pisciculture m.

hatchet, n. hachette f.

hate, vb. haïr.

hateful, adj. odieux.

hatred, n. haine f.

haughtiness, n. arrogance f., hauteur f.

haughty, adj. hautain.

haul, vb. traîner.

haunch, n. hanche f., cuissot m.

haunt, vb. hanter.

have, vb. avoir; (h. to, necessity) devoir.

haven, n. havre m.; (refuge) asile m.

haven't, vb. n'ont pas.

havoc, n. ravage m.

hawk, n. faucon m.

hawker, n. colporteur m., marchand ambulant m.

hawser, n. haussière f., amarre f.

hawthorn, n. aubépine f.

hay, n. foin m.

hay fever, n. fièvre des foins f.

hayfield, n. champs de foin m.

hayloft, n. fenil m., grenier m.

haystack, n. meule de foin f.

hazard, 1. n. hasard m. 2. vb. hasarder, risquer.

hazardous, adj. hasardeux.

haze, n. brume (f.) légère.

hazel, n. noisetier m.; couleur de noisette f.

hazy, adj. brumeux, nébuleux.

he, pron. il; (alone, stressed, with another subject) lui.

head, n. tête f.

headache, n. mal (m.) de tête.

headband, n. bandeau m.

headfirst, adv. la tête la première.

headgear, n. garniture de tête f., coiffure f.

head-hunting, n. chasse aux têtes f.

heading, n. rubrique f.

headlight, n. phare m., projecteur m.

headlong, adv. la tête la première.

headman, n. chef m.

headmaster, n. directeur m., principal m.

head-on, adj. and adv. de front.

headquarters, n. (mil.) quartier (m.) général; (comm.) bureau (m.) principal.

headstone, n. pierre angulaire f.

headstrong, adj. volontaire, têtu, entêté.

headwaters, n. cours supérieur (d'une rivière) m., eau d'amont f.

headway, n. progrès m.

headwork, n. travail de tête m., travail intellectuel m.

heady, adj. impétueux, capiteux.

heal, vb. guérir.

health, n. santé f.

healthful, adj. salubre.

healthy, adj. sain.

heap, 1. n. tas m. 2. vb. entasser.

hear, vb. entendre.

hearing, n. audition f.; ouïe f.

hearsay, n. ouï-dire m.

hearse, n. catafalque m., corbillard m.

heart, n. cœur m.

heartache, n. chagrin m., peine de cœur f.

heartbreak, n. déchirement de cœur m.

heartbroken, adj. avec le cœur brisé, navré.

heartburn, n. brûlures d'estomac f.pl., aigreur f.

heartfelt, adj. sincère, qui va au cœur.

hearth, n. foyer m., âtre m.

heartless, adj. sans cœur, insensible, sans pitié.

heart-rending, adj. à fendre le cœur, navrant, déchirant.

heartsick, adj. écœuré.

heart-stricken, adj. frappé au cœur, navré.

heart-to-heart, adj. à cœur ouvert, intime.

hearty, adj. cordial.

heat, 1. n. chaleur f. 2. vb. chauffer.

heated, adj. chaud, chauffé, animé.

heath, n. bruyère f., lande f.

heathen, adj. and n. païen m., païenne f.

heather, n. bruyère f., brande f.

heatstroke, n. coup de chaleur m.

heat wave, n. vague de chaleur f., onde calorifique f.

heave, vb. (lift) lever; (utter) pousser; (rise) se soulever, intr.

heaven, n. ciel m., pl. cieux.

heavenly, adj. céleste.

heavy, adj. lourd.

heavyweight, n. poids lourd m.

Hebrew, 1. n. (language) hébreu m. 2. adj. hébreu.

heckle, vb. poser des questions embarrassantes.

hectare, n. hectare m.

hectic, adj. (restless) agité.

hectograph, 1. n. hectographe

m., autocopiste m. 2. vb. hectographier, autocopier.

hedge, n. haie f.

hedgehog, n. hérisson m.

hedgehop, vb. voler à ras de terre.

hedgerow, n. bordure de haies f.

hedonism, n. hédonisme m.

heed, 1. n. attention f. 2. vb. faire attention à.

heedless, adj. étourdi, imprudent, insouciant.

heel, n. talon m.

hefty, adj. fort, solide, costaud.

hegemony, n. hégémonie f.

heifer, n. génisse f.

height, n. hauteur f.

heighten, vb. rehausser, augmenter.

heinous, adj. odieux, atroce, abominable.

heir, n. héritier m.

heir apparent, n. héritier présomptif m.

heirloom, n. meuble m. (or bijou m.) de famille.

heir presumptive, n. héritier présomptif m.

helicopter, n. hélicoptère m.

heliocentric, adj. héliocentrique.

heliograph, n. héliographe m.

heliotrope, n. héliotrope m.

helium, n. hélium m.

hell, n. enfer m.

Hellenism, n. hellénisme m.

hellish, adj. infernal, diabolique.

hello, interj. (telephone) allô.

helm, n. barre (f.) du gouvernail.

helmet, n. casque m.

helmsman, n. homme de barre m., timonier m.

help, 1. n. aide f. 2. vb. aider; (at table) servir. 3. interj. au secours!

helper, n. aide m.f.

helpful, adj. (person) serviable; (thing) utile.

helpfulness, n. serviabilité f., utilité f.

helping, 1. n. portion f. 2. adj. secourable.

helpless, adj. (forlorn) délaissé; (powerless) impuissant.

helter-skelter, adv. pêle-mêle, en désordre.

hem, 1. n. ourlet m. 2. vb. ourler.

hematite, n. hématite f.

hemisphere, n. hémisphère m.

hemlock, n. ciguë f.

hemoglobin, n. hémoglobine f.

hemophilia, n. hémophilie f.

hemorrhage, n. hémorragie f.

hemorrhoid, n. hémorroïde f.

hemp, n. chanvre m.

hemstitch, 1. n. ourlet m. 2. vb. ourler.

hen, n. poule f.

hence, adv. (time, place) d'ici; (therefore) de là.

henceforth, adv. désormais.

henchman, n. homme de confiance m., acolyte m., satellite m.

henequen, n. henequen m.

henna, 1. n. henné m. 2. vb. teindre au henné.

henpeck, vb. mener par le bout du nez.

hepatic, adj. hépatique.

hepatica, n. hépatique f.

her, 1. adj. son m., sa f., ses pl. 2. pron. (direct) la; (indirect) lui; (alone, stressed, with prep.) elle.

herald, n. héraut m.

heraldic, adj. héraldique.

heraldry, n. l'héraldique f.

herb, n. herbe f.

herbaceous, adj. herbacé.

herbarium, n. herbier m.

herculean, adj. herculéen.

herd, n. troupeau m.

here, adv. ici; (h. is) voici.

hereabout, adv. par ici, près d'ici.

hereafter, adv. dorénavant.

hereby, adv. par ceci, par ce moyen, par là.

hereditary, adj. héréditaire.

heredity, n. hérédité f.

herein, adv. ici; (h. enclosed) ci-enclus.

heresy, n. hérésie f.

heretic, n. hérétique m.f.

heretical, adj. hérétique.

hereto, adv. ci-joint.

heretofore, adv. jusqu'ici.

herewith, adv. avec ceci, ci-joint.

heritage, n. héritage m., patrimoine m.

hermetic, adj. hermétique.

hermit, n. ermite m.

hermitage, n. ermitage m.

hernia, n. hernie f.

hero, n. héros m.

heroic, adj. héroïque.

heroically, adv. héroïquement.

heroin, n. héroïne f.

heroine, n. héroïne f.

heroism, n. héroïsme m.

heron, n. héron m.

herpes, n. herpès m.

herring, n. hareng m.

herringbone, n. arête de hareng f.

hers, pron. le sien m., la sienne f.

herself, pron. elle-même; (reflexive) se.

hertz, n. hertz m.

hesitancy, n. hésitation f., incertitude f.

hesitant, adj. hésitant, irrésolu.

hesitate, vb. hésiter.

hesitation, n. hésitation f.

heterodox, adj. hétérodoxe.

heterodoxy, n. hétérodoxie f.

heterogeneous, adj. hétérogène.

heterosexual, adj. hétérosexuel.

hew, vb. couper, tailler.

hexagon, n. hexagone m.

heyday, n. apogée m., beaux jours m.pl.

hiatus, n. lacune f.

hibernate, vb. hiberner, hiverner.

hibernation, n. hibernation f.

hibiscus, n. hibiscus m.

hiccup, 1. n. hoquet m. 2. vb. hoqueter.

hickory, n. noyer (blanc) d'Amérique m.

hide, vb. cacher, tr.

hide, n. peau f.

hideous, adj. hideux.

hide-out, n. cachette f., lieu de retraite m.

hierarchical, adj. hiérarchique.

hierarchy, n. hiérarchie f.

hieroglyphic, adj. hiéroglyphique.

high, adj. haut.

highbrow, n. intellectuel m.

high fidelity, n. haute fidélité f.

high-handed, adj. arbitraire, tyrannique.

high-hat, vb. traiter de haut en bas.

highland, n. haute terre f.

highlight, 1. n. clou m. 2. vb. mettre en relief.

highly, adv. extrêmement.

high-minded, adj. à l'esprit élevé, généreux.

Highness, n. (title) Altesse f.

high school, n. lycée m.

high seas, n. haute mer f.

high-strung, adj. nerveux, impressionable.

high tide, n. marée haute f.

highway, n. grande route f.

hijacker, n. pirate de l'air m.

hike, n. excursion (f.) à pied.

hilarious, adj. hilare.

hilariousness, n. hilarité f.

hilarity, n. hilarité f.

hill, n. colline f.

hilt, n. poignée f., garde f.

him, pron. (direct) le; (indirect) lui; (alone, stressed, with prep.) lui.

himself, pron. lui-même; (reflexive) se.

hinder, vb. (impede) gêner; (prevent) empêcher.

hindmost, adj. dernier.

hindquarter, n. arrière-main m., arrière-train m.

hindrance, n. empêchement m., obstacle m., entrave f.

Hindu, 1. n. Hindou m. 2. adj. hindou.

hinge, n. gond m.

hint, 1. n. allusion f. 2. vb. insinuer.

hinterland, n. hinterland m., arrière-pays m.

hip, n. hanche f.

hippodrome, n. hippodrome m.

hippopotamus, n. hippopotame m.

hire, vb. louer; (servant) engager.

hireling, n. mercenaire m., stipendié m.

hirsute, adj. hirsute, velu.

his, 1. adj. son m., sa f., ses pl. 2. pron. le sien m., la sienne f.

Hispanic, adj. hispanique.

hiss, vb. siffler.

historian, n. historien m.

historic, adj. historique.

historical, adj. historique.

history, n. histoire f.

histrionic, adj. histrionique, théâtral.

histrionics, n. parade d'émotions f., démonstration peu sincère f.

hit, 1. n. coup m.; (success) succès m. 2. vb. frapper.

hitch, 1. n. (obstacle) anicroche f. 2. vb. (fasten) accrocher, tr.

hither, 1. adv. ici. 2. adj. le plus rapproché.

hitherto, adv. jusqu'ici.

hive, n. ruche f.

hives, n. éruption f., varicelle pustuleuse f., urticaire f.

hoard, 1. n. amas m. 2. vb. amasser; (money) thésauriser.

hoarse, adj. enroué.

hoax, n. mystification f.

hobble, vb. boitiller, clopiner, entraver.

hobbyhorse, n. dada m., cheval de bois m.

hobgoblin, n. lutin m., esprit follet m.

hobnail, 1. n. caboche f., clou à ferrer m. 2. vb. ferrer.

hobnob, vb. boire avec, fréquenter.

hobo, n. vagabond m., clochard m., ouvrier ambulant m.

hock, n. jarret m.

hockey, n. hockey m.

hocuspocus, n. passe-passe m.

hod, n. auge f.

hodgepodge, n. mélange confus m.

hoe, 1. n. houe f. 2. vb. houer.

hog, n. porc m.

hogshead, n. tonneau m., barrique f.

hog-tie, vb. lier les quatre pattes.

hoist, 1. n. treuil m., grue f. 2. vb. hisser.

hold, 1. n. prise f.; (ship) cale f. 2. vb. tenir; (contain) contenir; (h. back) retenir; (h. up) arrêter, détenir, entraver.

holdup, n. arrêt m., suspension f.; coup à main armée m.

hole, n. trou m.

holiday, n. jour (m.) de fête; fête f.; (h.s) vacances f.pl.

holiness, n. sainteté f.

Holland, n. les Pays-Bas m.pl., Hollande f.

hollow, adj. and n. creux m.

holly, n. houx m.

hollyhock, n. passe-rose f., rose-trémière f.

holocaust, n. holocauste m.

hologram, n. hologramme m.

holography, n. holographie f.

holster, *n.* étui *m.*

holy, *adj.* saint.

Holy See, *n.* Saint-Siège *m.*

Holy Spirit, *n.* Saint-Esprit *m.*

Holy Week, *n.* semaine sainte *f.*

homage, *n.* hommage *m.*

home, *n.* maison *f.;* (hearth) foyer (*m.*) domestique; (**at h.**) à la maison, chez soi.

homeland, *n.* patrie *f.*

homeless, *adj.* sans foyer, sans asile, sans abri.

homelike, *adj.* qui resemble au foyer domestique.

homely, *adj.* laid.

homemade, *adj.* fait à la maison.

home rule, *n.* autonomie *f.*

homesick, *adj.* nostalgique.

homespun, *n.* (étoffe) de fabrication domestique, fait à la maison, simple.

homestead, *n.* ferme *f.,* bien de famille *m.*

homeward, *adj.* de retour.

homework, *n.* travail fait à la maison *m.,* devoirs *m.pl.*

homicide, *n.* homicide *m.*

homily, *n.* homélie *f.*

homing pigeon, *n.* pigeon messager *m.*

hominy, *n.* bouillie de farine de maïs *f.,* semoule de maïs *f.*

homogeneous, *adj.* homogène.

homonym, *n.* homonyme *m.*

homosexual, *n. and adj.* homosexuel *m.*

Honduras, *n.* Honduras *m.*

hone, *vb.* aiguiser, affiler.

honest, *adj.* honnête.

honestly, *adv.* honnêtement, de bonne foi.

honesty, *n.* honnêteté *f.*

honey, *n.* miel *m.*

honeybee, *n.* abeille domestique *f.*

honeycomb, 1. *n.* rayon de miel *m.* **2.** *vb.* cribler, affouiller.

honeydew melon, *n.* melon *m.*

honeymoon, *n.* lune (*f.*) de miel.

honeysuckle, *n.* chèvre-feuille *m.*

honor, 1. *n.* honneur *m.* **2.** *vb.* honorer.

honorable, *adj.* honorable.

honorary, *adj.* honoraire.

hood, *n.* capuchon *m.;* (vehicle) capote *f.*

hoodlum, *n.* voyou *m.*

hoodwink, *vb.* tromper, bander les yeux à.

hoof, *n.* sabot *m.*

hook, 1. *n.* croc *m.;* (fishing) hameçon *m.* **2.** *vb.* accrocher.

hooked, *adj.* crochu, recourbé.

hooked rug, *n.* tapis à points noués simples *m.*

hookworm, *n.* ankylostome *m.*

hoop, *n.* cercle *m.*

hoop skirt, *n.* jupe à paniers *f.,* vertugadin *m.*

hoot, 1. *n.* ululation *f.,* hulule-

ment *m.,* huée *f.* **2.** *vb.* hululer, huer.

hop, 1. *n.* (plant) houblon *m.* **2.** *vb.* sautiller.

hope, 1. *n.* espérance *f.,* espoir *m.* **2.** *vb.* espérer.

hopeful, *adj.* plein d'espoir.

hopeless, *adj.* désespéré.

hopelessness, *n.* désespoir *m.,* état désespéré *m.*

hopscotch, *n.* marelle *f.*

horde, *n.* horde *f.*

horizon, *n.* horizon *m.*

horizontal, *adj.* horizontal.

hormone, *n.* hormone *f.*

horn, *n.* corne *f.;* (music) cor *m.*

hornet, *n.* frelon *m.,* guêpe-frelon *f.*

horny, *adj.* corné, calleux.

horoscope, *n.* horoscope *m.*

horrendous, *adj.* horrible, horripilant.

horrible, *adj.* horrible.

horrid, *adj.* affreux.

horrify, *vb.* horrifier.

horror, *n.* horreur *f.*

horse, *n.* cheval *m.*

horseback, *n.* (**on h.**) à cheval.

horsefly, *n.* taon *m.*

horsehair, *n.* crin *m.*

horseman, *n.* cavalier *m.*

horsemanship, *n.* équitation *f.,* manège *m.*

horseplay, *n.* jeu de mains *f.,* badinerie grossière *f.*

horsepower, *n.* puissance en chevaux *f.*

horseradish, *n.* raifort *m.*

horseshoe, *n.* fer à cheval *m.*

horsewhip, 1. *n.* cravache *f.* **2.** *vb.* cravacher, sangler.

hortatory, *adj.* exhortatif.

horticulture, *n.* horticulture *f.*

hose, *n.* (pipe) tuyau *m.;* (stockings) bas *m.pl.*

hosiery, *n.* bonneterie *f.*

hospitable, *adj.* hospitalier.

hospital, *n.* hôpital *m.*

hospitality, *n.* hospitalité *f.*

hospitalization, *n.* hospitalisation *f.*

hospitalize, *vb.* hospitaliser.

host, *n.* hôte *m.*

hostage, *n.* otage *m.*

hostel, *n.* hôtellerie *f.,* auberge *f.*

hostelry, *n.* hôtellerie *f.,* auberge *f.*

hostess, *n.* hôtesse *f.*

hostile, *adj.* hostile.

hostility, *n.* hostilité *f.*

hot, *adj.* chaud.

hotbed, *n.* couche *f.,* foyer ardent *m.*

hot dog, *n.* saucisse chaude.

hotel, *n.* hôtel *m.*

hot-headed, *adj.* impétueux, exalté, emporté.

hothouse, *n.* serre *f.*

hound, 1. *n.* chien (*m.*) de chasse. **2.** *vb.* poursuivre, pourchasser.

hour, *n.* heure *f.*

hourglass, *n.* sablier *m.*

hourly, *adv.* à chaque heure, à l'heure.

house, *n.* maison *f.;* (legislature) chambre *f.*

housefly, *n.* mouche domestique *f.*

household, *n.* (family) famille *f.;* (servants) domestiques *m.pl.*

housekeeper, *n.* gouvernante *f.*

housekeeping, *n.* ménage *m.,* économie domestique *f.*

housemaid, *n.* fille de service *f.,* bonne *f.,* femme de chambre *f.*

housewife, *n.* ménagère *f.*

housework, *n.* ménage *m.*

hovel, *n.* taudis *m.,* bicoque *f.*

hover, *vb.* planer.

hovercraft, *n.* aéroglisseur *m.*

how, *adv.* comment; (**h. much**) combien (de); (in exclamation) comme.

however, *adv.* (in whatever way) de quelque manière que; (with adj.) si . . . que; (nevertheless) cependant.

howitzer, *n.* obusier *m.*

howl, *vb.* hurler.

hub, *n.* moyeu *m.,* centre *m.*

hubbub, *n.* vacarme *m.,* tintamarre *m.*

huckleberry, *n.* airelle *f.*

huddle, 1. *n.* tas confus *m.,* fouillis *m.* **2.** *vb.* entasser.

hue, *n.* couleur *f.*

huff, 1. *n.* emportement *m.,* accès de colère *m.* **2.** *vb.* gonfler, enfler.

hug, 1. *n.* étreinte *f.* **2.** *vb.* serrer dans ses bras.

huge, *adj.* énorme.

hulk, *n.* carcasse *f.,* ponton *m.*

hull, *n.* coque *f.,* corps *m.*

hullabaloo, *n.* vacarme *m.*

hum, *vb.* (insect) bourdonner; (sing) fredonner.

human, humane, *adj.* humain.

humanism, *n.* humanisme *m.*

humanitarian, *adj.* humanitaire.

humanities, *n.* humanités *f.pl.*

humanity, *n.* humanité *f.*

humanly, *adv.* humainement.

humble, *adj.* humble.

humbug, *n.* blague *f.,* tromperie *f.,* fumisterie *f.*

humdrum, *adj.* monotone, assommant.

humid, *adj.* humide.

humidify, *vb.* humidifier.

humidor, *n.* boîte à cigares *m.*

humiliate, *adj.* humilier.

humiliation, *n.* humiliation *f.*

humility, *n.* humilité *f.*

humor, *n.* (wit) humour *m.;* (medical, mood) humeur *f.*

humorous, *adj.* (witty) humoristique; (funny) drôle.

hump, *n.* bosse *f.*

humpback, *n.* bossu *m.*

humus, *n.* humus *m.,* terreau *m.*

hunch, 1. *n.* bosse *f.;* pressentiment *m*. 2. *vb*. arrondir, voûter.

hunchback, *n*. bossu *m*.

hundred, *adj. and n*. cent *m*.

hundredth *n. and adj*. centième *m*.

Hungarian, 1. *n*. (person) Hongrois *m.;* (language) hongrois *m*. 2. *adj*. hongrois.

Hungary, *n*. Hongrie *f*.

hunger, *n*. faim *f*.

hungry, *adj*. affamé; (be h.) avoir faim.

hunk, *n*. gros morceau *m*.

hunt, *vb*. chasser.

hunter, *n*. chasseur *m*.

hunting, *n*. chasse *f*.

huntress, *n*. chasseuse *f*., chasseresse *f*.

hurdle, *n*. claie *f*.

hurl, *vb*. lancer.

hurricane, *n*. ouragan *m*.

hurry, 1. *n*. hâte *f.;* (in a h.) à la hâte. 2. *vb*. presser, *tr.;* se presser, *intr*.

hurt, *vb*. faire mal (à).

hurtful, *adj*. nuisible, pernicieux, préjudiciable.

hurtle, *vb*. se choquer, se heurter.

husband, *n*. mari *m*.

husbandry, *n*. agriculture *f*., économie *f*.

hush, 1. *interj*. chut! paix! 2. *vb*. taire, imposer silence à.

husk, 1. *n*. cosse *f*., gousse *f*. 2. *vb*. écosser, éplucher.

husky, *adj*. cossu; rauque, enroué.

hustle, *vb*. bousculer, se presser.

hut, *n*. cabane *f*.

hutch, *n*. huche *f*., clapier *m*.

hyacinth, *n*. jacinthe *f*.

hybrid, *n*. hybride *m*.

hydrangea, *n*. hortensia *m*.

hydrant, *n*. prise d'eau *f*., bouche d'incendie *f*.

hydraulic, *adj*. hydraulique.

hydrochloric acid, *n*. acide chlorhydrique *m*.

hydroelectric, *adj*. hydroéléctrique.

hydrogen, *n*. hydrogène *m*.

hydrophobia, *n*. hydrophobie *f*.

hydroplane, *n*. hydroplane *m*.

hydrotherapy, *n*. hydrothérapie *f*.

hyena, *n*. hyène *f*.

hygiene, *n*. hygiène *f*.

hygienic, *adj*. hygiénique.

hymn, *n*. (song, anthem) hymne *m.;* (church) hymne *f*.

hymnal, *n*. hymnaire *m*., receuil d'hymnes *m*.

hyperacidity, *n*. hyperacidité *f*.

hyperbole, *n*. hyperbole *f*.

hypercritical, *adj*. hypercritique.

hypersensitive, *adj*. hypersensible.

hypertension, *n*. hypertension *f*.

hyphen, *n*. trait d'union *m*.

hyphenate, *vb*. mettre un trait d'union à.

hypnosis, *n*. hypnose *f*.

hypnotic, *adj*. hypnotique.

hypnotism, *n*. hypnotisme *m*.

hypnotize, *vb*. hypnotiser.

hypochondria, *n*. hypocondrie *f*.

hypochondriac, *n. and adj*. hypocondriaque *m*.

hypocrisy, *n*. hypocrisie *f*.

hypocrite, *n*. hypocrite *m.f*.

hypocritical, *adj*. hypocrite.

hypodermic, *adj*. hypodermique.

hypotenuse, *n*. hypoténuse *f*.

hypothesis, *n*. hypothèse *f*.

hypothetical, *adj*. hypothétique.

hysterectomy, *n*. hystérectomie *f*.

hysteria, *n*. hystérie *f*.

hysterical, *adj*. hystérique.

I

I, *pron*. je; (alone, stressed, with another subject) moi.

iambic, *adj*. iambique.

Iberia, *n*. Ibérie *f*.

ice, *n*. glace *f*.

iceberg, *n*. iceberg *m.;* gros bloc de glace *m*.

ice-box, *n*. glacière *f*.

ice cream, *n*. glace *f*.

ice skate, 1. *n*. patin à glace *m*. 2. *vb*. patiner.

ichthyology, *n*. ichtyologie *f*.

icing, *n*. glacé *m*.

icon, *n*. icone *f*.

icy, *adj*. glacial.

idea, *n*. idée *f*.

ideal, *adj. and n*. idéal *m*.

idealism, *n*. idéalisme *m*.

idealist, *n*. idéaliste *m.f*.

idealistic, *adj*. idéaliste.

idealize, *vb*. idéaliser.

ideally, *adv*. idéalement, en idée.

identical (with), *adj*. identique (à).

identifiable, *adj*. identifiable.

identification, *n*. identification *f*.

identify, *vb*. identifier.

identity, *n*. identité *f*.

ideology, *n*. idéologie *f*.

idiocy, *n*. idiotie *f*., idiotisme *m*.

idiom, *n*. (language) idiome *m.;* (peculiar expression) idiotisme *m*.

idiot, *adj. and n*. idiot *m*.

idiotic, *adj*. idiot.

idle, *adj*. (unoccupied) désœuvré; (lazy) paresseux; (futile) vain.

idleness, *n*. oisiveté *f*.

idol, *n*. idole *f*.

idolatry, *n*. idolâtrie *f*.

idolize, *vb*. idolâtrer.

idyl, *n*. idylle *f*.

idyllic, *adj*. idyllique.

if, *conj*. si.

ignite, *vb*. allumer, mettre en feu.

ignition, *n*. ignition *f*., allumage *m*.

ignoble, *adj*. ignoble; (low birth) plébéien.

ignominious, *adj*. ignominieux.

ignoramus, *n*. ignorant *m*., ignare *m*.

ignorance, *n*. ignorance *f*.

ignorant, *adj*. ignorant; (be i. of) ignorer.

ignore, *vb*. feindre d'ignorer.

ill, 1. *n*. mal. 2. *adj*. (sick) malade; (bad) mauvais. 3. *adv*. mal.

illegal, *adj*. illégal.

illegible, *adj*. illisible.

illegibly, *adv*. illisiblement.

illegitimacy, *n*. illégitimité *f*.

illegitimate, *adj*. illégitime.

illicit, *adj*. illicite.

illiteracy, *n*. analphabétisme *m*.

illiterate, *adj*. illettré.

illness, *n*. maladie *f*.

illogical, *adj*. illogique.

illuminate, *vb*. illuminer.

illumination, *n*. illumination *f*., enluminure *f*.

illusion, *n*. illusion *f*.

illusive, *adj*. illusoire.

illustrate, *vb*. illustrer.

illustration, *n*. illustration *f.;* (example) exemple *m*.

illustrative, *adj*. explicatif, qui éclaircit.

illustrious, *adj*. illustre.

ill will, *adj*. mauvais vouloir *m.,* malveillance *f*.

image, *n*. image *f*.

imagery, *n*. images *f.pl*, langage figuré *m*.

imaginable, *adj*. imaginable.

imaginary, *adj*. imaginaire.

imagination, *n*. imagination *f*.

imaginative, *adj*. imaginatif.

imagine, *vb*. imaginer, *tr*.

imam, *n*. imam *m*.

imbecile, *n*. imbécile *m*.

imitate, *vb*. imiter.

imitation, *n*. imitation *f*.

imitative, *adj*. imitatif.

immaculate, *adj*. immaculé, sans tache.

immanent, *adj*. immanent.

immaterial, *adj*. immatériel, incorporel, sans conséquence.

immature, *adj*. pas mûr, prématuré.

immediate, *adj*. immédiat.

immediately, *adv*. immédiatement, tout de suite.

immense, *adj*. immense.

immerse, *vb*. immerger, plonger.

immigrant, *n*. immigrant *m.,* immigré *m*.

immigrate, *vb*. immigrer.

imminent, *adj*. imminent.

immobile, *adj*. fixe, immobile.

immobilize, *vb*. immobiliser.

immoderate, *adj*. immodéré, intempéré, outré.

immodest, *adj.* immodeste, impudique, présomptueux.
immoral, *adj.* immoral.
immorality, *n.* immoralité *f.*
immorally, *adv.* immoralement.
immortal, *adj. and n.* immortel *m.*
immortality, *n.* immortalité *f.*
immortalize, *vb.* immortaliser.
immovable, *adj.* fixe, immuable, inébranlable.
immunity, *n.* exemption *f.*, immunité *f.*
immunize, *vb.* immuniser.
immutable, *adj.* immuable, inaltérable.
impact, *n.* choc *m.*, impact *m.*
impair, *vb.* affaiblir, altérer, compromettre.
impale, *vb.* empaler.
impart, *vb.* donner, communiquer, transmettre.
impartial, *adj.* impartial.
impatience, *n.* impatience *f.*
impatient, *adj.* impatient.
impeach, *vb.* attaquer, accuser, récuser.
impede, *vb.* entraver, empêcher.
impediment, *n.* entrave *f.*, obstacle *m.*, empêchement *f.*
impel, *vb.* pousser, forcer.
impenetrable, *adj.* impénétrable.
impenitent, *adj.* impénitent.
imperative, 1. *n. (gramm.)* impératif *m.* 2. *adj.* impératif *(gramm.);* urgent, impérieux.
imperceptible, *adj.* imperceptible.
imperfect, *adj. and n.* imparfait *m.*
imperfection, *n.* imperfection *f.*
imperial, *adj.* impérial.
imperialism, *n.* impérialisme *m.*
imperil, *vb.* mettre en péril, exposer au danger.
imperious, *adj.* impérieux, arrogant.
impersonate, *vb.* personnifier, représenter.
impersonation, *n.* personnification *f.*, incarnation *f.*
impersonator, *n.* personnificateur *m.*
impertinence, *n.* impertinence *f.*
impervious, *adj.* impénétrable, imperméable.
impetuous, *adj.* impétueux.
impetus, *n.* élan *m.*, vitesse acquise *f.*
impinge, *vb.* se heurter à, empiéter sur.
implacable, *adj.* implacable.
implant, *vb.* inculquer, implanter.
implement, *n.* outil *m.*
implicate, *vb.* impliquer, entremêler.
implication, *n.* implication *f.*
implicit, *adj.* implicite.
implied, *adj.* implicite, tacite.

implore, *vb.* implorer.
imply, *vb,* impliquer.
impolite, *adj.* impoli.
imponderable, *adj.* impondérable.
import, 1. *n.* article *(m.)* d'importation; importation *f.* 2. *vb.* importer.
importance, *n.* importance *f.*
important, *adj.* important.
importation, *n.* importation *f.*
importune, *vb.* importuner.
impose (on), *vb.* imposer (à).
imposition, *n.* imposition *f.*
impossibility, *n.* impossibilité *f.*
impossible, *adj.* impossible.
impotence, *n.* impuissance *f.*
impotent, *adj.* impuissant.
impoverish, *vb.* appauvrir.
impregnable, *adj.* imprenable, inexpugnable.
impregnate, *vb.* imprégner, féconder.
impresario, *n.* imprésario *m.*
impress, *vb.* (imprint) imprimer; (affect) faire une impression à.
impression, *n.* impression *f.*
impressive, *adj.* impressionnant.
imprison, *vb.* emprisonner.
imprisonment, *n.* emprisonnement *m.*
improbable, *adj.* improbable.
impromptu, *adv., adj. and n.* impromptu *m.*
improper, *adj.* (inaccurate) impropre; (unbecoming) malséant.
improve, *vb.* améliorer, *tr.*
improvement, *n.* amélioration *f.*
improvise, *vb.* improviser.
impudent, *adj.* insolent, effronté, impertinent.
impugn, *vb.* attaquer, contester, impugner.
impulse, *n.* impulsion *f.*
impulsion, *n.* impulsion *f.*
impulsive, *adj.* impulsif.
impunity, *n.* impunité *f.*
impure, *adj.* impur.
impurity, *n.* impureté *f.*
impute, *vb.* imputer.
in, *prep.* en; (with art. or adj.) dans; (town) à.
inadvertent, *adj.* inattentif, négligent, involontaire.
inalienable, *adj.* inaliénable.
inane, *adj.* inepte, niais, bête.
inaugural, *adj.* inaugural.
inaugurate, *vb.* inaugurer.
inauguration, *n.* inauguration *f.*
Inca, *n.* Inca *m.*
incandescence, *n.* incandescence *f.*
incandescent, *adj.* incandescent.
incantation, *n.* incantation *f.*, conjuration *f.*
incapacitate, *vb.* rendre incapable, priver de capacité légale.

incarcerate, *vb.* incarcérer, emprisonner.
incarnate, 1. *vb.* incarner. 2. *adj.* incarné, fait chair.
incarnation, *n.* incarnation *f.*
incendiary, 1. *n.* incendiaire *m.* 2. *adj.* incendiaire, séditieux.
incense, *n.* encens *m.*
incentive, *n.* stimulant *m.*, aiguillon *m.*
inception, *n.* commencement *m.*, début *m.*
incessant, *adj.* incessant, continuel.
incest, *n.* inceste *m.*
inch, *n.* pouce *m.*
incidence, *n.* incidence *f.*
incident, *n.* incident *m.*
incidental, *adj.* fortuit.
incidentally, *adv.* incidemment, en passant.
incinerator, *n.* incinérateur *m.*
incipient, *adj.* naissant, qui commence.
incision, *n.* incision *f.*, entaille *f.*
incisive, *adj.* incisif, tranchant.
incisor, *n.* incisive *f.*
incite, *vb.* inciter, instiguer.
inclination, *n.* inclinaison *f.*, penchant *m.*
incline, *vb.* incliner.
inclose, *see* **enclose.**
include, *vb.* comprendre.
inclusive, *adj.* inclusif.
incognito, *adj. and adv.* incognito.
income, *n.* revenu *m.*
incomparable, *adj.* incomparable.
inconvenience, 1. *n.* inconvénient *m.* 2. *vb.* incommoder.
inconvenient, *adj.* incommode.
incorporate, *vb.* incorporer.
incorrigible, *adj.* incorrigible.
increase, 1. *n.* augmentation *f.* 2. *vb.* augmenter.
incredible, *adj.* incroyable.
incredulity, *n.* incrédulité *f.*
incredulous, *adj.* incrédule.
increment, *n.* augmentation *m.*, accroissement *m.*
incriminate, *vb.* incriminer.
incrimination, *n.* incrimination *f.*
incrust, *vb.* incruster.
incubator, *n.* incubateur *m.*
inculcate, *vb.* inculquer.
incumbency, *n.* période d'exercice *f.*, charge *f.*
incumbent, 1. *n.* titulaire *m.*, bénéficiaire *m.* 2. *adj.* couché, posé, appuyé.
incur, *vb.* encourir.
incurable, *adj.* incurable.
indebted, *adj.* endetté.
indeed, *adv.* en effet.
indefatigable, *adj.* infatigable, inlassable.
indefinite, *adj.* indéfini.
indefinitely, *adv.* indéfiniment.
indelible, *adj.* indélébile, ineffaçable.
indemnify, *vb.* garantir, indemniser, dédommager.

indemnity, n. garantie f., indemnité f., dédommagment m.

indent, vb. denteler, découper, entailler.

indentation, n. découpage m., renfoncement m., endentement m.

independence, n. indépendance f.

independent, adj. indépendant.

in-depth, adj. profond.

index, n. index m.

India, n. Inde f.

Indian, 1. n. Indien m. **2.** adj. indien.

indicate, vb. indiquer.

indication, n. indication f.

indicative, adj. and n. indicatif m.

indicator, n. indicateur m.

indict, vb. accuser, inculper.

indictment, n. accusation f., inculpation f., réquisitoire m.

indifference, n. indifférence f.

indifferent, adj. indifférent.

indigenous, adj. indigène.

indigent, adj. indigent, pauvre.

indigestion, n. dyspepsie f., indigestion f.

indignant, adj. indigné.

indignation, n. indignation f.

indignity, n. indignité f., affront m.

indirect, adj. indirect.

indiscreet, adj. indiscret.

indiscretion, n. imprudence f.

indiscriminate, adj. aveugle, qui ne fait pas de distinction.

indispensable, adj. indispensable.

indisposed, adj. peu enclin, peu disposé, indisposé, souffrant.

individual, 1. n. individu m. **2.** adj. individuel.

individuality, n. individualité f.

individually, adv. individuellement.

indivisible, adj. indivisible.

indoctrinate, vb. endoctriner, instruire.

indolent, adj. indolent, paresseux.

Indonesia, n. Indonésie f.

indoor, adj. d'intérieur.

indoors, adv. à la maison.

indorse, vb. endosser, appuyer sanctionner.

induce, vb. (persuade) persuader; (produce) produire.

induct, vb. installer, conduire.

induction, n. induction f.; installation f.

inductive, adj. inductif.

indulge, vb. contenter, favoriser.

indulgence, n. indulgence f.

indulgent, adj. indulgent.

industrial, adj. industriel.

industrialist, n. industriel m.

industrious, adj. travailleur.

industry, n. industrie f.; (diligence) assiduité f.

ineligible, adj. inéligible.

inept, adj. inepte, mal à propos.

inert, adj. inerte, apathique.

inertia, n. inertie f.

inevitable, adj. inévitable.

inexplicable, adj. inexplicable.

infallible, adj. infaillible.

infamous, adj. infâme.

infamy, n. infamie f.

infancy, n. (première) enfance f.

infant, n. enfant m.f.

infantile, adj. enfantin, infantile.

infantryman, n. soldat d'infanterie m., fantassin m.

infatuated, adj. infatué, entiché.

infect, vb. infecter.

infection, n. infection f.

infectious, adj. infectieux, infect, contagieux.

infer, vb. déduire.

inference, n. inférence f.

inferior, adj. and n. inférieur m.

inferiority complex, n. complexe d'infériorité m.

infernal, adj. infernal.

inferno, n. enfer m.

infest, vb. infester.

infidel, n. infidèle m., incroyant m.

infidelity, n. infidélité f.

infiltrate, vb. infiltrer.

infinite, adj. and n. infini m.

infinitesimal, adj. infinitésimal.

infinitive, n. infinitif m.

infinity, n. infinité f.

infirm, adj. infirme, faible, maladif.

infirmary, n. infirmerie f.

infirmity, n. infirmité f.

inflame, vb. enflammer, tr.

inflammable, adj. inflammable.

inflammation, n. inflammation f.

inflammatory, adj. incendiaire, inflammatoire.

inflate, vb. gonfler.

inflation, n. (currency) inflation f.

inflection, n. inflection f.

inflict, vb. (penalty) infliger.

infliction, n. infliction f., châtiment m.

influence, n. influence f.

influential, adj. influent.

influenza, n. grippe f., influenza f.

inform, vb. (tell) informer.

informal, adj. (without formality) sans cérémonie.

information, n. renseignements m.pl.

infringe, vb. enfreindre, violer.

infuriate, vb. rendre furieux.

ingenious, adj. ingénieux.

ingenuity, n. ingéniosité f.

ingredient, n. ingrédient m.

inhabit, vb. habiter.

inhabitant, n. habitant m.

inhale, vb. inhaler, aspirer, humer.

inherent, adj. inhérent.

inherit, vb. hériter.

inheritance, n. héritage m.

inhibit, vb. empêcher; (psychology) inhiber.

inhibition, n. inhibition f., défense expresse f., prohibition f.

inhuman, adj. inhumain.

inimical, adj. ennemi, hostile, défavorable.

inimitable, adj. inimitable.

iniquity, n. iniquité f.

initial, 1. n. initiale f. **2.** adj. initial.

initiate, vb. (begin) commencer; (admit) initier.

initiation, n. commencement m., début m., initiation f.

initiative, n. initiative f.

inject, vb. injecter.

injection, n. injection f.

injunction, n. injonction f., ordre m.

injure, vb. (harm) nuire à; (wound) blesser; (damage) abîmer.

injurious, adj. (harmful) nuisible; (offensive) injurieux.

injury, n. (person) préjudice m.; (body) blessure f.; (thing) dommage m.

injustice, n. injustice f.

ink, n. encre f.

inland, adj. and n. intérieur m.

inlet, n. entrée f., admission f., débouché m.

inmate, n. habitant m., hôte m., pensionnaire m.

inn, n. auberge f.

inner, adj. intérieur.

innocence, n. innocence f.

innocent, adj. innocent.

innocuous, adj. inoffensif.

innovation, n. innovation f.

innuendo, n. insinuation f., allusion malveillante f.

innumerable, adj. innombrable.

inoculate, vb. inoculer.

inoculation, n. inoculation f., vaccination préventive f.

input, n. informations fournies à un informateur f.pl.

inquest, n. enquête f.

inquire (about), vb. se renseigner (sur).

inquiry, n. (investigation) recherche f.; (question) demande f.; (official) enquête f.

inquisition, n. Inquisition f.; enquête f., recherche f.

inquisitive, adj. curieux, questionneur, indiscret.

inroad, n. incursion f., invasion f. empiétement m.

insane, adj. fou m., folle f.

insanity, n. folie f., insanité f., démence f.

inscribe, vb. inscrire, graver.

inscription, n. inscription f.

insect, n. insecte m.

insecticide, n. insecticide m.

inseparable, adj. inséparable.

insert, vb. insérer.

insertion, n. insertion f.

inside, 1. n. dedans m., 2. adj. intérieur. 3. prep. à l'intérieur de. 4. adv. (en) dedans.

insidious, adj. insidieux.

insight, n. perspicacité f., pénétration f.

insignia, n. insignes m.pl.

insignificance, n. insignifiance f.

insignificant, adj. insignifiant.

insinuate, vb. insinuer.

insinuation, n. insinuation f.

insipid, adj. insipide, fade.

insist, vb. insister.

insistence, n. insistance f.

insistent, adj. qui insiste, importun.

insolence, n. insolence f.

insolent, adj. insolent.

insomnia, n. insomnie f.

inspect, vb. examiner, inspecter.

inspection, n. inspection f.

inspector, n. inspecteur m.

inspiration, n. inspiration f.

inspire, vb. inspirer.

install, vb. installer.

installation, n. installation f., montage m.

installment, n. acompte m., versement partiel m., payement à compte m.

instance, n. exemple m.

instant, n. instant m.

instantaneous, adj. instantané.

instantly, adv. à l'instant.

instead, adv. au lieu de cela.

instead of, prep. au lieu de.

instigate, vb. instiguer.

instill, vb. instiller, faire pénétrer, inculquer.

instinct, n. instinct m.

instinctive, adj. instinctif.

institute, vb. instituer.

institution, n. institution f.

instruct, vb. instruire.

instruction, n. instruction f.

instructive, adj. instructif.

instructor, n. (mil.) instructeur m.; (university) chargé (m.) de cours.

instrument, n. instrument m.

instrumental, adj. instrumental, contributif (à).

insufferable, adj. insupportable, intolérable.

insufficient, adj. insuffisant.

insular, adj. insulaire.

insulate, vb. isoler.

insulation, n. isolement m.

insulator, n. isolant m., isolateur m.

insulin, n. insuline f.

insult, 1. vb. insulter. 2. n. insulte f.

insuperable, adj. insurmontable.

insurance, n. assurance f.

insure, vb. assurer.

insurgent, adj. and n. insurgé m.

insurrection, n. insurrection f., soulèvement m.

intact, adj. intact.

intangible, adj. intangible, impalpable.

integral, adj. intégrant.

integrate, vb. intégrer, compléter, rendre entier.

integrity, n. intégrité f.

intellect, n. (mind) esprit m.; (faculty) intellect m.

intellectual, adj. and n. intellectuel m.

intelligence, n. intelligence f.; (information) renseignements m.pl.

intelligent, adj. intelligent.

intelligentsia, n. l'intelligence f.

intelligible, adj. intelligible.

intend, vb. avoir l'intention de; (destine for) destiner à.

intense, adj. intense.

intensity, n. intensité f.

intensive, adj. intensif.

intent on, adj. (absorbed in) absorbé dans; (determined to) déterminé à.

intention, n. intention f.

intentional, adj. intentionnel, voulu, fait exprès.

intercede, vb. intervenir, intercéder.

intercept, vb. intercepter, capter.

intercourse, n. commerce m., relations f.pl., rapports m.pl.

interdict, vb. interdire, prohiber.

interest, 1. n. intérêt m. 2. vb. intéresser.

interesting, adj. intéressant.

interface, n. entreface f.

interfere, vb. (person) intervenir (dans); (i. with, hinder) gêner.

interference, n. (person) intervention f.

interim, adv. entre temps, en attendant.

interior, adj. and n. intérieur m.

interject, vb. lancer, émettre.

interjection, n. interjection f.

interlude, n. intermède m., interlude m.

intermarry, vb. se marier.

intermediary, n. intermédiaire m.f.

intermediate, adj. and n. intermédiaire m.f.

interment, n. enterrement m.

intermission, n. interruption f., relâche f.; (theater) entr'acte m.

intermittent, adj. intermittent.

intern, 1. n. interne m. 2. vb. interner.

internal, adj. interne.

international, adj. international.

nationalism, n. internationalisme m.

interne, n. interne m.

interpose, vb. interposer, tr.

interpret, vb. interpréter.

interpretation, n. interprétation f.

interpreter, n. interprète m.f.

interrogate, vb. interroger, questionner.

interrogation, n. interrogation f.

interrogative, 1. adj. interrogateur. 2. n. interrogatif m.

interrupt, vb. interrompre.

interruption, n. interruption f.

intersect, vb. entrecouper, intersecter, entrecroiser.

intersection, n. intersection f.

intersperse, vb. entremêler, parsemer, intercaler.

interval, n. intervalle m.

intervene, vb. intervenir.

intervention, n. intervention f.

interview, n. entrevue f.; (press) interview m. or f.

intestine, n. intestin m.

intimacy, n. intimité f.

intimate, adj. intime.

intimidate, vb. intimider.

intimidation, n. intimidation f.

into, prep. en; (with art. or adj.) dans.

intonation, n. intonation f.

intone, vb. entonner, psalmodier.

intoxicate, vb. enivrer.

intoxication, n. intoxication f., ivresse f.

intravenous, adj. intraveineux.

intrepid, adj. intrépide, brave, courageux.

intricacy, n. complexité f., nature compliquée f.

intricate, adj. compliqué.

intrigue, n. intrigue f.

intrinsic, adj. intrinsèque.

introduce, vb. (bring in) introduire; (present) présenter.

introduction, n. introduction f.; (presenting) présentation f.

introductory, adj. introductoire, d'introduction.

introspection, n. introspection f., recueillement m.

introvert, n. introverti m.

intrude on, vb. importuner.

intruder, n. intrus m.

intuition, n. intuition f.

intuitive, adj. intuitif.

inundate, vb. inonder.

invade, vb. envahir.

invader, n. envahisseur m., transgresseur m.

invalid, adj. and n. infirme m.f.

invariable, adj. invariable.

invasion, n. invasion f.

invective, n. invective f.

inveigle, vb. attirer, séduire, leurrer.

invent, vb. inventer.

invention, n. invention f.

inventive, adj. inventif, trouveur.

inventor, n. inventeur m.

inventory, n. inventaire m.

invertebrate, 1. n. invertébré m. 2. adj. invertébré.

invest, vb. investir; (money) placer.

investigate, vb. faire des recherches (sur).

investigation, *n.* investigation *f.*

investment, *n.* placement *m.*

inveterate, *adj.* invétéré, enraciné.

invidious, *adj.* odieux, haïssable, ingrat.

invigorate, *vb.* fortifier, vivifier.

invincible, *adj.* invincible.

invisible, *adj.* invisible.

invitation, *n.* invitation *f.*

invite, *vb.* inviter.

invocation, *n.* invocation *f.*

invoice, *n.* facture *f.*

invoke, *vb.* invoquer.

involuntary, *adj.* involontaire.

involve, *vb.* (implicate) impliquer; (entail) entraîner.

invulnerable, *adj.* invulnérable.

inward, *adj.* intérieur.

iodine, *n.* iode *m.*

Iran, *n.* Iran *m.*

Iraq, *n.* Irak *m.*

irate, *adj.* en colère, courroucé, furieux.

Ireland, *n.* Irlande *f.*

iridium, *n.* iridium *m.*

iris, *n.* iris *m.*

Irish, *adj.* irlandais.

Irishman, *n.* Irlandais *m.*

irk, *vb.* ennuyer.

iron, *n.* fer *m.*

ironworks, *n.* fonderie de fonte *f.*, usine métallurgique *f.*

irony, *n.* ironie *f.*

irrational, *adj.* irrationnel, déraisonnable, absurde.

irrefutable, *adj.* irréfutable, irrécusable.

irregular, *adj.* irrégulier.

irregularity, *n.* irrégularité *f.*

irrelevant, *adj.* non pertinent, hors de propos.

irresistible, *adj.* irrésistible.

irresponsible, *adj.* irresponsable.

irreverent, *adj.* irrévérent, irrévérencieux.

irrevocable, *adj.* irrévocable.

irrigate, *vb.* irriguer, arroser.

irrigation, *n.* irrigation *f.*

irritability, *n.* irritabilité *f.*

irritable, *adj.* irritable, irascible.

irritant, *n.* irritant *m.*

irritate, *vb.* irriter.

irritation, *n.* irritation *f.*

Islam, *n.* Islam *m.*

Islamic, *adj.* islamique.

island, *n.* île *f.*

isolate, *vb.* isoler.

isolation, *n.* isolement *m.*

isolationist, *n.* isolationniste *m.*

isosceles, *adj.* isoscèle.

Israel, *n.* Israël *m.*

Israeli, *n.* Israëli *m.*

issuance, *n.* délivrance *f.*

issue, 1. *n.* (way out, end) issue *f.*; (result) résultat *m.*; (question) question *f.*; (money, bonds) émission *f.* 2. *vb.* (come out) sortir; (publish) publier; (money) émettre.

isthmus, *n.* isthme *m.*

it, *pron.* (subject) il *m.*; elle *f.*; (object) le *m.*, la *f.*; (of it) en; (in it, to it) y.

Italian, 1. *n.* (person) Italien *m.*; (language) italien *m.* 2. *adj.* italien.

Italy, *n.* Italie *f.*

itch, 1. *n.* démangeaison *f.* 2. *vb.* démanger.

item, *n.* (article) article *m.*; (detail) détail *m.*

itemize, *vb.* détailler.

itinerant, *adj.* ambulant.

itinerary, *n.* itinéraire *m.*

its, 1. *adj.* son *m.*, sa *f.*, ses *pl.* 2. *pron.* le sien *m.*, la sienne *f.*

itself, *pron.* lui-même *m.*, elle-même *f.*; (reflexive) se.

ivory, *n.* ivoire *m.*

ivy, *n.* lierre *m.*

J

jab, *n.* coup *m.*, coup sec *m.* 2. *vb.* piquer, donner un coup sec.

jackal, *n.* chacal *m.*

jackass, *n.* âne *m.*; idiot *m.*

jacket, *n.* (man) veston *m.*; (woman) jaquette *f.*

jackknife, *n.* couteau de poche *m.*

jack-of-all-trades, *n.* maître Jacques *m.*, factotum *m.*, homme à tous les métiers *m.*

jade, *n.* rosse *f.*, haridelle *f.*; drôlesse *f.*, coureuse *f.*; jade *m.*

jaded, *adj.* surmené, éreinté, blasé, fatigué.

jagged, *adj.* déchiqueté, entaillé, dentelé.

jaguar, *n.* jaguar *m.*

jail, *n.* prison *f.*

jailer, *n.* gardien *m.*, geôlier *m.*

jam, 1. *n.* foule *f.*, presse *f.*, embouteillage *m.*; confiture *f.* 2. *vb.* serrer, presser.

jamb, *n.* jambage *m.*, montant *m.*, chambranle *m.*

jangle, 1. *n.* querelle *f.*, chamaille *f.*; cliquetis *m.* 2. *vb.* se quereller, se chamailler; cliqueter.

janitor, *n.* concierge *m.*

January, *n.* janvier *m.*

Japan, *n.* Japon *m.*

Japanese, 1. *n.* (person) Japonais *m.*; (language) japonais *m.* 2. *adj.* japonais.

jar, 1. *n.* (container) pot *m.*; (sound) son *m.*; discordant; (shock) secousse *f.* 2. *vb.* secouer, heurter.

jargon, *n.* jargon *m.*

jasmine, *n.* jasmin *m.*

jaundice, *n.* jaunisse *f.*

jaunt, *n.* petite excursion *f.*, balade *f.*

javelin, *n.* javelot *m.*, javeline *f.*

jaw, *n.* mâchoire *f.*

jay, *n.* geai *m.*

jaywalk, *vb.* se promener d'une façon distraite ou imprudente.

jazz, *n.* jazz *m.*

jealous, *adj.* jaloux.

jealousy, *n.* jalousie *f.*

jeans, *n.* jeans *m.pl.*

jeer, 1. *n.* raillerie *f.*; moquerie *f.*, huée *f.* 2. *vb.* se moquer de, huer.

jelly, *n.* gelée *f.*

jellyfish, *n.* méduse *f.*

jeopardize, *vb.* exposer au danger, mettre en danger, hasarder.

jeopardy, *n.* danger *m.*, péril *m.*

jerk, *n.* saccade *f.*

jerkin, *n.* justaucorps *m.*, pourpoint *m.*

jerky, *adj.* saccadé, coupé.

jersey, *n.* jersey *m.*, tricot de laine *m.*

Jerusalem, *n.* Jérusalem *m.*

jest, 1. *n.* plaisanterie *f.*, raillerie *f.*, badinage *m.* 2. *vb.* plaisanter, railler, badiner.

jester, *n.* railleur *m.*, farceur *m.*, bouffon *m.*

Jesuit, *n.* jésuite *m.*

Jesus, *n.* Jésus *m.*

jet, *n.* (mineral) jais *m.*; (water, gas) jet *m.*; (j. plane) avion (*m.*) à réaction.

jet lag, *n.* désorientation physiologique produite par le décalage d'heures.

jetsam, *n.* épaves *f.pl.*

jettison, *vb.* se délester.

jetty, *n.* jetée *f.*, môle *m.*

Jew, *n.* Juif *m.*, Juive *f.*

jewel, *n.* bijou *m.*

jeweler, *n.* bijoutier *m.*, jouaillier *m.*

jewelry, *n.* bijouterie *f.*

Jewish, *adj.* juif *m.*, juive *f.*

jib, *n.* foc *m.*

jibe, *vb.* être en accord, s'accorder.

jiffy, *n.* instant *m.*, clin d'oeil *m.*

jig, 1. *n.* gigue *f.*; calibre *m.*, gabarit *m.* 2. danser la gigue, sautiller.

jilt, *vb.* délaisser, plaquer, planter.

jingle, 1. *n.* tintement *m.*, cliquetis *m.* 2. *vb.* tinter, cliqueter.

jinx, *n.* porte-malheur *m.*

jittery, *adj.* très nerveux.

job, *n.* (work) travail *m.*; (employment) emploi *m.*

jobber, *n.* intermédiaire *m.*, marchandeur *m.*, soustant *m.*

jockey, *n.* jockey *m.*

jocular, *adj.* facétieux, jovial, rieur.

jocund, *adj.* enjoué.

jodhpurs, *n.* pantalon d'équitation *m.*

jog, 1. *n.* coup *m.*, secousse *f.*, cahot *m.* 2. *vb.* pousser, secouer, cahoter.

joggle, 1. *n.* petite secousse *f.* **2.** *vb.* secouer légèrement.

join, *vb.* (things) joindre; (group, etc.) se joindre à.

joiner, *n.* menuisier *m.*

joint, 1. *n.* joint *m.* **2.** *adj.* (in common) commun *m.*; (in partnership) co-.

jointly, *adv.* ensemble, conjointement.

joist, *n.* solive *f.*, poutre *f.*

joke, 1. *n.* plaisanterie *f.* **2.** *vb.* plaisanter.

joker, *n.* farceur *m.*, blagueur *m.*; joker *m.*

jolly, *adj.* joyeux.

jolt, 1. *n.* cahot *m.*, choc *m.*, secousse *f.* **2.** *vb.* cahoter, secouer, ballotter.

jonquil, *n.* jonquille *f.*

jostle, *vb.* coudoyer *tr.*

jounce, 1. *n.* cahot *m.*, secousse *f.* **2.** *vb.* cahoter.

journal, *n.* journal *m.*

journalism, *n.* journalisme *m.*

journalist, *n.* journaliste *m.*

journey, 1. *n.* voyage *m.* **2.** *vb.* voyager.

journeyman, *n.* compagnon *m.*

jovial, *adj.* jovial, gai.

jowl, *n.* mâchoire *f.*

joy, *n.* joie *f.*

joyful, *adj.* joyeux.

joyous, *adj.* joyeux.

jubilant, *adj.* réjoui, jubilant, exultant.

jubilee, *n.* jubilé *m.*

Judaism, *n.* judaïsme *m.*

judge, 1. *n.* juge *m.* **2.** *vb.* juger.

judgment, *n.* jugement *m.*

judicial, *adj.* judiciaire.

judiciary, *n.* judiciaire.

judicious, *adj.* judicieux, sensé.

jug, *n.* cruche *f.*

juggle, *vb.* jongler.

jugular, *adj.* jugulaire.

juice, *n.* jus *m.*

juicy, *adj.* juteux.

July, *n.* juillet *m.*

jumble, 1. *n.* brouillamini *m.*, fouillis *m.*, fatras *m.* **2.** *vb.* brouiller, mêler confusément.

jump, 1. *n.* saut *m.* **2.** *vb.* sauter.

junction, *n.* jonction *f.*; (rail) embranchement *m.*

juncture, *n.* jointure *f.*, jonction *f.*, conjoncture *f.*

June, *n.* juin *m.*

jungle, *n.* jungle *f.*, brousse *f.*

junior, *adj. and n.* (age) cadet *m.*; (rank) subalterne *m.*

juniper, *n.* genévrier *m.*, genièvre *m.*

junk, *n.* (waste) rebut *m.*

junket, *n.* jonchée *f.*; festin *m.*, partie de plaisir *f.*

jurisdiction, *n.* juridiction *f.*

jurisprudence, *n.* jurisprudence *f.*

jurist, *n.* juriste *m.*, légiste *m.*

juror, *n.* juré *m.*, membre du jury *m.*

jury, *n.* jury *m.*

just, 1. *adj.* juste. **2.** *adv.* (exactly) juste; (barely) à peine; (have j.) venir de.

justice, *n.* justice *f.*

justifiable, *adj.* justifiable, justifié.

justification, *n.* justification *f.*

justify, *vb.* justifier.

jut, *vb.* être en saillie.

jute, *n.* jute *m.*

juvenile, *adj.* juvénile.

K

kale, *n.* chou *m.*

kaleidoscope, *n.* kaléidoscope *m.*

kangaroo, *n.* kangourou *m.*

karakul, *n.* karakul *m.*, caracul *m.*

karat, *n.* carat *m.*

karate, *n.* karaté *m.*

keel, *n.* quille *f.*

keen, *adj.* (edge) aiguisé; (pain, point) aigu; (look, mind) pénétrant; **(k. on)** enthousiaste de.

keep, *vb.* tenir; (reserve, protect, retain) garder; (remain) rester; (continue) continuer à.

keeper, *n.* gardien *m.*

keepsake, *n.* souvenir *m.*

keg, *n.* caque *f.*, barillet *m.*, tonnelet *m.*

kennel, *n.* chenil *m.*

kerchief, *n.* fichu *m.*, mouchoir *m.*

kernel, *n.* (grain) grain *m.*; (nut) amande *f.*; *(fig.)* noyau *m.*

kerosene, *n.* pétrole *m.*

ketchup, *n.* sauce piquante à base de tomates *f.*

kettle, *n.* bouilloire *f.*

kettledrum, *n.* timbale *f.*

key, *n.* clef, clé *f.*; (piano, typewriter) touche *f.*

keyhole, *n.* entrée de clef *f.*

khaki, *n.* kaki *m.*

kick, 1. *n.* coup (*m.*) de pied; (gun) recul *m.* **2.** *vb.* donner un coup de pied à.

kid, *n.* (animal, skin) chevreau *m.*; (child) gosse *m.f.*

kidnap, *vb.* enlever de vive force.

kidnaper, *n.* auteur de l'enlèvement *m.*, ravisseur *m.*

kidney, *n.* rein *m.*; (food) rognon *m.*

kidney bean, *n.* haricot nain *m.*

kill, *vb.* tuer.

killer, *n.* tueur *m.*, meurtrier *m.*

kiln, *n.* four (céramique) *m.*, séchoir *m.*

kilocycle, *n.* kilocycle *m.*

kilohertz, *n.* kilohertz *m.*

kilowatt, *n.* kilowatt *m.*

kilt, *n.* kilt *m.*

kimono, *n.* kimono *m.*

kin, *n.* (relation) parent *m.*

kind, 1. *n.* genre *m.* **2.** *adj.* aimable.

kindergarten, *n.* jardin d'enfants *m.*, école maternelle *f.*

kindle, *vb.* allumer, *tr.*

kindling, *n.* allumage *m.*, bois d'allumage *m.*

kindly, *adv.* avec bonté.

kindness, *n.* bonté *f.*

kindred, 1. *n.* parenté *f.*, affinité *f.* **2.** *adj.* analogue.

kinetic, *adj.* cinétique.

king, *n.* roi *m.*

kingdom, *n.* royaume *m.*

kink, 1. *n.* nœud *m.*, tortillement *m.* **2.** *vb.* se nouer.

kiosk, *n.* kiosque *m.*

kipper, *n.* kipper *m.*, hareng légèrement salé et fumé *m.*

kiss, 1. *n.* baiser *m.* **2.** *vb.* baiser.

kitchen, *n.* cuisine *f.*

kite, *n.* cerf-volant *m.*

kitten, *n.* petit chat *m.*

kleptomania, *n.* kleptomanie *f.*

kleptomaniac, *n.* kleptomane *m.*

knack, *n.* tour de main *m.*, talent *m.*, truc *m.*

knapsack, *n.* havresac *m.*

knead, *vb.* pétrir, malaxer.

knee, *n.* genou *m.*

kneecap, *n.* genouillère *f.*

kneel, *vb.* s'agenouiller.

knell, *n.* glas *m.*

knickers, *n.* pantalon *m.*, culotte *f.*

knife, *n.* couteau *m.*

knight, *n.* chevalier *m.*

knit, *vb.* (with needles) tricoter.

knock, 1. *n.* coup *m.* **2.** *vb.* frapper.

knot, *n.* nœud *m.*

knotty, *adj.* plein de nœuds.

know, *vb.* savoir; (be acquainted with) connaître.

knowledge, *n.* connaissance *f.*; (learning) savoir *m.*

knuckle, *n.* articulation du doigt *f.*, jointure du doigt *f.*

kodak, *n.* kodak *m.*

Korea, *n.* Corée *f.*

L

label, *n.* étiquette *f.*

labor, 1. *n.* travail *m.*; (workers) ouvriers *m.pl.* **2.** *vb.* peiner.

laboratory, *n.* laboratoire *m.*

laborer, *n.* travailleur *m.*

laborious, *adj.* laborieux.

labor union, *n.* syndicat *m.*

laburnum, *n.* cytise *m.*

labyrinth, *n.* labyrinthe *m.*

lace, *n.* dentelle *f.*; (string) lacet *m.*

lacerate, *vb.* lacérer, déchirer.

laceration, *n.* lacération *f.*

lack, 1. *n.* manque *m.* **2.** *vb.* manquer de.

lackadaisical, *adj.* affecté.

laconic, *adj.* laconique.

lacquer, *n.* vernis-laque *m.*

lactic, *adj.* lactique.

lactose, *n.* lactose *f.*

lacy, *adj.* de dentelle.

ladder, *n.* échelle *f.*

ladle, *n.* cuiller à pot *f.*

lady, *n.* dame *f.*

ladybug, *n.* coccinelle *f.*

lag behind, *vb.* rester en arrière.

lagoon, *n.* lagune *f.*

laid-back, *adj.* décontracté.

lair, *n.* tanière *f.*, repaire *m.*

laissez faire, *n.* laissez faire *m.*

laity, *n.* les laïques *m.pl.*

lake, *n.* lac *m.*

lamb, *n.* agneau *m.*

lame, *adj.* boiteux.

lament, *vb.* se lamenter (sur); (mourn) pleurer.

lamentable, *adj.* lamentable, déplorable.

lamentation, *n.* lamentation *f.*

laminate, *vb.* laminer, écacher.

lamp, *n.* lampe *f.*

lampoon, 1. *n.* pasquinade *f.,* satire *f.* 2. *vb.* lancer des satires.

lance, *n.* lance *f.*

land, 1. *n.* terre *f.* 2. *vb.* (boat) débarquer; (plane) atterrir.

landholder, *n.* propriétaire foncier *m.*

landing, *n.* débarquement *m.,* mise à terre *m.*

landlord, *n.* propriétaire *m.f.*

landmark, *n.* borne *f.*

landscape, *n.* paysage *m.*

landslide, *n.* éboulement *m.*

landward, *adv.* vers la terre.

lane, *n.* (country) sentier *m.;* (town) ruelle *f.*

language, *n.* langue *f.;* (form of expression) langage *m.*

languid, *adj.* languissant.

languish, *vb.* languir.

languor, *n.* langueur *f.*

lanky, *adj.* grand et maigre.

lanolin, *n.* lanoline *f.*

lantern, *n.* lanterne *f.*

lap, *n.* genoux *m.pl.*

lapel, *n.* revers *m.*

lapin, *n.* lapin *m.*

lapse, 1. *n.* (of time) laps *m.;* (error) faute *f.* 2. *vb.* passer.

larceny, *n.* larcin *m.*, vol *m.*

lard, *n.* saindoux *m.*

large, *adj.* grand.

largely, *adv.* en grande partie.

largo, *n.* largo *m.*

lariat, *n.* lasso *m.*

lark, *n.* alouette *f.*

larkspur, *n.* pied d'alouette *m.,* delphinium *m.*

larva, *n.* larve *f.*

laryngitis, *n.* laryngite *f.*

larynx, *n.* larynx *m.*

lascivious, *adj.* lascif.

laser, *n.* laser *m.*

lash, 1. *n.* (whip) lanière *f.;* (blow) coup (*m.*) de fouet *f.* 2. *vb.* fouetter.

lass, *n.* jeune fille *f.*

lassitude, *n.* lassitude *f.*

lasso, *n.* lasso *m.*

last, 1. *adj.* dernier; (at l.) enfin. 2. *vb.* durer.

lasting, *adj.* durable.

latch, *n.* loquet *m.*

late, *adj.* and *adv.* (on in day, etc.) tard; (after due time) en retard; (dead) feu; (recent) dernier.

lately, *adv.* dernièrement.

latent, *adj.* latent, caché.

lateral, *adj.* latéral.

lath, *n.* latte *f.*

lathe, *n.* tour *m.*

lather, *n.* (soap) mousse *f.;* (horse) écume *f.*

Latin, 1. *n.* (person) Latin *m.;* (language) latin *m.* 2. *adj.* latin.

latitude, *n.* latitude *f.*

latrine, *n.* latrine *f.*

latter, *adj.* and *pron.* dernier.

lattice, *n.* treillis *m.*

laud, *vb.* louer.

laudable, *adj.* louable.

laudanum, *n.* laudanum *m.*

laudatory, *adj.* élogieux.

laugh, laughter, *n.* rire *m.*

laugh (at), *vb.* rire (de).

laughable, *adj.* risible.

launch, 1. *n.* (boat) chaloupe *f.* 2. *vb.* lancer, *tr.*

launder, *vb.* blanchir.

laundry, *n.* (works) blanchisserie *f.;* (washing) lessive *f.*

laundryman, *n.* blanchisseur *m.*

laureate, *adj.* and *n.* lauréat *m.f.*

laurel, *n.* laurier *m.*

lava, *n.* lave *f.*

la7aliere, *n.* lavallière *f.*

lavatory, *n.* lavabo *m.;* cabinet (*m.*) de toilette.

lavender, *n.* lavande *f.*

lavish, 1. *adj.* (person) prodigue; (thing) somptueux. 2. *vb.* prodiguer.

law, *n.* loi *f.;* (jurisprudence) droit *m.*

lawful, *adj.* légal.

lawless, *adj.* sans loi.

lawn, *n.* pelouse *f.*

lawsuit, *n.* procès *m.*

lawyer, *n.* (counselor) avocat *m.;* (attorney) avoué *m.;* (jurist) jurisconsulte *m.*

lax, *adj.* lâche, mou, relâché.

laxative, *n.* laxatif *m.*

laxity, *n.* relâchement *m.*

lay, *vb.* poser.

layer, *n.* couche *f.*

layman, *n.* laïque *m.*

lazy, *adj.* paresseux.

lead, 1. *n.* plomb *m.;* (pencil) mine *f.* 2. *vb.* mener, conduire.

leaden, *adj.* de plomb.

leader, *n.* chef *m.*

lead pencil, *n.* crayon à la mine de plomb *m.*

leaf, *n.* feuille *f.*

leaflet, *n.* feuillet *m.*

leafy, *adj.* feuillu.

league, *n.* (compact) ligue *f.;* (measure) lieue *f.*

League of Nations, *n.* La Société des Nations *f.*

leak, 1. *n.* (liquid) fuite *f.;* (boat) voie (*f.*) d'eau *f.* 2. *vb.* fuir; faire eau.

leakage, *n.* fuite d'eau *f.*

leaky, *adj.* qui coule, qui fait eau.

lean, 1. *adj.* maigre. 2. *vb. intr.* (l. against) s'appuyer sur; (stoop) se pencher. 3. *vb.tr.* appuyer.

leap, *vb.* sauter.

leap year, *n.* année bissextile *f.*

learn, *vb.* apprendre.

learned, *adj.* savant, docte.

learning, *n.* science *f.,* instruction *f.,* érudition *f.*

lease, *n.* bail *m.*

leash, *n.* laisse *f.,* attache *f.*

least, 1. *n.* (le) moins *m.* 2. *adj.* (le) moindre. 3. *adv.* (le) moins.

leather, *n.* cuir *m.*

leathery, *adj.* coriace.

leave, 1. *n.* permission *f.* 2. *vb.* laisser; (go away from) quitter.

leaven, 1. *n.* levain *m.* 2. *vb.* faire lever, modifier.

lecherous, *adj.* lascif, libertin.

lecture, *n.* conférence *f.*

lecturer, *n.* conférencier *m.*

ledge, *n.* bord *m.;* (of rocks) chaîne *f.*

ledger, *n.* grand livre *m.*

lee, *n.* côté (*m.*) sous le vent.

leech, *n.* sangsue *f.*

leek, *n.* poireau *m.*

leer, 1. *n.* oeillade *f.,* regard de côté *m.* 2. *vb.* lorgner.

leeward, *adj.* and *adv.* sous le vent.

left, *adj.* and *n.* gauche *f.;* (on, to the l.) à gauche.

leftist, *n.* gaucher *m.*

left wing, *n.* l'aile gauche *f.*

leg, *n.* (man, horse) jambe *f.;* (most animals) patte *f.*

legacy, *n.* legs *m.*

legal, *adj.* légal.

legalize, *vb.* rendre légal.

legation, *n.* légation *f.*

legend, *n.* légende *f.*

legendary, *adj.* légendaire.

legible, *adj.* lisible.

legion, *n.* légion *f.*

legislate, *vb.* faire les lois.

legislation, *n.* législation *f.*

legislator, *n.* législateur *m.*

legislature, *n.* législature *f.*

legitimate, *adj.* légitime.

legume, *n.* légume *m.*

leisure, *n.* loisir *m.*

leisurely, *adv.* à loisir.

lemon, *n.* citron *m.*

lemonade, *n.* citron (*m.*) pressé.

lend, *vb.* prêter.

length, *n.* (dimension) longueur *f.;* (time) durée *f.*

lengthen, *vb.* allonger, *tr.*

lengthwise, *adv.* en long.

lengthy, *adj.* assez long.

lenient, *adj.* indulgent.

lens, *n.* lentille *f.;* (camera) objectif *m.*
Lent, *n.* carême *m.*
Lenten, *adj.* de carême.
lentil, *n.* lentille *f.*
lento, *adv.* lento.
leopard, *n.* léopard *m.*
leper, *n.* lépreux *m.*
leprosy, *n.* lèpre *f.*
lesbian, 1. *adj.* lesbien. **2.** *n.* lesbienne *f.;* tribade *f.*
lesion, *n.* lésion *f.*
less, 1. *adj.* (smaller) moindre; (not so much) moins de. **2.** *adv.* **(l. than)** moins (de).
lessen, *vb.* diminuer.
lesser, *adj.* moindre.
lesson, *n.* leçon *f.*
lest, *conj.* de peur que . . . (ne).
let, *vb.* laisser; (lease) louer.
letdown, *n.* déception *f.*
lethal, *adj.* mortel.
lethargic, *adj.* léthargique.
lethargy, *n.* léthargie *f.*
letter, *n.* lettre *f.*
letterhead, *n.* en-tête de lettre *m.*
lettuce, *n.* laitue *f.*
levee, *n.* lever *f.*
level, 1. *adj.* (flat) égal; **(l. with)** au niveau de. **2.** *n.* niveau *m.*
lever, *n.* levier *m.*
levity, *n.* légèreté *f.*
levy, 1. *n.* levée *f.* **2.** *vb.* lever.
lewd, *adj.* impudique.
lexicon, *n.* lexique *m.*
liability, *n.* responsabilité *f.*
liable, *adj.* (responsible for) responsable de; (subject to) sujet à.
liar, *n.* menteur *m.*
libation, *n.* libation *f.*
libel, *n.* diffamation *f.*
libelous, *adj.* diffamatoire.
liberal, *adj.* libéral; (generous) généreux.
liberalism, *n.* libéralisme *m.*
liberality, *n.* libéralité *f.*
liberate, *vb.* libérer.
libertine, 1. *n.* libre-penseur *m.* **2.** *adj.* libertin.
liberty, *n.* liberté *f.*
libidinous, *adj.* libidineux.
libido, *n.* libido *m.*
librarian, *n.* bibliothécaire *m.*
library, *n.* bibliothèque *f.*
libretto, *n.* livret *m.*
license, *n.* permis *m.;* (tradesmen) patente *f.;* (abuse of freedom) licence *f.*
licentious, *adj.* licencieux.
lick, *vb.* lécher.
licorice, *n.* réglisse *f.*
lid, *n.* couvercle *m.*
lie, 1. *n.* mensonge *f.* **2.** *vb.* (fib) mentir; (recline) être couché; **(l. down)** se coucher; (be situated) se trouver.
lien, *n.* privilège *m.*
lieutenant, *n.* lieutenant *m.*
life, *n.* vie *f.*
lifeboat, *n.* bateau de sauvetage *m.*

life buoy, *n.* bouée de sauvetage *m.*
lifeguard, *n.* garde du corps *m.*
life insurance, *n.* assurance sur la vie *f.*
lifeless, *adj.* sans vie.
life preserver, *n.* appareil de sauvetage *m.*
life style, *n.* manière de vivre *f.*
lifetime, *n.* vie *f.,* vivant *m.*
lift, *vb.* lever.
ligament, *n.* ligament *m.*
ligature, *n.* ligature *f.*
light, 1. *n.* lumière *f.* **2.** *adj.* (not heavy) léger; (not dark) clair. **3.** *vb.* allumer, *tr.*
lighten, *vb.* (relieve) alléger, *tr.;* (brighten) éclairer, *tr.*
lighthouse, *n.* phare *m.*
lightly, *adv.* légèrement.
lightness, *n.* légèreté *f.*
lightning, *n.* (flash of) éclair *m.*
lightship, *n.* bateau-feu *m.*
lignite, *n.* lignite *m.*
likable, *adj.* agréable.
like, 1. *adj.* pareil. **2.** *vb.* aimer; plaire à. **3.** *prep.* comme.
likelihood, *n.* probabilité *f.*
likely, *adj.* probable.
liken, *vb.* comparer.
likeness, *n.* ressemblance *f.*
likewise, *adv.* de même.
lilac, *n.* lilas *m.*
lilt, 1. *n.* forte cadence *f.* **2.** *vb.* chanter gaiement.
lily, *n.* lis *m.;* **(l. of the valley)** muguet *m.*
limb, *n.* membre *m.;* (tree) grosse branche *f.*
limber, 1. *adj.* souple, flexible. **2.** *vb.* assouplir.
limbo, *n.* limbes *m.pl.*
lime, *n.* (mineral) chaux *f.;* (tree) tilleul *m.;* (fruit) lime *f.*
limelight, *n.* lumière oxhydrique *f.*
limestone, *n.* pierre à chaux *f.,* calcaire *m.*
limewater, *n.* eau de chaux *f.*
limit, 1. *n.* limite *f.* **2.** *vb.* limiter.
limitation, *n.* limitation *f.*
limitless, *adj.* sans limite, sans bornes.
limousine, *n.* limousine *f.*
limp, 1. *adj.* flasque. **2.** *vb.* boiter.
limpid, *adj.* limpide.
linden, *n.* tilleul *m.*
line, *n.* ligne *f.*
lineage, *n.* lignée *f.,* race *f.*
lineal, *adj.* linéaire.
linen, *n.* (cloth) toile *f.;* (sheets, etc.) linge *m.*
linger, *vb.* s'attarder.
lingerie, *n.* lingerie *f.*
linguist, *n.* linguiste *m.*
linguistic, *adj.* linguistique.
linguistics, *n.* linguistique *f.*
liniment, *n.* liniment *m.*
lining, *n.* (clothes) doublure *f.*
link, 1. *n.* (chain) chaînon *m.;* (fig.) lien *m.* **2.** *vb.* (re)lier.
linoleum, *n.* linoléum *m.*
linseed, *n.* graine de lin *f.*

lint, *n.* charpie *f.*
lion, *n.* lion *m.*
lip, *n.* lèvre *f.*
liquefy, *vb.* liquéfier.
liqueur, *n.* liqueur *f.*
liquid, *adj.* and *n.* liquide *m.*
liquidate, *vb.* liquider.
liquidation, *n.* liquidation *f.,* acquittement *m.*
liquor, *n.* boisson *(f.)* alcoolique.
lisle, *n.* fil d'Écosse *m.*
lisp, *vb.* zézayer.
list, 1. *n.* liste *f.* **2.** *vb.* enregistrer.
listen (to), *vb.* écouter.
listless, *adj.* inattentif.
litany, *n.* litanie *f.*
literacy, *n.* degré d'aptitude à lire et à écrire *m.*
literal, *adj.* littéral.
literary, *adj.* littéraire.
literate, *adj.* lettré.
literature, *n.* littérature *f.*
lithe, *adj.* flexible, pliant.
lithograph, *vb.* lithographier.
lithography, *n.* lithographie *f.*
litigant, *n.* plaideur *m.*
litigation, *n.* litige *m.*
litmus, *n.* tournesol *m.*
litter, *n.* (vehicle, animals' bedding) litière *f.;* (disorder) fouillis *m.;* (animals' young) portée *f.*
little, 1. *n.* and *adv.* peu *m.* **2.** *adj.* (small) petit; (not much) peu (de).
liturgical, *adj.* liturgique.
liturgy, *n.* liturgie *f.*
live, *vb.* vivre.
livelihood, *n.* vie *f.,* subsistance *f.,* gagne-pain *m.*
lively, *adj.* vif *m.,* vive *f.*
liven, *vb.* animer, activer.
liver, *n.* foie *m.*
livery, *n.* livrée *f.*
livestock, *n.* bétail *m.*
livid, *adj.* livide, blême.
lizard, *n.* lézard *m.*
llama, *n.* lama *m.*
lo, *interj.* voilà.
load, 1. *n.* (cargo) charge *f.;* (burden) fardeau *m.* **2.** *vb.* charger.
loaf, 1. *n.* pain *m.* **2.** *vb.* flâner.
loafer, *n.* fainéant *m.*
loam, *n.* terre grasse *f.*
loan, 1. *n.* (thing) prêt *m.;* (borrowing) emprunt *m.* **2.** *vb.* prêter.
loath, *adj.* fâché, peiné.
loathe, *vb.* détester.
loathing, *n.* dégoût *m.*
loathsome, *adj.* dégoûtant.
lobby, *n.* (hall) vestibule *m.*
lobe, *n.* lobe *m.*
lobster, *n.* homard *m.*
local, *adj.* local.
locale, *n.* localité *f.,* scène *f.*
locality, *n.* localité *f.*
localize, *vb.* localiser.
locate, *vb.* localiser.
location, *n.* placement *m.*
lock, 1. *n.* (door) serrure *f.;*

(hair) mèche f. 2. vb. fermer à clef.

locker, n. armoire f.; (baggage) consigne automatique f.

locket, n. médaillon m.

lockjaw, n. tétanos m.

locksmith, n. serrurier m.

locomotion, n. locomotion f.

locomotive, n. locomotive f.

locust, n. sauterelle f.

locution, n. locution f.

lode, n. filon m.

lodge, vb. loger.

lodger, n. locataire m.

lodging, n. logement m.

loft, n. grenier m.

lofty, adj. élevé; (proud) hautain.

log, n. (wood) bûche f.; (boat) loch m.

loge, n. loge f.

logic, n. logique f.

logical, adj. logique.

loins, n. reins m.pl.

loiter, vb. flâner.

lollipop, n. sucre d'orge m.

London, n. Londres m.

lone, lonely, lonesome, adj. solitaire.

loneliness, n. solitude f.

long, 1. adj. long m., longue f. 2. adv. longtemps.

longevity, n. longévité f.

long for, vb. désirer ardemment.

longing, n. désir ardent m.

longitude, n. longitude f.

longitudinal, adj. longitudinal.

look, 1. n. regard m.; aspect m. 2. vb. (l. at) regarder; (l. for) chercher; (l. after) soigner; (seem) paraître.

looking glass, n. miroir m.

loom, 1. n. métier m. 2. vb. se dessiner.

loop, n. boucle f.

loophole, n. meurtrière f., échappatoire f.

loose, adj. (not tight) lâche; (detached) détaché; (morals) relâché.

loosen, vb. desserrer.

loot, 1. n. butin m. 2. vb. piller.

lop, vb. élaguer, ébrancher.

loquacious, adj. loquace.

lord, n. seigneur m.; (title) lord m.

lordship, n. seigneurie f.

lorgnette, n. lorgnette f.

lose, vb. perdre.

loss, n. perte f.

lot, n. (fortune) sort m.; (land) terrain m.; (much) beaucoup.

lotion, n. lotion f.

lottery, n. loterie f.

lotus, n. lotus m., lotos m.

loud, 1. adj. fort; (noisy) bruyant. 2. adv. haut.

lounge, 1. n. sofa m.; hall m. 2. vb. flâner.

louse, n. pou m.

lout, n. rustre m.

louver, n. auvent m.

lovable, adj. aimable.

love, 1. n. amour m. 2. vb. aimer.

lovely, adj. beau m., belle f.

lover, n. amoureux m.

low, adj. bas m., basse f.

lowboy, n. commode basse f.

lowbrow, adj. terre à terre.

lower, vb. baisser.

lowly, adj. humble.

loyal, adj. loyal.

loyalist, n. loyaliste m.

loyalty, n. loyauté f.

lozenge, n. pastille f.

lubricant, n. lubrifiant m.

lubricate, vb. lubrifier.

lucid, adj. lucide.

luck, n. chance f.

lucky, adj. (person) heureux.

lucrative, adj. lucratif.

ludicrous, adj. risible.

lug, vb. traîner, tirer.

luggage, n. bagages m.pl.

lukewarm, adj. tiède.

lull, n. moment (m.) de calme.

lullaby, n. berceuse f.

lumbago, n. lumbago m.

lumber, n. bois (m.) de charpente.

luminous, adj. lumineux.

lump, n. (gros) morceau m.

lumpy, adj. grumeleux.

lunacy, n. folie f.

lunar, adj. lunaire.

lunatic, n. aliéné m.

lunch, 1. n. déjeuner m. 2. vb. déjeuner.

luncheon, n. déjeuner m.

lung, n. poumon m.

lunge, 1. n. botte f. 2. vb. se fendre.

lurch, 1. n. embardée f. 2. vb. faire une embardée.

lure, vb. (animal) leurrer; (attract) attirer.

lurid, adj. blafard, sombre.

lurk, vb. se cacher.

luscious, adj. délicieux.

lush, adj. luxuriant.

lust, n. luxure f.

luster, n. lustre m.

lustful, adj. lascif, sensuel.

lustrous, adj. brillant, lustré.

lusty, adj. vigoureux.

lute, n. luth m.

Lutheran, n. Luthérien m.

luxuriant, adj. exubérant.

luxurious, adj. (thing) luxueux.

luxury, n. luxe m.

lying, n. mensonge m.

lymph, n. lymphe f.

lynch, vb. lyncher.

lyre, n. lyre f.

lyric, adj. lyrique.

lyricism, n. lyrisme m.

M

macaroni, n. macaroni m.

machine, n. machine f.

machine gun, n. mitrailleuse f.

machinery, n. machines f.pl; (fig.) mécanisme m.

machinist, n. machiniste m.

machismo, n. phallocratie f.

macho, 1. adj. phallocrate. 2. n. homme phallocrate m.

mackerel, n. maquereau m.

mackinaw, n. mackinaw m.

mad, adj. fou m., folle f.

madam, n. madame f.

madcap, adj. and adj. écervelé.

madden, vb. exaspérer.

made, adj. fait, fabriqué.

mafia, n. mafia f.

magazine, n. revue f.

magic, 1. n. magie f. 2. adj. magique.

magician, n. magicien m.

magistrate, n. magistrat m.

magnanimous, adj. magnanime.

magnate, n. magnat m.

magnesium, n. magnésium m.

magnet, n. aimant m.

magnetic, adj. magnétique.

magnificence, n. magnificence f.

magnificent, adj. magnifique.

magnify, vb. grossir.

magnitude, n. grandeur f.

mahogany, n. acajou m.

maid, n. (servant) bonne f.; (old m.) vieille fille f.

maiden, adj. de jeune fille.

mail, 1. n. courrier m. 2. vb. envoyer par la poste.

mailbox, n. boîte (f.) aux lettres.

mailman, n. facteur m.

maim, vb. estropier, mutiler.

main, adj. principal.

mainframe, n. partie centrale d'un informateur f.

mainland, n. terre (f.) ferme.

mainspring, n. grand ressort m.; mobile essentiel m.

maintain, vb. maintenir; (support) soutenir.

maintenance, n. entretien m.

maize, n. maïs m.

majestic, adj. majestueux.

majesty, n. majesté f.

major, 1. n. (mil.) commandant m.; (school) sujet (m.) principal. 2. adj. majeur.

majority, n. majorité f.

major scale, mode, or key, n. ton majeur m., mode majeur m.

make, 1. n. fabrication f. 2. vb. faire.

make-believe, 1. n. trompe l'œil m. 2. vb. feindre.

maker, n. fabricant m.

makeshift, n. expédient m.

make-up, n. (face) maquillage m.

maladjusted, adj. mal adapté, mal ajusté.

maladjustment, n. mauvaise adaptation f.

malady, n. maladie f.

malaria, n. malaria f.

male, adj. and n. mâle m.

malevolent, adj. malveillant.

malice, n. méchanceté f.

malicious, adj. méchant.

malign, vb. calomnier.

malignant, *adj.* malin *m.*, maligne *f.*

malleable, *adj.* malléable.

malnutrition, *n.* mauvaise hygiène (*f.*) alimentaire.

malpractice, *n.* méfait *m.*

malt, *n.* malt *m.*

mammal, *n.* mammifère *m.*

man, *n.* homme *m.*

manage, 1. *vb. tr.* (administer) gérer; (conduct) diriger; (person, animal) dompter. 2. *vb. intr.* se tirer d'affaire; (**m. to**) réussir à.

management, *n.* direction *f.*

manager, *n.* directeur *m.*; (household) ménager *m.*

mandate, *n.* (politics) mandat *m.*

mandatory, *adj.* obligatoire.

mandolin, *n.* mandoline *f.*

mane, *n.* crinière *f.*

maneuver, *n.* manœuvre *f.*

manganese, *n.* manganèse *m.*

manger, *n.* mangeoire *f.*

mangle, *vb.* mutiler.

manhood, *n.* virilité *f.*

mania, *n.* (craze) manie *f.*; (madness) folie *f.*

maniac, *adj. and n.* fou *m.*, folle *f.*

manicure, *n.* (person) manucure *m.f.*; (care of hands) soin (*m.*) des mains.

manifest, 1. *adj.* manifeste. 2. *vb.* manifester.

manifesto, *n.* manifeste *m.*

manifold, *adj.* (varied) divers; (numerous) nombreux.

manipulate, *vb.* manipuler.

mankind, *n.* genre (*m.*) humain.

manly, *adj.* viril.

manner, *n.* manière *f.*; (customs) mœurs *f.pl.*

mannerism, *n.* maniérisme *m.*, affectation *f.*

mansion, *n.* (country) château *m.*; (town) hôtel *m.*

manslaughter, *n.* homicide involontaire *m.*

mantel, *n.* (framework) manteau *m.*; (shelf) tablette *f.*

mantle, *n.* manteau *f.*

manual, *adj. and n.* manuel *m.*

manufacture, 1. *n.* manufacture *f.*; (product) produit (*m.*) manufacturé. 2. *vb.* fabriquer.

manufacturer, *n.* fabricant *m.*

manure, *n.* fumier *m.*

manuscript, *adj. and n.* manuscrit *m.*

many, 1. *adj.* beaucoup de, un grand nombre de; (**too m.**) trop de; (**so m.**) tant de; (**how m.**) combien de. 2. *pron.* beaucoup.

map, *n.* carte (*f.*) géographique.

maple, *n.* érable *m.*

mar, *vb.* gâter.

marble, *n.* marbre *m.*

march, 1. *n.* marche *f.* 2. *vb.* marcher.

March, *n.* mars *m.*

mare, *n.* jument *f.*

margarine, *n.* margarine *f.*

margin, *n.* marge *f.*

marijuana, *n.* marijuana *f.*; marie-jeanne *f.*

marinate, *vb.* faire mariner.

marine, 1. *n.* (ships) marine *f.*; (soldier) fusilier (*m.*) marin. 2. *adj.* marin; (insurance) maritime.

mariner, *n.* marin *m.*

marionette, *n.* marionnette *f.*

marital, *adj.* matrimonial.

maritime, *adj.* maritime.

mark, 1. *n.* marque *f.*; (target) but *m.*; (school) point *m.* 2. *vb.* marquer.

market, *n.* marché *m.*

market place, *n.* place (*f.*) du marché.

marmalade, *n.* confiture *f.*

maroon, 1. *adj. and n.* rouge (*m.*) foncé. 2. *vb.* abandonner (dans une île déserte).

marquee, *n.* (tente) marquise *f.*

marquis, *n.* marquis *m.*

marriage, *n.* mariage *m.*

married, *adj.* marié.

marrow, *n.* moelle *f.*

marry, *vb.* épouser; se marier (avec).

marsh, *n.* marais *m.*

marshal, *n.* maréchal *m.*

marshmallow, *n.* guimauve (plant) *f.*

martial, *adj.* martial.

martinet, *n.* officier strict sur la discipline *m.*

martyr, *n.* martyr *m.*

martyrdom, *n.* martyre *m.*

marvel, 1. *n.* merveille *f.* 2. *vb.* (**m. at**) s'étonner de.

marvelous, *adj.* merveilleux.

mascara, *n.* mascara *m.*

mascot, *n.* mascotte *f.*

masculine, *adj.* masculin.

mash, *n.* (food) purée *f.*

mask, 1. *n.* masque *m.* 2. *vb.* masquer.

mason, *n.* maçon *m.*

masquerade, *n.* mascarade *f.*, bal masqué *m.*

mass, *n.* masse *f.*

Mass, *n.* messe *f.*

massacre, 1. *n.* massacre *m.* 2. *vb.* massacrer.

massage, *n.* massage *m.*

masseur, *n.* masseur *m.*

massive, *adj.* massif.

mass meeting, *n.* réunion *f.*

mast, *n.* mât *m.*

master, 1. *n.* maître *m.* 2. *vb.* maîtriser.

masterpiece, *n.* chef-d'œuvre *m.*

mastery, *vb.* maîtrise *f.*

masticate, *vb.* mâcher.

mat, *n.* (door) paillasson *m.*

match, 1. *n.* (for fire) allumette *f.*; (equal) égal *m.*; (marriage) mariage *m.*; (person to marry) parti *m.*; (sport) partie *f.* 2. *vb.* assortir, *tr.*

mate, *n.* (fellow-worker) camarade *m.f.*; (of pair) compa-

gnon *m.*; compagne *f.*; (boat) officier *m.*

material, 1. *n.* matière *f.*; (cloth) étoffe *f.* 2. *adj.* matériel.

materialism, *n.* matérialisme *m.*

materialize, *vb.* matérialiser, *tr.*; se réaliser, *intr.*

maternal, *adj.* maternel.

maternity, *n.* maternité *f.*

mathematical, *adj.* mathématique.

mathematics, *n.* mathématiques *f.pl.*

matinee, *n.* matinée *f.*

matriarch, *n.* femme qui porte les chausses *f.*

matrimony, *n.* mariage *m.*

matron, *n.* (institution) intendante *f.*

matter, 1. *n.* (substance) matière *f.*; (subject) sujet *m.*; (question, business) affaire *f.*; (**what is the m.?**) qu'est-ce qu'il y a? 2. *vb.* importer.

mattress, *n.* matelas *m.*

mature, 1. *adj.* mûr. 2. *vb.* mûrir.

maturity, *n.* maturité *f.*; (comm.) échéance *f.*

maudlin, *adj.* larmoyant.

mausoleum, *n.* mausolée *m.*

maxim, *n.* maxime *f.*

maximum, *n.* maximum *m.*

may, *vb.* pouvoir.

May, *n.* mai *m.*

maybe, *adv.* peut-être.

mayhem, *n.* mutilation *f.*

mayonnaise, *n.* mayonnaise *f.*

mayor, *n.* maire *m.*

maze, *n.* labyrinthe *m.*

me, *pron.* (unstressed direct and indirect) me; (alone, stressed, with *prep.*) moi.

meadow, *n.* (small) pré *m.*; (large) prairie *f.*

meager, *adj.* maigre.

meal, *n.* (repast) repas *m.*; (grain) farine *f.*

mean, 1. *n.* (math.) moyenne *f.*; (m.s financial) moyens *m.pl.*; (m.s way to do) moyen *m.* 2. *adj.* humble; (stingy) avare; (contemptible) méprisable. 3. *vb.* (signify) vouloir dire; (purpose) se proposer (de); (destine) destiner (à).

meaning, *n.* sens *m.*

meantime, meanwhile, *adv.* sur ces entrefaites.

measles, *n.* rougeole *f.*

measure, 1. *n.* mesure *f.* 2. *vb.* mesurer.

measurement, *n.* mesurage *m.*

meat, *n.* viande *f.*

mechanic, *n.* mécanicien *m.*

mechanical, 1. *adj.* mécanique. 2. *(fig.)* machinal.

mechanism, *n.* mécanisme *m.*

mechanize, *vb.* mécaniser.

medal, *n.* médaille *f.*

meddle, *vb.* se mêler (de).

media, *n.* organes de communication *m.pl.*

median, n. médian.
mediate, vb. agir en médiateur.
medical, adj. médical.
medicate, vb. médicamenter.
medicine, n. médecine m.
medieval, adj. médiéval.
mediocre, adj. médiocre.
mediocrity, n. médiocrité f.
meditate, vb. méditer.
meditation, n. méditation f.
Mediterranean, 1. adj. méditerrané. 2. n. (M. Sea) Méditerranée f.
medium, 1. n. milieu m.; (agent) intermédiaire m.; (psychic person) médium m. 2. adj. moyen.
medley, n. mélange m.
meek, adj. doux m., douce f.
meekness, n. douceur f.
meet, vb. rencontrer, tr.; (become acquainted with) faire la connaissance de; (expenses) faire face à.
meeting, n. réunion f.
megahertz, n. mégahertz m.
megaphone, n. mégaphone m.
melancholy, n. mélancolie f.
mellow, adj. moelleux.
melodious, adj. mélodieux.
melodrama, n. mélodrame m.
melody, n. mélodie f.
melon, n. melon m.
melt, vb. fondre.
meltdown, n. fusion f.
member, n. membre m.
membrane, n. membrane f.
memento, n. mémento m.
memoir, n. mémoire m.
memorable, adj. mémorable.
memorandum, n. mémorandum m.
memorial, 1. n. souvenir m., monument m. 2. adj. commémoratif.
memorize, vb. apprendre par cœur.
memory, n. mémoire f.
menace, 1. n. menace f. 2. vb. menacer.
menagerie, n. ménagerie f.
mend, vb. (clothes) raccommoder; (correct) corriger.
mendacious, adj. menteur.
mendicant, n. and adj. mendiant m.
menial, adj. servile.
menstruation, n. menstruation f.
menswear, n. habillements masculins m.pl.
mental, adj. mental.
mentality, n. mentalité f.
menthol, n. menthol m.
mention, 1. n. mention f. 2. vb. mentionner; (don't m. it) il n'y a pas de quoi.
menu, n. menu m.
mercantile, adj. mercantile.
mercenary, n. and adj. mercenaire m.
merchandise, n. marchandise(s) f.(pl.).
merchant, 1. n. négociant m. 2. adj. marchand.

merchant marine, n. marine marchande f.
merciful, adj. miséricordieux.
merciless, adj. impitoyable.
mercury, n. mercure m.
mercy, n. miséricorde f.; (at the m. of) à la merci de.
mere, adj. simple.
merely, adv. simplement.
merge, vb. fusionner.
merger, n. fusion f.
merit, 1. n. mérite m. 2. vb. mériter.
meritorious, adj. (person) méritant; (deed) méritoire.
mermaid, n. sirène f.
merriment, n. gaieté f.
merry, adj. gai.
merry-go-round, n. carrousel m.
mesh, n. maille f.
mesmerize, vb. magnétiser.
mess, 1. n. (muddle) fouillis m.; gâchis m.; (mil.) popote f. 2. vb. gâcher.
message, n. message m.
messenger, n. messager m.
messy, adj. (dirty) malpropre.
metabolism, n. métabolisme m.
metal, n. métal m.
metallic, adj. métallique.
metamorphosis, n. métamorphose f.
metaphysics, n. métaphysique f.
meteor, n. météore m.
meter, 1. n. (measure) mètre m.; (device) compteur m.
method, n. méthode f.
meticulous, adj. méticuleux.
metric, n. métrique.
metropolis, n. métropole f.
metropolitan, adj. métropolitain.
mettle, n. ardeur f.
Mexican, 1. n. Mexicain m. 2. adj. Mexicain.
Mexico, n. Mexique m.
mezzanine, n. mezzanine f.
microbe, n. microbe m.
microfiche, n. microfiche f.
microfilm, n. microfilm m.
microform, n. microforme f.
microphone, n. microphone m.
microscope, n. microscope m.
microscopic, adj. microscopique.
mid, adj. mi-.
middle, 1. n. milieu m. 2. adj. du milieu.
middle-aged, adj. d'un certain âge.
Middle Ages, n. moyen âge m.
middle class, n. classe moyenne f., bourgeoisie f.
Middle East, n. Moyen Orient m.
midget, n. nain m.
midnight, n. minuit m.
midriff, n. diaphragme m.
midwife, n. sage-femme f.
mien, n. mine f., air m.
might, n. puissance f.
mighty, adj. puissant.
migrate, vb. émigrer.

migration, n. migration f.
mild, adj. doux m., douce f.
mildew, n. rouille f.
mile, n. mille m.
mileage, n. kilométrage m.
milestone, n. borne routière f.
militarism, n. militarisme m.
military, adj. militaire.
militia, n. milice f.
milk, n. lait m.
milkman, n. laitier m.
milky, adj. laiteux.
mill, 1. n. (grinding) moulin m.; (spinning) filature f.; (factory) usine f. 2. vb. (grind) moudre; (crowd) fourmiller.
miller, n. meunier m.
millimeter, n. millimètre m.
milliner, n. modiste f.
millinery, n. modes f.pl.
million, n. million m.
millionaire, adj. and n. millionnaire m.f.
mimic, 1. n. mime m. 2. adj. mimique. 3. vb. imiter.
mince, vb. (chop) hacher.
mind, 1. n. esprit m.; (opinion) avis m.; (desire) envie f. 2. vb. (heed) faire attention à; (listen to) écouter; (apply oneself to) s'occuper de; (take care) prendre garde; (look after) garder; (never m.) n'importe.
mindful, adj. attentif.
mine, 1. n. mine f. 2. pron. le mien m., la mienne f.
mine field, n. champ de mines m.
miner, n. mineur m.
mineral, adj. and n. minéral m.
mine sweeper, n. dragueur de mines m.
mingle, vb. mêler, tr.
miniature, n. miniature f.
miniaturize, vb. miniaturiser.
minimize, vb. réduire au minimum.
minimum, n. minimum m.
minimum wage, n. salaire minimum m.
mining, n. exploitation minière f., pose de mines f.
minister, n. ministre m.
ministry, n. ministère m.
mink, n. vison m.
minnow, n. vairon m.
minor, adj. and n. mineur m.
minority, n. minorité f.
minstrel, n. ménestrel m.
mint, n. (plant) menthe f.; (place) Hôtel (m.) de la Monnaie.
minute, 1. n. minute f.; (of meeting) procès-verbal m. 2. adj. (very small) minuscule; (detailed) minutieux.
miracle, n. miracle m.
miraculous, adj. miraculeux.
mirage, n. mirage m.
mire, n. boue f., bourbier m.
mirror, n. miroir m.
mirth, n. gaieté f.

misadventure, n. mésaventure f., contretemps m.

misappropriate, vb. détourner, dépréder.

misbehave, vb. se mal conduire.

miscellaneous, adj. divers.

mischief, n. (harm) mal m.; (mischievousness) malice f.

mischievous, adj. espiègle; (wicked) méchant.

misconstrue, vb. mal interpréter, tourner en mal.

misdemeanor, n. délit m.

miser, n. avare m.f.

miserable, adj. (unhappy) malheureux; (wretched) misérable.

miserly, adj. avare.

misery, n. (affliction) souffrance(s) f.(pl.); (poverty) misère f.

misfit, n. vêtement manqué m.; inadapté m., inapte m.

misfortune, n. malheur m.

misgiving, n. doute m.

mishap, n. mésaventure f.

mislead, vb. tromper, égarer.

misplace, vb. mal placer.

mispronounce, vb. mal prononcer, estropier.

miss, vb. manquer; (I m. you) vous me manquez.

Miss, n. mademoiselle f.

missile, n. projectile m.

mission, n. mission f.

missionary, adj. and n. missionnaire m.f.

misspell, vb. mal orthographier.

mist, n. brume f.

mistake, 1. n. erreur f. 2. vb. (misunderstand) comprendre mal; (make a mistake) se tromper (de).

mister, n. monsieur m.

mistletoe, n. gui m.

mistreat, vb. maltraiter.

mistress, n. maîtresse f.

mistrust, 1. n. méfiance f. 2. vb. se méfier de.

misty, adj. brumeux.

misunderstand, vb. mal comprendre.

misuse, vb. (misapply) faire mauvais usage (de); (maltreat) maltraiter.

mite, n. denier m., obole f.

mitigate, vb. adoucir.

mitten, n. moufle f.

mix, vb. mêler, tr.

mixture, n. mélange m.

mix-up, n. embrouillement m.

moan, 1. n. gémissement m. 2. vb. gémir.

moat, n. fossé m.

mob, n. foule f.; (pejorative) populace f.

mobile, adj. mobile.

mobilization, n. mobilisation f.

mobilize, vb. mobiliser.

mock, vb. (m. at) se moquer de; (imitate) singer.

mockery, n. moquerie f.

mod, adj. à la mode.

mode, n. mode m.

model, n. modèle m.

moderate, 1. adj. modéré. 2. vb. modérer.

moderation, n. modération f.

modern, adj. moderne.

modernize, vb. moderniser.

modest, adj. modeste.

modesty, n. modestie f.

modify, vb. modifier.

modish, adj. à la mode.

modulate, vb. moduler.

moist, adj. moite.

moisten, vb. humecter.

moisture, n. humidité f.

molar, n. and adj. molaire f.

molasses, n. mélasse f.

mold, 1. n. (casting) moule m.; (mildew) moisissure f. 2. vb. (shape) mouler; (get moldy) moisir.

moldy, adj. moisi.

mole, n. (animal) taupe f.; (spot) grain (m.) de beauté.

molecule, n. molécule f.

molest, vb. molester.

mollify, vb. adoucir, apaiser.

molten, adj. fondu, coulé.

moment, n. moment m.

momentary, adj. momentané.

momentous, adj. important.

monarch, n. monarque m.

monarchy, n. monarchie f.

monastery, n. monastère m.

Monday, n. lundi m.

monetary, adj. monétaire.

money, n. argent m.; (comm.) monnaie f.

mongrel, n. métis m.

monitor, n. moniteur m.

monk, n. moine m.

monkey, n. singe m.

monologue, n. monologue m.

monoplane, n. monoplan m.

monopolize, vb. monopoliser.

monopoly, n. monopole m.

monosyllable, n. monosyllabe m.

monotone, n. monotone f.

monotonous, adj. monotone.

monotony, n. monotonie f.

monsoon, n. mousson f.

monster, n. monstre m.

monstrosity, n. monstruosité f.

monstrous, adj. monstrueux.

month, n. mois m.

monthly, adj. mensuel.

monument, n. monument m.

monumental, adj. monumental.

mood, n. humeur f.; (gramm.) mode m.

moody, adj. de mauvaise humeur.

moon, n. lune f.

moonlight, n. clair (m.) de lune.

moor, n. lande f.

mooring, n. amarrage m.

moot, adj. discutable.

mop, n. balai (m.) à laver.

moped, n. cyclomoteur m.

moral, 1. n. morale f.; (morals) moralité f. 2. adj. moral.

morale, n. moral m.

moralist, n. moraliste m.f.

morality, n. moralité f.; (ethics) morale f.

morally, adv. moralement.

morbid, adj. morbide.

more, 1. pron. en . . . davantage. 2. adj., adv. plus; (m. than) plus de; (no m.) ne . . . plus.

moreover, adv. de plus.

mores, n. mœurs f.pl.

morgue, n. morgue f.

morning, n. matin m.; (length of m.) matinée f.; (good m.) bonjour.

moron, n. idiot.

morose, adj. morose.

Morse code, n. l'alphabet Morse m.

morsel, n. morceau m.

mortal, adj. and n. mortel m.

mortality, n. mortalité f.

mortar, n. mortier m.

mortgage, 1. n. hypothèque f. 2. vb. hypothéquer.

mortician, n. entrepreneur de pompes funèbres m.

mortify, vb. mortifier.

mortuary, adj. mortuaire.

mosaic, 1. n. mosaïque f. 2. adj. en mosaïque.

Moscow, n. Moscou m.

Moslem, adj. and n. musulman m.

mosquito, n. moustique m.

moss, n. mousse f.

most, 1. n. le plus. 2. adj. le plus (de); la plupart (de). 3. adv. (with adj. and vb.) le plus; (intensive) très.

mostly, adv. pour la plupart; (time) la plupart du temps.

moth, n. (clothes) mite f.

mother, n. mère f.

mother-in-law, n. belle-mère f.

motif, n. motif m.

motion, n. mouvement m.; (gesture) signe m.; (proposal) motion f.

motionless, adj. immobile.

motion-picture, n. film m.

motivate, vb. motiver.

motive, n. motif m.

motley, 1. adj. bigarré. 2. n. livrée de bouffon m.

motor, n. moteur m.

motorboat, n. canot (m.) automobile.

motorist, n. automobiliste m.

motto, n. devise f.

mound, n. tertre m.

mount, 1. n. (hill) mont m.; (horse, structure) monture f. 2. vb. monter.

mountain, n. montagne f.

mountaineer, n. montagnard m., Alpiniste m.

mountainous, adj. montagneux.

mountebank, n. saltimbanque m., charlatan m.

mourn, vb. pleurer.

mournful, adj. triste.

mourning, n. deuil m.

mouse, n. souris f.

mouth, n. bouche f.

mouthpiece, n. embouchure f., embout m.

movable, adj. mobile.

move, vb. mouvoir, tr.; remuer; (stir) bouger; (affect with emotion) émouvoir; (change residence) déménager; (propose) proposer.

movement, n. mouvement m.

moving, 1. n. déménagement m. 2. adj. touchant.

mow, vb. faucher; (lawn) tondre.

Mr., n. M. m. (abbr. for Monsieur).

Mrs., n. Mme. f. (abbr. for Madame).

much, adj., pron. and adv. beaucoup (de); (too m.) trop (de); (so m.) tant (de); (how m.) combien (de).

mucilage, n. mucilage m.

muck, n. fumier m.

mucous, adj. muqueux.

mud, n. boue f.

muddy, adj. boueux.

muff, n. manchon m.

muffin, n. petit pain m.

muffle, vb. emmitoufler.

mug, n. gobelet m., pot m.

mulatto, n. mulâtre m.

mule, n. mulet m.

mullah, n. mollah m.

multicolored, adj. multicolore.

multinational, adj. multinational.

multiple, adj. multiple.

multiplication, n. multiplication f.

multiplicity, n. multiplicité f.

multiply, vb. multiplier, tr.

multitude, n. multitude f.

mummy, n. momie f.; maman f.

mumps, n. oreillons m.pl.

munch, vb. mâcher.

municipal, adj. municipal.

munificent, adj. munificent.

munition, n. munition(s) f.

mural, n. (painting) peinture (f.) murale.

murder, n. meurtre m.

murderer, n. meurtrier m.

murmur, 1. n. murmure m. 2. vb. murmurer.

muscle, n. muscle m.

muscular, adj. musculaire; (strong) musculeux.

muse, 1. n. muse f. 2. vb. méditer.

museum, n. musée m.

mushroom, n. champignon m.

music, n. musique f.

musical, adj. musical; (person) musicien.

musical comedy, n. comédie musicale f.

musician, n. musicien m.

Muslim, adj. and n. musulman m.

muslin, n. mousseline f.

must, vb. devoir; falloir (used impersonally, il faut que).

mustache, n. moustache f.

mustard, n. moutarde f.

muster, vb. rassembler, tr.

musty, adj. moisi, suranné.

mutation, n. mutation f.

mute, adj. muet.

mutilate, vb. mutiler.

mutiny, n. mutinerie f.

mutter, vb. grommeler.

mutton, n. mouton m.

mutual, adj. mutuel.

muzzle, n. muselière f.

my, adj. mon m., ma f., mes pl.

myopia, n. myopie f.

myriad, n. myriade f.

myrtle, n. myrte m.

myself, pron. moi-même; (reflexive) me.

mysterious, adj. mystérieux.

mystery, n. mystère m.

mystic, adj. mystique.

mystify, vb. mystifier.

myth, n. mythe m.

mythical, adj. mythique.

mythology, n. mythologie f.

N

nag, vb. gronder.

nail, 1. n. (person, animal) ongle m.; (metal) clou m. 2. vb. clouer.

naïve, adj. naïf m., naïve f.

naked, adj. nu.

name, 1. n. nom m. 2. vb. nommer.

namesake, n. homonyme m.

nap, n. petit somme m.

napkin, n. serviette f.

narcissus, n. narcisse m.

narcotic, adj. and n. narcotique m.

narrate, vb. raconter.

narrative, n. récit m.

narrow, adj. étroit.

nasal, adj. nasal.

nasty, adj. désagréable.

natal, adj. natal.

nation, n. nation f.

national, adj. national.

nationalism, n. nationalisme m.

nationality, n. nationalité f.

nationalization, n. nationalisation f.

nationalize, vb. nationaliser.

native, 1. n. natif m.; (primitive inhabitant, etc.) indigène m.f. 2. adj. natif; (place) natal; (language) maternel.

nativity, n. naissance f.

natural, adj. naturel.

naturalist, n. naturaliste m.

naturalize, vb. naturaliser.

naturalness, n. naturel m.

nature, n. nature f.

naughty, adj. méchant.

nausea, n. nausée f.

nauseous, adj. nauséeux.

nautical, adj. marin.

naval, adj. naval.

nave, n. nef f.

navigable, adj. navigable.

navigate, vb. naviguer.

navigation, n. navigation f.

navigator, n. navigateur m.

navy, n. marine f.

navy yard, n. arsenal maritime m.

near, 1. adj. proche. 2. adv. près. 3. prep. près de.

nearly, adv. de près; (almost) presque.

near-sighted, adj. myope.

neat, adj. propre.

neatness, n. propreté f.

nebula, n. nébuleuse f.

nebulous, adj. nébuleux.

necessary, adj. nécessaire.

necessity, n. nécessité f.

neck, n. cou m.

necklace, n. collier m.

necktie, n. cravate f.

nectar, n. nectar m.

need, 1. n. besoin m. 2. vb. avoir besoin de.

needful, adj. nécessaire.

needle, n. aiguille f.

needle point, n. pointe d'aiguille f.

needless, adj. inutile.

needy, adj. nécessiteux.

nefarious, adj. infâme.

negative, adj. négatif.

neglect, 1. n. négligence f. 2. vb. négliger (de).

negligee, n. négligée f.

negligent, adj. négligent.

negligible, adj. négligeable.

negotiate, vb. négocier.

negotiation, n. négociation f.

Negro, adj. and n. nègre m.

neighbor, n. voisin m.; (fellow man) prochain m.

neighborhood, n. voisinage m.

neither, 1. adj. and pron. ni l'un ni l'autre. 2. adv. non plus. 3. conj. (n. . . . nor) ni . . . ni.

neon, n. néon m.

neophyte, n. néophyte m.

nephew, n. neveu m.

nepotism, n. népotisme m.

nerve, n. nerf m.

nervous, adj. nerveux.

nervous system, n. système nerveux m.

nest, n. nid m.

nestle, vb. se nicher.

net, 1. n. filet m. 2. adj. net m., nette f.

Netherlands, the, n. les Pays-Bas m.pl., Hollande f.

network, n. réseau m.

neuralgia, n. névralgie f.

neurology, n. neurologie f.

neurotic, adj. and n. névrosé m.

neutral, adj. and n. neutre m.

neutron, n. neutron m.

neutron bomb, n. bombe à neutrons f.

never, adv. jamais.

nevertheless, adv. néanmoins.

new, adj. nouveau m., nouvelle f.; (not used) neuf m., neuve f.

news, n. (piece of news) nouvelle f.

newsboy, n. vendeur (m.) de journaux.

newscast, n. journal parlé m., informations f.pl.

newspaper, n. journal m.

newsreel, n. film d'actualité m.

New Testament, n. le Nouveau Testament m.

new year, n. nouvel an m.

next, 1. adj. prochain. 2. adv. ensuite. 3. prep. auprès de.

nibble, vb. grignoter.

nice, adj. (person) gentil; (thing) joli.

nick, n. entaille f.

nickel, n. nickel m.

nickname, n. surnom m.

nicotine, n. nicotine f.

niece, n. nièce f.

niggardly, adj. chiche.

night, n. nuit f.; (evening) soir m.

night club, n. boîte de nuit f., établissement de nuit m.

nightgown, n. chemise (f.) de nuit.

nightingale, n. rossignol m.

nightly, adv. tous les soirs; toutes les nuits.

nightmare, n. cauchemar m.

nimble, adj. agile.

nine, adj. and n. neuf m.

nineteen, adj. and n. dix-neuf m.

ninety, adj. and n. quatre-vingt-dix m.

ninth, adj. and n. neuvième m.

nip, 1. n. pincement m., pinçade f. 2. vb. pincer.

nipple, n. mamelon m.

nitrogen, n. nitrogène m.

no, 1. adj. pas de. 2. interj., adv. non.

nobility, n. noblesse f.

noble, adj. noble.

nobleman, n. gentilhomme m.

nobly, adv. noblement.

nobody, pron. personne.

nocturnal, adj. nocturne.

nod, 1. n. signe (m.) de la tête. 2. vb. incliner la tête.

node, n. nœud m.

no-frills, adj. simple.

noise, n. bruit m.

noiseless, adj. silencieux.

noisome, n. puant, fétide.

noisy, adj. bruyant.

nomad, n. nomade m. and f.

nominal, adj. nominal.

nominate, vb. (appoint) nommer; (propose) désigner.

nomination, n. (appointment) nomination f.; (proposal) désignation f.

nominee, n. personne nommée f., candidat choisi m.

nonaligned, adj. (in politics) non-aligné.

nonchalant, adj. nonchalant.

noncombatant, adj. and n. non-combattant m.

noncommissioned, adj. sans brevet.

noncommittal, adj. qui n'engage à rien.

nondescript, adj. indéfinissable.

none, pron. aucun.

nonentity, n. nullité f.

non-proliferation, n. non-prolifération m.

nonresident, n. and adj. non-résident m.

nonsense, n. absurdité f.

nonstop, adj. sans arrêt.

noodles, n. nouilles f.pl.

nook, n. coin m., recoin m.

noon, n. midi m.

noose, n. nœud coulant m.

nor, conj. ni; (and not) et ne ... pas.

normal, adj. normal.

normally, adv. normalement.

north, n. nord m.

North America, n. Amérique (f.) du Nord.

northeast, n. nord-est m.

northern, adj. du nord.

North Pole, n. pôle nord m.

northwest, n. nord-ouest m.

Norway, n. Norvège f.

Norwegian, 1. n. (person) Norvégien m.; (language) norvégien m. 2. adj. norvégien.

nose, n. nez m.

nosebleed, n. saignement du nez m.

nose dive, n. vol piqué m.

nostalgia, n. nostalgie f.

nostril, n. narine f.; (animals) naseau m.

nostrum, n. panacée f., remède de charlatan m.

not, adv. (ne) pas.

notable, adj. and n. notable m.

notation, n. notation f.

note, 1. n. note f.; (letter, finance) billet m.; (distinction) marque f. 2. vb. noter.

notebook, n. (small) carnet m.; (large) cahier m.

noted, adj. célèbre.

notepaper, n. papier à notes m.

noteworthy, adj. remarquable, mémorable.

nothing, pron. rien.

notice, 1. n. (announcement) avis m.; (attention) attention f.; (forewarning) préavis m. 2. vb. remarquer.

noticeable, adj. remarquable, apparent.

notification, n. notification f.

notify, vb. avertir.

notion, n. idée f.

notoriety, n. notoriété f.

notorious, adj. notoire.

notwithstanding, 1. adv. tout de même. 2. prep. malgré.

noun, n. substantif m.

nourish, vb. nourrir.

nourishment, n. nourriture f.

novel, n. roman m.

novelist, n. romancier m.

novelty, n. nouveauté f.

November, n. novembre m.

novice, n. novice m.f.

now, adv. maintenant; (n. and then) de temps en temps.

nowhere, adv. nulle part.

nozzle, n. ajutage m., jet m.

nuance, n. nuance f.

nuclear, adj. nucléaire.

nuclear physics, n. physique nucléaire f.

nuclear warhead, n. cône de charge nucléaire m.

nuclear waste, n. déchets nucléaires m.pl.

nucleus, n. noyau m.

nude, adj. and n. nu m.

nugget, n. pépite f.

nuisance, n. (thing) ennui m.; (person) peste f.

nuke, 1. n. arme nucléaire f. 2. vb. détruire avec des armes nucléaires.

nullify, vb. annuler, nullifier.

number, 1. n. nombre m.; (in a series, street, etc.) numéro m. 2. vb. compter, numéroter.

numerical, adj. numérique.

numerous, adj. nombreux.

nun, n. religieuse f.

nuncio, n. nonce m.

nuptial, adj. nuptial.

nurse, 1. n. (hospital) infirmière f.; (wet-n.) nourrice f. 2. vb. soigner; (suckle) allaiter.

nursery, n. (children) chambre (f.) des enfants; (plants) pépinière f.

nurture, 1. n. nourriture f. 2. vb. nourrir, entretenir.

nut, n. noix f.; (metal) écrou m.

nutcracker, n. casse-noix m.

nutrition, n. nutrition f.

nutritious, adj. nutritif.

nutshell, n. coquille de noix f.; (in a n.) en deux mots.

nylon, n. nylon m.

nymph, n. nymphe f.

O

oak, n. chêne m.

oar, n. rame f.

oasis, n. oasis f.

oath, n. serment m.; (curse) juron m.

oatmeal, n. farine d'avoine f.

oats, n. avoine f.

obdurate, adj. obstiné, têtu.

obedience, n. obéissance f.

obedient, adj. obéissant.

obeisance, n. salut m.

obelisk, n. obélisque m.

obey, vb. obéir à.

obituary, n. nécrologe m.

object, 1. n. objet m. 2. vb. objecter.

objection, n. objection f.

objectionable, adj. répréhensible.

objective, adj. and n. objectif m.

obligation, n. obligation f.

obligatory, adj. obligatoire.

oblige, vb. obliger.

oblivion, n. oubli m.

obnoxious, adj. odieux.

obscene, adj. obscène.

obscure, adj. obscur.

obsequious, adj. obséquieux.

observance, n. observance f.

observation, n. observation f.

observe, vb. observer.

observer, n. observateur m.

obsession, n. obsession f.

obsolete, adj. désuet.

obstacle, n. obstacle m.

obstetrician, n. médecin-accoucheur m.

obstinate, adj. obstiné.

obstreperous, adj. tapageur.

obstruct, vb. obstruer.

obstruction, n. obstruction f.

obtain, vb. obtenir.

obtrude, vb. mettre en avant.

obviate, vb. prévenir, éviter.

obvious, adj. évident.

occasion, n. occasion f.

occasional, adj. (not regular) de temps en temps.

occult, adj. occulte.

occupant, n. occupant m.

occupation, n. occupation f.; (vocation) métier m.

occupy, vb. occuper.

occur, vb. (happen) avoir lieu; (come to the mind) se présenter à l'esprit.

occurrence, n. occurrence f.

ocean, n. océan m.

o'clock, see clock.

octagon, n. octogone m.

octave, n. octave f.

October, n. octobre m.

octopus, n. poulpe m.

ocular, adj. oculaire.

oculist, n. oculiste f.

odd, adj. (not even) impair; (unmatched) dépareillé; (strange) bizarre.

oddity, n. singularité f.

odds, n. inégalité f., (betting) cote f.

odious, adj. odieux.

odor, n. odeur f.

of, prep. de.

off, 1. adv. (away) à . . . de distance; (cancelled) rompu. 2. prep. de.

offend, vb. offenser; (o. against the law) enfreindre la loi.

offender, n. offenseur m.; (law) délinquant m.

offense, n. offense f.; (transgression) délit m.

offensive, 1. n. offensive f. 2. adj. (mil., etc.) offensif; (word, etc.) offensant.

offer, 1. n. offre f. 2. vb. offrir.

offering, n. offre f., offrande f.

offhand, 1. adj. spontané. 2. adv. sans préparation.

office, n. (service) office m.; (function) fonctions f.pl.; (room) bureau m.

officer, n. (mil.) officier m.; (public) fonctionnaire m.

official, n. officiel.

officiate, vb. officier.

officious, adj. officieux.

offshore, 1. adv. vers le large. 2. adj. du côté de la terre.

offspring, n. descendant m.

often, adv. souvent.

oil, n. huile f.

oilcloth, n. toile cirée f.

oily, adj. huileux.

ointment, n. onguent m.

okay, interj. très bien.

old, adj. vieux (vieil) m., vieille f.; (how o. are you?) quel âge avez-vous?

old-fashioned, adj. démodé.

Old Testament, n. l'Ancien Testament m.

olfactory, adj. olfactif.

oligarchy, n. oligarchie f.

olive, n. (tree) olivier m.; (fruit) olive f.

ombudsman, n. (in France) médiateur m.; (in Quebec) protecteur du citoyen m.

omelet, n. omelette f.

omen, n. présage m.

ominous, adj. de mauvais augure.

omission, n. omission f.

omit, vb. omettre.

omnibus, n. omnibus m.

omnipotent, adj. omnipotent, tout-puissant.

on, prep. sur.

once, adv. une fois; (formerly) autrefois; (at o., without delay) tout de suite; (at o., at the same time) à la fois.

one, 1. adj. un; (only) seul. 2. n. un m. 3. pron. un; (indefinite subject) on, (indefinite object) vous; (the o.) celui; (this o.) celui-ci; (that o.) celui-là; (which o.) lequel.

oneself, pron. soi-même; (reflexive) se.

one-sided, adj. unilatéral.

onion, n. oignon m.

onionskin, n. pelure d'oignon f., (paper) papier pelure m.

only, 1. adj. seul. 2. adv. seulement.

onslaught, n. assaut m.

onward, adj. and adv. en avant.

opal, n. opale f.

opaque, adj. opaque.

open, 1. adj. ouvert. 2. vb. ouvrir.

opening, n. ouverture f.

opera, n. opéra m.

opera glasses, n. jumelles f.pl.

operate, vb. opérer; (put into operation) actionner.

operatic, adj. d'opéra.

operation, n. opération f.; (functioning) fonctionnement m.

operator, n. opérateur m.; (telephone) employé m.

operetta, n. opérette f.

opinion, n. opinion f.

opponent, n. adversaire m.f.

opportunism, n. opportunisme m.

opportunity, n. occasion f.

oppose, vb. (put in opposition) opposer; (resist) s'opposer à.

opposite, 1. adj. opposé. 2. adv.

vis-à-vis. 3. prep. en face de.

opposition, n. opposition f.

oppress, vb. opprimer.

oppression, n. oppression f.

oppressive, adj. oppressif; (heat, etc.) accablant.

optic, adj. optique.

optician, n. opticien m.

optimism, n. optimisme m.

optimistic, adj. optimiste.

option, n. option f.

optional, adj. facultatif.

optometry, n. optométrie f.

opulent, adj. opulent, riche.

or, conj. ou; (with negative) ni.

oracle, n. oracle m.

oral, adj. oral.

orange, n. orange f.

orangeade, n. orangeade f.

oration, n. discours m.

orator, n. orateur m.

oratory, n. art (m.) oratoire.

orbit, n. orbite f.

orchard, n. verger m.

orchestra, n. orchestre m.

orchid, n. orchidée f.

ordain, vb. ordonner.

ordeal, n. épreuve f.

order, 1. n. ordre m.; (comm.) commande f. 2. vb. ordonner; (comm.) commander.

orderly, adj. ordonné.

ordinance, n. ordonnance f.

ordinary, adj. and n. ordinaire m.

ordination, n. ordination f.

ore, n. minerai m.

organ, n. (music) orgue m.; (body) organe m.

organdy, n. organdi m.

organic, adj. organique.

organism, n. organisme m.

organist, n. organiste m.f.

organization, n. organisation f.

organize, vb. organiser.

orgy, n. orgie f.

orient, vb. orienter.

Orient, n. Orient m.

Oriental, 1. n. Oriental m. 2. adj. oriental.

orientation, n. orientation f.

origin, n. origine f.

original, adj. (new, unique) original; (from the origin) originel.

originality, n. originalité f.

ornament, n. ornement m.

ornamental, adj. ornemental.

ornate, adj. orné.

ornithology, n. ornithologie f.

orphan, n. orphelin m.

orphanage, n. orphelinat m.

orthodox, adj. orthodoxe.

orthopedics, n. orthopédie f.

osmosis, n. osmose f.

ostensible, adj. prétendu.

ostentation, n. ostentation f.

ostentatious, adj. plein d'ostentation.

ostracize, vb. ostraciser.

ostrich, n. autruche f.

other, adj. and pron. autre.

otherwise, adv. autrement.

ought, vb. devoir.

ounce, n. once f.

our, adj. notre sg., nos pl.

ours, pron. le nôtre.

ourself, pron. nous-même; (reflexive) nous.

oust, vb. évincer.

ouster, n. éviction f.

out, adv. dehors.

outbreak, n. (beginning) commencement m.; (insurrection) révolte f.

outburst, n. éruption f.

outcast, n. paria m.

outcome, n. résultat m.

outdoors, adv. dehors.

outer, adj. extérieur.

outfit, n. équipement m.

outgrowth, n. conséquence f.

outing, n. promenade f.

outlandish, adj. bizarre.

outlaw, vb. proscrire.

outlet, n. issue f.

outline, 1. n. contour m.; (general idea) aperçu m. **2.** vb. (drawing) tracer; (plan) exposer à grands traits.

out of, prep. hors de; (because of) par; (without) sans.

out-of-date, adj. suranné.

output, n. rendement m.

outrage, n. outrage m.

outrageous, adj. outrageant.

outrank, vb. occuper un rang supérieur.

outright, adv. complètement.

outrun, vb. dépasser.

outside, 1. adv. dehors. **2.** prep. en dehors de.

outskirts, n. limites f.pl.

outward, adj. extérieur.

oval, adj. and n. ovale m.

ovation, n. ovation f.

oven, n. four m.

over, 1. prep. (on) sur; (above) au-dessus de; (beyond) au delà de; (more than) plus de. **2.** adj. (all over) partout; (more) davantage; (finished) fini; (with adj.) trop.

overbearing, adj. arrogant.

overcoat, n. pardessus m.

overcome, vb. vaincre; (be o. by) succomber à.

overdue, adj. arriéré, échu.

overflow, vb. déborder.

overhaul, vb. examiner en détail, remettre au point.

overhead, 1. adj. (comm.) général. **2.** adv. en haut.

overkill, n. exagération rhétorique f.

overlook, vb (look on to) avoir vue sur; (neglect) négliger.

overnight, adv. pendant la nuit.

overpower, vb. (subdue) subjuguer; (crush) accabler.

overrule, vb. décider contre.

overrun, vb. envahir.

oversee, vb. surveiller.

oversight, n. inadvertance f.

overstuffed, adj. rembourré.

overt, adj. manifeste.

overtake, vb. rattraper; (accident, etc.) arriver à.

overthrow, vb. renverser.

overtime, n. heures (f.pl.) supplémentaires.

overture, n. ouverture f.

overturn, vb. renverser, tr.

overview, n. vue d'ensemble f.

overweight, n. excédent m.

overwhelm, vb. accabler (de).

overwork, vb. surmener, tr.

owe, vb. devoir.

owing, 1. prep. à cause de, en raison de. **2.** adj. dû.

owl, n. hibou m.

own, 1. adj. propre. **2.** vb. posséder; (admit) avouer; (acknowledge) reconnaître.

owner, n. propriétaire m.f.

ox, n. bœuf m.

oxygen, n. oxygène m.

oxygen mask, n. masque d'oxygène m.

oyster, n. huître f.

P

pace, 1. n. (step) pas m.; (gait) allure f. **2.** vb. arpenter.

pacific, adj. pacifique.

Pacific Ocean, n. océan Pacifique m.

pacifism, n. pacifisme m.

pacify, vb. pacifier.

pack, 1. n. paquet m.; (animals, persons) bande f. **2.** vb. emballer; (crowd) entasser.

package, n. paquet m.

pact, n. pacte m., contrat m.

pad, 1. n. (stuffing) bourrelet m.; (cotton, ink) tampon m.; (paper) bloc m. **2.** vb. (clothes) ouater; (stuff) bourrer.

padding, n. remplissage m., rembourrage m.

paddle, n. pagaie f.

paddock, n. enclos m.

pagan, adj. and n. païen m.

page, n. (book) page f.; (attendant) page m.

pageant, n. spectacle m.

pagoda, n. pagode f.

pail, n. seau m.

pain, 1. n. douleur f.; (trouble) peine f. **2.** vb. (hurt) faire mal (à); (distress) faire de la peine (à).

painful, adj. douloureux.

painstaking, adj. soigneux.

paint, 1. n. peinture f. **2.** vb. peindre.

painter, n. peintre m.

painting, n. peinture f.

pair, n. paire f.

pajamas, n. pyjama m.

palace, n. palais m.

palatable, adj. d'un goût agréable, agréable au palais.

palate, n. palais m.

palatial, adj. qui ressemble à un palais, magnifique.

pale, adj. pâle.

paleness, n. pâleur f.

palette, n. palette f.

pall, 1. n. drap funéraire m. **2.** vb. s'affadir.

pallbearer, n. porteur (d'un cordon du poêle) m.

pallid, adj. pâle, blême.

palm, n. (tree) palmier m.; (branch) palme f.; (hand) paume f.

palpitate, vb. palpiter.

paltry, adj. mesquin.

pamper, vb. choyer.

pamphlet, n. brochure f.

pan, n. (cooking) casserole f.

panacea, n. panacée f.

Pan-American, adj. panaméricain.

pancake, n. crêpe f.

pane, n. (window) vitre f.

panel, n. panneau m.

pang, n. angoisse f.

panic, n. panique f.

panorama, n. panorama m.

pant, vb. haleter.

pantomime, n. pantomime m.

pantry, n. office f.

pants, n. pantalon m.

panty hose, n. collant m.

papal, adj. papal.

paper, n. papier m.

paperback, n. livre broché m.

par, n. pair m., égalité f.

parable, n. parabole f.

parachute, n. parachute m.

parade, n. parade f.

paradise, n. paradis m.

paradox, n. paradoxe m.

paraffin, n. paraffine f.

paragraph, n. alinéa m.

parakeet, n. perruche f.

parallel, 1. n. (line) parallèle f.; (geography, comparison) parallèle m. **2.** adj. parallèle.

paralyze, vb. paralyser.

paramedic, n. assistant médical m.

parameter, n. paramètre m.

paramount, adj. souverain.

paraphrase, vb. paraphraser.

parasite, n. parasite m.

parcel, n. paquet m.; (p. post) colis postal m.

parch, vb. dessécher, tr.

parchment, n. parchemin m.

pardon, 1. n. pardon m. **2.** vb. pardonner.

pare, vb. (fruit) peler.

parent, n. père m.; mère f.; (parents) parents m.pl.

parentage, n. naissance f.

parenthesis, n. parenthèse f.

parish, n. paroisse f.

Parisian, 1. n. Parisien m. **2.** adj. parisien.

parity, n. parité f., égalité f.

park, 1. n. parc m. **2.** vb. stationner.

parley, n. conférence f., pourparler m.

parliament, n. parlement m.

parliamentary, adj. parlementaire.

parlor, n. petit salon m.

parochial, adj. paroissial; (limited in outlook) de clocher.

parody, n. parodie f.

parole, 1. *n.* parole *f.* **2.** *vb.* libérer conditionnellement.

paroxysm, *n.* paroxysme *m.*

parrot, *n.* perroquet *m.*

parsley, *n.* persil *m.*

parson, *n.* pasteur *m.*

part, 1. *n.* (of a whole) partie *f.;* (share) part *f.* **2.** *vb.* (divide) diviser; (share) partager; (of people) se séparer.

partake of, *vb.* participer à.

partial, *adj.* partiel; (favoring) partial.

participant, *adj. and n.* participant *m.*

participate, *vb.* participer.

participation, *n.* participation *f.*

participle, *n.* participe *m.*

particle, *n.* particule *f.*

particular, 1. *n.* détail *m.* **2.** *adj.* particulier; (person) exigeant.

parting, *n.* séparation *f.;* (hair) raie *f.*

partisan, *n.* partisan *m.*

partition, *n.* partage *m.;* (wall) cloison *f.*

partly, *adv.* en partie.

partner, *n.* associé *m.*

part of speech, *n.* partie (*f.*) du discours.

partridge, *n.* perdrix *f.*

party, *n.* (faction) parti *m.;* (social) réception *f.;* (group of people) groupe *m.;* (law) partie *f.*

pass, 1. *n.* (mountain) col *m.;* (permission) laissez-passer *m.* **2.** *vb.* passer.

passable, *adj.* traversable, passable, assez bon.

passage, *n.* passage *m.*

passenger, *n.* (land) voyageur *m.;* (sea, air) passager *m.*

passer-by, *n.* passant *m.*

passion, *n.* passion *f.*

passionate, *adj.* passionné.

passive, *adj. and n.* passif *m.*

passport, *n.* passeport *m.*

past, 1. *adj. and n.* passé *m.* **2.** *prep.* (beyond) au delà de; (more than) plus de; (half p. four) quatre heures et demie.

paste, 1. *n.* pâte *f.;* (glue) colle *f.* **2.** *vb.* coller.

pasteurize, *vb.* pasteuriser.

pastime, *n.* passe-temps *m.*

pastor, *n.* pasteur *m.*

pastry, *n.* pâtisserie *f.*

pasture, *n.* pâturage *m.*

pasty, *adj.* empâté, pâteux.

pat, *vb.* taper.

patch, 1. *n.* pièce *f.* **2.** *vb.* rapiécer.

patchwork, *n.* ouvrage fait de pièces disparates *m.*

patent, *n.* brevet (*m.*) d'invention.

patent leather, *n.* cuir (*m.*) verni.

paternal, *adj.* paternel.

paternity, *n.* paternité *f.*

path, *n.* sentier *m.*

pathetic, *adj.* pathétique.

pathology, *n.* pathologie *f.*

pathos, *n.* pathétique *m.*

patience, *n.* patience *f.*

patient, 1. *n.* malade *m.f.* **2.** *adj.* patient.

patio, *n.* patio *m.*

patriarch, *n.* patriarche *m.*

patriot, *n.* patriote *m.*

patriotic, *adj.* patriotique.

patriotism, *n.* patriotisme *m.*

patrol, *n.* patrouille *f.*

patrolman, *n.* agent (de police) *m.,* patrouilleur *m.*

patron, *n.* protecteur *m.;* (comm.) client *m.*

patronize, *vb.* protéger.

pattern, *n.* modèle *m.;* (design) dessin *m.*

pauper, *n.* indigent *m.,* pauvre *m.,* mendiant *m.*

pause, *n.* pause *f.*

pave, *vb.* paver.

pavement, *n.* pavé *m.;* (sidewalk) trottoir *m.*

pavilion, *n.* pavillon *f.*

paw, *n.* patte *f.*

pawn, 1. *n.* pion *m.* **2.** *vb.* mettre en gage, engager.

pay, 1. *n.* salaire *m.* **2.** *vb.* payer.

payment, *n.* payement *m.*

pea, *n.* pois *m.*

peace, *n.* paix *f.*

peaceable, peaceful, *adj.* paisible.

peach, *n.* pêche *f.*

peacock, *n.* paon *m.*

peak, *n.* sommet *m.*

peal, 1. *n.* retentissement *m.* **2.** *vb.* sonner, retentir.

peanut, *n.* arachide *f.*

pear, *n.* poire *f.*

pearl, *n.* perle *f.*

peasant, *n.* paysan *m.*

pebble, *n.* caillou *m.*

peck, *vb.* becqueter.

peculiar, *adj.* particulier; (unusual) singulier.

pecuniary, *adj.* pécuniaire.

pedagogue, *n.* pédagogue *m.*

pedagogy, *n.* pédagogie *f.*

pedal, *n.* pédale *f.*

pedant, *n.* pédant *m.*

peddle, *vb.* colporter.

peddler, *n.* colporteur *m.*

pedestal, *n.* piédestal *m.*

pedestrian, *n.* piéton *m.*

pediatrician, *n.* pédiatre *m.*

pedigree, *n.* généalogie *f.*

peek, 1. *n.* coup d'œil furtif *m.* **2.** *vb.* regarder à la dérobée.

peel, 1. *n.* pelure *f.* **2.** *vb.* peler.

peep, *vb.* regarder furtivement.

peer, 1. *n.* pair *m.,* pareil *m.* **2.** *vb.* scruter, regarder.

peevish, *adj.* irritable.

peg, *n.* cheville *f.*

pelt, 1. *n.* peau *f.,* fourrure *f.* **2.** *vb.* lancer, jeter.

pelvis, *n.* bassin *m.*

pen, *n.* plume *f.*

penalty, *n.* peine *f.*

penance, *n.* pénitence *f.*

penchant, *n.* penchant *m.*

pencil, *n.* crayon *m.*

pending, *prep.* pendant.

penetrate, *vb.* pénétrer.

penetration, *n.* pénétration *f.*

peninsula, *n.* péninsule *f.*

penitent, 1. *adj.* pénitent, contrit. **2.** *n.* pénitent *m.*

penknife, *n.* canif *m.*

penniless, *adj.* sans le sou.

penny, *n.* sou *m.*

pension, *n.* pension *f.*

pensive, *adj.* pensif.

pent-up, *adj.* refoulé.

penury, *n.* pénurie *f.*

people, 1. *n.* gens *m.f.pl.;* (of a country) peuple *m.* **2.** *vb.* peupler.

pepper, *n.* poivre *m.*

perambulator, *n.* voiture d'enfant *f.*

perceive, *vb.* apercevoir, *tr.*

percent, pour cent.

percentage, *n.* pourcentage *m.*

perceptible, *adj.* perceptible.

perception, *n.* perception *f.*

perch, 1. *n.* (for birds) perchoir *m.;* (fish) perche *f.* **2.** *vb.* se percher.

perdition, *n.* perte *f.*

peremptory, *adj.* péremptoire.

perennial, *adj.* perpétuel; (plant) vivace.

perfect, *adj.* parfait.

perfection, *n.* perfection *f.*

perforation, *n.* perforation *f.*

perform, *vb.* accomplir; (theater) jouer.

performance, *n.* (task) accomplissement *m.;* (theater) représentation *f.*

perfume, *n.* parfum *m.*

perfunctory, *adj.* fait pour la forme, superficiel.

perhaps, *adv.* peut-être.

peril, *n.* péril *m.*

perilous, *adj.* périlleux.

perimeter, *n.* périmètre *m.*

period, *n.* période *f.;* (full stop) point *m.*

periodic, *adj.* périodique.

periodical, *n.* périodique *m.*

periphery, *n.* périphérie *f.*

perish, *vb.* périr.

perishable, *adj.* périssable.

perjury, *n.* parjure *m.*

permanent, *adj.* permanent.

permeate, *vb.* filtrer.

permissible, *adj.* admissible.

permission, *n.* permission *f.*

permit, 1. *n.* permis *m.* **2.** *vb.* permettre.

pernicious, *adj.* pernicieux.

perpendicular, *adj.* perpendiculaire, vertical.

perpetrate, *vb.* perpétrer.

perpetual, *adj.* perpétuel.

perplex, *vb.* mettre dans la perplexité.

perplexity, *n.* perplexité *f.,* embarras *m.*

persecute, *vb.* persécuter.

persecution, *n.* persécution *f.*

perseverance, *n.* persévérance *f.*

persevere, *vb.* persévérer.

persist, *vb.* persister.

persistent, *adj.* persistant.

person, *n.* personne *f.*

personage, *n.* personnage *m.*

personal, *adj.* personnel.

personality, *n.* personnalité *f.*

personally, *adv.* personnellement.

personnel, *n.* personnel *m.*

perspective, *n.* perspective *f.*

perspiration, *n.* transpiration *f.*

perspire, *vb.* transpirer.

persuade, *vb.* persuader.

persuasive, *adj.* persuasif.

pertain, *vb.* appartenir.

pertinent, *adj.* pertinent.

perturb, *vb.* troubler.

peruse, *vb.* lire attentivement.

pervade, *vb.* pénétrer.

perverse, *adj.* entêté (dans l'erreur).

perversion, *n.* perversion *f.*

pessimism, *n.* pessimisme *m.*

pestilence, *n.* pestilence *f.*

pet, *n.* (animal) animal *(m.)* familier.

petal, *n.* pétale *m.*

petition, *n.* pétition *f.*

petroleum, *n.* pétrole *m.*

petticoat, *n.* jupon *m.*

petty, *adj.* insignifiant.

phantom, *n.* fantôme *m.*

pharmacist, *n.* pharmacien *m.*

pharmacy, *n.* pharmacie *f.*

phase, *n.* phase *f.*

phenomenal, *adj.* phénoménal.

phenomenon, *n.* phénomène *m.*

philanthropy, *n.* philanthropie *f.*

philosopher, *n.* philosophe *m.*

philosophical, *adj.* philosophique.

philosophy, *n.* philosophie *f.*

phobia, *n.* phobie *f.*

phonograph, *n.* phonographe *m.*

photocopier, *n.* photocopieur *m.*

photocopy, *n.* photocopie *f.*

photograph, photography, *n.* photographie *f.*

phrase, *n.* phrase *f.*

physical, *adj.* physique.

physician, *n.* médecin *m.*

physics, *n.* physique *f.*

pianist, *n.* pianiste *m.f.*

piano, *n.* piano *m.*

pick, *vb.* (choose) choisir; (gather) cueillir.

pickles, *n.* conserves *(f.pl.)* au vinaigre.

picnic, *n.* pique-nique *m.*

picture, *n.* tableau *m.;* (motion picture) film *m.*

picturesque, *adj.* pittoresque.

pie, *n.* tarte *f.*

piece, *n.* morceau *m.*

pier, *n.* jetée *f.;* quai *m.*

pierce, *vb.* percer.

piety, *n.* piété *f.*

pig, *n.* cochon *m.*

pigeon, *n.* pigeon *m.*

pigeonhole, *n.* (for papers, etc.) case *f.*

pile, 1. *n.* (construction) pieu *m.;* (heap) tas *m.* 2. *vb.* entasser.

pilgrim, *n.* pèlerin *m.*

pilgrimage, *n.* pèlerinage *m.*

pill, *n.* pilule *f.*

pillar, *n.* pilier *m.*

pillow, *n.* oreiller *m.*

pilot, *n.* pilote *m.*

pimple, *n.* bouton *m.*

pin, 1. *n.* épingle *f.* 2. *vb.* épingler.

pinch, *vb.* pincer.

pine, 1. *n.* pin *m.* 2. *vb.* languir.

pineapple, *n.* ananas *m.*

pink, *adj. and n.* rose *m.*

pinnacle, *n.* pinacle *m.*

pint, *n.* pinte *f.*

pioneer, *n.* pionnier *m.*

pious, *adj.* pieux.

pipe, *n.* tuyau *m.;* (smoking) pipe *f.*

piper, *n.* (bagpipe) joueur *(m.)* de cornemuse.

piquant, *adj.* piquant.

pirate, *n.* pirate *m.*

pistol, *n.* pistolet *m.*

piston, *n.* piston *m.*

pit, *n.* fosse *f.*

pitch, 1. *n.* (substance) poix *f.;* (throw) jet *m.;* (height) hauteur *f.;* (music) ton *m.* 2. *vb.* (throw) lancer.

pitcher, *n.* (vessel) cruche *f.;* (baseball) lanceur *m.*

pitfall, *n.* trappe *f.*

pitiful, *adj.* pitoyable.

pitiless, *adj.* impitoyable.

pity, 1. *n.* pitié *f.;* (what a p.!) quel dommage! 2. *vb.* plaindre.

pivot, *n.* pivot *m.,* axe *m.*

pizza, *n.* pizza *f.*

place, 1. *n.* endroit *m.;* (locality) lieu *m.;* (position occupied) place *f.* 2. *vb.* mettre.

placid, *adj.* placide.

plague, *n.* (disease) peste *f.;* (*fig.*) fléau *m.*

plaid, *n.* (blanket) plaid *m.;* (textile) tartan *m.*

plain, 1. *n.* plaine *f.* 2. *adj.* (clear) clair; (simple) simple; (of person) quelconque.

plaintiff, *n.* demandeur *m.*

plan, 1. *n.* plan *m.* 2. *vb.* faire le plan de.

plane, *n.* (surface) plan *m.;* (tool) rabot *m.;* (tree) platane *m.;* (airplane) avion *m.*

planet, *n.* planète *f.*

plank, *n.* planche *f.*

plant, 1. *n.* plante *f.* 2. *vb.* planter.

plantation, *n.* plantation *f.*

planter, *n.* planteur *m.*

plasma, *n.* plasma *m.*

plaster, *n.* plâtre *m.*

plastic, *adj.* plastique.

plate, *n.* plaque *f.;* (for eating) assiette *f.*

plateau, *n.* plateau *m.*

platform, *n.* plate-forme *f.;* (railroad) quai *m.*

platter, *n.* plat *m.*

plausible, *adj.* plausible.

play, 1. *n.* jeu *m.;* (drama) pièce (*f.*) de théâtre. 2. *vb.* jouer; (game) jouer à; (instrument) jouer de.

player, *n.* jouer *m.;* (theater) acteur *m.*

playful, *adj.* enjoué.

playground, *n.* (children) terrain *(m.)* de jeu.

playmate, *n.* camarade *(m.f.)* de jeu.

playwright, *n.* dramaturge *m.*

plea, *n.* défense *f.;* (excuse) excuse *f.*

plead, *vb.* plaider; (allege) alléguer.

pleasant, *adj.* agréable.

please, *vb.* plaire à; (satisfy) contenter; (if you p.) s'il vous plaît.

pleasure, *n.* plaisir *m.*

pleat, *n.* pli *m.*

pledge, *n.* gage *m.;* (promise) engagement *m.*

plentiful, *adj.* abondant.

plenty, *n.* abondance *f.*

pliable, *adj.* pliable.

pliers, *n.* pinces *f.pl.*

plight, *n.* état *m.*

plot, *n.* (literature) intrigue *f.;* (conspiracy) complot *m.*

plow, 1. *n.* charrue *f.* 2. *vb.* labourer.

pluck, *n.* courage *m.*

plug, *n.* tampon *m.;* (electric) prise (*f.*) de courant.

plum, *n.* prune *f.*

plumber, *n.* plombier *m.*

plume, *n.* panache *m.*

plump, *adj.* grassouillet.

plunder, *vb.* piller.

plunge, 1. *n.* plongeon *m.* 2. *vb.* plonger.

plural, *adj. and n.* pluriel *m.*

plus, *n.* plus *m.*

pneumonia, *n.* pneumonie *f.*

poach, *vb.* (of eggs) pocher.

poacher, *n.* braconnier *m.*

pocket, *n.* poche *f.*

pocketbook, *n.* sac *(m.)* à main.

poem, *n.* poésie *f.;* (long) poème *f.*

poet, *n.* poète *m.*

poetic, *adj.* poétique.

poetry, *n.* poésie *f.*

poignant, *adj.* poignant.

point, 1. *n.* point *m.;* (sharp end) pointe *f.* 2. *vb.* (gun, etc.) pointer; (indicate) désigner.

pointed, *adj.* pointu; (ironical) mordant.

poise, *n.* équilibre *m.*

poison, 1. *n.* poison *m.* 2. *vb.* empoisonner.

poisonous, *adj.* empoisonné; (plant) vénéneux; (animal) venimeux.

Poland, *n.* Pologne *f.*

polar, *adj.* polaire.

polar bear, *n.* ours *(m.)* blanc.

Pole, *n.* Polonais *m.*

pole, *n.* (geography) pôle *m.;* (wood) perche *f.*

police, *n.* police *f.*

policeman, n. agent (m.) de police.

policy, n. politique f.; (insurance) police f.

Polish, adj. and n. polonais m.

polish, vb. polir; (shoes) cirer.

polite, adj. poli.

politic, political, adj. politique.

politician, n. politicien m.

politics, n. politique f.

poll, n. (voting) scrutin m.

pollen, n. pollen m.

pollute, vb. polluer.

polygamy, n. polygamie f.

pomp, n. pompe f.

pompous, adj. pompeux.

pond, n. étang m.

ponder, vb. réfléchir.

ponderous, adj. pesant.

pony, n. poney m.

pool, n. mare f.; (swimming) piscine f.

poor, adj. pauvre.

pop, n. petit bruit (m.) sec.

pope, n. pape m.

popular, adj. populaire.

popularity, n. popularité f.

population, n. population f.

porch, n. véranda f.

pore, 1. n. pore m. 2. vb. (p. over) s'absorber dans.

pork, n. porc m.

pornography, n. pornographie f.

porous, adj. poreux.

port, n. (harbor) port m.; (naut.) bâbord m.; (wine) porto m.

portable, adj. portatif.

portal, n. portail m.

portfolio, n. portefeuille m.

portion, n. portion f.

portrait, n. portrait m.

portray, vb. (paint) peindre; (describe) dépeindre.

Portugal, n. Portugal m.

Portuguese, 1. n. (person) Portugais m.; (language) portugais m. 2. adj. portugais.

pose, 1. n. pose f. 2. vb. poser.

position, n. position f.

positive, 1. n. positif m. 2. adj. positif.

possess, vb. posséder.

possession, n. possession f.

possibility, n. possibilité f.

possible, adj. possible.

possibly, adv. il est possible que . . .; (perhaps) peut-être.

post, 1. n. (mail) poste f.; (wood) poteau m.; (place) poste m. 2. vb. (mail) mettre à la poste; (placard) afficher.

postage, n. affranchissement m.

postal, adj. postal.

post card, n. carte (f.) postale.

poster, n. affiche f.

posterior, adj. postérieur.

posterity, n. postérité f.

post office, n. bureau (m.) de poste.

postpone, vb. remettre.

postscript, n. post-scriptum m.

posture, n. posture f.

pot, n. pot m.; (saucepan) marmite f.; (marijuana) herbe f., kif m.

potato, n. pomme (f.) de terre.

potent, adj. puissant.

potential, adj. and n. potentiel m.

pottery, n. poterie f.

pouch, n. sac m.

poultry, n. volaille f.

pound, n. livre f.

pour, vb. verser; (rain) tomber à verse.

poverty, n. pauvreté f.

powder, n. poudre f.

power, n. pouvoir m.; (nation, mathematics) puissance f.

powerful, adj. puissant.

powerless, adj. impuissant.

practical, adj. pratique.

practically, adv. pratiquement.

practice, 1. n. (exercise) exercice m.; (habit) habitude f.; (not theory) pratique f. 2. vb. pratiquer; (piano, etc.) s'exercer (à).

practiced, adj. expérimenté.

prairie, n. savane f.

praise, 1. n. éloge m. 2. vb. louer.

prank, n. fredaine f.

pray, vb. prier.

prayer, n. prière f.

preach, vb. prêcher.

preacher, n. prédicateur m.

precarious, adj. précaire.

precaution, n. précaution f.

precede, vb. précéder.

precedent, n. précédent m.

precept, n. précepte m.

precious, adj. précieux.

precipice, n. précipice m.

precipitate, vb. précipiter.

precise, adj. précis.

precision, n. précision f.

preclude, vb. empêcher.

precocious, adj. précoce.

predecessor, n. prédécesseur m.

predestination, n. prédestination f.

predicament, n. situation (f.) difficile.

predict, vb. prédire.

predispose, vb. prédisposer.

predominant, adj. prédominant.

prefabricate, vb. préfabriquer.

preface, n. préface f.

prefer, vb. préférer.

preferable, adj. préférable.

preference, n. préférence f.

prefix, n. préfixe m.

pregnant, adj. enceinte.

prejudice, n. préjugé m.

preliminary, adj. préliminaire.

prelude, n. prélude m.

premature, adj. prématuré.

premeditate, vb. préméditer.

premier, n. premier ministre m.

première, n. première f.

premise, n. (place) lieux m.pl.; (logic) prémisse f.

premium, n. prix m.

preparation, n. préparation f.; préparatifs m.pl.

preparatory, adj. préparatoire.

prepare, vb. préparer, tr.

preponderant, adj. prépondérant.

preposition, n. préposition f.

preposterous, adj. absurde.

prerequisite, n. nécessité (f.) préalable.

prescribe, vb. prescrire.

prescription, n. prescription f.; (medical) ordonnance f.

presence, n. présence f.

present, 1. adj. and n. présent m. 2. vb. présenter.

presentable, adj. présentable.

presentation, n. présentation f.

presently, adv. tout à l'heure.

preservative, adj. and n. préservatif m.

preserve, 1. n. (jam) confiture f. 2. vb. (protect) préserver; (keep) conserver.

preside, vb. présider.

president, n. président m.

press, 1. n. presse f. 2. vb. presser; (iron) repasser.

pressure, n. pression f.

prestige, n. prestige m.

presume, vb. présumer.

presumptuous, adj. présomptueux.

pretend, vb. (claim, aspire) prétendre; (feign) simuler.

pretense, n. faux semblant m.

pretentious, adj. prétentieux.

pretext, n. prétexte m.

pretty, adj. joli.

prevail, vb. prévaloir; (p. upon) décider.

prevalent, adj. répandu.

prevent, vb. (impede) empêcher; (forestall) prévenir.

prevention, n. empêchement m.

preventive, adj. préventif.

previous, adj. antérieur.

prey, n. proie f.

price, n. prix m.

priceless, adj. inestimable.

prick, 1. n. piqûre f. 2. vb. piquer.

pride, n. orgueil m.

priest, n. prêtre m.

prim, adj. affecté.

primary, adj. premier; (school, geology) primaire.

prime, 1. n. comble m. 2. adj. premier, de première qualité. 3. vb. amorcer.

primitive, adj. primitif.

prince, n. prince m.

princess, n. princesse f.

principal, adj. principal.

principle, n. principe m.

print, 1. n. (mark) empreinte f.; (book) impression f.; (photo) épreuve f. 2. vb. imprimer.

printout, n. feuille imprimée produite par un ordinateur f.

priority, n. priorité f.

prism, n. prisme m.

prison, n. prison f.

prisoner, n. prisonnier m.

privacy, n. retraite f.

private, adj. particulier; (not public) privé.

privation, n. privation f.

privilege, n. privilège m.

prize, n. prix m.

probability, n. probabilité f.

probable, adj. probable.

probe, vb. sonder.

problem, n. problème m.

procedure, n. procédé m.

proceed, vb. procéder; (advance) avancer.

process, n. (method) procédé m.; (progress) développement m.

procession, n. cortège m.; (religious) procession f.

proclaim, vb. proclamer.

proclamation, n. proclamation f.

procure, vb. procurer.

prodigal, adj. and n. prodigue m.

prodigy, n. prodige m.

produce, vb. produire.

product, n. produit m.

production, n. production f.

productive, adj. productif.

profane, adj. profane.

profess, vb. professer.

profession, n. profession f.

professional, adj. professionnel.

professor, n. professeur m.

proficient, adj. capable.

profile, n. profil m.

profit, 1. n. profit m. 2. vb. profiter.

profitable, adj. profitable.

profound, adj. profond.

profuse, adj. (of thing) profus; (of person) prodigue.

program, n. programme m.

progress, n. progrès m.; (motion forward) marche f.

progressive, adj. progressif.

prohibit, vb. défendre.

prohibition, n. défense f.

prohibitive, adj. prohibitif.

project, 1. n. projet m. 2. vb. projeter; (jut out) faire saillie.

projection, n. projection f.; (jutting out) saillie f.

projector, n. projecteur m.

proliferation, n. prolifération f.

prolong, vb. prolonger.

prominent, adj. saillant.

promiscuous, adj. (indiscriminate) sans distinction.

promise, 1. n. promesse f. 2. vb. promettre.

promote, vb. (raise) promouvoir; (encourage) encourager.

promotion, n. promotion f.

prompt, adj. prompt.

pronoun, n. pronom m.

pronounce, vb. prononcer.

pronunciation, n. prononciation f.

proof, n. (evidence) preuve f.; (test) épreuve f.

prop, n. appui m.

propaganda, n. progagande f.

propagate, vb. propager, tr.

propeller, n. hélice f.

proper, adj. propre; (respectable, fitting) convenable.

property, n. propriété f.

prophecy, n. prophétie f.

prophesy, vb. prophétiser.

prophet, n. prophète m.

prophetic, adj. prophétique.

proportion, n. proportion f.

proportionate, adj. proportionné.

proposal, n. proposition f.; demande (f.) en mariage.

propose, vb. proposer, tr.

proposition, n. (proposal, grammar) proposition f.; (undertaking) affaire f.

proprietor, n. propriétaire m.f.

prosaic, adj. prosaïque.

proscribe, vb. proscrire.

prose, n. prose f.

prosecute, vb. poursuivre.

prospect, n. perspective f.

prospective, adj. en perspective.

prosper, vb. prospérer.

prosperity, n. prospérité f.

prosperous, adj. prospère.

prostitute, 1. n. prostituée f. 2. vb. prostituer.

prostrate, adj. prosterné.

protect, vb. protéger.

protection, n. protection f.

protective, adj. protecteur.

protector, n. protecteur m.

protégé, n. protégé m.

protein, n. protéine f.

protest, 1. n. protestation f.; (comm.) protêt m. 2. vb. protester.

Protestant, adj. and n. protestant m.

protocol, n. protocole m.

protrude, vb. saillir.

prove, vb. prouver; (test) éprouver.

proverb, n. proverbe m.

provide (with), vb. pourvoir (de), tr.

providence, n. (foresight) prévoyance f.; (divine) providence f.

province, n. province f.

provincial, adj. and n. provincial m.

provision, n. (stock) provision f.

provocation, n. provocation f.

provoke, vb. provoquer; (irritate) irriter.

prowess, n. prouesse f.

prowl, vb. rôder.

proximity, n. proximité f.

prudence, n. prudence f.

prudent, adj. prudent.

prune, n. pruneau m.

Prussia, n. Prusse f.

Prussian, 1. n. Prussien m. 2. adj. prussien.

pry, vb. fureter.

psalm, n. psaume m.

psychedelic, adj. psychédélique.

psychiatry, n. psychiatrie f.

psychoanalysis, n. psychanalyse f.

psychology, n. psychologie f.

psychological, adj. psychologique.

ptomaine, n. ptomaïne f.

public, 1. n. public m. 2. adj. public m., publique f.

publication, n. publication f.

publicity, n. publicité f.

publish, vb. publier.

publisher, n. éditeur m.

pudding, n. pouding m.

puddle, n. flaque f.

puff, n. (smoke etc.) bouffée f.

pull, vb. tirer.

pulley, n. poulie f.

pulp, n. pulpe f.

pulpit, n. chaire f.

pulsar, n. pulsar m.

pulsate, vb. battre.

pulse, n. pouls m.

pump, 1. n. pompe f. 2. vb. pomper.

pumpkin, n. potiron m.

pun, n. calembour m.

punch, 1. n. (tool) poinçon m.; (blow) coup (m.) de poing; (beverage) punch m. 2. vb. (pierce) percer; (pummel) gourmer.

punctual, adj. ponctuel.

punctuate, vb. ponctuer.

puncture, n. piqûre f.

punish, vb. punir.

punishment, n. punition f.

pupil, n. (school) élève m.f.; (eye) pupille f.

puppet, n. marionnette f.

puppy, n. petit chien m.

purchase, 1. n. achat m. 2. vb. acheter.

pure, adj. pur.

puree, n. purée f.

purge, vb. purger.

purify, vb. purifier.

purity, n. pureté f.

purple, adj. violet.

purpose, n. but m.; (to the p.) à propos.

purposely, adv. exprès.

purse, n. bourse f.

pursue, vb. poursuivre.

pursuit, n. poursuite f.; (occupation) occupation f.; (p. plane) avion (m.) de chasse.

push, 1. n. poussée f. 2. vb. pousser.

put, vb. mettre.

puzzle, 1. n. problème m. 2. vb. embarrasser.

pyramid, n. pyramide f.

Q

quadraphonic, adj. quadriphonique.

quail, n. caille f.

quaint, adj. (strange) étrange.

quake, vb. trembler.

qualification, n. (reservation) réserve f.; (aptitude) compétence f.; (description) qualification f.

qualify, vb. qualifier; (modify) modifier.

quality, n. qualité f.

qualm, n. scrupule m.

quantity, n. quantité f.

quarantine, n. quarantaine f.

quarrel, 1. n. querelle f. 2. vb. se quereller.

quarry, n. carrière f.

quarter, n. quart m.; (district, moon, beef) quartier m.

quarterly, adj. trimestriel.

quartet, n. quatuor m.

quartz, n. quartz m.

quasar, n. quasar m.

quaver, vb. chevroter.

queen, n. reine f.

queer, adj. bizarre.

quell, vb. réprimer.

quench, vb. éteindre.

query, n. question f.

quest, n. recherche f.

question, 1. n. question f. 2. vb. interroger; (raise questions) mettre en doute.

questionable, adj. douteux.

question mark, n. point (m.) d'interrogation.

questionnaire, n. questionnaire m.

quick, 1. adj. rapide; (lively) vif. 2. adv. vite.

quicken, vb. accélérer.

quiet, 1. n. tranquillité f. 2. adj. tranquille.

quilt, n. courtepointe f.

quinine, n. quinine f.

quip, n. mot (m.) piquant.

quit, vb. quitter.

quite, adv. tout à fait.

quiver, vb. trembloter.

quiz, 1. n. petit examen m. 2. vb. examiner.

quorum, n. quorum m.

quota, n. (share) quote-part f.; (immigration, etc.) contingent m.

quotation, n. citation f.; (comm.) cote f.

quote, vb. citer.

R

rabbi, n. rabbin m.

rabbit, n. lapin m.

rabble, n. tourbe f.

rabid, adj. enragé.

race, 1. n. (people) race f.; (contest) course f. 2. vb. lutter à la course (avec).

race-track, n. piste f.

rack, n. râtelier m.; (torture) chevalet (m.) de torture.

racket, n. (tennis) raquette f.; (noise) tintamarre m.

radar, n. radar m.

radiance, n. éclat m.

radiant, adj. radieux.

radiate, vb. irradier.

radiation, n. rayonnement m.

radiator, n. radiateur m.

radical, adj. and n. radical m.

radio, n. télégraphie (f.) sans fil (commonly T.S.F.).

radioactive, adj. radio-actif.

radish, n. radis m.

radium, n. radium m.

radius, n. rayon m.

raft, n. radeau m.

rafter, n. chevron m.

rag, n. chiffon m.

rage, n. rage f.

ragged, adj. en haillons.

ragweed, n. ambroisie f.

raid, n. (police) descente f.; (mil.) raid m.

rail, n. (bar) barre f.; (railroad) rail m.

railroad, n. chemin (m.) de fer.

rain, 1. n. pluie f. 2. vb. pleuvoir.

rainbow, n. arc-en-ciel m.

raincoat, n. imperméable m.

rainfall, n. chute (f.) de pluie.

rainy, adj. pluvieux.

raise, vb. (bring up, erect, promote) élever; (lift) lever; (plants) cultiver.

raisin, n. raisin (m.) sec.

rake, 1. n. râteau m. 2. vb. râteler.

rally, n. (mil.) ralliement m.; (meeting) rassemblement m.

ram, n. bélier m.

ramble, vb. rôder; (speech) divaguer.

ramp, n. rampe f.

rampart, n. rempart m.

rancid, adj. rance.

random, n. hasard m.

range, n. (scope) étendue f.; (mountains) chaîne f.; (distance) portée f.; (stove) fourneau m.

rank, 1. n. rang m. 2. vb. ranger, tr.

ransack, vb. (search) fouiller; (pillage) saccager.

ransom, n. rançon f.

rap, 1. n. coup m. 2. vb. frapper.

rapid, adj. and n. rapide m.

rapture, n. ravissement m.

rare, adj. rare.

rascal, n. coquin m.

rash, 1. n. éruption f. 2. adj. téméraire.

raspberry, n. framboise f.

rat, n. rat m.

rate, 1. n. taux m.; (speed) vitesse f.; (at any r.) en tout cas; (first-r.) de premier ordre. 2. vb. estimer.

rather, adv. plutôt.

ratify, vb. ratifier.

ration, n. ration f.

rational, adj. raisonnable; (mathematics, philosophy) rationnel.

rattle, n. (toy) hochet m.; (noise) fracas m.

rave, vb. délirer; (r. about) s'extasier sur.

raven, n. corbeau m.

raw, adj. cru.

ray, n. rayon m.

rayon, n. rayonne f.

razor, n. rasoir m.

reach, 1. n. portée f. 2. vb. atteindre; (extend) étendre, tr.; (arrive) arriver à.

react, vb. réagir.

reaction, n. réaction f.

reactionary, adj. réactionnaire.

read, vb. lire.

reader, n. (person) lecteur m.; (book) livre (m.) de lecture.

readily, adv. promptement.

ready, adj. prêt.

real, adj. réel.

realist, n. réaliste m.f.

reality, n. réalité f.

realization, n. réalisation f.

realize, vb. (notice) s'apercevoir de; (make real) réaliser, tr.

really, adv. vraiment.

realm, n. royaume m.

reap, vb. moissonner.

rear, 1. n. (hind part) queue f.; (mil.) arrière-garde f. 2. adj. situé à l'arrière. 3. vb. élever.

reason, 1. n. raison f. 2. vb. raisonner.

reasonable, adj. raisonnable.

reassure, vb. rassurer.

rebate, n. rabais m.

rebel, 1. adj. and n. rebelle m.f. 2. vb. se rebeller.

rebellion, n. rébellion f.

rebellious, adj. rebelle.

rebirth, n. renaissance f.

rebound, n. rebond m.

rebuke, 1. n. réprimande f. 2. vb. réprimander.

rebuttal, n. réfutation f.

recall, vb. (call back) rappeler; (remember) se rappeler.

recede, vb. s'éloigner.

receipt, n. (for payment) quittance f.

receive, vb. recevoir.

receiver, n. (phone) récepteur m.

recent, adj. récent.

receptacle, n. réceptacle m.

reception, n. réception f.; (welcoming) accueil m.

receptive, adj. réceptif.

recess, n. recoin m.; (Parliament) vacances f.pl.; (school) récréation f.

recipe, n. recette f.

reciprocate, vb. payer de retour.

recite, vb. réciter.

reckless, adj. téméraire.

reckon, vb. compter.

reclaim, v. (person) corriger; (land) défricher.

recline, vb. reposer, tr.

recognition, n. reconnaissance f.

recognize, vb. reconnaître.

recoil, vb. reculer.

recollect, vb. se rappeler.

recommend, vb. recommander.

recommendation, n. recommandation f.

recompense, n. récompense f.

reconcile, vb. réconcilier.

record, 1. *n.* (register) registre *m.;* (mention) mention *f.;* (known facts of person) antécédents *m.pl.;* (sports) record *m.;* (phonograph) disque *m.* **2.** *vb.* enregistrer.

record player, *n.* tourne-disques *m.*

recount, *vb.* raconter.

recover, *vb.* recouvrer; (from illness) se rétablir.

recovery, *n.* recouvrement *m.;* (health) rétablissement *m.*

recruit, 1. *n.* recrue *f.* **2.** *vb.* recruter.

rectangle, *n.* rectangle *m.*

rectify, *vb.* rectifier.

recuperate, *vb.* se rétablir, *intr.*

recur, *vb.* revenir.

recycle, *vb.* recycler.

red, *adj.* and *n.* rouge *m.*

redeem, *vb.* racheter.

redemption, *n.* rachat *m.;* (theology) rédemption *f.*

redress, 1. *n.* justice *f.* **2.** *vb.* redresser, réparer; faire justice à.

reduce, *vb.* réduire.

reduction, *n.* réduction *f.;* (on price) remise *f.*

reed, *n.* roseau *m.;* (music) anche *f.*

reef, *n.* récif *m.*

reel, *n.* bobine *f.*

refer, *vb.* référer.

referee, *n.* arbitre *m.*

reference, *n.* référence *f.*

refill, *vb.* remplir (à nouveau).

refine, *vb.* raffiner.

refinement, *n.* raffinement *m.*

reflect, *vb.* réfléchir.

reflection, *n.* réflexion *f.*

reform, 1. *n.* réforme *f.* **2.** *vb.* réformer, *tr.*

reformation, *n.* réforme *f.*

refractory, *adj.* réfractaire.

refrain from, *vb.* se retenir de.

refresh, *vb.* rafraîchir.

refreshment, *n.* rafraîchissement *m.*

refrigerator, *n.* frigidaire *m.*

refuge, *n.* refuge *m.*

refugee, *n.* réfugié *m.*

refund, 1. *n.* remboursement *m.* **2.** *vb.* rembourser.

refusal, *n.* refus *m.*

refuse, 1. *n.* rebut *m.* **2.** *vb.* refuser.

refute, *vb.* réfuter.

regain, *vb.* regagner.

regal, *adj.* royal.

regard, 1. *n.* égard *m.;* (regards, compliments) amitiés *f.pl.* **2.** *vb.* regarder.

regardless, *adj.* sans se soucier de.

regent, *adj.* and *n.* régent *m.*

regime, *n.* régime *m.*

regiment, *n.* régiment *m.*

region, *n.* région *f.*

register, 1. *n.* registre *m.* **2.** *vb.* enregistrer; (letter) recommander.

registration, *n.* enregistrement *m.*

regret, 1. *n.* regret *m.* **2.** *vb.* regretter.

regular, *adj.* régulier.

regularity, *n.* régularité *f.*

regulate, *vb.* régler.

regulation, *n.* règlement *m.*

regulator, *n.* régulateur *m.*

rehabilitate, *vb.* réhabiliter.

rehearse, *vb.* répéter.

reign, 1. *n.* règne *m.* **2.** *vb.* régner.

rein, *n.* rêne *f.*

reindeer, *n.* renne *m.*

reinforce, *vb.* renforcer.

reinforcement, *n.* renfort *m.*

reject, *vb.* rejeter.

rejoice, *vb.* réjouir, *tr.*

rejoin, *vb.* (join again) rejoindre; (reply) répliquer.

relapse, *n.* rechute *f.*

relate, *vb.* raconter; (have reference to) se rapporter (à); (relate to) entrer en rapport avec.

relation, *n.* relation *f.;* (relative) parent *m.*

relative, 1. *n.* parent *m.* **2.** *adj.* relatif.

relax, *vb.* relâcher.

relay, 1. *n.* relais *m.* **2.** *vb.* relayer.

release, 1. *n.* délivrance *f.* **2.** *vb.* libérer.

relent, *vb.* se laisser attendrir.

relevant, *adj.* pertinent.

reliability, *n.* sûreté *f.*

reliable, *adj.* digne de confiance.

reliant, *adj.* confiant.

relic, *n.* relique *f.*

relief, *n.* (ease) soulagement *m.;* (help) secours *m.;* (projection) relief *m.*

relieve, *vb.* (ease) soulager; (help) secourir.

religion, *n.* religion *f.*

religious, *adj.* religieux.

relinquish, *vb.* abandonner.

relish, 1. *n.* goût *m.* **2.** *vb.* goûter.

reluctant, *adj.* peu disposé (à).

rely upon, *vb.* compter sur.

remain, *vb.* rester.

remainder, *n.* reste *m.*

remark, 1. *n.* remarque *f.* **2.** *vb.* remarquer.

remarkable, *adj.* remarquable.

remedy, 1. *n.* remède *m.* **2.** *vb.* remédier à.

remember, *vb.* se souvenir de.

remembrance, *n.* souvenir *m.*

remind of, *vb.* rappeler à (person recalling).

reminisce, *vb.* raconter ses souvenirs.

remit, *vb.* remettre.

remnant, *n.* reste *m.,* vestige *m.,* (of cloth) coupon *m.*

remorse, *n.* remords *m.*

remote, *adj.* éloigné; (vague) vague.

removable, *adj.* transportable.

removal, *n.* enlèvement *m.*

remove, *vb.* enlever.

rend, *vb.* déchirer.

render, *vb.* rendre.

rendezvous, *n.* rendez-vous *m.*

renew, *vb.* renouveler.

renewal, *n.* renouvellement *m.*

renounce, *vb.* (give up) renoncer à; (repudiate) répudier.

renovate, *vb.* renouveler.

renown, *n.* renommée *f.*

rent, 1. *n.* loyer *m.* **2.** *vb.* louer.

repair, 1. *n.* réparation *f.* **2.** *vb.* réparer.

repay, *vb.* (give back) rendre; (refund) rembourser.

repeat, *vb.* répéter.

repel, *vb.* repousser.

repent, *vb.* se repentir (de).

repentance, *n.* repentir *m.*

repertoire, *n.* répertoire *m.*

repetition, *n.* répétition *f.*

replace, *vb.* (place again) replacer; (take place of) remplacer.

reply, 1. *n.* réponse *f.* **2.** *vb.* répondre.

report, 1. *n.* rapport *m.;* (rumor) bruit *m.* **2.** *vb.* rapporter; (inform against) dénoncer.

repose, *n.* repos *m.*

represent, *vb.* représenter.

representation, *n.* représentation *f.*

representative, 1. *n.* représentant *m.;* (politics) député *m.* **2.** *adj.* représentatif.

repress, *vb.* réprimer.

reprimand, *n.* réprimande *f.*

reproach, 1. *n.* reproche *m.* **2.** *vb.* faire des reproches à.

reproduce, *vb.* reproduire, *tr.*

reproduction, *n.* reproduction *f.*

reproof, *n.* réprimande *f.*

reprove, *vb.* réprimander.

reptile, *n.* reptile *m.*

republic, *n.* république *f.*

republican, *adj.* and *n.* républicain *m.*

repulsive, *adj.* répulsif.

reputation, *n.* réputation *f.*

repute, 1. *n.* renom *m.* **2.** *vb.* réputer.

request, 1. *n.* requête *f.* **2.** *vb.* demander.

require, *vb.* exiger.

requirement, *n.* exigence *f.*

requisite, *adj.* nécessaire.

requisition, *n.* réquisition *f.*

rescue, 1. *n.* délivrance *f.* **2.** *vb.* délivrer.

research, *n.* recherche *f.*

resemble, *vb.* ressembler à.

resent, *vb.* être froissé de.

reservation, *n.* réserve *f.*

reserve, 1. *n.* réserve *f.* **2.** *vb.* réserver.

reservoir, *n.* réservoir *m.*

reside, *vb.* résider.

residence, *n.* résidence *f.*

resident, 1. *n.* habitant *m.* **2.** *adj.* résidant.

resign, *vb.* résigner; (from post) se démettre (de).

resignation, *n.* résignation *f.;* (from post) démission *f.*

resist, vb. résister (à).
resistance, n. résistance f.
resolute, adj. résolu.
resolution, n. résolution f.
resolve, vb. résoudre.
resonant, adj. résonnant.
resort, 1. n. (resource) ressource f.; (recourse) recours m.; (place) lieu (m.) de séjour. 2. vb. avoir recours.
resound, vb. résonner.
resource, n. ressource f.
respect, 1. n. respect m.; (reference) rapport m. 2. vb. respecter.
respectable, adj. respectable.
respectful, adj. respectueux.
respective, adj. respectif.
respiration, n. respiration f.
respite, n. répit m.
respond, vb. répondre.
response, n. réponse f.
responsibility, n. responsabilité f.
responsible, adj. responsable.
rest, 1. n. (repose) repos m.; (remainder) reste m.; (the r., the others) les autres m.f.pl. 2. vb. se reposer.
restaurant, n. restaurant m.
restful, adj. qui repose.
restless, adj. (anxious) inquiet.
restoration, n. restauration f.
restore, vb. remettre; (repair) restaurer.
restrain, vb. contenir.
restraint, n. contrainte f.
restrict, vb. restreindre.
result, 1. n. résultat m. 2. vb. résulter.
resume, vb. reprendre.
résumé, n. résumé m.
resurrect, vb. ressusciter.
retail, n. détail m.
retain, vb. retenir.
retaliate, vb. user de représailles.
retard, vb. retarder.
reticent, adj. réservé.
retina, n. rétine f.
retire, vb. se retirer.
retort, n. riposte f.
retreat, 1. n. retraite f. 2. vb. se retirer.
retrieve, vb. recouvrer.
retrospect, n. renvoi m., (in retrospect) coup d'œil rétrospectif m.
return, 1. n. retour m.; (returns, comm.) recettes f.pl. 2. vb. (give back) rendre: (go back) retourner; (come back) revenir.
reunion, n. réunion f.
reveal, vb. révéler.
revel, vb. s'ébattre.
revelation, n. révélation f.
revelry, n. bacchanale f.
revenge, 1. n. vengeance f. 2. vb. (r. oneself) se venger.
revenue, n. revenu m.
reverberate, vb. réverbérer, réfléchir, répercuter.
revere, vb. révérer.
reverence, n. révérence f.

reverend, adj. révérend.
reverent, adj. respectueux.
reverie, n. rêverie f.
reverse, 1. n. (opposite) contraire m.; (defeat, medal) revers m.; (gear) marche (f.) arrière. 2. vb. renverser.
revert, vb. revenir.
review, n. revue f.
revise, vb. réviser.
revision, n. révision f.
revival, n. renaissance f.; (religious) réveil m.
revive, vb. revivre, intr.; faire revivre, tr.
revoke, vb. révoquer.
revolt, 1. n. révolte f. 2. vb. se révolter.
revolution, n. révolution f.
revolutionary, adj. révolutionnaire.
revolve, vb. tourner, intr.
revolver, n. revolver m.
reward, 1. n. récompense f. 2. vb. récompenser.
rheumatism, n. rhumatisme m.
rhinoceros, n. rhinocéros m.
rhubarb, n. rhubarbe f.
rhyme, 1. n. rime f. 2. vb. rimer.
rhythm, n. rythme m.
rhythmical, adj. rythmique.
rib, n. côte f.
ribbon, n. ruban m.
rice, n. riz m.
rich, adj. riche.
rid, vb. débarrasser.
riddle, n. énigme f.
ride, 1. n. promenade f. 2. vb. (horse) aller à cheval; (vehicle) aller en voiture.
rider, n. (on horse) cavalier m.
ridge, n. crête f.
ridicule, 1. n. ridicule m. 2. vb. se moquer de.
ridiculous, adj. ridicule.
rifle, n. fusil m.
rig, 1. n. (vessel) gréement m.; (outfit) tenue f. 2. vb. gréer.
right, 1. n. droit m.; (not left) droite f. 2. adj. (straight, not left) droit; (correct, proper) juste; (be r., of person) avoir raison; (all r.) c'est bien. 3. adv. (straight) droit; (not left) à droite; (justly) bien.
righteous, adj. juste.
righteousness, n. justice f.
right of way, n. droit de passage m., (automobiles) priorité de passage f.
rigid, adj. rigide.
rigor, n. rigueur f.
rigorous, adj. rigoureux.
rim, n. bord m.; (wheel) jante f.
ring, 1. n. anneau m.; (ornament) bague f.; (circle) cercle m.; (arena) arène f.; (sound) son m.; (phone) coup (m.) de téléphone. 2. vb. sonner.
rinse, vb. rincer.
riot, n. émeute f.

rip, 1. n. fente f. 2. vb. fendre, tr.
ripe, adj. mûr.
ripen, vb. mûrir.
ripoff, 1. n. vol m. 2. vb. voler.
ripple, 1. n. (on water) ride f. 2. vb. rider, tr.
rise, 1. n. (ground) montée f.; (increase) augmentation f.; (rank) avancement m. 2. vb. se lever.
risk, 1. n. risque m. 2. vb. risquer.
rite, n. rite m.
ritual, adj. rituel.
rival, 1. adj. and n. rival m. 2. vb. rivaliser avec.
rivalry, n. rivalité f.
river, n. fleuve m.
rivet, n. rivet m.
road, n. route f.
roam, vb. errer (par).
roar, vb. (person) hurler; (lion) rugir; (bull, sea) mugir; (thunder, cannon) gronder; (laughter) éclater de.
roast, 1. n. rôti m. 2. vb. rôtir.
rob, vb. voler.
robber, n. voleur m.
robbery, n. vol m.
robe, n. robe f.
robin, n. rouge-gorge m.
robot, n. automate m.
robust, adj. robuste.
rock, 1. n. rocher m. 2. vb. balancer; (child) bercer. 3. adj. (musique) rock.
rocker, n. (chair) chaise (f.) à bascule.
rocket, n. fusée f.
rocky, adj. rocheux.
rod, n. verge f.
rodent, adj. and n. rongeur m.
roe, n. (animal) chevreuil m.; (of fish) œufs (m.pl.) de poisson.
rogue, n. coquin m.
roguish, adj. coquin.
role, n. rôle m.
roll, 1. n. rouleau m.; (bread) petit pain m.; (list) liste f.; (r.-call) appel m.; (boat) roulis m. 2. vb. rouler.
roller, n. rouleau m.
Roman, 1. n. Romain m. 2. adj. romain.
romance, n. roman (m.) de chevalerie.
romantic, adj. romanesque; (poetry, music) romantique.
romp, 1. n. tapage m. 2. vb. batifoler.
roof, n. toit m.
room, n. (space) place f.; (private use) chambre f.; (public use) salle f.
roommate, n. camarade (m.f.) de chambre.
rooster, n. coq m.
root, 1. n. racine f.; (source) source f. 2. vb. enraciner, tr.
rope, n. corde f.
rosary, n. rosaire m.
rose, n. rose f.
rosin, n. colophane f.

rosy, *adj.* de rose.

rot, 1. *n.* pourriture *f.* 2. *vb.* pourrir.

rotary, *adj.* rotatoire.

rotate, *vb.* tourner.

rotation, *n.* rotation *f.*

rotten, *adj.* pourri.

rouge, *n.* rouge *m.*

rough, *adj.* rude; (sea weather) gros *m.,* grosse *f.*

round, 1. *adj.* rond; (r. trip) l'aller *(m.)* et le retour. 2. *n.* rond *m.;* (circuit) tournée *f.*

rouse, *vb.* (wake) réveiller; (stir up) secouer.

rout, *n.* (mil.) déroute *f.*

route, *n.* route *f.*

routine, *n.* routine *f.*

rove, *vb.* errer (par).

rover, *n.* rôdeur *m.*

row, 1. *n.* rang *m.;* dispute *f.* 2. *vb.* ramer.

rowboat, *n.* barque *f.*

rowdy, *adj.* tapageur.

royal, *adj.* royal.

royalty, *n.* royauté *f.;* (of author) droits *(m.pl.)* d'auteur.

rub, *vb.* frotter.

rubber, *n.* caoutchouc *m.*

rubbish, *n.* rebuts *m.pl.;* (nonsense) bêtises *f.pl.*

ruby, *n.* rubis *m.*

rudder, *n.* gouvernail *m.*

ruddy, *adj.* rouge.

rude, *adj.* (rough) rude; (impolite) impoli.

rudiment, *n.* rudiment *m.*

rue, *vb.* regretter.

ruffian, *n.* bandit *m.*

ruffle, *n.* (frill) fraise *f.*

rug, *n.* tapis *m.*

rugged, *adj.* (rough) rude; (uneven) raboteux.

ruin, 1. *n.* ruine *f.* 2. *vb.* ruiner.

ruinous, *adj.* ruineux.

rule, 1. *n.* règle *f.;* (authority) autorité *f.* 2. *vb.* gouverner; (decide) décider.

ruler, *n.* souverain *m.;* (for lines) règle *f.*

rum, *n.* rhum *m.*

Rumania, *n.* Roumanie *f.*

Rumanian, 1. *n.* (person) Roumain *m.;* (language) roumain *m.* 2. *adj.* roumain.

rumba, *n.* rumba *f.*

rumble, *vb.* gronder.

rumor, *n.* rumeur *f.*

run, *vb. intr.* courir; (of engine) marcher; (of colors) déteindre; (of liquids) couler; (r. away) s'enfuir.

run-down, *adj.* épuisé.

rung, *n.* échelon *m.*

runner, *n.* (person) coureur *m.;* (table) chemin *(m.)* de table.

rupture, *n.* rupture *f.*

rural, *adj.* rural.

rush, 1. *n.* (haste) hâte *f.;* (on-rush) ruée *f.;* (air, water) coup *m.;* (plant) jonc *m.* 2. *vb.* se précipiter, *intr.*

Russia, *n.* Russie *f.*

Russian, 1. *n.* (person) Russe

m.f.; (language) russe *m.* 2. *adj.* russe.

rust, 1. *n.* rouille *f.* 2. *vb.* rouiller, *tr.*

rustic, *adj.* rustique.

rustle, *n.* (leaves) bruissement *m.;* (skirt) frou-frou *m.*

rusty, *adj.* rouillé.

rut, *n.* ornière *f.*

ruthless, *adj.* impitoyable.

rye, *n.* seigle *m.*

S

Sabbath, *n.* sabbat *m.*

saber, *n.* sabre *m.*

sable, *n.* zibeline *f.*

sabotage, 1. *n.* sabotage *m.* 2. *vb.* saboter.

saboteur, *n.* saboteur *m.*

saccharin, *n.* saccharine *f.*

sachet, *n.* sachet *m.*

sack, 1. *n.* sac *m.* 2. *vb.* saccager.

sacrament, *n.* sacrement *m.*

sacred, *adj.* sacré.

sacrifice, 1. *n.* sacrifice *m.* 2. *vb.* sacrifier.

sacrilege, *n.* sacrilège *m.*

sad, *adj.* triste.

sadden, *vb.* attrister, *tr.*

saddle, *n.* selle *f.*

sadism, *n.* sadisme *m.*

safe, 1. *n.* coffre-fort *n.* 2. *adj.* sûr; (s. and sound) sain et sauf; (s. from) à l'abri de.

safeguard, *vb.* sauvegarder.

safety, *n.* sûreté *f.*

safety pin, *n.* épingle *(f.)* anglaise.

sage, *n.* (person) sage *m.;* (plant) sauge *f.*

sail, 1. *n.* voile *f.* 2. *vb.* naviguer; (depart) partir.

sailboat, *n.* canot *(m.)* à voiles.

sailor, *n.* marin *m.*

saint, *adj. and n.* saint *m.*

sake, *n.* (for the s. of) pour l'amour de.

salad, *n.* salade *f.*

salary, *n.* appointements *m.pl.*

sale, *n.* vente *f.*

salesman, *n.* vendeur *m.*

sales tax, *n.* impôt sur les ventes *m.*

saliva, *n.* salive *f.*

salmon, *n.* saumon *m.*

salt, 1. *n.* sel *m.* 2. *vb.* saler.

salute, 1. *n.* salut *m.* 2. *vb.* saluer.

salvage, *n.* sauvetage *m.*

salvation, *n.* salut *m.*

salve, *n.* onguent *m.*

same, 1. *adj. and pron.* même. 2. *adv.* de même.

sample, *n.* échantillon *m.*

sanatorium, *n.* sanatorium *m.*

sanctify, *vb.* sanctifier.

sanction, *n.* sanction *f.*

sanctity, *n.* sainteté *f.*

sanctuary, *n.* sanctuaire *m.*

sand, *n.* sable *m.*

sandal, *n.* sandale *f.*

sandwich, *n.* sandwich *m.*

sandy, *adj.* sablonneux.

sane, *adj.* sain d'esprit.

sanitary, *adj.* sanitaire.

sanitation, *n.* hygiène *f.*

sanity, *n.* santé (*f.*) d'esprit.

Santa Claus, *n.* Bonhomme Noël *m.*

sap, *n.* sève *f.*

sapphire, *n.* saphir *m.*

sarcasm, *n.* sarcasme *m.*

sardine, *n.* sardine *f.*

sash, *n.* ceinture *f.;* (window) châssis *m.*

satellite, *n.* satellite *m.*

satin, *n.* satin *m.*

satire, *n.* satire *f.*

satisfaction, *n.* satisfaction *f.*

satisfactory, *adj.* satisfaisant.

satisfy, *vb.* satisfaire.

saturate, *vb.* saturer.

Saturday, *n.* samedi *m.*

sauce, *n.* sauce *f.*

saucer, *n.* soucoupe *f.*

saucy, *adj.* impertinent.

sausage, *n.* saucisse *f.*

savage, *adj. and n.* sauvage *m.f.*

save, *vb.* sauver; (put aside) mettre de côté; (economize) épargner.

savior, *n.* sauveur *m.*

savor, *n.* saveur *f.*

savory, *adj.* savoureux.

saw, 1. *n.* scie *f.* 2. *vb.* scier.

say, *vb.* dire.

scab, *n.* croûte *f.,* gale *f.*

scaffold, *n.* échafaud *m.*

scald, *vb.* échauder.

scale, 1. *n.* (fish) écaille *f.;* (balance) balance *f.;* (series, graded system, map) échelle *f.;* (music) gamme *f.* 2. *vb.* escalader.

scalp, 1. *n.* cuir (*m.*) chevelu. 2. *vb.* scalper.

scan, *vb.* (examine) scruter; (verse) scander.

scandal, *n.* scandale *m.*

scandalous, *adj.* scandaleux.

Scandinavia, *n.* Scandinavie *f.*

Scandinavian, 1. *n.* Scandinave *m.f.* 2. *adj.* scandinave.

scant(y), *adj.* limité, faible.

scar, *n.* cicatrice *f.*

scarce, *adj.* rare.

scare, *vb.* effrayer.

scarf, *n.* écharpe *f.*

scarlet, *adj. and n.* écarlate *f.;* (s. fever) scarlatine *f.*

scathing, *adj.* cinglant.

scatter, *vb.* éparpiller.

scavenger, *n.* boueur *m.*

scenario, *n.* scénario *m.*

scene, *n.* scène *f.*

scenery, *n.* (theater) décors *m.pl.;* (landscape) paysage *m.*

scent, 1. *n.* parfum *m.,* odeur *f.* 2. *vb.* flairer, sentir.

schedule, *n.* plan *m.*

scheme, *n.* plan *m.*

scholar, *n.* savant *m.*

scholarship, *n.* (school) bourse *f.*

school, *n.* école *f.*

sciatica, *n.* sciatique *f.*

science, n. science f.
science fiction, n. science-fiction f.
scientist, n. homme (m.) de science.
scissors, n. ciseaux m.pl.
scoff at, vb. se moquer de.
scold, vb. gronder.
scoop out, vb. évider.
scope, 1. n. (extent) portée f.; (outlet) carrière f.
scorch, vb. roussir.
score, n. (games) points m.pl.; (twenty) vingtaine f.; (music) partition f.
scorn, 1. n. mépris m. 2. vb. mépriser.
scornful, adj. dédaigneux.
Scotch, Scottish, adj. écossais.
Scotchman, Scotsman, n. Écossais m.
Scotland, n. Ecosse f.
scour, vb. nettoyer.
scourge, n. fléau m.
scout, n. éclaireur m.; (boy s.) boy-scout m.
scowl, vb. se renfrogner.
scramble, vb. avancer péniblement.
scrap, 1. n. petit morceau m. 2. vb. mettre au rebut.
scrape, scratch, 1. n. égratignure f. 2. vb. gratter.
scream, 1. n. cri m. 2. vb. crier.
screen, n. écran m.; (folding s.) paravent m.
screw, 1. n. vis f. 2. vb. visser, tr.
screwdriver, n. tournevis m.
scribble, vb. griffonner.
scroll, n. rouleau m.
scrub, vb. frotter.
scruple, n. scrupule m.
scrupulous, adj. scrupuleux.
scrutinize, vb. scruter.
sculptor, n. sculpteur m.
sculpture, n. sculpture f.
scythe, n. faux f.
sea, n. mer f.
seabed, n. lit de la mer f.
seacoast, n. littoral m.
seal, 1. n. (animal) phoque m.; (stamp) sceau m. 2. vb. sceller.
seam, n. couture f.
seaport, n. port (m.) de mer.
search, 1. n. recherche f. 2. vb. chercher.
seasickness, n. mal (m.) de mer.
season, 1. n. saison f. 2. vb. assaisonner.
seat, 1. n. siège m. 2. vb. asseoir.
second, 1. n. seconde f. 2. adj. second, deuxième.
secondary, adj. secondaire.
secret, adj. and n. secret m.
secretary, n. secrétaire m.f.
sect, n. secte f.
section, n. section f.
sectional, adj. régional.
secular, adj. (church) séculier; (time) séculaire.
secure, 1. adj. sûr. 2. vb. (make

s.) mettre en sûreté; (make fast) fixer; (obtain) obtenir.
security, n. sûreté f.; (comm., law) caution f.; (finance, pl.) valeurs f.pl.
sedative, adj. and n. sédatif m.
seduce, vb. séduire.
see, vb. voir.
seed, n. semence f.; (vegetables, etc.) graine f.
seek, vb. chercher.
seem, vb. sembler.
seep, vb. suinter.
segment, n. segment m.
segregate, vb. séparer.
seize, vb. saisir.
seldom, adv. rarement.
select, vb. choisir.
selection, n. sélection f.
self, n. moi m., personne f.
selfish, adj. égoïste.
selfishness, n. ègoïsme m.
sell, vb. vendre, tr.
semantics, n. sémantique f.
semester, n. semestre m.
semicircle, n. demi-cercle m.
semicolon, n. point (m.) et virgule (f.).
seminary, n. séminaire m.
senate, n. sénat m.
senator, n. sénateur m.
send, vb. envoyer; (s. back) renvoyer.
senile, adj. sénile.
senior, adj. and n. (age) aîné m.; (rank) supérieur m.
senior citizen, n. personne du troisième âge f.
sensation, n. sensation f.
sensational, adj. sensationnel.
sense, n. sens m.
sensible, adj. (wise) sensé; (appreciable) sensible.
sensitive, adj. sensible.
sensual, adj. sensuel.
sentence, n. (gramm.) phrase f.; (law) sentence f.
sentiment, n. sentiment m.
sentimental, adj. sentimental.
separate, 1. adj. séparé. 2. vb. séparer, tr.
separation, n. séparation f.
September, n. septembre m.
sequence, n. suite f.
serenade, n. sérénade f.
serene, adj. serein.
sergeant, n. sergent m.
serial, n. roman-feuilleton m.
series, n. série f.
serious, adj. sérieux.
sermon, n. sermon m.
serpent, n. serpent m.
serum, n. sérum m.
servant, n. (domestic) domestique m.f.; (public) employé m.
serve, vb. servir.
service, n. service m.; (church) office m.
servitude, n. servitude f.
session, n. session f.
set, 1. n. ensemble m. 2. adj. fixe; (decided) résolu. 3. vb. tr. (put) mettre; (regulate) régler; (jewels) monter; (fix)

fixer. 4. vb. intr. (sun, etc.) se coucher; (s. about) se mettre à.
settle, vb. (establish) établir, tr.; (fix) fixer; (decide) décider; (arrange) arranger; (pay) payer; (s. down to, intr.) se mettre à.
settlement, n. (colony) colonie f.; (accounts) règlement m.
settler, n. colon m.
seven, adj. and n. sept m.
seventeen, adj. and n. dix-sept m.
seventh, adj. and n. septième m.
seventy, adj. and n. soixante-dix m.
sever, vb. séparer, couper.
several, adj. and pron. plusieurs.
severe, adj. sévère.
severity, n. sévérité f.
sew, vb. coudre.
sewer, n. égout m.
sex, n. sexe m.
sexism, n. sexisme m.
sexist, adj. sexiste.
sexton, n. sacristain m.
sexual, adj. sexuel.
shabby, adj. (clothes) usé; (person) mesquin.
shade, 1. n. ombre f.; (colors) nuance f.; (window) store m. 2. vb. ombrager.
shadow, n. ombre f.
shady, adj. ombragé; (not honest) louche.
shaft, n. (mine) puits m.
shaggy, adj. poilu, hirsute.
shake, vb. tr. secouer; trembler; (s. hands) serrer la main à.
shall, vb. (use future of verb).
shallow, adj. peu profond.
shame, n. honte f.
shameful, adj. honteux.
shampoo, n. schampooing m.
shape, 1. n. forme f. 2. vb. former.
share, 1. n. part f.; (finance) action f. 2. vb. partager.
shark, n. requin m.
sharp, adj. (cutting) tranchant; (clever) fin; (piercing) perçant; (music) dièse.
sharpen, vb. aiguiser.
shatter, vb. briser.
shave, vb. raser, tr.
shawl, n. châle m.
she, pron. elle.
sheaf, n. (grain) gerbe f.
shear, vb. tondre.
shears, n. cisailles f.pl.
sheath, n. étui m.
shed, 1. n. hangar m. 2. vb. verser.
sheep, n. mouton m.
sheet, n. (bed) drap m.; (paper, metal) feuille f.
shelf, n. rayon m.
shell, n. coquille f.; (of building) carcasse f.; (explosive) obus m.
shellac, n. laque f.

shelter, 1. *n.* abri *m.* **2.** *vb.* abriter.

shepherd, *n.* berger *m.*

sherbet, *n.* sorbet *m.*

sherry, *n.* xérès *m.*

shield, *n.* bouclier *m.*

shift, 1. *n.* (change) changement *m.;* (workers) équipe *f.;* (expedient) expédient *m.;* (shirt) chemise *f.* **2.** *vb.* changer; **(s. gears)** changer de vitesse.

shine, *vb.* briller, *intr.;* (shoes) cirer.

shiny, *adj.* luisant.

ship, *n.* navire *m.;* (large) vaisseau *m.*

shipment, *n.* envoi *m.*

shirk, *vb.* esquiver.

shirt, *n.* chemise *f.*

shiver, 1. *n.* frisson *m.* **2.** *vb.* frissonner.

shock, 1. *n.* choc *m.* **2.** *vb.* choquer.

shoe, *n.* soulier *m.*

shoelace, *n.* lacet *m.*

shoemaker, *n.* cordonnier *m.*

shoot, *vb.* tirer; (person) fusiller; (hit) atteindre; (rush) se précipiter.

shop, 1. *n.* boutique *f.;* (factory) atelier *m.* **2.** *vb.* faire des emplettes.

shore, *n.* rivage *m.*

short, *adj.* court.

shortage, *n.* manque *m.*

shorten, *vb.* raccourcir.

shorthand, *n.* sténographie *f.*

shot, *n.* coup *m.*

should, *vb.* devoir (in conditional).

shoulder, *n.* épaule *f.*

shout, 1. *n.* cri *m.* **2.** *vb.* crier.

shove, *vb.* pousser.

shovel, *n.* pelle *f.*

show, 1. *n.* (exhibition) exposition *f.;* (spectacle, performance) spectacle *m.;* performance) spectacle *m.;* (semblance) semblant *m.;* (display) parade *f.* **2.** *vb.* montrer, *tr.*

shower, *n.* averse *f.*

shrapnel, *n.* shrapnel *m.*

shrewd, *adj.* sagace.

shriek, *n.* cri *(m.)* perçant.

shrill, *adj.* aigu.

shrimp, *n.* crevette *f.*

shrine, *n.* châsse *f.*

shrink, *vb.* rétrécir, *tr.*

shroud, *n.* linceul *m.*

shrub, *n.* arbrisseau *m.*

shudder, 1. *n.* frisson *m.* **2.** *vb.* frissonner.

shun, *vb.* fuir.

shut, *vb.* fermer.

shutter, *n.* volet *m.*

shy, *adj.* timide.

sick, *adj.* malade.

sickness, *n.* maladie *f.*

side, *n.* côté *f.*

sidewalk, *n.* trottoir *m.*

siege, *n.* siège *m.*

sieve, *n.* tamis *m.*

sift, *vb.* cribler.

sigh, 1. *n.* soupir *m.* **2.** *vb.* soupirer.

sight, *n.* vue *f.;* (spectacle) spectacle *m.*

sightseeing, *n.* tourisme *m.*

sign, 1. *n.* signe *m.;* (placard) enseigne *f.* **2.** *vb.* signer.

signal, *n.* signal *m.*

signature, *n.* signature *f.*

significance, *n.* (meaning) signification *f.;* (importance) importance *f.*

significant, *adj.* significatif.

signify, *vb.* signifier.

silence, *n.* silence *m.*

silent, *adj.* silencieux.

silk, *n.* soie *f.*

silken, *adj.* de soie.

silly, *adj.* sot *m.*, sotte *f.*

silver, 1. *n.* argent *m.* **2.** *adj.* d'argent.

silverware, *n.* argenterie *f.*

similar, *adj.* semblable.

simple, *adj.* simple.

simplicity, *n.* simplicité *f.*

simplify, *vb.* simplifier.

simply, *adv.* simplement.

simultaneous, *adj.* simultané.

sin, 1. *n.* péché *m.* **2.** *vb.* pécher.

since, 1. *adv.*, *prep.* depuis. **2.** *conj.* (time) depuis que; (cause) puisque.

sincere, *adj.* sincère.

sincerity, *n.* sincérité *f.*

sinful, *adj.* (person) pécheur *m.,* pécheresse *f.;* (act) coupable.

sing, *vb.* chanter.

singer, *n.* chanteur *m.*

single, *adj.* (only one) seul; (particular) particulier; (not married) célibataire.

singular, *adj.* and *n.* singulier *m.*

sinister, *adj.* sinistre.

sink, 1. *n.* évier *m.* **2.** *vb.* enfoncer, *tr.;* (vessel) couler au fond; (diminish, weaken) baisser.

sinner, *n.* pécheur *m.*, pécheresse *f.*

sinus, *n.* sinus *m.*

sip, *vb.* siroter.

sir, *n.* monsieur *m.;* (title) Sir *m.*

sirloin, *n.* aloyau *m.*

sister, *n.* sœur *f.*

sister-in-law, *n.* belle-sœur *f.*

sit, *vb.* (s. down) s'asseoir; (be seated) être assis.

site, *n.* emplacement *m.*

situate, *vb.* situer.

situation, *n.* situation *f.*

six, *adj.* and *n.* six *m.*

sixteen, *adj.* and *n.* seize *m.*

sixteenth, *adj.* and *n.* seizième *m.*

sixth, *adj.* and *n.* sixième *m.*

sixty, *adj.* and *n.* soixante *m.*

size, *n.* grandeur *f.;* (person) taille *f.;* (shoes, gloves) pointure *f.*

skate, 1. *n.* patin *m.* **2.** *vb.* patiner.

skateboard, *n.* planche à roulettes *f.*

skeleton, *n.* squelette *m.*

skeptic, *n.* sceptique *m.f.*

skeptical, *adj.* sceptique.

sketch, 1. *n.* croquis *m.* **2.** *vb.* esquisser.

ski, 1. *n.* ski *m.* **2.** *vb.* faire du ski.

skill, *n.* adresse *f.*

skillful, *adj.* adroit.

skim, *vb.* (milk) écrémer; (book) feuilleter; (surface) effleurer.

skin, 1. *n.* peau *f.* **2.** *vb.* écorcher.

skip, *vb.* sauter.

skirt, *n.* jupe *f.*

skull, *n.* crâne *m.*

sky, *n.* ciel *m.*

skyscraper, *n.* gratte-ciel *m.*

slab, *n.* dalle *f.*

slack, *adj.* lâche.

slacken, *vb.* (slow up) ralentir; (loosen) relâcher.

slacks, *n.* pantalon *m.*

slander, 1. *n.* calomnie *f.* **2.** *vb.* calomnier.

slang, *n.* argot *m.*

slant, 1. *n.* (slope) pente *f.;* (bias) biais *m.* **2.** *vb.* incliner.

slap, *n.* claque *f.*

slash, *n.* taillade *f.*

slate, *n.* ardoise *f.*

slaughter, 1. *n.* (people) massacre *m.;* (animals) abattage *m.* **2.** *vb.* massacrer; abattre.

slave, *n.* esclave *m.f.*

slavery, *n.* esclavage *m.*

slay, *vb.* tuer.

sled, *n.* traîneau *m.*

sleep, 1. *n.* sommeil *m.;* **(go to s.)** s'endormir. **2.** *vb.* dormir.

sleepy, *adj.* somnolent; **(be s.)** avoir sommeil.

sleet, 1. *n.* grésil *m.* **2.** *vb.* grésiller.

sleeve, *n.* manche *f.*

sleigh, *n.* traîneau *m.*

slender, *adj.* mince; svelte.

slice, *n.* tranche *f.*

slide, 1. *n.* (sliding) glissade *f.;* (microscope) lamelle *f.;* (lantern) plaque (*f.*) de projection. **2.** *vb.* glisser.

slight, *adj.* léger; mince.

slim, *adj.* svelte.

sling, 1. *n.* fronde *f.;* (medical) écharpe *f.* **2.** *vb.* (throw) lancer; (hang) suspendre.

slip, 1. *n.* (sliding) glissade *f.;* (tongue, pen) lapsus *m.;* (mistake) faux pas *m.;* (paper) fiche *f.;* (garment) combinaison *f.* **2.** *vb.* glisser; (err) faire une faute.

slipper, *n.* pantoufle *f.*

slippery, *adj.* glissant.

slit, 1. *n.* fente *f.* **2.** *vb.* fendre.

slogan, *n.* mot *(m.)* d'ordre; (politics) cri *(m.)* de guerre.

slope, 1. *n.* pente *f.* **2.** *vb.* incliner.

sloppy, *adj.* (slushy) bourbeux; (slovenly) mal soigné.

slot, n. fente f.

slow, adj. lent; (clock) en retard.

slowness, n. lenteur f.

sluggish, adj. paresseux.

slumber, vb. sommeiller.

sly, adj. (crafty) rusé; (secretive) sournois.

smack, n. (a bit) soupçon m.; (noise) claquement m.

small, adj. petit.

smallpox, n. petite vérole f.

smart, 1. adj. (clever) habile; (stylish) élégant. 2. vb. cuire.

smash, vb. briser, tr.

smear, 1. n. tache f. 2. vb. salir.

smell, 1. n. odeur f. 2. vb. sentir.

smelt, 1. n. éperlan m. 2. vb. fondre.

smile, n., vb. sourire m.

smite, vb. frapper.

smoke, 1. n. fumée f. 2. vb. fumer.

smolder, vb. couver.

smooth, 1. adj. lisse. 2. vb. lisser.

smother, vb. étouffer.

smuggle, vb. faire passer en contrebande.

snack, n. casse-croute m.

snag, n. obstacle (m.) caché.

snail, n. escargot m.

snake, n. serpent m.

snap, 1. n. (bite) coup (m.) de dents; (sound) coup (m.) sec. 2. vb.tr. (with teeth) happer; (sound) faire claquer.

snapshot, n. cliché m.

snare, n. piège m.

snarl, vb. grogner.

snatch, vb. saisir.

sneak, vb. se glisser furtivement.

sneer, vb. ricaner.

sneeze, 1. n. éternuement m. 2. vb. éternuer.

snob, n. snob m.

snore, vb. ronfler.

snow, 1. n. neige f. 2. vb. neiger.

snug, adj. confortable.

so, adv. si; tellement; (thus) ainsi; (s. that) de sorte que.

soak, vb. tremper.

soap, n. savon m.

soar, vb. prendre son essor.

sob, 1. n. sanglot m. 2. vb. sangloter.

sober, adj. (moderate) sobre; (sedate) sérieux; (not drunk) qui n'est pas ivre.

sociable, adj. sociable.

social, adj. social.

socialism, n. socialisme m.

socialist, adj. and n. socialiste m.f.

society, n. société f.

sociology, n. sociologie f.

sock, n. chaussette f.

socket, n. douille f.

sod, n. motte f.

soda, n. soude f.; (s.-water) eau (f.) de Seltz.

sofa, n. canapé m.

soft, adj. doux m., douce f.; (yielding) mou m., molle f.

soften, vb. amollir, tr.

soil, 1. n. terroir m. 2. vb. souiller.

sojourn, 1. n. séjour m. 2. vb. séjourner.

solace, n. consolation f.

solar, adj. solaire.

soldier, n. soldat m.

sole, n. (shoe) semelle f.; (fish) sole f.

solemn, adj. solennel.

solemnity, n. solennité f.

solicit, vb. solliciter.

solicitous, adj. empressé.

solid, adj. and n. solide m.

solidity, n. solidité f.

solitary, adj. solitaire.

solitude, n. solitude f.

solo, n. solo m.

solution, n. solution f.

solve, vb. résoudre.

solvent, adj. (comm.) solvable.

somber, adj. sombre.

some, 1. adj. quelque; (partitive) de. 2. pron. certains; (with verb) en.

somebody, someone, pron. quelqu'un.

something, pron. quelque chose m.

some time, adv. (past) autrefois; (future) quelque jour.

sometimes, adv. quelquefois.

somewhat, adv. quelque peu.

somewhere, adv. quelque part.

son, n. fils m.

song, n. chant m.; (light s.) chanson f.

son-in-law, n. gendre m.

soon, adv. bientôt, tôt.

soot, n. suie f.

soothe, vb. calmer.

sophisticated, adj. blasé.

soprano, n. soprano m.

sordid, adj. sordide.

sore, adj. (aching) douloureux; (have a s. throat, etc.) avoir mal à. . . .

sorrow, n. douleur f.

sorrowful, adj. (person) affligé.

sorry, 1. adj. fâché; (be s.) regretter. 2. interj. pardon!

sort, 1. n. sorte f. 2. vb. trier.

soul, n. âme f.

sound, 1. n. son m. 2. adj. (healthy) sain, solide. 3. vb. sonner.

soup, n. potage m.

sour, adj. aigre.

source, n. source f.

south, n. sud m.

southeast, n. sud-est m.

southern, adj. du sud.

South Pole, n. pôle sud m.

southwest, n. sud-ouest m.

souvenir, n. souvenir m.

sow, vb. semer.

space, n. espace m.

space shuttle, n. navette spatiale f.

spacious, adj. spacieux.

spade, n. bêche f.; (cards) pique m.

Spain, n. Espagne f.

span, n. (hand) empan m.; (bridge) travée f.

Sapniard, n. Espagnol m.

Spanish, adj. and n. espagnol m.

spank, vb. fesser.

spanking, n. fessée f.

spare, 1. adj. (in reserve) de réserve. 2. vb. épargner.

spark, n. étincelle f.

sparkle, vb. étinceler.

sparrow, n. moineau m.

spasm, n. spasme m.

speak, vb. parler.

speaker, n. (public) orateur m.

special, adj. spécial.

specialist, n. spécialiste m.f.

specially, adv. spécialement.

specialty, n. spécialité f.

species, n. espèce f.

specific, adj. spécifique.

specify, vb. spécifier.

specimen, n. spécimen m.

spectacle, n. spectacle m.

spectacular, adj. spectaculaire.

spectator, n. spectateur m.

speculate, vb. spéculer.

speculation, n. spéculation f.

speech, n. (address) discours m.; (utterance) parole f.

speed, n. vitesse f.

speedy, adj. rapide.

spell, 1. n. (incantation) charme m.; (period) période f. 2. vb. épeler.

spend, vb. (money) dépenser; (time) passer.

sphere, n. sphère f.

spice, n. épice f.

spider, n. araignée f.

spike, n. pointe f.

spill, vb. répandre tr.

spin, vb. (thread) filer; (twirl) tourner.

spinach, n. épinards m.pl.

spine, n. épine f.; (backbone) épine (f.) dorsale.

spiral, 1. n. spirale f. 2. adj. spiral.

spirit, n. esprit m.

spiritual, adj. spirituel.

spiritualism, n. spiritisme m.

spit, 1. n. (saliva) crachat m.; (for roast) broche f. 2. vb. cracher.

spite, n. dépit m.; (in s. of) malgré.

splash, vb. éclabousser.

splendid, adj. splendide.

splendor, n. splendeur f.

splinter, n. éclat m.

split, vb. fendre.

spoil, 1. n. butin m. 2. vb. gâter.

sponge, n. éponge f.

sponsor, n. (law) garant m.

spontaneous, adj. spontané.

spontaneity, n. spontanéité f.

spool, n. bobine f.

spoon, n. cuiller f.

spoonful, n. cuillerée f.

sporadic, adj. sporadique.

sport, n. sport m.; (fun) jeu m.

spot, 1. n. (stain) tache f.;

(place) endroit *m.* **2.** *vb.* tacher; (recognize) reconnaître.

spouse, 1. *n.* époux *m.,* épouse *f.*

spout, 1. *n.* (teapot, etc.) bec *m.* **2.** *vb.* jaillir.

sprain, *n.* entorse *f.*

sprawl, *vb.* s'étaler.

spray, *n.* (sea) embrun *m.*

spread, 1. *n.* étendue *f.* **2.** *vb.* étendre, *tr.*

spree, *n.* **(be on a s.)** faire la noce.

sprightly, *adj.* éveillé.

spring, 1. *n.* (season) printemps *m.;* (source) source *f.;* (leap) saut *m.;* (device) ressort *m.* **2.** *vb.* (leap) sauter; (water) jaillir.

sprinkle, *vb.* asperger.

spry, *adj.* alerte.

spur, 1. *n.* éperon *m.* **2.** *vb.* éperonner.

spurious, *adj.* faux *m.*

spurn, *vb.* repousser.

spurt, 1. *n.* jet *m.* **2.** *vb.* jaillir.

spy, *n.* espion *m.*

squad, *n.* escouade *f.*

squadron, *n.* escadron *m.*

squalid, *adj.* misérable.

squall, *n.* rafale *f.*

squander, *vb.* gaspiller.

square, 1. *n.* (geom.) carré *m.;* (in town) place *f.* **2.** *adj.* carré.

squat, *vb.* s'accroupir.

squeak, *vb.* crier.

squeeze, *vb.* serrer; (lemon) presser.

squirrel, *n.* écureuil *m.*

squirt, *vb.* seringuer.

stab, *vb.* poignarder.

stability, *n.* stabilité *f.*

stable, 1. *n.* écurie *f.* **2.** *adj.* stable.

stack, *n.* (hay) meule *f.;* (pile) pile *f.;* (chimney) souche *f.*

staff, *n.* (stick) bâton *m.;* (mil.) état-major *m.;* (personnel) personnel *m.*

stage, *n.* (theater) scène *f.;* (in development) période *f.;* (stopping-place) étape *f.*

stagflation, *n.* stagflation *f.*

stagger, *vb.* (totter) chanceler.

stagnant, *adj.* stagnant.

stain, 1. *n.* tache *f.* **2.** *vb.* (spot) tacher; (color) teinter.

stairs, *n.* escalier *m.*

stake, 1. *n.* (post) pieu *m.;* **(at s.)** en jeu. **2.** *vb.* (gaming) mettre au jeu.

stale, *adj.* (bread) rassis.

stalk, *n.* tige *f.*

stall, 1. *n.* (stable, church) stalle *f.*

stamina, *n.* vigueur *f.*

stammer, *vb.* bégayer.

stamp, 1. *n.* timbre(-poste) *m.* **2.** *vb.* (letter) timbrer; (with foot) frapper du pied.

stampede, *n.* sauve-qui-peut *n.*

stand, 1. *n.* (position) position *f.;* (resistance) résistance *f.;* (stall) étalage *m.;* (vehicles) station *f.* **2.** *vb. tr.* (put)

poser; (endure) supporter. **3.** *vb. intr.* (upright) se tenir debout (be situated, be) se trouver; (stop) s'arrêter.

standard, *n.* (flag) étendard *m.;* (measure, etc.) étalon *m.;* (living, etc.) niveau *m.*

star, *n.* étoile *f.;* (movie) vedette *f.*

starch, *n.* amidon *m.*

stare, *vb.* regarder fixement.

stark, *adj.* pur.

start, 1. *n.* (beginning) commencement *m.;* (surprise, etc.) tressaillement *m.* **2.** *vb.* commencer, tressaillir.

startle, *vb.* effrayer.

starvation, *n.* faim *f.*

starve, *vb. intr.* mourir de faim.

state, 1. *n.* état *m.* **2.** *vb.* déclarer.

statement, *n.* déclaration *f.*

statesman, *n.* homme (*m.*) d'état.

static, *adj.* statique.

station, *n.* (railroad) gare *f.;* (bus, subway) station *f.*

stationary, *adj.* stationnaire.

stationery, *n.* papeterie *f.*

statistics, *n.* statistique *f.*

statue, *n.* statue *f.*

stature, *n.* stature *f.*

statute, *n.* statut *m.*

stay, *vb.* rester.

steady, *adj.* ferme; (constant) soutenu.

steak, *n.* bifteck *m.*

steal, *vb.* voler.

steam, *n.* vapeur *f.*

steamboat, *n.* bateau (*m.*) à vapeur.

steamship, *n.* vapeur *m.*

steel, *n.* acier *m.*

steep, *adj.* raide.

steeple, *n.* clocher *m.*

steer, 1. *n.* jeune bœuf *m.* **2.** *vb.* gouverner.

stem, *n.* (plant) tige *f.*

stenographer, *n.* sténographe *m.f.*

stenography, *n.* sténographie *f.*

step, *n.* pas *m.;* (of staircase) marche *f.*

stereophonic, *adj.* stéréophonique.

sterile, *adj.* stérile.

stern, *adj.* sévère.

stethoscope, *n.* stéthoscope *m.*

stew, *n.* ragoût *m.*

steward, *n.* (airline) garçon *m.*

stewardess, *n.* (airline) hôtesse de l'air *f.*

stick, 1. *n.* bâton *m.* **2.** *vb.* (paste) coller, *tr.;* (remain) rester.

sticky, *adj.* gluant.

stiff, *adj.* raide.

stiffness, *n.* raideur *f.*

stifle, *vb.* étouffer.

still, 1. *adj.* tranquille. **2.** *adv.* encore. **3.** *conj.* cependant.

stillness, *n.* tranquillité *f.*

stimulant, *n.* stimulant *m.*

stimulate, *vb.* stimuler.

stimulus, *n.* stimulant *m.*

sting, 1. *n.* piqûre *f.* **2.** *vb.* (prick) piquer; (smart) cuire.

stingy, *adj.* mesquin.

stir, 1. *vb.* remuer; (person, *intr.*) bouger. **2.** *n.* mouvement *m.*

stitch, 1. *n.* (sewing) point *m.;* (knitting) maille *f.* **2.** *vb.* coudre.

stock, *n.* (goods on hand) marchandises *f.pl.;* (finance) valeurs *f.pl.*

stockbroker, *n.* agent de change *m.*

stock exchange, *n.* Bourse *f.*

stocking, *n.* bas *m.*

stole, *n.* étole *f.*

stomach, *n.* estomac *m.*

stone, *n.* pierre *f.*

stool, *n.* escabeau *m.*

stoop, *vb.* se pencher.

stop, 1. *n.* arrêt *m.* **2.** *vb.* arrêter, *tr.;* (prevent) empêcher (de); (cease) cesser.

storage, *n.* emmagasinage *m.*

store, 1. *n.* (shop) magasin *m.;* (supply) provision *f.* **2.** *vb.* emmagasiner.

storm, *n.* orage *m.*

stormy, *adj.* orageux.

story, *n.* histoire *f.;* (floor) étage *m.*

stout, *adj.* gros *m.,* grosse *f.*

stove, *n.* fourneau *m.*

straight, *adj. and adv.* droit.

straighten, *vb.* redresser.

strain, 1. *n.* effort *m.* **2.** *vb.* (stretch) tendre; (filter) passer.

strait, *n.* (geographical) détroit *m.*

strand, *n.* plage *f.*

strange, *adj.* étrange; (foreign) étranger.

stranger, *n.* étranger *m.*

strangle, *vb.* étrangler.

strap, *n.* courroie *f.*

strategic, *adj.* stratégique.

strategy, *n.* stratégie *f.*

straw, *n.* paille *f.*

strawberry, *n.* fraise *f.*

stray, *adj.* égaré.

streak, 1. *n.* raie *f.* **2.** *vb.* rayer.

stream, *n.* courant *m.;* (small river) ruisseau *m.*

streamline, *vb.* caréner.

street, *n.* rue *f.*

strength, *n.* force *f.*

strengthen, *vb.* fortifier.

strenuous, *adj.* énergique.

streptococcus, *n.* streptocoque *m.*

stress, 1. *n.* force *f.;* tension *f.;* (gramm.) accent *m.* **2.** *vb.* accentuer.

stretch, *vb.* étendre, *tr.*

stretcher, *n.* brancard *m.*

strict, *adj.* strict.

stride, *n.* enjambée *f.*

strife, *n.* lutte *f.*

strike, 1. *n.* grève *f.* **2.** *vb.* frapper; (match, *tr.*) allumer; (clock) sonner; (workers) se mettre en grève.

string, *n.* ficelle *f.;* (music) corde *f.*

string bean, *n.* haricot vert *m.*

strip, 1. *n.* bande *f.* **2.** *vb.* dépouiller.

stripe, *n.* bande *f.;* (mil.) galon *m.*

strive, *vb.* s'efforcer (de).

stroke, 1. *n.* coup *m.* **2.** *vb.* caresser.

stroll, *n.* tour *m.*

strong, *adj.* fort.

structure, *n.* structure *f.*

struggle, 1. *n.* lutte *f.* **2.** *vb.* lutter.

stub, *n.* souche *f.*

stubborn, *adj.* opiniâtre, obstiné, têtu.

student, *n.* étudiant *m.*

studio, *n.* atelier *m.*

studious, *adj.* studieux.

study, 1. *n.* étude *f.;* (room) cabinet *(m.)* de travail. **2.** *vb.* étudier.

stuff, 1. *n.* (materials) matériaux *m.pl.;* (textile) étoffe *f.* **2.** *vb.* bourrer; (cooking) farcir.

stuffing, *n.* bourre *f.;* (cooking) farce *f.*

stumble, *vb.* trébucher.

stump, *n.* (tree) souche *f.*

stun, *vb.* étourdir.

stunt, *n.* tour *m.)* de force.

stupid, *adj.* stupide.

stupidity, *n.* stupidité *f.*

sturdy, *adj.* vigoureux.

stutter, *vb.* bégayer.

style, *n.* style *m.*

stylish, *adj.* élégant.

subconscious, *adj.* subconscient.

subdue, *vb.* subjuguer.

subject, 1. *n.* sujet *m.* **2.** *adj.* (people, country) assujetti; (liable) sujet. **3.** *vb.* assujettir.

sublimate, *vb.* sublimer.

sublime, *adj.* sublime.

submarine, *n.* sous-marin *m.*

submerge, *vb.* submerger.

submission, *n.* soumission *f.*

submit, *vb.* soumettre, *tr.*

subnormal, *adj.* sous-normal.

subordinate, *adj. and n.* subordonné *m.*

subscribe, *vb.* (consent, support) souscrire; (to paper, etc.) s'abonner.

subscription, *n.* souscription *f.;* (to paper, etc.) abonnement *m.*

subsequent, *adj.* subséquent.

subsidy, *n.* subvention *f.*

substance, *n.* substance *f.*

substantial, *adj.* substantiel; (well-to-do) aisé.

substitute, 1. *n.* remplaçant *m.* **2.** *vb.* substituer.

substitution, *n.* substitution *f.*

subterfuge, *n.* subterfuge *m.,* faux-fuyant *m.*

subtle, *adj.* subtil.

subtract, *vb.* soustraire.

suburb, *n.* faubourg *m.*

subversive, *adj.* subversif.

subway, *n.* métro(politain) *m.*

succeed, *vb.* (come after) succéder à; (be successful) réussir (à).

success, *n.* succès *m.*

successful, *adj.* heureux.

succession, *n.* succession *f.*

successive, *adj.* successif.

successor, *n.* successeur *m.*

succumb, *vb.* succomber.

such, *adj.* tel; (intensive, **s. a** + *adj.*) un . . . aussi + *adj.*

suck, *vb.* sucer.

suction, *n.* succion *f.*

sudden, *adj.* soudain.

sue, *vb.* poursuivre.

suffer, *vb.* souffrir.

suffice, *vb.* suffire.

sufficient, *adj.* suffisant.

suffocate, *vb.* suffoquer.

sugar, *n.* sucre *m.*

suggest, *vb.* suggérer.

suggestion, *n.* suggestion *f.*

suicide, 1. *n.* suicide *m.* **2.** *vb.* (commit s.) se suicider, *intr.*

suit, 1. *n.* (law) procès *m.;* (clothes) complet *m.;* (cards) couleur *f.* **2.** *vb.* convenir (à).

suitable, *adj.* convenable.

suitcase, *n.* valise *f.*

sum, *n.* somme *f.*

summary, 1. *n.* résumé *m.,* abrégé *m.* **2.** *adj.* sommaire, immédiat.

summer, *n.* été *m.*

summon, *vb.* (convoke) convoquer; (bid to come) appeler.

sun, *n.* soleil *m.*

sunburn, *n.* hâle *m.*

Sunday, *n.* dimanche *m.*

sunny, *adj.* ensoleillé.

sunshine, *n.* soleil *m.*

superb, *adj.* superbe.

superficial, *adj.* superficiel.

superfluous, *adj.* superflu.

superintendent, *n.* surveillant *m.*

superior, *adj. and n.* supérieur *m.*

superiority, *n.* supériorité *f.*

supernatural, *adj. and n.* surnaturel *m.*

supersede, *vb.* remplacer.

superstar, *n.* superstar *m.*

superstition, *n.* superstition *f.*

superstitious, *adj.* superstitieux.

supervise, *vb.* surveiller.

supper, *n.* souper *m.*

supplement, *n.* supplément *m.*

supply, 1. *n.* approvisionnement *m.;* (provision) provision *f.* **2.** *vb.* fournir (de).

support, 1. *n.* appui *m.* **2.** *vb.* soutenir; (bear) supporter; (back up) appuyer.

suppose, *vb.* supposer.

suppress, *vb.* supprimer.

suppression, *n.* suppression *f.*

supreme, *adj.* suprême.

sure, *adj.* sûr.

surface, *n.* surface *f.*

surge, *n.* houle *f.*

surgeon, *n.* chirurgien *m.*

surgery, *n.* chirurgie *f.*

surpass, *vb.* surpasser.

surplus, *n.* surplus *m.*

surprise, 1. *n.* surprise *f.* **2.** *vb.* surprendre.

surrender, *vb.* rendre, *tr.*

surround, *vb.* entourer.

survey, *n.* contempler; (investigate) examiner.

survival, *n.* survivance *f.*

survive, *vb.* survivre.

susceptible, *adj.* susceptible (de).

suspect, *vb.* soupçonner.

suspend, *vb.* suspendre.

suspense, *n.* incertitude *f.;* (in s.) en suspens.

suspension, *n.* suspension *f.*

suspicion, *n.* soupçon *m.*

suspicious, *adj.* soupçonneux; (questionable) suspect.

sustain, *vb.* soutenir.

swallow, 1. *n.* (bird) hirondelle *f.* **2.** *vb.* avaler.

swamp, *n.* marais *m.*

swan, *n.* cygne *m.*

swarm, *n.* essaim *m.*

sway, 1. *n.* (rule) domination *f.;* (motion) oscillation *f.* **2.** *vb.* gouverner.

swear, *vb.* jurer.

sweat, 1. *n.* sueur *f.* **2.** *vb.* suer.

Sweden, *n.* Suédois *m.*

Sweden, *n.* Suède *f.*

Swedish, *adj. and n.* suédois *m.*

sweep, 1. *n.* (bend) courbe *f.;* (movement) mouvement *(m.)* circulaire. **2.** *vb.* balayer.

sweepstakes, *n.* poule *f.*

sweet, *adj.* doux *m.,* douce *f.;* sucré.

sweetheart, *n.* amant *m.,* amante *f.*

sweetness, *n.* douceur *f.*

swell, *vb.* gonfler, *tr.;* enfler, *tr.*

swift, *adj.* rapide.

swim, *vb.* nager.

swindle, *vb.* escroquer.

swine, *n.* cochon *m.*

swing, *vb.* balancer, *tr.*

Swiss, 1. *n.* Suisse *m.* **2.** *adj.* suisse, helvétique.

switch, *n.* (electric) interrupteur *m.*

Switzerland, *n.* Suisse *f.*

sword, *n.* épée *f.*

syllable, *n.* syllabe *f.*

symbol, *n.* symbole *m.*

symbolic, *adj.* symbolique.

sympathetic, *adj.* compatissant.

sympathy, *n.* compassion *f.*

symphony, *n.* symphonie *f.*

symptom, *n.* symptôme *m.*

synchronize, *vb.* synchroniser, *tr.*

syndicate, *n.* syndicat *m.*

syndrome, *n.* syndrome *m.*

synonym, *n.* synonyme *m.*

synthetic, *adj.* synthétique.

syringe, *n.* seringue *f.*

syrup, *n.* sirop *m.*

system, *n.* système *m.*

systematic, *adj.* systématique.

T

tabernacle, *n.* tabernacle *m.*
table, *n.* table *f.*
tablecloth, *n.* nappe *f.*
tablespoon, *n.* cuiller *(f.)* à bouche.
tablet, *n.* tablette *f.*
tack, 1. *n.* (nail) broquette *f.* **2.** *vb.* clouer.
tact, *n.* tact *m.*
tag, *n.* étiquette *f.*
tail, *n.* queue *f.*
tailor, *n.* tailleur *m.*
take, *vb.* prendre; (lead) conduire; (carry) porter.
tale, *n.* conte *m.*
talent, *n.* talent *m.*
talk, 1. *n.* conversation *f.* **2.** *vb.* parler.
talkative, *adj.* bavard.
tall, *adj.* grand.
tame, *adj.* (animal) apprivoisé.
tamper, *vb.* toucher à.
tan, *n.* (leather) tan *m.;* (skin) hâle *m.*
tangible, *adj.* tangible.
tangle, *n.* embrouillement *m.*
tank, *n.* réservoir *m.;* (mil.) char *(m.)* d'assaut.
tap, 1. *n.* (water) robinet *m.;* (knock) petit coup *m.* **2.** *vb.* frapper légèrement.
tape, *n.* ruban *m.*
tape recorder, *n.* magnétophone *m.*
tapestry, *n.* tapisserie *f.*
tar, *n.* goudron *m.*
target, *n.* cible *f.*
tariff, *n.* tarif *m.*
tarnish, *vb.* ternir, *tr.*
task, *n.* tâche *f.*
taste, 1. *n.* goût *m.* **2.** *vb.* goûter.
tasty, *adj.* savoureux.
taut, *adj.* raide.
tavern, *n.* taverne *f.*
tax, 1. *n.* impôt *m.* **2.** *vb.* imposer.
taxi, *n.* taxi *m.*
taxpayer, *n.* contribuable *m.*
tea, *n.* thé *m.*
teach, *vb.* enseigner; (to do) apprendre à.
teacher, *n.* instituteur *m.;* (school) professeur *m.*
team, *n.* (animals) attelage *m.;* (people) équipe *f.*
teapot, *n.* théière *f.*
tear, 1. *n.* larme *f.;* (rip) déchirure *f.* **2.** *vb.* déchirer.
tease, *vb.* taquiner.
teaspoon, *n.* cuiller *(f.)* à thé.
technical, *adj.* technique.
technique, *n.* technique *f.*
tedious, *adj.* ennuyeux.
telegram, *n.* télégramme *m.*
telegraph, *n.* télégraphe *m.*
telephone, 1. *n.* téléphone *m.* **2.** *vb.* téléphoner.
telescope, *n.* télescope *m.*
televise, *vb.* téléviser.
television, *n.* télévision *f.*

tell, *vb.* dire; (story, etc.) raconter.
teller, *n.* (bank) caissier *m.*
temper, *n.* (humor) humeur *f.;* (lose one's t.) s'emporter; (anger) colère *f.;* (metals) trempe *f.*
temperament, *n.* tempérament *m.*
temperamental, *adj.* instable.
temperance, *n.* tempérance *f.*
temperate, *adj.* (habit) sobre; (climate) tempéré.
temperature, *n.* température *f.*
tempest, *n.* tempête *f.*
temple, *n.* temple *m.;* (forehead) tempe *f.*
temporary, *adj.* temporaire.
tempt, *vb.* tenter.
temptation, *n.* tentation *f.*
ten, *adj. and n.* dix *m.*
tenant, *n.* locataire *m.f.*
tend, *vb.* tendre, *intr.;* (care for) soigner.
tendency, *n.* tendance *f.*
tender, *adj.* tendre.
tenderness, *n.* tendresse *f.*
tendon, *n.* tendon *m.*
tennis, *n.* tennis *m.*
tenor, *n.* (music) ténor *m.*
tense, *adj.* tendu.
tension, *n.* tension *f.*
tent, *n.* tente *f.*
tentative, *adj.* tentatif, expérimental.
tenth, *adj. and n.* dixième *m.*
term, *n.* terme *m.;* (school) trimestre *m.;* (conditions) conditions *f.pl.*
terrace, *n.* terrasse *f.*
terrible, *adj.* terrible.
terrify, *vb.* terrifier.
territory, *n.* territoire *m.*
terror, *n.* terreur *f.*
test, 1. *n.* épreuve *f.* **2.** *vb.* mettre à l'épreuve.
testament, *n.* testament *m.*
testify, *vb.* témoigner (de); (declare) affirmer.
testimony, *n.* témoignage *m.*
text, *n.* texte *m.*
textile, *adj.* textile.
texture, *n.* texture *f.*
than, *conj.* que; (with numerals) de.
thank, *vb.* remercier; (t. you) merci.
thankful, *adj.* reconnaissant.
that *sg.,* **those** *pl.* **1.** *adj.* ce cet *m.,* cette *f.,* ces *pl.;* (opposed to this) ce . . . -là, etc. **2.** demonstrative pron. celui-là *m.,* celle-là *f.,* ceux-là *m.pl.* celles-là *f.pl.;* (object not named) cela, abbr. ça; (what is t.?) qu'est-ce que c'est que ça? **3.** relative pron. qui (subject); que (object). **4.** conj. que; (purpose) pour que.
the, *art.* le *m.,* la *f.,* les *pl.*
theater, *n.* théâtre *m.*
theft, *n.* vol *m.*
their, *adj.* leur *sg.,* leurs *pl.*

theirs, *pron.* le leur *m.,* la leur *f.,* les leurs *pl.*
them, *pron.* eux *m.,* elles *f.;* (unstressed, with verb) les (direct), leur (indirect).
theme, *n.* thème *m.*
themselves, *pron.* eux-mêmes *m.,* elles-mêmes *f.;* (reflexive) se.
then, *adv.* alors; (after that) ensuite.
thence, *adv.* (place) de là; (reason) pour cette raison.
theology, *n.* théologie *f.*
theoretical, *adj.* théorique.
theory, *n.* théorie *f.*
therapy, *n.* thérapie *f.*
there, *adv.* là; (with verb) y.
therefore, *adv.* donc.
thermometer, *n.* thermomètre *m.*
these, *see* this.
they, *pron.* ils *m.,* elles *f.*
thick, *adj.* épais.
thicken, *vb.* épaissir, *tr.*
thickness, *n.* épaisseur *f.*
thief, *n.* voleur *m.*
thigh, *n.* cuisse *f.*
thimble, *n.* dé *m.*
thin, *adj.* mince.
thing, *n.* chose *f.*
think (of), *vb.* penser (à).
thinker, *n.* penseur *m.*
third, 1. *n.* tiers *m.* **2.** *adj.* troisième.
Third World, *n.* Tiers Monde *m.*
thirst, *n.* soif *f.*
thirsty, *adj.* (be t.) avoir soif.
thirteen, *adj. and n.* treize *m.*
thirty, *adj. and n.* trente *m.*
this, *sg.* **these** *pl.* **1.** *adj.* ce, cet *m.,* cette *f.,* ces *pl.;* (opposed to that) ce . . . -ci, etc. **2.** demonstrative pron. celui-ci *m.,* celle-ci *f.,* ceux-ci *m.pl.,* celles-ci *f.pl.;* (object not named) ceci.
thorough, *adj.* complet.
those, *see* that.
though, *conj.* quoique.
thought, *n.* pensée *f.*
thoughtful, *adj.* pensif.
thousand, *adj. and n.* mille *m.*
thread, *n.* fil *m.*
threat, *n.* menace *f.*
threaten, *vb.* menacer.
three, *adj. and n.* trois *m.*
thrift, *n.* économie *f.*
thrill, 1. *n.* tressaillement *m.* **2.** *vb.* tressaillir, *intr.;* faire frémir, *tr.*
thrive, *vb.* prospérer.
throat, *n.* gorge *f.*
throne, *n.* trône *m.*
through, *prep. and adv.* à travers; (be t.) avoir fini.
throughout, *adv.* partout.
throw, *vb.* jeter.
thrust, *vb.* pousser.
thumb, *n.* pouce *m.*
thunder, 1. *n.* tonnerre *m.* **2.** *vb.* tonner.
Thursday, *n.* jeudi *m.*
thus, *adv.* ainsi.

thwart, vb. contrarier.

ticket, n. billet m.

tickle, vb. chatouiller.

ticklish, adj. chatouilleux.

tide, n. marée f.

tidy, adj. (person) ordonné; (thing) en bon ordre.

tie, 1. n. lien m.; (neck-t.) cravate f. **2.** vb. attacher; (bind) lier; (knot) nouer.

tier, n. gradin m.

tiger, n. tigre m.

tight, adj. serré; (drunk) gris.

tighten, vb. serrer.

tile, n. (roof) tuile f.

till, 1. prep. jusqu'à. **2.** conj. jusqu'à ce que.

tilt, vb. pencher.

timber, n. (building) bois (m.) de construction.

time, n. temps m.; (occasion) fois f.; (clock) heure f.; (what t. is it?) quelle heure est-il?; **(have a good t.)** s'amuser bien.

timetable, n. horaire m.

timid, adj. timide.

timidity, n. timidité f.

tin, n. étain m.

tint, n. teinte f.

tiny, adj. tout petit.

tip, 1. n. (money) pourboire m.; (end) bout m. **2.** vb. (money) donner un pourboire à; **(t. over)** renverser.

tire, 1. n. (car, etc.) pneumatique (abbr. pneu) m. **2.** vb. fatiguer.

tired, adj. fatigué.

tissue, n. tissu m.

title, n. titre m.

to, prep. à; **(in order** pour t.).

tobacco, n. tabac m.

today, adv. aujourd'hui.

toe, n. orteil m.

together, adv. ensemble.

toil, vb. travailler dur.

toilet, n. toilette f.

token, n. témoignage m.; (coin) jeton m.

tolerance, n. tolérance f.

tolerant, adj. tolérant.

tolerate, vb. tolérer.

tomato, n. tomate f.

tomb, n. tombeau m.

tomorrow, adv. demain.

ton, n. tonne f.

tone, n. ton m.

tongue, n. langue f.

tonic, adj. and n. tonique m.

tonight, adv. cette nuit; (evening) ce soir.

tonsil, n. amygdale f.

too, adv. trop; (also) aussi.

tool, n. outil m.

tooth, n. dent m.

toothache, n. mal (m.) de dents.

toothbrush, n. brosse (f.) à dents.

top, n. (mountain, etc.) sommet m.; (table) dessus m.

topcoat, n. pardessus m.

topic, n. sujet m.

torch, n. torche f.

torment, 1. n. tourment m. **2.** vb. tourmenter.

torrent, n. torrent m.

torture, 1. n. torture f. **2.** vb. torturer.

toss, vb. (throw) jeter; s'agiter, intr.

total, adj. and n. total m.

totalitarian, adj. totalitaire.

touch, 1. n. (touching) attouchement m.; (sense) toucher m.; (small amount) pointe f.; (contact) contact m. - **2.** vb. toucher.

tough, adj. dur.

tour, n. tour m.

tourist, n. touriste m.f.

tournament, n. tournoi m.

tow, vb. remorquer.

toward, prep. (place, time) vers; (feelings, etc.) envers.

towel, n. serviette f.

tower, n. tour f.

town, n. ville f.

toy, n. jouet m.

trace, n. trace f.

track, n. piste f.; (railroad) voie f.

tract, n. (space) étendue f.

tractor, n. tracteur m.

trade, 1. n. commerce m.; (job) métier m. **2.** vb. commercer.

trader, n. commerçant m.

tradition, n. tradition f.

traditional, adj. traditionnel.

traffic, n. circulation f.

tragedy, n. tragédie f.

tragic, adj. tragique.

trail, n. trace f.

train, 1. n. train m.; (dress) traîne f.; (retinue) suite f. **2.** vb. (sports) entraîner, tr.; (mil.) exercer, tr.

traitor, n. traître m.

tramp, n. (steps) bruit (m.) de pas; (person) chemineau m.

tranquil, adj. tranquille.

tranquility, n. tranquillité f.

transaction, n. opération f.

transfer, 1. n. transport m.; (ticket) billet (m.) de correspondance. **2.** vb. transférer, tr.

transform, vb. transformer.

transfusion, n. transfusion f.

transition, n. transition f.

translate, vb. traduire.

translation, n. traduction f.

transmit, vb. transmettre.

transparent, adj. transparent.

transport, transportation, 1. n. transport m. **2.** vb. transporter.

transsexual, adj. transsexuel.

transvestite, adj. travesti.

trap, 1. n. piège m. **2.** vb. prendre au piège.

trash, n. (rubbish) rebut m.

travel, 1. n. voyage m. **2/** vb. voyager.

traveler, n. voyageur m.

traveler's check, n. chèque de voyage n.

tray, n. plateau m.

treacherous, adj. traître.

tread, vb. marcher.

treason, n. trahison f.

treasure, n. trésor m.

treasurer, n. trésorier m.

treasury, n. trésor m.

treat, vb. traiter.

treatment, n. traitement m.

treaty, n. traité m.

tree, n. arbre m.

tremble, vb. trembler.

tremendous, adj. terrible.

trench, n. tranchée f.

trend, n. tendance f.

trespass, vb. empiéter.

triage, n. présélection f.

trial, n. (law) procès m.; (test) épreuve f.

triangle, n. triangle m.

tribulation, n. tribulation f.

tributary, 1. n. (river) affluent m. **2.** adj. tributaire.

tribute, n. tribut m.

trick, 1. n. ruse f. **2.** vb. duper.

tricky, adj. astucieux.

trifle, n. bagatelle f.

trigger, n. détente f.

trim, 1. adj. soigné. **2.** vb. (put in order) arranger; (adorn) garnir; (cut) tailler.

trinket, n. breloque f.

trip, 1. n. voyage m. **2.** vb. trébucher.

triple, adj. and n. triple m.

trite, adj. rebattu.

triumph, n. triomphe m.

triumphant, adj. triomphant.

trivial, adj. trivial.

trolley-car, n. tramway m.

troop, n. troupe f.

trophy, n. trophée m.

tropic, n. tropique m.

trot, 1. n. trot m. **2.** vb. intr. trotter.

trouble, 1. n. (misfortune) malheur m.; (difficulty) difficulté f.; (inconvenience, medical) dérangement m. **2.** vb. (worry) inquiéter, tr.; (inconvenience) déranger; (afflict) affliger.

troublesome, adj. gênant.

trough, n. auge f.

trousers, n. pantalon m.

trousseau, n. trousseau m.

trout, n. truite f.

truce, n. trêve f.

truck, n. camion m.

true, adj. vrai.

truly, adv. vraiment.

trumpet, n. trompette f.

trunk, n. (clothes) malle f.; (body, tree) tronc m.

trust, 1. n. confiance f.; (business) trust m. **2.** vb. se confier à; (entrust) confier.

trustworthy, adj. digne de confiance.

truth, n. vérité f.

truthful, adj. sincère.

try, vb. essayer; (law) mettre en jugement.

tryst, n. rendez-vous m.

T-shirt, n. maillot m.

tub, n. baignoire f.

tube, n. tube m.

tuberculosis, *n.* tuberculose *f.*

tuck, *n.* (fold) pli *m.*

Tuesday, *n.* mardi *m.*

tug, 1. *n.* (boat) remorqueur *m.* 2. *vb.* (pull) tirer; (boat) remorquer.

tuition, *n.* (prix de l')enseignement *m.*

tulip, *n.* tulipe *f.*

tumble, *vb.* (fall) tomber.

tumor, *n.* tumeur *f.*

tumult, *n.* tumulte *m.*

tuna, *n.* thon *m.*

tune, 1. *n.* air *m.*; (concord, harmony) accord *m.* 2. *vb.* accorder.

tunnel, *n.* tunnel *m.*

turban, *n.* turban *m.*

turf, *n.* gazon *m.*

Turk, *n.* Turc *m.*, Turque *f.*

turkey, *n.* dindon *m.*

Turkey, *n.* Turquie *f.*

Turkish, 1. *n.* turc. *m.* 2. *adj.* turc, turque f.

turmoil, *n.* tumulte m.

turn, 1. *n.* tour *m.*; (road) détour *m.* 2. *vb.* tourner.

turnip, *n.* navet *m.*

turret, *n.* tourelle *f.*

turtle, *n.* tortue *f.*

tutor, *n.* précepteur *m.*

twelfth, *adj. and n.* douzième *m.*

twelve, *adj. and n.* douze *m.*

twentieth, *adj. and n.* vingtième *m.*

twenty, *adj. and n.* vingt *m.*

twice, *adv.* deux fois.

twig, *n.* brindille *f.*

twilight, *n.* crépuscule *m.*

twin, *adj. and n.* jumeau *m.*, jumelle *f.*

twine, *n.* ficelle *f.*

twinkle, *vb.* scintiller.

twist, *vb.* tordre.

two, *adj. and n.* deux *m.*

type, 1. *n.* type *m.*; (printing) caractère *m.* 2. *vb.* taper à la machine.

typewriter, *n.* machine (*f.*) à écrire.

typhoid fever, *n.* fièvre (*f.*) typhoïde.

typical, *adj.* typique.

typist, *n.* dactylo(graphe) *m.f.*

tyranny, *n.* tyrannie *f.*

tyrant, *n.* tyran *m.*

U

udder, *n.* mamelle *f.*

ugliness, *n.* laideur *f.*

ugly, *adj.* laid.

ulcer, *n.* ulcère *m.*

ulterior, *adj.* ultérieur.

ultimate, *adj.* dernier.

umbrella, *n.* parapluie *m.*

umpire, *n.* arbitre *m.f.*

unable, *adj.* incapable; (u. to) dans l'impossibilité de.

unanimous, *adj.* unanime.

uncertain, *adj.* incertain.

uncle, *n.* oncle *m.*

unconscious, 1. *n.* inconscient *m.* 2. *adj.* (aware) inconscient; (faint) sans connaissance; (u. of) sans conscience de.

uncover, *vb.* découvrir.

under, 1. *prep.* sous. 2. *adv.* au-dessous.

underestimate, *vb.* sous-estimer.

undergo, *vb.* subir.

underground, *adj.* souterrain.

underline, *vb.* souligner.

underneath, *adv.* en dessous.

undershirt, *n.* gilet (*m.*) de dessous.

understand, *vb.* comprendre.

undertake, *vb.* entreprendre.

undertaker, *n.* entrepreneur (*m.*) de pompes funèbres.

underwear, *n.* vêtements (*m.pl.*) de dessous.

undo, *vb.* défaire.

undress, *vb.* déshabiller, *tr.*

uneasy, *adj.* gêné.

uneven, *adj.* inégal.

unexpected, *adj.* inattendu.

unfair, *adj.* injuste.

unfit, *adj.* peu propre (à).

unfold, *vb.* déplier.

unforgettable, *adj.* inoubliable.

unfortunate, *adj.* malheureux.

unhappy, *adj.* malheureux.

uniform, *adj. and n.* uniforme *m.*

unify, *vb.* unifier.

union, *n.* union *f.*

unique, *adj.* unique.

unisex, *adj.* unisexuel.

unit, *n.* unité *f.*

unite, *vb.* unir, *tr.*

United Nations, *n.* Nations Unies *f.pl.*

United States, *n.* États-Unis *m.pl.*

unity, *n.* unité *f.*

universal, *adj.* universel.

universe, *n.* univers *m.*

university, *n.* université *f.*

unleaded, *adj.* sans plomb.

unless, *conj.* à moins que . . . ne.

unlike, *adj.* dissemblable.

unload, *vb.* décharger.

unlock, *vb.* ouvrir.

untie, *vb.* dénouer.

until, *conj.* jusqu'à ce que.

unusual, *adj.* insolite.

up, *prep.* vers le haut de.

uphold, *vb.* soutenir.

upholster, *vb.* tapisser.

upon, *prep.* sur.

upper, *adj.* supérieur.

upright, *adj.* droit.

uproar, *n.* vacarme *m.*

upset, *vb.* renverser.

upstairs, *adv.* en haut.

uptight, *adj.* tendu.

upward, 1. *adj.* dirigé en haut. 2. *adv.* en montant.

urge, *vb.* (beg) prier.

urgency, *n.* urgence *f.*

urgent, *adj.* urgent.

us, *pron.* nous.

use, 1. *n.* usage *m.* 2. *vb.* employer; se servir de.

useful, *adj.* utile.

useless, *adj.* inutile.

usher, *n.* huissier *m.*

usual, *adj.* usuel.

utensil, *n.* ustensile *m.*

utilize, *vb.* utiliser, se servir de.

utmost, 1. *n.* le plus; (all one can) tout son possible. 2. *adj.* (greatest) le plus grand.

utter, 1. *adj.* absolu. 2. *vb.* prononcer; (cry) pousser.

utterance, *n.* émission *f.*

V

vacancy, *n.* vide *m.*, vacance *f.*

vacant, *adj.* vide.

vacate, *vb.* quitter, évacuer.

vacation, *n.* vacances *f.pl.*

vaccinate, *vb.* vacciner.

vaccine, *n.* vaccin *m.*

vacuum, *n.* vide *m.*; (v. cleaner) aspirateur *m.*

vagrant, *n.* vagabond *m.*

vague, *adj.* vague.

vain, *adj.* vain.

valiant, *adj.* vaillant.

valid, *adj.* valide.

valise, *n.* valise *f.*

valley, *n.* vallée *f.*

valor, *n.* valeur *f.*

valuable, *adj.* de valeur.

value, 1. *n.* valeur *f.* 2. *vb.* évaluer.

value-added tax, *n.* taxe à la valeur ajoutée *f.*

valve, *n.* soupape *f.*

vandal, *n.* vandale *m.f.*

vanguard, *n.* avant-garde *f.*

vanilla, *n.* vanille *f.*

vanish, *vb.* s'évanouir.

vanity, *n.* vanité *f.*

vanquish, *vb.* vaincre.

vapor, *n.* vapeur, *f.*

variation, *n.* variation *f.*

varied, *adj.* varié.

variety, *n.* variété *f.*

various, *adj.* divers.

varnish, *n.* vernis *m.*

vary, *vb.* varier.

vase, *n.* vase *m.*

vasectomy, *n.* vasectomie *f.*

vassal, *n.* vassal *m.*

vast, *adj.* vaste.

vat, *n.* cuve *f.*

vault, *n.* voûte *f.*

vegetable, *n.* légume *m.*

vehement, *adj.* véhément.

vehicle, *n.* véhicule *m.*

veil, *n.* voile *m.*

vein, *n.* veine *f.*

velocity, *n.* vitesse *f.*

velvet, *n.* velours *m.*

vengeance, *n.* vengeance *f.*

vent, *n.* ouverture *f.*

ventilate, *vb.* ventiler.

venture, 1. *n.* aventure *f.* 2. *vb.* hasarder, *tr.*

verb, *n.* verbe *m.*

verbose, *adj.* verbeux.

verdict, *n.* verdict *m.*

verge, n. bord m.

verify, vb. vérifier.

versatile, adj. versatile.

verse, n. vers m.pl.; (line of poetry) vers m.

version, n. version f.

vertical, adj. vertical.

very, adv. très.

vessel, n. vaisseau m.

vest, n. gilet m.

veteran, n. vétéran m.

veto, n. véto m.

vex, vb. vexer.

viaduct, n. viaduc m.

vibrate, vb. vibrer.

vibration, n. vibration f.

vice, n. vice m.

vicinity, n. voisinage m.

vicious, adj. méchant.

victim, n. victime f.

victor, n. vainqueur m.

victorious, adj. victorieux.

victory, n. victoire f.

videodisc, n. vidéodisque m.

videotape, n. bande vidéo f.

view, n. vue f.

vigil, n. veille f.

vigilant, adj. vigilant.

vigor, n. vigueur f.

vile, adj. vil, abominable.

village, n. village m.

villain, n. scélérat m.

vindicate, vb. défendre.

vine, n. vigne f.

vinegar, n. vinaigre m.

vineyard, n. vigne f.

vintage, n. (grapes gathered) vendange f.; (year of wine) année f.

violate, vb. violer.

violation, n. violation f.

violence, n. violence f.

violent, adj. violent.

violet, 1. n. violette f. 2. adj. violet.

violin, n. violon m.

virgin, n. vierge f.

virile, adj. viril.

virtual, adj. vrai.

virtue, n. vertu f.

virtuous, adj. vertueux.

virus, n. virus m.

visa, n. visa m.

visible, adj. visible.

vision, n. vision f.

visit, 1. n. visite f. 2. vb. visiter.

visitor, n. visiteur m.

visual, adj. visuel.

vital, adj. vital.

vitality, n. vitalité f.

vitamin, n. vitamine f.

vivacious, adj. vif m., vive f.

vivid, adj. vif m., vive f.

vocabulary, n. vocabulaire m.

vocal, adj. vocal.

vogue, n. vogue f.

voice, n. voix f.

void, adj. (law) nul.

volcano, n. volcan m.

volume, n. volume m.

voluntary, adj. volontaire.

volunteer, 1. n. volontaire m. 2. vb. s'engager.

vomit, vb. vomir.

vote, 1. n. vote m. 2. vb. voter.

voter, n. votant m.

vouch for, vb. répondre de.

vow, n. vœu m.

vowel, n. voyelle f.

voyage, n. voyage m.

vulgar, adj. vulgaire.

vulnerable, adj. vulnérable.

W

wade, vb. traverser à gué.

waffle, n. gaufre (américaine) f.

wag, vb. agiter.

wage, vb. (war) faire la guerre.

wages, n. salaire m.

wagon, n. chariot m.

wail, vb. gémir.

waist, n. taille f.

wait (for), vb. attendre.

waiter, n. garçon m.

wake (up), vb. réveiller, tr.; s'éveiller, intr.

walk, 1. n. promenade f. 2. vb. marcher; (take a w.) se promener.

wall, n. mur m.

wallcovering, n. tenture f.

wallet, n. portefeuille m.

wallpaper, n. papier peint m.; papier à tapisser m.

walnut, n. noix f.

walrus, n. morse m.

waltz, n. valse f.

wander, vb. errer.

want, 1. n. besoin m. 2. vb. vouloir.

war, n. guerre f.

ward, n. (hospital) salle f.; (charge) pupille m.f.

ware, n. marchandises f.pl.

warlike, adj. guerrier.

warm, 1. adj. chaud; (be w.) avoir chaud. 2. vb. chauffer.

warmth, n. chaleur f.

warn, vb. avertir.

warning, n. avertissement m.

warp, vb. détourner.

warrant, 1. n. mandat m. 2. vb. garantir.

warrior, n. guerrier m.

warship, n. navire (m.) de guerre.

wash, vb. laver, tr.

washing machine, n. laveuse mécanique f.

washroom, n. salle de bain f.

wasp, n. guêpe f.

waste, 1. n. (money) gaspillage m.; (time) perte f.; (rubbish) déchets m.pl. 2. vb. gaspiller, perdre.

watch, 1. n. (timepiece) montre f.; (guard) garde f. 2. vb. veiller, garder.

watchful, adj. vigilant.

watchmaker, n. horloger m.

watchman, n. gardien m.

water, n. eau f.

waterbed, n. aqualit m.

water color, n. aquarelle f.

waterfall, n. chute (f.) d'eau.

waterproof, adj. imperméable.

wave, 1. n. (sea) vague f.; (sound) onde f.; (permanent w.) ondulation (f.) permanente. 2. vb. agiter; (hair) onduler.

waver, vb. vaciller.

wax, n. cire f.

way, n. (road) chemin m.; (distance) distance f.; (direction) côté m.; (manner) manière f.

we, pron. nous.

weak, adj. faible.

weaken, vb. affaiblir.

weakness, n. faiblesse f.

wealth, n. richesse f.

wealthy, adj. riche.

weapon, n. arme f.

wear, vb. porter.

weary, adj. las.

weasel, n. belette f.

weather, n. temps m.

weave, vb. tisser.

weaver, n. tisserand m.

web, n. (fabric) tissu m.; (spider) toile f.

wedding, n. noces f.pl.

wedge, n. coin m.

Wednesday, n. mercredi m.

weed, n. mauvaise herbe f.

week, n. semaine f.

weekday, n. jour (m.) de semaine.

week end, n. week-end m., fin de semaine f.

weekly, adj. hebdomadaire.

weep, vb. pleurer.

weigh, vb. peser.

weight, n. poids m.

weird, adj. mystérieux.

welcome, adj. bienvenu.

welfare, n. bien-être m.

well, 1. n. (water) puits m. 2. adv. bien.

well-known, adj. bien connu.

west, n. ouest m.

western, adj. de l'ouest.

westward, adv. vers l'ouest.

wet, 1. adj. mouillé; (weather) pluvieux. 2. vb. mouiller.

whale, n. baleine f.

what, 1. adj. quel. 2. pron. (relative, that which) ce qui (subject), ce que (object); (interrogative) qu'est-ce qui; quoi. 3. interj. quoi!

whatever, 1. adj. quelque . . . qui (subject), . . . que (object). 2. pron. quoi qui (subject), . . . que (object).

wheat, n. blé m.

wheel, n. roue f.

when, conj. quand.

whenever, conj. toutes les fois que.

where, conj. où.

wherever, conj. partout où.

whether, conj. soit que; (if) si.

which, 1. adj. quel. 2. pron. (relative) qui; lequel; (interrogative) lequel.

whichever, pron. n'importe lequel.

while, conj. pendant que; (whereas) tandis que.

whim, *n.* caprice *m.,* lubie *f.*

whip, *n.* fouet *m.*

whirl, *vb.* faire tourner, *tr.;* tourner sur soi, *intr.*

whirlpool, *n.* tourbillon *(m.)* d'eau.

whirlwind, *n.* tourbillon *(m.)* de vent.

whisker, *n.* (man) favori *m.;* (animals) moustache *f.*

whiskey, *n.* whiskey *m.*

whisper, *vb.* chuchoter.

whistle, 1. *n.* sifflet *m.* **2.** *vb.* siffler.

white, *adj.* blanc *m.,* blanche *f.*

who, *pron.* qui.

whoever, *pron.* qui que.

whole, *adj.* entier.

wholesale, *adj. and adv.* en gros.

wholesome, *adj.* sain.

wholly, *adv.* entièrement.

whom, *pron. (relative)* que; lequel; *(interrogative)* qui.

whose, *pron. (relative)* dont; *(interrogative)* de qui.

why, *adv.* pourquoi.

wicked, *adj.* méchant.

wickedness, *n.* méchanceté *f.*

wide, *adj.* large.

widen, *vb.* élargir, *tr.*

widespread, *adj.* répandu.

widow, *n.* veuve *f.*

widower, *n.* veuf *m.*

width, *n.* largeur *f.*

wield, *vb.* manier.

wife, *n.* femme *f.*

wig, *n.* perruque *f.*

wild, *adj.* sauvage.

wilderness, *n.* désert *m.*

wildlife, *n.* faune *f.*

will, 1. *n.* volonté *f.;* **(last w.)** testament *m.* **2.** *vb.* vouloir; (bequeath) léguer.

willful, *adj.* obstiné.

willing, *adj.* bien disposé.

wilt, *vb.* flétrir.

win, *vb.* gagner.

wind, *n.* vent *m.*

window, *n.* fenêtre *f.;* (shop) devanture *f.*

windy, *adj.* venteux.

wine, *n.* vin *m.*

wing, *n.* aile *f.*

wink, 1. *n.* clin *(m.)* d'œil. **2.** *vb.* clignoter.

winner, *n.* gagnant *m.*

winter, *n.* hiver *m.*

wipe, *vb.* essuyer.

wire, *n.* fil *(m.)* de fer.

wireless, *n.* télégraphie *(f.)* sans fil *(abbr.* T.S.F.).

wisdom, *n.* sagesse *f.*

wise, *adj.* sage.

wish, 1. *n.* désir *m.* **2.** *vb.* désirer.

wit, *n.* esprit *m.*

witch, *n.* sorcière *f.*

with, *prep.* avec.

withdraw, *vb.* retirer, *tr.*

wither, *vb.* flétrir.

withhold, *vb.* refuser.

within, *adv.* dedans.

without, *prep.* sans.

witness, *n.* témoin *m.*

witty, *adj.* spirituel.

wizard, *n.* sorcier *m.*

woe, *n.* malheur *m.*

wolf, *n.* loup *m.*

woman, *n.* femme *f.*

womb, *n.* matrice *f.*

wonder, *vb.* (ask oneself) se demander; (be surprised) être étonné.

wonderful, *adj.* merveilleux.

woo, *vb.* faire la cour à.

wood, *n.* bois *m.*

wooden, *adj.* de bois.

wool, *n.* laine *f.*

woolen, *adj.* de laine.

word, *n.* mot *m.*

work, 1. *n.* travail *m.* **2.** *vb.* travailler.

worker, *n.* travailleur *m.*

workman, *n.* ouvrier *m.*

world, *n.* monde *m.*

worldly, *adj.* mondain.

world-wide, *adj.* mondial.

worm, *n.* ver *m.*

worn, *adj.* usé.

worry, 1. *n.* souci *m.* **2.** *vb.* tracasser, préoccuper, *tr.*

worse, 1. *adj.* pire. **2.** *adv.* pis.

worship, 1. *n.* culte *m.* **2.** *vb.* adorer.

worst, 1. *adj.* (le) pire. **2.** *adv.* (le) pis.

worth, *n.* valeur *f.;* (be w. while to) valoir la peine de.

worthless, *adj.* indigne; (without value) sans valeur.

worthy, *adj.* digne.

would, *vb.* vouloir.

wound, 1. *n.* blessure *f.* **2.** *vb.* blesser.

wrap, *vb.* envelopper.

wrapping, *n.* couverture *f.*

wrath, *n.* courroux *m.*

wreath, *n.* couronne *f.*

wreck, *n.* (ship) naufrage *m.;* (remains) débris *m.pl.*

wrench, *vb.* tordre.

wrestle, *vb.* lutter.

wretched, *adj.* misérable.

wring, *vb.* tordre.

wrinkle, *n.* ride *f.*

wrist, *n.* poignet *m.*

wrist watch, *n.* montre-bracelet *f.*

write, *vb.* écrire.

writer, *n.* écrivain *m.*

writhe, *vb.* se tordre.

wrong, 1. *n.* tort *m.* **2.** *adj.* faux *m.,* fausse *f.;* **(be w.)** avoir tort.

X, Y, Z

x-rays, *n.* rayons X *m.pl.*

xylophone, *n.* xylophone *m.*

yacht, *n.* yacht *m.*

yam, *n.* igname *f.*

yard, *n.* (house, etc.) cour *f.;* (lumber, etc.) chantier *m.;* (measure) yard *m.*

yarn, *n.* fil *m.*

yawn, 1. *n.* bâillement *m.* **2.** *vb.* bâiller.

year, *n.* an *m.;* (duration) année *f.*

yearly, *adj.* annuel.

yearn for, *vb.* soupirer après.

yell, *vb.* hurler.

yellow, *adj. and adv.* jaune *m.*

yes, *adv.* oui; (after negative question) si.

yesterday, *adv.* hier.

yet, 1. *adv.* encore. **2.** *conj.* néanmoins.

yield, *vb.* (resign, submit) céder; (produce) produire.

yoke, *n.* joug *m.*

yolk, *n.* jaune *m.*

you, *pron.* vous; (familiar, *sg.*) tu.

young, *adj.* jeune.

your, *adj.* votre *sg.,* vos *pl.;* (familiar form) ton *m.sg.,* ta *f.sg.,* tes *pl.*

yours, *pron.* le vôtre; (familiar form) le tien *m.,* la tienne *f.*

yourself, *pron.* vous-même; (familiar form) toi-même; (reflexive) vous, te.

youth, *n.* jeunesse *f.*

youthful, *adj.* (young) jeune; (of youth) de jeunesse.

zap, *vb.* frapper d'une façon soudaine et inattendue.

zeal, *n.* zèle *m.*

zealous, *adj.* zélé.

zebra, *n.* zèbre *m.*

zero, *n.* zéro *m.*

zest, *n.* entrain *m.;* (taste) saveur *f.*

zip code, *n.* code postal *m.*

zone, *n.* zone *f.*

zoo, *n.* jardin *(m.)* zoologique.